Contents

Introduction

Keynotes

Papers

Introduction

Tuğrul İlter

The following is the selected proceedings of the **Second International Conference on Communication and Media Studies: Communication in Peace/Conflict in Communication** hosted by the Faculty of Communication and Media Studies at Eastern Mediterranean University in Famagusta, Northern Cyprus.

Located on the northern half of a multi-cultural but divided island, Cyprus, and in a wider region, Middle East, that has been prone to conflict, with peace taking a very long time coming, reflection on Peace and Conflict is an ongoing concern for its inhabitants. It was not surprising, therefore, that Peace and Conflict were pressing concerns for us, the conference organizing committee, in deciding this year's conference theme. With the recent Peace Journalism Conference and institutional initiatives along those lines at our Faculty, it seems that we have also become a contributor to a what is fast becoming a Faculty tradition.

However, we were also concerned about how Peace and Conflict were commonly understood as polar opposites. In a polarized opposition there is no place for conflict in peace, and peace, the privileged term of the binary opposition, needs to be pure and homogeneous, cleansed of any unlicensed differences and contradictions. Yet, a radically plural and democratic politics *must* harbor conflicting and antagonistic views of things; opposition is internal to it; and its view of freedom says that "freedom is always the freedom of those who think differently." By contrast, the ideal of a homogeneous, selfsame, indivisibly unified society, as we keep hearing about these days, is totalitarian and repressive of the very differences that make a society, *any society*, possible.

We thought that a deconstructive and feminist framework that destabilizes the entrenched certainties of polar oppositions and an ethical response to the irreducible otherness of the other, as well as to one's own alterity, would be very appropriate and relevant in our times for rethinking these issues, and relied on that framework in formulating the theme of our conference as "Communication in Peace/Conflict in Communication" to emphasize the interrelationship of the two parts separated by the slash, as well as the formulation of the subtopics that were listed in the call for papers.[1]

We invited Gary Hall, Meyda Yeğenoğlu, Wilhelm Kempf, and Mahmut Mutman as keynote speakers. We had recently discovered, and were very much impressed by Gary Hall's work in cultural studies, deconstruction and new media technologies as well as his

1 The call for papers can be viewed in the appendix to this introduction. The conference website can be reached at: http://fcms.emu.edu.tr/cpcc/

initiatives concerning open access publishing and archiving. His "Country X" experiment, where a "country" is formed by using the resources of the Net, and more specifically his "Hyper Cyprus" project named after our conference and the title of his keynote speech, challenged us to rethink our received understanding of identity and politics based on national and international territorialization. Meyda Yeğenoğlu, a longtime friend and colleague, specializes in orientalism, globalization, postcolonial theory, cultural studies and migrancy. Her book Colonial Fantasies was hailed as an important contribution to postcolonial theory by its double refusal of the marginalization of questions of gender and sexual identity in accounts of orientalism, and certain kinds of feminist approach whose assumptions are themselves implicated in orientalist ideas of "otherness" and which aspires to supplement "the orientalist lack" experienced by men who are refused access to the "forbidden inner space of the Orient." Wilhelm Kempf, a familiar name in peace journalism circles, has contributed to the formation and development of the field, and specializes in nonviolent conflict resolution and the construction of social reality by the mass media. Mahmut Mutman, another longtime friend and colleague, specializes in cultural and media theory and was going to talk on "States of Exception: Sovereign Terror," using Giorgio Agamben's concept of "state of exception" as a point of departure. Unfortunately, he had to cancel his trip at the last minute due to a medical emergency.

We were very pleased with the enthusiastic international response and with the proposals submitted to our conference. Academics from ten different countries responded to our call and presented highly stimulating and thought provoking papers discussing various aspects of the issues posed by our call for papers. The conference thus provided a great opportunity for both regional and global exchange of ideas, to establish new academic relations, and to make new friends[2]. I would like to take this opportunity to thank them all once again for contributing to the success of our conference.

In addition to our participants and keynote speakers, many people worked very hard to make our conference possible on and behind the scenes. The Faculty of Communication and Media Studies (FCMS), and the Eastern Mediterranean University (EMU), hosted and facilitated the conference. The Dean of FCMS, Sevda Alankuş, has been an enthusiastic supporter of the conference from the start and has assisted us at every stage of the conference. I believe that the non-hierarchical, non-regimented, thus more "peaceful" way of conducting the conference that impressed many of our international participants would not have been possible without her being the Dean. The organizing committee consisted of myself, Nurten Kara, Melek Atabey, Yetin Arslan, and Müge Orun. Our colleague Hanife Aliefendioğlu assisted in the preparation of the slide-music show seen at the beginning of the conference. The FCMS Administrative Officer Emine Alpsoy played a pivotal role in the organization of the conference. The British Council, the Friedrich Ebert Stiftung, and the Turkish Airlines provided crucial and much appreciated support. Our assistant Serkan Şen mobilized his "Event Management" class to work on our conference as a class project, and his students took turns behind the conference desk in the Palm Beach Hotel where our guests stayed and at other points of contact. Erdem Dağdemir and Can Bekcan worked on the design of the conference literature and posters. The Tourism, Publicity and Marketing Department of the Ministry of Economy and Tourism provided tourist brochures to the area. Our computer specialists Yunus Bayır, Ümit Pil, Tangül Keleş, Fikret Vefa and Ecevit Aşıkoğlu helped with the computer and sound set up where available. The staff of EMU-TV and Radio Eastern Mediterranean made the live broadcast of our conference possible. And finally, Fırat Tüzünkan, Roya Alagheband, Shahryar Mirzaalikhani, and Ümit İnatçı provided invaluable help with this book's design and its readiness for printing. Let me reiterate my heartfelt thanks to all.

2 Some missed this opportunity to engage in an ongoing discussion on peace building. One colleague from a university in the Southern part of the island, who was interested, could not attend due to a conflicting engagement. With no participants from the South, the other side of the island was represented by expatriates living in the North who identify themselves as "Cypriots." Maybe the timing of our conference was a factor as it coincided with efforts by the Republic of Cyprus government to prevent Eastern Mediterranean University's inclusion in the Bologna Process. EMU is a full member of the European Universities Association. What made Gary Hall's "Hyper Cyprus" all the more remarkable in this context was that it forced us to rethink these particular "Cypriot" burdens of representation and our relationship to the Other(s) within.

Appendix: Call for Papers

Second International Conference in Communication and Media Studies:
Communication in Peace/Conflict in Communication
Keynote speakers: Gary Hall, Meyda Yeğenoğlu, Wilhelm Kempf, Mahmut Mutman

Dates: 2- 4 May 2007
Venue: Eastern Mediterranean University
Faculty of Communication and Media Studies
Famagusta, North Cyprus

The Faculty of Communication and Media Studies at Eastern Mediterranean University invites paper, panel and event proposals addressing the general theme of *"Communication in Peace/Conflict in Communication."* The Second International Conference, which will be held at the EMU campus in Famagusta, North Cyprus between May 2-4, 2007, aims at bringing together scholars to present their research and exchange ideas in a wide range of topics under the general theme including but not limited to:

- Peace Journalism
- Media and Mediation in Conflict
- Conflict Resolution
- Forgiveness and Reconciliation
- Gender, Ethnicity, Nationality, Race, Religion, Age and Peace/Conflict
- Communication Education and Peace
- Communication Ethics and Peace
- Film and Peace/Conflict
- Peaceful Films, Disturbing Films
- Adcult, Ad-diction, Adbusting
- Communication and Miscommunication
- Miscommunication in Communication
- Peace/Conflict in Intercultural Communication
- Self-Other Communication and Ethnocentrism
- Epistemic Violence in Communicating With the Other
- Love and Friendship
- Citizenship and Cosmopolitanism
- Migrancy, Exile, Diaspora
- Communication in Divided Cities/Lands
- Borders that Divide/Unite
- Enclosure of the Net in the Age of Access

The language of our international conference will be both English and Turkish.

The deadline for submitting proposals is 14 February 2007. Please send your abstracts (not more
than 300 words) by Wednesday 14 February 2007 to:

Assoc. Prof. Dr. Tuğrul İlter
e-mail: tugrul.ilter@emu.edu.tr

or
Assist. Prof. Dr. Melek Atabey
e-mail: melek.atabey@emu.edu.tr

or
Assist. Prof. Dr. Nurten Kara
e-mail: nurten.kara@emu.edu.tr

An electronic submission form is also provided at the conference web site. The deadline for submitting full papers is 06 April 2007.

Submissions are subject to blind peer review at every stage. Notifications of acceptance together with a paper style sheet will be sent on 28 February 2007. Abstracts and papers will be accessible to all participants on the conference web site once the complete program is set.

Hyper-Cyprus: On Peace and Conflict in the Middle East*

Gary Hall
Coventry University
gary@garyhall.info

Peace and Conflict: The 6 Step Programme

I've been asked to speak today about how the kind of analysis I've performed elsewhere in my work—one described as destabilizing 'the entrenched certainties of polar oppositions and attempting to develop an ethical response to the irreducible otherness of the other as well as to one's own alterity'—might help us to rethink ideas of peace and conflict. And, in particular, how it might do so in relation to the multi-cultural but divided island of Cyprus and the wider region of the Middle-East.

Contents

* [Editors' note] The distinctive format of Gary Hall's keynote article is deliberate. It was written in line with his wiki-theme, and "is meant to mimic a wikipedia entry (or at least remind the reader of one)."

6. Hyper-Cyprus
    6.1 Wikimedia
    6.2 The geopolitics of knowledge
    6.3 University-generated media

Peace and Conflict: The 6-Step Programme

The following is by now a tried and tested method for doing so, one that offers simple yet effective treatment of such issues, using a set of 6 easy-to-follow, step-by-step instructions:

The 6-Step Programme

Step 1 - show how any would-be unified self – be it an individual, a culture, a nation – can only establish and maintain its identity by distinguishing itself from and excluding that which it is *not*;

Step 2 - demonstrate that any such self cannot be positioned in terms of a simple conflict or oppositional relationship with those identified as being 'outside' and 'other' to it; for at the same time as it rejects and condemns those others, it also needs them and their difference to establish and maintain its own identity;

Step 3 - reveal that any such self depends upon and even contains many of the attributes it otherwise ascribes to its others;

Step 4 - show that it *is* just another form of what it accuses those others of being;

Step 5 - argue that, rather than attempting to 'de-other' itself by getting rid of whatever it is that its others represent, what the prospective self-identical entity needs to do is recognise that this relation represents an internal dislocation. (The idea here is for it to stop imagining itself as constituting some kind of integral totality at the same time as it continually fears its own immanent dissolution at the hands of 'others');

Step 6 - explain that this internally dislocated nature, rather than representing a crisis or threat, is just what it is; that any would-be unified self just *is* constitutively non-identical to itself; that this is what makes it possible (and of course impossible) in the first place.[1]

Can such an approach be adopted with regard to the situation of Cyprus, thereby providing us with a means of responding to the issues of peace and conflict in communication that are being raised by this conference? I would maintain that it can (although, as you'll see, I also have problems with doing so—but that's for later…).

At this point I want to move away from broad generalisations, as despite the impression I may have given with my playful opening, I don't want to suggest analyses conducted along these lines are all the same. Part of what I'm trying to do in my work is develop an ethics which retains a relation of infinite responsibility to an unconditional hospitality even when it comes to the reading of other texts. For this reason I'm going to turn now to focus on a specific instance of such an analysis: that provided by the political philosopher Chantal Mouffe, who is one of the most interesting contemporary theorists of the relation between peace and conflict, in her recent books *The Democratic Paradox* (2000) and especially *On the Political* (2005).

On the Political

In keeping with the analysis sketched above, Mouffe views the political in terms of a conflict and antagonism that is irreducible. Reading the philosopher Carl Schmitt against himself, Mouffe argues that the political '"can be understood only in the context of the friend/enemy grouping"'.[2] 'By showing that every consensus is based on acts of exclusion, [Schmitt] reveals the impossibility of a fully inclusive "rational" consensus' (p. 11). This is because of what Mouffe calls the '"constitutive outside"' whereby, when it comes to the 'field of collective identities, we are always dealing with the creation of a "we" which can exist only by the demarcation of a "they"' (p. 15)—the ethnic minority, the immigrant, the asylum seeker, the religious or political extremist, the terrorist and so on. From this point of view we can't ever achieve peace: not internally within a culture or society; nor externally between different cultures and societies. Instead, we need

1 For one analysis along these lines, see my 'Coca-colonised Thinking?', *The Oxford Literary Review*, No. 28, forthcoming. Also available in the Cultural Studies Open Access Archive (CSeARCH) at http://www.culturemachine.net/csearch

2 Carl Schmitt, *The Concept of the Political* (New Brunswick: Rutgers, 1976), p. 35; cited in Chantal Mouffe, *On the Political* (London: Routledge, 2005), p. 11. All other references to Mouffe are to the latter text unless otherwise indicated.

to acknowledge the 'antagonistic dimension' that is 'constitutive of "the political"' (p. 2) and give up on the fantasy of ever arriving at a completely united and harmonious world in which all 'power, sovereignty and hegemony' is 'overcome' (p. 130).

Now, it's important not to see the irreducibility of conflict as a purely negative thing, as it might be, say, by liberal thought, which has as one of its central tenets 'the rationalist belief in the availability of a universal consensus based on reason' (p. 11). In fact, far from placing democracy at risk, a certain degree of confrontation constitutes the very possibility of its existence, for Mouffe. As far as she is concerned, 'a well functioning democracy calls for a clash of legitimate democratic political positions' (p. 30). It's thus far more dangerous *not* to acknowledge this irreducible antagonism, as this lack of acknowledgement leads to negative forms of conflict in the arenas of both domestic and international politics. Mouffe explains this by referring to the various affective forces, which she calls '"passions"': i.e. those drives, desires and fantasies which make people want to become part of a crowd, group, community or nation and which 'are at the origin of collective forms of identification' (p. 24). Unless these passions and the forms of conflict they give rise to have a legitimate democratic means of expressing themselves, then there is a danger that they will 'be replaced by a confrontation between essentialist forms of identification or non-negotiable moral values', with all the attendant negative consequences (p. 30). For Mouffe, 'democratic institutions can contribute to [the] disarming of the libidinal forces leading towards hostility which are always present in human societies' by providing positive channels for their expression (p. 26).

From Political to Moral

Mouffe's emphasis on the constitutive nature of political conflict leads her to argue strongly against the *post-political* vision of the world that has been attributed to sociologists such as Ulrich Beck and Anthony Giddens. Revising ideas of the 'post-industrial society' and the 'end of ideology' from the 1960s, they argue that conceptions of politics built around shared, large-scale group identities have become irretrievably old-fashioned and outmoded (p. 35). For them, Western societies are currently experiencing a '"second modernity" in which individuals liberated from collective ties can now dedicate themselves to cultivating a diversity of lifestyles, unhindered by antiquated attachments' such as those associated with the ideological divisions of left and right (p. 1). Liberal democracy has thus won out over communism, and consensus is held as being now achievable through dialogue rather than political conflict and antagonism.

For Mouffe, however, what we are seeing at the moment is not the 'disappearance of the political in its adversarial dimension... What is happening is that nowadays the political is played out in the *moral register*' (p. 5). So after the events of 9/11, North Korea, Iran and Iraq were famously positioned by George W. Bush in terms of an 'axis of evil';[3] an axis which was soon expanded to take in Cuba, Libya and Syria, too.[4] Similarly, in 2002, Cherie Blair, the human rights lawyer and wife of the British Prime Minster, was made to apologise for saying that 'as long as young people [in Palestine] feel they have got no hope but to blow themselves up you are never going to make progress'. She had to apologise for saying this because nowadays people in her position are expected to condemn actions such as suicide bombing as morally wrong and thus incomprehensible to all right-minded people; not interpret them as Cherie Blair did as a political issue, and hence understandable.

The problem with this moralistic approach is that no dialogue or discussion is possible with anything that is 'evil'. Evil—as is clearly the case with regard to Osama bin Laden, the Taliban, Saddam Hussein—just *has to be condemned and destroyed*. Yet not only does this playing out of the political in moral terms lead those on the side of 'good' to be perhaps just as violent as those they accuse of being morally wrong; it also results in that which is repressed returning in illegitimate, violent forms, since it has no legitimate outlet.

Cyprus

Can an approach such as that offered by Mouffe, and inspired by the philosophy of Jacques Derrida and Carl Schmitt, be adopted with regard to Cyprus, then?

Cyprus's situation is a singular one for many reasons. Nevertheless, it's a particularly interesting and appropriate place to address issues of this kind, given that it has formed a part—sometimes an extremely important part—of so many Empires, which have all left their traces to produce a multiple, hybrid culture: Greek, Persian, Roman, Byzantine, Ottoman, British. Divided between North and South, could we not say that Cyprus occupies a strategic place (given the location of the conference hotel next to the Green Line, I'm tempted to say a border point or part of the frontier), between Turkey and Greece, yes; but also between Asia and Europe, East and West, not to mention the Islamic and Christian, religious and secular worlds?

3 George W. Bush, 'President Delivers State of the Union Address', The White House, Office of the Press Secretary, January 29, 2002; available at: http://www.whitehouse.gov/news/releases/2002/01/20020129-11.html; accessed 12.04.2007.
4 'US Expands "Axis of Evil"', *BBC News*, Monday, 6 May, 2002; available at: http://news.bbc.co.uk/2/hi/americas/1971852.stm; accessed 12.04.2007.

(I'm aware that's all a bit of a cliché. You must get tired of people coming here and describing it as 'a land of contrasts' and so on. Perhaps another way of approaching this issue is, if conflict *is* constitutive of the political, then perhaps one of the most interesting places to think about peace is one in which the irreducibility of antagonism is very apparent. From this standpoint, rather than being a 'backward region' not worth paying attention to because it is always locked in political turmoil—as a recent article in *Prospect* magazine indeed maintains—the fact that it is the scene of so much violence and antagonism is precisely what makes the Middle East so interesting and important when it comes to exploring how different people can live together.)[5]

Mouffe certainly raises a number of issues that are relevant to us here today, I think, regarding peace and conflict in communication.

Terrorism

For instance, we could use her argument to interpret events such as the 7/7 bombings in London as the reactions of Islamic fundamentalists to the globalizing advance of Western, liberal democracy. From this perspective, terrorism is not simply the 'work of isolated groups of fanatics'. It is 'the product of a new configuration of the political which is characteristic of the type of world order being implemented around the hegemony of a single hyper-power': that of the US (p. 81). In fact, as far as Mouffe is concerned, 'the lack of political channels for challenging the hegemony of the neo-liberal model of globalization is… at the origin of the proliferation of discourses and practices of radical negation of the established order' (p. 82), among which we could also presumably include the recent car-bombings in Baghdad as well as all those events associated with the name al-Queida.

Hrant Dink

Could we develop a similar analysis, then, with regard to the assassination earlier this year of the Armenian-Turkish journalist Hrant Dink? Was Dink killed because he was seen as being wrong in *moral* rather than *political* terms? Did the ultra-nationalist far right in Turkey perceive him as an evil enemy to be destroyed because they lack other channels for challenging the hegemony of the Western, liberal democratic model of globalization, channels that would have enabled them to see Dink instead as a *political* opponent?

The Question of Europe (and Cosmopolitanism)

Although of course she does not mention Dink, Mouffe nevertheless insists that it is a mistake to think neo-liberal globalisation can be best resisted on a nationalist or even national level. Instead, she argues for the creation of a strong political Europe, at least to counter the US and 'oppose the violations of international law and human rights by the Bush government' (p. 129). But she is careful to emphasise that this should not be regarded as merely the first stage in the creation of a cosmopolitan world order based on the universalization of the European liberal democratic worldview: one which presents the latter as 'the only just and legitimate regime, whose institutions would, in idealized conditions, be chosen by all rational individuals' (p. 83); and anyone who does not choose it—those associated with Islam, for instance—as irrational, uncivilised or morally and culturally backward. Too often the choice nations outside the West are faced with—especially when it comes to joining organisations such as the European Union—is that they can retain their traditional culture, religions, and ways of life but then *not* take part in the economic modernization and prosperity associated with the West. Or they can join in with this so-called progressive modernization and reformation on the economic level, but then also have their traditional culture, religions and ways of life transformed into a liberal, democratic, individualistic order. Consequently, rather than cosmopolitanism, Mouffe argues for a multipolar world, with ideas, decisions and critiques being generated in a plurality of places: not just America or Europe but lots of different centres of power. One can easily imagine such centres including the Middle East as well as South America (perhaps under Hugo Chavez, who yesterday announced that he is pulling Venezuela out of the World Bank and the International Monetary Fund), China, East Asia, India…

On the Anti-Political

So, yes, all this is interesting and useful with regard to some of the issues relating to peace and conflict we are thinking about. Not least because it enables us to understand that the Middle East is not a state of exception; that conflict in the region is not natural, timeless and without foreseeable end. The Middle East can only be viewed in this way if history and politics are excluded from our analyses. Instead, we can now see that conflict and antagonism are constitutive of the political and irreducible aspects of it. The point is not to search for the complete resolution of all conflict and the associated reconciliation between the different conflicting parties—that is impossible—but to find more constructive ways of expressing it.

5 Edward Luttwak, 'The Middle of Nowhere', *Prospect*, May, 2007: pp. 26-29.

Yet—somewhat surprisingly perhaps—adopting an approach of this kind is *not* what I want to suggest we do here: partly for reasons that are specific to Mouffe's analysis; but also for reasons that are applicable to this kind of theoretical approach in general. The reasons that are specific to Mouffe have to do with the way in which her theory, for me, is *not* political, and I would even say is in fact *anti-political.* This is apparent from her attempt to tame and domesticate the conflict and violence which, following Schmitt, she regards as inherent to the political.

Antagonism vs. Agonism

For Mouffe, the main question of democratic politics is not how to eliminate issues to do with power and conflict so that we end up in a state of perpetual peace, Kantian or otherwise. The question is rather: how can power and conflict assume a form that is compatible with democratic values? As far as she is concerned, a pluralist democracy can achieve this only through the establishment of a set of institutions and practices by which domination and violence 'can be limited and contested'.[6] To this end Mouffe identifies two different forms in which antagonism can emerge: antagonism and what she calls agonism. 'While antagonism is a we/they relation in which the two sides are enemies who do not share any common ground, agonism is a we/they relation where the conflicting parties, although acknowledging that there is no rational solution to their conflict, nevertheless recognize the legitimacy of their opponents. They are "adversaries" not enemies' (p. 20). We can thus now begin to think the problem of democratic politics somewhat differently; for from the viewpoint of 'agonistic pluralism', the goal of democratic politics is to transform *antagonism* into *agonism.* In this way, Mouffe is able to produce an account of society that acknowledges the irreducibility of conflict and violence, but not to such an extent that it destroys any democratic political association.

My concern, however, is that this leads her to offer a consensual vision of society that is almost as free from political conflict as that of the liberals she positions her theory very much against. For Mouffe is still drawing a line between those with whom 'we have a shared adhesion to the ethico-political principles of liberal democracy', and those with whom we don't; between those we disagree with, but can nevertheless treat as legitimate opponents and so include within the democratic political association, and those we cannot treat as legitimate and who therefore remain enemies to be excluded.

To argue that Mouffe is adopting the same strategy she criticises others for employing on the grounds that it:

a. is impossible
b. denies the pluralism she regards as constitutive of modern liberal democracy
c. implies the eradication of the political which has to do precisely with conflict and antagonism

would be to get ahead of ourselves, however. Mouffe's political philosophy is not necessarily inconsistent on this point. For one thing, a certain amount of pluralism and conflict is still possible here: it has just been transformed from antagonism into agonism. For another, Mouffe has no problem with placing limits on pluralism or with the exclusion of what she considers to be illegitimate forms of politics—just so long as it is clear that this is 'an eminently *political* decision' (p. 25), not an expression of a 'universal morality' (p. 121). In marked contrast to the liberalism of Jürgen Habermas and John Rawls, then, Mouffe *does* appear to be providing the basis for including the kind of conflict and pluralism over politics that might otherwise be considered to be eliminated from her philosophy. Witness the way she emphasises that 'the drawing of the frontier between the legitimate and the illegitimate is always a political decision, and that it should therefore always remain open to contestation' (p. 121). From this perspective, Mouffe has made a *political decision* in favour of the founding ethico-political principles of liberal democracy and against those who think differently enough to want to challenge these principles. She stresses however that, being *political,* this decision is an inherently violent one that always remains open to political conflict and contestation.

My question, though, is *does it*? For all that Mouffe emphasises the importance of making *a political decision,* it seems to me that a number of the decisions she makes do not remain open to challenge at all. Let me draw attention to three of the most important of these: important, not just for Mouffe's philosophy, but for the kind of analysis we might develop regarding of peace and conflict.

The Others of Democracy

To begin with, there is the notion that other forms of sociality don't permit the kind of legitimation of conflict Mouffe ascribes to democracy.

The reason Mouffe makes a *political decision* in favour of liberal democracy is because she regards the latter, for all its

6 Chantal Mouffe, *The Democratic Paradox* (London: Verso, 2000), p. 22.

problems, as preferable to other forms of social organisation, such as fascism, totalitarianism, religious fundamentalism and so on, due to the fact that it recognises and permits a degree of antagonism. "What is specific and valuable about modern liberal democracy", she writes, "is that... it creates a space in which... confrontation is kept open, power relations are always being put into question and no victory can be final" (p. 15). Still, while it may be true that democracy *does* allow for conflict, and certain other forms of sociality including those associated with totalitarianism, fascism and religious fundamentalism do not, is that to say *all* other possible forms of sociality do not? Really? Is this something that has been thoroughly and rigorously investigated? Or has it just been adopted nowadays as something of a philosophical and political truism? Is this decision on Mouffe's part not based on precisely the kind of stereotypes—about democracy (that it does allow for political contestation); about of other forms of sociality (that they do not); and about other forms of (non-democratic) conflict—that have been used by some to justify the universalization of democracy as the "modern", "progressive" way to go?

Democracy

The second of Mouffe's uncontestable decisions concerns democracy itself rather than its others. For Mouffe, there can be conflict within democracy over the way 'the institutions constitutive of the democratic political association' are to be interpreted, but not over the continuing existence of those democratic institutions in some shape or form. In other words, the nature of those institutions can be contested; what cannot be contested is the shared symbolic space—i.e. democracy—that is necessary for that contestation to take place. The democratic system cannot be replaced by a communist one, for example. Something similar happens on the international plane. Here 'different vernacular models of democracy' from that of the Western liberal version are perfectly acceptable, and are even to be encouraged (p. 129). Yet for all her talk of the dangers of the universalization of the Western or European cosmopolitan world-view, Mouffe is still quite happy to universalize democracy, as these all have to be models of democracy of some kind. While the nature of particular *forms* of democracy can be challenged, then—which means Islamic countries, say, don't necessarily *have* to adopt the Western liberal model—what can't be challenged is democracy itself.

I should just stress, I'm saying this *not* because I suffer from what Jacques Rancière has recently described as a 'hatred of democracy'.[7] I'm not maintaining that a political decision *cannot* be taken to the effect that democracy is the best—or least worst—system to adopt in a given situation. (I can appreciate that democracy must appear particularly attractive in circumstances such as those experienced in Turkey at the weekend when the military again, as they have so many times before, threatened to get involved in the running of civil society.)[8] What it is to say is that, if the political for Mouffe is a decision taken in an undecidable terrain, which it is, then such a political decision is not available to be taken in her work, not regarding democracy anyway (2000, p. 130).

Hegemony

This brings me to the third of Mouffe's unchallengable decisions: that politics is always hegemonic. Quite simply, 'there is no "beyond hegemony"', for Mouffe. 'Every order is *by necessity* a hegemonic order' (p. 106).

Now I would agree that political antagonism is 'ineradicable'—to the extent that we shouldn't be searching for complete reconciliation between the various conflicting parties in the Middle East (or absolute 'unity, togetherness and solidarity', as the Turkish Prime Minister put it in his speech to the nation the other day in response to the army's intervention). But does that mean politics *always* takes a hegemonic form? After all, hegemony is not universal: it is a *particular* form of politics. What, then, of other kinds of politics? Interestingly, Mouffe positions her 1985 book with Ernesto Laclau, *Hegemony and Socialist Strategy*, as having acknowledged 'that politics is now taking place in a multiplicity of domains hitherto considered as non-political'.[9] Mouffe is thus clearly in favour of 'enlarging the domain of politics' (p. 53). Just not so much to be capable of making a political decision in favour of struggles which cannot be apprehended through the category of hegemony.

Mouffe as Anti-Political Liberal (and not all that pluralistic)...

This does not mean I agree with Beck and Giddens that we *have* entered a 'post-political' era, and that I consider viewing politics in terms of hegemony to be completely out of date. Again, I'm not maintaining that a responsible decision *cannot* ever be taken to the effect that hegemony *is* an appropriate concept to use when attempting to understand, analyse and resist a particular situation. I'm just drawing attention to the fact that Mouffe has a transcendentalised and festishized notion of hegemonic politics which is in her own terms universally moralizing and anti-political, as she does not appear to

7 Jacques Rancière, *Hatred of Democracy* (London: Verso, 2007).

8 I am not going to detail them here, but for a succinct English language account of the events that took place in Turkey on the weekend immediately preceding the conference, see 'The Battle for Turkey's Soul', *The Economist*, May 5, 2007: p. 9.

9 Ernesto Laclau and Chantal Mouffe, *Hegemony and Socialist Strategy: Towards a Radical Democratic Politics* (London: Verso, 1985).

be willing to make an actual political decision about any of this. Not one that remains open both to contestation and to the actual complexities of a given social or cultural situation: to the incalculable, the other, *the undecidable*, and especially to the possibility that politics may not always appear as she presents it. As a result, I would argue that Mouffe's theory of politics is *not political* even according to her own criteria. What's more, *it's not all that pluralistic either*, since she is clearly leaving little room here for political positions that conflict with her own.

In fact the whole thrust of Mouffe's politics is to establish a democratic society that will allow for agonism but not '*antagonism* properly speaking'. But as I say, she can only do this: firstly, by distinguishing between antagonism and agonism; and then, secondly, by excluding or marginalizing antagonism - that which she cannot tame or transform 'into *agonism*' (p. 117), and which therefore *really* is conflicting with her own values - outside this (radical) liberal-democratic realm. Of course, aware that there is a danger here of herself excluding political confrontation and conflict to a 'constitutive outside' of her own making in an attempt to eradicate it from democratic society and thereby maintain a degree of relative peacefulness and reconciliation, Mouffe stresses, as we have seen, that 'the drawing of the frontier between the legitimate and the illegitimate is always a political decision, and that it should therefore always remain open to contestation' (p. 121). However, as we have also seen, the decision as to what forms of conflict to consider legitimate and therefore include in democratic society and what to consider illegitimate and therefore exclude is in actual fact *not* always kept open to conflict and contestation by Mouffe. On the contrary, this decision is foreclosed, certainly when it comes to democracy and hegemony. Like the liberals she criticizes, then, Mouffe too, it seems, cannot envisage political conflict, antagonism and pluralism *within* democratic society.

... Western, American and bourgeois

Somewhat ironically, Mouffe's political philosophy thus turns out to be another form of the liberalism she positions her theory against. All of which brings me to the more general reasons I want to suggest that we *don't* adopt an analysis along these lines at this conference. For Mouffe's adherence to the 6 step programme I outlined earlier means her political philosophy is all too easily incorporated into those 'modernist', 'liberal' and 'American' ways of thinking Timothy Clark has recently identified as being built into the institution of academic criticism. According to Clark, the problem with these ways of thinking, for all that they are more or less ubiquitous in literary and cultural theory, is that they tend to be:

a. reductive - in that they have at their foundation one unacknowledged but 'all-determining norm': that there is a natural desire for identity, 'one whose self-realisation' is aggressive 'assertion against others';[10]

b. insufficiently critical - for example, the assumption that there is a universal drive for unified identity is never interrogated;

c. liberal - underpinned as they are by notions of sovereign, unified identity and subjectivity, such apparently 'radical' critical projects effectively reiterate the very terms of the bourgeois, liberal, humanist discourse they are attempting to place in question.

WikiNation

On Historical Movements, Moments, Eras, Trends and Turns

Having said all that, I don't want to leave you with the impression that we should now turn our backs on that tradition of thought which has concerned itself with the study of various attempts to establish identity through aggressive self-assertion against others. It is a tradition of thought which, for me, *has* been, and very much continues to be, incredibly interesting and important. So none of this is about intellectual fashion, looking for the next big thing, or pronouncing the end of one thing and the beginning of something else. It's not about dividing the history of thought into historical movements, moments, eras, trends or turns: from hegemony to post-hegemony; culture to complexity; ideology to affect; representation to flows; or language and textuality to science and technology. Nor is it about, say, Bergson, Badiou, Deleuze and Latour somehow superseding Heidegger, Barthes, Derrida and Lacan. I think we need to be more generous, hospitable and responsible than that. My argument concerns more the manner in which this tradition—which includes not just Mouffe and Heidegger *et al*, but also Agamben, Spivak, Bhabha, Said, Foucault, Fanon and Sartre, stretching as far back at least as Freud and Hegel—has often been taken up: the way analyses of this kind have become something of a programme, and in the process *have* been too easily incorporated into uncritical, reductive, liberal and American ways of thinking, closing 'off the force of debate and contestation', and severely reducing the complexity that is intrinsic to situations such as that of Cyprus, Turkey, the Middle East and indeed Europe.[11]

10 Timothy Clark, *The Poetics of Singularity: The Counter-Culturalist Turn in Heidegger, Derrida, Blanchot and the Later Gadamer* (Edinburgh: Edinburgh University Press, 2005).

11 Timothy Clark, ibid.

Thinking Schmitt against Schmitt and Mouffe against Mouffe

For instance, it's not hard to understand why Mouffe has to foreclose the decisions I detailed above. If she didn't, the antagonistic values she tries to exclude would threaten to bring into question the very concepts of democracy and hegemony she is anxious to defend. Nevertheless, what for me is so interesting about Mouffe's philosophy is the way at the same time it also shows us that 'bringing a deliberation to a close always results from a decision which excludes other possibilities and for which one should never refuse to bear responsibility by invoking the commands of general rules or principles' (p. 105)—a state of affairs which would presumably include her own general principles regarding agonistic pluralism, liberal democracy and hegemony. Instead, such a political decision has to be taken in relation to 'specific practices' in 'particular contexts' (2005, p. 121). It is also one that has to remain open to political conflict and contestation.

From this point of view, the question Mouffe's work pushes us to ask—even if she is not willing or able to raise it herself—is that, if we *really* want to be political, then don't we have to take the risk of remaining open to those who *are* different; those with whom we *don't* 'have a shared adhesion to the ethico-political principles of liberal democracy', and whom we *cannot* necessarily treat as legitimate political adversaries? We cannot decide against them always and forever, by invoking general rules or principles in advance:

a. because that would not be to take a decision in an undecidable terrain, and so would not be political;

b. because a specific practice or particular context may arise where we may need to take a decision in favour of such different politics and antagonistic 'enemies'.

To be sure, doing so might risk challenging many of our own strongly held ideas – including those of liberal-democracy, and of hegemony. But what Mouffe shows—and I'm thinking *with* Mouffe *against* Mouffe here, just as she thinks Schmitt against Schmitt—is that this is precisely the point. If the political *is* a decision taken in an undecidable terrain, then it *must* involve remaining open to the possibility of bringing even our ideas of democracy and hegemony into question.

Creating, Inventing, Experimenting

What this means is that, in order to be political, we need to be committed to both politics *and* what I elsewhere call—partly following Mouffe in doing so—*hyperpolitics*.[12] The latter names a refusal to consider the question of politics as closed or decided in advance, and an associated willingness to open up an unconditional space for thinking about politics and the political beyond the way in which they have been traditionally conceived—a thinking of politics which is *more than politics*, while still being political. This in turn means not *just producing yet another analysis or critique* of the politics of others. We have to do this, since without rigorous analysis we risk uncritically repeating the reductive adherence to democracy and hegemony and bourgeois liberal humanism I've identified in Mouffe, and Clark identifies in academic criticism more widely. So we can't just shift the balance *away* from critique and *onto* 'affirmative methods', as Brian Massumi has suggested.[13] (Which is why I've spent so long carefully working through Mouffe's political philosophy.) But along with critique we *also* have to be prepared to go *beyond* what can be discerned and predicted by means of analysis. For we can now see that what it means to be political is not something that can, on the basis of either my own philosophy, or that of others, be decided once and for all *a priori* by means of analysis. Politics is not merely about the kind of intended consequences and affects that can be predicted, foreseen and articulated in advance. Politics is *also* something that has to be invented and created in relation to specific practices, in particular situations and contexts, by performing the associated decisions, and otherwise doing things that may be unanticipated and unpredictable, and thus *beyond* analysis.

Country X

It is opportunities for doing this—for making affirmative, performative, affective political interventions by creating singular situations in which people are required to take responsible political decisions—that I've been experimenting with in recent years. Examples include country x, which was a creative collaboration between Matthew Herbert, Robert Smith and myself. We took our cue for country x from the way in which, by their 'nation building' in Afghanistan and Iraq, Bush and Blair have shown what many philosophers and political theorists have argued for a long time: that nations are not fixed or 'natural', but *can be constructed and invented.* So we devised a project to explore the possibility of creating a new concept for a country; one which owed its heterogeneous emergence to a widespread dissatisfaction with the politics, policies, borders and conflicts of the existing nation states. For example, while country x did not have an identity based on a particular geographical location or common history, what it did have is an unlimited immigration and emigration policy. We made a decision that anyone, anywhere, could become a citizen of country x irrespective of gender, religion, race, ethnicity, age, health, family history, social background, education, income, credit rating, employment status…

12 See my *Digitize This! The Politics of New Media, or Why We Need Open Access Now* (Minneapolis: University of Minnesota Press, 2008).
13 Brian Massumi, *Parables for the Virtual: Movement, Affect, Sensation* (Durham and London: Duke University Press, 2002), p. 17.

Hyper-Cyprus

Could *we* do something similar at this conference? Could *we* use some of what I've said about peace and conflict today, *not just to generate more critiques* of the relationships between North and South, Turkey and Greece, East and West, Islam and Christianity, traditional and modern, past and present and so on? Could we also begin to work co-operatively and affirmatively to invent new ways of organising institutions, cultures, communities, countries, in all their complexity, uncertainty and multiplicity? What if we devised our own community or country as a way of creating an actual, affective point of potentiality and transformation - not least in order to counter the hyper-power of Western liberal democracy? One characterised precisely by a hyper-political willingness to open up an unconditional space for thinking about politics and the political—and with them ideas of peace and conflict—beyond the way in which they have conventionally been conceived?

A Hyper-Cyprus, if you like!

WikiMedia

To enable us to begin experimenting along these lines, I've set up a wiki (along with Steve Green of *Culture Machine*). You can find this at:
http://rime.tees.ac.uk/wiki/theUniversity3G/

This consists of material you are entirely free to add to, edit, delete, and creatively remix, reconstruct, reformat and reinvent however you see fit. (Basically, it works like Wikipedia, except it's a way for us to experiment with generating different notions of culture, community, the nation etc. rather than a free encyclopaedia).

It is important that we should use digital media to do this, I think. In his book *Imagined Communities*, Benedict Anderson showed how modes of communication are central to ideas of the nation; and how writing in particular was central to the formation of the *modern* nation.[14] But if the mode of communication begins to change—from writing on paper to digital, say—does this not offer us a chance to raise some important questions regarding how the modern nation is conceived, and to begin to think the nation differently, and reimagine and reinvent it?

It is also important that, within this, we should use the wikimedia mode of communication specifically. For this enables us to experiment with ideas that are:

- User-generated—so everyone will be able to create and contribute to this 'nation' and directly participate in its organisation and running;

- Distributed in structure—what I am calling Hyper-Cyprus will have no *one* point of control;

- Not limited to geographical, cultural or national boundaries—and which instead have the potential to be inter- and trans-nationally inclusive, even global in scope if we wish;

- Continually in process—identity here will not be fixed and unified but fluid, emergent, constantly in the process of becoming;

- Highly responsive—Hyper-Cyprus will be able to respond quickly to citizen's/users' demands: for new features, institutions, philosophies and so forth.

As such, the wikified mode of communication can help us to avoid simply repeating the Western, liberal models of culture, community, the nation and indeed academic work and the institution of academic criticism. It can do so by virtue of the way in which the project's wikimedia form means that Hyper-Cyprus will not be:

a. simply made up of the contributions of autonomous, unified, sovereign, liberal subjects. This is what's interesting about wikimedia specifically. Whereas a lot of 'Web 2.0' such as MySpace and Facebook is very humanist and individualistic, wikis tend to be the product of anonymous groups or networks of people working co-operatively and collaboratively to produce hard-to-recreate resources for free. As the example of Wikipedia illustrates, by harnessing collective intelligence and the power of the crowd, wikimedia has the potential to provide an alternative model of social organisation to that of neo-liberal global capitalism, one which offers a way of thinking individuality *and* collectivity,

14 Benedict Anderson, *Imagined Communities: Reflections on the Origin and Spread of Nationalism* (London: Verso, 1983).

singularity *and* commonality together;

b. but Hyper-Cyprus also won't be owned and controlled by a limited number of authors, editors, publishers or institutions. Instead, 'producers' (such as myself and Steve Green) create the basic idea and framework and then gift it to everyone else open access to build upon and develop;

c. finished or even finishable—rather it will be constantly edited, added to, up-dated, revised, re-worked. Along with b. (above), this will assist us in keeping Hyper-Cyprus open to continual political conflict and contestation;

d. single, centralised or unified—Hyper-Cyprus's networked, distributed structure means anyone, anywhere, can potentially join in, publish and participate. It therefore has the potential to be extremely pluralistic. We could even have a multi-locational, multi-polar institution, community or country, if we so wish.

The Geopolitics of Knowledge

This last point is especially important with regard to something else that was mentioned in my invitation to speak at this conference: that coming here would enable me to 'establish some international links outside "the usual Anglo/Australian/ American nexus"' as the journal I co-edit, *Culture Machine*, puts it. When we made this claim in *Culture Machine*, we were trying to avoid reproducing the centre/periphery model of the geopolitics of knowledge. It is a model in which there are a few nations at the centre who are exporting, and in effect universalising, or at least globalizing, their knowledge; and a whole host of nations outside the 'centre', who may be able to import 'universal theory', but who don't have the opportunities to publish, export or even develop such 'universal' theories of their own.

The wikifmedia mode of communication can be of assistance with this, it seems to me. Not by placing more emphasis on the so-called periphery. But by making it possible to produce a multiplicitous academic and publishing network; one with a far more fluid, pluralistic, distributed and de-centred structure. And again Cyprus itself could be said to have an important strategic position or role to play in any such publishing network, given it is the location of so many electronic monitoring facilities which are used to check and keep a watch on communications around the world.[15]

University-Generated Media

In view of the above I don't want to be prescriptive and establish a set of rules, norms, principles or procedures for any such new community. I don't even want to designate what we should call it. I've given it the same title as this talk—'Hyper-Cyprus'—but you're perfectly free to change this. Perhaps we wouldn't want it to assume the conventional form of a country or nation, with all that implies (i.e. that it is restricted to a particular national territory, geographical location, social demographic, common identity, history, language, race, ethnicity, religion, ancestry or a system of beliefs). That would possibly be too limiting, and would risk restricting any such potential community primarily to those with a specific interest in Cyprus, Turkey or the Middle East. There might also be a danger of Hyper-Cyprus degenerating into the sort of polarised exchanges that have characterised discussions of the 'Cyprus problem' elsewhere on the web.

One thing that *is* certain about this emergent community is that it's not something I *can simply tell you about and show you*: it's something that has be invented and created by all of us. However, just to get the ball rolling I have placed something in the wiki: this is an initial proposal—in the form of a mission statement—for a new university that could perhaps be part of any reconceived nation.

I'm not going to run through all this now. You can read it on the wiki. And, again, you are all completely free to add to, edit, delete, distribute and mash-up this text however you wish.[16] Suffice it to say that I wanted to start with a mission statement for the university: partly because of the central role the university plays in global capitalism's knowledge economy; and partly to show that this isn't a libertarianism of the kind that is often associated with the internet—that we do still need institutions, for example, and perhaps even the state. But also because the university is a place where most of us work. It's certainly where we all are today. And it seemed to me to be appropriate strategically to try to start from where we are: in *Cyprus*, in the *university*.

15 Brendan O'Malley and Ian Craig, *The Cyprus Conspiracy: America, Espionage and the Turkish Invasion* (London: I.B.Taurus, 1999

16 I'll also place a copy of this text in there, subject to the same open content conditions.

Muslim Europeans, European Imaginary and the Limits of Liberal Tolerance

Meyda Yeğenoğlu
Middle East Technical University
Department of Sociology
meyda@metu.edu.tr

European Imaginary

Modernity's secularist narrative, which is based on the progressive distancing of the secular from the religious, is now highly questionable. Despite the prevailing secularist argument's relegation of religion to the domain of the private, religion has never ceased to appear in the public space. The secularist thesis represents the West as exemplary in relegating religion to the private sphere of individually held beliefs and thereby distancing the realms of culture and politics from religion. This fantasized relation with religion, goes hand in hand with the *displacement* of the increasing prominence of religion in the Euro-American public space to issues of culture and cultural identity.

The presence of millions of Muslim Europeans, especially after September 11 exacerbate the deep-seated Orientalist anxieties in Europe. This Orientalist unease with Islam goes hand in hand with the interest in bringing to fore the so-called distinctive European characteristics and thereby distinguishing the Europeanness of Europe. The recurring Orientalism in the discourse of European cultural identity can be traced in the expulsion of Islam from what is deemed to be the proper identity of Europe.

The discourse of the European identity and the appraisals and rankings offered whether people with Muslim religious belonging are qualified to be considered European enough can be seen as a symptom of a discourse whose agenda is the preservation of the so-called European tradition by maintaining its purity. The discourse of integration and unity that is incarnated in the discourses about the European Union is fundamentally about defining a common or harmonious European identity that is based on the principle of shared European values. These values function not only as the benchmark to judge whether certain countries are eligible to accede to the Union, but also organize the individual and collective imaginings of borders and zones that demarcate the European and non-European people, cultures, morality, and institutional practices. Of course this imaginary is materialized and translated into geographical and physically and legally designated borders through the institutions of citizenship.

The idea of Europe, based on the understanding of a common European identity, constitutes an imaginary of Europe that is exclusionary and elitist, as Gail Lewis (2006) notes. However, this fantasized unity is shot with a horror of division. The fantasy of Europe as a civilized continent as compared to the barbarians outside its borders is the founding moment of Orientalist thinking on which Europe's history has been based. The search for a common identity and shared values are laid out in relation to those who are culturally different.

In mapping the Europeanness of Europe, the assessment of the compatibility of different cultures and life styles becomes a central issue as it is against to those who are culturally (and religiously) different that the fantasized unity of Europe is imagined. What is believed to make Muslim people external to the essence of Europe is the attribution of an irreconcilable difference to the values, culture and life style of Europeans and Muslims. Their presence is feared to constitute a threat to the Europeanness of Europe. As Sherene Razack (2004) suggests, the notion of European superiority designates "the West as a place without culture but with values, thereby locating Westerners firmly within modernity and on the terrain of the universal, a logic that has been hegemonic since the enlightenment" (p. 148).

Such a model, where West is figured as having *values* and Muslims as having *culture* (Razack 2005, p. 6), ensures designating who is entitled to have membership in the European identity. In demarcating who is inside and who is outside of Europe, the old anxieties and fears about Islam and Muslims in Europe have re-surfaced. This anxiety is about "the presence of Muslim communities and Islamic traditions within the borders of Europe" (Asad 2002, p. 209). As Muslims and their cultures, approaches and ways of life are so far from the European culture that they cannot claim Europeanness. They do not share the civilizational essence with Europeans. Because of their lack of this civilizational essence, not all inhabitants of the European continent are "really" or "fully" European" (Asad 2002, p. 217). Muslims' co-habitation of the geography called Europe together with Europeans cannot be envisaged as their existence carries the potential risk of the annihilation of Europe by way of its Islamization. Hence the continual demarcation of the boundary between Islam and Western civilization.

When Islam prominently figures as the antitheses of the values of Western civilization, the nature of the cultural difference between the West and Islam is framed as a culture clash. In this age of war of cultures, while it is the principles of freedom and tolerance that are used to define Europe, it is the excessive weight attributed to the religious affiliation that comes to define the Muslims of Europe. As Aziz-al Azmeh (cited in Talhami 2004, p. 153) calls it, this ensures the over-Islamization of Muslims.

Islam remains external to Europe although it is a significant aspect of it. Not only its externality is emphasized by resorting to the purity and specificity of a specifically European identity, but also it is posed as an ever present danger within its borders, achieving the notoriety of being fanatic, irrational and extreme. It is the critique of Islamic fundamentalism that acts as bedrock for a renewed definition of European identity. The representation of Islam as inherently prone to fanaticism and fundamentalism enables the imagining of diverse nations and groups as a community united in European values. This functions as an insignia under which groups as diverse as feminists, Christian conservatives, social democrats, liberals, nationalists and the left can be united. The narrative of an Islamic threat to the fundamental European values generates two related claims regarding Muslim culture: while some underline the incompatibility of Muslim culture with European cultures, others denounce it for its inability to adjust to Europe's open and universalist civility (Henkel 2006, p. 5). The important aspect of this narrative, whether put as a result of the incompatibility of two cultures or the failure of existing Muslim groups to adjust to the European civilization and values, is that it becomes, in Henkel's (2006) words "an emblem that marks religious Muslims as fundamentalist and thus as categorically unfit for democratic society" (p. 5). This, in turn, is used to confirm the fundamental discrepancy and mutual exclusiveness between Islam and the West

Religious Component in the European Identity

The role of religion in shaping the boundary between Islam and the West (while one is a religious and the other is a geographical identification) can be traced to the historic relationship between Europe and Islam. Although Europe always designated the other as the religious one, ironically religion has historically been a powerful binding force in the emergence and consolidation of Europe as a unified identity. It is primarily the opposition to an imagined Islamic threat and the desire to block its advancement within Europe that gave and continues to give a sense of identity to Europeans.

With the Enlightenment that what became effective was no longer fundamentally a religious term of identification, but a secular one through which Europe was attributed the role of a universal civilizational project. However, the formation of secularized versions of the idea of Europe did not imply a radical break from the Christian world view. Despite the increasing secularization of the terms with which Europe came to identify itself, the Christian world-view remains as the dominant cultural motif by which European civilisation could identify itself.

Despite the prevailing modernist secularist narrative's distancing of the secular from the religious and its relegation of religion to the domain of the private, religion has never ceased to appear in the public space. The authority and force secularism held implied that the space religion occupied in the public domain is defined and regulated by this modernist narrative. It is thus not possible to imagine secularism without its other. The very act of separating religion from other domains, in particular from the domain of politics and culture, is a product of the coercive power of secularism. Indeed, it is not only the concept of the secular but the very distinction between the religious and the secular is produced by the latter (Asad 2002, p. 193). The production of religion by the very forces of secularist narrative does not imply that religion's mode of presence is simply enclosed by secularism, especially in the context of the geopolitics of today's globalized world. Perhaps this is the reason that lead many intellectuals to talk about the "return of the religious" or the "resurgence of the religion".

While Asad emphasizes how the religious itself is produced by secularism, Derrida (2002) alerts us to another problematic layer in the way in which the religious is delimited and separated from the political and other domains:

> To determine a war of religion *as such*, one would have to be certain that one can distinguish all the predicates of the religious.... One would have to dissociate the essential traits of religious as such from those that establish, for example, the concepts of ethics, of the juridical, of the political or of the economic. And yet, nothing is more problematic than such a dissociation. The fundamental concepts that often permit us to isolate or to pretend to isolate the political...remains religious or in any case theologico-political. (p. 63)

However untenable the convictions of the Western modernist secularist doctrine are and no matter how much we recognize the force of the return of the religious, it is not possible to suggest that the secularist narrative no longer holds the upper hand or has given up its pretensions to represent itself as the foundation of universally valid values. What we need to examine is the mode in which religion enters today's public sphere and the way this entrance is regulated and redefined. It is perhaps possible to talk about a new articulation of religion with the political and cultural. The field of politics, culture and religion are now interconnected with each other more powerfully than what secularism has tried to persuade us. It is therefore highly important that we stop seeing the "return of the religious" as a pre-modern remnant or as a regressive force.

However, whenever the prominence of religion in the contemporary world is evoked, it is almost automatically assumed that what is being referred to is the "resurgence of Islam" or the "fundamentalist" or "political Islam" (highly problematical notions). This assumption is indeed an indicator of the force of the secularist thesis which represents the West as exemplary in attaining modernity and managing to progressively distance its other realms from religion and thereby succeeding to relegate Christianity to the private sphere of individually held beliefs. Hence the chain of association goes: the resurrection of religion is nothing but a residue of pre-modernity and it is associated with Islam. This fantasized relation with the other (religion) goes hand in hand with the *displacement* of the increasing prominence of the religion in the Euro-American public space to other issues and concerns. But, we cannot understand the increasing importance religion has started occupying in the constitution of cultural identities in Euro-America by simply gathering information about church attendance or pointing to the manifestly religious metaphors or discourses. This will be a limited approach as the religious elements might not be appearing as religious *per se*, but displaced to and articulated with issues of culture and cultural identity. That is to say, the negotiation and articulation between religion and the constitution of cultural identity is much more complicated than the clear-cut delimitation and dissociation secularism has offered.

In the new fashioning of European identity, we might question whether the privileged position Christianity holds as a unifying theme in Europe is decisively over or not. Perhaps it is not the discourse of Christianity *per se* but the secularized versions and consequences of which are now displaced to "cultural difference" and "lifestyle" that are active in the constitution of a European identity. The religious component entrenched within the discourse of the European Union provides a discursive universe for rendering a new border between Europe and its Others. In other words, the identity that is called European is also very much based on religion and specifically on Christianity. The Christian values and heritage of Europe is either implicity and in many cases explicitly evoked to proclaim (promulgate) the externality of European Muslims to Europe.

Muslim Woman and the Headscarf Dispute

One of the controversial and suspect issues that has aggravated the relations between Muslim immigrants and Europeans has been the question of women's dress. The veil is one of the historically charged items through which the suspicion of Muslims and their culture's alienness to the essence of Europe has been debated and illustrated. It is seen as the sign of female oppression and more recently (particularly after *September 11*) an allegiance to a militant ideology. In a world where the relegation of religion to the realm of private life and personal choice is privileged as the sign of embracing secularism, the wearing of the veil comes to stand as a symbol of a dangerous faith, since religion needs to remain a matter of personal and private choice. As Talhami (2004) notes, "a veiled woman...is an open advertisement of a belief system that is still regarded as alien and we might add, threatening to the prevailing religions of the land" (p. 158). The prohibition brought to the wearing of the veil is legitimized on the grounds that it endorses women's subordinated status in Islam and therefore it is incongruous with gender equality. Hence, any expression of Muslim identity in the public realm is taken as a regressive tendency and the demands to cleanse the public sphere from the traces of this so-called religious element. This encapsulation of the veil to the domain of the private realm is rationalized with reference to the principle of secularism whose universal authority is deemed to be beyond any doubt.

It is the principles of freedom, respect and tolerance for private life that are offered as the distinguishing characteristics and essential difference of Europe from that of non-Europeans. The lack of secularization and modernity is what defines the non-European culture. However, as Gail Lewis (2006) notes, this claim for Europe's specificity is translated into a claim of socio-political advancement and superiority. This constitutes a symbolic universe which ensures for the West the position of universal standard of humanity. It is the freedom of Western women that is presented as illustrating the advanced gender order of the civilized West as opposed to the oppression of women in Islam, who is symbolized with the immigrant Muslim women in Europe. In other words, the imaginary of Europe and the fantasy of its gender order are constitutive of each other. Europe's gender order and its apparent equality and the imaginary of Europe as the land of freedom and tolerance are mutually implicated in each other (Gail Lewis). And similarly, the lack of secularization and modernity that is endemic to Muslim culture is the reason attributed to Muslim woman's disparaging status. The representation of the Western women as emblematic of the European civilization and its advanced status in turn shapes the nature of the relation between different femininities and the women of the East and West. It is with the aid of discourses of racial, ethnic and religious otherness that the oppositional positioning of Western and Muslim immigrant women is secured. It is not only the veil but also many other practices that are deemed to be Islamic are condemned as indicators of violence against women. Hence what is at stake is the benevolence to salvage Muslim women from their tribal and feudal culture. In other words, gender becomes the link that secures the strong relation established between the idea of culture clash and women's rights. In Sherene Razack's (2004) words, "naming violence against Muslim women is a principal weapon in the 'War on Terror'" (p. 130). It is the rising of Islam within the borders of Europe that enables this violence to flourish on European soil. So, women's rights are deemed to require extensive and close attention including the tightening of the borders of Europe. Hence the idea of a shared Europeannes is constituted through gender (Razacak 2005, p. 14). Sherene Razack vividly shows us how a strange nexus had emerged in contemporary geopolitics between Western feminism and racism (2005, p. 5). To quote her: "in an era of heightened interest in Muslim women's bodies, when the marines landing in Afghanistan can be considered in the press a feminist event, Western feminists on both ends of the political spectrum can find themselves making arguments that complement racist state agendas" (Razack 2004, p. 134). Here I am not suggesting that the complicity between a certain Western feminist gesture and racist/colonialist gesture are cohabiting the same universe for the first time in history. That kind of complicity has been endemic to Europe since colonialism. Women's bodies, as the site upon which the truth of culture is inscribed, has historically been a powerful metaphor in colonial discourse's justification of the protection of women from their own culture. What is unique and specific to today's mingling of racism and feminism is that it enables the exclusion and marking of millions of European Muslims as external to Europe by emphasizing their unassimilability and alienness to European culture and civilization.

However, the immigrant Muslim woman, whose oppression is symbolized in her headscarf/veil is almost a test case of European tolerance that is used as the defining characteristic of European civilization. As Gail Lewis (2006) notes, the non-alignment between self-defined womanhood of the other woman and the figure of the immigrant woman inscribed in the imaginary of Europe exposes the limits of liberal tolerance precisely because her visibility is to be erased. "The dilemma becomes one of whether the immigrant Muslim woman will be divested of her visibility through the process of assimilation, or is she to be allowed to demonstrate her difference and abjection and thus display the contamination in our midst…in which case Europe's civilizing mission is undermined. Either way, the figure of the immigrant woman both bespells and exposes the limits of Europe". (Lewis 2006, p. 95).

What About a New Europe: A Multicultural Europe?

Will the Muslim presence in Europe be allowed to transform what Europe is and what is has managed to be so far? To put the question differently, will Islamophobia win and hence the myth of Europe founded on Judeo-Christian values be reinforced and Muslims will remain external and alien in a Christocentric Europe, to use Gabriella Marranci's term (2004). Or will Europe be prepared to accept Muslims to become part of Europe and hence will there be a real multicultural contact between the cultures of Muslim and non-Muslim Europeans? Will Europe be capable of opening itself to the other so that Muslims will not be simply in Europe but will become European Muslims? Or are they going to continue to be treated as the enemies within? From Huntington's thesis of clash of civilizations, to Gisgard d"Estaing's decsription of Europe as a Christian club, to the Dutch media presenter Pim Fortuyn's book entitled *Against Islamization of Our Culture*, to Le Pen's presentation of himself as the last defense against Islamization of Europe and France, to the Somali immigrant Hirsi Ali's authentic narratives about the dangers of Islam for women, an Islamophobic culture is well and alive. The fear of Islam, that is, the fear of being invaded by Muslims and the resultant Islamization of Europe is indeed about the fear of multiculturalism. As Marranci (2004) suggests, Islamophobia is a phobia of multiculturalism.

In various occasions Derrida has addressed the question of Europe. The rethinking of Europe Derrida suggests can be understood with what he considers a "paleonym", an old word with a new meaning grafted onto it. With this we actively attend to a new Europe that is yet undetermined. Derrida (1992) suggests that Europe must go beyond jumping to the other heading and recall ourselves to the other of the heading. The attempt to redefine Europe or the grafting of the new Europe onto the old one requires that we attend to the European memory, its inheritance, its legacy by breaking its Western monopoly and control. So, if the European identity has to be rethought and renewed differently from the previous European programs, the "today" of Europe has to be thought differently. Derrida suggests that if the "today" of Europe is going to be questioned, altered and thought differently, then Europe will have to distance itself from the assumption that today's Europe can refer to a single, undivided experience of the present. That is, the present Europe can be thought anew only when its presence to itself is regarded as not entirely present to itself. European identity needs to be understood as inhabited by its yesterday and tomorrow. Derrida warns us that the task of thinking today's Europe demands that we ask the question of Europe in a new way. But the redefinition of European identity cannot be a search for a completely new Europe beyond all the programs of Eurocentrism and anti-Eurocentrism. This redefinition requires the opening of Europe to Otherness or responsibility to the other. This new Europe will emerge precisely in not closing itself off in its own identity but by advancing itself toward what it is not.

Rejecting an easy or programmatic solution of either complete unification or total dispersion, Derrida underlines the necessity of working with and from the Enlightenment values of liberal democracy while at the same time underlying that these values are never enough to ensure respect for the other. Rather, we should take them as that which can never be completely taken for granted. The duty, the responsibility that comes with the experience of this aporia dictates, for Derrida (1992), the "opening of Europe, opening it onto that which is not, never was and never will be Europe" (p. 77) as well as "welcoming foreigners in order not only to integrate them, but recognize and accept their alterity" (p. 77).

It is clear that Derrida's suggestion to rethink the "today" of Europe by thinking its past and tomorrow is about bringing the memory of colonialism back into picture. I would like to suggest that any gesture that reminds how European memory has colonialism inscribed in it has to address how the rethinking of colonialism has been accompanied at the same time with its delinking from racism. Today, this serves Europe not only to assert its purity in the wake of its growing Muslim population but also reinstitute Europe as the home of whiteness and Christianity which in turn enables the Europeans "to define themselves over and against Muslims from North Africa and the Middle East" (Goldberg 2006, p. 353) once more.

In addressing the importance of the specific way in which colonialism can be brought as part of the European memory, I suggest that as long as colonialism is thought as something that happened outside of Europe, in places other than Europe, then colonialism is effaced as part of Europe's history. By this way the legacy of colonialism is not recognized as an integral part of Europe, but, in Theo Goldberg's (2006) formulation, "dissipates if not disappears" (p. 336). The future determination of European identity must include the struggles of those people subjugated by European colonialism who are now the millions of laborers living and working in Europe.

If we are to think Europe's yesterday it is essential to think about the Holocaust and to think how the tomorrow necessitates about thinking the Mussulmans of Europe. To fully address the legacy of colonialism, that is to address how the modern and contemporary Europe has been made by its colonial history and how colonialism did not take place outside of Europe and its targets were nor far removed from European soil is to address today the very living embodiment of this legacy, that is, the Moroccans in Belgium and the Netherlands, Algerians in France, Turks in Germany, Pakistanis and Bangladeshis in Britain, that is the Mussulmans of the camps.

Theo Goldberg (2006) directs our attention to the subtle means by which the colonial legacy has been denied. The privileging of anti-semitism in Europe functions as an alibi in the radical delinking of the intellectual and political histories of colonialism and racism. He points to how European racial denial is related to the desire of the race to implode and erase itself" (p. 334). However, despite this impossible wish for the evaporation of the racial, it has always lingered, always, already returned and haunting, but buried and silenced (p. 334). Goldberg asks a simple question: why has it been very difficult to raise issues of race and racism in the European context? The answer lies in the Holocaust being the defining event or the mark par excellence of race and racially inscribed history (p. 336). With Holocaust, Europe managed to reduce the racial to the Jewish question and hence Holocaust functioned as the instance of the evaporation of the question of the racial and racism in Europe. This privileging instance enabled Europe to ask itself the ethico-political question of racism in a peculiar way: how did we manage to do it people who are (pretty much) like us, to those who were among us and indeed those who are us? The very question that addresses the impossibility of doing it to those who are similar, for Goldberg, is the condition for making it possible to imagine doing it to people who are different. If we attempted the annihilation of difference among us, then it becomes easier to do it to those who are at a distance, to those who are neither among us nor part of us or can ever be part of us. The very assertion of universal here (we were the same) requires the sacrifice of the different. However, in remembering Holocaust, it is important that we must remember that it was not only the Jews but also the Gypsies, gays, lesbians, disabled, communist and political progressives who were targeted. It was not solely about the Jewish experience in Europe. However, the natives belonged to other lands and therefore alien and foreign. Jews, Gypsies, gays were part of us. By accepting anti-semitism as the sum of Europe's only experience of racist past, a strong alibi is constituted. But we must also remember that, the Holocaust had its foreign element as well. As Agamben notes, the foreigner in the camp was the name for those Jews that had left life but had not yet given in to death. They were called Mussulman. The Mussulman existed alongside death, just prior to death, lacking dignity and self-control. Goldberg says, Mussulmans in the camp, are now the Muslims in Europe: the foreigners, unwanteds and untouchables within. The Mussulman within us now is the fanatic, fundamentalist Muslim men who is prone to violence, war, militancy, terrorism. Someone who belongs to his traditions vehemently, which is displayed in the terrible oppression the Muslim women go through, which is symbolized in the headscarf that they are forced to put on. They are here in Europe but don't really or fully belong there. Their presence is temporary. Perhaps they are born in there but are not part of Europe.

Race is not about false views about biology or skin colour. Nor is it simply about religion. Race is the invisible border designating who belongs or does not belong. In asserting the Europeanization of Europe, Europe is designated as the place of and for Europeans. Historically this Europe presumes Europeans to be white and Christian. People of different colour and religion in Europe might be in Europe but they are not European nor can they become fully or properly European or belong there. Europeans have come once more to define themselves over and against Muslims (Goldberg 2006, p. 353). Nor the European racism is about the racially perceived foreigners. It is about identifying the foreign, keeping the foreign as foreign and making sure that those racially, culturally and religiously non-European remain forever as foreign. As Goldberg (2006) states "the backing off from Turkish membership of the European Union is the latest case in point. No matter how seemingly reformed and romancing democracy is, a nation identified as overwhelmingly Islamic will conjure up anxieties for those taking their values, their invented continental civilization and civilities at root Christian" (p. 354). Hence borders in Europe are constituted racially. Etienne Balibar (2004), notes that alongside with the formation of "European citizenship" a European apartheid is being formed (p. 9 & 121), one that could block the construction of a democratic European community. The construction of a European apartheid is the other face of the development of the European Union in its pursuit of a new identity. Such a situation favors the development of forms of specifically European racism whose defining characteristics is its displacement from skin colour to issues of cultural difference.

References

Asad, Talal. (2002). Muslims and European identity: Can Europe represent Islam? In Anthony Pagden (Ed.) *The idea of Europe: From antiquity to the European Union* (pp. 209-228). Cambridge: Cambridge University Press.

Balibar, Etienne. (2004). *We, the people of Europe?: Reflections on transnational citizenship* (J. Swenson, Trans.). Princeton and Oxford: Princeton University Press.

Derrida, Jacques. (1992). *The other heading: Reflections on today's Europe* (P. A. Brault and M. B. Naas, Trans.). Bloomington and Indianapolis: Indiana University Press.

Derrida, Jacques. (2002). Faith and knowledge: The two sources of "religion" at the limits of reason alone. In Gil Anidjar (Ed.), *Acts of Religion* (pp. 42-101). New York: Routledge.

Goldberg, David Theo. (2006). Racial Europeanization. *Ethnic and Racial Studies*, 29(2) March, 331-364.

Henkel, Heiko. (2006). The journalists of *Jyllands-Posten* are a bunch of reactionary provocateurs. *Radical Philosophy, 137,* May/June, 2-7.

Lewis, Gail. (2006). Imaginaries of Europe: Technologies of gender, economics of power. *European Journal of Women's Studies, 13(2),* 87-102.

Marranci, Gabriella. (2004). Multiculturalism, Islam and the clash of civilizations theory: Rethinking Islamophobia. *Culture and Religion, 5(1),* 105-117.

Razack, Sherene. (2004). Imperilled Muslim women, dangerous Muslim men and civilized Europeans: Legal and social responses to forced marriages. *Feminist Legal Studies, 12,* 129-174.

Razack, Sherene. (2005). Geopolitics, culture clash and gender after 911. *Social Justice, 32(4),* 11-31.

Talhami, Chada Hashem. (2004). European, Muslim and female. *Middle East Policy,* XI(2), Summer, 152-168.

Peace Journalism: Between advocacy journalism and constructive conflict coverage

Wilhelm Kempf
University of Konstanz
Department of Psychology
PeaceResearchKN@aol.com

1. Journalism or Public Relations?

The term "Peace Journalism" combines two elements that are difficult to harmonize: "Peace" and "Journalism."

Journalism is a form of public communication that is subject to professional norms. Because of these norms it differs from other types of public communication, for example, Public Relations.

The professional norms of good journalism include in particular the following: truthfulness, objectivity, neutrality and detachment. For Public Relations these norms are at best irrelevant. The only thing that matters is success. And this success is measured in terms of achieving specific communication aims which are "externally defined by a client, host organization or particular groups of stakeholders" (Hanitzsch, 2007, p. 2). Typical aims are, e.g., to convince the public of the attractiveness of a product, of the justice of one's own political goals or also of the wrongfulness of a political opponent.

Good Journalism differs from Public Relations precisely because it does not aim to influence the public, but rather pursues only the goal of reporting truthfully about reality. As David Loyn (2003), a BBC correspondent and prominent critic of Peace Journalism, has maintained: "Our task is always to seek to find out what is going on, not carrying any other baggage" (n. p.).

Good Journalism has just one aim: to represent reality accurately. The other characteristics of good journalism—objectivity, neutrality and detachment—are means to reach this aim (Loyn, 2007).

Peace Journalism combines journalism with peace as an external aim. It understands itself as "a normative mode of responsible and conscientious media coverage of conflict <u>that aims at</u> contributing to peacemaking, peacekeeping, and changing the attitudes of media owners, advertisers, professionals, and audiences towards war and peace" (Shinar, 2007).

A goal conflict arises out of this that arouses concern that Peace Journalism "could compromise the integrity of journalists and confuse their role as neutral disseminators of facts" (Loyn, 2003).

This concern is all the more justified because some supporters of Peace Journalism seem all too inclined to underrate values like objectivity, neutrality and detachment (e.g., Mc Goldrick, 2006; Peleg, 2007) and to lump Peace Journalism together with other terms (e.g., Shinar, 2007) "that refer to advocacy models of reporting—such as the 'journalism of attachment' (Bell, 1997), 'victim journalism' (Hume, 1997), 'justice journalism' (Messman, 2001), and 'engaged journalism' (Lynch, 2003)." According to Lynch & McGoldrick (2005), "Peace Journalism is when editors and reporters make choices—of what stories to report, and how to report them."

The two together, disregarding the tools of good journalism and understanding peace journalism as a form of advocacy journalism, create a dangerous mix which is prone to abuse the noble goal of peace as a legitimation for biased coverage. Journalism of this kind "will not stand neutrally between good and evil, right and wrong, the victim and the oppressor" (Bell, 1997, 8). Where this can ultimately lead has been shown in a fateful manner by the journalism of attachment.

When journalists go on a "crusade against conventional reporting" (Peleg, 2007), they all too easily become recruits for the propaganda war (Kempf, 2003). But Peace Propaganda is nothing other than propaganda either, and a Peace Journalism that crosses the border to propaganda does not deserve to bear the name of journalism. According to a proposal by Thomas Hanitzsch (2007), it ought to be banished to the domain of Public Relations.

A Peace Journalism that deserves the name is only conceivable as good journalism and requires more than just good will and a moral impetus.

2. Journalistic Responsibility

Impartiality and objectivity are indispensable tools of good journalism, and David Loyn is right when he concludes that the reporter's tools need to be sharpened, not altered. "Rather than disregard the concept, it is more fruitful to consider the structures that support better or worse practice" Loyn, 2007, n. p.).

As soon as we call for better practice, however, it turns out that truth or truthfulness are not values in themselves. The striving for truth in particular meets an obvious practical need. Truthfulness makes it possible to add to our knowledge stock the experiences of others as guides for our own actions. Since we draw on them all the time, reliance on the assertions of others is an indispensable element of our own everyday life practice. That is, there is a justified interest in being sure that only statements will be made that can be defended in every case (and not just to uncritical or uninformed opponents) (cf. Kambartel, 1968).

This applies in particular to the assertions of journalism, and even more so to conflict journalism. War and peace are events of existential significance that no one can disregard.

When Jörg Becker (2002) maintains that the media have a political obligation to participate in and stand up for peace of their own accord, this is not just the opinion of a German political scientist, but rather the consensus of the legal framework and codes of conduct established by international and national law, trade unions and responsible media institutions.

Art. 3 of the 1978 UNESCO Media Declaration, for instance, states that, "the mass media have an important contribution to make to the strengthening of peace and international understanding and in countering racialism, apartheid and incitement to war" (UNESCO, 1979, p. 102). Also the numerous ethical codes for journalists that apply in almost all the countries of the world give expression to similar self-imposed obligations and contain the obligation to act for peace and against any kind of war propaganda (cf. Becker, 2004).

David Loyn (2007) also honors these codes of conduct for providing a framework which enables journalists to engage in robust skeptical inquiry, but also to comply with libel laws and remain on the right side of civilized discourse.

Even if he fears that "highly prescriptive rules might inhibit good journalism," Loyn has thereby approached a perspective that sees no insurmountable conflicts between objectivity and normativity. And with the insight that "a side-effect of my reporting may be that it makes conflict resolution harder or easier," Loyn comes closer to peace journalism than he thinks.

Journalists are responsible for the way, for <u>how</u> they report; and even the creation of "opportunities for society at large to consider and to value non-violent responses to conflict," as called for by Lynch & McGoldrick (as quoted in McGoldrick 2006, p. 4), is not an external goal imposed on journalism from outside. The obligation to create these opportunities results directly from the role assigned to journalism in democratic societies.

In that Loyn regards the above-named "side-effects" of journalistic work as mere 'collateral damage' which is to be investigated later, "after our reporting" (Loyn, 2007), he thereby not only distances himself from the concept of – however understood – peace journalism, but rather also attacks the model of good journalism that he intends to defend against it.

Of course professional journalists do not set out to reduce conflict. They seek to present accurate and impartial news coverage. But it is often through good reporting that conflict is reduced (Howard, 2003), and what is demanded is no more than responsible journalism. Without responsibility, good journalism is inconceivable.

Thus we replace David Loyn's (2007) provocative dichotomy of "good journalism <u>or</u> peace journalism" with the normative formula "good journalism = responsible journalism = peace journalism."

3. War Discourse vs. Peace Discourse

Implying that both good journalism and peace journalism need a more sophisticated approach, this formula is no less provocative. Indeed, the idea behind this formula has inspired the work of generations of media researchers and journalists who have criticized the media for falling into the propaganda trap.

David Loyn has a point when he argues that journalistic practices which commit themselves to the adoption of particular perspectives are bound to be less objective than others. But the proximity of mainstream conflict coverage and war propaganda shows that it is not peace journalism which is tied to the adoption of a particular perspective, but on the contrary: the traditional tools of journalism are not sufficient to guarantee good journalism. While "reporters live in a social context and share a language and certain assumptions with their audience" (Loyn, 2007, p. 5), "propaganda sets out precisely to penetrate and transform shared language and assumptions" (Lynch, 2007, p. 3).

While in principle conflict is open to interpretation as either a competitive (win-lose) or a cooperative (win-win) process (Deutsch, 1973), conventional war discourse, as initiated by political and military elites and adopted by mainstream journalism and its public, is all about the questions: "Who is the aggressor?" and "How can he be stopped?"

Whether deliberately or not, by adopting this particular perspective, societal discourse reduces conflict to a zero-sum game and becomes a motor of conflict escalation (Kempf, 2003).

Only if it goes beyond such win-lose scenarios can journalism contribute to the transformation of war discourse into a more constructive form of discourse which is guided by questions like: "What is the problem?" and "How can it be resolved?" Broadening the perspective on conflict and opening it to peaceful alternatives, therefore, is the very essence of de-escalation oriented conflict coverage, which I have suggested as a first step of peace journalism (cf. Kempf, 2003).

This is neither a highly prescriptive rule which might inhibit good journalism, nor does it imply that we should adopt a particular perspective. On the contrary, it is a rule which only forbids the unacceptable. It is a rule which enjoins journalists to not limit their perspective to that of the war-making elites. It is a rule which prohibits volunteering on the propaganda front.

If this is how we understand it, peace journalism is not an antipode, but rather a necessary prerequisite of good journalism.

If this is what we aim at, we must make clear, however, that our understanding of peace journalism is completely different from the way some of its adherents and critics have interpreted Galtung's demand that journalists should become active participants, playing a part in the complex 'cat's cradle' that makes up a conflict.

David Loyn (2007) is right when he states that reporting and peacemaking are different roles, and that peacemaking is simply not the journalist's role. In addition, it cannot be the function of journalism to mediate between conflict parties, to sit down at a negotiating table with them and moderate their disputes (Kempf & Jaeger, 2005).

Journalism and the media do, however, play an essential role in the societal construction of reality that can be fulfilled in different ways: Through the type of news coverage chosen they can give an impetus either to the escalation or to the de-escalation of conflicts.

So viewed, journalism also does not have to be first an active participant playing a part in the complex 'cat's cradle' that makes up a conflict. It already is and always will be. What peace journalism demands of it is merely to assume responsibility for how it fulfills this role.

4. New Wine in Old Bottles?

Already Gjelten (2001) pointed out that there is no necessity for journalists to place their professional abilities in the service of either conflict resolution or prevention: They must simply do their work better – in the frame of the traditional standards of their profession. But if peace journalism is nothing other than good journalism, isn't this just old wine in new bottles, as Thomas Hanitzsch (2007) has criticized? No, it is not. For the fulfillment of these standards presupposes specific conflict competencies, and whether journalists possess or acquire these competencies should not be left to chance (Kempf & Jaeger, 2005).

To study the conditions and possibilities under which journalists can actually perform their work better, even in war and crisis situations, and to provide the necessary competencies: this is how I understand the program of peace journalism.

David Loyn (2007) also claims that journalists need methods for a more complex understanding of context and would be more likely to be accurate and impartial if they, and their editors, had an understanding of their own psychology and blind spots, and of the psychology of the news story and its actors.

Journalists are themselves members of society and are subject not only to certain institutional pressures (Bläsi, 2006), but also to the same social-psychological mechanisms as other people, particularly to the competitive misperceptions (Deutsch, 1973) which, so to speak, adjust automatically with their own involvement in escalating conflict (Kempf, 2002, KEMPF 2003).

Although Thomas Hanitzsch (2007) is right in claiming that there are manifold nuances in the media, it cannot be ignored that typical mainstream coverage reduces conflicts to force and violence. It contains little knowledge of the dynamics of conflict and no ideas for alternatives to violence. Even journalists who feel committed to traditional standards of truth and objectivity tend to paint pictures in black and white, often reducing conflicts to simple antagonisms in order to make news stories more exciting, and the conflict more understandable for their public.

Intractable conflicts are demanding, stressful, painful, exhausting and costly in both human and material terms. This requires that societal members develop conditions to facilitate successful coping. One aspect of the conditions provided by war culture is a psychological infrastructure that consists, for example, of commitment to one's own side and its leadership, the maintenance of its objectives, high motivation to contribute, perseverance and readiness for personal sacrifice (Bar-Tal, 1998).

All these mechanisms lend plausibility to an escalation-prone misrepresentation of reality which is typical of mainstream conflict coverage and requires special efforts to overcome.

Thomas Hanitzsch (2004a) also agrees: "What we need is more quality in journalism" (p. 205). Nothing needs to be added to this other than that it is precisely in conflict coverage that this quality does not establish itself on its own. Professional norms are necessary, but not sufficient to guarantee good journalism and a more constructive mode of conflict coverage (Shinar, 2007). In order to produce good journalism, journalists need knowledge, competencies and qualifications that go beyond traditional journalistic training and enable them to counteract the escalation-prone misperceptions of reality I mentioned before.

5. Misrepresentation of Reality?

While truthfulness is a shared goal which unites most adherents (e.g., Lynch, 2007) and critics (e.g., Loyn, 2007) of peace journalism, it has been challenged by Thomas Hanitzsch (2007), who insists that any objections to a 'media-biased reality' miss the point.

Hanitsch's arguments are inconsistent and contradictory, however. While he originally held that the version of reality constructed by war reporting is as compatible with classical standards of truth as countless other versions (Hanitzsch, 2004b, 185), he now draws on Schudson (2003) and claims that "every representation of the world is inevitably biased" (Hanitzsch, 2007, p. 5).

The only thing consistent in Hanitzsch's arguments is that he uses the social construction of reality as grounds to dispute the right to any critique of the media.

But can subjective realities – and particularly the one version of reality which is constructed by war reporting – really not be criticized? Can we really not speak meaningfully of misrepresenting reality?

As I have shown elsewhere (Kempf, 2006a), Hanitzsch's argumentation is based on a large number of methodological errors: It is based on an inadequate and logically incorrect understanding of truth and reality, and on a lack of differentiation between facts and meanings, between truth and beliefs, and between objective and subjective realities.

In particular, it is wrong to label the reality constructed by the media as true or false per se. The media construction of reality is a matter of meaning-making, and a dispute about its adequacy can only be a dispute which relates it to something outside itself: the facts upon which it rests, the goals it serves and/or the rules it follows.

Only the first of these criteria, the factual basis of media-constructed reality, has to do with truthfulness and objectivity. And as far as facts are concerned, Hanitzsch (2007) is right that media accounts of the facts can be substantiated in everyday journalism only through their coherence with other facts, that is, with what we already know. But this is just as little a counter-argument as the circumstance that we base our constructions of reality on a factual foundation which always remains incomplete.

To criticize the media because they do not possess pure and complete truth would be quite naïve. But this is not the point when Galtung (2002) criticizes the media for reducing conflict to a zero-sum game, or when Jake Lynch (2007) asserts that journalism needs some practical way to analyze and address its own role in creating realities, etc.

What peace journalism criticizes about the media is, to be sure, that specific facts are systematically concealed. But even here the critique is not primarily of the facts themselves, but rather of the escalation potential that unfolds from ascribing meanings that translate the mix of reported and suppressed facts into a comprehensible narrative.

Conflict is an interactive process, and like all human actions it involves (at least) three different kinds of reality. There is one party's subjective reality and the subjective reality of an opponent. While both these realities can only be assessed from within the respective party's perspective, the third kind of reality can only be assessed from an external perspective and shows how subjective realities interact with each other.

In order to evaluate the escalation or de-escalation potential of the conflict parties' reality constructions, an external perspective is needed. And from this external perspective, we may well criticize some reality constructions as biased toward promoting conflict and appreciate others as more balanced and open-minded.

When Thomas Hanitzsch (2007) claims that such an external perspective is neither needed nor possible, he is thereby not just throwing overboard the claim to deliver a balanced and comprehensive account of conflict. He is also depriving editors of any basis upon which they could fulfill their role to make a judgement without siding with one particular version of reality (Loyn, 2007). Not just peace journalism, but any type of good journalism is thereby rejected.

6. Naive and Illusory?

In order to support his rejection, Hanitzsch (2007) imputes to peace journalism an "overly individualistic and voluntaristic perspective, which seems to suggest that journalists only need to change their attitudes and behaviors, and as a result they will produce conflict coverage that embraces the values of peace journalism" (p. 5).

There are in fact many structural constraints which shape and limit the work of journalists: constant time pressure, chronic lack of space, limited budget, censorship and disinformation, editorial staff expectations, the needs of the public, the laws of the market, etc. On the basis of a systematic analysis of the process of producing conflict coverage and a great number of expert interviews with experienced conflict reporters from radio, television and the print media, Burkhard Bläsi (2004, 2005, 2006) has dealt in great detail with this and studied the suitability of peace journalistic models for practice. Constructive conflict coverage proves accordingly to have future prospects that can, however, only gain broader influence through permanent changes in specific journalistic routines, attitudes and competencies.

Robert Hackett (2006) has also thought critically about the prospects of realizing the principles of peace journalism in practice. His theoretical study considers three conceptual frameworks for analyzing the relationship between journalism and other relations and institutions of power in order to identify the tasks, challenges and potential strategies for the peace journalism movement: Herman & Chomsky's (1988) propaganda model, Shoemaker & Reese's (1996) hierarchy of influences model and Pierre Bourdieu's (1998) notion of journalism as a field. According to Hackett's analysis, the barriers to peace journalism include the difficulties of constructing 'peace' as a compelling narrative, the national basis (and biases) of much of the world's news media and their publics, the ideological and structural links between media corporations and states, and the embeddedness of dominant media and states in relations of inequality. Nonetheless, he concludes that there are many niches in the system where it is possible to practice and find a constituency for different and experimental forms of journalism.

Peace journalism is not as naïve as Hanitzsch assumes. But Hanitzsch (2007) has taken account neither of the work of Bläsi and Hackett nor of the basic research on the acceptance and effects of peace journalism.

One of his chief arguments is that "the mainstream media can ill afford to abandon news values, as this would jeopardize the economic base on which they are forced to operate" (p. 5). This is a serious argument, and peace journalistic basic research has been working on this already for some time – not only theoretically, but also with a range of empirical and experimental studies. Even if a final assessment can still not be made, it appears that Hanitzsch's recommendation of holding to traditional news factors is based, on the one side, on an inaccurate portrayal of news factors as absolute and, on the other side, on a naturalistic error.

Recent studies of news coverage on the Middle East conflict during the Israeli-Palestinian peace process (Annabring, 2000; Kempf, 2003) and of German press coverage of France after the Second World War (Jaeger, 2003, 2004, 2005) have shown that news factors are not rigid entities, but rather are dealt with by the media in quite flexible ways.

Beyond this, it is logically inadmissible to infer from the way media news coverage is that this is what the media public wants. Even if one thinks that news factors are "selection structures of public communication whose scope includes not only journalism, but also its public" (Hanitzsch, 2004b, 188), this cannot obscure the fact that news factors theory was only derived from the content analytic study of media news coverage and not, for example, from a study of public preferences.

Recent studies show, however, that the public is much less oriented in its preferences to news factors like simplification, negativism and personalization than is commonly assumed. Thus Wolling (2002) found that information quality is an essential factor for the evaluation of news coverage programs, and as Eilders (1997) has shown, the better they are already informed, the less readers orient themselves to traditional news factors.

As experimental studies have demonstrated (Bläsi, Jaeger, Kempf & Spohrs, 2005; Jackson, 2006; Kempf, 2005, 2006b; Möckel, 2007; Schaefer, 2006; Sparr, 2004, Spohrs, 2006), traditional escalation-oriented conflict coverage is in fact not better suited to awakening reader interest, but rather de-escalation oriented peace journalism has the same potential. De-escalation oriented coverage is not only perceived by recipients as more balanced, it also awakens greater interest in further information.

Not only the media, but also the public are much more flexible than news factors theory claims, and peace journalism does have a public. Recipients are also more competent and more interested in differentiated conflict representation than is commonly assumed.

7. Conclusions

In conclusion, it can be maintained that there are definite chances for the practical implementation of the peace journalistic program, and it can make an urgently needed contribution to assuring the quality of conflict and crisis journalism. That in the foreseeable future peace journalism will remain in a minority position need not represent an obstacle. Even from this position it can contribute to structuring media discourse on conflicts in a more transparent and balanced way and to protecting conflict coverage from the fateful propaganda traps into which traditional war reporting seems to be continually falling (Jaeger, 2002).

As preconditions for this I see only two things: First, there is a need for a further intensification of basic peace journalistic research and the critical examination of so many myths which journalism shares with media studies. News factors and public preferences are, for one thing, two different things which must be kept separate; good journalism is not a description of the current state of conflict coverage, but is, in contrast, only practiced by relatively few journalists, and the professional norms and tools of journalism are, of course, indispensable, but not sufficient to ensure good journalism.

Second, however, caution is imperative, so that the critique of the journalistic mainstream does not throw the baby out with the bath-water. Thus it is not only appropriate, but also urgently necessary to question the conventional journalistic understanding of objectivity (see McGoldrick, 2006), to free it of its inadequacies and constructively further develop it. To radically turn away from the call for objectivity, as suggested by Lynch & McGoldrick (2005) or Hackett (2006), not only endangers the acceptance of the peace journalistic project in the journalistic community, however, but also twists peace journalism into a form of advocacy journalism, which leads directly to PR and propaganda and can squander the trust bonus which its recipients grant to peace journalism.

References

Annabring, U. (2000). *Protagonisten und Konfliktkonstellationen im israelisch-palästinensischen Friedensprozeß*. Universität Konstanz: Psychol. Diplomarbeit.

Bar-Tal, D. (1998). Societal beliefs in times of intractable conflict: The Israeli case', *International Journal of Conflict Management 9(1)*, 22–50.

Becker, J. (2002). Medien im Krieg. In Albrecht, U., Becker, J. (Eds.), *Medien zwischen Krieg und Frieden*. Baden-Baden: Nomos, 13-26.

Becker, J. (2004). Contributions by the media to crisis prevention and conflict settlement. *Conflict & Communication Online*, 3/1+2.

Bell, M. (1997). TV News: how far should we go? *British Journalism Review 8(1)*, 7–16.

Bläsi, B. (2004). Peace journalism and the news production process. *Conflict & Communication Online*, 3/1+2.

Bläsi, B. (2005). Produktionsbedingungen konstruktiver Konfliktberichterstattung. In: Projektgruppe Friedensforschung Konstanz (Ed.), *Nachrichtenmedien als Mediatoren von Peace-Building, Demokratisierung und Versöhnung in Nachkriegsgesellschaften* (pp. 257-276). Berlin: Regener.

Bläsi, B. (2006). *Keine Zeit, kein Geld, kein Interesse ...? Konstruktive Konfliktberichterstattung zwischen Anspruch und medialer Wirklichkeit.* Berlin: Regener.

Bläsi, B., Jaeger, S., Kempf, W., Spohrs, M. (2005). Glaubwürdigkeit und Attraktivität von eskalations- und deeskalationsorientierten Nachrichtentexten. In Projektgruppe Friedensforschung Konstanz (Ed). *Nachrichtenmedien als Mediatoren von Peace-Building, Demokratisierung und Versöhnung in Nachkriegsgesellschaften* (pp. 203-234). Berlin: Regener.

Bourdieu, P. (1998). *On television.* New York: New Press.

Deutsch, M. (1973). *The resolution of conflict.* New Haven: Yale University Press.

Eilders, C. (1997). *Nachrichtenfaktoren und Rezeption. Eine empirische Analyse zur Auswahl und Verarbeitung politischer Information.* Opladen: Westdeutscher Verlag.

Galtung, J. (2002). Peace journalism – A challenge. In: Kempf, W., Luostarinen, H. (Eds.), *Journalism and the New World Order.* Vol. II. Studying War and the Media, (pp. 259-272). Göteborg: Nordicom.

Gjelten, T. (2001). Finding the right "Moral Attitude": Journalists can best serve victims by balancing humanity and professionalism. *Media Studies Journal, 15(1)*, 72-76.

Hackett, R.A. (2006). Is peace journalism possible? Three frameworks for assessing structure and agency in news media. *Conflict & Communication Online*, 5/2.

Hanitzsch, Th. (2004a). The peace journalism problem. In Hanitzsch, T., Löffelholz, M., Mustamu, R. (Eds.), *Agents of peace. Public Communication and Conflict Resolution in an Asian Setting*, (pp. 185-209). Bonn: Friedrich Ebert Stiftung.

Hanitzsch, Th. (2004b). Journalisten zwischen Friedensdienst und Kampfeinsatz. In Löffelholz, M. (Ed.), *Krieg als Medienereignis II. Krisenkommunikation im 21. Jahrhundert* (pp. 169-193). Wiesbadsen: Verlag für Sozialwissenschaften.

Hanitzsch, Th. (2007). Situating Peace Journalism in Journalism Studies: a critical appraisal. *Conflict & Communication Online*, 6/2.

Herman, E.S., Chomsky, N. (1988). *Manufacturing consent: The political economy of the mass media.* New York: Pantheon Books.

Howard, R. (2003). *Conflict sensitive journalism.* Copenhagen: International Media Support & Institute for Media Policy & Civil Society.

Hume, M. (1997). *Whose war is it anyway? The dangers of the journalism of attachment.* LM Special, InformInc.

Jackson, L.E. (2006). *Moral disengagement. How media use can affect the support of war.* Berlin: VDM Verlag

Jaeger, S., 2002. Compatibility of peace and news media. *Communicator, 37/1*, 27-30.

Jaeger, S. (2003). Die deutsche Zeitungsberichterstattung über Frankreich nach dem zweiten Weltkrieg - Beiträge zur Aussöhnung. *Conflict & Communication Online*, 2/2.

Jaeger, S. (2004). The German press coverage on France after World War II. *Conflict & Communication Online*, 3/1-2.

Jaeger, S. (2005). Themenauswahl in der Nachkriegsberichterstattung. In Projektgruppe Friedensforschung Konstanz (Ed). *Nachrichtenmedien als Mediatoren von Peace-Building, Demokratisierung und Versöhnung in Nachkriegsgesellschaften* (pp. 51-80). Berlin: Regener.

Kambartel, F. (1968). Was ist Logik? In Kambartel, F. *Theorie und Begründung* (pp. 95-110). Frankfurt/Main: Suhrkamp.

Kempf, W. (2002). Conflict coverage and conflict escalation. In: Kempf, W., Luostarinen, H. (Eds.). *Journalism and the New World Order.* Volume II: Studying war and the media (pp. 59-72). Göteborg: Nordicom.

Kempf, W. (2003). *Constructive conflict coverage. A social psychological approach.* Edited by the Austrian Study Center for Peace and Conflict Resolution. Berlin: Regener.

Kempf, W. (2005). Two experiments focusing on de-escalation oriented coverage of post-war conflicts. *Conflict & Communication Online*, 4(2).

Kempf, W. (2006a). Social constructionism and its implications for critical media studies. *Conflict & Communication Online*, 5/1.

Kempf, W. (2006b). Acceptance and impact of de-escalation-oriented conflict coverage. Diskussionsbeiträge der Projektgruppe Friedensforschung Konstanz, Nr. 60. Berlin: Verlag Irena Regener.

Kempf, W., Jaeger, S. (2005). Konstruktive Nachkriegsberichterstattung - Ein Forschungsbericht. Diskussionsbeiträge der Projektgruppe Friedensforschung Konstanz, Nr. 58. Berlin: Verlag Irena Regener.

Loyn, D. (2003). Witnessing the truth. openDemocracy.net, 20 February, URL: http://www.opendemocracy.net/articles/ViewPopUpArticle.jsp?id=2&articleId=993.

Loyn, D. (2007). Good journalism or peace journalism? *Conflict & Communication Online*, 6/2.

Lynch, J. (2003). "Journalists need to think: a reply to David Loyn" in Open Democracy Journalism & War Debate, www.opendemocracy.net/media-journalismwar/article_1037.jsp

Lynch, J. & McGoldrick, A. (2005). *Peace journalism*. Stroud, UK: Hawthorn Press.

McGoldrick, A. (2006). War journalism and "objectivity". *Conflict & Communication Online*, 5/2.

Messman, T. (2001). Justice journalism: Journalist as agent of social change. *Media File*, 20 (4), autumn. http://www.media-alliance.org/mediafile/20-4/justice.html

Möckel, J. (2007). News from the Holy Land - Akzeptanz und Wirkung von Konfliktberichterstattung im Fernsehen. Universität Konstanz: Psychol. Diplomarbeit.

Peleg, S. (2007). In defense of peace journalism: A rejoinder. *Conflict & Communication Online*, 6/2.

Schaefer, C.D. (2006). The effects of escalation vs. de-escalation-orientated conflict coverage on the evaluation of military measures. *Conflict & Communication Online*, 5/1.

Schudson, M. 2003. *The sociology of news*. New York: W. W. Norton.

Shinar. D. (2007). Epilogue: Peace journalism – The state of the art. *Conflict & Communication Online*, 6/1.

Shoemaker, P., Reese, S. D. (1996[2]). *Mediating the message: Theories of influences on mass media content*. White Plains, NY: Longman.

Sparr, J. (2004). Konfliktberichterstattung! Wer mag's konstruktiv? Zur Akzeptanz konstruktiver Konfliktberichterstattung durch die Leserschaft. Universität Konstanz: Psychol. Diplomarbeit.

Spohrs, M. (2006). Über den Nachrichtenwert von Friedensjournalismus - Ergebnisse einer experimentellen Studie. *Conflict & Communication Online*, 5/1.

UNESCO (1979). Records of the general conference. Twentieth session. Paris, 24 October to 28 November 1978. http://unesdoc.unesco.org/images/0011/001140/114032Eb.pdf.

Wolling, J. (2002). Aufmerksamkeit durch Qualität? Empirische Befunde zum Verhältnis von Nachrichtenqualität und Nachrichtennutzung. In Baum, A., Schmidt, S. J. (Eds.) *Fakten und Fiktionen. Über den Umgang mit Medienwirklichkeiten* (pp. 202-216). Konstanz: UVK.

War, Media In Former Yugoslavia And Education In The Region

Aleksandra Petrovic
Institute for Educational Research
apetrovic@rcub.bg.ac.yu

Media and Education in the Former Yugoslavia

When the Federal Republic of Yugoslavia disintegrated in 1991, nationalistic forces in each ex-republic took over the control of the media. Leading media management cadres and journalists, as their executors, are responsible for spreading falsehoods about other ethnic groups. Nevertheless, representatives of other nations were relieved from the media (Baksic, SEE Portal), by which the preconditions for spreading hate towards those who did not belong to the same nation were formed. Numerous reports of various international organizations testify to this. As the most prominent deficiencies of reporting from Bosnia they highlight: negative selection of information, use of scarce information sources, state judgements without arguments, use of hate-speech and inadequate language expression in general (Media Plan Institute, 1997).

The media representatives extended their role of war agitators to the role of the creator of national identity – Serbian, Croat, Bosnian (earlier: Muslim), but also Slovenian and Macedonian. They often explored the themes related to the history of each particular ethnic community in the former Yugoslavia. Most commonly they presented false historical facts to prove that a particular ethnic group, in majority on a particular territory, had the exclusive right on common cultural heritage – the heritage belonging to a number of other national communities as well.

The nations of former Yugoslavia suddenly became minorities in newly formed separate states - ex-republics of Yugoslavia, and many ethnic groups were forced to migrate from their places of residence.

"Popular" history, as is presented in newspapers or on TV, as well as the one that pretends to be scientific – in education, omits the facts related to the presence of other ethnic communities on a particular territory.

Ms Diana Johnstone, ex-press representative of the Greens in the European Parliament, writes about the history of the former Yugoslavia and presents untrue arguments and negative attitudes towards other ethnic groups: the Croats are labelled secessionists and, according to her, Albanians and Muslims were volunteers in the German SS divisions in the Second World War (Johnstone, 1998). Ms Johnstone concludes that the rights of minorities are nowhere else respected as much as in Serbia and Montenegro (Johnstone, 1998).

Undoubtedly, if representing democratic media, foreign reporters should not publish any texts with untrue statements on the conflicts in particular countries, let alone take sides or imitate those media that had agitated for the war in the former Yugoslavia.

Falsified facts from national history or the history of the former Yugoslavia belong to political propaganda present not only in the media but in school textbooks, too. Some journalists often cited the works of university professors and researchers from scientific institutions as their sources of information, by which the responsibility for spreading nationalistic hate of some members of the institutions of high education becomes obvious. The media and school textbooks were full of horrible persecution and tormenting of civilians, for which the other party in the war was blamed. The other party was the exclusive culprit for initiating armed conflicts and mass murders and persecutions. Such contents were aimed at mobilizing additional forces from the population in order to either engage them directly in military forces or to provide support for the war policy as the only solution to all the problems. The truth is that the war served well to some, first to gain power, then to strengthen their positions, all in the name of defending the people and national boundaries. Both the media and school were engaged and used to that purpose.

Feminism, Media and the War in the former Yugoslavia

"Women are, in accordance to their nature, against war"

The existence of feminism in the former Yugoslavia cannot be denied, but can justifiably be a matter of discussion on the extent to which women took part in antiwar propaganda, or how women were included in the war machinery of the media. For example, the feminist movement was significantly developed in Slovenia, but it is questionable whether the members of the feminist movement took part in the antiwar campaign, and how they fought against nationalism in their own community. There were organizations that acted against the war in public (Zajovic, 2007). In spite of that, the impression is that potentials carried by the feministic movement were not used against nationalism.

When the war started one could see pictures of women in military uniforms either as volunteers or reporters on fields of operations (Slapsak, 1996). Otherwise, women were engaged in providing for and taking care of the refugees and organizing various forms of help to suffering population. Nongovernmental female organizations were engaged in the sphere of informal education, too. Besides various nongovernmental organizations for the rights of women, still active within alternative education are Female Studies whose fundamental aim is to improve the position of women in the society. It is, however, one thing to propagandize gender equality, and quite another to fight against nationalism in one's own environment and oppose to the prevailing nationalistic policy. That exactly is the sphere in which the engagement of female organizations was insufficient, especially in the early nineties when major conflicts in the former Yugoslavia started. Some research results indicate to the fact that some members of the feminist movement accepted the nationalistic option in the war-stricken society (Knezevic, 1994). In their analyses of the position of women and the activities of female organizations in the war, the feminists state that only men led the war, while the position of women in those conditions is not defined precisely. Men are accused that they led the war in Yugoslavia, and that women were in a subordinate, passive position. Those who were active in such conditions founded various pacifistic organizations (Ivekovic, 1995; Petkovic, 2005; Slapsak, 1996).

Although female organizations were engaged in the sphere of informal education, when the national curriculum was changed and nationalistic contents were implemented and all the facts related to common history and culture of the nations of ex-Yugoslavia were omitted, female organizations in Serbia did not raise their voice against it in the media, nor did they try in any other way to influence the authorities to make corrections in the curricula. One of the essential problems of current nongovernmental feminist organizations, primarily of those active on the territory of the Republic of Serbia, is that they overtly support particular political options. By doing so they put women in a subordinate position to men who are exclusive leaders of all political parties in Serbian society.

Democratization of Media and the Education System

The European Union financed independent media in the former Yugoslavia in the nineties of the last century in order to help the development of civic societies. The education systems were democratized, primarily structurally. However, the contents with nationalistic implications have not vanished from the curricula (Agicic 2003; Kevereski, 2003; Petrovic, 2003). Especially carefully censured are those parts of the textbooks or reference books which would indicate to the guilt of the own nation in the wars on the territory of the former Yugoslavia. In contrast to the sphere of education, which is still governed by conservative nationalistic streams when, at least, the contents of national school subjects are concerned, there are a number of independent media that have a critical approach in their analyses of the problems of war in the former Yugoslavia. The state owned televisions have been transformed into public services, but still have remained under the control of the ruling structures.

References

Agicic, D. (2003). History teaching in Croatia – situation and development prospect. In *Round table on Educational collaboration between former Republics of Yugoslavia: Textbooks and curricula of History, Geography, Language and Literature and Civics* (pp. 16-18). Zagreb: Forum za slobodu odgoja.

Baksic, H. (n.d.). Stampani mediji u BiH – roditeljska paznja. *SEE Portal – Southern Slavic,* Retrieved February 12, 2007, from http://ssla.oneworld.net/article/view/93988/1/

Ivekovic, R. (1995). *Zene, nacionalizam i rat: Vodite ljubav, a ne rat.* Retrieved February 23, 2007, from http://www.women-war-memory.org/hr/rada_ivekovic

Johnstone, D. (1998). Seeing Yugoslavia Through a Dark Glass: Politics, Media and the Ideology of Globalization. *Covert Action Quarterly, 65* (Fall). Retrieved April 28, 2007, from http://ourworld.compuserve.com/homepages/grattan_healy/johnston.htm

Kevereski, Lj. (2003). Aspects of intercultural education in the Republic of Macedonia. In *Round table on Educational collaboration between former Republics of Yugoslavia: Textbooks and curricula of History, Geography, Language and Literature and Civics* (pp. 28-33). Zagreb: Forum za slobodu odgoja.

Knezevic, Dj. (1994). "Mi" nasuprot "Ja" ili problemi politickog identiteta u feministickom, odnosno zenskom, "pokretu" u Hrvatskoj, *Kruh i ruze, 1* (proljece 1994). Retrieved March 17, 2007, from http:/www.zinfo.hr/hrvatski/stranice/izdavastvo/kruhiruze/kirl/kirl.html

Media Plan Institut (1997). *Mediji u BiH – Osvajanje demokratije*. Retrieved February 12, 2007, from www.mediaonline.ba/ba/arhiva/arhiva_izvestaja/izvestaji/osvajanjedemokratije97.pdf

Petkovic, S. (2005). *Mir, demokratija i rodna jednakost*. Kotor: Zenski informativno - edukativni centar Crne Gore. Retrieved February 23, 2007, from http://zinecanima.cg.yu/zinec%20br%2010.pdf

Petrovic, A. (2003). Curricular changes in the Republic of Serbia from 1991 until 2002. In *Round table on Educational collaboration between former Republics of Yugoslavia: Textbooks and curricula of History, Geography, Language and Literature and Civics* (pp. 21-23). Zagreb: Forum za slobodu odgoja.

Slapsak, S. (1996). Zene i rat u bivsoj Jugoslaviji, *Republika, 145*. Retrieved February 23, 2007, from www.yurope.com/zines/republika/arhiva/96/145/145-16.html

Zajovic, S. (2007). *Uvek neposlusne*. Beograd: Zene u crnom.

İletişim Çatışmalarının Çözümünde Anahtar Kavram: Duygusal Zekâ

Ayhan Doğan
İletişim Fakültesi
Atatürk Üniversitesi
ayhan25@yahoo.com

Fatma Geçikli
İletişim Fakültesi
Atatürk Üniversitesi
fgecikli@atauni.edu.tr

Giriş

Çatışma, standart karar verme mekanizmalarında meydana gelen bir bozulmadır (March ve Simon, 1988, s. 112-13). "Çatışma birbirleriyle uyuşmayan iki veya daha fazla güdünün aynı anda bireyi etkilemesiyle ortaya çıkar, güdülerin türüne, şiddetine, içinde bulunulan ortama göre değişik görüntüler sergiler (Cüceloğlu, 1991, s. 282). Bu tanımlardan hareketle iletişim çatışması, iki veya daha fazla kişi arasında biliş, algı, duygu, gereksinim, kişisel özellikler, kültürel özellikler, statü ve roller, sosyal ve fiziki faktörler ile mesajın niteliği gibi birçok nedenden kaynaklanan anlaşmazlık olarak ifade edilebilir. Anlaşmazlık, ters düşme, zıtlaşma, bozulma ve uyuşmazlık çatışmanın temel unsurlarındandır.

İnsan, ilişkiler ağı içerisinde yaşamını devam ettiren bir canlıdır. İletişim bu ağ içerisinde insan yaşamının olmazsa olmaz olgusudur. Aynı zamanda, insanların hem iş hem de özel yaşamında başarı ve mutluluğun en önemli anahtarlarından biridir ve her geçen gün önemi artmaktadır. İletişim sadece bilgi, duygu, düşünce ve tutumların aktarıldığı tek yönlü bir süreç değil, insanların birbirlerini anlamaları ve yakınlaşmalarında etken olan ve toplumsal değişmeyi çok yönlü bir şekilde etkileyen bir uygulamalar bütünü olarak değerlendirilmektedir. L. Lawrence Kincard "İletişimi insanlar arasında yakınlaşma aracı olarak değerlendirmekte ve karşılıklı anlayışa ulaşmak amacıyla bilginin katılımcılar tarafından paylaşıldığı yakınlaşma süreci " olarak ifade etmektedir (aktaran Tabak, 1999, s. 3). Karşılıklı anlayışa ulaşmak, kişilerin kendi duygularını anlaması ve yönlendirmesi, başkalarının duygularını sezebilmesi ve algılayabilmesi ile mümkündür. Bu duygusal zekâyı geliştirmekle mümkün olabilir. Duygusal zekâ insanın duygularına ne kadar hükmedebildiğini ve onları nasıl daha verimli kullanabileceğini açıklayan değişken bir faktördür. Duygusal güçleri gerektiği gibi kullanmasını bilen, yani duygusal zekâsı yüksek kişiler iş ve özel yaşamlarını kendilerine kolaylaştırmakta, çevresindekilerin ve kendi hislerinin farkında olarak güncel yaşamda karşılaşılan iletişim çatışmalarının üstesinden gelebilme potansiyellerini artırmaktadır (Konrad ve Hendl, 2005, s. 15).

Çalışmamızda, iletişim çatışmalarının çözümünde etkili olan duygusal zekâ kavramı incelenmektedir. Çatışma ve iletişim çatışmalarının nedenleri hakkında bilgi verilmekte, duygusal zekâ kavramı, anlamı ve önemi üzerinde durulmakta ve çatışmanın çözümündeki rolü incelenmektedir.

1. Çatışma, İletişim Çatışmaları ve Nedenleri

Çatışma, "birey ve grupların içindeki ve aralarındaki uyuşmazlık, anlaşmazlık ya da ters düşme biçiminde kendini gösteren bir etkileşim durumu" (Rahim, 1985, s. 81) olarak tanımlanmaktadır.

Çatışma iletişimin bütün kullanım alanlarında görülebilir. Çatışmaların tamamında bireye inmek gerekir. Kişinin kendi içindeki çatışma, kendisinden ne beklendiğinden emin olmadığı, çelişkili şeyler düşündüğü durumlarda ortaya çıkan ve kişiyi rahatsızlığa, kızgınlığa ve baskı altında kalmaya sevk eden çatışmadır. Kişilerarası çatışma, iki kişinin çeşitli konularda anlaşmazlığa düşmesidir, kişiler - gruplar arasındaki çatışma, daha çok kişilerin grup tarafından belirli kuralları kabule zorlanmaları ile oluşmaktadır. Bütün bu çatışmaların temelinde insan faktörü vardır. Dolayısıyla, kişilerarası çatışmaları en aza indirgemek için bu duruma ağırlık vermek gerekir.

Çatışma çeşitli şekillerde sınıflandırılabilir.

1.Yıkıcı ve Yapıcı Çatışmalar
Yıkıcı çatışma bireylerin amacına ulaşmasını engelleyen veya geciktiren çatışmalardır.

Yapıcı çatışma ise ; bireylerin amacına katkıda bulunan çatışmalardır.

2. Ortaya Çıkış Şekillerine Göre Çatışmalar

Dökmen (1996) çatışmaları çıkış şekillerine göre aşağıdaki gibi sınıflandırmaktadır (ss. 47-59):

- **Aktif Çatışma:** Çatışma halindeki tarafların fiilen gösterdikleri davranışları kapsar.

  Kişiler arasındaki iticilik, birbirlerinden hoşlanmama, herhangi bir nedenle kızgın oluşları, geçmiş yaşantıları içerisindeki anlaşmazlıkları aktif çatışmaya zemin hazırlayan unsurlardır. Bu çatışma, karşılıklı ağır sözler kullanma şeklinde başlar, fiziksel güç kullanımına kadar devam edebilir.

- **Pasif Çatışma:** Kişilerin çekindikleri veya küs oldukları için birbirleriyle aktif iletişim kuramadıkları zaman ortaya çıkar.

- **Varoluş Çatışması:** Taraflardan biri diğerinden gelen bilgi, duygu ve düşünceleri, sözel veya sözsüz anlamda, yanlış anlarsa, ya da onun ifadeleri ile ilgisi olmayan bir mesaj gönderirse bu duruma varoluş çatışması adı verilir. Bu çatışma da kişi dikkatini, karşısındakine değil kendisine yöneltmiştir.

- **Tümden Reddetme:** Kişi_kendisine gönderilen mesajı tamamen reddeder, tam karşıtı bir fikir ileri sürer ve savunursa tümden reddetme çatışması ortaya çıkar.

- **Önyargılı Çatışma:** Kişiler belirli bir konuda tartışmaya başlamadan önce o konuda belli bilgiler ve fikirler edinerek bir hüküm oluştururlar ve tartışma sırasında ısrarlı bir şekilde önyargılı fikirleri savunurlar ve tartışma onların kararlarını değiştirmez.

- **Yoğunluk Çatışması:** İki kişinin düşünceleri ve fikirleri arasında kısmen uyuşma var ise, yoğunluk çatışması söz konusu demektir. Örneğin ; bir kadının güzel bulduğu elbisesi için, diğeri, güzeldi ama o kadar da değil derse, bu bir yoğunluk çatışmasıdır.

- **Alıkoyma Çatışması:** Kişinin mesajı isteyerek yada istemeyerek değişikliğe uğratması durumunda ortaya çıkan çatışmadır. Bir kişi karşısından gelen bilgi, fikir, duygu ve düşünceleri tam olarak anlar, fakat üçüncü bir kişiye doğru olarak ifade etmez. Bu kişiler, aldıkları bilginin sadece bir kısmını diğerine aktarır.

- **Kısmi Algılama Çatışması:** Alıcı konumundaki kişi kaynaktan gelen mesajlardan bir kısmını algılar, diğerlerini algılamazsa kısmi algılama çatışması ortaya çıkar.

Kişilerarası iletişim çatışmalarının niteliğini belirleyen, başlangıç ve sonuç faktörleri şeklinde gruplandırılan iki ana faktör vardır. Başlangıç faktörleri, sonuç faktörlerinin özünü ve iletişim çatışmalarının esas nedenini oluşturan faktörlerdir (Dökmen, 1996, s. 83).

Başlangıç faktörleri şu şekilde gruplandırılabilir.

- Biliş (cognition)
- Algı (perception)
- Duygu
- Gereksinimler
- İletişim becerisi
- Kişisel faktörler
- Kültürel faktörler
- Roller
- Sosyal ve fiziksel faktörler
- Mesajın niteliği

- **Biliş;** duyu organlarından organizmaya ulaşan uyarıcıların algılanması, anlamlandırılması, depolanması , hatırlanması ve kullanılması sürecine verilen addır. Kişiler ilişkiler ağı içerisinde sağlıklı iletişimler kurabilmek ve bunları sürdürebilmek için güçlü ve zengin bir bilişsel yaşantıya gereksinim duyarlar. Örneğin yerine göre şakalar yapmak, arasıra görüşse bile kişilerin, isimlerini unutmamak yani güçlü bir hafıza, kişilerarası iletişimde önemlidir. Bu özellikler bilişsel bir etkinliktir. Psikolojik danışma / psikoterapi alanındaki yaklaşımlardan birisi "Bilişsel-Davranışçı (Cognitive-Behavioral)" yaklaşımdır. Bu yaklaşıma göre düşüncelerimiz, duygularımızı ve davranışlarımızı etkiler ve yönlendirir. Akılcı ve gerçekçi olmayan bazı negatif düşünceler, ruhsal bozuklukların temel nedenidir ve düşünceler değiştirilerek yol açtıkları ruhsal sorunlar giderilebilir. Düşünceler kalıplaşmış hale gelirse değişik iletişim çatışmalarına ortam hazırlayabilir. Örneğin ; aşırı genellemeci ve değiştirme gayreti olan kişinin, önyargılı ve tümden reddedici çatışmalara yol açması, Ana baba tavrı takınarak karşısındakini savunuculuğa itmesi, kişiselleştirme eğilimi yüksek olan kişinin pasif çatışma sergilemesi, küserek kabuğuna çekilmesi mümkün olabilir (Dökmen, 1996, s. 85-97). Kişilerin sahip olduğu önyargılı ve kalıplaşmış düşünceleri çatışmalara yol açıyorsa, bu çatışmaları azaltmanın yolu hem gönderici hem de alıcıdaki önyargılı yaklaşımı azaltmaktır. Önyargıyı yok etmek için her iki tarafın duygu ve düşüncelerini kontrol altına alması gerekir.

• **Algı;** Algı, duyu organlarından beyine gelen verilerin örgütlenmesi, yorumlanması, anlamlandırılması süreci olarak ifade edilebilir (Dökmen, 2000, s. 7). Duyu organlarına ulaşan iletiler algılama olmadan bir anlam ifade etmezler, çevreden gelen verilere algılama sonucunda tepkiler verilmektedir (Güney, 2000, s. 7). Algılama kişinin inanç ve değer yargıları, içinde bulunduğu durum, geçmiş yaşantıları, beklentileri gibi birçok faktör tarafından etkilenir. Bu durum algıda seçiciliği beraberinde getirir. Kişiler bazı mesajları veya mesajın bir kısmını bilerek ya da bilmeyerek algılamayabilir. Eğer kişiler önyargılı iseler, belirli kaynaklardan gelen iletileri ya hiç algılamayacaktır ya da kaynağın kastettiğinden farklı algılayacaklardır (Gannon, 1979; Koçel, 2003, s. 544). Bu durum, kişilerin duymak istediklerini duyacakları anlamına gelir (Stoner, 1978 ; Koçel, 2003, s. 544). Zekâ, yaş, sosyo-kültürel ve fiziksel çevre eğitim ve gereksinimler kişinin algılama gücünü etkileyen değişkenlerdir. "Kelimeler bile anlamlarını onların kullanımından çok alıcının algılama yeteneğine göre alır" (Bone & Kurtz, 1978, s. 465). Kişiler, farklı inanç ve değer yargıları, örf ve adetlere, geleneklere, farklı fikir yapısına, farklı tecrübeye sahip ise aynı mesajı farklı algılayabilirler ve böylece iletişim çatışmalarına yol açabilirler. Çatışmaların üstesinden gelmek için, duygusal zekâ geliştirilebilir ve karşı tarafın bakış açısından bakılırsa sorun ortadan kaldırılabilir.

• **Duygu;** Duygu yoğunlukları da iletişim çatışmalarına yol açmaktadır. " Duygu hislerde ve zihinsel tutumda fizyolojik değişiklikler ve açıklayıcı davranışlarla birlikte ortaya çıkan bir "hareket" tir (Barutçugil, 2004, s. 73). Gerek sözlü, gerekse sözsüz iletişim sırasındaki davranışlar " niyet edilenler ve niyet edilmeyenler" olarak ikiye ayrılır. Niyet edilmeksizin yapılan davranışlar, duygusal davranışlardır (Dökmen, 1996, s. 101). Duygular jest, mimik ve ses tonu ile ifade edilir.

• **Gereksinimler;** Güdüleri, istekleri, arzuları, gereksinimleri, dürtüleri ve ilgileri kapsayan genel bir kavramdır. Açlık, susuzluk, cinsellik gibi fizyolojik kökenli güdülere dürtü (drive) adı verilir. İnsanlara özgü başarma isteği gibi yüksek dürtülere de gereksinme denir. Güdüler organizmayı (1) uyarır ve faaliyete geçirir; (2) organizmanın davranışını belirli bir amaca doğru yöneltir. Organizmanın davranışında bu iki özellik gözlendiği zaman organizmanın güdülenmiş olduğu söylenir" (Cüceloğlu, 2000, s. 230). Kişiler güdüleri doğrultusunda birtakım davranışlar gösterebilirler, ya da bazı güdülerin etkisiyle çatışmalara girebilirler. Örneğin ; bazı gereksinimlerin karşılanması engellendiği zaman kişi saldırganlaşır ve gereksinimleri de kapsayan güdüler iletişim çatışmalarına zemin hazırlar.

• **İletişim Becerisi;** Kişilerarası iletişimin gerçekleşmesi için kaynakta ve alıcıda temel iletişim yetenekleri olması gerekir. Bu yetenekler konuşma-dinleme ; okuma yazma ve düşünme şeklinde gruplandırılmaktadır. Ayrıca beden dilinin kullanıldığı yerde el ve kol hareketleri, yüz ifadeleri ve ses tonunu ayarlayabilmek iletişim yetenekleri içinde yer almaktadır. İletişim becerisi bu yeteneklerin etkili bir şekilde kullanılması ile elde edilebilir. Örneğin ; telaffuz bozukluklarını gidermek yanlış anlamaları önleyebilir. Konuşurken göz teması oluşturmak, çok eski ve çok yeni sözcüklere yer vermemek, aşırı yavaş ya da aşırı hızlı konuşmak, çok alçak veya çok yüksek sesle konuşmak iletişim engelini oluşturur ve çatışmalara neden olur. Görünüşte dinleme, tuzak kurucu dinleme, saplantılı dinleme ve konuşanın sürekli sözünü kesmek de yine iletişim sorunlarına ortam hazırlar. Yerli yersiz jest ve mimikleri kullanmak, ses tonunu kırıcı bir şekilde ayarlamak iletişim engeli olarak karşımıza çıkabilir.

• **Kişisel Faktörler;** İletişim çatışmalarına neden olan kişisel faktörler cinsiyet, fiziksel görünüm ve tutumlar başlıkları altında değerlendirilmektedir. Cinsiyet, araştırmaları kadınlar ve erkekler arasında algılayış ve iletişim biçimleri arasında farklılık olduğunu göstermektedir. Örneğin ; sıkıntılı süren evliliklerdeki kadınlar eşlerindeki duygusal değişikliklere, erkeklere oranla daha fazla tepki göstermektedirler. Erkekler, eşlerinden kendilerine yönelen sözsüz mesajları değerlendirmemektedirler (Dökmen, 1996, s. 343).

• **Fiziksel Görünüm;** Kişilerarası ilişkilerde kime nasıl davranılması gerektiğine karar verme sürecinde eldeki ilk bilgi, karşıdakinin fiziksel görünümüdür. İnsanları kendinize yakın veya uzak hissetmenizde de etkilidir. Fiziksel görünüm hem iletişimi başlatan kaynak hem de mesajın hedefindeki alıcı için önemlidir. " İnsanlar yeni karşılaştıkları birisinin dış görünüşüne kısa bir süre baktıktan ve o kişiyi zihinlerdeki bilişsel kalıplardan birisine yerleştirdikten sonra, ona "efendi, bey, beyefendi, hemşeri, bacı, bayan ya da hanımefendi" demeye karar verirler. Ancak insanlar birbirlerini, derilerinin rengine, cinsiyetlerine, milliyetlerine ya da kıyafetlerine göre bir takım katı sınıflara ayırırlarsa, fiziksel görünüm ipucu olmaktan çıkıp bir çatışma kaynağı haline gelebilir" (Dökmen, 1996, s. 110). "İnsanların sadece dış görünüşlerine bakarak olumsuz davranışlar geliştirilirse, sonu gelmeyen çatışmaların ortaya çıkması sağlanmış olur. İnsanların görünüşleri ne kadar farklı olursa olsun; içleri birbirine benzer, kalp sesinin cinsiyeti, gözyaşının milliyeti yoktur" (Dökmen, 1996, s. 110).

• **Tutumlar;** "Tutum bireyin psikolojik bir obje ile ilgili düşünce, duygu ve davranışlarını düzenli bir şekilde oluşturma eğilimidir. Kişisel tutumlar, kişinin yetişme tarzı ve yaşam boyu geçirilen tecrübeler sonucu oluşmakta ve kişiyi diğer insanlardan ayıran özellikler arasında yer almaktadır" (Özkalp & Kırel, 1996; Şimşek vd., 2001, s. 52). Günlük yaşamda kişilerle kurulan dostluklarda, arkadaşlıklarda ya da tartışmalarda ve kavgalarda tutumların payı çoktur. Tutumların özellikle kalıplaşmış yanlış bilgilere dayanması kişilerarası çatışmalara neden olmaktadır.

• **Kültürel Faktörler;** Farklı yaşam biçimleri, ortak yaşantının azlığı, dil, toplumsal kurallar iletişim çatışmalarına neden olabilirler. Her toplumda yazılı olmadığı halde çoğunluk tarafından bilinen ve kişiler arasındaki iletişimi etkileyen toplumsal kurallar vardır. Bu kurallar kültürün bir parçasıdır ve insanların nerede, nasıl davranacaklarını belirler. Kişiler içinde yaşadıkları toplumun kurallarına uymadıklarında çevrelerinden gelen doğrudan ve dolaylı baskılarla karşılaşırlar (Dökmen, 1996, s. 113). Örneğin ; Büyüklerin yanında bacak, bacak üstüne atmak, babanın karşısında sigara içmek, saygı çerçevesinde değerlendirilir. Bu kurallara uyulmadığında iletişim çatışmaları ortaya çıkabilir.

Kültürün bir parçası olan dil iletişimin temel unsurudur. Dil, göstergelerden ve sembollerden oluşur. Dil, duygu, düşünce ve hissedileni ifade etmede de sembol kullanma yöntemidir (Strauss ve Sayles, 1972, s. 187). Kullanılan sembollere birden fazla anlam yüklenmesi iletişim çatışmalarına neden olmaktadır. Gönderici ve alıcının sembollere aynı anlamı yüklememesi karışıklıklara ortam hazırlamaktadır.

• **Roller;** Kişilerarası iletişim çatışmalarının en önemli kaynaklarından biride rollerdir. "Grup içinde belli bir pozisyonda bulunan kişiden beklenen davranışlara" rol adı verilir (Dökmen, 1996, s. 120). Kaynak çevresiyle iletişim kurmaya çalışırken üstlendiği rolün niteliğinden ötürü dikkat etmelidir. Rolüne uygun düşmeyen mesaj gönderdiğinde alıcı üzerinde tutum ve davranış değişikliğine yol açmaz. Rollerin niteliğinden dolayı kişiler çatışmalar yaşarlar. Yeteneklerine ve ilgilerine uygun olmayan bir rolü üstlenme zorunda kalan kişi ile rol arasında uyuşmazlık durumu yaşanır. Bir kişinin sahip olduğu roller bireyle çatışıyorsa, bu çatışmayı algılayan kişi iç çatışma yaşayabilir (Dökmen, 1996, s. 120-126). Her iki durumda da olay kişilerarası iletişim çatışmalarına kadar gidebilir.

• **Sosyal ve Fiziksel Çevre;** Sosyal ve fiziksel çevre ile kişilerin davranışları arasında bir takım paralellikler bulunması çevre ile kişilerarası iletişim arasında da paralellik bulunduğu anlamına gelmektedir. İçinde yaşanılan çevre kişilerarası iletişimi ve dolayısıyla çatışmaları etkileyebilir. Kalabalık ve aşırı müdahaleci ortamlar bu çatışmaya örnek verilebilir.

• **İletinin Niteliği;** İletinin anlamlılık, doğruluk, gerçekçilik, açıklık, anlaşılabilirliği önemlidir. İletinin beklenen düzeyde algılanması, anlaşılması, kavranması, ve benimsenmesi anlamlılığına bağlıdır. İletiyle ilgili üç çeşit anlamdan bahsedilebilir: Çağrımsal anlam, kavramsal anlam ve hiyerarşik anlam. Çağrımsal anlam iletinin biçim ve içeriğiyle neleri hatırlatması gerektiği ile ilgilidir. Kavramsal anlam, bilgi unsurlarının ilişkileri ve gruplandırılması sonucunda ortaya çıkar. Hiyerarşik anlam ise, bilgi unsurlarının sistematik olarak düzenlenmesi ile ilgilidir (Tabak, 1999, s. 203). İletinin anlamı kasten çarpıtılabilir ve farklı biçimlerde ortaya çıkabilir. Amaçlı yalanlar buna örnek oluşturabilir (Aldag ve Stearns, 1987, s. 481). Bu anlamsal özellikler yani mesajın niteliği, çatışmanın kaynağını oluşturmaktadır.

• **Sonuç Faktörleri;** Çatışmaya neden olan bu faktörler doğrudan gözlenen çatışmaların yüzeysel nedenleri içinde yer almaktadır. Sonuç faktörleri dört grupta değerlendirilebilir (Dökmen, 1994, s. 79).

- Kişinin kendisine bakış açısı.
- Kişinin karşındaki kişiye bakış açısı
- Kişinin kendine gönderilen mesaja bakış açışı.
- Kişinin iletişim stili.

Bu faktörler gündelik yaşamda ortaya çıkan çatışmalarda şu şekilde kendini göstermektedir (Dökmen, 1994, s. 80).

- Kişi, kendisine gönderilen iletiyi, iletinin gönderilme şeklini ya da iletiyi göndereni, kendisine uygun bulmayabilir.
- Kişi, kendisine gönderilen iletiyi, iletinin gönderiliş şeklini ya da iletiyi göndereni, kendisine uygun bulabilir.
- Kişi iletiyi dinleyebilir
- İletiyi dinlemeyebilir.
- İletiyi yanlış anlayabilir.
- İletiyi doğru anlayabilir.
- İletiye karşı olabilir.
- İletiye katılabilir.
- Bu iletiye ilişkin verdiği geribildirim karşındaki kişiye uygun olmayabilir.
- Bu iletiye ilişkin verdiği geribildirim karşındaki kişiye uygun olabilir.

İletişim süreci çerçevesinde, kaynağın bilgisi, becerisi, konu ve alıcıya yönelik tutum inanç ve değer yargıları, sosyo-kültürel kimliği ve bakış açısı, toplumsal rol ve statüsü ; güvenilirliği, prestij sahibi olması, saygınlığı ve uzmanlığı, kişilik yapısı ve kendine olan güveni gibi faktörler gönderdiği iletinin alıcı üzerinde etkili olmasını sağladığı gibi çatışmaya da neden olabilmektedir. Aynı faktörler, alıcı içinde geçerlidir. Alıcının sahip olduğu özellikler iletişim sürecini etkileyecek zaman zaman çatışmaların ortaya çıkmasına zemin hazırlayacaktır. Yukarıda bahsi geçen, mesajın anlamı yine süreci etkileyecektir. Kanalda oluşan psikolojik ya da fiziksel gürültü ve geribildirim yetersizlikleri de çatışmalara yol açabilir. Tablo I de kaynak ve alıcıda görülen özelliklerin de iletişim sürecinde önemli rol oynadığı ifade edilebilir.

Kaynak →	Alıcı
. Amaçları	. Bilgisi
. Geçmiş tecrübeleri	. Yeteneği
. Tutumu	. Geçmiş tecrübeleri
. Teknik bilgisi	. Dünya görüşü
. Alıcıya olan güveni	. Değer yargıları
. Değer yargıları	. Bekleyişleri
. Dünya görüşü	. Benlik anlayışı
. İşe/ kişiye verdiği önem	. Kuvvetli ve zayıf yönleri
. Endişeleri	. Endişeleri
. Kuvvetli / zayıf yönleri	. Gönderici hakkındaki düşünceleri
. Alıcının imajı	. Olay hakkındaki bilgisi
. Empatisi	. Başkalarından duydukları
. Motivasyonu	. Dinleyici olabilme özelliği
	. Göndericinin genel imajı
	. Motivasyonu
	. Göndericiye güven

Tablo I, İletişim Sürecindeki Gönderici ve Alıcı (Koçel, 2003, s. 541).

Kişilerin iletişim stilleri de iletişim sürecinde belirleyici olmaktadır. Tablo II.de çatışmacı, baskın ve kaçışçı iletişim stillerine yer verilmektedir.

Çatışmacı ⇦	Baskın	⇨ Kaçış
(Agresif davranışlar)	(Güven içeren Davranışlar)	(İtaatkar Davranışlar)
. Karşı saldırı ve İncitme	. Kendine ve diğerlerine saygı göstermek	. Kendine ve diğerlerine yönelik saygıdan eksiklik.
. Başkasının zamanına, mekanına, değerlerine, gereksinimlerine ve ilgilerine saldırı	. Kişilerin gereksinimlerini uygun bir şekilde karşılama . Kişilerin uygun zaman ve mekanını bekleme (zaman ve mekana yönelik taciz girişiminin bulunmaması)	. Gereksimleri, duyguları, değerleri ve ilgileri yanıtlama da dürüst bir yaklaşım sergilememe

Tablo II. Çatışmacı, baskın, kaçışçı iletişim stili (Weiss, 1996, s. 120)

İletişim kurarken agresif hareketlerde bulunan kişi veya kişiler sürekli bir saldırı halindedir. Bu kişilerin bakışları çok serttir, konuşurken yumruklarını sıkarlar, insanlara oldukça yakın hareket ederler, küfrederler, çok ağır sözcüklerin yer aldığı bir dil kullanırlar, tehditlerde bulunur ve aşağılayıcı bir tavır sergilerler.

Baskın davranışları sergileyenler, diğerlerinin zamanını, mekânını, kişisel duygularını koruyan ve saldırı içeren davranışlardan uzak duran kişilerdir. İletişimlerinde dürüst, güvenilir ve doğru sözlüdürler. Jest ve mimiklerini etkin bir şekilde kullanır, ses tonuna dikkat ederler. Değişime açık kişilerdir. Sen yerine ben ve biz kullanımına önem verirler. Sen sözcüğü tehdit ve suçlamaya açıktır.

Kaçışçı iletişim stilinde kişiler diğerlerinden uzak durmaya çalışırlar. Bu davranışlarda kendini reddetme ve kendini engelleme söz konusudur. Bu kişiler çok zayıf bir ses tonuyla konuşurlar, göz temasından kaçınır yere bakarlar ve bunalımlı bir haldedirler.

İletişim Çatışmalarına Karşı Duygu Odaklı İletişim:

Duygusal Zekâ (EQ)

Duygusal zekâ kavramı ilk olarak 1990 yılında Yale ve New Hampshire Üniversitesinden psikologlar Peter Salovey ve John Mayer tarafından ortaya atılmıştır. Yüksek başarı elde eden kişilerin doğuştan getirdiği bazı özelliklerinin olduğuna inanılır, ancak neden bazı kişiler sahip olduğu yetenekleri zaman içinde geliştirirken, bazıları yetenekli oldukları halde sonradan körelip gittikleri? Sorusunun yanıtı merak konusu olmuştur. Bunun üzerine 25 yaşında çok başarılı olacağı izlenimi veren, ancak sonraki on yılda beklenilen ölçüde başarılı olamayan genç yöneticiler üzerine bir araştırma yapılmıştır. Araştırmada çarpıcı sonuçlar ortaya çıkmıştır. Bu kişilerin başarılı olan eşitlerine göre dört özelliği göze çarpmaktadır (Batlaş, 2001, s. 65).

- İnsan ilişkilerinde başarısız olmak
- Otoriter olmak
- Üst yönetimle çatışmak
- Fazla hırslı olmak

Bu çalışma sonrasında IQ'nun tek başına yeterli olmadığı, başarılı olmak için duygusal zekaya gereksinim olduğu ileri sürülmüştür.

Yirminci yüzyılın sonlarına kadar tanıma, anlama ve uyum yeteneğinin, bilişsel zekâ (BZ) olarak ifade edilen zihinsel yeterlilikle mümkün olduğu sanılıyordu. Oysa edebiyat, sanat, ilişki yönetimi ve diğer birçok alanda farklı zihinsel fonksiyonların rol aldığının bilinmesi duygusal zekânın (DZ) ön plana çıkmasına neden oldu (Batlaş, 2006, s. 5). Artık yaşam kalitesinin yükseltilmesinde duygusal zekânın bilişsel zekâ kadar önemli olduğu kabul edilmektedir.

Biri duygusal, biri akılcı olan iki zekâ genellikle bir uyum içinde ve farklı bilinç biçimlerini birbirleriyle kaynaştırarak yaşamda yol alınmasına yardımcı olur. Çoğunlukla duygusal ve akılcı zihin denge halindedir. Duygu, akılcı zihnin işleyişine katkıda bulunur, akılcı zihin ise duygusal verileri şekillendirir ve bazen de reddeder. Ancak, yine de her ikisi de yarı bağımsız melekelerdir, beyindeki farklı ama birbirleriyle bağlantılı devrelerin işlemesini sağlar (Goleman, 2005, s. 23-24). Bilişsel zeka ve duygusal zeka arasındaki dengeyi oluşturan kişi kimliğini ve itibarını kaybetmeden var olabilir. Bir ressamın eserinde tuvale yansıttığı form bilişsel zekâ, renk ışığın kesişmelerinde ise ortaya çıkan duygusal zekâdır (Batlaş, 2006, s. 5). Bilişsel zekâ kişinin daha çok zeka katsayısını vermektedir. Buna karşılık duygusal zeka, kişinin duygularından haberdar olması, duygusal sentez yapabilmesi ve buna benzer fonksiyonları ortaya koymasıdır (Özdilek, 2002, s. 7). Her iki zekâ da birbirinin karşıtı değil tamamlayıcısıdır.

Mayer ve Salovey'e göre, duygusal zekâ " kendinin ve başkalarının duygularını hissetmek, düşünceleri desteklemek için duyguları ortaya koymak, anlamak, zihinsel ve duygusal gelişimi geliştirmek için duyguları etkili bir biçimde yönetme yeteneği"dir (Mayer ve Solavey, 1993, s. 433). Bradberry ve Greaves'e göre ise,"duygusal zekâ herkesin içinde var olan ve birazda soyut olan "bir şey"dir. Davranışlarımızı "nasıl yöneteceğimizi sosyal karışıklarla nasıl baş edeceğimizi ve olumlu sonuçlar elde edecek kişisel kararlar almamızı sağlayan bir unsurdur" şeklinde tanımlamaktadırlar (Bradberry ve Greaves, s. 45).

Tanımlarda duygusal zekânın dört boyutu göze çarpmaktadır.

- Kişinin kendi duygularını tanıması ve anlaması.
- Başkalarının duyguları için empati göstermesi ve anlaması.
- Duygularıyla başa çıkması.
- Duygularını yaşam kalitesini yükseltecek şekilde kullanması.

Geçmişte duygular, insanın zayıf yanının bir simgesi olarak görülürdü. Ancak günümüzde duyguların gücü anlaşılmaya başlandı. Artık duyguları tanımamak, anlamamak, düzenleyememek ve yönetememek büyük hata ve kayıplara yol açmaktadır. Duygularını yönetemeyen insan, aklını da yönetememektedir (Atabek, 1999, s. 11).

"İnsan doğasında olumlu ve olumsuz duygular vardır. Bununla beraber iyiyi, doğruyu ve mükemmeli sevebilme özelliği de mevcuttur. Yapıcı duygular, insandaki temel duygulardandır. Sevgi, ümit, güven, şefkat, iyimserlik, mutluluk bunlardan bazılarıdır" (Tarhan, 2006, s. 65). Duyguların alınganlık, acı, keder, neşesizlik, hor görme, aşağılama, küçümseme gibi kümeleri de vardır. Tüm bu duyguların kontrolü zordur ama imkânsız değildir. Duygusal zekâsı gelişmiş insanlar duyguların görülen yanlarının yan ısıra görülmeyenleri de sezebilmektedirler. Bu durum iletişim çatışmalarının çözümlemesinde avantaj olarak görülmektedir. Duygusal zekâ kişisel ve mesleki başarı için sahip olunması gereken en önemli yetkinliktir. Bu yetkinlik insan ilişkilerini güçlendirmek için ve iletişimi geliştirmek için gerekli teknikleri ve yöntemleri kişiye vermektedir.

Duygusal zekâ kapsamına giren beş temel yetenek vardır. Bu yetenekler, özbilinç, duyguları yönetebilme, kendini harekete geçirebilme, başkalarının duygularını anlayabilme ve ilişkileri yürütebilme olarak sınıflandırılmaktadır (Goleman, 1996, s. 61-62).

▪Özbilinç

"Duygusal benlik bilinci" olarak da anlamlandırılmaktadır. Benlik bilinci kişinin kendi duygularını tanıması, etkilerini fark etmesi, duygularıyla baş edebilmesi ve karşısındaki kişileri doğru değerlendirme yetkinliğidir. Kişi eğer gerçek duygularının farkına varmazsa, tamamen karşısındakinin insafına kalabilir. Oysa duygularını tanıyan kişiler, karar gerektiren karmaşık konularda veya ortamlarda ne düşündüklerinden emin oldukları için, kendilerine olumlu bir yol bulabilirler. Yani tehditleri fırsata dönüştürebilirler. Bu kişiler, iletişim kurarken de açık sözlü, içten, esnek, hoşgörülü olabilmektedirler.

Duygusal farkındalığı yüksek kişi, ne hissettiğini bilir, duygularını anlar, düşünceleriyle sözleri ve sözleriyle hissettikleri arasında bağlantı kurar, duygu dünyasının performansını nasıl etkilediğini tanımlar, değerlerinin ve hedeflerinin kendisine nasıl yön verdiğinin farkındadır (Batlaş, 2006, s. 20).

▪Duyguları Yönetebilme

Duyguları uygun biçimde yönetebilme yeteneği özbilinç temeli üstünde gelişir. Kişinin sahip olduğu dürtüleri, istekleri, tutkuları kontrol etmesi, yönetmesi ve denetleyebilmesidir. Kişinin dürüst ve tutarlı olması, beklenmedik durumlarla baş edebilmesi, yeni fikirlerden rahatsızlık duymaması, otokontrol sistemini çalıştırarak, olaylar sonrasında kendini de mercek altına alması ancak duygularını yönetebilmesi ile mümkündür.

▪Kendini Harekete Geçirebilme

Kişinin duygularını bir amaç etrafında toparlaması, dikkat edebilme, kendini harekete geçirebilme, kendine hâkim olabilme ve yaratıcılık için gereklidir.

Başarı yönelimi, bağlılık, girişimcilik ve iyimserlik bu yetkinliğin bir parçasıdır. Duygusal özdenetim-doyumu erteleyebilme ve ani ortaya çıkan davranışları kontrol edebilme- her başarının altında yatan temel özelliktir. Engeller karşısında tıkanıp kalmamak her türlü yüksek performansa olanak sağlar. Kendini harekete geçirebilen kişiler iş ve özel yaşamlarında daha üretken ve etkili olabilmektedirler.

▪ Başkalarının Duygularını Anlayabilme

Empati yapabilme yani kişinin kendisini karşısındakinin yerine koyması, o kişinin duygu ve düşüncelerini doğru olarak anlaması, hissetmesi ve bu durumu ona iletmesi sürecidir (Dökmen, 1996, s. 170). Duygusal özbilinç temeli üzerine inşa edilen empati kişilerarası ilişkilerde temel beceridir. Karşısındakinin ne hissettiğini sezebilmenin anahtarı ses tonu, jest ve mimikler gibi sözsüz ifadeleri okuyabilmekten geçer. Duygusal gerçek ne söylendiğinde değil, nasıl söylendiğinde saklıdır. Empatik kişiler başkalarının neye gereksinim duyduğunu, ne istediğini gösteren belli belirsiz sosyal sinyallere karşı daha duyarlıdır. İnsanlar kendi duygularını tanımada ve anlamada ne kadar başarılıysa, başkalarının duygularını anlama da o kadar başarılıdır.

▪ İlişkileri Yürütebilmek

Sosyal beceriler olarak da ifade edilmektedir. Bu beceriler, başkalarının harekete geçirilmesine, teşvik edilmesine ve ikna edip etkileyerek rahatlamasına olanak sağlar. Kişi istediklerini zorlamadan ve zorlanmadan elde edebilir. "Sosyal beceriler: İletişim (Kişinin karşısındaki kişiyi anlamak için dinlemesi ve karşındaki kişiyi ikna etmesi) , Etki yaratma ve etkileme (Kişinin karşısındaki kişi ve grupta istek uyandırıp heyecan yaratması). Çatışma çözümü (Kişinin anlaşmazlıkları müzakere ederek ve uzlaşarak çözüme yönelmesi). İşbirliği (Kişinin başka insanlarla ortak amaçlar doğrultusunda işbirliği yapmaktan zevk duyması) , Ekip çalışmasına yatkınlık (Kişinin bir grupla birlikte olduğu zaman ortak amaçlar doğrultusunda sinerji yaratacak bir çalışmaya girebilmesi) , Liderlik (Kişinin başka insanları ikna etmesi, ilham vermesi, heyecan yaratması ve harekete geçirmesi) , İlişki kurma (Kişinin aile, sosyal ve iş çevresiyle anlamlı ve doyumlu ilişkiler kurması, gündelik ilişkilerde insanlarla ilişki kurma ve geliştirme konusunda zorluk çekmemesi) (Batlaş, 2001, s. 73) şeklinde gruplandırılabilir.

Yukarıdaki faktörler dikkate alındığında ilişkilerde etkili olmayı sağlayan sosyal becerilerdir. Bu becerilerdeki eksiklik yaşam kalitesinde yetersizliğe ve ilişkilerde tekrar tekrar felakete yol açar hatta en parlak zekâlı kişilerin ilişkilerin berbat ederek, ukala, itici ya da duyarsız olarak algılanmalarına neden olur.

İlişkiler yönetimi, ilk üç duygusal zekâ yetisi olan öz –farkındalık, öz-yönetim ve sosyal yeterliğin bir ürünüdür. Kişiler kendilerinin ve başkalarının duygularından haberdar olarak başarılı iletişim kurabilirler. Bu yeteneği kullanmak açık ve net görüşmeyi garanti ederken çatışmaların da etkili bir şekilde çözümünü sağlar. İlişkiler yönetimi, kişinin zaman içinde diğerleri ile kendi arasında kurduğu bir bağdır. İnsanlarla olan ilişkilerini iyi yöneten kişiler kurdukları ilişkilerin değerini bilir ve farklı birçok insanla hatta sevmedikleri kişilerle bile iletişim içinde olmanın faydalarını görürler. Sağlam açık, güvenilir ilişkiler arayıp bulunması ve üzerine titrenmesi gereken değerlerdir. Bu ilişkiler kişilerin karşısındakini nasıl anladığı ve nasıl davrandığının bir sonucudur (Bradberry ve Greavers, 2006, s. 51-52). J. Freedman'a göre duygusal zeka insanlara farklı bakmanın ve geliştirici ilişki kurmanın yolunu açar.

Önce insan felsefesinden hareket edildiğinde elbetteki duygular ön plana çıkmaktadır. Duyguların iletişim gücü önemlidir. Mutluluk, kızgınlık, öfke, korku, nefret ve tiksinti gibi duygular yüz ifadeleri ile aktarılır. Elbetteki bu içten gelen bir durumdur. Ancak bireyler kendi duygularını anlamaya çalışıp olumlu bir şekilde yönlendirebilirse iletişim çatışmalarını en aza indirgeyebilirler. İfade edilmek istenen, duyguların bastırılması değil, anlaşılması ve yönlendirilmesidir. İletişim çatışmaları daha çok duyguların kontrol edilmesinde sorun yaşandığında ortaya çıkar. Kendi kişisel değerlerini, fikir ve düşüncelerini, deneyimlerini, ani olaylarda tepkilerini değerlendirerek, duygular kontrol edilebilir.

Güçlü duyguları yönetme tekniklerinden bazıları şunlardır (Barutçugil, 2004, s. 90-91):

- Kendinizin ve karşınızdaki kişinin duygularını anlayın ve tanımlayın. Örneğin kızgın mısınız yoksa yalnızca heyecanlandınız mı ? Karşınızdaki üzüldü mü yoksa aşırı bir korku içinde mi?

- Duyguların kaynağını belirleyin. Şu andaki tepkiler geçmişteki olumsuz bir deneyimden mi yoksa bulunduğunuz durumdan mı kaynaklanıyor? Yoksa başka bir olaya kızgınlığınız mı bu duruma neden oldu?

- Duygularınızı ifade edin. Onları bastırmak ya da inkar etmek yoluna gitmeyin, duygularla doğrudan yüzleşmek gerekir. Aynı şekilde, karşıdakinin açık ve doğrudan ifade etmesi için cesaretlendirilmesi gerekir.

- Duyguları çatışmacı olmayan bir biçimde ifade edin. Sen yerine ben ya da biz sözcüğünü kullanabilirsiniz.

- Karşınızdakinin duygularını anladığınızı ve önem verdiğinizi ona söyleyin. Olay hakkında farklı düşünseniz de karşınızdakinin duyguları gerçektir. Onların varlığını inkar etmek yalnızca bu duyguları besler ve güçlendirir. Onların açıklanmasına izin vermek ve anlamaya çalışmak yoğunluğunun azalmasına yardım eder. Böylece, çatışmanın özündeki konuları çözmek kolaylaşır.

- Duygusal patlamalara duygusal tepki vermeyin. Aktif ve yansıtıcı dinleme becerilerini kullanarak durumu kontrol altına almak kolaylaşır. Bu süreçte siz de duygusal tepki verirseniz çatışmanın tırmanmasına yol açarsınız. Eğer sakin kalmakta zorlanıyorsanız ortamı terk ederek sakinleşmek ve düşünmek için zaman kazanabilirsiniz.

- Sembolik jestler kullanın. Üzgün olduğunuzu ifade eden bir not göndermek, özür dilemek, birlikte bir yemek yemek hatta bir el sıkışması, saygıyı ifade etmek ve olumsuz duyguları gidermek için maliyeti olmayan jestlerdir.

Duygusal zekânın insan ilişkilerinin temeli olan iletişime etkisini de yadsımak olanaksızdır. " Vücudumuzda dolaşan kan ne ise, iletişimde de duygu o anlama gelir. Duygudan yoksun bir iletişim kalıcı olmayacaktır" (Tarhan, 2006, s. 70). Bu noktada, duygusal zeka, iletişim kurmayı, odaklanmayı, ikna etmeyi ve ilişkileri yönlendirmeyi sağlayacaktır (Tekinay, 1999, s. 44). İletişim çatışmalarının çözümünde kişinin duygusal tepkilerine odaklanması, kendi duygularını kontrol edebilmesi ve diğerleriyle empatik iletişim geliştirerek anlamaya çalışması ilişkilerinde esnek ve hoşgörülü olması etkili olabilir. Bu bağlamda, duygusal zekanın tüm yetkinlikleri dikkate alınarak çatışmacı ve duygusal zekaya sahip kişilerin iletişim özellikleri tablo III teki gibi oluşturulabilir.

ÇATIŞMACI İLETİŞİM STİLİ	DUYGUSAL ZEKÂYA SAHİP İLETİŞİM STİLİ
. Yargılayıcı,	. Anlamaya çalışan,
. Karşı saldırı ve incitme,	. Sakin ve soğukkanlı,
. Yıkıcı eleştiren,	. Yapıcı eleştiren,
. Empatiden yoksun,	. Empati yapabilen,
. Özgüvenden yoksun,	. Özgüven sahibi,
. Müzakere etmeye karşı,	. Müzakere ederek anlaşma,
. Otokontrol sistemini çalıştırmayan,	. Otokontrol sistemini çalıştıran,
. Zaman ve mekana saldıran,	. Zaman ve mekâna göre iletişimi şekillendirir,
. İnanç ve değer yargılarına saldıran,	. İnanç ve değer yargılarına saygı duyan,
. Katı	. Esnek,
. Güvenirliği ve inanırlığı olmayan,	. Güvenilir ve inanılır,
. Tutarsız jest ve mimikler,	. Tutarlı jest ve mimikler,
. Sözlü ve sözsüz iletişim arasında tutarsızlık olan iletişim stili,	. Sözlü ve Sözsüz İletişimin birbirini tamamladığı iletişim stili,

Tablo III, Çatışmacı ve Duygusal Zekâya Sahip İletişim Stili

Kişilerin yaşamlarının büyük bölümünü işgal eden iletişim çatışmaları üstesinden gelinemediği veya etkin bir şekilde yönetilemediği zaman insan yaşamında yıkıcı etkilere neden olmaktadır. Kişilerin strese girmesine, motivasyonsuzluğa, yaşamdan zevk almama ve amaçlara ulaşamama gibi birçok olumsuzluğa yol açmaktadır.

Çatışmanın yıkıcı etkilerini ortadan kaldırmak ve çatışmayı yönetebilmek için duyguları kontrol altına almak ön koşuldur. İnsan yaşamını tehdit edecek boyuta gelmediği sürece, çatışma kaçınılmazdır. Çatışmaları olumlu hale getirmek için duygusal zekâ itici güç olabilir.

Duygusal zekâ iletişimde nasıl itici güç olabilir? Bu soruya yanıt vermeden önce iletişim kavramının tanımını yapmak gerekir. "İletişim bilgi, duygu, düşünce, tutum ve kanaatlerin sözlü ve sözsüz iletiler aracılığıyla kaynaktan alıcıya iletilmesi, alıcının da bu iletileri biyolojik ve psiko-sosyal süreçlerden geçirerek tekrar kaynağa geri göndermesi sürecine" denir. İletişim sürecinde, iletişimi başlatan kaynak, ileti, iletilerin hedefindeki kişi alıcı, kanal ve geribildirim gibi unsurlar yer almaktadır. İletişim sürecinin üç ana aktörü kaynak, ileti ve alıcıdır.

Kişilerarası iletişim çatışmalarının etkili bir şekilde çözümlenmesi kaynak ve alıcının bakış açılarıyla yakından ilgilidir. Elbetteki her konuda uzlaşmaya varılacak diye bir şey söz konusu değildir. Her iki tarafında kendi duygularını anlaması, karşılıklı olarak birbirlerinin duygularını anlamaya çalışması, gereksinim ve beklentilerine yanıt verecek biçime dönüştürmeleri mümkün olabilir.

Kaynak ve alıcı olumsuzlukların ön plana çıktığı karamsar bakış açılarına şartlanmazsa ve olumlu düşünürse, davranış ve tepkilerini takip ederek duygusal anlarını algılayıp ve neler hissettiğini anlamaya çalışırsa, duygularını kabul eder ve paylaşırsa, duygu yoğunluğunu kontrol edip sakin olabilirse, neden bazı olaylarda gereğinden fazla panik yapıp tepki gösterdiğini düşünürse aynı şekilde karşısındakinin de duygularını anlamaya çalışırsa, iletişim çatışmasının yaratılması için nedenleri ortadan kaldırmış olur.

. "İnsanı iyi hayat arkadaşına,, nazik bir komşuya, anlayışlı bir ebeveyne veya karizmatik bir patrona dönüştüren şey, duygusal zekadır " (Konrad& Hendl, 2005, s. 10)

Duyguların gücüne inanmak, onları anlamak ve yaşam kalitesini yükseltecek şekilde yönlendirmek gerekir. T. Moore duyguların gücünü aşağıdaki dörtlükte açık bir şekilde vurgulamıştır.

> Hiçbir şey yitip gitmez onun gözünde,
> Duyguların gözüyle bakabiliyorsa eğer.
> Onun için her meltemde bir öykü vardır,
> Her dalgada bir resim...

Duygusal zekâya sahip olmayan ve olumsuz düşünen kişiler iletişim sürecinde kaybetmeye mahkumdurlar. Kaybedenler ve kazananların bazı belirgin özellikleri şu şekilde gruplandırılabilir (Çobanoğlu, 2005, s. 230-231).

Kaybedenler	Kazananlar
Sorunları büyütür ve sürekli sorunlardan bahsederler.	Fırsatlar üzerinde durur.
Gerekli şeyleri yarım bırakır, gereksiz şeyler için ısrarcı olur	Ne zaman isteyip ne zaman geri duracağını bilir.
Başkalarını eleştirir ve aleyhlerinde konuşur	Diğer insanların yetenek ve başarılarını takdir eder, onları model alır.
Çok meşguldür ve hiçbir işe yetişemez	Çok çalışır ve zamanı boşa harcamaz.
Kendini aklamak için zaman harcar.	Kendini geliştirmek için zaman ayırır.
Gerçek düşüncelerini söylemediğinden yakınır.	Düşüncelerini rahatça ifade eder.
Özür ve mazeretlere sığınır.	Çözümler üretir.
Başkalarını değiştirmek için uğraşır.	Kendi davranışlarını değiştirebilir.
Kendinden farklı insanlara hoşgörü göstermez.	İnsanların farklılıklarını kabul eder.
Hayatına kurallar ve önyargılar şekil verir.	Esnektir, yeni koşullara uyum sağlar.
Sıkça kıskançlık duygusu hisseder.	Samimi ve yardımseverdir.
	Hatalarından ders alır.

Sonuç

İletişim çatışmalarının ortaya çıkmasına kişisel, kültürel ve sosyal birçok faktör yol açmaktadır. Çözümünü ise, insana verilen değer içerisinde düşünmek gerekir. İnsan odaklı düşünmek için ise duygusal zekâya gereksinim vardır. Duygusal zeka, kişisel ve sosyal yetkinlikten meydana gelir. Kişisel yetkinlik, kişinin duygularının farkına varması ve davranışlarını, eğilimlerini kontrol etme kabiliyeti olan duyguların farkında olma ve yönetme yetkinliklerinin bir sonucudur. Sosyal yetkinlik ise başkalarının duygularını, davranışlarını anlama ve ilişkileri kontrol etme yeteneği olan sosyal yeterlik ve sosyal farkındalıkların bir sonucudur.

İnsanların duygu ve düşünceleri birbirinden oldukça farklıdır. Bu anlamda olaylara ve konulara bakış tarzlarıda birbirine benzememektedir. Farklılıklar huzursuzlukları ve anlaşmazlıkları da beraberinde getirir. Olumsuzlukları ortadan kaldırmak ve farklılıkları yönetmek duygusal zekaya sahip olmak ve geliştirmekle mümkündür. Duyusal zeka, kim olduğunu bilmek, kendi duygularını anlamak, anlamlandırmak ve olumlu sonuçlar alabilmek için yönlendirmek, öfke, üzüntü, korku, utanç, şaşkınlık gibi duygu ve ruh hallerini dengeleyebilmek, başkalarının duygularını anlamak ve onlara hissettirmek gibi yetkinlikler içeren duygusal kalitenin bir kompozisyonudur. Bu yetkinlikler ilişki kalitesini belirlemekte ve yetkinliklere sahip olmamak ise çatışmalara zemin hazırlamaktadır.

İletişimde kaybedenler ve çatışmacı kişilerin kendine dönük, sabırsız, fevri, kurgulayıcı, itici, kendini önemseyen, başkalarını eleştiren bir yaklaşım sergileyen ve karşısındakinin duygularına, sorunlarına ilgi göstermeyenler oldukları bilinmektedir. İletişimde kazananlar ise sabırlı, hem kendini hem de başkalarını anlamaya çalışan, esnek, çözümler üreten ve hatalardan ders çıkaran gibi özelliklere sahiptir.

İletişim yönetiminde duygusal zekâ göstergelerini aşağıdaki gibi gruplandırabiliriz.

- İletişimde amaçları belirlemek ve duyguların katkısını ortaya koymak.
- Mevcut duyguları gözden geçirmek, güçlü ve zayıf yönlerini belirlemek.
- İnsanların zayıf yönlere sahip oldukları kadar, güçlü yönlere de sahip olduklarını bilmek.
- Kişilerin tutum ve davranışlarının duygularıyla yakından ilgili olduğunu ve güçlü bir duygusal zekânın kişilerin tutum ve davranışları üzerinde belirleyici olduğunu, ilişkilerinde onların tatmin düzeylerini belirlediğini bilmek.
- Duyguların yönetiminin, bir kişiyi bir bütün olarak çevresiyle uyumlu tutmak ve iletişimde istenen hedeflere ulaşmak için birbirlerine bağlı olarak yürütülen belirli çabaları ifade ettiğini bilmek.
- Başkalarının duygularını ve hislerini hesaba katmak gerektiğini bilmek, empati göstermek.
- Duyguların dili olan beden dilinin etkin bir şekilde nasıl kullanılacağını bilmek.

İnsan beyni üzerinde çalışan psikologlar, insan zekasını gerçek ölçütünün bilişsel zeka(IQ) olsa bile yaşam kalitesini yükseltmek ve ilişkileri düzenlemek için duygusal zekanın etkili olduğunu ifade etmektedirler. Kişiler duygularını ustaca ifade edebilir ve karşısındakinin duygularını ne kadar doğru anlayabilirlerse iletişim çatışmalarını çözmeleri o kadar kolay olacaktır.

Kaynakça

Atabek, E. (1999). *Bizim duygusal zekâmız.* İstanbul: Altın Kitaplar Yayınevi.

Aldag, R. J. ve Stearns, T. M. (1987). *Management.* Cincinnati, Ohio: South-Western Publishing Co.

Baltaş, A. (2001). *Ekip çalışması ve liderlik.* İstanbul: Remzi Kitabevi.

Baltaş, Z. (2006). *Duygusal zeka.* İstanbul: Remzi Kitabevi.

Barutçugil, İ. (2004). *Duyguların yönetimi.* İstanbul: Kariyer Yayıncılık.

Boone, Lurs E., Kurtz, David, L. (1978). *Management.* New York: Random House Business Division.

Bradberry, T., ve Greaves, J. (1999). *Duygusal zekanızı keşfedin.* (Çev. Sevda Kubilay) İstanbul: T. Truva Yayınları.

Çobanoğlu, Ş. (2005). *Mobbing.* İstanbul: Timaş Yayınları.

Dökmen, Ü. (1996). *İletişim çatışmaları ve empati.* İstanbul: Sistem Yayıncılık.

Strauss, G., ve Sayles, L.R. (1972). *Personnel, the human problems of management.* , Englewood Cliffs, NJ: Prentice Hall.

Goleman, D. (1996). *Duygusal zeka.* (Çev, Banu Seçkin Yüksel). İstanbul: Varlık Yayınları.

Koçel, T. (2003). *İşletme yöneticiliği* (9. Basım). İstanbul: Beta Yayınları.

Konrad, S., ve Hendl, C. (2005). *Duygularla güçlenmek.* (Çev. Meral Taştan) İstanbul: Hayat Yayıncılık.

Mayer, J. D., ve Salovey, P. (1993). The intelligence of emotional intelligence. *Intelligence, 17*(4).

Özdilek, O. (2002). EQ'n kadar konuş! *Posta Gazetesi,* 15 Nisan Pazartesi.

Rahim , M. A. (1985). A strategy for managing conflict in complex organizations. *Human Relations, 38.*

Stoner, J. A.F. (1998). *Management.* Englewood Cliffs, NJ: Prentice-Hall Inc.

Şimşek, Ş., Akgemci, T. ve Çelik, A. (2001). *Davranış bilimlerine giriş ve örgütlerde davranış.* Ankara: Nobel Yayınları.

Tabak, S. (1996). *Sağlık iletişimi.* İstanbul: Literatür Yayıncılık.

Tarhan, N. (2006). *Duyguların dili.* İstanbul: Timaş Yayınları.

Tekinay, N. A. İnsan kaynaklarının rolü değişiyor. *Capital Dergisi, 7*(4), Nisan, 144-147.

Weiss, J. W. (1996). *Organizational behavior & change.* Minneapolis/St. Paul: West Publishing Company.

Toplumsal İletişim Sürecinde "Öteki" ve Söylemsel-Epistemik Şiddet

Barış Çoban,
Uluslarası Kıbrıs Üniversitesi
barishc@gmail.com

Giriş

Toplumsal yapı bütünsel değildir, ancak bütünselmiş gibi görünme çabası içerisindedir. Toplumu üst-belirleyen iktidar yapısının söylemsel ve eylemsel müdahalesi ile toplum bütünsel bir yapılanım gibi kurgulanır. Bu sahte bütünlük aslında daha çok iktidarın, söylemsel-epistemik şiddete dayanan, ideolojik aygıtları aracılığıyla, ama her zaman için—doğrudan şiddet kullanan—zor aygıtlarının gizil müdahalesi tehdidi ile yaratılır. Toplumsal yapıyı denetim altında tutan grup, diğer grupları—ve aslında aynı süreçte kendini de—"öteki"leştirerek kendilerini sınırları belli, ayrı yapılanımlar olarak var ederler. Bu grupların oluşumunun temelinde sınıfsal—politik—etnik, kültürel, dinsel, cinsel vb. farklılıklar yatar, bu farklılıklar toplumsal söylem ve pratiklerle ifade edilir.

Toplum birbirine "öteki" olarak bakan bir çok farklı yapılanımların örgülenmesinden oluşur ve heterojen bir görünüme sahiptir. Toplumun bu parçalı yapısı iktidarın işleyişi açısından olumsal bir görünüm arz etmez, iktidar tüm bu grupları denetim altında tutmak için değişik ve değişken toplumsal politikalar üretir. Buna rağmen toplumsal yaşam içerisinde parçalanma, süreksizlik ve yerinde çıkmalar sonucunda iktidar kendisini hiçbir zaman tam olarak yeniden-üretemez. Bu anlamda egemen sınıfın etnik, dinsel, kültürel vb. kimlikleri gizil şiddet içeren ideolojik söylemle, tüm topluma dayatılmaya ve toplumsal parçalanmanın aşılması—daha doğrusu üzerinin örtülmesi—söylemsel şiddete dayalı tektipleştirme süreci ile gerçekleşirilmeye çalışılır. Tüm bunlara karşın toplum farklı direniş biçimleri ile bu tektipleştirmeye direnir, kendi etnik kimliğini, dilini, dinini, kültürünü, cinsel tercihini yaşamaya, yeniden-üretmeye çalışır. Bu süreç içerisinde iktidar çoğunluk olarak tanımladığı topluluğu ideolojik aygıtlarıyla, en çok da kitle iletişim araçları ile azınlık olarak tanımlanan "öteki"lere karşı konumlandırır. Toplumsal bilinç "öteki"nin toplumsal bütünlüğe bir tehdit oluşturduğu düşüncesi ile hastalanır ve toplum bu düşünce ile gerçekten sağlıksız bir parçalanma sürecine girer. Söylemsel alanda başlayan parçalanma ve çatışma gündelik toplumsal pratiklere taşınır, baskın grubun söylemsel şiddetini dillendiren kitle iletişim araçları, şiddete dayalı toplumsal pratiklerin de meşrulaştırılarak toplumsal yaşamın doğal, sıradan pratikleri olarak kabul edilmesini sağlar. Toplumsal iletişim süreci iletişimselliğinden soyunur, şiddete dayalı baskıcı iktidarın ideolojisini toplumsal bilinçyapısına taşır.

"Öteki", Özne, İktidar

İktidarın toplumsal yapıyı biçimlendirme süreci, toplumsal özne ve "öteki" ilişkisi bağlamında anlamlandırılabilir. "Öteki" öznenin dölyatağıdır. Öteki ben'in varolmasının önkoşullarından bir tanesidir, "özne özkimliğine ulaşmak için, kendini imgesel öteki ile özdeşleştirmeli, kendini yabancılaştırmalıdır" (Zizek, 2002, s. 121). İnsanın kendisini tanıyabilmesi öteki dolayımıyla olasıdır, öteki benliğin görülebildiği tek yerlemdir: "insan kendi kendisinin karşısında iken, onun karşısında olan ötekidir" (Marx, 1993, s. 148). Toplumsal ilişkiler sisteminde öznenin varoluşunu yaratan da ötekinin varoluşudur, yapısal bütün içerisinde özne diğer öznelerle kurduğu ilişki içerisinde bir anlam kazanabilir. "Özne her zaman onu öteki için temsil eden bir gösterene raptedilmiş, mıhlanmıştır ve bu mıhlama sayesinde simgesel bir görev yüklenir, öznelerarası simgesel ilişkiler ağı içinde bir yer edinir" (Zizek, 2002, s. 129). Bu öznelerarasılık "öteki"nin varlığını önvarsayar. Bu yüzden özne "kendisinin Öteki karşısındaki dışsal konumunun Öteki'nin kendisine içsel olduğunu kavramak zorundadır... Özneyi Öteki'den dışlarmış gibi görünen özelliğin kendisi zaten Öteki'nin "düşünümsel bir belirlenimi"dir; tam da Öteki'den dışlanmış olduğumuz için, çoktan onun oyununun bir parçasıyızdır" (Zizek, 2002, s. 139-140). Bu gerçeklik bizim varoluşumuzun imlendiği noktaya gönderme yapar. Özneyi vareden önce ötekinin bizdeki içsel konumudur, biz kendiliğimizi bu dışsal olanın içsel yansımasında bulmaya çalışırız, kendi varlığımız başka varlıkla anlamlandırılabilir bir yapılanım gösterir; "...her birey kendisi için varlık olunca başkası için varlık olarak oluşur ve kendisi için varlık olunca başkası onun için varlık olur... bu karşılıklılık zorunlu bir olgudur" (Marx, 1999, s. 165-166). Bu bağlamda "öteki" özne için olmazsa olmazdır, kendi varoluşunun yeniden-üretimi de ötekiyle girdiği iletişim içerisinde olası hale gelir. Toplumsal iletişimsel süreçleri bu bağlamda birbirlerine "öteki" olarak konumlanmış özneleri önvarsayar, iletişim süreci "öteki" olmadan gerçekleşemez.

"Öteki"nin sorunsal haline gelmesi temel olarak iktidar ilişkilerinin yapısından kaynaklanmaktadır, iktidarın çoğunluğu baskı altında tutan azınlık grubunun elinde olması, iktidar ilişkileri bağlamında toplumun süreğen bir denetim altında tutulmasını zorunlu kılar. Bu süreç parçalanmaların yaratılması ve bu durumun "disiplin ve cezalandırma" aygıtınca toplumsal denetim sürecinde iktidar hesabına kullanılmasını içerir. Toplumsal yapının iktidarına sahip olan devlet, toplumu ben ve "öteki" olarak bölümler ve iktidarı içselleştiren "ben"ler, iktidarın içselleştirmeyen\içselleştiremeyen "öteki"lere karşı konumlandırılır.

Devlet, iktidar ilişkileri bağlamında toplumun belli sınırlar içersine alınarak anlamlandırılmasını olanaklı kılan bir yapılanımdır, ancak dayattığı parçalanmışlık, "öteki"nin reddi yabancılaşmaya neden olur: "Devlet, aslında, insanın insana başka bir anlam yüklemesi, emretme/itaat etme bölünmesinde bir küme insanın bir diğer küme insana yabancılığı anlamına gelmektedir" (Gauchet, 2000, s. 36). Toplumsal yapıyı belirleyen iktidar aygıtı olarak devlet aslında olanaksız bir homojenlik istemine—"öteki"sizliğe—gönderme yapar ve bu olanaksızlık tarafından belirlenir, bu "eksiğin" etrafında örgülenir. Devletin kendisini "öteki"lerin olmadığı bütünsel bir yapı olarak kurgulamasına rağmen, gerçeklik bu kurguyu parçalar. Devlet temel olarak baskı üzerine kuruludur, bu bağlamda devletin söylemsel ve eylemsel yapısı egemen olan grubun diğer grupları, "öteki"leri denetim altında tutmasına hizmet eder: "...Gerçeklikte devlet, bir sınıfın bir başka sınıf tarafından bastırılmasına yarayan bir makineden başka bir şey değildir..." (Lenin, 1990, s. 31). Devlet bu anlamda şiddet üzerine temellenir ve şiddet üreten bir makinedir, bu söylemsel ve eylemsel şiddet, toplumsal pratikler üzerinden kendisini var eder.

Devletin kurguladığı toplumsal yapı belli sınırlar içerisine kapatılmış—bu sınırla bütünselleştirilmeye çalışılan—parçalanmaya işaret eder. "Nihai olarak sahip olduğumuz, başarısız bir bütünlüktür, ele geçirilemez bir tamlığın mekanıdır. Bütün, hem olanaksız hem de zorunlu nesnedir. Olanaksızdır çünkü, ne kadar kararsız olursa olsun bir tür kapanma olmadıkça hiçbir anlamlandırma ve hiçbir özdeşlik olmayacaktır" (Laclau, 2007, s. 88). Tüm devletler birden fazla etnik, dinsel vb. gruplar barındırmaktadır, ancak devletlerin tümellik yaratma isteği ve buna bağlı olarak geliştirdikleri söylem ve eylemler toplumsal yapı ve iletişim biçimlerinde parçalanma ve yerinden çıkmalar yaşanmasına neden olur. Buna karşın toplumsal iletişim süreci "öteki"nin yeniden tanımlanması ve önyargıların aşılması için etkin bir araç olarak da kullanılabilir. Yaşanılan durumun dayatması sonucunda homojen bir yapı istemi parçalanır, kimlik sorununun aşırı vurgulanması baskılanan kimliklerin tepkisellik ve şiddet içeren bir biçimde yeniden-doğuşuna neden olur. Bu nedenle de her tümellik girişimi, ötekinin reddi olduğu için ve ona karşı gizil de olsa şiddet içerdiği için, ister istemez parçalanmanın yolunu açar. Tarihsel bağlama dayandırılan düşmanlıklar, önyargılar vb., buna bağlı olarak, "öteki"lere uygulanan toplumsal baskı, söylemsel-epistemik şiddet toplumsal yapıda parçalanmalar yaşanmasına neden olur. Toplum "ötekileştirilmiş" kimlikler üzerinden kendini ifade eden, çatışan yapılardan oluşan bir bütünlük olarak iktidarın aygıtlarınca baskı ile birarada tutulur. Bu süreçte, tüm diğer ideolojik aygıtlardan daha etkin olan kitle iletişim araçlarının da önemli işlevleri vardır. "Öteki"ne yönelik toplumsal önyargıların, söylemsel şiddetin belirlenmesinde ve vurgulanmasında kitle iletişim aaraçları oldukça etkilidir. Toplumsal iletişim gerçekte öznelerin tüm farklılıklarına rağmen kendilerini var ettikleri, ifade ettikleri bir alan olduğunda anlam kazanır. İletişim toplumsal bağlamda şiddetin üretimi için kullanılabileceği gibi toplumsal dayanışma ve barışın yaratılması için de kullanılabilir. Bu süreç toplumsal düşünüş ve söylemin önyargı ve şiddetten arındırılarak yeniden-anlamlandırılması ile olasıdır.

İktidar toplumsal bilinçyapısını (bilinç ve bilinçdışını) belirleme sürecinde toplumsal belleğe müdahale eder. Toplumsal bellek ideolojik bir yüklemlenime sahiptir. İdeolojik bağlamda toplumsal belleği belirlemek toplumsal düşünüş ve eylemleri de belirlemek anlamına gelir. Çünkü "toplumsal olarak paylaşılan inançlar toplumsal bellek"in temelini oluşturur, ideoloji "gruplar tarafından paylaşılan temel inançlar ise" ideolojiyi "toplumsal bellek olarak tanımladığımız yere, toplumsal bilgi ve tutumlar ile yanyana" (van Dijk, 2003, s. 22-24) koyabiliriz. Toplumların, kendi toplumsal yapılanımları içerisinde yer alan diğer azınlık gruplarına ve diğer toplumlara ilişkin düşünüş ve tutumları toplumların kendilerini nasıl gördüğünün ve görmek istediğini gösterir, ancak bu süreç iktidarın üst-belirlediği bir süreçtir.

Toplumsal bellek toplumsal bilinçyapısının düğüm noktalarından bir tanesidir, toplumsal belleği belirleyenler bu bağlamda toplumsal bilinç alanını da belirlemiş olurlar. Toplumsal düşünüş ve eylemlerin temelinde toplumsal belleğin belirleyiciliği yatar. Toplumsal kültür gündelik yaşam pratikleri içerisinde öznelere taşınır, ancak bu süreç egemen ideolojik yapıdan bağımsız değildir, egemen ideoloji toplumsal iletişim sürecinde öznelerin bilinçyapılarına müdahil olabileceği tüm toplumsal pratiklerde kendisini üretme ve yeniden-üretme çabasını gösterir. Toplumsal belleğin belirlenmesi de bu anlamda oldukça önemli bir süreçtir. Toplumsal bellek kurgusal bir yapıya sahiptir, iktidarın ideolojisinin belirlediği bu kurgusal yapılanım toplumsal düşünüş, söylem ve eylemlerin çıkış noktasını oluşturur. Toplumsal belleğin kurgusunu belirlemek, aslında toplumun yapısını belirlemektir. Bu nedenle her iktidar, örneğin "tarih yazıcılığı" sorununu bağlamında tarihi ve tarihsel metni belirleyerek toplumsal belleğin, bilinçyapısının ve böylelikle toplumun tüm düşünüş ve eylem pratiklerinin de belirlenmesi için çaba gösterir. Toplumsal belleğe iktidar tarafından kazınan, "öteki"ne karşı öfke ve nefret içeren tüm tutum ve yaklaşımlar sonucunda, gündelik yaşam içerisinde iktidardan farklı düşünenlere karşı iktidar aygıtlarından önce toplumun müdahalesini ve şiddetinin uygulanması bu gerçeklikten kaynaklanır. Toplumlara iktidar tarafından, gelenek olarak yerleştirilen davranış, düşünce ve ritüeller iktidarı yeniden-üretirken, toplumsal özgürleşmeyi kesintiye uğratır, toplumsal muhalefet üzerinde baskı kurar. Ancak iktidar toplumsal belleği bütünsel olarak belirleyemez, her zaman için toplumsal anlamda iktidara karşı direnenlerin kendilerini varedebilecekleri bellek alanları da vardır, bu da karşı düşünce ve karşı-tarihin—muhalif tarih söyleminin—olanaklılığını yaratır. Toplumsal bellek bir iktidar mücadelesi alanıdır. Kitle iletişim araçları toplumların belleklerinin belirlenmesinde ve tarihsel olanın geçerli ideoloji bağlamında yeniden-anlamlandırılması süreçlerinde önemli işlevlere sahiptir.

Toplumsal belleğin ve bilinçyapısının belirlenmesi süreci—Althusserci anlamıyla—ideolojik aygıtlar ile gerçekleştirilir. Bu süreçte kitle iletişim araçları etkin bir biçimde işgörür. Egemen sınıfın ideolojisi toplumsal iletişim pratiklerini üst-belirlediği için, iktidar ilişkilerinin parçalıyıcılığı iletişimsel süreçte de kendisini yeniden-üretir. İletişimsel süreç toplumsal yapının parçalanmışlığını yeniden-üretirken, "öteki"lere karşı söylemsel-epistemik şiddet uygular. Toplumsal iletişim sürecinde egemen yapıya bağlı çoğunluk grubunun "öteki"ler hakkında olumsal olmayan düşünceleri, önyargıları toplumsal ilişkilerde parçalanma yaşanmasına neden olur, bu süreç gündelik yaşamın tüm pratiklerinde kendisini yansıtır. Kısacası iktidarın toplumsal yapılanıma ilişkin kurgusu iletişimsel süreçleri ön-belirler. İktidar ilişkilerinin toplumsal iletişim sürecindeki yansıması olan söylemsel-epistemik şiddet, toplumsal özgürleşmeyi, gerçek iletişimsel biçimlerin geliştirilmesini engeller.

Toplumsal İletişim: Şiddet ve Öteki

İletişim için "öteki" olmazsa olmazdır, zorunluluktur, "öteki"nin olmadığı bir iletişimsel süreçteten sözetmek olası değildir. Toplumsal yapının "öteki"siz bir bütünlük haline getirilmesi, aslında toplumun ortadan kaldırılmasıdır. Bastırma yoluyla "öteki"nin üzerinin örtülmesi yanılsamalı bir bütünlük yaratır, gerçekte ise bastırılmış olan herşey farklı bir biçimde de olsa mutlaka geri döner, toplumsal yapıda kopma, yerinden çıkma ve parçalanmalar yaratan sorunlar bağlamında, kendisini bir düğüm noktası—*point de capiton*—olarak dayatır.

Toplumsal alanda "öteki" öznenin varoluş koşullarını yaratır, ancak toplumsal yapının değişim süreci ile birlikte "öteki"ne dair toplumsal düşünüş radikal değişim ve dönüşümler geçirmiştir. "Öteki" ile olan iletişimsel süreçlerin kırılması, kesintiye uğraması ve yerinden çıkması sonucunda "özne"ler, toplumlar kendi varoluşlarının merkezi olan "öteki"ne şiddet uygulamaya söylemsel ya da eylemsel olarak onu yoketmeye yönelmiştir. İletişimsel anlamda, söylemsel olarak "öteki"ne uygulanan şiddet, öznelerin kendilerine yönelen yoketme isteğini ifade eder. Çünkü, her zaman için özne "öteki"nde kendisini görür, özneler, daha doğrusu toplumlar, kendilerine olan öfkelerini—eksikliklerini, hastalıklarını—"öteki" üzerinden bastırmaya, gidermeye çalışır. Toplumsal ilişkiler bağlamında temel belirleyen olan iktidarın ideolojisi, bunu topluma taşıyan ideolojik aygıtlar ve temel olarak da kitle iletişim araçları, toplumsal bağlamda "öteki"ne yönelik söylemsel-epistemik şiddeti toplumu daha kolay denetlenebilecek parçalanmış bir yapının üretimi ve yeniden-üretimi için kullanır. Toplumsal özgürlük gerçekte "öteki" ile gerçekleştirilecek iletişime dayanır, ancak toplumsal önyargıların yaratılması ve bunların söylemsel şiddet ile ifade edilmesi, toplumsal barışın engellenmesine ve çok etnik yapı barındıran toplumların kırılan yapısının daha da zayıflatılmasına neden olur.

Toplumsal yaşam sürecinde şiddet iktidar ilişkileri bağlamında anlamlandırılabilir. Toplumun içinde yaşadığı dönemin üretim biçimi, ilişkileri ve buna bağlı olarak kültürel siyasal yapısı toplumsal yapıyı üst-belirler. Toplumsal yapının iktidar ilişkileri egemen iktidarın ideolojik aygıtlara ve zor aygıtlarına gönderme yapılmadan çözümlenemez. Toplumsal bilinçyapısı egemen iktidarın ideolojik olarak belirlediği bir yapı olmasına rağmen bir çok parçalanma, yerinden çıkma ve kopuntu nedeniyle tümel bir yapılanıma sahip değildir. Bu nedenle iktidar ılışkılerı bağlamında farklı sınıf ve grupların kendını ifade edebilecekleri "eksikler" ve boşluklar sözkonusudur. İktidar ilişkileri egemen iktidardan topluma doğru yönelen etkileşimsel bir sürece gönderme yapar, bu süreç her zaman için iktidarın şiddetini de barındırır.

Şiddet toplumsal bağlamda doğal değildir, iktidar ilişkilerinden kaynaklanır, ideolojinin üst-belirlediği söylemsel ve eylemsel bir yapılanım gösterir. "Şiddet, bir dünya görüşünün parçasıdır ve 'ironik bir episteme'yle, çoğu zaman 'anlaşılması' açısından daha derinlerde yatan bir şeyin belirtisidir" (Hobart, 1996). Şiddetin anlaşılması toplumsal yapıyı –bilinçyapısı, pratikler vb.—iktidar ve ideoloji bağlamında derinlemesine çözümlemekle olası hale gelir. İktidar ilişkilerinin akılcılığı da aslında şiddetin aranması gereken yeri işaret eder. İktidarın ve bunun yansıması olarak toplumun düşünsel yapısı söylemsel şiddeti reddetmez, aksine onu içselleştirmiştir: "tüm insan davranışları akılcılık yoluyla planlanır ve programlanır... Hatta en şiddet içerenlerin de bile akılcılık mevcuttur. Şiddette en tehlikeli olan da şiddetin bu akılcılığıdır. Tabi ki şiddetin kendisi berbat bir şeydir. Ancak şiddetin en derin kökü ve sürekliliği onun bizim tarafından kullanılan akılcı biçiminden kaynaklanır. Eğer akıl çağında yaşıyorsak şiddeti reddedebiliriz düşüncesi vardır. Bu görüş kesinlikle hatalıdır. Şiddet ile akılcılık arasında uyuşmazlık yoktur" (Foucault, 1996, s. 299). Bu bağlamda, şiddetin de yoğun olarak içerildiği toplumsal pratiklerin iktidarın akılcılığından kaynaklandığı ileri sürülebilir. "Öteki"ne yönelik tüm düşünce ve söylemler akılcı açıklamalarla meşrulaştırılır. Toplumsal sorunların nedenleri olarak görülen "öteki"lerin ortadan kaldırılması sorunların da ortadan kalkacağı düşüncesini beraberinde getirir, bu anlamda söylemsel-epistemik şiddet için akılcı, meşru bir iletişimsel ortamda yaratılmış olur. Bu acımasız akılcılık, gerçekliğin tahrif edilmiş bir biçimde görülmesinde ve bu tahrif edilmiş görüntü içerisinde tahrifin nedeni olarak kodlananın yokedilmesi—tahrifi—ile sorunun aşılacağı çıkarımı, şiddetin meşruluğunu da akılcı bir biçimde ortaya koyar. Tarihsel olarak bir çok soykırımda akılcı düşüncelere, söylemlere dayandırılmıştır. Ancak "öteki"ler yokedildiği halde toplumsal sorunlar daha da ağırlaşarak devam etmiştir. Toplumsal anlamda "öteki" toplumun kendisinde görüp korktuğu tüm eksiklik, aşağılık duygusu vb.den kurtulmak için yokettiği kendi ikizi gibi işgörür, intihar etme cesaretine sahip olamayanlar, kendilerinde nefret ettikleri herşeyi "öteki"ne—onlara ayna tutan ikizlerine—yüklerler ve onu yokederek bu lanetten kurtulduklarını düşünürler, ancak içlerindeki karanlık azalacağına giderek artar.

Şiddet iktidar için vazgeçilmezdir, iktidar biçimleri karmaşıklaştıkça şiddet biçimleri de çeşitlenir ve karmaşıklaşır. Bu bağlamda söylemsel-epistemik şiddet yeni emperyal dönemdeki ulus-devletlerinin olağan düşünüş ve söyleminin en önemli parçası haline gelmekte ve meşrulaştırılarak toplumsal söylemin öğesine dönüştürülmekte, toplumsal yapı bu düşünüş ve söylemlerle parçalanmakta, azınlık haline getirilen gruplar iktidarın etkisi altındaki toplumsal gruplarca baskı altına alınmaktadır.

Gündelik yaşam içerisinde düşünsel ve söylemsel şiddet "sıradanlaşmakta", "sıradan faşizm" kitlelerin gündelik yaşamının ideolojisi haline gelmektedir. Gündelik yaşamın şiddet üreten bir biçim alması ise temel olarak kitle iletişim araçlarının etkili—ama kesinlikle olumsal olmayan—biçimlendirme yöntemlerinin sonucunda gerçekleşmektedir. Gündelik hayattaki şiddet doğallaştırılmış, normalleştirilmiş ve bunun sonucunda "sosyal darwinizm" olarak adlandırılan faşizan anlayış meşrulaştırılmıştır, buna göre kalabalık olanın, güçlünün şiddeti etkin şekilde kullanıp toplumsal yapı içersindeki azınlıkları, "öteki"leri denetim altına alanların hayatta kalıp diğerlerinin yokolması doğanın kanunu olduğu gibi toplumun doğasının da kanunudur. Toplumsal yapı karşılaştığı sorunları çözemedikçe şiddete eğilim göstermekte ve giderek kendisine daha da yabancılaşmakta, şiddet anlamsızca toplumsal özneler tarafından birbirlerine yöneltilmekte ve iktidarın toplumsal yapı üzerindeki denetimi de zor aygıtlarına bırakılmaktadır. Bunun sonucunda toplum elinde kalan son insani değerleri yitirdiği gibi, özerk iktidar alanlarını da, son özgürlüklerini de iktidarın ellerine teslim etmek zorunda kalmaktadır. Toplumsal parçalanma şiddeti yaygınlaştırmaktadır: "Şiddet, düzenin parçalandığı rejimlerde ya da vatandaşların temel etnik, dinsel veya ulusal ayrımlamalarla bölündüğü durumlarda güç kazanır" (Tarrow, 1996). Ancak, iktidar bu bölünmelerin aşılması için uğraşmak yerine parçalanmayı hızlandıracak şekilde hareket etmektedir, iktidarın söylemsel ve eylemsel şiddeti "öteki"nin şiddetini çağırır ve toplumsal yaşam çatışkan bir biçim almaya başlar. "Öteki"nin şiddeti iktidarın şiddetine karşı kendisini konumlandırır, kendi söylemsel yapısını iktidarın şiddetine göre biçimlendirir, söylemsel alandaki iktidar mücadelesi şiddet de içeren bir biçim alır ve parçalanmışlık söylemsel alanda yeniden-üretilmiş olur. "Öteki"nin şiddeti iktidarın şiddeti yanında daha etkisiz ve "meşru müdafa" gibi görünür, iktidarın baskısına karşı meşru bir direniş olarak kendisini vareder. Bu bağlamda, İdeolojik aygıtlar ve zor aygıtlarının şiddeti, toplumsal alandaki bir çok diğer şiddet biçimlerinin de beslendiği yer olarak yorumlanabilir. Sonuç olarak iktidar aygıtları şiddet üreten aygıtlardır.

İdeolojik aygıtlar genelde "rıza" üreten bir yapıya sahip olsalar da, her zaman için epistemik şiddeti etkin olarak kullanırlar. Egemen ideolojiye direnenler iktidarın düşünsel, söylemsel baskısını ve şiddetini gündelik yaşam içerisinde hissederler. İktidarın muhalif toplumsal düşünüş biçimlerine karşı geliştirdiği ideolojik baskı her zaman için devletin zor aygıtlarının baskısını da hissettirir. Başka bir deyişle iktidar, ideolojisini rıza üretim süreci içerisinde aktarma çabasında iken, toplumsal çatışmanın yaşandığı dönemlerde zor aygıtlarını etkin olarak kullanır, muhalifleri toplumdan koparmaya çalışır, farklı düşünüş biçimlerini marjinal kılacak söylemsel ve eylemsel şiddet biçimleri geliştirir. Bu bağlamda, toplumsal söylemin faşizan yapısı, toplumsal yaşam alanlarında iktidarın ürettiği faşizan baskı biçimleri ile şiddetin doğallaştırıldığı bir sistemin göstergesidir. Toplumsal düşünüş ve söylemin şiddeti meşrulaştırması, güçlü olanın haklı olduğunun genel kabulü, iktidarı ve iktidarın desteklediği legal ya da illegal şiddet aygıtlarının tüm yaşam alanlarında etkin olmaya başlaması toplumsallığın yokolmasını da beraberinde getirir. Toplum tüm özgür, özerk iletişimsel olanaklarını yokeder, iktidarın teksesli yapısının karanlığında estetize edilmiş söylemsel ve eylemsel şiddet biçimleri ile yanılsamalar içerisinde gerçekliğini yitirir. Toplum bu süreçte kendisini reddeder, yokeder; süreç gerçek anlamda toplumsal intihar olarak da okunabilir. Tarihsel bağlamda Almanya'da faşizm dönemi toplumsal intihar olarak yorumlanabilir.

Söylemsel şiddet gizil bir biçimde ardında eylemsel şiddetin olduğunu da hissettirir. Buna göre, "Öteki"ne yönelik bu tehditkar söylem aslında "öteki"lere iktidarın arzuladığı toplumsal kurgu içerisinde kendilerinin içerilmediğini anlatmaktadır. Azınlık olarak görülen politik, etnik, dinsel, cinsel gruplar söylemsel olarak sürekli taciz edilir, sıradan insanın faşizan söylemi "öteki"ni temel hedef olarak görür ve kendi yaşadığı bir çok sorunun kaynağı olarak da "öteki"ler imlenir. Ancak, toplumsal yaşam bağlamında temel sorun kaynağı olan üretim ilişkileri ve iktidar ilişkilerini sorgulamak ve aşmak için mücadele etme sorumluluğundan kaçınan toplumlar, "öteki"lere karşı şiddet içeren düşünce, tutum ve söylemlerle kendilerini aldatan yanılsamalar, geçici rahatlamalar yaşamayı tercih eder. Başka bir deyişle, iktidarı karşısına alamayan toplumsal çoğunluk azınlıkları hedef alarak, aslında kendi bastırılmışlığının intikamını alır, yanılsamalı bir rahatlama yaşarken, kendisini daha da içinden çıkılmaz hastalıklı bir durumun içerisine sokar. İktidarın hedef alınması, toplumun iktidar yapısı karşısında "öteki"leşmesini ve iktidarın şiddetiyle karşı karşıya gelmesine neden olacağı için, kaçınılması gereken bir durum olarak görülür.

Toplumsal parçalanmışlığın şiddet yoluyla aşılacağı düşüncesi, toplumu ve toplumsal bilinçyapısını sakatlarken, gündelik yaşam içerisinde de kendisini gösterir. Gündelik yaşam pratikleri içerisinde iktidar ilişkileri yeniden-üretilirken çoğunluk olarak tanımlanan toplumsal grubun söylemi aslında "sıradan faşizm"in söylemidir; yani kendisine benzemeyen herşeyden korkar ve onun yokedilmesi gerektiğini düşünür. Toplumun kendine olan güvensizliği—tekinsizlik—"öteki"ne yüklemlenir: "Tekinsiz Julia Kristeva'nın ırkçılık ve milliyetçilik çözümlemesinin temel özelliğidir... unheimlich'in—tekinsizliğin—karakteristik figürlerini anımsatan dış dünyadaki Öteki (sınıf, ırk, millet, cins) olmaktan daha çok içdünyamızdaki Öteki'dir, 'kendimize olan yabancılığımızdır'" (Cohen, 2002). Diğer bir deyişle kendi parçalanmışlığını, komplekslerini, eksikliklerini ve aşağılanmışlıklarını "öteki"ne yükler ve onu yoketme düşü kurarak kendi hastalıklarından kurtulacağı yanılgısına kapılır. "Nüfusun bir kısmının şeytanileştirilmesi yoluyladır ki bir toplum kendi tutarlılığına dair bir anlayışa varır... grup üyeleri arasında karşılıklı bir özdeşleşmeyi mümkün kılan unsur, bir şeye ya da birisine duyulan ortak nefrettir" (Laclau, 2007, s. 88). Toplum "öteki"ne karşı oluşturduğu birlikle kendisini bir bütünlük olarak duyumsar, kendi imgesel dağılmışlığının sınırlarını ötekine yönelik söylemsel ve eylemsel şiddetle çizmeye, kendi imgesini yakalamayı, "öteki"nin simgesel ve varoluşsal yokoluşuna bitiştirir. Ancak, aslında durup düşünse ve gerçekliğini anlayabilecek bir çıplaklıkla kendisine aynada bakabilse herşey paramparça olur. Toplum kendi gerçekliğinden, parçalanmışlığından büyük bir korku duyar. Bu korku nedeniyle de toplum genellikle kendisine ayna tutan entellektüellerden nefret eder, farklı ya da muhalif düşüncelerden korkar. İktidarın onu rahatlatan yanılsamalarını tercih eder, kendi gerçekliğinin karanlığını "öteki"ne yüklemleyerek aşmaya yönelir.

Söylemsel Şiddet ve Irkçılık

Toplumsal yaşam sürecinde "öteki" olarak konumlandırılanlara karşı geliştirilen söylemsel ve eylemsel şiddet içeren ırkçı ideolojik tutumlar, toplumsal iletişim sürecinde egemen ideoloji tarafından topluma aktarılır. Irkçılığı doğallaştıran bu süreç, ırkçılığın genel kitlenin bilinçyapısına ve sonrasında da günlük dil kullanımlarına, yani söylem yapılarına taşınmasına yol açar. "Irkçıklık söylemde dahil, ayrımcı toplumsal pratikler tarafından yerel (mikro) düzeyde ve kurumlar, örgütler ve genel grup ilişkilerinde küresel (makro) düzeyde üretilen ve ırkçı ideolojiler tarafından bilişsel olarak desteklenen etnik bir eşitsizlik sistemidir" (van Dijk, 2003, s.54). Kitle iletişimi bu eşitsizlik sisteminin toplumsal bilince aktarımı ve söylemsel yeniden-üretimine hizmet eder. Bu süreç gündelik hayatımızı etkileyecek kadar etkindir; "ırkçılığın medya tarafından bildirilen oldukça pervasız biçimlerde ve yalnızca ara sıra meydana geldiğini vurgulamak için bu sisteme 'gündelik hayattaki ırkçılık' denir" (van Dijk, 2003, s. 52). Toplum bilinçsizce kendisi gibi olmayan "öteki"leri söylemsel olarak aşağılar, tüm toplumsal pratikler içerisinde sıradan insan bu ırkçılığı normal bir düşünüş olarak görmeye başlar. "Ayrımcılığın günlük toplumsal pratikleri Ötekiler hakkındaki olumsuz inançların bilişsel temelini önvarsayar: Irkçı ideolojiler tarafından yapılandırıldıkları için kalıplaşmış fikirler, önyargılar, ırkçı tutumlar ya da diğer toplumsal olarak paylaşılan düşünceler" (van Dijk, 2003, s. 53) toplumsal çatışmalara neden olur. Egemen ideoloji ile "öteki"lerin ideolojileri arasında gündelik yaşam pratikleri bağlamında yaşanan çatışma, kitle iletişim araçlarını etkin kullanan iktidarın lehinedir. Toplumsal yapının bu parçalanmış halini gündelik yaşam pratikleri bağlamında üreten ve yeniden-üreten iktidar, toplumu bu şekilde, yani "öteki"—başka bir deyişle bölünme, parçalanma—korkusuyla daha kolay denetim altında tutar. Buna bağlı olarak da iktidarın zor aygıtlarının süreğen bir şekilde toplumsal yaşama müdahil olması meşrulaştırılmış olur.

Gündelik yaşam içinde ırkçılık, söylemler aracılığıyla yeniden-üretilmektedir. "Gündelik konuşmalar gündelik popüler ırkçılığın doğal yerlemleridir... etnik klişeler ve önyargılar böylelikle, söylentiler gibi, daha hızlı yayılırlar" (van Dijk, 2002). Ayrıca, gündelik söylemler toplumsal düşünüşün yapısını yansıtırlar. Diğer bir deyişle, toplumsal yaşam sürecinde, tüm toplumsal pratikler iktidarın ideolojisi tarafından belirlenmiş olan ırkçı düşünüş, söylem ve eylemlerin sıradanlaşmış bir biçimde tekrarlandığı ve yeniden üretildiği süreçler olarak da görülebilir. "Gündelik hayattaki ırkçılığın temel karakteristikleri şöyle özetlenebilir: Gündelik hayattaki ırkçılık 1) toplumsallaşmış ırkçı kavramların toplumsal pratikleri tanımlanabilir ve yönetilebilir kılan anlamlarla birleştiği 2) ırkçı imalar taşıyan pratiklerin kendi içlerinde alışıldık ve tekrarlanır hale geldiği 3) temel ırksal ve etnik ilişkilerin bu rutin ya da gündelik hayattaki benzer pratikler tarafından gerçekleştirildiği ve desteklendiği bir süreçtir" (Essed, 2002). "Öteki"nin bu dışsallaştırımı ve toplumsal yaşamın ırkçı düşünüş ve eylemlerle şiddet içeren bir biçim alması, gündelik yaşamın çatışma alanı haline gelmesini beraberinde getirir. Böylelikle söylemsel ya da eylemsel ırkçı şiddet meşrulaştırılır. Toplumsal pratik olarak ırkçılık "öteki"ne karşı açık ve gizli, doğrudan ya da dolaylı bir saldırıyı barındırır. "Gündelik hayattaki ırkçılık doğrudan ya da dolaylı olarak deneyimlenir... Gündelik hayattaki ırkçılık, çoğunlukla da saklı ve saptanması güç olan, toplu pratikleri içerir... ırkçılık gündelik hayatta üç önemli süreç üzerinden işler: ırksal ve etnik grupların marjinalleştirilmesi, (atfedilmiş) grup karakteristikleri ve kültürlerinin sorunsallaştırılması ve (olası) karşı eylemin bastırılması" (Essed, 2002). Böylece, egemen toplumsal grupların, azınlıkları kendi toplumsal düşünüşlerinin sınırının dışına atarak marjinalleştirmesi temel olarak söylemsel-epistemik şiddet yoluyla gerçekleştirilir ve tüm kitle iletişim araçları da bu şiddeti yayar ve—kitleselleştirerek—meşrulaştırır. Ayrıca, azınlık grubunun tüm toplumsal yapısı ve kültürü egemen grubun kültürüne göre aşağı bir düzeyde konumlandırılır ve azınlıkların kendilerini ifade etmelerine, bu baskıya karşı direniş biçimleri geliştirmelerine hem toplumsal yapı hem de iktidar aygıtları tarafından izin verilmez.

Geleneksel ırkçı yaklaşım "öteki"nin biyolojik varoluşuna yönelir ve "öteki"leri toplumsal yapıyı sakatlayan hastalıklar olarak görür ve gerçek tedavi "öteki"lerin yokedilmesidir. Buna karşın "yeni ırkçılıkta azınlıklar biyolojik olarak aşağılık değildir ama farklıdır. Azınlıkların, bir çok bakımdan "eksiklikleri" ve düzeltilmesi gereken "patolojileri" olmasına rağmen, farklı bir kültürü vardır" (van Dijk, 2000). Ne var ki, bu farklılık tahammül edilmesi gereken toplumsal bir zenginlik olarak değil bütünlüğü tehdit eden bir saldırı olarak algılanır. Van Dijk tarafından vurgulandığı gibi "yeni ırkçılığın", ince ve simgesel doğası nedeniyle, bir çok biçimi söylemseldir. Yeni ırkçılık, geleneksel ırkçığın doğrudan, açık şiddetinden uzak durur, daha "seçkin" bir söylem kullanır. Bu söylemler tüm kitle iletişim araçları ve sonrasında gündelik iletişim içerisinde "normal ve doğal" bir görünüm içerisinde kullanılır ve egemen çoğunluk grubunun sessizce kabul ettiği meşru ideoloji ve tutumlara dayanan etnik hegemonyayı üretir. "Irkçılığın toplumsal pratiği olarak söylem, aynı zamanda insanların ırkçı inançlarının ana kaynağıdır. Medyanın gücü ilkin söylemsel ve simgeseldir. Medya söylemi toplumun bilgisinin, tutumlarının, ideolojilerinin ana kaynağıdır" (van Dijk, 2000). Van Dijk'ın da ifade ettiği gibi bu bağlamda, kitle iletişim araçlarının yeni ırkçılığın üretimi ve yeniden-üretiminde etkin bir rol oynadığı da söylenebilir. Egemen ideolojinin aktarıcısı olarak işlev gören kitle iletişim araçları toplumsal yapıda "öteki"lerin belirlenmesi, anlamlandırılması ve onlara karşı söyleme dayanan ırkçılık biçimleriyle saldırılmasının yolunu açabilir. "Gündelik yaşamdaki azınlıklar üzerine yapılan konuşmaların çoğu kitle iletişim araçlarından esinlenmiştir. Konuşanlar genelde etnik azınlıklarla ilgili bilgi ve görüşlerinin kaynağı (ve otoritesi) olarak televizyon ya da gazetelere gönderme yaparlar... Ötekilere ilişkin tüm inançlarımız kitle iletişim araçlarının söyleminden, edebiyattan, ders kitaplarından, yazılardan ya da diğer seçkin söylem biçimlerinden gelir... kitle iletişim araçları günümüzde toplumdaki etnik bilgi ve düşüncelerin temel kaynağıdır" (van Dijk, 2002). Kitle iletişim araçlarının azınlıklara, farklı olana karşı şiddet içeren söylemi gündelik hayattaki faşizmi besler ve faşizmin giderek söylemsel anlamda doğallaşması ile birlikte toplum "öteki"ne uygulanan şiddeti meşru görmeye başlar ve sonrasında "linç toplulukları" oluştuğunda toplum linç kültürü içerisinde "öteki"leri yoketmek için eyleme geçer. Etnik, dinsel vb. sorunların yaşandığı coğrafyalarda kitle iletişim araçları önyargıların ve çatışmaları daha da keskinleşmesine neden olabildiği ve toplumların bir arada, barış içerisinde yaşamlarını olanaksızlaştırdığı görülmektedir.

Yeni teknolojik gelişimlerle etkisini daha da arttırmış olan kitle iletişim araçları küresel bağlamda etkili hale gelir, ancak bu durum demokratikleşme ve özgürleşmeyi değil iktidar yapılarının daha da etkin bir şekilde söylemsel ve eylemsel şiddeti kullanabilmesinin olanaklarını üretir. Bu süreç küreselleşme bağlamında yoğun bir biçimde yeniden-biçimlendirilmiş olan ulus-devlet yapılarının yeni biçimine gönderme yapar. Küresel egemen iktidar bu baskıcı ulus-devletler aracılığıyla toplumları "rıza"dan çok "şiddet" ve "baskı" ile yönetmeye başlar. "Öteki"leri hedef alan "anti-terör" yasaları ve şiddet içeren küresel ya da yerel iktidarların müdahaleleri ile tüm dünyadaki "öteki"ler—muhalifler—bastırılmaya, sindirilmeye çalışılır. Küresel sermaye bu ulus-devlet yapılarını serbest pazarlar olarak kullanmaya devam eder, "öteki"lerden kaynaklanan yerel sorunlar ise—şiddeti etkin bir biçimde kullanma yetkisi ve gücüyle donatılmış olan—ulus-devlet yapıları tarafından çözümlenir. Gelecek, toplum için bir "kara-ütopya"ya dönüştürülür, iletişim tek-yönlü baskıcı bir şiddet biçimine dönüştürülür yani yokedilir, bunun sonucunda toplumsal özgürleşme bilinmeyen bir geleceğe ertelenir. Ancak toplum her zaman için iktidarlara ve onların yarattığı olumsuzluklara karşı kendi direnme biçimlerini geliştirirler, "öteki"ler kendilerini yeniden-üretecek iletişim biçimlerini yaratma gücüne sahiptirler.

Sonuç

"Öteki"ne yönelik şiddete karşı toplumsal barışı savunan toplumsal muhalefet, tüm farklılıkları zenginlik olarak gören ve bütünsel bir yapı istemi ve tektipleşme yerine, tüm toplumsal öznelerin kendilerini ifade edebildiği özgür-demokratik bir yapının gerekliliği, yani "barış içerisinde birarada yaşama"nın mümkün olduğunu savunur. Toplumsal gerçekliğin yeniden-biçimlendirilmesinin gerekliliği vurgusuna sahip olan muhalif düşünce "öteki"nin yaşam hakkını ve toplumsal yaşam alanında herkesin eşit haklara sahip olduğunu, iktidarın tüm baskılarına karşı topluma kitle iletişim sürecine müdahil olarak aktarmaya çalışır.

"Kolektif bedende—kendine yabancılaşmanın—"yarık"ın ifade edilişi olan azınlık kimliklerinin üretimi olarak kültürel farklılığın anlaşılması" (Bhabha, 1995, s. 3) gerekir, çokkültürlülüğün, kültürel farklılıkların kabulü toplumsal yapının parçalanmasını değil parçalanmanın aşılmasını beraberinde getirir. Aynı zamanda, toplumun kendine yabancılaşmışlığının da aşabilmesi, ancak kendi hastalığının merkezi olarak konumlandıdığı bu yarığın, "öteki"nin, kendi varoluşunun bir parçası olarak kabul edilmesi ile olasıdır. Bu süreç toplumun kendini daha sağlıklı bir biçimde inşa edebileceği demokratik yapılanımın zorunluluklarındandır. Toplumsal belleğe kazınmış önyargıların aşılması da bu sürece bağlı olarak gerçekleştirilebilir. Toplumsal iletişim sürecinin, tüm toplumsal grupların sesini aktaran ve kültürünü, dilini, dinini vb. yaşatmasına, yeniden-üretmesine olanak verecek bir biçimde yeniden-düzenlenmesini savunur ve kendi olanakları dahilinde toplumsal iletişime müdahale eder. Muhalifler, yani toplumsal sorunları "öteki"leri yokederek değil, "öteki"lere yönelik tüm şiddet biçimlerini yokederek aşılacağına inananlar, iktidarın olumsal olmayan yaklaşımlarını parçalayacak söylem ve eylemleri toplumun gündelik yaşamına taşıyıp, ırkçı, faşist söylem ve eylemlerin sorgulanması ve toplumsal yapıdan sökülmesi için çaba gösterir. Muhalif düşünüş, iktidar ilişkileri bağlamında iktidarın toplumlar için varolduğunu ve toplumsal yaşamı bir savaş alanı haline getirmek yerine, toplumsal yapının tüm parçalanmışlığı ile kabul edilip, bu parçalı bütünlüğün herkes için yaşanılabilir kılınması gerektiğini savunur. Söylemsel-epistemik şiddetin toplumsal iletişim sürecinden, gündelik yaşamdan sökülüp atılması uzun süreli bir politika ve mücadele gerektirir. Söylemsel-epistemik şiddetin gündelik yaşam pratikleri içerisinde doğallaşıp, normalleştirilmesi, sıradanlaşması ve sonrasında eyleme dönüşmesi toplumsal çatışmanın başlangıç noktasını imler. Bu sürecin yaşanmaması, toplumsal iletişimin çoksesli kılınması ve kitle iletişim araçlarının tüm baskılara rağmen farklılıklara ve "öteki"lere yönelik yaklaşımları olumsallaştıracak iletileri örgülemesi ile mümkündür. Toplumsal yapının parçalanacağı korkusuna dayanan toplumsal söylemler ve bunlar kitle iletişim araçlarıyla toplumsal bilinçyapısına taşınması sonucunda, toplumsal yaşam alanlarında bu parçalanma kurgusal olmaktan çıkar, gerçeklik olarak yaşantılanmaya başlanır. Başka bir deyişle, söylemin belirleyici olduğu gündelik yaşamda parçalanma kuvveden fiile çıkar, somutlaşır.

Kitle iletişim araçlarının "balkanlaştırıcı" etkisinin ortadan kaldırılması, günümüzde en büyük toplumsal sorun halini almaktadır. Tüm toplumlar "öteki"lere yönelik şiddet içeren söylem ve eylemleri gündelik yaşam pratiklerinden başlayarak ortadan kaldırmak zorundadır. Hiçbir iktidar ve bu anlamda iktidara bu süreçte destek veren ya da sessiz kalarak destek veren toplum, "öteki"ne karşı işlediği suçların hesabını tarih önünde vermekten kaçamamıştır. Tarih söylemi bu anlamda iktidarların—toplumların—işlediği suçların ve bazı toplumların—toplulukların—da kurban edilmesinin tarihi olmaktan çıkarılmadıkça, gerçek bir toplumsal barıştan, özgürleşmeden sözetmek olanaklı hale gelemeyecektir. Toplumsal iletişim toplumsal barışı öngerektirir, toplumun "öteki"lerle varolabileceği ve "öteki"nin toplumsal anlamda vazgeçilmezliği kabul edildiğinde, gerçek anlamda toplumsal barış elde edilebilir.

Kaynakça:

Althusser, L. (2003). *İdeoloji ve Devletin İdeolojik Aygıtları.* (A. Tümertekin, Çev.). İstanbul: İthaki Y.

Bhabha, H. K. (1995). *The Location of Culture.* London: Routledge.

Cohen, P. (2002). "Psychoanalysis and Racism: Reading the Other Scene." *A Companion to Racial and Ethnic Studies.* (D. T. Goldberg & John Solomos, Eds.). Blackwell Publishing. Blackwell Reference Online. Retrieved March 31, 2007, from http://www.blackwellreference.com/subscriber/tocnode?id=g9780631206163_chunk_g97806312061319

Essed, P. (2002). "Everyday Racism." *A Companion to Racial and Ethnic Studies.* (D. T. Goldberg & J. Solomos, Eds.). Blackwell Publishing. Blackwell Reference Online. Retrieved March 2007 from http://www.blackwellreference.com/subscriber/tocnode?id=g9780631206163_chunk_g978063120616320

Foucault, M. (1996). Truth is in the future. *Foucault Live (Interviews, 1961-1984)* (2nd Edition). (S. Lotringer, Ed.). (L. Hochroth & John Johnston, Trans.). New York: Semiotext.

Gauchet, M. (2000). "Anlam Borcu ve Devletin Kökenleri. İlkellerde Din ve Siyaset". *Devlet Kuramı* (C.A. Bakal, Der. ve Çev.). Ankara: Dost Kitabevi Yayınları.

Hobart, M. (1996). "Şiddet ve Susku: Bir Eylem Siyasasına Doğru". *Cogito: Şiddet.* Sayı: 6-7. İstanbul : YKY.

Laclau, E. (2007) *Popülist Akıl Üzerine.* (N. B. Çelik, Çev.). Ankara: Epos.

Lenin, V.İ. (1990). *Ekim Devrimi Dosyası: Sovyet Yönetiminin Örgütlenmesi.* Ankara: Ekim Y.

Marx, K. (1993). *Ekonomi Politiğin Eleştirisine Katkı.* (S. Belli, Çev.). Ankara: Sol Yayınları.

Marx, K. (1999). *Grundrisse.* (A. Gelen, Çev.). Ankara: Sol Yayınları.

Tarrow, S. (1996). *Power in Movement.* New York: Cambridge University Press.

van Dijk, T. (2000). New(s) Racism: A Discourse Analytical Approach. In S. Cottle (Ed.), *Ethnic Minorities and the Media* (pp. 33-49). Buckingham, UK & Philadelphia, USA: Open University Press.

van Dijk, T. (2002) Discourse and Racism. *A Companion to Racial and Ethnic Studies.* (D. T. Goldberg & J. Solomos, Eds.). Blackwell Publishing, Blackwell Reference Online. Retrieved on March 31, 2007 from http://www.blackwellreference.com/subscriber/tocnode?id=g9780631206163_chunk_g978063120616317

van Dijk, T. (2003). "Söylem ve İdeoloji". *Söylem ve İdeoloji* (B. Çoban & Z. Özarslan, Der., N. Ateş, Çev.) İstanbul: Su.

Zizek, S. (2002). *İdeolojinin Yüce Nesnesi.* (T. Birkan, Çev.) İstanbul: Metis.

Public Relations and Nation-Building Under Political Isolation: The Case of Northern Cyprus

Baruck Opiyo
Department of Public Relations & Advertising
Faculty of Communication & Media Studies
Eastern Mediterranean University
baruck.opiyo@emu.edu.tr

Serra İnci Çelebi
Department of Public Relations & Advertising
Faculty of Communication & Media Studies
Eastern Mediterranean University
serra.celebi@emu.edu.tr

Introduction

The importance of a good image for a nation cannot be overemphasized. Both international PR scholars and Political scientists agree that a good image is important for countries, much like good reputation and credibility are important for individuals and corporations. This recognition has caused many nations worldwide to resort to skillful communication campaigns to both create and seek to maintain the kind of reputation and image they wish to carve for themselves, and made this activity integral part of their policymaking and public diplomacy (see James, 1996, Kunczik, 1990; Kotler, et al., 1993; Taylor & Kent, 2006; Yack, 1999, Starck & Kruckeberg, 2001).

This paper builds on the above understanding of national promotion and publicity, and uses Northern Cyprus as a case, to explore and examine its communication with international publics as part of its "public diplomacy" efforts which Wang (2006) argues, generally refers to a government's process of communicating with foreign publics in an attempt to bring about understanding for its nation's ideas and ideals, its institutions and culture, as well as its national goals and current policies (p. 91).

The creation of a national identity – which is defined as the conscious identification of a group of people with shared national goals - is foundational to nation-building process, an activity whose importance and relevance for nations has been documented by many PR scholars and political scientists (see Taylor & Botan, 1997; Taylor, 2000; Scott, 1966; Taylor & Kent, 2006, among others). As early as 1993, Grunig had argued that in view of a seeming close relationship between public diplomacy and Public Relations, public diplomacy could be analyzed from public relations perspective, and suggested possible applicable conceptual models that could be used.

While not all of these concerns may be of interest and relevance to Northern Cyprus, the country has its own unique reasons to warrant interest in promotion as well as the academic interest in the manner and means through which the country is promoted in and to the outside world. As a country, Turkish Republic of Northern Cyprus is not recognized as a nation state, except by Turkey and Azerbaijan, and is, in fact officially isolated from the community of nations by a UN-imposed embargo which prohibits political and diplomatic ties, as well as trade, business, social, cultural and educational ties between TRNC and the rest of the UN-member states. Turkish Republic of Northern Cyprus (TRNC) thus does not belong to the UN or any of its agencies, and is forbidden from operating or receiving direct international flights or doing direct, legal trade with nearly all countries of the world except those that recognize it, especially Turkey. The social, economic, political and humanitarian consequences of these historical events on the peoples of North Cyprus are far-reaching and worthy of a separate investigation and analysis. The scope of the current study is only to trace and document the efforts that North Cyprus government has made under these circumstances to publicize and promote itself to the outside world, including its side of the story of the division of Cyprus and the decades-old search for peace on the island.

Different historical circumstances of different nations present equally different causes and issues to which public relations efforts are often directed. Taylor & Kent (2006) have suggested that nations could and often use international PR to cultivate and foster national identity of citizens, create and maintain national unity in a country, and to build relationships with both national and international publics, among other uses. In a previous study, Taylor (2000) examined how one country, Malaysia, had used PR in nation-building and forging national unity among its different ethnic groups. Similarly, countries like the East-Central African state of Rwanda, after experiencing the 1994 genocide which left nearly a million people dead, have had to use international communication campaigns not only to re-unite its people, but also to re-brand the post-genocide Rwanda in a bid to distance itself from a particularly unpleasant past. Much of post-genocide Rwanda's PR effort has gone into re-branding the country by portraying it as a place where justice (can still) prevail and the two main communities, the Hutus and Tutsis can live and work together in harmony, although under a newly-designed national flag which was created as part of national reconciliation strategy to symbolize the birth of a new nation.

Method

Authors on methodology often argue that a scholar's research question or questions should be the key determinant of method employed in research (see Babbie, E., 2004; Wimmer & Domminick, 2007; Sparks, G.G., 2006). Considerations of other factors such as demographics, social setting, or type of research investigation further influence choice of appropriateness of research procedures such as probability or nonprobability sampling techniques, ethnographic, symbolic interaction as methods, would be most appropriate.

In comparison to many countries, Turkish Republic of Northern Cyprus is a fairly small state, occupying only 3355 sq Kms out of the 9251 square kilometres covered by the entire island of Cyprus (http://www.cyprusive.com). Official population of the country as of April 2007 Census was 264,000 out of which nearly half were foreigners or settlers. Turkish Cypriots were only about half of the entire population. (TRNC Census, 2007; Cyprus Today, May 5-11, 2007).

Perhaps partly due to the size and population of the country, the Turkish Cypriot culture is based largely on personal interactions, and access to government officials, Ministers, Prime Minister or President does not require procedure and protocal that is characteristic of scheduling appointment with or interviewing such public figures ordinarily entail in many other countries and societies.

Nonprobability sampling technique of snowball sampling was therefore considered most appropriate and selected in this study to reach nearly all current and former government officials who held key portfolios in government PR and Public Communications. An 18-point interview schedule (whose copy appears in Appendix A) was administered to the 20 key informants whose portfolios appear in Apendix B. The interview schedule was personally administered by a professional researcher, a native Turkish speaker, in Turkish language, and follow-up questions were asked where necessary to seek clarifications or to articulate interview questions to respondents. Turkish language was preferred because it is the official *lingua franca* of Northern Cyprus, and also to facilitate accuracy, completeness and conciseness of expression of thought. Questions were read out to respondents orally and proceedings of the entire interview session tape-recorded on tape and later transcribed and translated into English for analysis and interpretation. Responses were grouped according to similarity of ideas in response to interview questions to determine or elicit the most recurrent themes. It was based on these themes that findings have been categorized, analyzed and interpreted.

Findings

Respondents gave answers to the variety of questions which appear as Appendix A. Only answers to questions to questions which fell within the scope of this paper are summarised here. Broadly, it emerged that promotional activities of the government of TRNC fall into two main categories: a) political publicity that is mainly conducted by members of Foreign Ministry, and b) publicity connected with tourism, which is conducted by the members of the Ministry of Tourism. Foreign Press Club is the main player in promoting the TRNC abroad. Problems most frequently enountered while promoting North Cyprus, according to most respondents, were mainly financial and legal in nature. Although concerns about isolation and embargoes were persistently raised, it also emerged that TRNC participated in nearly all international exhibitions it wished to participate in, seemingly without limitations.

It was gathered that North Cyprus has representative offices and consulates in two cities in Turkey—Istanbul and Izmir. For other countries, TRNC's interests are served by Embassies of Turkey, and through trade delegation visits to mosly Organization of the Islamic Conference (OIC) member states by TRNC government representatives. Further, TRNC has designated "Tourist Information Centers" in Turkey, England, Germany, Italy, and Sweden in which only Cypriot Turks are employed. The Centers get financial support from the TRNC government and in terms of the type and volume of the activity they conducted, they make contracts with a professional PR/ Advertising firms in those countries.

In spite of these efforts, or perhaps because of TRNC's recognition by Turkey, the bulk of tourists to TRNC come from Turkey (60-65%), with all other nations together accounting only for the remaining 35-40%). Because of Turkey's big potential as source of tourists, TRNC promotional offices are located in three cities in Turkey—Antalya, Izmir and Istanbul.

With regard to international promotion of TRNC, the President of the county and (his) team of advisors are responsible for promoting the country in North America and Europe, while the Ministry of Foreign Affairs is responsible for dealing with the other countries including Asia and Africa. This is remarkedly different from what the situation was until 2002-2003, when the (former President), Rauf Denktas, was the only responsible person for meeting with the leaders of other nations.

With regard to the manner or methods of promoting the country, rspondents stated that PIO (Public Information Office) sometimes commissioned or only purchased books written on behalf of the TRNC and distributed them to major libraries, corporations, and individuals as well as offices abroad. For a while, this arrangement was found to work well; however, some unimportant books were also purchased, leading the PIO to lose credibility in its function in promoting the activities with regard particularly to the Cyprus issue in recent years.

Undue politicization of the issue of Cyprus, especially within the EU, was cited as one of the major challenges to promotional efforts of the TRNC. It was also observed that the workers of PIO (Public Information Office) couldn't do their jobs efficiently and effectively due to frequent changes of political parties, their leaders, and subsequently, government. "With the every single political change; efficient, skilled, experienced, and qualified staff's position changes," one respondent said. "This makes strategic approach to publicity both for promoting the country or solving the Cyprus problem through public communication difficult," he added.

But experiences of success stories were shared as well. In the words of one interviewee, "In 2005 a group from England and a group from North Cyprus had worked together and organized a function in Brussels to publicize the need for lifting embargoes on North Cyprus. The chamber of Industry had supported the effort, and the result was considered fairly successful. Very successful demonstrations were conducted outside the EU parliament in Brussels!" Another promotional effort in the same year involved TRNC publicity team accompanying the Turkish Prime Minister Mr. Tayyip Erdoğan to Moscow together with Turkey's stock exchange and other trade executives. At this meeting, the representative from the TRNC's Chamber of Industry had been also presented alongside the Russian President and other businessmen, and the Cyprus issue brought to everyone's attention in the presence of the world press too.

Targetted Publics

Those who carry out TRNC's publicity acknowledged that until recently there had not been a particular age group that they had been targetting. Then they realized that an age group around 50-55 years old was interested in the coming to North Cyprus due to its nature. They saw that the world's trend was changing from mass tourism to more specialized tourism, and they wanted to tailor their efforts to conform to this reality. As a result, they improved the walking trails in North Cyprus, and generated greater awareness to the caves in the country. These efforts were mostly focused on the areas of Tatlısu, Taşkent, Buffeuvento, Karpaz, Yeni Erenköy which are ideal nature sights and trails. They were also targetting pensioners through the strategy of B&B (Bed and Breakfast) lodging arrangements in 16 villages around Karpaz, 21 in total, some were already in use that were undergoing restorations, and others were being developed from scratch, and were new but were in compliance with that particular areas architecture, design and materials. These were all being built in the villages. The aim here is for the tourists to get a feel/taste of real village way of life, by introducing them to the village culture and food.

TRNC Promotion Tomorrow

Various suggestions were made by respondents in response to the questions of what new, better or additional steps could be taken to make promotion of the TRNC more effective. One suggestion was to make traditional products of the country famous. Colorful baskets, laces, the art of engraving wooden wares with cultural heritages. It was further suggested that supporting hand-made arts and introducing them at stands in international hand-made arts fairs could significantly contribute to the promotion of the country. The Turkish Cypriots also had varieties of odd and interesting local products which might be brought together in outstanding and hygienic transparent jars with a brochure in it, that could be delivered or sold in national and international airports.

Another idea was about encouraging (more) international visitors into TRNC so they could discover and experience the beuty of the place first-hand. Having people visit TRNC would make them aware of the realities and facts on the ground in North Cyprus without being biased by any of the anti-TRNC propaganda that often comes form the South. Since Turkish Cypriots do not have official voice or representation within the international community, much of the information on the situation in Cyprus in the international arena is one-sided. Self-experiment and experience, it was suggested, would give them the possibility of hearing from the North. As one interviewee put it, "People believe what is written in newspapers, but newspapers don't write the real or whole story."

Obstacles to Promotion

One of the major obsacles to promotion cited by respondents had to do with the fact that except in Azerbaijan and Turkey, the name Turkish Republic of Northern Cyprus (TRNC) could not be used in international tourism and promotional fairs. Using the name in any other country often resulted in swift and orchestrated response from the "Republic of Cyprus" which considers Turkish Cypriot state illegal. For a while, they were included in such events under the name of "Northern Cyprus", but later even that became problematic because it was construed to indicate existence of another country.

In a fair in Russia in the year of 2000, Cypriot Turks were barred from distributing brochures mainly because the name "Northern Cyprus" had been written on them at the stand. In an effort to overcome this problem, Cypriot Turks based in England started to work with a company called the "North Cyprus Tourism Centre Ltd.". A Cypriot Turkish staff was working and doing business in England under that name. When they took part in exhibitions, they appeared under the name of "North Cyprus Tourism Centre Ltd." One participant from Foreign Ministry shared his experience and said that he went to Vienna as a guest of TAYEX which is about courses and programs in internal services and is available to EU members and future members. Participants were introduced to each other and were given forms to fill in regarding their position, country etc., and then they were given the program. There was a Greek Cypriot spokesman in the organization who was a TAYEX and an EU member. Due to influence and protests of the Greek Cypriot delegate, during the last few days the the exhibition, the Turkish Cypriot member realized he was being referred to only as "an expert," and not as Head of Tourism, Planning and Economics Minister. It was reported that those who went to international arenas to promote TRNC often encountered such problems.

Technology

The main among several new communication technologies used in the promotion of TRNC include satellite press conferences, and satellite media tours. They were also other less commonly used but important communication technologies, with the internet being the most widely-used when compared to the other new communication technologies. But lack of command of multi-lingual skills and training among government staff was frequently cited as a major obstacle to efficient use of the internet, and thus its impact. The officers were considered slow to reply to incoming e-mails because they were not proficient in the language in which an in-coming e-mail was written, for example. So, training in other languages was cited as one of the areas that ought to be priority for the TRNC government in its publicity efforts. In addition, some respondents complained about out of date interactive web page of the TRNC and suggested that it needed to be updated regularly.

Discussion of Findings & Conclusions

This paper traced the various methods used by the government of Northern Cyprus to publicize or promote itself abroad against the background of its international political and economic isolation. To do so, interviews were conducted with nearly all of the people currently involved in the government's promotional effort as well as a few prominent ones among those who have since retired from their posts.

Findings show that Northern Cyprus makes systematic efforts to promote itself as a tourist destination especially in a select group of Western countries, especially United Kingdom, Austria, Sweden, and Germany as well as for business, investment and trade through organizations such as Organization of the Islamic Conference (OIC) mainly at trade fairs and exhibitions. It became evident through the interviews that publicity of Northern Cyprus government is primarily aimed at achieving two objectives: 1). Lobbying international community and nations against perceived injustices of political and economic isolation of North Cyprus, and 2). Marketing North Cyprus as a potential tourist destination, especially in countries considered important origin nations of tourists, especially in Western Europe.

The study discovered that although Northern Cyprus is home to 65% of the island's places of historical, archaeological and other touristic interests, the full rwards in tourism revenue from these places of interest are yet to be fully realized, mainly due to some significant problems that have hindered development of tourism in North Cyprus to its full potnetial. These include, but are not limited to, the fact that public relations and publicity work is carried out by government officers who not only lack professional training and outlook but also lack motivation, creativity, results-based performance, and are also not trained to carry out PR or public communication work. Further, the study discovered the existence of systematic counter-efforts to TRNC promotion by Greek Cypriot government in the South as one of the major sources of problems that tend to stiffle promotion of Northern Cyprus abroad. The arising conflict between the two governments has often played out into courts of Law both at home and abroad – in countries as far away as Cyprus's colonial power, England which also happens to be an important country of origin for many tourists visiting North Cyprus. In 2004 there was a protracted court battle between Greek Cypriot government through its Embassy in London, and the City of London, over adverts in underground train stations and London buses publicizing North Cyprus as a holiday destination. It also emerged that Greek Cypriot government has also resorted to trading practices of undercutting and/or sabotaging efforts by North Cyprus by offering to pay more money to private sector agencies found to be promoting Northern Cyprus if they agreed not to mention the name "Northern Cyprus" in publicity materials being designed for the island of Cyprus.

Generally, the problems encouneterd in the process of TRNCs promotion were found to emanate from both legal and practical constraints. Legally, the name "Turkish Republic of Northern Cyprus" cannot be used outside TRNC, Turkey and Azerbaijan where the country is recognized. Elsewhere in the world, only the Republic of Cyprus is recognized, making promoting TRNC particularly difficult without being able to mention it by name. By extension, this legal situation means that TRNC cannot be given a web site ending with the suffix, "gov," and has had to contend with not having a legal "gov" web-presence – having to use "org" instead, a situation which causes many browsers looking for information on Northern Cyprus to end up with information on their nemesis, the South instead!

At the practical level, lack of sufficient economic resourses – caused and perpetuated by the tade embargoes and isolation means Northern Cyprus has comparatively less money to spend on its publicity or tourism promotion efforts. For example, government communication efforts of the Greek Cyprus is staffed with 300 mostly professional staff, in comparison to just between 12-13 people in the North. While most of those engaged by the Greek Cypriot administration are well-paid communication professionals, the few working for TRNC are civil servants who do not always have specialized training in Communication. In addition, there is a big difference in tourist hotel bed capacity between the South and North. While there are 30,000 beds on the Southern part of the island, there are only 14,000 in the North, causing an increase in the number of tourists who visit the north only on day basis and cross over back to the South for the night – thereby depriving Northern Cyprus the much needed revenue.

A number of those interviewed admitted that doubling as tourism promoters who are also dealing with trade issues make them "generalists" with no special expertise – feeeling neither like government cardre officers nor business and trade experts. The effects of this jack-of-all trade and master of none approach to government publicity became clearly evident in lack of systematic, strategic, result-based approach to publicity in Northern Cyprus. Not only are the places of historical interests not professionally reserved but they are also run on what seemed like ad-hoc basis. As one respondent pointed out, "North Cyprus is one of the very few places where museums and other places of historical interests can get closed over the weekend!" And it is intesting that in spite of this lack of professional approach by the TRNC government, Greek Cypriot administration has a sound, professional strategy to counter and frustrate approaches to promotion by the North.

Findings of this study necessitate urgent remedial measures by the TRNC government, given especially that tourism accounts for about 42% of its annual revenue, a percentage that can see a quantum leap if many of the issues in this study would be dealt with and some of the suggestions adopted. Ironically, the resulting increase in tourism income would also offset substantial part of the economic impacts of TRNC's multi-faceted isolation which has been in place for decades.

References

Babbie, E. (2004). *The Practice of Social Research* (10th ed.). Belmont, CA: Wadsworth.

Benoit, W. L. (1997). Image repair discourse & crisis communication. *Public Relations Review, 23*(3), 177-186.

Dodd, C. H. (1993). Cyprus: Historical introduction. In Dodd, C. H. (Ed.), *The Political, Social, and economic development of Northern Cyprus* (pp. 1-13). Huntingdon, Cambridgeshire, England: Eothen Press.

Hoftede, G. (2005).*Cultures and organizations: Software of mind.* New York: McGraw Hill Company.

Holt, B. (2004). *How brands become icons: The principles of cultural branding.* Cambridge, MA: Harvard Business School Publishing Company.

Ingham, B. (2003). *The wages of spin.* London, England: John Murray.

Jaffe, E. D., Nebenzahl, I. D. (2006). *National image & competitive advantage: Theory & practice of place branding* (2nd ed.). Copenhagen, Denmark: Copenhagen Business School Press.

Jefkins, F. (1998). (5th Ed.) *Public relations.* Essex, England: Pearson Education.

Kent, L. M., & Taylor, M. (2007). Beyond excellence: Extending the generic approach to international public relations: The case of Bosnia. *Public Relations Review, 33*(2), 10-20.

Kotler, P., Haider, D. H., Rein, I. (1993). *Marketing places: Attracting investment, industry, and tourism to cities, states and nations.* New York, NY: Free Press.

Kunczik, M. (1990). *Images of nations and international public relations.* Bonn, Germany: Friedrich-Ebert Stiftung.

L'Etang, J. (2006). Public relations as diplomacy. In L'Etang, J., & Pieczka, M. (Eds.), *Public Relations: Critical debates and contemporary practice* (pp. 373-388). Mahwah, NJ: Lawrence Erlbaum.

Martinelli, D. K. (2006). Strategic public information: Engaging audiences in government agencies' work. *Public Relations Quarterly, 2,* 37-40.

Meech, P. (2006). Corporate identity and corporate image. In L'Etang, J., & Pieczka, M. (Eds.), *Public Relations:*

Critical debates and contemporary practice (pp. 389-403). Mahwah, NJ: Lawrance Erlbaum.

Ouma, O. I. (2007, May 21). Why I'll never become president. *Daily Nation* (p. 5). Nairobi, Kenya.

Sparks, G.G. (2006). *Media effects research: A basic overview.* Belmont, CA: Wadsworth.

Starck, K., & Kruckeberg, D. (2001). Public relations and community: A rconstructed theory revisited. In R. L. Heath & G. Vasquez, *Handbook of public relations* (pp. 51-60). Thousand Oaks, CA: Sage.

Taylor, M. (2000). Toward a public relations approach to nation-building. *Journal of Public Relations Research, 12*(2), 179-210.

Taylor, M., & Kent, M. L. (2006). Public relations theory and practice in nation building. In Botan, C. & V. Hazleton (Eds.), *Public relations theory II* (pp. 341-359). Mahwah, NJ: Lawrence Erlbaum.

Wang, J. (2006). Managing national reputation and international relations in the global era: Public diplomacy revisited. *Public Relations Review, 32*(2), 91-96.

Wimmer, R.D., & Dominick, J.R. (2007). *Mass media research: An introduction* (8th ed.). Belmont, CA: Wadsworth.

Zhang, J., & Cameron, G. T. (2003). China's agenda building and image polishing in the US: Assessing an international public relations campaign. *Public Relations Review, 29*(1), 13-28.

Wang, J. (2006). Managing national reputation and international relations in the global era: Public diplomacy revisited. *Public Relations Review, 32*(2), 91-96.

Wimmer, R.D., & Dominick, J.R. (2007) (8th Ed.) *Mass media research: An introduction.* Belmont, CA: Wadsworth.

Zhang, J., & Cameron, G. T. (2003). China's agenda building and image polishing in the US: Assessing an international public relations campaign, *Public Relations Review, 29*(1), 13-28.

APENDIX A

Name of the Interviewee: ______________________

Title: ______________________

Institution: ______________________

How many years have you worked in this position/office?

____

Q1: How does the Turkish Republic of North Cyprus (TRNC), which is officially under UN embargo with problems of international isolation, promote itself in the global world? Does it have any politics or strategies in promoting itself?

Q2: Does the TRNC evaluate its efforts? How does it evaluate its failure or its success?

Q3: Are there any obstacles or any legal restrictions that the government faces for promoting the TRNC?

Q4: Are there any public relations/advertising firm or firms that promote the TRNC abroad? How do you decide to have an office and in which country?

Q5: How does the TRNC undertake promotional activities with regard to the Cyprus issue? Please reply to this question in the light of important stakeholders and regions you are taking into consideration.

Q6: Do the promotional efforts target any groups or publics? (e.g., tourists, students)

Q7: Is there a turning point that changed the mentality and process of publicity and PR activities for the TRNC?

Q8: Can you compare and contrast the pre-referenda and post-referenda period in terms of promotional objectives of the TRNC? Was there any differences? And who was responsible for what?

Q9: What are the most frequently used tactics and vehicles to promote the TRNC?

Q10: Can you say whether a certain mode of communication should be used and is more effective for promoting the TRNC? Why? (Such as advertising, publicity, public relations activities or one-to-one communication)

Q11: What are the roles of new communication technologies (e.g., the Internet, satellite press conference, satellite media tours) for promoting the TRNC?

Q12: Under what conditions and to what extent are these new communication technologies being used?

Q13: Does change in government affect how the TRNC is promoted, and if so, how?

Q14: The credibility and efficacy of the communication coming from a foreign government are often viewed with suspicion and is not perceived as credible by people. Is there such an obstacle for the TRNC?

Q15: Do you evaluate the roles of NGOs, the UN, and multinational companies in PR and publicity of the TRNC?

Q16: Are there any activities undertaken in promoting the TRNC which you think could be done differently and better than the present ones? If so, what are they?

Q17: We understand that the TRNC's interests are represented by the Turkish Embassies in many countries. Is this in all countries where there are Turkish Embassies?, and what exactly do the [Turkish Embassies] do for the TRNC?

Q18: Any additional comments you would like to make?

Q19: Could you give names of other people or agencies that we could interview for the topic we are working on?

Q20: We would be very happy if you could provide us with any document(s) on the promotion of the TRNC.

THANK YOU VERY MUCH FOR GIVING YOUR USEFUL TIME AND SHARING YOUR INVALUABLE OPINION ON THE PROMOTION OF TRNC.

The Uighur Condition: Negotiating Nation, Identity, and Culture in Modern China

Briar Smith
Annenberg School for Communication
University of Pennsylvania
bsmith@asc.upenn.edu

In his discussion of English national culture, Donald (1988) argues that nationalism can be

> understood as an intersection of mentalities and ideologies and that the apparatuses of discourse, technologies and institutions (print capitalism, education, mass media, and so forth) which *produces* what is generally recognized as "the national culture"...implies the nation is an effect of these cultural technologies, not their origin. A nation does not express itself through its culture: it is cultural apparatuses that produce "the nation". What is produced is not an identity or a single consciousness...but (hierarchically organized) values, dispositions, and differences. (p. 32)

This is a particularly succinct (but by no means exhaustive) explanation of the cultural production of the nation that can be used as a backdrop for analyzing the "Uighur[1] Condition" in China. If the nation is constituted by cultural apparatuses, then a large nation such as China, encompassing diverse ethno-religious minorities but not necessarily committed to the protection or perpetuation of this diversity, should therefore regard the apparatuses of minority cultural production with suspicion and circumspection. China's ethnic Uighur minority is a salient example of this nation's traditional mistrust of its ethnic minorities,[2] a mistrust that is compounded by the fact that the Uighurs are Muslim and have historically resisted Han dominance, making them the most politically sensitive ethnic group in China (Mackerras, 2004). Apprehensive about the implications of a cultural difference and wishing to secure a hegemonic national order, China is systematically circumscribing or "declawing" the cultural apparatuses that contribute to sustaining this ethnic minority culture within China. This paper is an analysis of the ways in which the Chinese government, through its official policies, attitudes, and unofficial practices, is attempting to effectively dismantle Uighur identity in order to contain or extinguish the "Uighur threat" and the various means by which Uighurs sustain and reifying their culture with respect to China's commitment to ideological homogeneity and hegemonic order.

Who are the Uighurs?

The history of this second largest ethnic Muslim minority in China is convoluted and fraught with ambiguity and contestation between the bodies that seek to define it. As far back as the 8th century, the term Uighur defined a group of formally nomadic, later settled, oasis dwelling people who spoke a Turkish dialect. Originally Buddhist, they trace their origin to the Uighur Empire (744-840 c.e.) in northwestern Mongolia, and primarily settling in the Turpan Basin and Ili Valley, Uighur identity is historically elusive and subject to multiple interpretations. As an example of the historical convolution surrounding the Uighur ethnogenesis, some scholars argue that the Uighur identity did not coalesce until the 15th century when the Uighurs converted to Islam, at which point the term fell out of use for 500 years until China began to use it to further its designs in the region.[3] Justin Rudelson's (1997) comprehensive ethnography of Uighur identity discusses how the term Uighur came to be used by Uighurs themselves. Ethnic tensions in the region were manipulated between the Dungan (modern day Hui[4]) and the Turkic Muslims (now known as the Uighurs) in order to buttress Chinese military and agricultural

1 This paper will use both spellings Uighur and Uyghur. There is no consensus in the literature about spelling and both were encountered equally. Any documents or sources from the Chinese government use the spelling Uygur.

2 For a detailed historical account of China's policies towards ethno-religious minorities, see Mackerras (2003).

3 For an example of the ambiguity surrounding the ethnic designation, see Gladney (2004, pp. 207-209).

4 The Hui are known as Chinese Muslims. The important distinction is that the Hui are ethnically Chinese while the Uighur are ethnically Turkic.

interests in the region. The Turkic Muslims established an independent government called the Turkish Islamic Republic of East Turkistan, which was later demolished by China's military leader in Xinjiang, Sheng Shicai, with the assistance of the Soviets and Dungan troops. Despite the fact that the Dungans were also Muslim, the Turkic Muslims of Xinjiang associated them with the Han Chinese administration which had used them to maintain their rule in the region and were therefore enemies; this suspicion and distrust of the Hui has lasted until present day. The ethnic acrimony in the region prompted Chinese officials to implement the kind of Soviet ethnic policy and classification system used in Soviet Central Asia, which gave each group certain political rights accompanying their minority status. The timing of this ethnic designation helped Turkic Muslims conceptualize themselves as a single group, distinguished from other ethnic groups in the region, such as the Kazakhs, Hui, and Han (Rudelson, 1997). [5] Another extremely important consequence of this ethnic minority designation was that the Uighurs, by far the largest population in Xinjiang, could compete with the other ethnicities in the region as a *nationality*, distinct from the Hans and the Hui Muslims. It should be stressed here that what is understood as contemporary Uighur identity is a confluence of many historical factors and as a "gradual evolution through successive stages of interaction with the Chinese nation state" (Gladney, 2004, p. 210).

Xinjiang

Xinjiang, formally termed the Xinjiang Uyghur Autonomous Region (XUAR) [6] in 1955, was the first of five autonomous regions in China and constitutes 1/6 of the entire Chinese landmass. It shares a border with eight other countries: Mongolia, Russia, Kazakhstan, Kyrgyzstan, Tajikistan, Pakistan, Kashmir, and Afghanistan. Not surprisingly, Xinjiang has many ethnic minorities besides the Uighur, such as Kazakhs, Tajiks, Kyrghyz, Tartars, and Uzbeks, the majority of whom identify as Muslims. XUAR is a site of geographical contestation between the ethnic minorities who have historically inhabited the region and the Chinese nation-state.

Both the Uighurs and the Chinese government assert narratives of a longstanding claim to the land. The Chinese maintain that the territory has been an inseparable part of the Chinese nation since the Western Han Dynasty (206 BC-24 AD) when China had military outposts in the region, but it was not until 1759 that the Manchu Qing Dynasty (1644-1911) exerted formal control over the region they named Xinjiang, or literally, New Dominion, and it was not until 1884 that Xinjiang became a province (Millward & Perdue, 2004). In chronicling the political history after Xinjiang became a province, James Millward and Nabijan Tursun (2004) reflect on how reactions to the Qing Dynasty's ethnocentric political sentiment in the region set the stage for the continued ethnic and religious discord. Instead of continuing the eighteenth century policies of allowing political diversity in territories recently brought into the Chinese empire, the Qing court favored an assimilative approach that sought:

> political integration by means of Chinese-style administration in Xinjiang, development of solidly ethnic Han officialdom in Xinjiang instead of local Turkic begs (headsmen), intensified promotion of Chinese immigration to Xinjiang and reclamation of land there, and cultural assimilation of a segment of the Uyghur population through Confucian education. (p. 63)

The mid-nineteenth century brought a dramatic increase in Han immigration to

Xinjiang in an effort to better incorporate it into China, resulting in the Uighurs uniting against the perceived dominant hegemony. Three revolts lead to short-lived independent states: the Kashgar Emirate (1864-1877), the Turkish Islamic Republic of Eastern Turkistan (1933-1937, mentioned above), and taking advantage of China's civil war, the Eastern Turkistan Republic was established between 1944-1949. Each of these independent states was eventually pulled back into China by Chinese forces. Notably, the Eastern Turkistan Republic leaders flew to Beijing for a meeting with the newly instituted CCP government and died in a mysterious plane crash on the way back to Xinjiang. Attempts at rebellion and self-rule have continued until present day, demonstrating that the "Uighurs in Xinjiang have never fully accepted Chinese domination" (Kung, 2006, p. 380).

Evidence of the continued resistance to Chinese rule has manifested in outbreaks of violence across the region, particularly in the 1990's after the CCP relaxed some of its harsh policies towards religion and cultural expression. Coinciding with the collapse of the Soviet Union, the proximity of the newly independent central Asian states invigorated a new wave of Uighur nationalism and a spate of separatist violence in the region (Forney, 2002). Attracting the immediate attention of the CCP, the separatist inclinations of Uighur independence groups were met with a series of ferociously named crackdowns aimed at extinguishing this disloyalty to the nation-state of China. In 1996, it was evident that Uighur separatism had a religious dimension, and the CCP implemented the first "Strike Hard" campaign which targeted "splittism," stirring up trouble," and illegal religious activities. In 1997, it was the "Rectification of Social Order" and the 1998 "People's War." After Jiang Zemin inspected Xinjiang, a "Focused Rectification of Religious Places" was launched

5 Rudelson (1997) argues that the Chinese learned this system of bestowing ethonyms from the Soviets who had had a lot of practice in Central Asia defining ethnic minorities living in the USSR. Here, the term Uighur is intended to redescribe and reinscribe a group of people who had been referring to themselves by the name of the oasis in which they lived in which they inhabited, such as Kashgarlikhs, Urumqiliks, Aksulikhs, Lobniks.

6 China has 155 ethnic autonomous areas. Forty-four of the 55 designated ethnic minorities in China have their own ethnic autonomous areas.

in 2001, and a two-year "Strike Hard" ("Strike Hard, High Pressure" after September 11th) campaign which "came in the context of increased repression by the Chinese authorities, in whose eyes the concepts "separatism", "religious extremism", and "terrorist activity" had become interchangeable" (Kung, 2006, p. 386). This conflation of nationalist movements with terrorism manifested itself in a sharp discursive shift in Chinese media rhetoric from separatists to Islamic terrorists. [7]

In May 2003, China released a ten-part white paper on Xinjiang Uygur Autonomous Region (XUAR)[8] which described the genesis of the supposed Uighur terrorist groups, and detailed numerous incidents of violence attributed to East Turkistan independence movements that resulted in 162 deaths and included attacks on police stations, communications infrastructure, bombings of buses, assassinations of judges, and strikes against military bases. Although after September 11 the US State Department and the UN both recognized the inclusion of Uighur groups on the list of international terrorists,[9] the reports of mass arrests, high numbers of executions, flimsy evidence, and a tendency to over-include all Uighur separatist groups prompted President Bush to warn Jiang Zemin that the "War on Terror" was not an excuse to persecute ethnic minorities in China. In 2004, when China released a list of four organizations and eleven people it claimed to be terrorists, the U.S. did not endorse it (Lawrence, 2004, pp. 30-32). Dru Gladney's (2003) investigation of Uighur separatism makes an important distinction between terrorism and the type of violent incidents in Xinjiang:

> Despite on-going tensions and frequent reports of isolated terrorist acts, there has been no evidence that any of these actions have been aimed at disrupting the economic development of the region. Most confirmed incidents have been directed against Han Chinese security forces, recent Han Chinese émigrés to the region, and even Uyghur Muslims perceived to be too closely collaborating with the Chinese Government. (p. 4)

It wasn't until September 11 which focused the world's attention on Islamic terrorism that China took the opportunity to overtly conflate the Uighur's religious identification with separatist activities in the region. In an example of China's paranoia about the Uighur's destabilizing potential, the only "separatist attack" since September 11 was the arrest of a young unemployed Uighur at concert hall in Kashgar who recited an "independence-minded poem." Local party officials told foreign journalists that he had "attacked government policy" regarding ethnic minorities and "wanted to destroy unity between the Uighur and Han. We regard this as terrorism in the spiritual form" (Marquand, 2003, p. 2).

Mass resettlement of the Han Chinese into Xinjiang has created serious problems for the Uighurs and is remains one of the largest source of tension in the region. In 1949, the Han population in Xinjiang was around 300,000, or 7% of the population. According to the 2000 Chinese census, the Han population had increased to 38.7% while the Uighurs maintained a slim population majority at 45% (8.4 million). However, these population estimates are misleading[10] and if continuing immigration is included, the Han are actually the largest ethnic group in Xinjiang. The "Develop the West" campaign, initiated in 2000, directed billions of dollars to rural and impoverished western regions. It has resulted in an economic shift in Xinjiang, especially in Urumqi, but the benefits of new infrastructure, jobs, and a robust provincial economy have largely benefited the Hans and have had very little impact on the Uighurs' living conditions (Lim, 2003). In many cases, living conditions have deteriorated for Uighurs as property and rent rates rise, forcing them from their buildings and neighborhoods as well as drastically increasing the emigration from Xinjiang to other provinces as Uighurs search for work in the rest of the country. Xinjiang is rich in natural resources such as oil and natural gas, and being strategically located next to Central Asia and the Middle East, Xinjiang's geographic position has become extremely important to China's economy. Although creating abundant work opportunities, Han Chinese control the vast majority of the Xinjiang public and private sector economies and widely discriminate against Uighurs in their hiring practices, rationalizing that Uighur are largely unqualified for many jobs due to their low "education and cultural level," (Lim, 2003, p. 1) which is compounded by a linguistic divide as many Uighurs have limited or no Mandarin skills. While government related industries have a quota system which requires them to hire a small number of bilingual Uighur employees, the private sector has no such mandate and is free to have an exclusively Han work force or use discriminatory wage systems, leaving the impression among the Uighurs that the Han are "foreign overlords who take land and jobs from local people" and that "they have become second-class citizens in their own land" (Mackerras, 2004, p. 5). Although labeled an Autonomous Region, which means the government head for the region must be chosen from the ethnic group, the most powerful body in China is the CCP, and the Party head in Xinjiang is Han. Discrimination and suspicion towards Uighurs manifests itself at this level by requiring that some Uighur civil servants attend daily ideology classes valorizing the CCP and national unity, while penalizing poor performance on weekly political thought quizzes by skimming paychecks (Mangier, 2006, p. 5)

7 For a full analysis of this discursive shift, see Gladney (2003).

8 For the full report, see http://news.xinhuanet.com/english/2003-05/26/content_887198.htm

9 In 2004 U.S. officials disclosed that 22 Uighurs are among the nearly 600 prisoners being held on suspicion of terrorism at the U.S. detention centre at Guantanamo Bay, Cuba

10 The census does not include employees and families of the Production and Construction Corp or members of the People's Liberation Army, which would be around 3.5 million together.

Resisting the increasing Han demographic dominance and coping with the fairly egregious economic bias in favor of the Hans has resulted in deep resentment toward the Han presence, seen as "diluting local culture and ensuring Beijing's control" (Dillon, 2004, p. 75). Since the beginning of the government-encouraged immigration to Xinjiang and in an effort to avoid socio-religious conflict, the Han primarily settle in new developments, called "New Towns," adjacent to Uighur "Old Town" neighborhoods, which tend to have better infrastructure and running water. By settling in land not occupied by Uighurs or in towns adjacent to older Uighur communities, Han immigration practices are perceived as "encirclement" (Rudelson, 1997, p. 38). Although some Uighurs are willing to live in these primarily Han "New Towns," pervasive and intense social segregation is the norm.

Because Uighurs are prohibited from organizing protests or any kind of alternative political assembly, they are essentially powerless to address their discontent with China's policy to encourage Han immigration into the region in any explicitly political way. Resistance to the socio-economic changes threatening Uighur culture is expressed through other means. Deploying various identitarian practices in order to articulate collective difference between themselves and the Han, the Uighurs reinforce social boundaries through "the demarcation of a complex system of ethnic boundaries...symbolic (cultural differences that are given symbolic meaning in patterns of interaction) and concrete (ensuring spatial and social segregation)" (Smith, 2000, p. 158). For instance, the nation of China, despite spanning multiple time zones, insists upon a unified time system, so that all provinces operate on Beijing time. Despite having to calculate the time difference, most Uighurs leave their watches set to "local time," or "Xinjiang time" rather than "Beijing time," which is consistent with Xinjiang's topological position, but which also "represents a symbolic rejection of Han Chinese hegemony and administration" and "draws a symbolic boundary between the 'original' Central Asian inhabitants and the Han Chinese and Hui Muslim 'newcomers'" (Smith, 2000, p. 161). Other symbolic boundaries maintained include the Uighur-enforced taboo on intermarriage between Uighur and Han. Interestingly, intermarriage happened frequently in the past but was unacceptable by the 1990's with Uighurs attributing the taboo to differences in religious and cultural practices (Mackerras, 2004, p. 11)[11] The historical discontinuity of the taboo underscores that ethnic boundaries are mobilized in response to evolving socio-cultural conditions.

Another way in which Uighurs endeavor to spatially segregate themselves from the imperiling Han presence that curtails expression of Uighur national culture is by laying a deliberate emphasis on the Islamic avoidance of pork. Surpassing an uncomplicated adherence to dietary restrictions, the Uighurs mobilize this difference to enact a symbolic wall around their culture. However, the Uighurs are constantly negotiating this boundary, which is permeated with contradictions, and concessions made in particular circumstances.[12] Joanne Smith's (2000) ethnography describes some of these practices employed in avoiding pork,[13] which left her with "the distinct impression that urban Uighurs exaggerated their disgust regarding pigs and pork in order to better articulate their dislike for the Han Chinese" and that although these "social borders may appear invisible from the outside, but they become salient in structuring interethnic social, religious, and commercial interactions" (p. 167). Underscoring the fact that dietary practices can attest more to a social and political climate than religious doctrine, some Uighurs who live in Kazakhstan have trouble turning pork down when it is offered to them as guests by Russian friends. The Kazakhstani Uighurs tend to have a more permissive attitude towards drinking alcohol because of their protracted proximity to Russian culture (Roberts, 1998). Han immigration in Xinjiang has served to redefine the ways in which Uighur identity politics are practiced. Obscuring the historical practice of identity based on oasis association,[14] contemporary Uighur identity is reinscribed as a monolithic but historically inconsistent ethno-religious identification in response to their contested existence in China.

Education and Islam

Historically, China's language policy has been one of the most flexible and responsive to local conditions. Well-received by both party officials and the national minorities, China's integrationist (instead of assimilative) language policy contributed to national stability as well as helped preserve ethnic minority cultures and traditions and was central to China's nation building project.[15] However, language, clearly central to racial/ethnic identity, has increasingly been subjected to the PRC's shift from accommodation to assimilation in both covert and overt language policies, which threaten a sustained Uighur

11 Mackerras also notes that a survey conducted in 2000 found that 77.9% of Han in Xinjiang believed that intermarriage between Han and Uighurs was all right, but only 32.4% of Uighurs did.

12 See for example Cesaro (2000).

13 Such as exaggerating the Hans' ritual uncleanliness (since they come into contact with pork products) as an explanation of why the two groups do not intermingle while simultaneously eating with Han co-workers during lunch at *qingzhen* restaurants when it was necessary to eat with co-workers. University campuses generally have separate dining halls for Muslim students and Han students, as well as segregated dorms to manage dietary differences, but Uighurs sometimes choose to live in the Han dormitories in order to be able to practice their Chinese more frequently. *Qingzhen* is Chinese for "pure" and "true" and denotes dietary practices that are *halal* as well as describing one who practices Islam as the pure and true faith. On a 2006 trip to China, I noticed these characters on prepackaged food in supermarkets, such as yogurt, to denote that the food was *halal* and contained ingredients that can be consumed by Muslims. This is a fairly recent development, since I do not recall ever seeing this on prepackaged food in 2001 and I think it is extraordinarily significant that this religious consideration be a part of consumer choices. I personally witnessed the *qingzhen* food carts and serving hatches in the campus cafeteria on the Beijing University campus in July 2006. A Han Chinese student told me that the food cart managers will not even serve Han students *qingzhen* food as they do not want their utensils, plates, etc contaminated.

14 Rudelson (1997) gives examples of important oases, including Kashgar, Khotan, Turpan, Hami, Ili, and Urumqi, the capital of Xinjiang.

15 For a detailed discussion of China's linguistic policies in border regions, see Dwyer (2005).

identity by bringing "yet more monoculturalism in the form of Han favoritism and cultural assimilation" (Dwyer, 2005, p. 37).

After formally integrating Xinjiang into China, schools in Xinjiang were divided into Chinese-language schools and ethnic-language schools. The ethnic language schools taught courses delivered in Uighur while mainly using textbooks that were directly translated from Chinese books. These schools also required Chinese language instruction starting in third grade. The ethnic language curriculum included more Uighur culture, music, and dance than the Chinese language schools.[16] Since the mid-1990s, linguistic policies at the primary, secondary and university education levels have been implemented with the ostensible goal of increasing Chinese use by non-Hans in order to integrate them into the dominant Han society.[17] Instead of Chinese language instruction starting in 3rd grade, a 2004 change now requires 1st graders to begin instruction in Chinese language and receive their courses in Chinese as well. The Chinese educational system in Xinjiang requires all students to pass a test on the PRC official history of Xinjiang, clearly biased towards the Han narrative of events, and social studies classes do not include information on periods of Uighur independence prior to 1949 (Benson, 2004, p. 198). Since curriculum differences between the Chinese and ethnic language schools are being dismantled, the government has begun a policy of merging schools in order to streamline and modernize education in the region, as well as increase opportunities for Uighurs to be hired for jobs from which they would otherwise be disqualified due to the language divide (Lim, 2003). In 2002, professors at Xinjiang University had to stop teaching their courses in Uighur and use Mandarin, handicapping and embarrassing the classroom as many professors and students alike cannot speak Mandarin at an advanced level. Although China's official policy guaranteeing ethnic minorities the right to attend schools taught in their own language has not changed, it has been effectively reversed in Xinjiang, indicative of China's mercenary aspirations: "This is not a random phenomenon…It is a well-planned and systematic direct attack on Uyghur culture... Their purpose is to eradicate Uyghur culture, and close the cultural differences between the Uyghur nation and the Chinese nation" ("China Imposes Chinese Language on Uyghur Schools, 2004, para. 9).

Uighurs demonstrate a strong preference for using Uighur, as it is seen as central to their identity and history and is mobilized as a form of resistance to Han hegemony. Demarcating ethnic difference from the Han, it can be an insult to accidentally address a Uighur in Chinese and profuse apologies are made to repair the social damage of addressing someone in Mandarin (Smith, 2000, p. 160). Indeed, language plays a crucial role in defining divisions in Xinjiang society as evidenced by the Uighur subgroup communities of *Minkaohan* and *Minkaomin*.[18] While ethnically Uighur, the *Minkaohan* take on many Han Chinese characteristics and play a unique socio-political role in Xinjiang society. They tend to have a higher educational level since the language divide does not hinder entrance to university; they have access to better jobs as a result of their linguistic abilities in the workplace and make up the vast majority of minority government employees. However, the *Minkaohan* pay a high cost: they negotiate a social tightrope as language and education become central to withstanding the corrosion of Uighur cultural production. They are generally excluded from the larger *Minkaomin* community and "the butt of jokes and the targets of sharp criticism…labeled traitors and sell-outs" (Taynen, 2006, p. 57), while at the same time, they are socio-economically discriminated against by the Han and feel the Uighur condition more acutely as a result of their linguistic and cultural hybridity. The division between *Minkaohan* and *Minkaomin* and Han in Xinjiang underscores the importance of language and education in Uighur identity politics. Chinese educational policies reflect this as they unofficially and officially shift to prohibit Uighur language instruction in schools and merge Han and Uighur schools. Curtailing Uighur cultural production in an educational environment and enforcing proximity accelerates Uighur assimilation and conversion to Han culture. However, these policies are backfiring, and according to Dwyer's (2005) assessment, "official language polices are often overlooked as critical factors in conflict over ethnic nationalism" and China's hard-line policies against multilingualism and cultural pluralism "are only serving to reinforce and sustain Uyghur nationalism and separatist movements" (p. 124).

Recent religious policies in the region have been especially harsh, contributing to deep resentment over the repression of this central defining feature of Uighur identity. As stated above, the 1980's brought a relaxation of CCP policies toward religious practices in China, which allowed China's 20 million Muslims greater freedom to practice Islam, build mosques, and educate children in *madrassahs*. In XUAR, however, the backlash over separatist violence in the 1990's and the crackdowns on "terrorism" after 9/11, have subjected these loci of cultural production to policies and practices that seek to undermine their influence in Uighur society. Fewer than half of Xinjiang's approximately 24,000 mosques are authorized to hold Friday prayers and holiday services ("International Religious Freedom Report," 2006). Imams in major mosques are employees of the state, sermons must be pre-approved by the regional government, Uighur cadres are not allowed to attend

16 See Benson (2004, pp. 190-216) for a detailed account of the educational system in Xinjiang.

17 This practice of "encouraging" ethnic minorities in China to learn Chinese in order to improve their economic standing and increase job opportunities is not particular to the Uighurs. This is a growing trend in China in which linguistic policies are enacted that, while claiming to be to the ethnic minority's benefit, actually accelerate Han hegemony and cultural assimilation. To see a discussion of the same linguistic policies happening in another region to China and to another ethnic minority, the Miao, see Magistad (2006).

18 *Minkaohan* means a minority who studies Chinese, and is used as a label to describe someone who received his education in the Han school system. Conversely, *Minkaomin* means a minority who has been educated in the minority language educational system.

religious services, prayers and fasting are not allowed at the university level, boys younger than 18 are not allowed to attend mosque, and children under 18 are not allowed to receive religious instruction, even private Koranic study at home (Eranosian, 2005, p. 13). Female Uighur students are required to take off their Muslim headscarves and shorten their long skirts "violat[ing] their religion's fundamental notions of female modesty, in order to attend public schools" (Fuller & Lipman, 2004, p. 335). Obviously, the extremely short leash with which Uighurs are able to practice their religion is the subject of much resentment and bitterness directed at the Han administration, inspiring the very type of separatist violence and desire for an independent Uighur nation these policies are intended to stifle.

In an incisive investigation into Chinese conceptions of patriotism, nationalism, and religion, Lap-Yan Kung (2006) explains that religion in China is more of a political issue than an ideological one: Chinese sovereignty is challenged by religion because it competes for loyalty with the state. Patriotism, which downplays ethnicity and culture and emphasizes fidelity to the state, is proffered by the Chinese government as a civil religion intended to dilute ethno-religious identities and result in devotion to the motherland and CCP rule. In this sense, the practice of Islam can be a highly symbolic means of confronting Chinese administration because

> Islam permeates all realms of Uighur life-political, social and economic. The term "Muslim" refers not only to religious persons, but is used to refer to all native Central Asians. In other words, there is clear symbiosis between national identity and religious identity....there is a growth of Islamic tradition at the local level that may deepen the sense of separation...the ties between Muslim communities and foreign Muslims across the borders in recent years has become a potential threat to Chinese authorities (p. 381).

Cognizant of religion's power to unite and mobilize among minorities and across national boundaries, the PRC requires Muslim imams to attend patriotic education classes intended to buttress loyalty to the socialist system and Communist party leaders and face having their accreditation revoked if they aren't convincing enough. Because Uighurs are not ethnically Han Chinese, and by extension, less devoted to the Chinese nation-state, they face significantly more religious suppression than other Muslim groups in China. For instance, the ethnically Han Hui Muslims encounter far less suppression of their religious practices than the Uighurs, and as China busily cracks down on religious expression in Xinjiang, money from Saudi Arabia is pouring into China, building mosques and Islamic schools in Hui communities and sending Saudi imams on talking tours to preach their conservative brand of Wahabiism (Magistad, 2006).

In addition to the blatantly ideological turn in educational policies, and the vice-grip on religious expression, Chinese officials continue their assault on other modes of cultural production. Uighur novels are subject to intense censorship, and books highlighting their versions of history have been banned. Uighur journals are closely scrutinized by censors and the editor responsible for each article is listed in code at the bottom for easy reference. On the other hand, the CCP makes sure its messages reach as broad an audience as possible with 41 radio transmission stations reaching 91.3% of Xinjiang's population and 826 television transmission stations reaching 90.1% of the population ("White Paper on the History and Development of Xinjiang Uygur Autonomous Region," 2006). Broadcasts in minority languages were at their peak in the 1990's and have been steadily declining with formerly all Uighur language Xinjiang TV and Xinjiang Broadcasting reduced to just eight hours a day, with the remaining broadcasts in Mandarin and programming biased towards Han Chinese concerns and interpretations. Although some local newspapers (closely monitored) are originally written in local minority languages, most newspapers in the region are direct translations from the original Chinese and retain their Han-centrism. Xinjiang publishing houses, while producing a sizeable amount of Uighur language literature in the form of novels, ballads/prose poems, dictionaries, and quasi-academic journals, are closely monitored. The internet, which is subject to oversight and censorship throughout China, has been used in recent years for "soft" assimilative purposes by way of a national information sharing network that provides access to decidedly Han cultural resources found in eastern Chinese libraries, museums and art galleries (Dwyer, 2005, p. 45). It is clear that the CCP recognizes the ability of media industries to provide a "space of identification, not just an evocation of a common memory, but rather, the experience of encounter and of solidarity" (Morley & Robbins, 1996, p. 67). China hopes to prevent separatist aspirations and insurrections by asphyxiating these spaces of identity, common memories, and solidarity. Broadly circumscribing access to cultural artifacts such as indigenous media, literature, art, and music, while simultaneously thrusting the Han versions on locals has only increased the acuteness with which Uighurs feel their inability to express an ethno-religious identity.

Although the PRC may not always be overt or mechanical in its policies geared towards rectifying the Xinjiang problem, the effort to dismantle Uighur nationalism is manifested in their process of cultural deproduction. To ensure Sinicization in Xinjiang, and by extension, neutralize separatist inclinations, each locus of Uighur identity production is under scrutiny, control, or manipulation. Massive Han immigration to Xinjiang over the last six decades has diluted the fabric of Uighur culture as Han presence permeates the region. Income inequality and discrimination are constant reminders of the Uighur's status in China's Han-centric climate. Literacy and education, central to China's nationalist project of integration, are manifested in linguistic and educational policies that force young Uighurs to learn and speak Mandarin since "literacy inculcates not only Chinese language, but Chinese culture, *wenhua*, into those minorities who are to become Chinese" (Gladney, 2004, p. 263). Islam is oppressively controlled in the hope that weaning Uighurs from a central node of cultural production will result in the transformation of religious piety into nation-state devotion. Uighurs are not free to represent themselves through mass media, a site of ethno-religious imagination. Expressions of Uighur identity are subversive and threatening to the national order in that they nourish an idea of ethnic, social, and religious difference. Restricting Uighurs from what can be called the "production and consumption of difference" is intended to preclude ideologies associated with an independent nation. As China's ties to the West grow, and with increasing international scrutiny on their human rights record in the lead up to the Olympics, the Uighurs will remain a thorn in China's side as it negotiates its image in world opinion.

References

Benson, L. (2004). Education and social mobility among minority populations in Xinjiang. In S. F. Starr (Ed.), *Xinjiang: China's Muslim borderland* (pp. 190-216). London: M.E. Sharpe.

Cesaro, C. M. (2000). Consuming identities: Food and resistance among the Uyghur in contemporary Xinjiang. *Inner Asia, 2*, 225-238.

China Imposes Chinese Language on Uyghur Schools. (2004, March 16). *Radio Free Asia*. Retrieved April, 14 2007 from http://www.rfa.org/english/news/social/2004/03/16/130822/

Dillon, M. (2004). *Xinjiang: China's Muslim far Northwest*. London and New York: RoutledgeCurzon.

Donald, J. (1988). How English is it? Popular literature and national culture. *New Formations, 6*, 32-47.

Dwyer, A. (2005). The Xinjiang conflict; Uyghur identity, language policy and political discourse. *Policy Studies, 15*. Retrieved April 18, 2007 from http://www.eastwestcenterwashington.org/publications/psseriespdf15.htm

Eranosian, N. (2005). Chinese national unity vs. Uyghur separatism: Can information and communication technologies integrated with a customized development plan help avoid cultural collision? *Tufts University Fletcher School Masters of Arts in Law and Diplomacy Masters Theses Collection*. Retrieved April 10, 2007 from http://fletcher.tufts.edu/research/2005/Eranosian.pdf

Forney, M. (2002, March 25). One nation-Divided. *Time International*, Retrieved April 12, 2007, from http://www.time.com/time/asia/features/xinjiang/cover.html.

Fuller, G. E., & Lipman, J. N. (2004) Islam in Xinjiang. In S. F. Starr (Ed.), *Xinjiang: China's Muslim borderland* (pp. 320-353). London: M.E. Sharpe.

Gladney, D. C. (2003). China's minorities: The case of Xinjiang and the Uyghur people. *United Nations Commission on Human Rights, Sub-Commission on Promotion and Protection of Human Rights*. Retrieved April 14, 2007 from http://www.unhchr.ch/Huridocda/Huridoca.nsf/(Symbol)/E.CN.4.SUB.2.AC.5.2003.WP.16.En?Opendocument

Gladney, D. C. (2004). *Dislocating China: Muslims, minorities and other subaltern subjects*. Chicago: University of Chicago Press.

Kung, L. Y. (2006). National identity and ethno-religious identity: A critical inquiry into Chinese religious policy, with reference to the Uighurs in Xinjiang. *Religion, State and Society, 34*(4), 375-391.

Lawrence, S. V. (2004). Why China fears this Uyghur exile. *Far Eastern Economic Review, 167*(28), 30-32.

Lim, L. (2003). China's Uighurs lose out to development. *BBC News*. Retrieved April 13, 2007 from http://news.bbc.co.uk/2/hi/asia-pacific/3330803.stm.

Mackerras, C. (2003). *China's ethnic minorities and globalisation*. London: RoutledgeCurzon.

Mackerras, C. (2004). Ethnicity in China: The case of Xinjiang. *Harvard Asia Quarterly, VIII*(1), 5-15.

Magistad, M. (2006, September 12). Muslims in Western China. *Public Radio International: The World*. Retrieved April 7, 2007 from http://www.theworld.org/?q=node/4500.

Magistad, M. (2006, November 28). Chinese Miao Report. *Public Radio International: The World*. Retrieved April 7, 2007 from http://www.theworld.org/?q=node/6169.

Magnier, M. (2006, October 23). Muslims feel the long arm of Beijing. *Los Angeles Times Online*. Retrieved April 10, 2007 from http://fairuse.100webcustomers.com/fuj/latimes100.htm.

Marquand, R. (2003, September 29). Pressure to conform in west China. *Christian Science Monitor*. Retrieved April 20, 2007 from http://www.csmonitor.com/2003/0929/p06s01-woap.htm

Millward, J. A., & Perdue, P. (2004). Political and cultural history of the Xinjiang region through the late nineteenth century. In S. F. Starr (Ed.), *Xinjiang: China's Muslim borderland* (pp. 27-63). London: M.E. Sharpe.

Millward, J. A. & Tursun, N. (2004). Political history and strategies of control, 1884-1978. In S. F. Starr (Ed.), *Xinjiang: China's Muslim borderland* (pp. 63-101). London: M.E. Sharpe.

Morley, D. & Robins, K. (1996). *Spaces of identity: Global media, electronic landscapes and cultural boundaries*.

London: Routledge.

Roberts, S. P. (1998). Negotiating locality, Islam, and national culture in a changing borderlands: the revival of the *Mäshräp* ritual among young Uighur men in the Ili valley. *Central Asian Survey, 17*(4), 673-699.

Rudelson, J. (1997). *Oasis Identities: Uyghur nationalism along China's Silk Road.* New York: Columbia University Press.

Smith, J. (2000). Making culture matter: Symbolic, spatial and social boundaries between Uyghurs and Han Chinese, *Asian Ethnicity, 3*(2), 153-174.

Taynen, J. (2006). Interpreters, arbiters or outsiders: The role of the Min Kao Han in Xinjiang society. *Journal of Muslim Minority Affairs, 26*(1), 45-62.

U.S. Department of State. (2006). International religious freedom report. Retrieved April 20, 2007 from http://www.state.gov/g/drl/rls/irf/2006/71338.htm.

White Paper on the History and Development of Xinjiang Uygur Autonomous Region Part six: "Progress in Education, Science and Technology, Culture and Health Work. (2003, May 26). Retrieved April 13, 2007 from http://news.xinhuanet.com/english/2003-05/26/content_887295.htm

Çizgi Roman Uyarlaması "Son Osmanlı: Yandım Ali" Filminde Barış-Savaş Karşıtlığı

Bülent Küçükerdoğan
Sanat ve Tasarım Fakültesi, İletişim Tasarımı Bölümü
İstanbul Kültür Üniversitesi
b.kucukerdogan@iku.edu.tr

Selçuk Hünerli
Sanat ve Tasarım Fakültesi, İletişim Tasarımı Bölümü
İstanbul Kültür Üniversitesi
s.hunerli@iku.edu.tr

Si vis pacem, para bellum.
Barış istiyorsanız savaşa hazır olun.
Vegetius

1.Giriş

"İnsanoğlu tarihin başlangıcından beri, hiç bitmeyen bir kargaşa içindedir. Sürekli amaçlarına erişebilmek için mücadele vermektedir: Yaşamak, soyunu sürdürebilmek, yiyecek bulmak, barınacak yer sağlamak... Tarih ilerledikçe, yaşamak ve soyunu sürdürebilmek adına başlatılmış olan bu mucadeleler gitgide amacından şaşmış; insanlar kendilerini, ailelerini diğer insanların hayatlarını görmezden gelip, bir avuç toprak uğruna katliamlar yapmaya başlamışlardır. Savaşlar, dünyanın en önemli öğesi haline gelmiştir zamanla. İnsanlar çocuklarına ilk olarak bu savaşların tarihlerini öğretmeye başlamışlardır. Militarizmin getirmiş olduğu savaş etrafında yeniden yapılanma ilkesi, "katiller"i gitgide "kahramanlar"a dönüştürmeye başlamıştır. Günümüzde artık barış değil, savaş ödüllendirilmektedir. En çok prim yapan filmler savaş teması üzerine kurulmuş olanlardır. Gerek efektleriyle, gerek oyuncularıyla, gerekse senaryolarıyla seyirciler sinema salonlarına çekilmekte, savaş olağan bir şey gibi gösterilmektedir." (Işın, 2003, ss. 9-12). Son Osmanlı: Yandım Ali filmi de işgal altındaki Osmanlı İmparatorluğu'nu, yani savaşı anlatan bir filmdir. Yandım Ali'ye geçmeden önce kısaca çizgi roman'dan sinemaya yapılan uyarlamalar konusuna değinmek gerekir:

İlk canlandırma sinemacıları, özellikle de Amerika Birleşik Devletleri'ndekiler, çizgi roman karakterlerini canlandırmaya başlamışlardır. Örneğin 1916-1917 yılları arasında George Herman'ın *Crazy Cat (Çılgın Kedi)* isimli kahramanı, C.Nolan, Fare İgnatz, Leon Searl, Frank Moser, Bert Green, Edward Greenham, H.E. Hancook isimli çizerlerce 19 adet film yapılmıştır (Stephenson, 1973, ss. 30-31).

Bunun tam tersi durumlar da gerçekleşmiştir. Avustralya'lı Pat Sullivan'ın canlandırma filmi için yarattığı *Felix The Cat (Kedi Felix)*, 1917'de sinemada, 1923'te ise gazete ve dergilerde yerini almıştır. *Felix The Cat* halen bir çok dergi ve gazetede çizgi roman olarak yayımlanmakta, adına dergiler yayımlanmaktadır.

Dünya sinemaları çizgi romanların uyarlanmalarını hemen hemen sinemanın ilk dönemlerinden beri önemli bir tür olarak uygulayagelmişlerdir. Önceleri, kişilerin benzerleri, uzam ve sürem uyumunun tutturulması, öykünün de sinema anlatımına göre küçük değişiklikler içermesi yeterli sayılmış, çizgi roman uyarlamaları bu biçimiyle bile izleyicilerin ilgisini çekmişlerdir.

İlk olarak 1991 yapımı çizgi roman uyarlaması "Dick Tracy" filminde çizer M. Kilian'ın biçemini yansıtmaya çalışan yönetmen Warren Beatty, oyuncuların fiziksel özelliklerini makyaj yöntemleriyle değiştirerek ilk biçem uyarlama örneğini oluşturmuştur. Ardından gelen Spiderman dizisi iki filmde de, özellikle Spiderman'in uçuş sahneleri çizgi romandaki perspektif ve derinlik korunarak yansıtılmaya çalışılmıştır.

Ancak Frank Miller uyarlaması Sin-City filminde Robert Rodriguez ve Frank Miller ortak çalışarak hem kişi özellikleri, hem uzam, hem sürem, hem de siyah-beyaz leke dengesi üzerine kurulmuş ve renklerin simgesel anlamını kullanan çizgi romanın neredeyse birebir benzerini gerçekleştirerek önemli bir adım attılar. Sin City filminde çizgi romandaki planlar aynı biçimde sinema planlarına aktarıldı. Bu filmin hemen ardından yine Frank Miller'in 300 adlı çizgi romanındaki biçem birebir korunarak mükemmel bir uyarlama örneği daha gerçekleştirildi.

2. Son Osmanlı: Yandım Ali Fimi Genel Betimlemesi

"Yandım Ali, denizci olarak yaptığı askerlik sırasında Alman bir subayı dövünce kaçak duruma düşmüş bir osmanlı kabadayısı olarak karşımıza çıkar. Gayrımüslüm bir silah kaçakçısıyla evli bir sevgilisi vardır ve tek arzusu biraz para kazanıp sevgilisini kaçırarak Viyana'ya gitmektir. Ancak Yandım Ali'nin yolu bir gün Mustafa Kemal'le kesişir. O anda tüm düşüncesi değişir ve Yandım Ali, vatanın kurtuluşunun en önemli konu olduğunun ayırdına varır. Artık yaşam Yandım Ali için çok farklı olacaktır" (www.sonosmanli-yandimali.com).

Çizgi romancı Suat Yalaz'ın "Son Osmanlı: Orient Ekspres" adıyla Sabah gazetesinde 200 yılının nisan ayında başlayan çizgi dizisinin kahramanı olan "Yandım Ali" kahramanının nasıl milli mücadeleye katılmaya karar verişinin şiddet, ibret ve ihanet dolu öyküsü. Yapımcıları tarafından son dönemlerin önemli trendi olan çizgi roman uyarlaması tanıtımlarına çok uyan bir çalışma olarak gözükmüyor "Son Osmanlı: Yandım Ali" filmi. Yalnızca ana kahraman ve birkaç yardımcı kahraman filmde yer almış. Yalaz'ın çizdiği Yandım Ali, Ermeni sorunlarıyla, milli mücadeleyle çok yakından ilgilendiği gibi, karşısına çıkan tüm yabancı dilberleri de elde ettiği bir yapısı var. Çalışmanın ileriki bölümlerinde ayrıntılı biçimde incelenecek olan filmin sonundan da anlaşılacağı üzere Son Osmanlı: Yandım Ali filmi devam filmlerinin yalnızca basit bir habercisi olarak gözlemlendi. Film Suat Yalaz'ın 1960'lı yıllarda yaptığı ve başrollerini Kartal Tibet'in oynadığı "Karaoğlan" serisi filmlere benzememekte, ancak kahraman "Yandım Ali" "Karaoğlan"ın 19. Yüzyıl yansıması olarak dikkati çekmektedir.

Klasik Türk çizgi romanlarının, anlattıkları dönemin kötü kişilerine karşı devletin yanında tek başına verdikleri mücadelelerden beslenen bir yapısı var. Fatihin Fedaisi Kara Murat, Malkoçoğlu, Karaoğlan nasıl dönemlerinin derin devlet görevlileri olarak görev yapmaktaysa, Yandım Ali'nin de "Polat Alemdar"dan farkı yok gibi görülüyor. Tam da Türk toplumunun Avrupa Topluluğu, Amerika Birleşik Devletleri, yakın komşularında yaşananlarla ilgili girmiş olduğu zor dönemin gereksinimi olan ulusalcılık bu filmde yoğun olarak işlenmektedir.

Film gösterime girdikten hemen sonra Almanya'da 18 yaş altına gösterilmemesine ilişkin bir karar alındı. Bu kararın ardından, itiraz eden filmin yapımcı şirketi Özen Film'in açıklamasına göre, söz konusu filmi izleme yaşı, Almanya'daki ilgili makamlara yapılan başvurular sonucunda düşürüldü. Oluşturulan kurul, "oy birliğiyle filmde milliyetçilik yapılmadığı ve işgal altındaki bir ulusun işgal kuvvetlerine karşı kullandığı sözcüklerin doğal olduğuna karar verdi." Bu haberler Almanya'da filmi daha çok kişinin izlemesine neden olmuştur.

Bu bağlamda "Son Osmanlı: Yandım Ali" filmi görsel ve işitsel göstergeler ile anlatı yerlemleri üzerinden savaş/barış karşıtlığı konusu göz önünde tutularak çözümlenecek ve ele alınacaktır.

"Son Osmanlı: Yandım Ali" Filminin Künyesi

Eser: Suat Yalaz

Yapımcı: Mehmet Soyarslan

Müzik: Hasan Saltuk

Görüntü Yönetmeni: Zekeriya Kurtuluş

Sanat Yönetmeni: Filiz Ekinci

Yürütücü Yapımcı: Ömer Can- Berna Akpınar

Ses Teknisyeni: Onur Yavuz

Sanat Yönetmeni: Hakan Dündar

Müzik Koordinatörü: Mehmet Soyarslan

Müzik: Kalan Müzik

Kostüm Tasarım: Nalan Türkoğlu

Film Öyküsü: Mehmet Soyarslan

Dekor: Erhan Akgün

Yapım: Özen Film

2.1. Anlatı Yerlemleri

2.1.1. Kişi

"Film aslında, ülkenin kurtuluşuna tanıklık eden bir süreci Yandım Ali karakteri üzerinden anlattığı için, ülkenin içinde bulunduğu zor durumu belirli karşıtlıklar üzerinden betimlemeye çalışır: ülkesini sevenler- sevmeyenler, ülkesini satanlar- satmayanlar, mert insanlar- çıkarcılar vb. ve bu durumu perçinlemek için iki karakter net bir biçimde öne çıkartılır: Rum Dimitri ve İngiliz subay. Zaten zor günler yaşayan Osmanlı'nın tamamıyla yok olması için elinden gelen her şeyi yapabilecek karakterde olan İngiliz General Subay, o dönemde var olan dış tehdidin ciddiyetinin hatırlatılmasıdır" (Gürses, 2007). Filmdeki ana ve yardımcı kişiler aşağıdaki gibidir:

Ali

Filmin ana kişisi "Yandım Ali" adıyla tanınan Ali'dir. Ali ne yapacağına tam karar verememiş, donanmadan bir Alman subay dövdüğü için atılmış, evil bir kadınla ilişkisi olan bir külhanbeyidir. Ali tüm bu olumsuz özelliklerinin yanında ezilenin tarafında olan bir yapı da çizer. Örneğin, sevgilisi ve kendisine bir gelecek kurmak için çaldığı paraların tümünü, Osmanlı İmparatorluğu teslim olduğu için evlerine dönmek zorunda kalan zor durumdaki askerlere vermesi, Çukurçeşmeli Osman'ın tek başına dövüştüğü 6 kişi arasına yine hiç düşünmeden dalması ve onun kim olduğunu bilmeden yalnızca mazlum oduğu için kurtarması bunun en iyi örneklerindendir. Yandım

Ali lakabı da zaten sıkışan insanlara yardım ettiği için çevresindekilerce takılan bir isimdir. Yandım Ali diyene yetişmektedir Ali. Ali düşmanları sorgulamadan kovalar, dostlara da sorgulamadan yardım eder. Ali cesur, güçlü, çapkın ve yakışıklıdır.

Ali Suat Yalaz tiplemelerine klasik bir örnektir. Temel olarak bakıldığında dünya görüşü ve yaşam biçemi "Karaoğlan" ya da Yurt dışında bilinen adıyla "Kebir"e çok benzer. Filmin çizgi roman uyarlaması olduğunu anlatan en önemli öğe "Yandım Ali" tiplemesinin oyuncu "Kenan İmirzalıoğlu"na çok benzemesidir.

Mustafa Kemal

Yandım Ali'nin karşılaştıktan sonra yaşama bakışını değiştiren, olayı geçtiği dönemle ilgili önemli ipuçlarını yakaladığımız ve filmin tarihsel bir gerçekçilik taşımasına katkıda bulunan bir kişi olarak filmde yer alır. Mustafa Kemal'in filmlerde bu kadar açık yer alması ve olay örgüsü içinde kullanılması Türk Sinemasında sık karşılaşılan bir durum değildir.

Defne

Zengin bir Rum'la isteği dışında evlenmek zorunda kalmış bir kadındır. Ali'nin eski sevgilisidir, ancak gönlü hala ondadır. Ali de Defne'yi sever ancak sevgisi başka kadınlarla birlikte olmasına engel değildir. Kocası sayesinde elde ettiği silahları milli mücadeleye bağışlaması Ali'ye olan sevgisinin bir ürünüdür.

Celal

Boğazda teknesiyle insanları karşıdan karşıya geçirerek geçimini sağlayan Celal önce Ali'yle dövüşür ancak onun mertliğini görünce Ali'nin en yakın dostlarından biri olur. Celal film içinde Alinin en önemli yardımcılarındandır.

Çukurçeşmeli Osman

Ali'ye can borcu olan, yine Ali'nin yaşamını kurtaran çete reisi bir kişidir. Osmanlı'ya ve Ali'ye ihanet etmesinin nedeni ailesi için duyduğu kaygıdır. Ölmeden önce Ali'den ihanetinden kimsenin haberi olmaması için istekte bulunur.

Dimitri

Dimitri, Ali'nin sevgilisi Defne'nin Rum kocasıdır. Osmanlının düştüğü zor durumdan ve işgal güçlerinden çıkar sağlamak amaçlı çalışmalar yapar. Ali ve Defne arasındaki ilişkinin de farkındadır.

İngiliz Subay

İşgalci güçlerin komutanıdır. Osmanlıyı çökertmek en önemli çabalarının başında gelir. Aynı zamanda Defne'yi de elde etmeye çalışan yılışık, çirkin bir kişidir.

Mösyö Gouraut

Ali'nin boks hocası ve eski sevgilisinin kocasıdır. Ali ile yakaladığı sevgilisini yanlışlıkla öldürdükten sonra bundan Ali'yi sorumlu tutmuş ve onu öldürmek için çalışmıştır.

2.1.2. Uzam

Uzam 1918'in İstanbul'udur. İstanbul İngilizlerin işgali altındadır. Tam anlamıyla karmaşık bir ortam söz konusudur. Azınlıklar işgalcilerle işbirliği içinde ve Osmanlıya karşıdırlar. İşgalcilerin bulunduğu uzamlar gösterişli ve varsıllığı anlatırken, Türkler yoksulluk içinde ve viranelerde yaşamaktadırlar.

İşgal dönemini anlatmak için İstanbul Boğazı 3 boyutlu bilgisayar grafikleri aracılığıyla işgalcilerin gemileri ve kimi binalar yerleştirilmiştir. Filmdeki uzam kullanımı 1918 İstanbulu'nu iyi yansıtmaktadır.

2.1.3. Sürem

Film 1918 yılında geçer. Giysi, bezem ve tarihi olayların olay örgüsündeki yeri izleyiciye bu zaman dilimini verir. Film Ali'nin milli mücadele için çalışmaya karar verme sürecini anlatır. 1 aylık bir zaman dilimi ele alınmıştır. Alinin geçmişle ilgili anlattıkları geridönüş yöntemiyle canlandırılmıştır. Filmde dizisel nitelikte eşsüremli bir anlatı sözkonusudur.

2.2. Görsel Nitelikli Göstergeler

2.2.1. Beden Dili Göstergeleri

Beden dilinin çeşitli işlevleri bulunmaktadır. Bunlardan birincisi *etkileşimi yönlendirme* işlevidir. Bu durumda kişiler farklı ortamlardaki değişik davranışlarıyla karşısındaki kişilerle olan ilişkilerinin durumunu belirlerler. Bir diğer işlev de *duyguların açığa vurulması* işlevidir. Duyguların açığa vurulmasında "Bazı tür anlamları, özellikle duyguları sözsüz iletişimle daha etkili ve dolaysız biçimde ifade etme olanağı vardır" (Cüceloğlu, 1996, s. 34) Üçüncü işlevse *iletişimsizliği olanaksız kılması* durumudur. Söz gelimi, susmanın da bir iletişim biçimi olduğu durumlar vardır. Kimi zaman diğer kişi ya da kişilerin iletişim kurma isteği karşısında bir isteksizlik belirtisi olarak susulur, kimi zaman kızıldığı için susulur, kimi zaman da mimiklerin anlaşma için yeterli olduğu durumlarda susulur; ancak iletişim sürer.

Filmde özellikle Osmanlı vatandaşı müslüman ya da müslüman olmayan erkekleri ceketi omuzlarına atan ve genellikle külhanbeyi davranışlarında bulunan kişiler olarak betimlenmiştir. Yandım Ali ve arkadaşları da aynı biçimde görülür. Yandım Ali'nin Osmanlı'ya ve Türk Bayrağına saygısızlık edenlere ne olursa olsun tepki verdiği anlaşılmaktadır.

İşgal güçlerinin askerleri kazanmışlığın verdiği güvenle İstanbul'da son derece küstah tavırlar sergilemektedirler. Her iki kesimin tavırları düşünüldüğünde kuşkusuz barış dolu bir ortam beklenemez. Hemen hemen tüm karşılaşmalar kavga ya da küçük çatışmalara döner.

2.2.2. Teknik Açıdan Görsel Nitelikli Göstergeler *Kamera Devinimleri*

Temel kamera devinimleri arasında yatay-dikey-aşağı-yukarı çevrinme, ileri-geri,sağa-sola kaydırma, dikey yükselme, düşey alçalma ve optik kaydırmayı sayabiliriz. Kamera devinimi göstergeleri aşağıdaki gibidir (Berger, 1997, s. 117):

Gösteren	Tanım	Gösterilen (anlam)
aşağı çevrinme	kamera aşağı bakar	bakanın güçlülüğü
yukarı çevrinme	kamera yukarı bakar	bakanın zayıflığı
optik öne kaydırma	kamera yaklaşır	gözlemleme
açılma	görüntü ekranda belirir	başlangıç
kararma	görüntü ekrandan kaybolur	bitiş
kesme	bir görüntüden diğerine geçilir	heyecan, telaş

Filmin tümünde kamera devinimlerinden anlatım için yararlanıldığı gözlemlenmiştir. Uzam tanımlamalarında sağa ve sola kaydırma, vinç hareketleri en çok kullanılanlardır. Barış ve savaş karşıtlığı açısından bakıldığında, kavga planlarında kameranın hızla devinimlendiği görülmüştür. Kavganın hızı ve karmaşıklığı kamera devinimlerine de yansır. Buna karşıt filmin içindeki ender huzur dolu planlarda kamera devinimleri sakinliği dinginliği yansıtacak oranda yavaş ve düzenlidir.

Çekim Ölçekleri

Çekim ölçekleri, görüntüsel süreci anlamlandırmada belirli işlevler yüklenmektedir (Berger, 1993, s. 35):

Gösteren	Tanım	Gösterilen (anlam)
yakın çekim	yalnızca yüz	samimiyet
orta çekim	bedenin çoğu	kişisel ilişki
uzak çekim	dekor ve kişiler	bağlam, alan, kamusal uzaklık
genel çekim	kişinin bütün bedeni	toplumsal ilişki

Film içinde çekim ölçekleri değerlendirildiğinde genel geçer anlamların dışında bir kullanıma rastlanmamıştır. Duyguların önem kazandığı planlarda yakın planlar, uzamsal tanımlarda uzak ve genel çekimler gözlemlenmiştir.

Kamera Açısı:

İzleyicinin bakış noktasını ve çekimin çerçevelediği alanı sınırlayan kamera açısı ya da kamera konumunun değişmesiyle izleyicinin bakış noktası da değişir. Kamera açısının doğru seçilmesi, birbirini izleyen görüntülerin bütünlüğündeki sürekli ilgi üzerinde önemli bir etkisi vardır: Öykünün görselleştirilmesini çarpıcı kıldığı gibi, inanırlığı da vurgular.

Özellikle Mustafa Kemal'in gösterildiği planlarda kamera açısı alt açı olarak belirlendiğinden, Mustafa Kemal'in kararlılığı, ortama egemen oluşu ve lider yapısı vurgulanmaktadır. Bu sahnelerin dışında kamera göz düzeyi açısı olup, izleyicilerin kendilerini olayın içinde duyumsamaları sağlanmış...tır.

Görüntüsel Geçişler

Kurgunun en önemli öğelerinden olan görüntüsel geçiş yöntemleri çekim, sahne, ayrım ve bölümleri birbirinden ayırmayı sağlar. Bu anlamda, "Bir kameradan ya da resim kaynağından ötekine geçmek için kullanılan yöntem, yapımla ilgili koşullara ve yönetmenin izleyicilere aktarmak istediği özel izlenimlere bağlıdır" (Gökçe, 1997, s. 139) Temel geçiş yöntemleri kesme, zincirleme, bindirme, kararma, açılma ve silmedir.

Filmin bütününde çoğunlukla kesme geçiş kullanılmış ve olayın akışını engelleyecek görsel etkilerden görüntüsel geçişlerde az kullanılmıştır. Yalnızca birkaç planda çizim ve fotoğraf görüntü durdurulmuş, bu görüntüler üzerinden gerçek görüntülere geçiş sağlanmıştır. Bu geçişler geçmişte yaşananları göstermek amaçlı kullanılmıştır. Örneğin Çukurçeşmeli'nin Ali tarafından kurtarılışını anlattığı planda ve Ali'nin Fransız spor hocasıyla yaşadığı olaylar anlatılırken bu yöntem uygulanmıştır. Filmin bir çizgi roman uyarlaması olduğunu anımsatacak tek görsel kullanım da bu tür geçişlerdir.

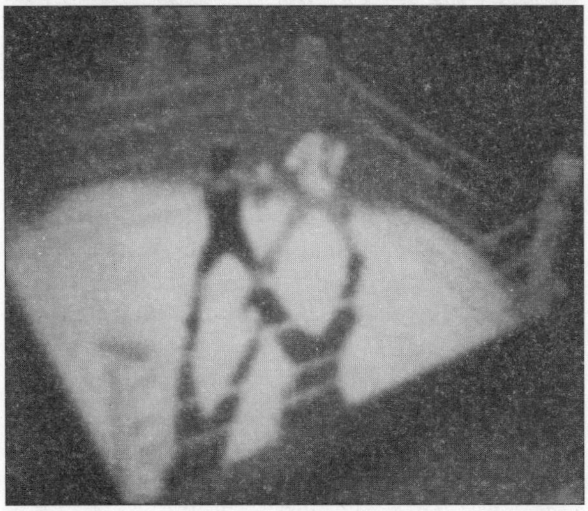

Uzamsal ve zamansal geçişlerde kararma ve açılma yöntemi kullanılmıştır. Genellikle uzun zaman ya da uzak mekan geçişlerinde kullanılan bir yöntem olan kararma ve açılmanın bu biçimde kullanılması dramatik etkiyi artırmak açısından kullanılmıştır. Tüfeğinin dipçiğiyle sıradan bir Osmanlı vatandaşına vuran işgal gücü askerinden sonra görüntünün kararması son derece olağandır.

2.2.3. Işık

Aydınlatma izleyici üzerinde etkiler bırakır. Aydınlık ve güneşli bir hava; sevinç, canlılık; karanlık, yağmurlu bir hava, keder ve durgunluk duygusu yaratmaktadır. Böylelikle, çevreyi tanıtan ve anlamlandıran, görüntüdeki nesnelerin ya da kişilerin zaman ve uzamda ilişkilerini düzenleyen ve görsel sürekliliği etkili kılan, izleyiciye aktarılmak istenen iletiyi vurgular nitelikli aydınlatmanın organik, kompozisyonel, duygusal işlevlerini yerine getiren bir yöntem benimsenmiş olur (Kılıç, 1984, s. 17).

Film dönemsel etkiyi vermek için özellikle gece planlarında az ışık kullanılmış olup kişi yüzleri adınlatılmıştır. Burada özellikle Mustafa Kemal'in göründüğü planlarda yüzünün ışıl ışıl aydınlık olduğu gözlemlendi. Ayrıca yine çizgi roman etkisini artırmak için aydınlık ve gölge dengesinin korunmaya çalışıldığı anlaşılmaktadır. Ancak, yine dönemin Türk ulusu için karanlık bir dönem olması filmin büyük bir bölümünün karanlıkta geçmesinin nedenidir.

2.2.4. Renk

Sinema filmi, yönetmenin düş gücüyle oluşturduğu çekimler ve seçtiği renklerle oluşur. Dolayısıyla renklerin estetik olarak ve anlam yüklenerek kullanıldığı en önemli sanat dallarından biridir. Renkler evrensel ya da yerel simgeler olarak çok eskiden beri kullanılmaktadır. Sinema filmlerinde de kullanılan bu simgeler kimi zaman sanatçıların farklı bakış açılarıyla yeniden anlamlandırılabilmektedir. Tan Oral "Renk, karikatürde vazgeçilmez bir unsurdur. Karikatür, renksiz basıldığında anlamını yitiriyorsa o renkli, yitirmiyorsa boyalı karikatürdür" (aktaran Çeviker, 1998, s. 206) sözleriyle rengin simgesel kullanımının önemini belirtmektedir.

Çizgi romanı siyah beyaz olarak basılan film renkli çekilmiştir. Bu bağlamda çizgi romanın filmle uyum sorunu söz konusudur. Renkli olarak çekilen filmde renk düzeltmesi sonucu sepya tonların egemenliği söz konusudur. Bu biçimde de zamansal bir çağrışım ve yakın Türk tarihinin görünümü verilmeye çalışılmıştır. Filmin sepialığının yanında kırmızı ve beyaz renkler son derece vurguludur. Buradan da Türk bayrağına göndermeler yapılır. Ali'nin Türk bayrağını korumak uğruna yaşamını tehlikeye attığı sahnede bunun en önemli örneklerindendir. Ayrıca kırmızı şiddetin ve tutkunun da rengi olarak dikkati çeker. Filmde kanlı sahnelerde kan gösterilmesinden kaçınılmamıştır. Ayrıca kırmızı ve kan kullanımıyla "savaş", "mücadele", anlamları da aktarılmak istenmektedir.

2.3. İşitsel Göstergeler

Sinema alanında, izler kitlenin çoğunluğu görüntünün önemini vurgulasa bile en az onun kadar önemli olan bir unsur daha vardır: ses. Ses ve görüntünün uyumlu birlikteliği sinemayı görsel-işitsel bir sanat dalına dönüştürmektedir. Ses, müzik, efekt ve konuşmalardan oluşmaktadır. Bu üç öge de birbirini tamamlar ve önem sıralamasında kol kola durmaktadır. Bir çok filmde ses, öyküyü destekleyen, tamamlayan, hatta kimileyin tek başına anlamı olan bir bütünü oluşturur.

"Sinemanın sadece görsel değil, görsel-işitsel bir sanat olduğunu sık sık unutuyoruz. Dahası ses de kendi içinde hiyerarşiye tabii tutuluyor. Sesin bileşenlerinden söz, müzikten; müzik ise gürültü olarak görülen ses efektlerinden daha önemli sayılıyor. Gelgelelim kimi filmler tüm anlatımlarını, ses öğesinin kullanımına yaslayabiliyorlar" (http://www.sinematek.org/ses.htm).

Sinemasal anlatımda, görüntüyle desteklensin ya da desteklenmesin, ses aracılığıyla seyirci üzerinde istenilen etki sağlanabilir. İzleyenlerde şüphe, kuşku, coşku ya da korku duygusu yaratmak kullanılacak dipses ve müzik parçalarıyla çok kolaylaşmıştır.

Ses, uzamı yapılandıran ve zamansal gelişimi vurgulayan anlatısal bir öğedir. Sinemasal dil söz konusu olduğunda müzik temel bir öğe biçiminde karşımıza çıkar. Bu bağlamda müzik filmin ruhuyla uyum içinde olabildiği gibi o filmi mahvedebilir de. Adrei Tarkovski "müzik yalnızca görüntüye eklenen yalın bir öğe değildir. Filmin ruhu, kavramıyla müzik arasında mükemmel bir bileşimin varolması gerekmektedir" (aktaran Hureau, 2005, s. 64) der

"Göz gibi kulak da "seçme" işlemi yapar. Gözün ve kulağın seçtiği görüntüler ve sesler, bir insanın herhangi bir sahne üzerindeki yoğunlaşmasını gösterir. Bu nedenle, bir film yapımında tüm seslerin değil de en gerekli olanların seçilerek kullanılması insan tabiatına yaklaşım yönünden doğru bir uygulamadır. Çevredeki tüm seslerin kullanılması bir karmaşaya neden olur ve vurguyu azaltır. Eş deyişle , filmsel anlatıda ses öğesinin başarıyla kullanılması filmin dramatik kuruluşu yönünden adeta bir zorunluluktur"(Sözen, 2003, s. 184).

2.3.1. Ses Kullanımı

Konuşma ve Dipses

Film, konuşma ve dipses yoğunluklu bir yapıdadır. Bu konuşmalar çoğunlukla diyaloglar biçiminde olsa da çok sayıda karakterin konuştuğu sahneler de bulunmaktadır. Diyaloglar İngilizce, Türkçe kimi zaman ise Rumcadır. Diyalogların arkasında duyulan dipses genellikle söz konusu döneme ait şarkılar ya da savaş dönemini anımsatacak uçak, kalabalık ya da askerlerin ayak seslerinden oluşmaktadır. Sessel bağlantılar çoğunlukla müzikler ya da diyaloglar arasındaki sürekliliği sağlamaktadır. Konuşmalarda özellikle Yandım Ali tam bir külhanbey ağzı kullanır. Bayrağa ya da Türklüğe hakaret eden biri olursa küfürlü konuşmaktan kaçınmaz.

Müzik Kullanımı ve İşlevi

"Ses bandı ve görüntü bandı, her ikisi de ayrı ayrı ancak birbirine uygun biçimde düzenlenir ve filmin iki önemli yapısını oluşturur. Film yalnızca planların birbiriyle bütün içinde olmalarıyla değil, bu iki etmenin yani ses ve görüntü bantlarının birlikteliğiyle önem kazanır. Anlatının okunurluğu ve dramatik iç uyumu bu ikilinin düzenlenmesine bağlıdır"(Amiel, 2002, s. 22).

Yandım Ali Son Osmanlı filminde de tüm diyalogların dipsesi olarak askeri marşlar ya da İstanbul gibi ülkenin belli bir bölgesini işaret eden oraya özgü müzikler kullanılmıştır. Hem sahnenin anlamına uygundur hem de sahneyi destekleyici niteliktedir.

Karşılıklı konuşmaların olduğu sahnelerde bile dipses olarak müzik kullanılmıştır. Eğer konuşma hüzünlüyse çok derinden gelen müzik, savaş ile ilgili diyaloglara geçildiğinde daha ritmik hale dönüşmektedir. Kahramanların tek başlarına bulundukları sahneler görüntüye daha derin bir anlam katmak amacıyla özellikle müzikle desteklenmiştir.

Sahneye başka bir karakter geldiğinde müzik ya dipses olarak geri planda devam etmekte ya da yavaş yavaş azalarak yok olmaktadır.

Müzikler Kurtuluş Savaşı günlerinin ezgilerinden oluşmaktadır; hangi bölgede ya da hangi kentteki sahneyi izlediğimiz şarkılar ile belirtilmiştir. Açılış sahnesi İstanbul'da geçmektedir; Rumca şarkı söyleyen bir azınlığın meyhanedeki görüntüleri ile süslenmiştir. Öte yandan askeri olaylar ya da ordu ile ilgili bir monolog ya da diyalog olduğunda örneğin Ali elindeki gazeteden Atatürk'ün resmini gördüğünde Atatürk konuşmaya başlar, dipseste askeri tınılar duyulur, konuşma bittiğinde yeniden ağır bir müzik tonuna geçilir. Yine dövüş sahnelerinde izleyiciyi filmin içine çekmek için hem efektler yüksek dozda kullanılmış; hem de dipses ritmi yoğun bateri ile desteklenmiştir.

Müzik parçaları, sahnelerin durumuna göre dikkatle seçilmiştir. Böylece ortama uygun duygular elde edilmiştir. Hareketin yoğun olduğu sahnelerde ayak seslerine eşlik eden müzikler daha ritimli iken romantik sahnelerde daha yavaş ve duygusal müzikler kullanılmıştır. Yine aynı ayrım savaş sahneleri ile savaşın acılarını yansıtan sahnelerde de bir karşıtlık olarak karşımıza çıkmaktadır. Savaş sahnelerinde savaşı, gücü simgeleyen ve izleyiciyi savaşın içine çeken güçlü ritimler kullanılırken; savaşın getirdiklerinin ve savaşın götürdüklerinin vurgulandığı sahnelerde ise yumuşak ve izleyiciyi bu kez de acının içine çeken müzikler dikkati çekmektedir. Ayrıca herhangi bir kahramanlık öyküsü anlatılırken de yine fonda yaşanan acıyı ortaya koyabilmek amacıyla uygun bir müzik parçası verilmektedir.

Ses Efektleri ve Kullanımı

"Ses ve görüntü kurgusu kimi zaman anlatısal bir açıklama yaparmışçasına işlev görür, öyküyü aktarır" (Amiel, 2002, s. 22). Film boyunca top, tüfek gibi silah sesleri, orduların yürüyüş sesleri, kavga sahnelerinde kırılan bardak ve yumruk sesleri, kılıç sesi, yaradan kurşunun çıkarılma sesi efekt olarak kullanılmıştır. Görüntülerin inandırıcılığını desteklemek, öyküyü güçlendirmek, izleyicinin filmin akışına kapılmasını sağlamak amacıyla bu yola gidilmiştir.

3. Sonuç

"Son Osmanlı: Yandım Ali" sinema filmi yapımcılarının duyurduğu gibi tam bir çizgi roman uyarlaması sayılmaz. Ancak çizgi romandan esinlenilmiş ve çizgi romanda aktarılmak istenen anlam kimi yerlerde çizgi roman özelliklerini koruyarak verilmiştir. Uyarlamada ana unsur çizgi romanın kendisi değil ana kişisi Yandım Ali'dir. Ayrıca filme konu olan gerçekte çizgi romanın siyah/beyazdır, ancak film renkli çekilmiştir. Film içinde yalnızca birkaç geçiş sahnesinde çizgi romanı anımsatacak planlar kullanılmıştır.

"Barışın, savaşın karşıtı olduğu konusu üzerinde hiçbir kuşku yoktur. Ama, barışın kapsamının ne olduğu tartışma konusudur. Dar anlamda, barışı savaş koşullarından uzakta olmak biçiminde algılayanlar olduğu gibi; geniş anlamda, gerçek barışın, silahlı çatışmalardan uzak kalmanın ötesinde, ancak yeterli gelir, istihdam, eğitim, sağlık, beslenme, kültür ve çevre koşullarında sağlanabileceği görüşünde olanlar vardır" (Ruşen, www.tarihikentlerbirligi.org)

Filmin ana izleği (tema) "işgal altındaysanız savaşmak zorundasınız" iletisini taşımaktadır. Bu bağlamda da "gerçek barış"tan söz etmek olası değildir hiç kuşkusuz. Savaş-barış karşıtlığı kapsamında Ali'nin destekleyicileri ve engelleyicileri vardır. Destekleyicilerin işlev değiştirmesi ya da engelleyicilerin destekleyici konumuna geçmesi film içinde Ali'nin yalnız kalmasına neden olur. Ali'nin tek destekçisi gerçek aşkı Defne'dir. Filmde Türk ulusunun geçmişte yaşadıklarının gösterilmesiyle günümüz arasında bağlantı kurulabilir. Günümüzde işgal değişik biçimlerde tanımlanmakta ve yorumlanmaktadır. Filmin "ulusalcılık" imgesi aktardığını söylemek doğrudur. Ancak Türk ulusu işgal altındayken azınlıkların tümü Türklere ihanet etmiş midir? Oysa filmde ne kadar azınlık varsa tümü Türklere düşmanca tavırlar sergilemektedir. İyi niyetli olanları bile yine işgalcilerle işbirliği içindedir. Ancak günümüz ortamında "ulusalcılık" imgesinin bu türden aktarımının da aşırı bir tepki olduğunu düşünebilir miyiz? Halkı azınlıkllara karşı kışkırtmak yerine "bilinçli olmaya", "geçmişi unutmaya", "geçmişten ders aktarmaya" bir yönlendirme olarak düşünebilir miyiz?

Mustafa Kemal'in filmde kullanılması gerçek bir dönem filmi olduğunu vurgulamak amaçlı göstergelerden birisidir. Ancak film bir kurmacadır ve anlatısını güçlendirecek değişiklikleri de içermektedir.

Film yönetmeninin de söylediği gibi ulusalcılık duygularına gereksinim duyulan bir dönemde gerçekleştiğinden yüksek bir izleyici kesimine ulaşmış ve amacını yerine getirmiştir. Temel olarak Türk çizgi romanı kahraman kişiliğine uygun bir kişilik olan Yandım Ali'nin günümüz dizilerinde görülen derin devlet kahramanlarına benzediği söylenebilir. Gerçekte tarihin hangi dönemini anlatırsa anlatsın, Türk Çizgi Roman kahramanlarının derin devletle ilişkili olduğunu söylemek yanlış olmaz.

Kaynaklar

Amiel, V. (2002). *Esthétique du Montage.* Paris: Nathan.

Berger, A. (1993). *Kitle iletişiminde çözümleme yöntemleri,* (Çev. Nazmi Ulutak). Eskişehir: Anadolu Üniversitesi.

Berger, A. *Narratives: In Popular culture, media and everday life.* London: Sage Publications.

Cüceloğlu, D. (1996). *Yeniden insan insana,* (12. Basım). İstanbul: Remzi Kitabevi.

Çeviker, T. (1998). *Karikatür üzerine yazılar.* İstanbul: İris Yayıncılık.

Gökçe, G. (1997). *Televizyon program yapımcılığı ve yönetmenliği*. İstanbul: Der Yayınları.

Gürses, İ. (2007). Sonosmanlı - Yandım Ali. http://www.film.gen.tr/ 11.04.2007.

http://www.sinematek.org/ses.htm/ 14.4.2007.

http://www.sonosmanli-yandimali.com/14.4.2007.

Hureau, N. (2005). *Raconter en images ou l'art du montage*. Paris: Scope Editions.

Işın, G., (2003), Savaş - barış ve Alfred Nobel. *PiVOLKA, 2*(10), 9-12.

Keleş, R. (2007) Barışın güvencesi tarih ve Çanakkale. http://www.tarihikentlerbirligi.org/icerik/yerelKimlikDetay.asp?sayi=16&makale=121/ Son erişim 12.04.2007.

Kılıç, L. (1984). Işık ve aydınlatma. *Afsad Fotoğraf Dergisi, 1*(04) 17-25.

Sözen, M. (2003). *Sinemada ses kullanımı*. Ankara: Detay Yayınları.

Stephenson, R. (1973). *The animated film*. London, New York: The Tantivy Press/ A.S. Bannes.

Modern Bride / Modem Bride: Filipina Mail-Order Brides on the Internet and the Circuit of Culture

Christine Anne R. Cox
Ataneo de Manila University
xtincox@yahoo.com

Filipinas: "Queen of the Mail-Order Brides"

"I'm looking for a man who's willing to help me in my studies," Ana wrote in her profile on an Internet matchmaking site for Filipino women. "I'm just a poor girl and all I want is to finish my studies and find a good job so that I can help my father, especially now that he is getting old."

The 22-year old from Cebu City, Philippines is among an estimated 50,000 to 100,000 Filipinas who sign up with international marriage brokers (IMBs) to find and marry Western men. In a recent report, the U.S. Immigration and Naturalization Service estimated that the number of marriages between Filipinas and American men through the Internet had doubled in the past decade, now totaling nearly 6,000 every year (Scholes, 2001). It is no surprise then, that Filipinas have earned the title "queen of the mail-order brides".

Every year, thousands of women enter marriage with men that they have met through marriage agencies. Women from poor families in third-world nations are transported from their homes like delivered products, to men from first-world countries like the United States, Canada and Europe. This practice has created a host of problems for both the "import" and "export" nations, including the exploitation of women, creation of immigration problems, the perpetuation of stereotypes and domestic violence.

This study will examine the mail-order bride industry by using theorist Stuart Hall's Circuit of Culture, from the "production" of the mail-order bride, the "identity" of the Filipina, "representation" in cyberspace,"consumption" by the men, and finally "regulation" of the industry. While it may seem that there is nothing wrong with helping Western men find the women of their dreams, the mail-order bride industry can easily become a tangled web of lies, deceit, and misrepresentation brought about by racialized images of Filipinas on the Internet.

Production: From Paper Catalogs to Online Catalogs

Before the Internet, IMBs took a great deal of time and money in searching for and promoting mail-order brides in catalogues. With the help of technology, the whole process becomes less rigorous and cheaper. Some dot-com companies charge less than $10.00 per domain name, and the web makes it easier to update pictures and information. With the web becoming more and more accessible through Internet cafes, it is easier for one to become a mail-order bride. A site called "A Filipina Bride," for example, has an online form and a link to a downloadable application form where ladies fill in basic information like their name, contact numbers, birth date, religion and nationality, as well as more personal information like eye color, hair color, astrological sign, blood type and whether they drink or smoke. A Filipina Bride urges the applicant to invite her friends to apply and attach "two or more beautiful pictures of yourself."

One IMB explains why the Internet is his preferred marketing location: "So when the World Wide Web came along, I saw that it was a perfect venue for this kind of business. The paper catalogs were so expensive that the quality was usually very poor; but on the Web you can publish high-resolution full-color photos which can be browsed by everyone in the WORLD" (Hughes, 2004). There is a huge market for women who are eager to meet and marry Western men, and the laws of supply and demand, as well as the efficiency of the Internet, has encouraged many newcomers to enter the industry every year (Lloyd, 2000, p. 346).

The websites contain thousands of women's profiles, and

to access this information, users pay around $5 to $10 for every mailing address or telephone number, plus a handling fee, or for a larger sum they can become members and access more details. The IMBs encourage "bulk" buying so that the men will have more to choose from. There are tour packages to different provinces in the Philippines which include airfare, hotel accommodation and dinner parties. For additional costs, "extras" might include express mailforwarding, language translations, a personal tour guide, a car with driver, mobile phone rental and side trip adventures like scuba diving, volcano exploring and water skiing.

These are only a fraction of the usual services offered by the one-stop-shop agencies, because the men can also avail of the following: stamps, discounted phone cards, gift items like flowers and chocolates and even engagement rings--all of which can aid them in their quest for the ideal wife. Since the enactment of stricter laws, the websittes add the services of investigators who do background checks and lawyers for expedited visa and immigration assistance. Clearly, there is a lot of money to be made in the mail-order bride business. It is not surprising that these kinds of services have mushroomed on the Internet, with the earnings of some estimated to be as high as $2 million a year (Checkoway, 2000).

Interestingly, most Filipina mail-order bride businesses were started by those who were themselves involved in mail-order marriages. For example, Delaney Davis, a native of Florida who runs filipinalady.com and filipinawife.com, started his online business in 1999 after meeting his Filipina wife, Josie Ponio. They were wed in Cebu in January 29, 2001, when she was just 18 years old. According to Davis, he decided to set up his online business as a tribute to Josie. He recalls that when he uploaded their pictures on the web, he began to receive letters from men wanting to find out how to meet and marry a Filipina. Like other IMB's he claims that "Filipina Lady" is an introduction service that aims to fulfill the fantasy of Western men to meet and marry "beautiful island girls."

Identity: Who is the Filipina?

Domestic worker. Sex-worker. Mail-order bride. To the close-minded and unaware, these are the images attributed to the Filipina. Why do these stereotypes continue to persist? Researchers have found out that pre-Spanish colonization, Filipina women enjoyed a more egalitarian status with men. Among the rights of pre-Spanish Filipino women are to be treated as an equal by her husband and to share his honors, to be consulted or informed by her husband about his business affairs and contracts, and to divorce her husband in case of non-support or maltreatment (Hunt, 2002). Then four hundred yeares of Spanish colonization has embedded a patriarchal system in the cultural context. The Philippnes today is a predominantly Catholic country, where personal and community values are male-centered. Most Filipinos are brought up to frown on sex before marriage and divorce. Traditionally, the man of the house has the role of "breadwinner" or financial provider, while the "ilaw ng tahanan" (light of the home) is the woman who usually stays at home to do housework. But challenging times and economic difficulties has forced women to seek paid work outside of the home, even out of the country. Currently, an estimated 7 million Filipinos are working in more than a hundred countries the world over, with a trend showing more women going abroad to bring home the dough (Hunt, 2002). In Cyprus, Filipinas and Sri-Lankans make up the bulk of domestic workers (Thomson, 2006). The huge export of Filipino women working mostly as caregivers and domestic helpers in first-world countries has led to the persistent global image of the Filipina maid. "The Phillippines has virtually become a country of maids..." says former Labor Secretary Franklin Drillon, "...cheap domestic labor to clean up the rest of the world" (quoted in Glodova & Onizuka).

In Canada, another of the leading recipients of Filipina mail-order brides, immigration policies such as the 20-year-old Caregiver program has had a negative impact on the image and identity of Filipinas. Filipinas make up more than 80 percent of all domestic workers in Canada (Diocson, 2000), which over time led to the stereotype of the women being docile, obedient, subservient and old-fashioned. Cecilia Diocson (2000), the head researcher of the Phillippines Women's Center of British Columbia said that

> the husbands of mail-order brides are mostly middle-aged, very dependent, have had previous relationships and even children. What is really on their agenda is to have a woman who can cook, wash their clothes, have children and care for the children they already have. It's not a question of love but entirely of self interest.

In one case, an American man who was quadriplegic petitioned for a young Filipina. It was very obvious to Embassy representatives that the primary reason he wanted her was for him to have a nursemaid (Glodova & Onizuka, 1994).

Another association for the Filipina stems from decades of American colonization and military presence in the Phillippines. During their stays, the soldiers usually develop strong perceptions of Filipinas as bar girls and sex workers. Prostitution flourished around the Subic naval base and Clark air force base, where racialized sex was a way of marking out national identity, shaping military men's attitudes to local culture and local women (Pettman, 1997). These cultural differences indicate the boundaries in power relationships between male and female. First World and Third World, the colonizer and the colonized, and the rich and the poor. The Philippines' reputation as sex centers not only tolerates but institutionalizes the women's place in the entertainment and hospitality industry. National identity becomes part of the advertising of international tourism, and the IMBs are all too happy to exploit it.

Representation: The Social Construction of the Filipina Bride

What's in a name? The words "mail-order bride" immediately conjure up an image or a concept that helps a person interpret the world and make sense of certain meanings, even though that person has never met a mail-order bride in real life. In the Internet, Asians are frequently associated with images of Japanese geishas, China dolls, domestic helpers and comfort women or prostitutes. Both scholarly literature and popular culture are replete with images of the Asian bride, from the negative stereotype of the submissive to the romanticized ideal of the uncomplaining homemaker. The fact remains that Asian brides are sought the world over because IMBs advertise them as committed, devoted and trustworthy. The Filipina is even more in demand because the Catholic religion strictly forbids divorce and frowns upon separation, so foreign men would view this as a plus factor. The images that portray brides allow the viewer to false affirm that these representations are accurate descriptions of reality (Epstein, 2007).

World Class Service (WCS), a company which is based in Brandon, Florida, has gained notoriety over the past few years because of its claim to the domain name www.filipina.com. Despite the bad press in the local media, World Class Service remains a remarkably popular place for both Filipina bride hopefuls and men in the market for Filipina wives. Since World Class Service has moved to its new address at www.filipinas.us, it still has its fair share of visitors: 1,178,714 as of last count.

Like most Philippine mail-order bride websites, WCS uses a fairly simple layout, but beyond the colorful graphics and background music, texts like "How do I order?" and "Free Wives - Hundreds of Listings" reminds the user that WCS is in the business of commodifying women. The site constitutes the viewer as specifically male and Western, a sort of "White knight in shining armor" who will rescue Filipina women from the deprived material conditions of their homelands through marriage. According to WCS, their mission, "for over a fifteenth of a century, has been to introduce girls from the Philippines who would like to correspond with, meet, and marry Western men." It is the man's duty, therefore, to "Date Locally, Marry

Globally," their adopted slogan. Citations like "Commended by the National Right-to-Wife Committee," "Featured in the critically acclaimed A Bride Too Far," and "Focus of a front-page article in The Philippine Inquirer" serve to highlight their infamous name and legitimize their undertaking.

Clicking on the photo catalogs will bring the user to a page where he can do a customized search of the women by age, weight, and height, (WCS claims they are the first in the industry) or access only the newer brides. A bride's information page contain the following: her age, her desired aged for the men she wants to meet, whether or not she has children, height, weight, geographical location, education, career, a description of her hobbies and what she looks for in a man, including what nationalities she prefers, A user can click on the photos of the women to get a larger view. The addresses of the Filipinas sell for $2 to $4 each, but as of date, the owner of WCS, who identifies himself as Larry Pendarvis, says that you can no longer buy addresses at the site, and that soon all addresses will be displayed free of charge because all he wants is for the girls to find good husbands.

While most of IMB websites are run by Western men who have married mail-order brides, a site called Everlasting Love is run by a Filipina named Jean, who advertisers her fellow Filipinas using the same hegemonic blueprint used by Westerners. Jean, who met her American husband Teri through a pen-pal site, wanted to help her friends in meeting foreign men, and when the demand grew, she used the Internet to tap a larger audience. The pictures of happy couples and testimonials of the men are proof of the success of her endeavor. Jean says that, "We may not be matchmakers or have fancy search engines like Asiandate, Cherry Blossoms, Filipina Wife, Singles, American Singles or One and Only but unlike classifieds, bars, lounges or mail order bride agencies," but that they do have "beautiful Pinay [sic] who are educated, petite, thrifty, obedient, docile, submissive, virgins, tender, elegant, family oriented, adult, not AARP (American Association of Retired Persons, a nonprofit membership organization dedicated to addressing the needs and interests of persons 50 and older) but mature, and lust filled lovers," She tells her male audience:

> ...take your Viagra, Prozac and vitamins before you get married and drive off with your gorgeous, intelligent, desirable wife and companion in your Volvo on your honeymoon so you handle the May December sex and find true happiness.

Several signifying practices can be made out from this lengthy meaning-riddled discourse about the participants. One depiction found in other websites is that of Filipinas being petite, young virgins who are docile and submissive. The symbolic words are used to define the place of the woman and deprive her of the same power allotted to the man. The mention of Viagra, Prozac and Volvo signify that the patrons are usually rich, mature sexually-active men who were probably disillusioned by their first wives and are interested in finding someone who will cater to their whims.

The site's main speaker, who is a Filipina herself, uses her voice to lend an air of authenticity to the site's claims.

Talking about her own experiences with her friends and family, she comes to represent just how a typical Filipina would act and think:

> ...frankly we take pleasure in being submissive to the reasonable demands of our husband. Western men make us feel comfortable, and even protected, as we naturally look to Western men for high moral and spiritual integrity...we are raise [sic] with high vales of honesty, fidelity, and do not feel the need to control our men. (Why do women want to control man?)

This narrative paints a picture of the Filipinas as weak-willed, entrusting all the power to the highly regarded and well-respected Western man. Although many will not agree with the way genders are represented, the predominance of such representations is a powerful socializing agent, in that people come to know the Filipina through these patriarchal discourses.

In order to facilitate the screening of potential brides, the site introduces the "Filipina Theater"—a showcase of "choice ladies" who, according to the site's owner, have passed medical and background checks. The Filipina Theater is but an unusual means of extending the voyeur in the viewer, juxtaposing the star, which is the mail-order bride, in the surreal setting of a theater. The viewer can unobtrusively watch the flow of images from behind the computer screen, allowing him to window shop from the comfort and privacy of his home. The theater comes to represent the blurring of reality and fantasy, eradicating geographic boundaries and rupturing the political identities of the Filipina as the viewer marks all Filipina bodies with similar attributes, and these bodies are framed as ideal objects and marked as authentic. The website does more than objectify and commodify the women by such presentations; it takes advantage of the interactivity and multimedia feature offered by the Internet to enhance the whole buying experience for the men.

Consumption: Chasing the Dream of the Exotic Bride

There is not a lot of information on the men who purchase mail-order brides, as IMBs are privy to information about their clients and hardly do background checks on the men. The men who use these websites are primarily from the most industrialized nations: United States, Australia, Canada, and Western Europe, particularly Germany, Sweden and Norway (The International Mail-Order Bride Industry: An Increasing Threat to Women, 2004).

For both American men and Filipinas, idealized images influence the decision to seek one another. The American men imagine the Filipina to be the epitome of the traditional wife, while a kind of internalized colonial mentality influences the Filipinas' preference for American men. The testimonials of these consumer husbands on IMB websites make it clear that that the men are seeking a relationship in which the woman is an obedient wife and there is deference to the man as "head of the household" (The International Mail-Order Bride Industry: An Increasing Threat to Women, 2004). Filipinas can easily become the natural "second choice" of men whose egos have been bruised by Western women. Many of the men talk about their bad relationships with women from their country. A mail-order bride customer said: "I wanted a wife who isn't career-oriented, who participates very little in the world outside, who does not have high aspirations, who is useful and whose life revolves around me" (Halulalani, 1995).

A quick browse of the profiles of the men seeking Filipinas in Cebuanas.com will show that most of the men are over the age of 40, have been through divorce and are seeking loyal, sensual, loving women. It is not unusual to find couples with age differences of 20 to 30 years, as men are likely to desire young women and the women are hoping to find older men who are financially secure and more experienced. Some are very specific when it comes to physical features: one wrote that the woman should be slim and have very long black hair, while another wanted a woman who would love his kids no matter what, and know how to cook and clean the house. "Koolheart," a resident of California, United States, posted in his profile that he wanted a woman who would be submissive to him in the bedroom. A new member who calls himself "heGman444's" is a divorced 49-year old truck driver from Canada. He says that finds North American women:

> phony, with ugly hearts...they appear to be only out for themselves, you can never spend enough [sic] on them, have enough to give them, do enough for them, make enough money to keep them, are completely blameless, as it is always someone else's fault for their difficulties, especially yours, are faultless, liars, decievers [sic], de-moralizers, cheaters, players and plastic.

Obviously, heGman444 has been burned from a previous relationship with a Western woman and is now looking for a serious partner who is "devoted, committed, and trustworthy."

A 53-year old boat captain from Florida nicknamed "wordsmithereen's" takes a very forward approach in advertising himself, using his status as green-card giver: "Do you want to come to the US? I have been on this site for a while. I see the same thing almost every time. Almost to a number you say you are simple, and god-fearing, and you want a good man. If you want to get my attention, tell me something I don't know about you. Send me a message and tell me what makes you different. Otherwise, frankly it comes down to if you are prettier than the one before, and the size of your breast. I am here in the US, and you aren't. I know that makes a difference. If you want to come live with me, don't lie, tell me. If you think you can love me, tell me that too. I seriously hope for love but don't require it."

These sites represent the exploitation of poverty, with the power dynamics in favor of the Western men. IMB sites are built on the commodification of women, where men can hand-pick their woman of choice by age, height, weight, religion and measurements. The websites feature links with "Order Now" "Favorites" "Check Out" and "View Shopping Cart" that further objectify the mail-order brides. The fact that the men has all the resources and the buying power and the women's goals are centered around leaving their current situation gives the men considerable power in the transaction (Lloyd, 2000, p. 348). The men, as paying customers, feel as if they had bought a product and are free to do whatever they wish with it, and that is where the trouble begins. Says an article entitled "Why Western Men Like Philippine Women" from a link in WCS:

> Generally, the Filipina will be willing to buckle down and work alongside her man. They want opportunity in the West. But most do not expect a free ride. Especially as they want to remit money back home to help their sibs with education and to help their parents share in her prosperity. This can create problems depending on the attitude of the husband. But mostly, the man is so pleasured by his acquisition that he willingly agrees to help her family in some way.

Regulation: Legal Loopholes in Cyberspace

While many who use the marriage broker services result in happy unions, some are not as lucky. There are cases of domestic abuse among couples who meet via these brokers, although there is very little documentation because the women fear deportation. While the IMBs provide their Western clients more than enough information about the women, the brides will only have access to information which the man wishes to share. Some sites do offer background checks, but only for the women; the women have no way of knowing if the supposed man of their dreams has a history of violent behavior. She is even more at risk of danger because when she immigrates, she is isolated from her family and friends and has no one to depend on. The men freely wield power over the women which they have "bought," to the point that some cases of abuse have ended in cold-blooded murder.

One such case is that of Susanna Blackwell. Susanna met her husband Timothy through "Asian Encounters" and in 1994, left the Philippines to marry him in Washington, United States. During their short-lived marriage, Timothy regularly abused Susanna. There was even an incident where he choked her the day after their wedding. After a few months, she left him and began to report the abuse to the police and file divorce proceedings. The Blackwells were separated for more than a year when Timothy learned that Susanna was pregnant with another man's child. While awaiting divorce proceedings outside of a Seattle courtroom, the pregnant Susanna and two of her female friends were shot to death. Timothy was convicted of murdering all three (Illustrative Cases of Women and Their Children Exploited and Abused through the International Marriage Broker Industry, 2005).

The need for protection for mail-order brides have spawned all kinds of effort from government agencies, non-profit agencies and independent women's groups and advocates, but there exists many legal loopholes in this kind of industry, especially one that takes place online. The Philippines, in 1990, enacted Republic Act Number 6955 (Anti-Mail-Order Bride Law), which is "an act to declare unlawful the practice of matching Filipino women for marriage to foreign nationals on a mail-order basis and other similar practices including the advertisement, publication, printing or distribution of brochures, fliers and other propaganda materials in furtherance thereof and providing penalty therefore" (http://www.preda.org/work/resolution/repact.htm). The Anti-Mail-Order Bride law regulated the traditional catalog-based agencies, but it was difficult to lay charges against companies based overseas who use the Internet. According to Philippine Senator Loren Legarda, new ways of marriage matching using cyberspace and other forms of communication technology are beyond the reach of the law:

> The law is flawed because of its failure to designate a specific agency that would monitor and ensure enforcement. Since the servers of these on-line agencies are obviously based in the US, we we cannot prosecute them here for lack of territorial jurisdiction. But what we could go after are their local partners or agents.

The United States, for its part, passed the International Marriage Broker Regulation Act of 2005, or IMBRA. IMBRA provides foreign women with information they need to make informed choices. Specifically, the Act: prohibits an IMB from profiling girls under the age of 18; requires IMBs to conduct background and criminal checks on the men; obtain a signed consent form from the women allowing information about her to be sent to the man; and give pamphlets with information for the women about U.S. laws and her rights. The law also halts the practice of Americans simultaneously seeking visas for multiple fiancees and provides a lifetime cap of two fiancee visas per U.S. Petitioner (Miller-Muro, 2006). This legislation is definitely a step in the right direction, but there is still a long way to go, as many men (and brokers) will find away around the law. The scope is only limited to U.S. Citizens, and the U.S. does not regulate how companies treat the women they commodify. The laws of the import countries simply do not complement or support the laws of export countries (Mallare, 2006, p. 19).

It is understandable that Filipino women are aggressively

seeking a brighter future by taking their chance as a mail-order bride, but in their eagerness, some have fallen into the trap of sexual exploitation of women. The current trafficking of women through the mail-order bride industry sells the women into bondage, which "subordinates women by uniting men with power to women without it" (Epstein, 2007). The purpose of some of the agencies is not to find lifetime partners for women but supply foreign men with a wife to be treated as a sex object and all-around maid. Philippine Senator Ernesto Maceda argued that "by making Filipina brides a marketable commodity and flaunting them as such like cattle in tawdry and revolting advertisements, this business has gravely insulted all that we, as a nation, hold sacred" (Lloyd, 2000, p. 352).

There is a very real problem within the mail-order bride industry that needs to be addressed, and this problem is not just the problem of the export countries who supply mail-order brides or the import country whose men participate in mail-order bride transactions. It is an international problem, which, on a larger scale is contributing to violence, prostitution rings and the flesh trade. International regulation, transnational cooperation and a working legal framework is necessary because the forces of supply and demand exist beyond any national, or even physical borders.

Conclusion

The circuit of culture has shown that the dominant discourses about Filipinas in the websites present a rather homogenous and superficial image of Filipinas and creates very ideal expectations from the men. Such typification disregards any realistically diverse characteristics of Filipinas who have histories, varied experiences and who are alive and real. On the Internet, race itself may not be fixed or finite, but racial stereotypes—or "cybertypes" are hardwired into our online interactions (Nakamura, 2002). This kind of stereotyping tends to occur where power inequalities exist, and the World Wide Web is just the place with imbalances and complications. In the real world, one way to wield power is physical exploitation but in the online web there is another power: symbolic power, or the power to represent someone in a certain way.

The Internet is a powerful tool for constructing a global image of Filipino women. Type in the word "Filipina" and the top search engine results would still lead to mail-order bride, dating and sex sites. But it must be noted that search engines are not the enemy; after all, they reflect the reality of cyberspace. The Filipina mail-order brides are not the enemy either; they have every right of being called Filipinas as much as other Filipinas. The real enemy is indifference: lack of concern from the nations who participate and tolerate the practice of marketing women using sexual, racial and ethnic labels. It is also the narrowmindedness of people who refuse to see the Filipina beyond perceptions of the past and beyond the power inequalities in the real world and in the online world which do not reflect the diverse facets of the modern Filipina. Even in a generally peaceful country like the Philippines there exists a kind of conflict in which the Filipina struggles with a negotiated identity, a conflict of meanings at play. Filipinas remain largely the "defined" rather than the "definers" of their own identity. This makes it ever so important for Filipinas here and all over the world in challenging the status quo and "owning" the world "Filipina" in cyberspace.

References

Checkoway, J. (June 7, 2000). Ordering brides on the web: Old business, new source. *The New York Times*. Retrieved September 13, 2002 from http://partners.nytimes.com/library/tech/00/06/biztech/technology/07chek.html

Diocson, C. (2000). Canada: The new frontier for Filipino mail-order brides. *Status of Women Canada (SWC) Website*. Retrieved August 24, 2002 from http://www.swc-cfc.gc.ca/pubs/pubspr/0662653343/200011_0662653343_e.pdf

Epstein, D. (January 25, 2007). Romance is dead: The consumer husband marries a surrogate corpse and the mail-order bride industry invites feminism to the wedding. *Social Science Research Network Website*. Retrieved March 14, 2007 from http://ssrn.com/abstract=959534

Glodova, M. & Onizuka, R. (1994). Mail-order Brides: Women for Sale. Fort Collins: Alaken, Inc.

Halualani, R.T. (1995). The interesting hegemonic discourses of an asian mail-order bride catalogue: Pilipina "oriental butterfly" dolls for sale. *Women's Studies in Communication, 18*(1), 45-64.

Hughes, D. (2004). Human trafficking: Mail-order bride abuses. Paper presented at the Subcommittee on East Asian and Pacific Affairs Senate Foreign Relations Committee, July 13, 2004. *United States Senate Website*. Retrieved March 1, 2007 from http://www.senate.gov/~foreign/testimony/2004/HughesTestimony040713.pdf

Hunt, D.D. & Sta. Ana-Gatbonton, C. (2002). Filipino women and sexual violence: Speaking out and providing services. *Immigrant Women's Support Service Website*. Retrieved March 3, 2007 from http://www.iwss.org.au/public/forumpapers/philippines.pdf

Illustrative Cases of Women and Their Children Exploited and Abused through the International Marriage Broker Industry (2005). *Tahirih Justice Center Website*. Retrieved March 3, 2007 from http://tahirih.org/legal/docs/IMBRACasesfor2005Intro(SHORT).DOC

Inquirer News Service. (January 14, 2002). Probe of e-mail order bride service urged. *PREDA Foundation, Inc.*

Website. Retrieved September 13, 2002 from http://www.preda.org/archives/research/digest/digest13.html

Lloyd, K. (2000). Wives for sale: The modern international mail-order bride industry. *Northwestern Journal of International Law and Business*. Retrieved February 23, 2007 from http://www.popcenter.org/problems/Supplemental_Material/trafficked_women/Lloyd_2000.pdf

Mallare, M.L. (May 2006). Mail-order brides: A closer look at U.S. & Philippine relations. *Asia Pacific Perspectives: An Electronic Journal*, *VI*(1). Retrieved March 14, 2007 from http://www.pacificrim.usfca.edu/research/perspectives

Miller-Muro, L. (January 5, 2006). Historic law signed by president Bush to prevent the abuse of foreign women through international marriage brokers. *Tahirih Justice Center Website*. Retrieved March 1, 2007 from http://tahirih.org/legal/docs/IMBRAPressReleaseJan52006.pdf

Nakamura, L. (2000). Race in/for cyberspace: Identity tourism and racial passing on the internet. *University of California, Irvine School of Humanities Website*. Retrieved September 16, 2002 from http://www.humanities.uci.edu/mposter/syllabi/readings/nakamura.html

Pettman, J.J. (1999). Sex tourism: The complexities of power. In *Culture and Global Change* (pp. 109-116). London Routledge.

Scholes, R.J. (2001). The "Mail-Order" Bride Industry and its Impact on U.S. Immigration. *U.S. Citizen and Immigration Services Website*. Retrieved August 27, 2002 from http://www.uscis.gov/files/article/MobRept_AppendixA.pdf

The international mail-order bride industry: An increasing threat to women (Summer 2004). *Making theConnection: News and Views on Sexuality, Education, Health and Rights*. Volume *3*(2). Retrieved February 23, 2007 from http://www.siecus.org/inter/connection/connection3_2.pdf

Thomson, M. (June 2006). Migrants on the edge of Europe: Perspectives from Malta, Cyprus and Slovenia. *Sussex Centre for Migration Research Website*. Retrieved May 14, 2007 from http://www.sussex.ac.uk/migration/documents/mwp35.pdf

Mail-Order Bride Websites

A Filipina Bride

http://www.afilipinabride.com

Filipina Lady

http://www.filipinalady.com

Filipina Wife

http://www.filipinawife.com

World Class Service

http://www.filipinas.us

Everlasting Love

http://www.everlastinglove.com

Cebuanas.com

http://www.cebuanas.com

Eşitlik Arayışında Bir Adım: "Birarada Yaşam" Girişimi ve Medyada Temsili

Emel Baştürk Akca
İletişim Fakültesi
Kocaeli Üniversitesi
eakcatr@yahoo.com

Özet

Farklı etnik ve dini grupları içinde barındıran Türkiye Cumhuriyeti, kuruluşundan bu yana,—tüm ulus-devletler gibi—bu farklılıkları tek bir kimlik altında birleştirmeye, homojen bir kimlik yaratmaya çalışmıştır. Bu homojen kimlik arayışında farklılıklar ve hatta "İslam" da ulusal kimliği ve birliği tehdit eden unsurlar olarak görülür. İslam, Türk ulusunun unsurları arasında görülse de milli kimliği önceleyen biçimde kendini yalnızca "Müslüman" olarak tanımlamak, "laik" rejim açısından tehlikelidir ve bu nedenle İslam da resmi milliyetçi söylemin "ötekileri" arasında yerini alır. Ancak özellikle 1990'lı yıllardan bu yana Türkiye'de "ötekileştirilen" bu farklı kesimlerin kendilerini ifade etme ve ötekiler arasında bir diyalog kurma çabası gözlenmektedir. Özel radyo ve televizyonların yayın hayatına girmesiyle, kamusal alanda temsil edilme imkânı bulamayan farklılıklar, kendi medyalarını kurarak, kendi dilleri içinden konuşmaya başlarlar. Bu konuşmalarda, öncelikle devletin bütünlüğü ve diğer kesimler için tehdit oluşturmadıklarını anlatma çabası dikkati çeker. Bu mesaj ilk olarak 90'lı yıllarda İslami kesimde "Birlikte Yaşam" düşüncesi ya da sloganıyla ortaya çıkar. Değişen siyasal konjonktür içinde aynı düşünce 2000'li yıllarda bu kez Özgürlük ve Dayanışma Partisi (ÖDP) tarafından "Birarada Yaşam Girişimi" adıyla yeniden gündeme gelir. Bu çalışmada, Türk milliyetçiliğinin doğası, ulusçu söylem, Türkiye'de farklı kamuların temsili, çok kültürlülük gibi anahtar kavramlar üzerinden "Birlikte Yaşam Girişimi"nin kendini nasıl ifade ettiği ve farklı basın organlarında nasıl temsil edildiği analiz edilmeye çalışılmıştır.

Giriş: "Ötekiler" Konuşuyor...

Ulus inşası, ulusal sınırlar içinde yer alan toplulukları ortak bir kimlik ve kültür altında birleştirme çabasına dayanır. Tek bir etnik kimlik üzerine temellenmiş olsun ya da olmasın tüm uluslar, farklılıkları, homojen bir kimlik algısında birleştirme çabası içindedir. Farklı etnik kimlik ve dinlere mensup grupları içinde barındıran Türkiye Cumhuriyeti de, çok etnili ve dinli bir imparatorluktan, bir ulus-devlet oluşturma çabasına girmiş ve bunun için de farklılıkları, Türk kimliği altında birleştirmeye çalışmıştır. Türk ulusal söylemi, "birlik" ve "beraber"liğe vurgu yaparken, farklılıkların birlikteliğini değil, farklılıklarından arınmış, "laik Türk vatandaşları" yaratma isteğini ifade etmiştir. Bu çerçevede azınlıklar, "Müslümanlar" ve farklı etnik gruplar, bu homojen kimlik tasavvuru, dolayısıyla Türkiye Cumhuriyeti'nin bütünlüğü için bir tehdit olarak algılanırlar. Ancak özellikle 90'lı yıllardan itibaren, Türkiye'deki farklı gruplar—kendi hakları için siyasi iktidarla çatışmaktan öte—çeşitli kanallarla kendilerini diğer gruplara ve özellikle resmi söylemin temsilcilerine anlatma yoluna gitmiştir. Bunda özel radyo ve televizyon yayınlarının başlamasıyla, farklı grupların kendilerini ifade edebilecekleri mecralara kavuşmasının etkisi büyüktür. Başka bir ifade ile bu gruplar, medyayı da kullanarak kamusal alanda görünür olmaya ve kendi dillerinden konuşmaya başlamıştır. Bu kendini ifade etmede daha çok, devlet, rejim ve diğer gruplar için bir tehdit olmadıkları mesajı vardır. Bu mesaj ilk olarak 1990'ların başında İslami çevreler tarafından "Birlikte Yaşam" sloganı ya da fikriyle ortaya konmuştur.

Farklı kesimlerden aydınların da desteğini alan bu düşünce, yeni medya ortamlarında dile getirilmiş ve akademik tartışmalara da konu olmuştur. Özel radyo ve televizyon yayıncılığının—getirdiği pek çok olumsuzluğa rağmen—özellikle radyo aracılığıyla Türkiye'de çok sesliliğin kapısını araladığını söylemek mümkündür. O güne dek TRT'nin devlet denetimli yayınlarında temsil edilme imkanı bulamayan kesimler hızla kendi radyolarını kurmaya ve "konuşmaya" başlar. Radyo yayıncılığının, daha az maliyetli bir yayıncılık alanı olmasının da etkisiyle 90'lı yıllarda—deyim yerindeyse—bir özel radyo patlaması yaşanır.

Özel radyo ve televizyonlar, o güne dek TRT'nin tekelinde bulunan yayın alanından dışlanan kesimlerin kamusal alanda görünür kılınmasını sağlar. TRT'de kendisine yer bulamayan arabesk ve protest müzik gibi "alternatif" kültür ürünleri, televizyon ekranları ve radyolarla buluşur. Bu değişim, farklı kesimlerin birbirinden haberdar olmasını, onunla karşılaşmasını sağlar. Konuşmaya başlamanın bir sonraki adımı ise, farklılıkların tanınması, konuşma özgürlüğünün devamının sağlanması yolundaki çabalar olur. Bu çabalar da farklı kesimlerin birbirleriyle uyum içinde yaşayabileceği tezlerinin seslendirilmesi biçiminde karşımıza çıkar. 90'larda İslami kesimde dillendirilen "Birlikte Yaşam" sloganı, 2000'lere gelindiğinde siyasal perspektifin bir başka ucundan gelir. Bu çalışmada Özgürlük ve Dayanışma Partisi'nin başlatmış olduğu "Birarada Yaşam Girişimi"nin kendini nasıl temsil ettiği ve farklı yayın organlarında nasıl temsil edildiği analiz edilmeye çalışılmıştır. Çalışmada, farklılıkların bir arada yaşaması girişiminin söylemsel analizi çerçevesinde, Türk milliyetçiliğinin doğası, ulusçu söylem, Türkiye'de farklı kamuların temsili, çok kültürlülük gibi kavramlar da tartışılır.

90'lı yılların tüm dünyada büyük anlatıların, modernleşme projelerinin sorgulanmaya başlandığı bir dönem olduğu da gözden kaçmamalıdır. Bozdoğan ve Kasaba (2005), kimilerince postmodern çağ olarak adlandırılan bu dönemi "şimdiye kadar bastırılmış yeni seslerin ilk kez duyulduğu, hayatın her boyutunda yerleşik kabullerin kökünden ve sanıyoruz ki geri dönülmez biçimde sorgulandığı, çok hareketli ve çoğulcu bir ortam" olarak tanımlarlar (s. 1). Bu ortamda Türk modernleşmesi de çeşitli kesimler tarafından eleştirilir, Türk ulusçuluğunun homojen yapısına karşı, "çeşitlilik" ve "kültürel kimlik" gibi kavramlar ön plana çıkar.

Ulusal Söylemde Farklılıkların "Ötekileştirilmesi"

Türk ulusçuluğu, içerisinde farklı etnik kimlikler ve dini grupları barındırmakla birlikte, tek bir etnik kimlik etrafında kurulmuş bir milliyetçiliktir. Bu yönüyle Türk milliyetçiliğinin "kültürel" bir milliyetçilik olduğunu söylemek mümkündür. Kültürel milliyetçilik ya da kültür devleti, "bir etnik grubu (halkı), bir anadili ve bir anayurdu esas alır". II. Dünya Savaşı sonuna kadar bu türden devlet deneyimleri, milliyetçi tek parti iktidarlarının önderliğinde "ulusal birliği" inşa etme sürecini yaşamışlardır. Bu tür bir devlet modeli içinde "ulusal birlik", "kültür birliği" anlamındadır (Aydın, 1998, s. 40).

Türk ulusçuluğunun tanımlanmasında Şerif Mardin'in ulusçuluk sınıflamasını da dikkate almak gerekir. Mardin iki tip ulusçuluktan söz eder; modernist ulusçuluk ve geleneksel ulusçuluk. Yazara göre her iki tip ulusçuluk da Türkiye'de yaşanmıştır. Modernist ulusçuluk anlayışı, Türk toplumunu çağdaş uygarlıklar düzeyine getirmeyi ve bu şekilde ülkeyi güçlendirmeyi amaçlamaktadır (aktaran Konyar, 1998, s. 151). 1930'lu yılardan itibaren de "geleneksel milliyetçilik" denebilecek ikinci tür bir milliyetçilik ortaya çıkmıştır. Bu "milliyetçilik türü, birincisine göre *milliyetçi ruh* ve *kültürel bilinç* konusuna çok daha fazla önem" vermektedir" (1998, s. 151). "Geleneksel milliyetçilik" tipi sözü edilen dönemden itibaren "modernist milliyetçilik"in yanında önemli bir konumda yerini almıştır.

Mardin, "modernist" ve "geleneksel" milliyetçilikten söz ederken, Türk milliyetçiliğinin –ve aslında Batı milliyetçiliklerinin de- yaşadığı değişimi açıklar. Taner Timur, Batı burjuvazilerinin devrimci niteliklerini kaybettikten sonra Batı'da milliyetçiliğin çoğu kez şoven ve ırkçı bir görünüm kazandığını ve sömürge rejimlerini meşrulaştırıcı yönde kullanıldığını söyler (1994, s. 26). Balkanlar'daki ulusçuluk anlayışından etkilenen ya da nesnel koşulları nedeniyle bu anlayışı benimsemek durumunda kalan Türk ulusçuluğu romantik bir yapıya sahiptir. Balkan ulusçuluğu ise Alman ve Rus ulusçuluğunun halkçılık hareketlerinden etkilenmiş ve aydınlar, "ulus bilinci"ni halka "aşılamayı" amaç edinen bir "Halka Doğru" hareketi başlatmışlardır. Bu hareketi desteklemek için de önce kendi halklarının "ulusal kimliği"ni (*volksgeist'ını*) keşfetmeye yönelirler (1998, s. 49). Alman "entelijensiyası" "ulusal birlik"ten yoksundur ve bu nedenle ulusu oluşturmanın ve birarada tutmanın yolu olarak başka kavramlara dayanmak zorunda kalmıştır: "kültür" ve "devlet" kavramları. "Alman romantikleri daha sonra 'kültür' kavramı ile yer değiştiren *vokslgeist* kavramıyla işe başlamışlar" (1998, s. 37). Hegel'in temellendirdiği "iyi devlet"in sınırlarını, Almanca konuşanların ya da bu ortak dili konuşanların paylaştığı varsayılan ortak "kültür"ün coğrafi sınırı belirleyecektir. Böylelikle ulusal devlet ile etniklik ya da belirli bir kültür arasındaki ilişki de kurulmuş olur. Aynı zamanda "soydaşlık" ile "yurttaşlık" arasında da bir koşutluk inşa edilir. Dolayısıyla böyle bir ulus tasavvuruna dayanarak devlet kurmaya kalkışanlar için milliyetçilik, bu türden bir devlete kavuşmanın ideolojik aracı haline gelir.

"Halka Doğru" projesinin sözcülüğünü önce Selanik'te çıkan ve sonra İstanbul'a taşınan *Genç Kalemler* dergisi üstlenir. Masami Arai, dergide, "Türklük"ten kastedilenin hep "Anadolu halkı—Anadolu köylüsü" olduğunu belirtir (aktaran Aydın, 1998, s 50). Hareket, *Halka Doğru* dergisiyle kurumlaşmıştır. Bu eğilimin savunuculuğunu Ziya Gökalp'in yazılarında buluruz. Herder'in *volksgeist* olarak adlandırdığı olguya—kültüre—Gökalp (1998) "hars" demiş ve aydınların "halka giderek" ondan harsı öğrenmesi gerektiğini, böylece oluşacak bilincin ulusal kimliğin temeli olacağını savunmuştur (s. 50). Halka Doğru Projesinin uzantıları—aynı ismi taşımamakla birlikte—Cumhuriyet döneminde de devam etmiştir.

Ziya Gökalp'in "müşterek kültür" olarak tanımladığı ulusçuluk ilkesini yeni Türk Cumhuriyeti de benimsemiş ve "kültürün, halkın yaşayışının içinden çıkartılarak sistematik bir kültür politikasıyla işlenebileceği varsayılmıştır" (Mardin, 1990, s. 204). Kemalizmin gelişimi, "bu öğenin Atatürk tarafından ne kadar ciddiye alındığını gösteren örneklerle doludur. Folklor araştırmaları, dilin araştırılmasında yerel kaynaklara inilmesi bu örneklerin bazılarını belirler." (s. 204).

Özellikle 1930'lu yıllar bu çabaların yoğunlaştığı yıllar olur. Bu dönemde savaşlar bitmiş, devrimler büyük ölçüde tamamlanmış ve sıra bunların halka benimsetilmesine gelmiştir. İşte bu dönemde Kemalizmin benimsediği halkçılık ideolojisi doğrultusunda "halkın" eğitimine yönelik kurumlar oluşturulmaya başlanır. Bunlardan en önemlileri Halkevleri, Millet Mektepleri ve Köy Enstitüleridir. Ulusçu ideoloji ve söylem ders kitaplarına da yansır ve özellikle tarih kitapları Türk tarih tezini yeni kuşaklara öğretmenin en önemli araçları haline gelir. Özetlemek gerekirse Cumhuriyetle birlikte kurulan yeni Türk devleti, "Batıdaki örneklerine uygun olarak, kendisini meşrulaştıracak bir 'ulus' aramaya ve bu ulusun pragmatik sınırları meydana çıktıktan sonra da çerçevesini bu sınırların çizdiği bir kimliği benimsetmeye" (Aydın, 1998, s. 109) girişmiştir.

Anderson (1995) milleti, "inşa edilmiş birliktelik", "hayali bir cemaat" olarak tanımlarken, her ulusun uluslaşma süreci ve sonrasında ulusal bir kültür yaratmaya çalıştığına işaret eder. Türk milliyetçiliği de Türkiye Cumhuriyeti'nin kuruluşundan hemen sonra gündeme gelen "devrimler"le, önce Osmanlı'dan kalan kurumları ortadan kaldırmaya, sonra da Türk Dil Kurumu ve Türk Tarih Kurumu gibi kurumlar aracılığıyla yeni ulusun kültürünü inşa etmeye çalışır. Çelik'in (2002) ifade ettiği gibi "Türkiye Cumhuriyeti'nin resmi ve kurucu ideolojisi olarak tanımlanan Kemalizm'in siyasal toplumsal projesi, yeni bir vatan, yeni bir toplum, yeni kimlik ve bu yaratılmış olan ulus için yeni bir tarih" tanımlamıştır (s. 75). Foucault'nun üzerinde durduğu bilgi ve iktidar ilişkisi üzerinden gidersek, bu kurumlar Türkiye Cumhuriyeti ve Türk ulusuna dair "bilgi"yi oluşturacak olan kurumlardır. Resmi standart eğitim kurumları ve basın da bu bilgiyi ve ulus olma bilincini halka taşıyacak kurumlar olarak karşımızda durur.

Milli Mücadele, hem içte hem de dışta savaş vermiş, başka bir deyişle "bir taraftan işgal kuvvetleri ile savaşırken, diğer taraftan da yerli işbirlikçileri", saray çevresi ile mücadele etmek zorunda kalmıştır. Bu nedenle Milli Mücadele döneminde ve hatta Cumhuriyetin ilk yıllarına kadar Türk milliyetçiliği, farklı kesimlerle uzlaşma içinde olma yoluna gitmiştir. Birinci Meclis'te İslami kesimlerden, Turancılık gibi daha radikal bir milliyetçiliği savunanlara, Lazlar ve Çerkezler gibi farklı etnik kimliklerini açıkça telaffuz edenlere kadar farklı kesimler bir araya gelmiştir. Ancak, devrimlerin gerçekleştirilmesinin ardından, bu devrimlerin topluma benimsetilmesi ve toplumun bu yeni idealler ışığında yeniden biçimlendirilmesi sürecinde, artık farklılıklardan değil, ortak tek bir kültürden söz etmek gerekmektedir.

Yeni Cumhuriyetin Osmanlı İmparatorluğu ya da daha doğrusu eski sistemle her türlü bağlantısını kopartabilmek için İmparatorluk'tan kalan tüm kurumların ortadan kaldırılması gerekmektedir (saltanatın, hilafetin kaldırılması, tekke ve zaviyelerin kapatılması gibi). Çünkü yine Timur'un (1994) ifadesi ile "bir devrim sadece egemen konumdaki bir toplumsal sınıfın ayrıcalıklarına son vermekten ibaret değildi. Onun bu ayrıcalıklarını *meşru kılan dünya* görüşünü ve siyasal mekanizmaları da yok etmeyi zorunlu" kılmaktaydı (s. 283). Reformlarla gerçekleştirilmeye çalışılan şey de buydu. İşte yukarıda sözü edilen "kültürel milliyetçilik" ya da Mardin'in sınıflandırmasıyla "geleneksel milliyetçilik" tam da bu çabalarla ortaya çıkmaktaydı.

Türk modernleşme projesi, modernizmin temelinde yatan "Batı tipi ilerleme modeli" ya da başka bir ifadeyle "çizgisel tarih anlayışı"yla hareket eder. Bu anlayışa göre, imparatorluktan ulus-devlet modeline geçmek, bir ilerleme/gelişmedir ve imparatorluk dönemine ait kurumlar ve kültürel yapılar ise geri kalmışlığın ürünleridir. Kemalist söylemin sıkça tekrarladığı, Türkiye Cumhuriyeti ile birlikte "ümmet zihniyetinden, millet zihniyetine" geçilmiş olduğu düşüncesi, hem kamusal alanda görünür olan bir İslam anlayışını ötekileştirmekte, hem de Osmanlı'yla olan bağları koparmaya hizmet etmektedir. Ayrıca ümmetten millete geçiş, ulus içindeki farklı etnik kimliklerin Türk kimliği altında birleştirilmesini de beraberinde getirir. Artık farklı etnik kimliklerden söz etmek mümkün değildir. Tüm bu kimlikler, bölgesel, kültürel farklılıklara indirgenir.

Resmi milliyetçi söylem, bir noktaya kadar İslami bir söylemi de içerdiği için, İslam'ın resmi milliyetçiliğin ötekilerinden biri olduğu uzun süre görünür hale gelmemiştir. Hatta 60, 70 ve 80'lerde komünizmle mücadele, devlet kurumları ve İslami kesim arasında ittifaklar doğurmuş, Türk-İslam sentezi hakim güç olmuştur. Devletin, Diyanet İşleri Başkanlığı gibi bir kurum aracılığıyla Sünni İslam'a hizmet ettiği, Sünni İslam'ı egemen dini yapı olarak kurduğu görüşü hakimdir. Ancak bu durum 90'lı yıllarda farklı kamuların kendini temsil etme süreciyle birlikte Türkiye'de İslami bir yükselişin yaşanmasıyla değişime uğrar. İslami kesimler, Diyanet İşleri Başkanlığı gibi kurumlar aracılığıyla, "resmi bir İslam" anlayışının kendilerine dayatıldığını dillendirmeye başlarlar. Onlara göre, devlet, her şeyin olduğu gibi Müslüman olmanın sınırlarını da belirlemektedir. Devletin izin verdiği ölçülerin dışına çıkmak istemek, "gericilik", "çağ-dışılık" ve "irtica" olarak tanımlanır. 1990'larda İslami kesimde dillendirilmeye başlanan "Birlikte Yaşam" teorisi, İslam'ın tüm topluma İslami kuralları dayatmak isteyen bir anlayış olmadığını, farklı kesimlerle bir arada yaşayabileceğini ifade etmektedir. Başörtüsü yasağının kamusal alan tartışmalarıyla birlikte genişletilmesi, dini eğitim konusundaki kısıtlamalar,

İslami kesimleri de "mağdur" konumuna getirmiş ve başörtüsünü de bir "hak mücadelesi"ne dönüştürmüştür. İslam, Türk ulusunun unsurları arasında görülse de milli kimliği önceleyen biçimde kendini yalnızca "Müslüman" olarak tanımlamak, "laik" rejim açısından tehlikelidir ve bu nedenle İslam da resmi milliyetçi söylemin "ötekileri" arasında yerini alır

Benzer şekilde Kürt milliyetçiliğinin yükselişe geçtiği 1980'li yıllarda, devletin politikası Kürt varlığını reddetmek yönünde biçimlenir. Ayrıca, Kürtlerin farklılıklarını dile getirecek biçimde siyaset yapmasının önü de kapatılır. Bu süreçte Kürt sorunu, PKK terörüyle mücadele kapsamında tartışılabilmektedir. Ancak 1990'lı yıllar, dünya siyasetinde olduğu kadar, Türkiye'de de önemli değişikliklere sahne olur. 1980'lerde başlayan serbest piyasa ekonomisine geçiş süreci 90'larda kapitalist sistemin ülkede yerleşmesiyle devam eder. Postmodernite, küreselleşme gibi kavramlar toplumsal yapıyı da etkiler. Keyman'ın (1998) ifadesiyle "1980'lerin anahtar kavramı postmodernite iken, 1990'lı yıllarda globalleşme" anahtar kavram olmuştur (s. 39). Küreselleşme, yalnızca dünya ekonomisi ve dünya politikasını etkilemekle kalmamış, "günlük yaşam deneyim ve patriklerinin kurucu öğelerinden biri olarak" karşımıza çıkmıştır. Başka bir ifadeyle küresel kapitalizm yalnızca ekonomik yapıyı değil, toplumsal yapıyı da etkilemiştir. Özel radyo ve televizyon yayınlarının başlamasını mümkün kılan ekonomik, teknolojik ve siyasi bir dönüşüm söz konusudur. Türkiye'nin Avrupa Birliği ile ABD ile ilişkileri de daha liberal politikaların uygulanmasını teşvik eder. Türkiye, 2000'li yıllara gelindiğinde bir yandan yükselen bir milliyetçiliğe, diğer yandan da farklılıkların kendilerini ifade etme çabasına sahne olmaktadır.

Türkiye'de Kimlik Politikaları...

1990`lı yıllar, Türkiye`nin Kürt gerçekliğiyle yüzleşmek zorunda kaldığı yıllardır. İsmi bile telaffuz edilmek istenmeyen Kürtler`den söz etmek, ancak 90`larda mümkün olabilir. AB sürecinde demokratikleşme yolunda atılan adımlar, Kürt halkı ve aydınlarında sorunun demokratik yollarla çözülebileceği inancını/ umudunu arttırır. Kürt sorununda gelinen çözümsüzlük noktasında, başından bu yana Kürt varlığını tanımak istemeyen, "egemen milliyetçilik"in ve sorunu şiddet yoluyla "çözebileceği"ni düşünen PKK terörünün payı vardır. Ancak Türkiye'de Kürt varlığının tanınmasının, Türkiye'yi son tahlilde bölünmeye götürecek yıkıcı bir "taviz" olduğunu düşünmeyen Türkler kadar, PKK'nın şiddete dayalı yapısını eleştiren geniş bir Türkiyeli Kürt topluluğu ortaya çıkmakta ve görüşlerini dilendirecek mecralar aramaktadır. İnsel'in (2006) belirttiği gibi, "derin devlet" ve PKK ikilisinin oluşturduğu şiddet sarmalından kurtulabilmek, bu ikilinin toplumun bütününü sürüklediği ölümcül dansı etkisiz kılmak konusunda Türkiyeli Kürtlerin adına konuşanların omzuna ağır bir yük binmektedir. Bu gelişmeler, Türk resmi söylemi tarafından ötekileştirilenlerin hak ve özgürlük mücadelesi noktasında ortak bir zeminde buluşması ve diyalog yolunda adımlar atmasının önünü açar. Bu nedenle birlikte yaşam konusundaki girişimlerin,—tarafların birbirini anlaması ve hak ve özgürlükler adına ortak adımlar atabilmesi için daha çok yol kat edilmesi gerekse de—sağ ve sol kesimden gelmesi şaşırtıcı değildir. Bu iki kesim, anti-emperyalizm noktasında da ortak bir söylemi paylaşır.

"Globalleşme sürecinin ortaya çıkarttığı belirsizlik durumunu simgeleyen en önemli gelişmelerden biri de *faklılıkların tanınmasına dayalı kimlik siyasetinin* siyasal söylemi belirleyici duruma gelmesi"dir (Keyman, 1998, s. 40). Keyman (1998), Türkiye'de 21. yüzyıla girerken siyasal yaşama anlam verme gücünde olan iki farklı siyaset anlayışından söz edebileceğimizi söyler: "Bir taraftan 'çoğulculuğa karşı aynı'lığı ve tek'liği savunan', milliyetçi bir siyaset anlayışının giderek güçlenmesi", diğer taraftan da "bu milliyetçi siyaset anlayışına karşı güçlendirilmesi gereken liberal demokrasiyi savunan, fakat bunu yaparken liberal demokrasinin çoğulcu toplum yapısına uygun" biçimde "yeniden kurulması gerektiğini" vurgulayan yeni bir siyaset anlayışına çağrılar var (ss. 40, 41). Bu çağrılar, kimlik politikalarına vurgu yaptıkları kadar, Türkiye'deki siyasal yapıya ilişkin değişimler de talep etmektedir.

Türkiye'de 2000'li yıllara gelindiğinde—akademik çevrelerle sınırlı kalsa da—"çokkültürlülük" kavramı tartışılmaya başlanır. Çok-kültürlülük Avrupa ülkeleri ve ABD'de de oldukça tartışmalı konulardan biridir. Farklı etnik ve kültürel kimliklerin tanındığı ülkelerde bile çokkültürlü bir toplum yapısının oluşturulması noktası sorunsuz değildir. Avrupa, "hem Avrupa Birliği çerçevesindeki serbest dolaşım hakkı, hem de üçüncü ülkelerden aldığı göçmen işçiler nedeniyle farklı kültürdeki insanların bir arada yaşadığı bir kıta haline gelmiştir. ABD ve Kanada gibi geleneksel olarak göç alan ülkelerden farklı biçimde Avrupa, bu yeni durumu tam olarak kabullenememiş ve dolayısıyla gerekli düzenlemeleri de gerçekleştirememiştir" (Altınbaş, 2006, s. 52). Altınbaş (2006), özellikle 1980'li yıllardan bu yana çokkültürlülük konusunun Avrupa'nın önemli gündem konularından birini oluşturduğunu ve bunda da "o zamana kadar uygulanmaya çalışılan asimilasyoncu politikaların başarısızlığının" etkili olduğunu söyler (s. 53). Çokkültürlülük farklı (ya da farklı olduğunu iddia eden) kesimlerin, bu farklılıklarının tanınması ve sürdürülmesi amacıyla gündeme getirilmiş bir konudur. Bu çalışmanın konusu doğrudan çokkültürlülük olmadığı ve/veya Türkiye'de birarada yaşam girişimleriyle açıkça çokkültürlülüğün telafuz edilmemesi nedeniyle bu konu daha geniş olarak tartışılmayacaktır. Ancak farklılıkların birlikte yaşayabilmesinin nasıl mümkün olabileceği sorusunun yanıtlanmasında çokkültürlülük ve çoğulculuk gibi kavramların tartışılması gerektiği belirtilmelidir.

Avrupa ve ABD'de yaşanan tartışmalara bakıldığında bu konunun Avrupa için de oldukça sorunlu bir mesele olduğu görülür. Bu nedenle Bauman'ın çokkültürlülüğü bir bilmeceye benzeten yaklaşımı dikkate değerdir. Bauman'a

(1999) göre çok kültürlülük; "tekleştirilmiş bir ulusal kültüre inananlar, kültürlerinin izini etnik kimliklerde arayanlar ve dinlerini kültürleri olarak görenlerden oluşan üç tarafın adalet ve eşitlik durumunu nasıl sağlayabileceğini" soran bir bilmecedir (s. 7). Bu bilmeceye yanıt bulabilmek için, kültürün inşası ve anlamı hakkında yeniden düşünmek gerekir. Bauman, modern ulus-devlet yapısı içinde belirlenen kültüre ilişkin algılarımızı ve tanımlamamızı gözden geçirmemizi söylerken, mevcut tanımlama içinden bakıldığında, farklılıkların sayısı kadar farklı kültürden söz edilmesi gerektiğini, bunun da bizi bir çıkmaza sürükleyeceğini söyler. Çokkültürlülüğün tanımlanması da oldukça zordur; bir ideoloji ya da toplumsal politika olarak farklı tanımlarından söz etmek mümkündür. Bunun yanı sıra çokkültürlülüğe getirilen eleştiriler de fazladır. Bassam Tibi'ye göre "başarılı bir entegrasyon için mutlaka paylaşılması gereken ortak bir kültür bulunmalıdır; ancak bu çokkültürlülükle mümkün olamamaktadır. Çünkü, bu sistemde kültürel gettolarda herhangi bir kaynaşmaya izin verilmemektedir (aktaran Altınbaş, 2006, s. 55).

Ahmet İnsel (2006) de Tibi'ye benzer biçimde, çokkültürlülüğün kabulüyle birlikte, "her alanda ve özellikle siyasal alanda çoğulculuk ilkesinin yerini çokkültürlülüğün almasının yol açabileceği özgürlük kısıtlaması" riskinden söz eder: "İnsani varoluşun bir kültürel varlığın korunması ilkesine indirgenmesi tehlikesidir bu. 'Sen Türksün, Türk kalacaksın' veya 'sen Kürtsün, Kürt kalmalısın' anlayışı, normatif bir çokkültürlülük uygulamasının olası sonuçlarından biridir. Bu durum, kültürel-etnik ilkeyi birincil kılar, insanı ise o ilkenin bir aracı konumuna dönüştürür. Oysa özgürleşmenin öznesi kimlik değil, insandır, kişidir." Çokkültürülük ve/veya çoğulculuk üzerine tartışmalar, uzun soluklu bir çalışmanın konusu olacak kadar geniştir. Buradan Türkiye'de farklı kesimlerin, farklılıklarının tanınması talebine dönersek, Türkiye'nin kendi özgün koşulları içinde bir çözüm yolunun bulunması gereği ortaya çıkar. "Birlikte Yaşam" ve "Birarada yaşamı savunalım" girişimi bu talebi dile getiren girişimlerdir. Ancak ÖDP'nin başlattığı "Birarada yaşamı savunalım" kampanyasının farklı görüşlere sahip olan iki gazetede (*Yeni Şafak* ve *Birgün*) nasıl temsil edildiği, çoğulculuk, hak ve özgürlükler adına nerede olduğumuzu görmek açısından önemlidir.

"Birarada Yaşamı Savunalım"

1990'lı yıllarda Ali Yaşar Sarıbay ve Ali Bulaç gibi yazarların öncülüğünde akademik çevreler ve aydınlar arasında seslendirilmeye başlanan "birlikte yaşam" tartışmaları, daha çok Müslüman ve Müslüman olmayanların, birbirleri için bir tehdit oluşturmaksızın bir arada yaşayabilecekleri fikrine odaklanır. Hz. Muhammed zamanında Medine'de yaşayan Müslüman ve gayri-Müslimler arasında imzalanan ve birbirlerinin haklarını tanıdıklarını gösteren "Medine Vesikası", İslam'ın diğer dinlerle barış içinde yaşayabileceğinin kanıtı ve "birlikte yaşam"ın modeli olarak sunulur. Ancak birlikte yaşam girişimi, Türkiye'deki farklı kesimlerin birbirlerine duyduğu "korku"yu gidermek ve birbirleri arasında bir diyalogu başlatmak için yeterli olmamıştır. "Birlikte yaşam" fikri daha sonra, "dinler arası hoşgörü/diyalog" adı altında İslam'ın diğer tek tanrılı dinlerle uyum içinde yaşayabileceği (yaşadığı) tezine sıkışıp kalmış, ülke içindeki "laik" ve "Müslüman" kesimler arasındaki gerilimi ortadan kaldırmak adına adımlar atılamamıştır. Avrupa Birliği'ne üyelik müzakerelerinin yoğunlaştığı son yıllarda ise "dinlerarası diyalog", "medeniyetler ittifakı" söylemiyle birleşerek, daha çok AB ülkelerine yönelik, "Müslüman Türkiye'nin gayri-Müslim topluluklarla uyum içinde yaşabileceği" mesajına dönüşmüştür. ÖDP öncülüğünde başlayan "Birarada Yaşam" girişimi[1] ise Türkiye içindeki farklılıkların temsiline yönelik bir söylemle kaşımıza çıkmaktadır.

"Birarada Yaşamı Savunalım" kampanyası bazı illerde belirli aralıklarla mitingler düzenleyerek ve bir web sitesi aracılığıyla sesini duyurmaya çalışır. Girişimi desteklemek için bir grup vatandaş tarafından kurulan web sitesinde (www.biraradayasam.net), bir imza kampanyası başlatılmış ve 2006 yılı Mayıs, Haziran ve Temmuz ayları boyunca çeşitli illerde yapılacak mitingler duyurulmuştur. Yaklaşık 6 bin kişinin imzaladığı metinde "*Yeterince acının yaşandığı bu topraklarda, yeni acılar yaşamak istemiyorum. Farklılığımızı zenginlik olarak görüyor, eşit, özgür demokratik bir Türkiye'de birarada yaşamı savunuyorum*" ifadeleri yer alır. Sitede, metni imzalayanların görüşlerine de yer verilmekte ve bu görüş ya da yorumlar dolayımıyla birarada yaşam girişiminin temellendiği düşünce daha açık olarak ortaya konmaktadır. Girişim 26 Mayıs'ta İstanbul'daki ilk mitingin ardından 14 Haziran 2006'da İstanbul'daki daha geniş katılımlı ikinci mitingini gerçekleştirir. Bu tarihten önce Mersin ve Ankara'da da birer miting gerçekleştirilmiştir.

İstanbul, Taksim'deki miting, 15 Haziran 2006 tarihli *Birgün* gazetesinde "Birarada Yaşamayı savunanlar buluştu" başlığıyla ilk sayfada yer alır. Gazete, girişimin diğer mitinglerini de haberleştirmiş ancak, bu tarihe kadar buna ilişkin haberler ilk sayfaya taşınmamıştır. İstanbul'daki üçüncü miting ise bundan yaklaşık on gün sonra 25 Haziran 2006 tarihinde gerçekleşir. *Birgün* haberinde, İstiklal Caddesi'nde "insan zinciri" eylemi gerçekleştirildiğini, "birarada yaşamı savunanların" elele yürüdüğünü söyler. Girişime ilişkin haberler, büyük ölçüde ÖDP yetkilileri ve eyleme katılanların görüşleriyle biçimlenir. *Birgün*'ün haberinde ÖDP İstanbul İl Başkanı Sinan Tutal'ın açıklamasına yer verilmektedir. Gazete Tutal'ın girişimin amacını ve talebini özetleyen şu sözlerini alıntılar;

1 "Birarada Yaşamı Savunalım" basında ve hazırladıkları web sitesinde "kampanya" olarak nitelendirilmektedir. Ancak "kampanya", yalnızca ÖDP'nin seçmenlerine yönelik bir hareketten çok farklı kesimleri buluşturmayı amaçladığı için "girişim" olarak adlandırmanın daha uygun olduğu düşünülmektedir. Bu nedenle makale boyunca "kampanya" yerine, "girişim" sözcüğü kullanılacaktır.

Türkiye toplumunun parçalanmasına, giderek laik-anti laik, Türk-Kürt gibi suni bir çatışma sürecine sokulmasına karşı, bu parçalanmaya ve çatışmaya dur demek ve bir arada yaşamı savunmak için ellerimizi birleştiriyoruz. "Ya sev ye terket" diyerek adliye koridorlarında, sokakta yüzümüze bağıran ırkçı ve milliyetçilere karşı, devlet yönetiminde kişinin kafasının içine değil de eşinin kafasının dışına bakmayı adet edinen veya başörtüsü ile okumak isteyenlere "Sudii Arabistan'a gitsin" diyen siyasetçilere karşı, "Kürtler Kuzey Irak"a yerleşsin diyen Kızılelmacılara karşı, sağa sola bomba koyarak birarada yaşamı tahrip etmek isteyenlere karşı, Susurluk, Şemdinli, Sauna, Atabey ve Danıştay baskınında ortaya çıkan çetelere karşı bir arada yaşamı savunuyoruz.

Tutal'ın sözleri, "birarada yaşamı savunalım" mitinglerinin Türkiye'de yükselen milliyetçiliğe ve bunun getirdiği "cepheleşmelere" karşı bir girişim olduğunu açık etmektedir. Gerek, imza kampanyasının organize edildiği web sayfasında, gerekse de *Birgün* gazetesinin aktardığı açıklamalarda etnik farklılıklar açıkça zikredilir. Bunun yanı sıra başörtüsü sorununa da değinilmekte ve bu sorunlara, onları ülke dışına atmak, başka bir ifadeyle "yok etmek" biçimindeki "çözümlere" tepki gösterilmektedir. *Birgün*'ün 15 Haziran tarihli haberinde 25 Haziran'da Kadıköy'de yapılacak miting de duyurulmakta ve Tutal'ın ağzından halk, mitinge davet edilmektedir.

Birgün gazetesinde girişimle ilgili çok sayıda köşe yazısı da yer almış, özellikle imza kampanyasına katılanların mesajları köşe yazıları aracılığıyla aktarılmıştır. Gazetenin yazarlarından Doğan Tılıç, girişime en çok yer veren isimlerdendir. Tılıç, "Birarada yaşamaya giden yolun taşları, birarada yaşayacakların karşılıklı olarak öykülerini birbirlerine anlatabilmeleriyle, birbirlerini dinlemeleriyle döşenecek" diyerek, farklı etnik ve dini gruplardan insanların öykülerine yer verir. Köşe yazılarına taşınan mesajlarda, Kürt, Türk, Alevi, Sünni, Gayr-i Müslim farklı kesimlerin birbirleriyle ortak anılarına yer verilmekte ve daha "demokratik" bir ülkede haklarına sahip olarak birlikte yaşama istekleri dile getirilmektedir.

Yeni Şafak gazetesinde ise "Birarada Yaşam" girişiminin İstanbul'daki üçüncü mitingine kadar, konuyla ilgili bir habere rastlanmaz. 25 Haziran'daki miting öncesinde 20 Haziran 2006'da ÖDP Genel Başkanı Hayri Kozanoğlu ile geniş bir röportaja yer verilir. "*Gerilimi yumuşatmak solcuların da görevi*" başlığıyla verilen röportajda, ÖDP'nin "Birarada Yaşamı Savunalım" sloganıyla 25 Haziran'da Kadıköy'de "meydana çıkacağı" belirtilir. *Yeni Şafak*'ın röportajında, mitingler farklı kesimlerden insanların bir araya geldiği bir "halk girişiminden" çok ÖDP'nin mitingi olarak sunulur. Röportajı yapan Fadime Özkan, Kozanoğlu'na açıkça, "bu atılımın seçim stratejilerinin bir parçası" olup olmadığını sorarken, girişimin gerçek amacını da sorgulamaktadır. Arkasından da "Eşit özgür ve birarada yaşama söylemi hemen her partinin programında var. Hiçbir parti aksini söylemiyor. Söylem aynı, eylem de farklılaşılıyor. Sizi diğer partilerden ayıran ne?" sorusu yöneltilir. Gazete bu sorgulamanın ardından Kozanoğlu'nun kampanyanın, ÖDP'nin seçim stratejisiyle ilgisi olmadığı, "toplumdaki gerilimlerin, çatışmaların ortadan kaldırılması için bir yurttaş sorumluluğu" olduğu açıklamasına da yer verir. Röportajda girişimin amacından çok, seçimler ve diğer siyasi partilerle ilişkiler üzerine yoğunlaşılmaktadır.

Yeni Şafak'taki girişimle ilgili ilk geniş haber, mitingin ardından 26 Haziran 2006 tarihinde yer alır: *"Cephecilere Türkiye mozaiğinden cevap"* başlıklı haber, altın gün önce yayımlanan röportaja kıyasla daha olumlu ve destekleyici niteliktedir. Haberin spotunda *"Türk toplumunda cepheleşme yaratma peşindeki bazı siyasilerin ayrımcı girişimine Lazı-Kürdü, başörtülüsü-başı açığının oluşturduğu Türkiye mozaiği, 'Birarada Yaşamı Savunalım' mitinginde buluştu"* sözleri yer alır. *Birgün* gazetesindeki haber ve yorumlarda olduğu gibi bu haberde de Türkiye'de resmi söylem aracılığıyla kurulan ikili karşıtlıklar (başı örtülüsü-başı açığı, Türkü-Lazı-Kürdü, Doğulusu-Batılısı) sıralanmakta ve bu karşıtlıkların "icat edilmiş" karşıtlıklar olduğu mesajı verilmektedir. Haberde yine ÖDP Genel Başkanı Kozanoğlu'nun konuşmasına yer verilmekte ve Kozanoğlu'nun "hoşgörüden, barıştan, diyalogdan yana bir seçeneği yaygınlaştırmak için çaba gösterecekleri" yönündeki açıklaması ön plana çıkartılmaktadır. Yukarıda da değinildiği gibi "hoşgörü, barış ve diyalog" çağrısı 1990'lı yılların ortalarından beri İslami kesimde de sıkça dile getirilen bir mesajdır. Gazetenin, kendi okur kitlesi için olumlu çağrışımları olan bu sözleri seçmiş olması tesadüf değildir.

Düzenlenen mitinglere farklı inanç ve kültürleri temsil eden sivil toplum örgütlerinin katılımı ve söz hakkının sağlanmış olması, girişimin eşitlik ve özgürlük talebini destekler niteliktedir. *Yeni Şafak*, mitinge katılanların yaptığı konuşmalar arasından öncelikle yazar Adalet Ağaoğlu'nun sözlerine, sonra da Mazlum-Der adına konuşan yazar Yıldız Ramazanoğlu'nun görüşlerine yer verir. Gazetenin aktardığı Ramazanoğlu'nun "tarih boyunca farklı inançtan, kimlikten insanların bu topraklarda eşit ve özgür yaşadıkları, bundan sonra da yaşayabileceğine" ilişkin sözleri, İslami kesimin "Birarada yaşam" girişimine bakışını özetlemektedir. Osmanlı'nın fetihlerle genişleyen bir imparatorluk olmasına rağmen, feth ettiği halkın dinini değiştirmek yönünde bir baskı yapmadığı, gayr-i Müslimlerin dinlerini özgürce yaşadığı söylemi, İslami kesimde "hoşgörü ve diyalogdan yana" olanların sıkça vurguladığı bir söylemdir.

Yeni Şafak, haberinde *"apoletliler tanık da sanık da olabilmeli"* alt başlığıyla, Türk siyasal yapısı içerisinde TSK'nın en etkin güçlerden biri olmasını da eleştirmektedir. Haberde Kozanoğlu'nun *"apoletlerine bakılmaksızın, herkesin tanık da olabildiği, sanık da olabildiği, genç subayların görüşlerinden çok, genç sivillerin görüşlerine önem verildiği bir Türkiye istiyoruz. Bazıları başörtülülere Suudi Arabistan'ın, bazı etnik kökenden gelenlere de Irak'ın yolunu gösteriyor. Bu görüşte olanlar bir zamanlar da 'Komünistler Moskova'ya' diye bağırıyorlardı*" sözleri alıntılanır. Kozanoğlu'nun sözlerinde Türkiye Cumhuriyeti'nin kurucu sınıflarına bir eleştiri ve demokrasi talebi vardır. Türk Silahlı Kuvvetleri, homojen bir toplum oluşturma çabasının önemli kurumlarındandır.

Yeni Şafak, mitinge köşe yazılarında da yer vermekte ve bu yazılarda Türkiye'de bir "hoşgörüsüzlük ve tahammülsüzlük" ortamının yaygınlaştığına değinilmektedir. Koray Düzgören'in 26 Haziran tarihli yazısında, *Birgün* gazetesinde Doğan Tılıç'ın yaptığı yorumlara benzer yorumlar yer alır. Yorumlarda dikkati çeken nokta, Ermeniler, Kürtler ve Müslüman kesimlere olan hoşgörüsüzlüğün kaynağının resmi devlet söyleminde aranmasıdır. Her iki gazete de birinci bölümde, Türk modernleşmesi ve resmi devlet söylemi üzerine yapılan tespitlerle örtüşür biçimde, Türkiye'de resmi söylemin "ötekiler" yarattığını ima etmekte, kimi zaman da açıkça dile getirmektedir. Düzgören yazısında "cepheleşmeyi körükleyenlerin" "devletin resmi görüşü"nü benimsediklerini ve baktıkları bu pencere içinden, "askerlerin eleştirilmesine, Atatürk'çülüğün tartışılmasına, Ermeni meselesinde resmi tezlerin dışına çıkılmasına razı" olamadıklarını söyler.

Birgün gazetesi ise 25 Haziran tarihli mitingi, *"Binler 'birarada' yaşamı savundu"* başlığıyla verir. Haberde 7 binden fazla kişinin, "daha fazla özgürlük ve demokrasi talebiyle bir araya geldiği", "halaylar, horonlar ve türküler eşliğinde özgürlük istediği" söylenir. Gazetede mitingde konuşan aydınlar ve sivil toplum örgütü temsilcilerinin sözlerine de yer verilir. *Birgün* de *Yeni Şafak* gazetesi gibi önce yazar Adalet Ağaoğlu'nun sözlerini aktarır, ancak Mazlumder'in görüşlerine yer vermez. *Birgün*'de Mazlumder yerine Alevi Bektaşi Federasyonu Genel Başkan Yardımcısı Ali Kenanoğlu'nun sözleri yer almaktadır. Ayrıca mitinge katılan sivil toplum örgütleri sıralanırken de yalnızca, SODEV, DİSK, KESK, Eğitim-Sen, TMMOB, İHD ile 78'liler Girişimi gibi örgütlerin adları geçer. Mitingi destekleyen sivil toplum örgütleri arasında Mazlumder'in ismine yer verilmemesi kadar, farklı ideolojik görüşleri temsil eden örgütlerin mitinge destek vermemesi de düşündürücüdür.

Birgün gazetesinin bu haberinde de, "Kürtler, Türkler, Çerkezler, Lazlar" gibi Türkiye coğrafyasındaki farklı etnik kimliklerin zikredildiği görülür. Gazetede ayrıca "yaşasın barış" sloganlarının yanı sıra Kürtçe sloganlara da yer verilmektedir. Gazetenin, bu ifadeler aracılığıyla farklılıkları, yalnızca etnik kökenler üzerinden kurduğu görülür. Çokkültürlülük konusundaki çekincelerden biri de İnsel'in (2006) dikkat çektiği gibi "insani var oluşun bir kültürel varlığın korunması ilkesine indirgenmesi", bir din ya da etnik kökene ait olma ile sınırlandırılması tehlikesini içinde barındırır.

Sonuç ve Değerlendirme

ÖDP'nin öncülüğünde başlayan "Birarada Yaşamı Savunalım" girişimi, 1990'lardan bu yana Türkiye'de farklılıkların temsili ve farklı kesimler arasında diyalogun başlatılması adına umut verici gelişmelerden biri olarak değerlendirilebilir. Ancak düzenlenen mitinglerin *Birgün* ve *Yeni Şafak* gazetelerinde temsil edilme biçimleri, Türk resmi söyleminin "ötekileri"nin de "Birarada Yaşamı" savunurken bile diğerlerini dışarıda bırakmaya devam ettiklerini göstermektedir. Her iki gazete de öncelikle kendilerine "yakın" olan kesimlere ve söylemlere yer vermiş, farklı görüşlerin seslerini ikinci plana itmiştir. Başka bir ifadeyle *Birgün* gazetesi yazarlarından Doğan Tılıç'ın "birarada yaşamaya giden yolun taşları, birarada yaşayacakların karşılıklı olarak öykülerini birbirlerine anlatabilmeleriyle, birbirlerini dinlemeleriyle döşenecek" sözlerine rağmen, gazetelerin haberlerinde ortaya çıkan tablo, her kesimin yine öncelikle kendi sesini dinlemeye çalıştığı biçimindedir.

Haberler ve köşe yazılarında seçilen sözcükler ve görüşlerine başvurulan kaynaklar her iki kesimin öncelikle kendi seslerini duyduklarını ve duyurmaya çalıştıklarını gösterir. Ayrıca, ÖDP'nin 3 Kasım 2002 genel seçimlerinde 100 binden fazla oy aldığı[2] düşünüldüğünde, mitinglere katılanların sayısının 7 bin kişiyi aşmaması, girişimin, ÖDP tabanının bile desteğini alamadığı anlamına gelir. Ortaya çıkan bu tablo, resmi milliyetçi söylemin, kendi "ötekileri"ni yaratırken, toplumdaki farklılıkların birbirleriyle uzlaşma kültürünü ya da zeminini de yok ettiğini gösterir.

Avrupa Birliği'ne üyelik çabalarıyla birlikte devletin farklılıklara karşı politikalarında değişiklikler gözlense de bu değişim, farklılıkların "Türkiye mozaiği"ni oluşturduğu gibi ayrılaştırıcı bir mantığın dışına çıkamaz. Tüm bu ayrılaştırma çabalarına rağmen de Türkiye toplumunun "laikler", "İslamcılar", "Kürtler", "sosyalistler", "gayrimüslümler"... olarak kompartımanlara ayrıldığı ve popüler milliyetçilikle birlikte bu ayrımların da giderek keskinleştiği gözlenir. Böyle bir ortam içinde bir arada, özgürce yaşama adına yapılan girişimler de bu kesimlerin birbirlerini anlamaya çalışarak dinledikleri zeminler oluşturmaya yetmiyor.

Bauman'ın (2006) belirttiği gibi "sivil haklar hareketleri yabancıları dışlar, etnik haklar hareketleri sözde o etnik kökenden olmayanları ya da yarı-etnik kökenlileri dışlar ve dini haklar hareketleri inançsızları dışlar" (s. 13). "Birarada Yaşamı Savunalım" kampanyasının iki farklı görüşü temsil eden gazetelerde çerçevelenme biçimi böyle bir dışlamayı bize göstermiştir. Kampanyada, herhangi bir dine inanmayanlar, kendilerini etnik kökenleri üzerinden

2 10 Kasım 2002 günlü ve 24932 sayılı Resmi Gazete'de açıklanan seçim sonuçları http://www.tesav.org.tr/2002.htm, adresli siteden alınmıştır.

temsil etmek istemeyenler ve eşcinseller ise hiç anılmaz. Bütün bu farklılıkların demokratik ve barışçıl bir toplumda birlikte yaşamalarını sağlayacak siyasal yapılanmanın nasıl olması gerektiği konusu da oldukça tartışmalı ve çetrefilli bir konudur. Avrupa ülkelerinde 1980'li yıllardan bu yana çokkültürlülük üzerine tartışmalar devam etmektedir. Ama şunu belirtmek gerekir ki birarada yaşamanın siyasal formülü üzerinde düşünmek de ancak farklılıkların varlığını ve farklılığını kabul etmekten geçer. Bunun için de öncelikle tüm korku ve baskılardan uzak biçimde Türk modernleşmesiyle yüzleşmek, tarihe başka bir perspektiften bakmak gerekir. Bu gerçekleştirilemediği için Türkiye'de çokkültürlülük ve çoğulculuk üzerine yapılan tartışmalar, akademik çevrelerde bile oldukça sınırlıdır. Başkasının sesini de en az kendimizinki kadar "iyi" duyamadığımız sürece "Birarada Yaşam"ı gerçekleştirmek mümkün görünmemektedir.

Kaynaklar:

Altınbaş, D. (2006). Avrupa ve çokkültürlülük: Fransa örneği. *Stratejik Analiz Dergisi*, Ekim 2006, 52-61.

Anderson, B. (1995). *Hayali cemaatler, Milliyetçiliğin kökenleri ve yayılması*, İ. Savaşır (Çev.), İstanbul: Metis Yayınları.

Aydın, S. (1998). *Kimlik sorunu, ulusallık ve "Türk kimliği"*, İstanbul: Öteki Yayınevi.

Bauman, G. (2006). Çok Kültürlülük bilmecesi: Ulusal, etnik ve dinsel kimlikleri yeniden düşünmek, I. Demirakın (Çev.). İstanbul: Dost Kitabevi

Bozdoğan, S. & Kasaba, R. (2005). Giriş. *Türkiye'de Modernleşme ve Ulusal Kimlik*, Bozdoğan, S. & Kasaba, R (Der.) içinde ss. 1-11. İstanbul: Tarih Vakfı Yayınları.

Çelik, N. B. (2002). Kemalizm: Hegemonik bir söylem. *Modern Türkiye'de siyasi düşünce, kemalizm* (Cilt 2) içinde ss. 73-91. İstanbul: İletişim Yayınları.

İnsel, A. (2006). Çokkültürlülük, milliyetçilik, özgürlük. *Birikim Dergisi*, http://www.birikimdergisi.com/birikim/makale.aspx?mid=150 (Son erişim 03.16.2007).

Keyman, F. (1998) Globalleşme ve Türkiye: Radikal demokrasi olasılığı. *Küreselleşme, sivil toplum ve islam*, E. F. Keyman ve A. Y. Sarıbay (Der.) içinde ss. 34-55. Ankara: Vadi Yayınları.

Konyar, H. (1998). *Çok partili hayata geçiş sürecinde ulus gazetesi; CHP ve Kemalist ilkeler*, Yayınlanmamış Doktora Tezi, İ.Ü. Sosyal Bilimler Enstitüsü.

Mardin, Ş. (1990). *Türkiye'de toplum ve siyaset, makaleler 1*, M. Türköne ve T. Önder (Der.). İstanbul: İletişim Yayınları.

Timur, T. (1983). Osmanlı ve "batılılaşma." *Cumhuriyet dönemi Türkiye ansiklopedisi* içinde ss. 139-146. İstanbul: İletişim Yayınları.

Timur, T. (1994), *Türk devrimi ve sonrası*. Ankara: İmge Kitabevi.

Peace or Conflict? Turkish and Greek Press Discourse on Football Matches[*]

Emre Gökalp
Department of Sociology
Anadolu University
egokalp@anadolu.edu.tr

Nikos Panagiotou
Department of Social Policy
Democritus University of Thrace
nikpanagio@yahoo.com

It is evident that the press coverage of international sport/football events plays a crucial role in consolidating nationalist discourses and the public perceptions about the Other. Rhetoric of "us" and "other" is ubiquitous in the press coverage of international sport/football events. The case of Turkish and Greek press is mainly significant since there has been a historical and current "hostility" between two states. In this regard, the aim of this study is to make a comparative analysis from 1988 to 2006 through the representation of football matches in three high-circulated daily newspapers and two daily sports newspapers in Turkey and Greece, in regard to reconstructing nationalist discourses

1-The Theoretical Framework: Football, Nationalism and the Press

The inter-relationship between (the media coverage of) sports/football games and nationalism have been examined by a number of studies (Alabarces, Tomlinson and Young, 2001; Blain, N., Boyle, R. & O'Donnell, H, 1993; Bishop and Jaworski, 2003; Crolley and Hand 2002; Duke and Crolley 1996; Giulinotti, 1999; Maguire, Poulton and Possamai, 1999a; Maguire, Poulton and Possamai, 1999b; Poulton, 2004; Rowe, 1999)[1], and the connection between the media sport and nationalism has proved to be a fertile area of study. The close relationship between sport and nationalism is especially visible in the international sporting events.

As the national sport in many countries, football is the mirror of the notion of "imagined communities" (Anderson, 1983) especially in the matches between two national teams since it is too easy to imagine the nation through those 11 football players (Duke and Crolley, 1996, p. 4). As Hobsbawm (1990) argues, "the imagined communities of millions seem more real as a team of eleven named people" (p. 143). "Sportsmen representing their nation or state" became "primary expressions of their imagined communities."

The state of "encounter" in football matches reflects the most natural and "innocent" appearance of nationalist/ essentialist "us" and "other(s)" distinction. It thus provides a *mimetic* representation of the struggle between nations which is constructed as "history's engine" by nationalist ideologies. This encounter equips the struggle between nations with precise and statistical representations of victory (Bora, 2001, p. 559). Therefore sportive victories are experienced as if they were political victories; defeats on the other hand cause deep disillusionment (Colome, 1993, p. 126).

Needless to say, there is also a clear articulation between press and nationalism. Anderson has mainly underlined

1 For the relationship between nationalism and football in Turkey, see Bora, 2001; Bora and Erdoğan, 1993; Erdoğan, 1993; Kozanoğlu, 1999 and Gökalp, 2006. For this connection in Greece, see Tzanelli, 2006.

* We would like to thank Ioannis N. Grigoriadis and Umut Özkırımlı for their comments on an earlier draft of this paper

the role of newspapers in the daily reproduction of nationhood. In explaining how a nation is collectively imagined, Anderson (1983) speaks of newspaper reading as a "mass ceremony which is repeated by thousands of people at daily intervals" (p. 35). Whatever the impact of globalizing trends, as Guibernau (1996) argues, mass media will continue to play a prominent role in the reconstruction and dissemination of nationalist discourses (p. 148). As Billig (1995) argues, there is no doubt that sports news flags nationalism quite strongly (pp. 119-126). "All the papers, whatever their politics, have a section in which the flag is wawed with regular enthusiasm. This is the sports section" (p. 119). Through the coverage of international sport/football tournaments, the media reinforce identifications, so making the nation more "real" than "imagined" (Poulton, 2004, p. 452).

Nevertheless, nationalism in the field of sports cannot totally eliminate divisions/tensions within nations. That is to say, it is not always possible to fulfil the ideological construction of national unity through sports/football. The reproduction of dominant ideologies and discourses through the field of sports is neither irresistible nor free of contradiction. In the field of sports, local or particular belongings may sometimes outweigh the construction of national unity (Giulianotti, 1999, pp. 32, 66-68).

However, as the significance of national identities and the hegemonic positions of nationalist discourses are effective at present in spite of the erosion of nation-state and national identity because of globalisation process, the crucial connection between football and nationalism will definitely continue to bear importance in different forms. "The nation state remains a powerful image and central point of reference for the invoking of group identity of the (implied) readers. Moreover, the imagery of the nation has been shown to rest on common sense, unproblematic and unproblematized notions of uniformity and conformity" (Bishop and Jaworski, 2003, p. 266). In this sense, it is possible to argue that the Rhetoric of "us" and "other" is omnipresent in the news texts focused on the international football matches.

2-Methodology

Our study aims to examine the reconstruction of Turkish and Greek nationalist discourses from 1988 to 2006 through the press coverage of football matches among the national and club teams of the two countries through the textual analysis. This comparative study is based on news stories of three high-circulated daily newspapers and two daily sports in both countries. The Greek newspapers that were selected and examined are: 1) *To Vima* 2) *Eleftherotypia* 3) *Eleftheros Typos* 4) *Athlitiki Iho* 5) *Filathlos*. The Turkish newspapers that were selected and examined are: 1) *Hürriyet* 2) *Sabah* 3) *Posta* and *Zaman* 4) *Fotomaç* 5) *Fanatik*.

National teams and club teams of the two countries played nine (seven of them is official) matches between 1988 and 2006. Additionally, four matches were played between a Turkish team (Trabzonspor) and the Greek Cypriot teams (APOEL FC and Anorthosis Famagusta).

The comparison of the Greek and Turkish press through in depth analysis demonstrates that same events are portrayed and interpreted in a similar way. As Entman (1991) underlined, comparing news coverage of same events is crucial since "the critical textual choices that frame the story" are revealed (p. 6) However, our study does not explore how Greek and Turkish readers perceived the games coverage. However it is possible to argue that the selected newspapers may have constituted "an important element in shaping the rang and impact of opinion" (Chang, 1989, p. 34). In a word, the news discourse about the matches between Greek and Turkish teams plays an undeniable role in modifying and consolidating the public perceptions about the "Other".

The best way to understand the role of the media in politics is to view them as part of the overall political system and of the relations between the two countries. Media is an important component which "foreign policy decision-makers take into considerations as they develop their policies" (Naveh, 2002, p. 2) since it both constrains leaders and officials yet provides them with opportunities to advance their goals (Gilboa, 2002).

Our approach is founded on the premise that mass media role in the construction and reconstruction of nationalist discourses is of high importance. Furthermore, as recent studies demonstrate (Wolfsfeld, 2004; Panagiotou, 2005), mass media play a central role both in the promotion of conflict and peace.

We've examined the headlines and leads of the news texts focused on the pre - and after the football games related to these thirteen matches in the ten dailies in total. Our study does not explore how Greek and Turkish audiences perceive the news coverage. However it is evident that the news discourse about the matches between Greek and Turkish teams plays an undeniable role in modifying and consolidating the public perceptions about the "Other." It is also certain that "the national media have been among the many factors that have contributed to the aggravation and perpetuation of tension between the two countries" (Özgüneş and Terzis, 2000, p. 405). As in the words of Rumelili (2005),

> In Greek-Turkish relations, the media plays a dual mediating role between the governments and public opinion: it "manufactures consent" for government policies towards the "Other"; and it plays an important role in shaping the public opinion that leaders have to take into consideration. Until recently, the Greek and Turkish media has exercised this dual influence

in a conservative, conflict-enhancing direction (p. 9).

In this context, thus, it might be argued for the beginning that the press coverage of football matches among the national and club teams of the two neighbouring countries play an undeniable role in the reproduction of nationalist discourses. But we should bear in mind the fact nationalism has never been a monolithic phenomenon. In other words, each nationalism have been made of discourses of nationalism that compete with each other, while presenting permeability to an important extent. Therefore, the question that needs to be answered first of all in this study is: What kind of nationalism is being reconstructed in the press of the two countries? Is it a kind of patriotism that offers pride in one's home country? Or do news discourse of both print media reproduce sentiments of national superiority? Briefly, this study is constructed around the following questions: Do they derogate/pejorate the "rival" team by way of rude jargon and glorify their own team/country? Do they use ethnic stereotypes and negative images in the news discourse? Do they "other" the "rival" football team and its nation/ country as "enemy" by means of metaphors related with militarism and violence. In general, do they contribute to the increasing friendship and peace between the two countries especially after the earthquakes of 1999? Or, do they contribute to the deepening and consolidating the tension?

3- Analysis and the Research Findings

As it is evidenced from these headlines, the long-standing political and military rivalry between Turkey and Greece makes football matches between the two countries particularly crucial and "sensitive" occasions for the sports press.

Measures taken in fear of violent actions (November 5, 2003-*Vima*)

Fear of episodes in the game overshadow the game (August 3, 2005-*Vima*)

Football lost, politics won Turkey-Greece: 3-1 (September 21, 1988-*Eleytherotypia*)

The two foreign ministers watched the game as a move to downplay the tension Fenerbahçe-Panathinaikos 1-1 (October 31, 2002-*Vima*)

Fear of events: The demonstrations in Fener Patriarchate the other day tightened the atmosphere before Greece-Turkey match tomorrow. (September 7, 2004-*Sabah*)

Two neighbours keep a stiff upper lift tonight (September 8, 2004-*Zaman*)

As it will be seen in the following part, the mass circulated press coverage of the football matches between the two countries reinforce and consolidate the nationalist discourses. The print media of the two countries underlines "we" identification of the both sides with their own nations. On the other hand, they both stress the otherness of each other and confirm and disseminate a fear of the "other."

3-a (Nationalist) Historical References

"Sport is a crucial component instrumental in 'keeping alive' nations' 'dreams of their special charisma'." International sporting contests tend to reawaken "sleeping memories" and renew deeply laden national habitus codes. As such, they tend to fuel the historic and ongoing strains and tensions (Maguire, Poulton and Possamai, 1999, pp. 439, 441). In this sense, throughout the Turkish and Greek press coverage of the football matches between the two countries, there are many references to past national and military histories of the countries. As it is evidenced from these headlines, the emotional power that the headlines exercise in these games is strongly connected with the past of the two countries.

Let's go for victory: We are coming across to Greece against whom we have always won (March 29, 1989-*Hürriyet*)

They choose special stadium: Karaiskaki stadium is of great importance to Greece. It bears the name of their national hero who initiated rebellion against the Ottoman Empire in the 1800's. By taking the match to this stadium, Greeks aimed to ignite their audience and to make repress Turkey (September 9, 2004-*Hürriyet*)

Severe Provocation: Many newspapers published in Turkey today will write headlines such as "May friendship win." We ask them: Which friendship? The name of the stadium Greeks chose for this match is Georgios Karaiskaki. Who is this Karaiskaki? The defeated general in the battle of independence against the Ottomans... The Greek Federation did not conceal their intentions to ignite audience in the choice of this stadium... And the press kept abreast with the federation... Some newspapers wrote, "Turks are our primordial enemy." (September 8, 2004-*Fotomaç*)

The first match is played in Karaiskaki Stadium in Piraeus. Karaiskaki is the name of the general rebelled against the Ottoman Empire. The second match will be played today in İnönü Stadium bearing the name of a Turkish commander who forced the Greeks to submission. Let's see who wins (June 4, 2005-*Sabah*)

***Ayşe* shall go on vacation:** As a result of the peace operation initiated with this password, Turkey brought peace to the Turks and Greeks in Cyprus in July 20, 1974. Precisely 31 years later Trabzonspor is bringing peace and friendship both to the Turks and the Greeks. (July 26, 2006-*Sabah*)

As it is evidenced from these headlines, the emotional power that the headlines exercise in these games is strongly connected with the past of the two countries.

3-b Eventful matches or banner and flag crisis in the tribunes

In this study, we have paid specific attention to the "eventful" matches since a group of fanatics of both sides have managed to manipulate not only the news discourse but also the discursive space of the two countries. In short, because of these groups, nationalist winds blow in the two countries at least in our context. Especially in Fenerbahçe-Panathninaikos matches (October 31, 2002), a group of Greek fanatics opened a map demonstrating Cyprus just as a Greek island. They also opened a banner saying that "*The best Turk is a dead Turk*" and "*Constantinoupolis is the Capital of Greece.*"

... "*The best Turk is a dead Turk*" banner was opened before the match, but the banner was immediately removed on warnings by Panathinaikoks authorities (November 15,2002-*Zaman*)

Grim photograph: Greek supporters opened yellow Cypriote flag in the tribunes, and beat tempo with "*Cyprus is ours and ours it shall it remain*" demonstrating their rage (November 6, 2003-*Star*)

Double Provocation: Fanatics obscure demonstrations of friendship When Greek fanatics provoked FB supporters by opening the flag of Cyprus demonstrating Cyprus as a Greek island, FB fans responded by opening a poster of Mehmet the Conqueror (November 1, 2002-*Sabah*)

Conquest poster raised: Fenerbahçe supporters hung a conquest poster on the marathon tribune. The poster, which read "*Istanbul since 1453*" and demonstrated Mehmet the Conqueror on a ramping horseback, yielded the reactions of Greek supporters. The banner was removed on UEFA observer's request (November 1, 2002-*Fanatik*)

On the other hand, a group of Turkish fanatics opened a poster's of Istanbul's conquest demonstrating Mehmet the Conqueror on a ramping horseback. They also opened a Cyprus map on which was written "*If you want peace you should recognize Turkish Republic of Northern Cyprus.* Although the majority in tribunes ignored fanatics and applauded friendship, these actions of handful fanatics shadowed the friendship atmosphere and caused one-sided and biased reporting in the news texts of the two countries.

Scandal: The banners the Greeks hanged on the tribunes: *Sh... shall pour on Atatürk's grave, Istanbul is the capital of Greece, Cyprus is one and ours.* (November 6, 2003-*Sabah*)

They demonstrate their rage: We constantly give messages of friendship and end the tension between the two countries. But with no avail... Because Greek citizens take up the issues of Cyprus, Istanbul and most importantly the Great Leader Atatürk in every chance they have, and they try our patience. They've also turned the Olympiakos-Galatasaray match played in Rizoupolis Stadium to a political arena (November 6, 2003-*Fanatik*)

Grim Provocation by the Greeks!: Greek supporters assaulted to the busses carrying GS team and press members all along the way and opened banners on which was written "*Istanbul is the capital of Greece*" (November 6, 2003-*Hürriyet*)

It is possible to note that these events are magnified by media to further support existing bias and prejudices. For that reason, it might be argued that the discourse of sports pages tends to fuel the historic and ongoing strains and tensions by making historical references.

The Turks have shown their real face again (*Eleytheros typos*)

The Turkish media emphasized the political aspects of the game (*Eleytherotypia*)

Provocative claims by Fenerbahce (*Eleytherotypia)*

Turks provoked. They have waived flags of the Turkish-Cypriot pseudo-state, (*Filathlos*)

The fans were provoked by Fatih Akyel, while they were shouting in favor of PKK, (*Eleytheros typos*)

The Turkish fans has provoked by opening banners on which was written "İstanbul 1453" and "do you remember my grandfather" (October 21, 2003-*Vima*)

The Turkish provocation. "We" go to the next round (November 5, 2003-*Eleytherotypia)*

A climate of terror by the "Grey Wolfs" (August 24, 2006-*Eleytheros typos*)

The fear for violence overshadow the game (*Vima*)

Greece-Turkey peace (?) (September 8, 2004-*Vima)*

While the newspaper coverage of the international football matches usually evoke past and present hostilities, it is possible to point out that the situation is quite different in our case. As it is seen from these examples, historical hostilities are generally evoked by a group of ultra-nationalist fanatics, and then they are represented and disseminated by the press. In other words, Turkish and Greek sports press are neither directly responsible from this hate speech nor the unique source of this discourse. Yet, it is obvious that the Turkish and Greek journalists are the main actors in highlighting, manipulating and sensationalizing these events in such an ultra-nationalist discourse.

Grim Provocation by the Greeks!: (November 6, 2003-*Hürriyet*)

A game with a lot political implications (January 7, 2004-*Athlitiki Iho*)

Is it football or a political game? Galatasaray-Olympiakos 1-0 (October 21, 2003- *Filathlos*)

This friendship does not serve us well (June 5, 2005-*Zaman*)

Ardent and fanatic Greek audience does not cause exuberance (September 9, 2004-*Sabah*)

Increasing nationalism in Greece has revived fanaticism (September 7, 2004-*Sabah*)

Nationalistic fever of the Turkish media: They hail the victory of the national team as a political one (*Vima*)

The Turks have shown their real face again (*Eleytheros typos*)

The Turkish fans provoked us by waving Turkish Cypriot Flags August 11, 2006-*Eleytheros typos*)

The Turks are following "hooligans policy" (June 4, 2005-*Eleytheropia)*

In the name of the country. Trabzonspor-Apoel FC (*Eleytheros typos*)

Being the most typical characteristic/presupposition of nationalism throughout the world, the stereotyping/ generalization of a particular act to the whole nation is a presupposition continually used by Turkish and Greek sports press. In this way, on the one hand, the representation of national identities as the fixed and unique possible subject of identity has been provided. On the other hand, within an ethnocentric and essentialist context, the Turkish and Greek national identity and nationalism are projected towards future by the continuous discursive construction of a monoblock of categories/nations that have always existed and been hostile to "us"

3-c (Metaphorical) Militaristic headlines

In sports press, the representation of football matches with lexical choices that are unrelated to football, especially those including violence and militarism, is, of course, not particular to Turkey and Greece. On the contrary, this situation is prevalent in other countries too.

We've precipitated Greek defense (September 22, 1988-*Sabah*)

Athenian torture 4-1 (November 15, 2002-*Fanatik*); **An eye for an eye** (November 14, 2002-Fotomaç) ; **Victory time** (September 21, 2003-*Fotomaç*)

The Lions (GS) lie in ambush in Athens (November 5, 2003-*Hürriyet*)

Anatolian Blaze on the other side of the coast (September 8, 2004-*Sabah*)

The Great Attack (September 8, 2004-*Fotomaç*)

We'll hit like the Russians (Sports Supplement-H) (June 3, 2005-*Zaman*)

Victory at this dawn: No passage to Greece! (June 4, 2005-*Posta*)

Let's go for victory (June 4, 2005-Sabah) **Greek coup in Trabzon** (July 27, 2005-*Fotomaç*)

Epic time (August 3, 2005-*Fotomaç*)

However, the fact that Greece and Turkey achieved their nation-state status through armed struggles against one another has been particularly important in this context. "The two peoples, in order to hold on to the best defined part of their identity—their nationhood—have to continue recalling their national liberation struggles in history textbooks, national celebrations, religious services and the media, thus bringing conflicts and clashes to the fore and nourishing distrust" (Özgüneş and Terzis, 2000, p. 408).

A more than welcomed victory (*Filathlos*)

We believed in victory. Greece-Turkey: 0-1 (March 29, 1989-*Athlitiki Iho)*
Slogans shouted in the stadium saying that: Greeks has won a gold metal in Smirni at 1922 (*Vima)*
Greece is seeking victory over Turkey's match (March 29, 1989-*Athlitiki Iho)*
A historical victory (July 26, 2005-*Eleytherotypia*)
The heroes conquered Trapezounta (August 5, 2005-*Vima*)
Heroes have managed to get draw in the most "heated" stadium. Turkey-Greece: 0-0 (June 4, 2005-*Athlitiki iho)*
Committed to fight and win (*Eleytheros typos)*
A climate of terror by the "Grey Wolfs" (August 24, 2006-*Eleytheros typos*)
We have avoided a Greek-Turkish war (Greece-Turkey: 0-0 08/09/2004), *Vima*

3-d Distribution of uniforms and flags in matches

One of the most significant national(istic) icons, flags of the both countries have been frequently used as a visual material since the 1990's in the sports pages of newspapers. However, there is an issue which much more important than the use of Turkish and Greek flag as a visual material: Especially in the 2000's, football federations started to distribute flags and national uniforms. Following are the headlines and leads of newspapers related to this issue:

Greek Federation distributes 27 thousand uniforms: Before the Greece-Turkey match, Greek Federation distributed 27 thousand uniforms to the audience in the tribunes. It was noteworthy that Greek authorities gave a uniform to each audience as a present (September 9, 2004-*Zaman*)

Free uniforms: The sponsors of Greek national team worked a lot before the Turkey match... It was stated that around 30 thousand uniforms were distributed to audience in the stadium entrance (September 9, 2004-*Fanatik*)

Red and White Everywhere: National team uniforms and Turkish flags were distributed to each audience in the match (June 5, 2005-*Hürriyet*)

Welcome to banquet: 10 thousand burgundy-blue balloons will fly into the air in the Anorthosis match, and 20 thousand Northern Cypriote and Turkish flags will be distributed (August 3, 2005-*Fanatik*)

Needless to say, this practice or "invented tradition" plays a crucial role in the "nationalist mobilization" of not only the supporters in the stadiums but of the whole nations of the two countries.

3-e Headlines emphasizing friendship

We must underline that the "negative" or the nationalist examples examined so far are the only examples of the representations in the sports press of the two countries. On the other hand, especially Turkish sports press emphasized friendship in a sensible manner. It is certain that this situation is very much related with the changing government policies and with the relatively softening diplomatic relations.

Our national team is playing against Greece after 40 years' time: "May the match of friendship shall be played in a friendly atmosphere" (September 21, 1988-*Hürriyet*)

The new step to friendship that started with "the Spirit of Davos" is taken in İnönü Stadium (September 21, 1988-*Sabah*)

We beat Greece in a friendly way. 3-1: Everything is nice... The weather is nice... The match is nice and above all, this "friendship" is nice. (September 22, 1988-*Sabah*)

A Welcome with flowers: Preparing to host the 2008 championship, the flags of Turkey and Greece are unfurled. The two countries give a message of friendship to the world (October 31, 2002-*Hürriyet*)

Turkish-Greek friendship has not been dissolved: 1-1 (November 1, 2002-*Zaman*)

Third Bridge on the Bosphorus: Breeze of friendship blew in the İstanbul Bosphorus yesterday (October 31, 2002-*Fanatik*)

Turks and Greeks hand in hand, heading to 2008 (October 31, 2002-*Fotomaç*)

***Kalimera*!** (October 21, 2003-*Star*)

Match Ends, Friendship Remains (September 8, 2004–*Posta*)

Our neighbor hasn't upset us (September 8, 2004-*Posta*)

Friendship has won (September 9, 2004-*Posta*)

An Affair of Friendship (September 9, 2004-*Hürriyet*)

Friendship is not spoilt in the Aegean Sea (September 9, 2004-*Zaman*)

Friendship wins. Greece 0 – Turkey 0 (September 9, 2004-*Sabah*)

May friendship win! (June 4, 2005-*Sabah*)

Nobody can ruin our friendship (p. 33) (June 5, 2005-*Hürriyet*)

Things left to be resolved (August 10, 2006-*Vima*)

The two national teams confront each other in the shadow of Davos spirit. Turkey-Greece: 3-1 (September 21, 1988-*Eleytherotypia*)

The match has underlined the rapprochement between the two nations Greece-Turkey: 0-1 (March 29, 1989-*Filathlos*)

A draw in the game a victory in the rapprochement of the two nations (Greece-Turkey: 0-0 (September 8, 2004-*Eleytherotypia*)

A draw in the game a victory of the fanatics Fenerbache-Panathinaikos 1-1 (October 31, 2002-*Vima*)

A chance for friendship not war Greece-Turkey: 0-0 (September 8, 2004-*Eleytherotypia*)

The rapprochement at stake Galatasaray-Olympiakos 1-0 (October 21, 2003-*Filathlos*)

Moreover, as shown in the headlines quoted below, we should not underestimate that a number of football matches between Turkey and Greece are also reported fairly neutral way.

Landmark match for Galatasaray (GS): GS is hosting Greece's Olympiakos in Istanbul today. (October 21, 2003-*Hürriyet*)

The lions (GS) revive hope: (October 22, 2003-*Hürriyet*)

GS has revived 1-0 (October 22, 2003-*Sabah*)

Even Zeus cannot be saviour (June 4, 2005-*Fotomaç*)

For the first time in history a Greek Cypriote team is playing against a Turkish team (July 26, 2005-*Posta*)

The first official match with the Greek Cypriotes (July 26, 2005-*Hürriyet*)

All for each other (August 3, 2005-*Fanatik*)

Trabzonspor: 1- Apoel: 0 (August 24 10, 2006- Hürriyet; August 24 10, 2006-*Sabah*)

May first friendship and then Trabzon win (July 26, 2005-*Fanatik*)

Turkey-Greece: 2-0 (January 8, 2004-*Athlitiki Iho)*

Greece-Turkey: 0-1 (March 30, 1989-*Athlitiki Iho)*

Panathinaikos is to write history today (November 14, 2002-*Athlitiki Iho*)

Olympiakos is looking for a new start in İstanbul (October 21, 2003-*Eleytherotypia*)

However, the newspapers of the two countries make use of the rhetoric of "us" and "them" even in the headlines seems to be quite neutral, as evidenced in the headlines quoted below:

Our national team is playing against Greece as a return match of the 3-1 score for the sake of "the Spirit of Davos" (March 29, 1989-*Sabah*)

Our national team has won Greece with ease once again (March 30, 1989-*Hürriyet*)

May this be our night of victory in Europe! (October 31, 2002- *Zaman*)

We are ready for *sirtaki*! (November 5, 2003-*Star*)

We've missed victory: Greece 0- Turkey 0 (September 9, 2004-*Posta*)

We deserved to win. Turkey-Greece: 0-0 (June 4, 2005-*Filathlos)*

They have disgraced us (referring to the stance of Panathinaikos team) **Fenerbache-anathinaikos 1-1** (October 31,2002-*Eleytherotypia*)

A Stolen victory. Turkey-Greece: 2-0 (January 8,2004-*Eleytherotypia)*

Disgrace the Greek team was harassed in the Turkish stadium (August 03, 2005-*Vima*)

4- Concluding Remarks

Our findings demonstrate that the football matches between Turkey and Greece are being used by the mass circulated Turkish and Greek dailies to reconstruct an intense form of nationalist discourse rather than increasing friendship and peace between the two countries. For both cases, it is clearly evident that the political climate between the two states influences the way that sports events are reported. In times of crisis or tension, not only the headlines but also the news discourses are articulated into more essentialist, parochial and fanatic nationalism.

We do consider that the images displayed regarding the sports events between the two countries are crucial in any attempts of reconciliation. The way that the other is presented in the Greek newspapers is following the dominant ethnocentric approach of Greek Turkish relation in its most extreme though we have to note.

For the Greek case, there is a major difference between the quality press and the sports press since the latter is much more ethnocentric in orientation. Another difference between the way that the sport and the other papers have covered the events is that the latter is influenced by the government policies or their ideological preferences while this is not the case for the sport press. The prevalence of militaristic or negative headlines especially in the case of the sport press we have to bear in mind that it is connected with the way that these newspapers operate, regarding the coverage of sports events. Especially in the case of the Greek press this is a tactic that aims to attract readers and a choice that is commonly used even in games between Greek teams.

Our study shows the framework in which the Greek-Turkish relations takes place is more complex, since the "enmity" between the two nations have influenced the whole spectrum of their between relations. As Millas (2004) argues "due to historical reasons each party conceives the 'other' as a prospective threat or as a challenge to its identity and interprets teach of his actions accordingly, creating a vicious circle where the national perceptions and the negative images concerning the other dictate the vigilant attitude of 'our' and which in turn also aggravates the attitude to the 'other'" (p. 53).

As Millas (2004) revealed this argument in his study on the Greek and Turkish schoolbooks, this explanation is also relevant in press coverage of the football events, through the discourse which strengthening the strong "we" and "other" distinction. In a word, united "us" against the "Other." On the other hand, the discursive strategies are employed in the coverage of the football matches in such a way that places them into a package "that is culturally resonant and professionally valuable." Since football is a "valuable consumer commodity which has to be packaged in an attractive and therefore marketable linguistic form" (Crolley and Hand, 2002), the deregulation of the media sector in Turkey and Greece in the 1990s led to fierce competition among the news media and nationalist reporting helped to keep the ratings and circulations up (Rumelili, 2005, p. 10).

References

Alabarces, P., Tomlinson, A., & Young, C. (2001). Argentina versus England at the France .98 World Cup: Narratives of nation and the mythologizing of the popular. *Media, Culture & Society, 23*, 547-566.

Anderson, B. (1983). *Imagined communities: Reflections on the origin and spread of nationalism*. London, New York: Verso.

Blain, N., Boyle, R. & O'Donnell, H. (1993). *Sport and national identity in the european media*. Leicester University Press

Bishop, H. and Jaworski, A. (2003). We beat "em": Nationalism and the hegemony of

homogeneity in the British press reportage of Germany versus England During Euro 2000," *Discourse & Society, 14*(3), 243-271.

Bora, T. (2001). Türkiye'de futbol ve milliyetçilik. S. Yarasimos, et al (Eds.) *Türkiye'de Sivil Toplum ve Milliyetçilik* içinde ss. 559-581. İstanbul: İletişim).

Bora, T. & Erdoğan, N. (1993). Dur tarih, vur Türkiye. Türk milletinin milli sporu olarak futbol. T. Bora & R. Horak (Eds.) *Futbol ve kültürü* içinde ss. 221-240. İstanbul: İletişim.

Chang, T.K. (1989). Access to the news and U.S. foreign policy: The case of China, 1950-1984. *Newspaper Research Journal, Fall*, 33-44.

Crolley, L. & Hand, D. (2002). *Football, Europe and the Press*, London: Frank Cass

Duke, V. & Crolley, L. (1997). *Football, nationality and the state*. London & New York: Longman.

Entman, R. M. (1991). Framing U.S. coverage of international news: Contrasts in narratives of the KAL and Iran Air incidents. *Journal of Communication, 41*(4), 6–27.

Gilboa, E. (2002). Global communication and foreign policy. *Journal of Communication, 52*, 731–48.

Gilboa, E.(2002), *Media and Conflict*. New York: Transnational Publishers.

Giulianotti, R. (1999). *Sociology of the Global Game*. London: Routledge.

Gökalp, E. (2006). Beware the Turks Are Coming! Reproducing Turkish nationalism(s) through the press coverage of football games. *RAMSES Series on Europe and the mediterranean, Working Paper 7/06*, October, 1-20. Accessed 04.04.2007 from http://www.sant.ox.ac.uk/esc/ramses/gokalp.pdf

Hobsbawm, E. (1990). *Nations and nationalism since 1780*. Cambridge: Cambridge University Press.

Kozanoğlu, C. (1999). Beyond Edirne: Football and the national identity crisis in Turkey. In G. Armstrong and R. Giulianotti (Eds.), *Football Cultures and Identities*, (pp. 117-125). London: McMillan Press.

Maguire, J., Poulton, E. & Possamai, C. (1999a). WELTKRIEG III? Media coverage of England versus Germany in Euro 96. *Journal of Sport & Social Issues, 23*(4), 439-54.

Maguire, J., Poulton, E. & Possamai, C. (1999b). The war of the words? Identity politics in Anglo-German press coverage of Euro 96. *European Journal of Communication, 14*(1), 61-89.

Millas, H. (2004). National perceptions of the "other" and the persistence of some images. In M. Audin and K. Ifantis (Eds), *Turkish-Greek Relations: The security dilemma in the Aegean*, (pp. 53-66). London: Routledge.

Naveh, C. (2002). The role of the media in foreign policy decision-making: A theoretical framework. *Conflict and Communication Online, 1*(2), 1-12.

Ozgunes, N and Terzis, G. (2000). Constraints and remedies for journalists reporting national conflict: the case of Greece and Turkey. *Journalism Studies, 1*(3), 405-426.

Panagiotou, N. (2005). *The role of the press in foreign policy: A critical discourse analysis of the Greek press coverage of the Greek-Turkish relations*. Unpublished PhD Thesis, Aristoteleio University of Thessaloniki, Department of Journalism and Mass Communication (In Greek).

Poulton, E. (2004) Mediated patriot games: the construction and representation of national ıdentities in the British television production of Euro "96." *International Review for the Sociology of Sport 39*(4), 437–55.

Rowe, D. (1999) *Sport, culture and the media*. Maidenhead: Open University Press.

Rumelili, B. (2005). The European Union and cultural change in Greek-Turkish relations. *Working Papers Series in EU Border Conflicts Studies 17*, 1-31. Accessed 04.04.2007 from http://www.euborderconf.bham.ac.uk/publications/files/WP17_Turkey-Greece.pdf

Tzanelli, R. (2006). Impossible is a fact.: Greek nationalism and international recognition in Euro 2004. *Media, Culture & Society, 28*, 483-503.

Wolfsfeld, G. (2004). *Media and the Path to Peace*. Cambridge University Press.

Cartoon Metaphors of Arafat: Conflicting Constructions of Social Reality: Editorial Cartoonists Frame the Death of Yasser Arafat

Fran Hassencahl
Department of Communication and Theatre Arts
Old Dominion University
fhassenc@odu.edu

This paper continues a line of research and publication that investigated the use of metaphor in the print news coverage of the death of Yasser Arafat. Hassencahl (2006) examined the news coverage by *The Jerusalem Post* (Israel), *The New York Times* (US) and *The Guardian* (UK) of the last days of Arafat's life and found four dominant myths, which were expressed as metaphors. The majority of the news stories used the metaphor of Arafat as a scapegoat for the failure of the peace process in the Middle East. In the absence of concrete information about Arafat's illness reporters created the metaphor of the mysterious illness. The stories also discussed Arafat's handling of funds and created the metaphor of stacks of cash hidden in secret bank accounts. The fourth metaphor covered in the news stories portrayed Arafat's wife, Suha, as a greedy, contentious and somewhat hysterical, shrew.

Research Questions

RQ 1: Do the four metaphors of scapegoat, death under mysterious circumstances, hidden stashes of cash and a shrew/ wife reappear in the cartoon images of Arafat?

RQ 2: Do other metaphors appear?

RQ 3: Is the frequency of the appearance of the cartoon metaphors similar or dissimilar to the metaphors used in the news stories?

Methods

Sample

Sixty-seven cartoons were drawn from the online database, Daryl Cagle's Professional Cartoonist Index, at http://cagle.com that contains the work of 97 American editorial cartoonists. Cartoons were not drawn from *The Guardian* or *The Jerusalem Post*, because their cartoons are strips and rely more on verbal explanation rather than the visuals used in single frame cartoons. Like the previous study of news coverage, cartoons were taken from October 29, 2004 when Arafat traveled by helicopter from his compound in Ramallah to a Paris hospital to his death on November 11, 2004. Three of the cartoons were discarded, because they did not contain any metaphors, leaving a total N of sixty-four cartoons. Verbal and the visual metaphors were identified and analyzed to see whether they fit into the four established categories or if additional categories emerged.

Metaphor as a Model of Analysis

Early scholars of metaphor held that metaphors were stylistic devices, the tools of poets and rhetoricians. We now know from research on cognitive processing that metaphors are not just decoration; they convey meaning. Scholars "re-discovered [metaphor] as an instrument of thought" (Radman, 1995, p. 2). Gibbs (1994), Lakoff (1993), and Seitz (1998) drew from cognitive theory and found empirical evidence that metaphor is not just an element of language, but is a characteristic of thought itself. Metaphor is a way of knowing; it performs an epistemological function. Miller (1995) explained that the viewer of a visual metaphor makes an association, which is based upon prior knowledge and experience, in order to navigate the meaning. The interpretation of the image "is jointly negotiated by producers and viewers" (El Refaie, 2003, p. 81). We can navigate this tension between the empirical and the poetic, because "metaphor mediates intuitive and symbolic cognition, it is able to function as an organ of reason" (Otabe, 1995, p. 24).

Lakoff and Johnson (1980) and Edelman (2001) observed that metaphors are commonplace in every day conversation and shape our thinking. Cartoonists, who work in a medium of pictures and few words, recognize that metaphor helps to convey their message. Pulitzer Prize winning cartoonist Nick Anderson explained why he uses metaphor, "When you're communicating with pictures...it's best to use a metaphor because it...surprises the reader" and helps the reader "see things in a different way" (McClure, 2005, p. 51). Lakoff and Johnson (1980) noted that when we compare two elements we highlight the similarity between the two elements, but we also mask other ways that the two elements are dissimilar. To say, "Arafat is a terrorist" highlights ways in which the two elements are similar, but this comparison also detracts from important ways in which the two elements differ.

In addition to metaphors being commonplace and shapers of our thought, metaphors can justify our actions. Within the context of international relations, foreign policy and war, metaphors are commonplace and are used to justify policies and actions (Lakoff, 1991; Chilton & Lakoff, 1995). Lakoff (1991) examined the metaphors the George Bush, Sr. administration used during the Gulf War and argued that those metaphors helped to justify the military actions that the U.S. and coalition forces took during the war. The "state is a person" metaphor suggested, "war is a fight between two people" and framed the war as a struggle between Bush and Saddam Hussein. With this use of metaphor in foreign policy rhetoric, Lakoff observed that we lost sight of the realities of the war. With its focus on one individual (Hussein) the metaphorical framework masked the death and damage that the war brought to Iraqi citizens.

Many editorial cartoonists turned the verbal metaphors from President Bush's speeches and press conferences into visual metaphors in their artwork. Hart & Hassencahl (2002), Ivie (1980, 1984, 1996, 2005), and Lakoff (2001) stated that the metaphors used by past and present presidents served to justify war. In *Moral Politics*, Lakoff (1996) argued that we use metaphors" to frame moral issues: to interpret them, understand them, and explore their consequences", and that metaphors "play an absolutely central role in our judgments about what is good behavior and what is bad, what is the right thing to do and what is wrong" (p. 44).

How do cartoonists, as rhetors, use visual metaphor to influence a reader's viewpoint? Three studies (DeSousa, 1984; Conners, 1998; Hart & Hassencahl, 2002) specifically used metaphorical analysis to study depictions of enemies in editorial cartoons during times of war. DeSousa (1984) found that cartoonists drew upon commonplace images within American culture to explain what was happening to American citizens held during the 1979-1980 U.S.-Iran hostage crisis. Metaphors such Khomeini-as-madman and Khomeini-as-religious-fraud gave the American public a venue for venting their hostilities in a situation where little else could be done.

The other three visual metaphor studies drew upon Keen's (1986) analysis of how we dehumanize the enemy with visual metaphors. Keen found that in times of war we dehumanized the enemy by framing them as animals and barbarians. Conners (1998) concluded from her analysis of cartoons from the 1991 Gulf War that these cartoons, "reflected Bush administration rhetoric labeling Hussein as a threat that the United States needed to control" (p. 110). Hassencahl and Hart (2004) examined 1300 war-related cartoons that depicted Saddam Hussein and found that the prominent metaphors of enemy-as-aggressor, enemy-as-death, and enemy-as-criminal served to dehumanize the enemy and justify his removal.

Yasser Arafat, (1929-2004), Chairman of the Palestinian Liberation Organization and the President of the Palestinian National Authority, a tireless and controversial advocate, also can be considered as a metaphor for the effort to found a Palestinian state. After he appeared in November of 1974 at the General Assembly of the United Nations in New York wearing a pistol, holding an olive branch and warning the world to not let the olive branch drop from his grasp, he became an instantly recognizable image for the Palestinian cause. Whether shaking hands with Yitzhak Rabin on the lawn of the Carter White House, sharing the Nobel Peace Prize in 1994 or meeting various heads of states seeking solutions for peace between Palestine and Israel, his presence and persona exemplifies what some journalists have referred to as " Mr. Palestine". Arafat became a visual metaphor and easily caricatured world political leader who wore tan military fatigues and covered his balding pate with the black and white checked *kaffiya*, which has become an emblem of the Palestinian cause. Cartoonists exaggerated his large nose and his need for a valet to provide him with a shave and a pressing of his uniform.

Findings

Scapegoat Metaphor

The myth of the scapegoat comes from the Biblical practice of the high priest symbolically placing the sins of the congregation upon the head of a goat, which is then released to perish in the wilderness. The participants in this act attempts to absolve the collective society of the guilt for past injustices inflicted upon others or even upon themselves and is commonly discussed particularly in the context of Nazi Germany and the Jews in World War II. Literary and rhetorical critic, Kenneth Burke (1982) in *A Grammar of Motives* noted that the "scapegoat is a vessel of vicarious atonement" (p. 407). The perpetuators of the act of ritual cleansing load "the burden of their own iniquities upon it" (p. 406).

The issue of one state or two states in a location that has remained contested since the Balfour Declaration in 1917 remains unresolved, despite wars and guerilla action, the interference and advice of the great powers, and funds given above and under the table to arm both sides. Suffice it to say that the dispute between Israel and Palestine continues and each side blames the other for the failure to achieve a viable two-state solution. Within these dialectical opposites of good and evil, it becomes possible to establish an innocent victim and the evil villain. It is not the focus of this paper to discuss and or take sides in this dispute.

The cartoonists; however, did take sides and placed the blame for the problems of the Middle East at Arafat's feet. Cartoonists portrayed Arafat as the scapegoat for a failed peace process in the Middle East some fifty-two times. Some also blamed him for the current rise in terrorism in the world. These cartoonists focused upon cultural and religious shared metaphors about Heaven and Hell. We see Heaven to be a beautiful and comfortable place, a suitable reward, for those who have lived a good life. We reserve Hell as the opposite unpleasant place for those who have not lived a good life. One cartoon showed the traditional Devil with horns and a forked tail who carries a pitchfork and leads Arafat down a steep and curving set of steps to Hell, which is captioned as Arafat's "New Homeland." Only one cartoonist expressed ambivalence about Arafat's final destination and showed him as a two-headed individual wearing both a halo and horns.

All of the cartoonists suggested that Arafat's deeds prevent his entry into Heaven. Several cartoonists showed Arafat being denied entrance into Heaven. One showed an angel wearing a military uniform and wings and sitting in a guardhouse. He asks Arafat to wait while he looks for Arafat's name in his book. Signs at the gate indicate that this is a restricted area and there will be no unauthorized entry. As Arafat stands among the fluffy clouds, his gaze goes to the guardhouse, and he says, "Uh-Oh", because he sees the Israeli flag unfurled above the guardhouse. Another cartoon featured a angel who tosses Arafat out of Heaven after pointing out the locations in heaven for the 11 Israeli athletes killed at the Munich Olympics, Leon Klinghoffer, who was thrown overboard from the Achille Lauro cruise ship, and "the countless" murdered Israelis. All of these acts are attributed to Arafat, who then is thrown from the cloud.

It is customary to recount the accomplishments and virtues of the deceased. If this person is an historic person, there may be some discussion of his or her legacy. None of the cartoons in this category suggested that Arafat has done anything other than to bring pain and suffering to his people. In one cartoon a Palestinian family walks down a street, which is named "Terrorism" The buildings are pocked by the bullets of war and the conversation bubble above the father's head says, "He led us to the very end." Behind them is a street sign that says, "Dead End." Another street metaphor was the Yasser Arafat Memorial Highway which stretched out into the horizon past the bombed out shells of Palestinian houses. A directional sign labeled "Nowhere" is placed at the edge of the highway. Five cartoons used this road/street metaphor to suggest that death and violence for Middle Eastern drivers lie ahead on the Arafat road.

Another cartoon showed Arafat in a hospital bed receiving a transfusion of either nutrients or medications. The cord attached to his wrist runs up to the standing hook where usually the plastic drip bag is hung. In place of the bag is a barefoot individual who could represent either sex and is labeled "Palestinians." The small person is attached to the post by a hook in its back and connected to Arafat with tubing, which looks much like any transfusion. The person looks passively at the floor and depending upon one's interpretation is being drained by Arafat or is sacrificing to keep him alive.

Arafat's legacy is shown as a large pile of skulls and as bloodstains on walls and on maps of Israel and Palestine. A badly mangled and burned bus, representing the acts of Palestinian suicide bombers in Israel, has the street name of Legacy posted above the windshield where one would expect to find a street name or a route number. The bus pulls a military caisson with Arafat's coffin on it. The cartoonists did not see a legacy of peace in the Middle East.

A common visual metaphor for peace is the dove that carries an olive branch in its beak and the cartoonists have these doves flying through out the cartoons. The cartoonists suggested that the dove of peace has experienced a hard life under Arafat. Doves appear as suicide bombers who are carried in Arafat's right hand. In Arafat's other hand is the detonator for the bomb belt tied about the doves' plump waists. In this parade of multiple images of Arafat and the doves it is clear that the doves are under Arafat's control. In another cartoon a dove is held prisoner against Arafat's chest. In two cartoons doves wait patiently on a tree branch above Arafat's gravestone; another dove lies dead upon Arafat's grave.

Three cartoonists suggested that there could be renewed hope for the peace dove. One also used a metaphor of two doors. In another cartoon a dove flies away from Arafat's bedside after falling from the now deceased Arafat's grasp. The dove looks back and says, "Finally." Another optimistic dove peers through Arafat's empty *kaffiya* and the caption reads "an opening." A cartoonist represents Arafat's death as the skeleton key that will liberate the dove of peace that is held prisoner by a huge padlock hanging about its neck. The implication is that the errors of the past may be placed upon the back of the scapegoat. Starting fresh in the peace endeavor may in the future bring better things.

Other cartoonists are less optimistic and showed a dove holding two suitcases and the obligatory olive branch. The dove is at an intersection. On the one wall is a poster of Arafat, which is labeled "The Devil You Know." On the other side is the poster of a future leader, whose face is blocked out by a sign, which says "Coming Soon (after nasty protracted power struggle)". Above this unknown replacement for Arafat is the caption "The Devil You Don't." A plump dove at a similar juncture in another cartoon looks up at President Bush and Prime Minister Sharon. Each leader portends danger for the dove; both have huge hungry falcons on their outstretched arms.

Norris, Kern & Just (2003) argued that reporters often take their cues from Presidential statements and behavior. President Bush never trusted Arafat or tried to work with him. At a press conference on March 30, 2002 at his ranch in Texas he insisted that Arafat should and could control terrorist activity by Palestinians against Israel. He called Arafat a supporter of terrorists and refused to meet with him or even converse with him on the telephone. In the press release issued by Bush on November 10, 2004 he called the death of Arafat "a significant moment in Palestinian history." After offering condolences, Bush focused upon the future and his hopes that the future would bring peace and an independent and democratic Palestine. Nothing was said about Arafat's efforts to bring about those ends, too.

Eleven cartoons labeled Arafat as a terrorist. Three cartoons used the epithet of "The Father of Modern Terrorism." In one case the cartoonist drew a grave marker and its legend designates Arafat as "The Father of Modern Terrorism." Another cartoon displayed Arafat's empty checkered *kaffiya* with the label of "Father of Modern Terrorism" written upon it. Another cartoon showed a framed picture of Arafat with black mourning ribbons draped above it. The caption underneath Arafat's picture is "Our Founder". What did Arafat found? The answer is in the cartoon's caption, which says "Global Terror Inc."

Metaphor of Death from Mysterious Causes

When Arafat was taken by helicopter from his compound in Ramallah to a Paris military hospital he was alert and waving to his supporters who were told that he suffered from the flu. After Arafat reached Paris his health deteriorated. Arafat had not designated a successor and since the nature of his illness was initially was unknown by the doctors, there were many who optimistically predicted his recovery and return to Palestine. Arafat's wife also insisted that he would get better and she raised a curtain of secrecy between Arafat and the press. With no concrete information and great confusion (the Belgian press prematurely announced Arafat's death), the press speculated that he was dying of cancer, liver disease, a severe infection of unknown causes and even AIDS. After Arafat's death *The New York Times* ran a story on November 12, 2004 by Elizabeth Rosenthal, a medical doctor, who states that he "died mysteriously, surrounded by secrecy." She suggests that Arafat's inner circle wanted to keep his cause of death a secret, because Arafat "suffered from a disease that they considered embarrassing" or that the doctors in Ramallah had missed a treatable condition and had allowed him to deteriorate beyond what could then be remedied in Paris. The immediate cause of Arafat's death appears to be a brain hemorrhage, but in the absence of concrete information the press felt free to conjecture that the reason for secrecy was that Arafat was dying of a less socially acceptable disease.

Rumors about Arafat being poisoned are not substantiated. Blood tests ruled out poisoning, but it is of interest that a news story ran in *The Jerusalem Post*, which suggested that the Israelis could have poisoned Arafat had they wished to do so (Lahoud, 2004). None of the cartoonists focused on the cause of Arafat's death and only six cartoons deal with his illness. A cartoonist shows a balding buzzard named "Palestinian Infighting" perched above Arafat's hospital bed. Next to it sits another ubiquitous dove with an olive branch in its beak. If we look closely at the scene, we see a get-well card on the nightstand. Instead of the customary greeting, the card requests that Arafat "Don't get well soon." As mentioned earlier, there were no succession plans and there was intense speculation at home and abroad over the nature of his illness and possible successor.

Metaphor of Suha the Shrew

Yasser Arafat was 62 years old when he married a 28 year-old journalist and publicist, Suha Tawil. Seven news stories covered Suha; only one story quotes anyone who expressed any sympathy for his wife and daughter. The reporters characterized Suha as a shrew. Shrews are tiny mouse like mammals that tend to live solitary lives and aggressively defend their territory. After Shakespeare's play, *The Taming of the Shrew*, the term shrew was used to describe an ill tempered and scolding wife. All of the stories characterized Suha as Arafat's aggressive, not assertive, protector, who stood at his bedside and withheld information about the nature of and the day-to-day progression of his illness. Under French privacy laws, she was not required to release information to the press or to any public. It is not known whether she withheld information due to a desire for privacy, control, or for cultural reasons.

Only four cartoons portrayed Ms. Arafat and none of these are complimentary. All of them link to her desire for power and money. The cartoon, which shows her desire for power, has her dressed in Arafat's uniform and arranging his *kaffiya* upon her head. A second cartoon shows Suha and a member of the PNA kneeling at the bedside of a comatose Arafat. They request that "The Holy Father of Terrorism" tell them in which Swiss bank accounts he has stashed "Palestinian billions." Another cartoon suggested that Suha with her clutch of portfolios, bank records, stocks and keys to bank deposit boxes already has access to those funds. This same cartoon contrasts the past leadership which shows Yasser Aarafat holding up a pistol and saying "Allah Akbar" (God is Great) and the present leadership, which shows Suha saying "Moolah Akbar" (Money is Great) and holding up the keys to safety deposit boxes. Suha is reduced to being the acquisitive shrew that aggressively guards her territory and her cash.

Metaphor of the Stash of Billions of Dollars

Nine cartoons dealt with Arafat's money. The cartoonists see this the money as belonging to the people of Palestine. No one accuses Arafat of having a lavish personal life style. They do question his wife's expenditures. Press stories raised questions about the location of Arafat's money and whether it will be found. A hidden stash implies that the money may have been gotten illegally. Arafat's PLO political party was originally a guerrilla group and never developed a system of transparency or accounting for the funds they generated through bribes, fees, donations and investments. The label "Father of Palestine" in many ways mirrors or serves as a metaphor for the financial relationship Arafat had with his people. If a child is short on funds, he or she may turn to Dad with a request for help. Good children are thankful for what Dad has given and do not ask about the amount or source of those funds.

The cartoons suggested that the "billions" are a secret that will die with Arafat. One cartoonist drew a picture of an associate who has rushed to the bedside of Arafat and instead of inquiring about his health asks, "Where's the money?" Another cartoonist suggested that the money is ill gotten gains by showing Arafat sitting among bags of money in a bank vault. Arafat is grinning and we can see that under his *kaffia* he is sprouting two horns. Arafat has become the devil with his hidden billions. In a third cartoon Arafat's head is turned into a funnel and millions of dollars are being funneled in to a storage bottle while a group of Palestinian men and a child stand to watch this event on the street in front of their homes. Trash and water in the street suggests a lack of municipal services for this neighborhood. A caption inside the frame of the cartoon says, "Father of the Palestinians." The word "Father" is crossed out and the word "Funnel" is substituted, which also reinforces the idea that Arafat has taken the money of his people.

The bulk of the metaphors used by the cartoonists to describe Arafat's final days are those that portray him as a scapegoat. The cartoonists used no other metaphors in addition to the four categories in this study. Figures 1 and 2, although not totally comparable, since Hassencahl (2006) examined press coverage and the unit used number of words rather than images and words or metaphors used in this study, do show that the combined news and editorial cartoon coverage used the image of Arafat as scapegoat. Sixty-nine percent of the total metaphors in the cartoons present his legacy as a scapegoat, not only for the failure to gain peace between the Israelis and the Palestinians, but also for the terrorism occurring in the in other parts of the world.

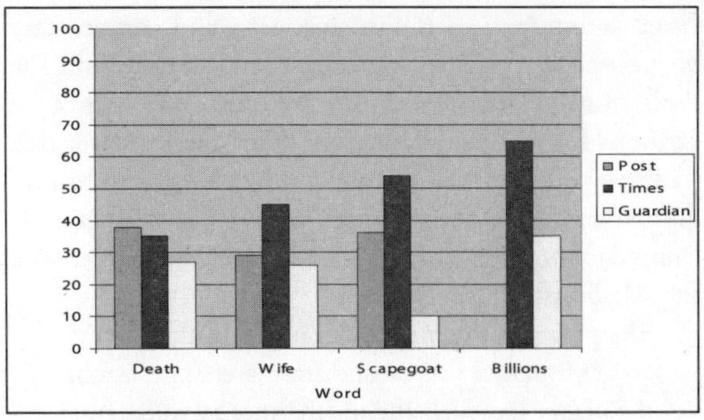

Figure 1. Comparison of press coverage of myths

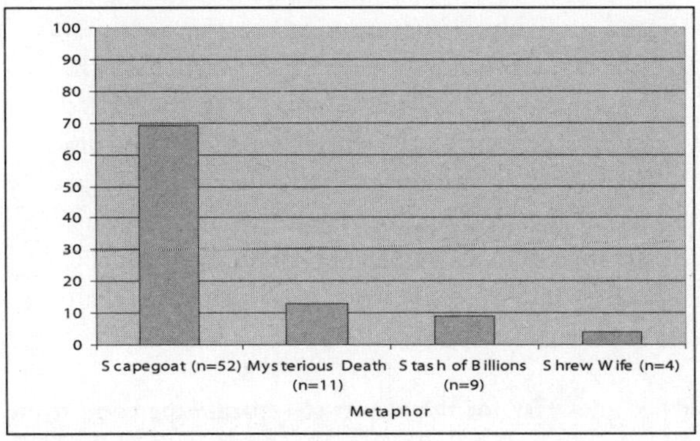

Figure 2. Cartoon metaphor frequency expressed in percentages; total N =75

Conclusion

The four metaphors: Arafat as the scapegoat, Arafat's mysterious death, the stashed billions of dollars, and Suha, the mean spirited shrew, are present in the two weeks of news coverage by the *New York Times*, *The Jerusalem Post* and *The Guardian* and the cartoon sample from the same period of time. The bulk of the news stores and the editorial cartoons focused upon the metaphor of Arafat as the scapegoat for peace.

It is difficult to determine whether editorial cartoonists can change the attitudes of those who can view them in daily papers or on the web where the cartoons can be revisited and shared with friends. We do know that metaphors are commonplace, and that they function as part of our cognitive process; we think with metaphors. Metaphors draw upon our shared values and experiences. We utilize those metaphors to make judgements about what is good and bad, about who are our friends and who are our enemies. We use the metaphor of the scapegoat and the missing billions to describe the legacy of Arafat. We loose sight of the charitable work and the contributions of Suha Arafat. At a difficult transition in her life, we offer no sympathy, but label her a shrew. The story of Arafat's death becomes a tale about the struggle over political power and money. We see only Arafat's Palestinian critics; these metaphors mask the very real grief that millions of Palestinians expressed at his death.

Cartoonists do see themselves as rhetors, who create the

visual counterpart of the written news and commentary of newspapers. Cagle, cartoonist and creator of The Professional Cartoonist Index web site, the source of cartoons for this study, observes that America has a rich tradition of editorial cartoons. He views cartoons as more than humor and considers cartoonists to be graphic commentators (Hays, Morris & Willis, 2003). DeSousa and Medhurst (1982) believe:

> The power of the metaphor lies not in the specific artist's intent or success at fostering change, but in the degree to which and the manner by which, the cartoonist taps into the collective consciousness of readers and thereby reaffirms cultural values and individual interpretation of those values. The cartoonist does not create from whole cloth, but, instead, articulates a frame from the artist's unique percept to the shared experiences of the readers. The cartoon generally functions not as a change agent, but as a statement of consensus, an invitation to remember cultural values and beliefs and, by implication, to participate in their maintenance. (p. 85)

It becomes easy for the viewer to separate the good from the evil, particularly when cartoonists show angels barring Arafat's entry into heaven. Yasser Arafat was a complex individual. To his followers he was the father of his country, a freedom fighter, a survivor, the little guy, an irreplaceable symbol and a statesman. To his detractors he was corrupt, a thief, a manipulator and trickster, an incorrigible terrorist, an opportunist and a man who created world terrorism. The press and President Bush depict Arafat as the scapegoat for terrorism. Norris, Kern and Just (2003) argue that the press takes their cues from the political leadership. When President Bush uses the terrorism metaphor he frames Arafat's struggle to achieve a Palestinian state as a terrorist act. When he refuses to meet with Arafat blame for the situation in the Middle East is placed upon Arafat's shoulders. This becomes the dominant discourse and places "events into ideologically preferred frames" Karim (2000, p. 6). These American cartoonists are free to connect their images to the dominant social myths. In this case the dominant metaphors of Arafat as a scapegoat, death under mysterious circumstances, stashes of cash and a shrew for a wife become hegemonic discourses both in the news coverage and in the editorial content of the cartoons.

References:

Burke, K. (1962). *A grammar of motives and a rhetoric of motives*. Cleveland, OH: World Publishing.

Bush, G. W. (2002, March 30) Remarks by the President on the Middle East. [On-Line]. Available: http://www.whitehouse.gov/news/releases/202/03/print/200203301-.html

Bush, G. W. (2004, November11) President's statement on Yasser Arafat. [On-Line]. Available: http://www.whitehouse.gov/news/releases/2004/11/print/20041111.html

Cagle, D. (2007).Daryl Cagle's Professional Cartoonist Index. At http://www. cagle.com/

Chilton, P. & Lakoff, G. (1995). Foreign policy by metaphor. In C. Schaffner & A.L. Wenden (Eds.), *Language and peace* (pp. 309-59). Amsterdam: Harwood Academic.

Conners, J. L. (1998). Hussein as enemy: The Persian Gulf War in political cartoons. *Harvard international journal of press/ politics 3*(3), 96-114.

DeSousa, M.A. (1984). Symbolic action and pretended insight: The Ayatollah Khoumeini in U.S. editorial cartoons. In M. J. Medhurst & T.W. Benson (Eds.), *Rhetorical dimensions in media: A critical casebook* (pp. 204-230). Dubuque, Iowa: Kendall/Hunt.

DeSousa, M.A. (1982). Political cartoons and American culture: Significant symbols of campaign 1980. *Studies in visual communication, 8*, 84-97.

Edelman, M. (2001). *The politics of misinformation*. Cambridge: Cambridge University Press.

El Refaie, E. (2003). Understanding visual metaphor: The example of newspaper cartoons, *Visual communication, 2*(1), 75-95.

Gibbs, R. W. (1994). *The poetics of mind: Figurative thought, language, and understanding*. Cambridge: Cambridge University Press.

Hart, W. B. & Hassencahl, F. (2002). Dehumanizing the enemy in editorial cartoons. In B.S. Greenberg (Ed.), *Communication and terrorism: Public and media responses to 9/11* (pp. 137-151). Creskill, NJ: Hampton Press.

Hart, W. B. & Hassencahl. F. (2004). Culture as persuasion: Metaphor as weapon. In L. Artz & Y. Kamalipour (Eds.), *Bring `em on: Media and politics in the U.S. War on Iraq* (pp. 85-100). Landham, NJ: Rowman & Littlefield.

Hassencahl, F. (2004). American and European political cartoonists pen/pin Saddam Hussein: An analysis of U.S.-Iraq war editorial cartoons. In Y. Passadeos (Ed.), *Mass media in transition: An international compendium* (pp. 337-351). Athens, Greece: Athens Institute for Education and Research.

Hassencahl, F. (2006). Framing the death of Yasser Arafat: Conspiracy or natural causes. In Yuksel, E. (Ed.), *4th international symposium on communication in the millennium* (pp. 87-94). Eskişehir, Turkey: Anadolu University Press.

Hays, K., Morris, V. & Willis, G. (2003, March 19). Editorial cartoonists draw on a fine line during times of war. *The flipside*. Atlanta, GA. Retrieved April 6, 2006, from Lexis/Nexis database.

Ivie, R. L. (1980). Images of savagery in American justification for war. *Communication monographs, 47*, 278-292.

Ivie, R. L. (1984). Speaking "common sense" about the Soviet threat: Reagan's rhetorical stance. *The western journal of speech communication, 48*, 39-50.

Ivie, R. L. (1996). Tragic fear and the rhetorical presidency: Combating evil in the Persian Gulf. In M.J. Medhurst (Ed.), *Beyond the rhetorical presidency* (pp. 153-178). College Station, Texas: Texas A &M University Press.

Ivie, R. L. (2005). *Democracy and America's war on terror.* Tuscaloosa, AL: University of Alabama Press.

Karim, K. H. (2000). *Islamic peril: Media and global violence.* Montreal, Canada: Black Rose Books.

Keen, S. (1986). *Faces of the enemy: Reflections of the hostile imagination.* New York: Harper & Row.

Lahoud, L. (2004, November 8). Aide alleges Israel poisons Arafat. *Jerusalem Post.* Retrieved April 6, 2006, from Factiva database.

Lakoff, G., & Johnson, M. (1980). *Metaphors we live by.* Chicago: University of Chicago Press.

Lakoff, G. (1991). Metaphor and war: The metaphor system used to justify war in the Gulf. *Peace research. 23*(2/3), 25-32.

Lakoff, G. (1993). The contemporary theory of metaphor. In A. Ortony (Ed.), *Metaphor and thought* (2nd ed.) (pp. 202-51). Cambridge: Cambridge University Press.

Lakoff, G. (1996). *Moral politics: What conservatives know that liberals don't.* Chicago: University of Chicago Press.

McClure, L. (2005). Battle lines: political cartoonists take on Iraq. *Current Events, a weekly reader publication, 105*(4), S1.

Miller, A. I. (1995). Imagery and metaphor: The cognitive sciences connection. In Z. Radman (Ed.), *From a metaphorical point of view: A multidisciplinary approach to the cognitive content of metaphor* (pp. 199-224). Berlin, Germany: Walter de Gruyter.

Norris, P., Kern, M., & Just, M. (Eds.). (2003). *Framing terrorism: The news media, the government and the public.* New York: Routledge.

Otabe, T. (1995). From "clothing" to "organ of reason": An essay on theories of metaphor in German philosophy in the age of enlightenment. In Z. Radman (Ed.), *From a metaphorical point of view: A multidisciplinary approach to the cognitive content of metaphor* (pp. 7-25). Berlin, Germany: Walter de Gruyter.

Radman, Z. (1995). Introduction. In Z. Radman (Ed.), *From a metaphorical point of view: A multidisciplinary approach to the cognitive content of metaphor* (pp. 1-4). Berlin, Germany: Walter de Gruyter.

Rosenthal, E. (2004, November 12). Secrecy by aides and silence by doctors persist, and what killed Arafat is still a mystery. *New York Times.* Retrieved April 6, 2006, from Factiva database.

Seitz, J. A. (1998). Nonverbal metaphor: A review of theories and evidence. *Genetic, social and general psychology monographs, 14*(1), 95-119.

Talking to the Enemy or Talking to the Media? Thoughts on Dialogues in a Situation of Conflict

Gabriella Rossetti
Anthropology, Communication Studies
University of Ferrara
rfg@unife.it

"Talking" and "The Enemy"

"Talking to the enemy" has been the key sentence used to frame activities aimed at non violent conflict resolution, reconciliation or post conflict reconstruction of mutual trust and coexistence in conflict or war torn societies.

"Talking to the enemy" was used for quite a long time as title for encounters between Palestinians and Israelis, or , to be more accurate, between citizens of Israelis and inhabitants of the West Bank and Gaza (occupied territories).

Here I intend to offer for discussion some thoughts and comments which I developed, with other interested partners and researchers, as participant to several events (workshops, seminars) in which, according to an agreed program, Palestinian and Israelis women met. The conversion among them, the roles which were played and exchanged, can be reported by a participant (and committed) observer as I was; it was possible to identify the patterns of communication and of role taking (although through the brokerage of translators who were, inevitably, also mediators). It was also possible to see that, during the process, other interlocutors were called into the conversation, when the "Media", with a capital "M" where evoked or addressed directly or indirectly, thus serving as scapegoats for what went wrong in the communication process or, vice versa, as ultimate judges and problem solvers, a sort of *deus ex machina*, to which the positive conclusion of the process was entrusted.

The particular meetings I refer to are not part of the well nown People to People Norwegian supported program[1], from which they differ in some important features; they were designed by women's associations which had a long tradition in this kind of meetings; so long, in fact, that most of the staff and participants active in the last two years, were too young to be able to recall, as a personal experience, the times when programs of this kind had started: around the year 1991. Apparently, there was a fracture, due also to the events of recent history and politics, which cancelled the memory of or the will to remember what was done before the beginning of the second Intifada. Yet, the story of People to People programs had built some kind of tradition, so that, whenever new programs are and will be designed under the headline of "peace and conflict resolution" (just to quote some lines of support (finance) of the European Union) things develop in a similar line and perspective. If we can say this it is because, contrary to what happens usually when aid projects are concerned, there has been, recently, a sort of public evaluation of those programs to which we can refer while reflecting on the more recent experiences.[2]

"Talking to the enemy" refers to communication when there has been a communication breakdown. Just by putting the two words side by side, "talking" and "enemy" we create some kind of oximore and the first (*talking*) expands into the positive semantic spheres of friendliness and openness; it becomes capable of reversing a relationship of conflict and mistrust, magically transforming hate into care, distance into proximity. On the other hand, the word "enemy", in this context, immediately looses most of its objective correlations to the facts of a history of armed conflicts, war, killings, imprisonments, and expands its meaning towards the subtleties of the psychological and

1 Two hundred and twenty two Israeli and 204 Palestinian organizations, 29 "mixed", 5 Norwegian and 5 from other areas were involved in projects financed with US $ 20-25 million between 1993 and 2000.

2 2 General Discussion moderated by Ziad AbuZyyad, (2006), PIJ Co-Editor, "People-to-People What Went Wrong & How to Fix it", in *Journal of Politics, Economics and Culture*, *12*(4) & *13*(1).

cultural processes of "construction" of a stereotyped image, by definition far from the actual personalities of those who were labelled as enemies. The images evoked by this catchphrase are of peaceful, affectionate moving of two partners towards each other, embracing and "getting over" by turning a page in history. "Healing" is the verb often underlying all this, as if the conflict had been a disease and the "talking" could, in itself with no added components, be the cure.

Palestine/Israel: a Long Story, Almost a Tradition

In reality, "talking to the enemy" could be the description of several different events. The very table of official political negotiations between two conflicting parts is the public place in which enemies talk to each other; traders or business people belonging to parties at war might be talking to each other forgetting for a while the conflict in the name of the interests of their business; something similar might happen among artists or sportsmen whose activities may be performed in a niche which is imagined as part of a different world wider than the one torn by a conflict. After the Oslo agreements, in fact, different activities were developed at all these levels; the ones we refer to now are mainly those which were defined as "dialogues": part of a process of peace/reconciliation. Projects under this heading dealt with "history, identity, trauma, tolerance, non violence," etc... Groups belonging to the two conflicting parties met: the meetings were "encounters" in the sense that the very fact of seeing each other and sharing a room, sitting around the same table, "breathing the same air" as someone put it, was considered an event worthy to be mentioned in one's biography.

The very definition of encounters as dialogues produced many interesting discussions and problems which are still felt in the new wave (very low and timid indeed) of programs which is being developed in the present situation.

The first problem was, typically, the relationship between what was going on at the level of politics and among the main actors involved in the conflict (armies, political leaders, armed forces) and the worlds of the encounters. While the first was depicted as the "real", wide, effective world, the others became immediately, by contrast and comparison, worlds of the "lesser gods", fragmented, less real, almost fictional places, although there were undoubtley real people involved in it, although the goals and principles which inspired the dialogues were accepted by the value systems of the two societies much more than those at work at the other, official level. A pre given assumption of impotence shaped this representation; a very contradictory one, since those who embarked into the dialogues saw themselves as brave and courageous individuals, often strengthened by their belonging to groups or associations, approved and supported by third parties from all over the "real world" and yet they also depicted themselves (and were perceived from outside) as fragile, marginal and doomed to un-effectiveness. The power of producing change and effectiveness was assigned only to those individuals active at the "official" level, while the dialogues failed to be seen in the frame of any "official", public light; the power which the individuals engaged in the dialogues exerted over themselves producing transformations in their attitudes towards the "enemies" were often perceived as useless, since the criteria and indicators of success of the encounters were those borrowed from the level of the "big" politics. If there was a breakdown in the peace process and violence erupted on one side or another, then a failure judgement was passed over to the process of dialogues too. There were those who wondered whether the dialogues had to be considered "as meetings between nations or individuals, attempts for systemic social change or down to earth relationship building". Of course one might ask, in turn, whether "nations" can communicate as such and whether systemic social change can happen apart from "down to earth relationship building" and *how* do "nations" communicate, in case they do. We can see how many key issues are at stake here in just this very simple, naïve question. It is a question which refers to the interplay of "systems" and subjects, of structures which are man made, but are perceived as superior to the sums of the individuals involved and capable to shape their feelings, thoughts and behaviour. In other words, it is assumed that the power of a "treaty" in shaping the "nations" minds (and hearts) is superior to the sum of the intentions and wills of millions of individual citizens.

The leader of one of the most committed organizations in the programmes of People to People rapprochement once stated that 90% per cent of the Palestinians and Israelis were in favour of a peaceful agreement, and 90 % were against it. He meant precisely that on one hand a "system" had to be put in place to allow the "nations" (the two societies) to express their good will for peace, and, on the other hand, that humans are capable of a wide range of attitudes (opinions, feelings, emotions) and can choose from time to time to "tune" into one key or another. Thus the responsibility of "communication" between nations is assigned at the same time to individuals and to structures or systems put in place by a special group of citizens: the leaders, the strongest. The differential of power among the different layers of citizens was therefore seen as the source of the apparent failures. But the underlying problem was, I believe, also that, having identified this gap, those involved in the dialogues often abandoned the process of assigning value to what they were doing as a source of power of a different kind.

A second problem identified as cause of the weakness of these experiments in communication was the difference in the investments and agendas of the two parties. The typical pattern of communication and role taking was the one in which the Palestinians came to the meetings with the declared goal of lobbying upon the Israelis in order to "persuade them to persuade" their leaders in the government to change their politics, while the Israelis' goal was to show to the Palestinians that the front of their enemies was more diversified than they might think. The first brought their sufferings, the latter their strength as opposition. This difference in agendas reversed the official pattern of the relationship: here the "one top" position was held by Palestinians, while Israelis occupied the "one down"

Was this difference a sign of one or both parties having a "wrong" perception of what the dialogues could be, or was it the result of a "down o earth" objective situation which had to be seen as that of a confrontation between an oppressor and an oppressed? If these are the roles pre-assigned by the *true* nature of the situation, then anything which might blur them will be seen as a dangerous deviance from the objective truth. "We are opposed to people-to-people programs in principle, and to the whole ideal of dialogue. This touches upon the asymmetry of power…. We work a lot with Palestinian organizations, but we are working to end the occupation…..That's what creates equality in the working relationship" (Halper, 2006, p. 101)[3]. Here the process of communication is on one hand made simple: it is just a matter of "telling the truth", while on the other hand it is moved directly on the big stage where "it is the powerful side which frames and directs the dialogue". The responsibility, from this point of view, resides entirely with the Israelis, at all levels: the dialogues are only organizational meetings aimed at agreeing on the activities of campaigns. If "enemies" get together it is just because, in this particular situation, they have decided that they are not such anymore, since they move towards the same goal. No matter if and how there might still be feelings of mistrust and personal dislikes: people are tools in the system of machinery with one goal. This referring to a real, objective situation, although it is depicted in a way which is deeply different (practically the opposite) from the official one, leaves no space for complexities and ambiguities, for breaches in the roles of the main actors: the villain and the victim, one completely guilty, the other completely innocent. Once the parts are assigned in this way, the Israelis who come to these meetings align themselves on the side of the victims, distancing from the rest of their fellow citizens. Apparently they become the losers in this game, but not as much as one might imagine, as we shall see later on. As far as communication is concerned, the real problem behind this one is that dialogues are perceived as useless, because there is nothing new one could expect to discover by "talking to the enemy" since the general picture of the relationship is already given as labelled as "the truth".

The third problem is somehow related to the last one: the fact that those who accept to take part into programs of Dialogues between enemies are already convinced. But convinced of what? Answering this question would require more in depth research and, most of all, researchers interested in discovering which kinds of convictions, feelings, thoughts and behaviours *passed* through the lives of the participants at that time. The general impression from what an outsider might guess is that participants were interested in bringing to the meetings their ideal selves, or, better, that 90% of their pro-peace, pro-non violent resolution attitudes and convictions, leaving out of the door the other 90%, just to follow the paradox quoted above. The good image of the programme had to be preserved, at the cost of cancelling those differences which make communication meaningful and useful, while underscoring similarities and points of agreements. All this and much more accounted for the declaration of failure of the Dialogues which took place between 1993 and the year 2000.

Officially, the drawbacks were ascribed to the influence of the macro level changes but very little was done to understand the kind of communication that flew between the parts and even less to understand the role played by the third party (Norwegian participants mostly, but also many others, among whom Italians were numerous with different programmes aimed at youth and women, when the methodology was that of dialogues, but also several professional encounters linked to exchanges of technical know how between institutions.)

A better understanding of the processes developed inside the relationship of dialogues was possible during the recent revivals of encounters between enemies. When the whole experiment had been ruled out as deceptive if not even hypocritical and dangerous for the cause of the assessment of truth (a precondition, we learned, for any reconciliation process) new programmes were started, during the past two years: the ones I draw my comments from regard women's associations.

Today: Women in Dialogues

From the beginning, the dialogues' goal was, officially, "to cultivate grassroots' contacts between Israeli and Palestinians and lay the foundations for a culture of peace and coexistence…in an attempt to change the dehumanised and stereotyped perceptions of "the other" society and nurture empathy, personalization and recognition of each others' goals and needs". In the same recent text in which these goals are recalled, the authors state, bluntly, that "It has become conventional wisdom that People-to People efforts did not achieve their goals…". This conventional wisdom was based on the "clearly observable fact that the support for peace and non violent resolution was affected, in both societies, by *measures on the ground* which could not prevent the breakdown of the peace process."

Just when these statements circulated widely in both societies, one of the most vibrant and original experiences intertwined with the people-to-people programmes, but

3 Jeff Halper, Coordinator of Israeli Committee against House Demolitions.

developed independently, the associations of the Jerusalem Link, (particularly supported by some parts of the Italian women's movement) managed to gather some twenty women (ten from Israel and ten from Palestine), organizing meetings in Italy and then developing a new programme in Israel and Palestine which is being implemented at present.

I am not in a position of talking on behalf of these women. I position myself as a third party which participated into some of the activities and intends to go deeper into the understanding of the experience.

"Talking to the enemy" when initiated by women, has a particular meaning: first of all, it used to be based on the assumption that for women crossing borders between conflicting fields was a way to state their uneasiness in identifying with nations, ethnicities, governments in which they were not given full citizenship, or, worse, which were based and developed on their exclusion from decision making levels. Also, women's secular exclusion from warfare was often used as an asset for claiming particular merits in the field of peace making and vocal opposition to armed confrontations. During the past twenty years there have been a number of important ground breaking experiences of women getting together to cross armed borders and meet with the other part. One powerful assumption had been, on a theoretical level that alliances across borders were possible and desirable because women shared common interests in changing the structure not only of their own, but of all existing societies in as much as they are base on the inferiorization and exclusion of the female half. "We are all traitors of any nationalism" was a common phrase pronounced by women in former Yugoslavia during the wars of the 90's. A lot has been written on all this and on what was baptized "transversal politics" of women's "rooting" in their own place, but "shifting" their attention (and often their bodies, by physically going there) towards others' difficult places (Cockburn, 2007). This is not the place to discuss these issues. What I want to discuss here is the type of communication which flows between the parts during these last, more recent dialogues.

Guilt, Blame and Innocence

Apparently, the pattern described above, is repeated identical. Palestinian women come to the meetings with one shared, expressed goal: to lobby on the Israelis in order to persuade them to persuade their government to "end the occupation". On the other side, Israelis women (in this particular case, mostly young women in their twenties and thirties) come again to show that they want peace, but this time there is a new stress on "guilt" which was not as important or as evident in the previous experiences. By "confessing" the guilt of their part, they pay the price necessary to enter the relationship with their partners but they also do more than that. The background of the conflict has changed: we know all the events which changed the picture during the past seven years. There is one piece of the picture though, which sheds a new light on the communication's flows in the dialogues among these women. It has to do with the role the media played in the coverage of the re-occupation of the West Bank. Daniel Dor, an Israeli journalist and writer, published a brilliant analysis of three newspapers during the period of "Operation Defensive Shield" started in the year 2002. On the back cover, we read: "in the three years that have passed since Operation Defensive Schield, one fact remains uncontroversial: never, until the operation, had there been such a wide breach between the Israeli collective consciousness and international public opinion." This breach was filled with *blame* and the fear, almost terror, of it. When reporting about one Terror Attack which took place on Monday, February 23, 2004 on the bus N. 14, while Israel was being judged at The Hague tribunal for the separation wall, "What the (two) newspapers mostly did was express, reflect, impress and highlight a certain collective sensibility: a sarcastic, angry, irritated sense of siege, of course, but also, and much more significantly a *mental siege*. More than anything else, what reverberated from the papers much more than the fear or the anger or the mourning for the victims of the suicide attack, was the insult of *blame*." What was at stake was "the desperate need to suppress, to dismiss, to fend off guilt. ...The suppression of guilt is a much wider phenomenon than the mere suppression of information that potentially implies guilt."(Dor, 2004, pp. 2-3). Here we see the media getting into a frame similar to that of the dialogues: not as much selecting facts and news, may be with some bias, but to work on the thick, blurred level of self representation, of identities and presentation of self to others. Now we can see that the sense of guilt presented by the Israeli women in the most recent dialogues was reflecting a new twist in the representation of the conflict in their society to which they responded by admitting guilt. But what they did actually was to separate themselves from the rest of the Israeli society preserving, only for themselves, the image of the innocent. On the contrary, the Palestinian women, at least during the first turns of the conversation (when the leaders of the two groups plus one representative of the third party (from Italy) introduced the dialogue *in front of the local television*) wanted to stress that they were there as a "people" (one, united people with no fractures inside) so that, whatever they said about their desire for peace and peaceful coexistence was to be meant as uttered by the one voice of all those who named themselves Palestinians.

Whom to Talk to: Different Levels of Communication

Here, in the first sequence of the dialogue, the two parties presented themselves as deeply different: there were apparently very meagre possibilities of mutual recognition as individuals who share some sort of common experience, let alone as women sharing common marginality inside their respective societies. It was suddenly clear that the dialogue was not happening between the participants sitting in that room: others absent interlocutors were evoked. The Palestinians were addressing their words to the media (their own television which was reporting the initial stage of the event and all possible media in the known world), while the Israeli were invited to address not so much those particular individuals who were sitting in the room, but the whole collective people for whom those women from the West Bank said they stood for or, as second choice, their own leaders and ruling parties. The third party, the women from Italy, addressed the group referring to movements of solidarity back home and to the challenge of influencing public opinion and public interest (back home): how to open some channel for a communication which could bridge the gap between official media and/or superficial ideological positions and the complexities of life experience of those who lived inside the conflict. In a way, they could have represented that wider world whose attitudes towards Israeli/ Palestine were changing according to most analysts, its media, local and international, but also a group of selected committed and active observers who, in Italy as in other parts of the world, claimed they were sharing interests as women to stop armed conflicts and "expel war from history"[4]. The space for this third party's voice was almost cancelled for a number of reasons including the intensity of the emotions accompanying the encounter (a first time experience for many participants) of the two main parties and the non irrelevant fact the third party was also perceived mainly as the mediator with the funding agency: the European Union.

What is interesting though is that, once the official opening was over and participants split into groups, the situation changed. The groups had decided to discuss the classic issues of the negotiation (right of return, the settlements, Jerusalem, etc.) but, instead of entering a discussion on strategies and tactics, future scenarios and interpretations of the chain of causes and effects in the past, they offered a stream of stories. Communication *shifted* towards narration of life stories. First person narratives, in most cases, but also third person: in all cases individual actors were given a voice and it was clear, immediately, that the stories introduced a different code of communication. On one hand the narrations avoid controversial discourse: especially when they are told in the key of personal autobiographical stories, little or no space is left for contradictory interpretations; on the other hand, especially when they are told orally, in a face to face encounter, they activate passions[5], not necessarily compassion and sympathy, but empathy. In a short time, there was a shift from an extreme of "collectiveness" to the one of "individuality", from impersonal statements to personal experiences, from the rituals with which the Conflict and its well known structures were evoked to the unknown events of single lives, real "*news*" since they were heard (and in some cases also told) fir the first time and therefore worth of being told and listened to. On one hand the meaning which is officially built and on the other another meaning, the one *which allows and justifies the face to face encounter.*

In this second phase, the third party, a committed participant, but mainly still an observer , played the role of reinforcing the "active listening" by both parts.

A third phase in the communication was opened when comments were given and evaluations and forward looking plans were attempted. Now the other interlocutors evoked in the first phase, the media, were mentioned again by many participants, but with a completely different meaning; no more as symbols of the collective identities of both parties, spoke persons of "the nations", but, on the contrary, as powerful producers of hate, responsible of the "construction of the enemy". "It is all in the media", said a woman from Jenin referring to the image of Palestinians as supporters of a violent approach. "News build the enemy" replied a young woman from Israel. Here the media are used as "recipients" of all the unpleasant bad feelings and images which fuel mistrust, suspicion or even reciprocal hatred. The result is the creation of a space in which on one hand the outer world is re-interpreted and, on the other, the life experience of the participants acquires a new meaning while "the enemy" is transformed, for a while, into an active listener.

Now the question might be: who will be interested in saving this space and giving it the legitimacy and visibility which might transform it from a private into a public space as meaningful as others which "hit the news"?

The women who are engaged in these encounters are now facing a dilemma: going on with the dialogues, getting deeper and deeper into what they called the "mental obstacles" in the face to face communication knowing that this small world might remain such, an island of meanings which contradict the official discourse or suspending the encounters and engage in the efforts to access the "real" official stage of representation. Palestinian women insist, at times, that the other part should produce some kind of public "action", possibly accessing the media, in order to prove their commitment and good faith.

We don't know now which choice will be made. What we can observe, as third parties, is that it is extremely difficult for these women, in spite of their commitment and real bravery, to give value to the communication and change they experience in the face to face encounters where they engage in "talking to the enemy". The split and

4 Namely the organization called "women in black", particularly active in solidarity movement, rallies and vigils whose very ambitious slogan is "let us expel war from history". In Italy Raffaella Lamberti of the women's association Orlando, based in Bologna and Elisabetta Donini from Torino organised meetings with women from Palestine and Israeli since the first Intifada, when, as they state: "we shared a common political agenda as women".

5 Patrizia Violi, personal communication , commenting the recent experience of a project, mediated by the Italian Orlando, in support of the Jerusalem Link (two women's organizations , one from Israel (Bat Shalom) the other from East Jerusalem (Jerusalem Woman's Center) active in "bridge building" since the years of the first Intifada.

the gap between the personal experience (although made possible by a group, several associations and the support of powerful multilateral institutions) and the power of those who "make the history" is as wide as ever. Now it is more and more clear, also to the "grassroots", that not only governments, leaders, armies and militants make history, but also the media. It is a relatively new consciousness, in comparison with the first phase of "people-to-people" encounters; it might worsen the sense of powerlessness and impotence; it might shift too much the attention to the world of media as the only real power in the field; but it might also produce a change in the way the whole conflict is represented. As Daniel Dor revelead in his analysis of the Israel press, if what is at stake is , more than a naïve trust in the possibility of telling the truth, the process of shaping the feelings of belonging and identity (by suppressing guilt or by strengthening victimhood) then this matter might be seen as something on which everybody can act: what happens in the face to face dialogues will at last be given the importance and relevance of an "action" and "visibility" might be granted although it passes through the embodied gaze of women sitting and talking in a small room.

References:

Cockburn, C. (2007). *From where we stand, War, Women's Activism & Feminist Analysis*. London: Zed Books.

Dor, D. (2004). *The Supression of Guilt, the Israeli Media & the Reoccupation of the West Bank* .London: Pluto Press.

Halper, J. (2006, Moderator). People-to-People, what went wrong & how to fix it?. *Palestine-Israel Journal, 12*(4) & *13*(1), 101. Retrieved from http://www.pij.org/details.php?id=408

AbuZayyad, Z. (2006, Moderator). People-to-People, what went wrong & how to fix it?. Journal of Politics, Economics and Culture, *12*(4) & 13(1).

Türkiye'de Barış Hareketinde İnternetin Kullanımı: Küresel BAK Örneği

Gülüm Şener
Beykent Üniversitesi
gulumsener@yahoo.com

Giriş

İnternet, yeni toplumsal hareketler için geleneksel iletişim araçlarından farklı olarak "alternatif" bir medya olmayı vaat etmektedir. Kitle iletişim araçlarının sermaye gruplarının elinde yoğunlaşması sonucunda kamusal alanda seslerini duyurma imkanı bulamayan yeni toplumsal hareketler için internet; ucuzluğu, zaman ve mekan sınırı tanımaması, geleneksel hiyerarşik yapılarını kırarak "yatay iletişim"e dayanmasıyla söz konusu hareketlerin haberleşme, örgütlenme ve eylem kapasitelerini arttırmakta ve küreselleşmesine yardımcı olmaktadır. Yeni toplumsal hareketler; iletişimlerini kurdukları sanal gruplar aracılığıyla yürütmekte, yine internet aracılığıyla aktivist toplamakta, belirli sorunlar etrafında toplanan "sanal cemaatler" yaratmakta, aktivistlerini bilgilendirmek ve harekete geçirmek için websiteleri, haberleşme listeleri, bülten panoları, sohbet odaları gibi araçlardan yararlanmaktadırlar.

Ancak, internetin kullanımının birçok ülkede üst-orta gelir gruplarıyla sınırlı kalması (sayısal uçurum), bu kullanımın da iş ve boş zaman ekseninde biçimlenmesi, internetin içeriğinin giderek ticarileşmesi ve enformasyonun fragmanlaşması, internet kullanıcıları arasındaki kültürel ve dilsel farklılıklar gibi etkenler yeni toplumsal hareketlerin seslerini internet üzerinden geniş kitlelere duyurabilmeleri açısından başlıca engelleri oluşturmaktadır.

Bu çalışmada, internetin yeni toplumsal hareketlere sağladığı katkılar ve sınırlılıklar, Türkiye'den Küresel Barış ve Adalet Koalisyonu (Küresel BAK) hareketi üzerinden anlaşılmaya çalışılmıştır. Türkiye'de savaş karşıtı hareketler içerisinde en geniş aktivist kitlesine sahip olması, yeni toplumsal hareketlerin özelliklerini içermesi hareketin seçilmesinde önemli etkenlerdir. Saha araştırmasında birçok yöntem bir arada kullanılmıştır. Harekete bir önaraştırmanın ardından, hareketin yürüttüğü etkinlik ve kampanyalara katılınarak yerinde gözlemlerde bulunulmuş, hareketin internet sitesi ve *Yahoo* üzerindeki haberleşme grubu incelenmiştir. Bunun yanısıra hareketin çekirdeğinde yer alan sözcülerle yapılan öngörüşmelerle Küresel BAK üzerine daha ayrıntılı bilgi edinilmiştir. Son olarak, haberleşme grubuna üye aktivistlerin internet kullanımını ölçen bir on-line anket uygulanmıştır.

Internetin Yeni Toplumsal Hareketler İçin İmkanları ve Sınırlılıkları

1990'ların başından itibaren küreselleşme sürecine bir tepki olarak ortaya çıkan ve "üçüncü kuşak hareketler" olarak da adlandırılan yeni toplumsal hareketler, yeni enformasyon ve iletişim araçları aracılığıyla küresel düzeyde ve kollektif örgütlenen ve eylemde bulunan hareketlerdir. Yeni toplumsal hareketler; küresel şirketlere meydan okumakta, küresel sermaye sınıfına karşı çıkmakta, tüketim karşıtı bir kültürün ve ideolojinin öncülüğünü yapmaktadırlar (Guedes, 2002, s. 4). Kimlik temelli olması, "çoğulculuk" ve "farklılık" kavramlarını öne çıkarması, eylemi bireysel ve kollektif kimliklerin bir karışımı olarak görmesi, şiddet yerine uzlaşmaya dayanması, esnek ve ademimerkezi yapılara sahip olması gibi özellikleriyle önceki toplumsal hareketlerden ayrılan yeni toplumsal hareketler (Johnston, Larana ve Gusfield, 1994, ss. 6-9), birçok nedenden ötürü neoliberal küreselleşmeyi eleştirerek cinsiyete, yaşa, etnik gruba, ulusa, dine dayalı kimliklerin onaylanmasını, ulus-devletin yeniden kurgulanmasını, "üçüncü-kuşak haklar" olarak anılan çevre, toplumsal cinsiyet, iletişim, yerel ve ulusüstü mekan ve etnik kimliği ilgilendiren hem bireyleri hem de kollektif yapıları içine alan bir vatandaşlık kavramının yaygınlaşmasını kapsamaktadır" (Leon, Burch ve Tamayo, 2001).

Internet, yeni toplumsal hareketler için de geleneksel iletişim araçlarından farklı olarak "alternatif" bir medya olmayı vaad etmektedir. Geleneksel kitle iletişim araçlarının sermaye gruplarının elinde yoğunlaşması sonucunda kamusal alanda seslerini duyurma imkanı bulamayan yeni toplumsal hareketler için Internet; ucuzluğu, zaman ve mekan sınırı tanımaması, geleneksel hiyerarşik yapıların dayattığı "dikey iletişim" yerine "yatay iletişim"e dayanmasıyla sözkonusu hareketlerin haberleşme, örgütlenme ve eylem kapasitelerini arttırmakta ve küreselleşmesine yardımcı olmaktadır. Kimlik temelli hareketler olarak görülen yeni toplumsal hareketler; iletişimlerini büyük oranda kurdukları sanal gruplar aracılığıyla yürütmekte, yine Internet aracılığıyla aktivist toplamakta, belirli sorunlar etrafında toplanan "sanal cemaatler" yaratmakta, aktivistlerini bilgilendirmek ve harekete geçirmek için websiteleri, haberleşme listeleri, bülten panoları, sohbet odaları gibi araçlardan yararlanmaktadırlar (Langman ve Morris, 2005).

Ancak tüm bu özellikler, Interneti ayrıcalıklı kılsa da Internetin dünyaya yayılmasının tarihsel olarak tek ideolojinin egemenliğini dayattığı ve bireylerin büyük ideolojilere, siyasete ve demokrasiye güvenini kaybedip kayıtsızlaştığı bir dönem olan Soğuk Savaş sonrası döneme rastlaması, Internet'in kullanımının birçok ülkede üst-orta gelir gruplarıyla sınırlı kalması (sayısal uçurum), bu kullanımın da iş ve boş zaman ekseninde biçimlenmesi, Internetin içeriğinin giderek ticarileşmesi (hem küresel sermaye grupları tüketime ilişkin verilerin toplanması açısından etkin bir gözetleme aracı olması hem de Internetin tüketim ekonomisinin başat sektörlerinden reklam için yeni bir mecra oluşturması), Internet kullanıcıları arasındaki kültürel ve dilsel farklılıklar gibi etkenler yeni toplumsal hareketlerin seslerini geniş kitlelere duyurabilmeleri açısından başlıca engelleri oluşturmaktadır. Internetin toplumsal kullanımına ilişkin bu genel çerçevenin yanısıra yeni toplumsal hareketlerin grup dinamiği açısından konuya yaklaştığımızda ise enformasyonun ve yeni teknolojilerin denetiminin belirli kişilerin elinde toplandığını görmekteyiz. Yeni enformasyon ve iletişim teknolojileri yeni toplumsal hareketler için haberleşme ağı oluşturmakla birlikte diğer iletişim yöntem ve araçlarıyla ele alındığında anlam kazanmaktadır.

Küresel BAK Aktivistlerinin İnterneti Kullanımı

Bu çalışmada internetin teknolojik potansiyelinin sınanması için Türkiye'den Küresel Barış ve Adalet Koalisyonu (Küresel BAK) hareketinin örneklem olarak seçildiği bir saha araştırması yürütülmüştür. Türkiye'de savaş karşıtı hareketler içerisinde en geniş aktivist kitlesine sahip olması, yeni toplumsal hareketlerin özelliklerini içermesi hareketin seçilmesinde önemli etkenlerdir. Saha araştırmasında birçok yöntem birarada kullanılmıştır. Araştırmacı, harekete ilişkin bilgi-belge toplamanın yanı sıra, hareketin yürüttüğü etkinlik ve kampanyalara katılarak yerinde gözlemlerde bulunmuş, hareketin İnternet sitesi ve Yahoo! üzerindeki haberleşme grubunu incelemiştir. Bunun yanı sıra hareketin çekirdeğinde yer alan sözcülerle yapılan öngörüşmelerle Küresel BAK üzerine daha ayrıntılı bilgi edinilmiştir. Son olarak, haberleşme grubuna üye aktivistlerin İnternet kullanımını ölçen anket İnternet üzerinden uygulanmıştır.

Küresel BAK Hareketine İlişkin Genel Bilgi

Küresel BAK'ın işleyişi ve örgütlenmesi hakkındaki genel bilgiler, Yürütme Kurulu üyesi ve haberleşme grubu moderatörü Yıldız Önen, Yürütme Kurulu üyesi Hakan Tahmaz, BAK sekreteri Arife Köse, aktivist Ayşegül Önen ve Filiz Ülgüt'le yapılan kişisel görüşmeler ile BAK'ın İnternet sitesinden alınan bilgilerden derlenmiştir.

Hareketin Ortaya Çıkışı ve Gelişimi

Küresel Barış ve Adalet Koalisyonu (Küresel BAK) 10 Haziran 2003'te kurulmuştur. Ancak, Küresel BAK'ın öncesinde 2000'de düzenlenen Prag kampanyası, 2001'de Cenova kampanyası, Savaşa Hayır Platformu, 2002'de Irak'ta Savaşa Hayır Koordinasyonu yer almaktadır. Küresel BAK; başta Tarık Ali, Howard Zinn, Marcos olmak üzere muhaliflerin Küresel Barış ve Adalet Koalisyonu'nun (Global Peace and Justice Coalition) kurarak internet üzerinden dünyada imzaya açtığı metni alarak Türkiye'de imzaya açmışlar, Haziran 2003'te yazar Adalet Ağaoğlu'nun katıldığı bir basın toplantısıyla faaliyete geçmişlerdir. İmza metni ilk etapta 212 kişi tarafından imzalanmış; sokaklarda açılan standlar ve internet üzerinden de yeni aktivisler kazanılarak hareket kitleselleşmiştir.

Yürütme Kurulu üyesi Hakan Tahmaz, Savaşa Hayır Platformu'ndan Küresel BAK'a geçişi şöyle açıklamaktadır: "Irak'ta Savaşa Hayır Platformu, örgütler ittifakı gibi algılanıyor ve sol içi çekişmelere sahne oluyordu. Bunu aşmak için daha geniş bir toplumsal zemin yaratma arayışına girdik" (Kişisel Görüşme, Mart 2005). Savaşa Hayır Platformu'nda çeşitli şiddet olaylarının da yaşandığına dikkat çeken Tahmaz, şiddeti aşmak ve yalnızca kurumların değil, bireylerin de temsil edilebileceği tek konulu bir kampanya yürütmenin gerekliliğinden Küresel BAK'ı hazırlayan sürecin doğduğuna işaret etmektedir.

Küresel BAK'ın öncelikli üç hedefi bulunmaktadır:

1-Türkiye çapında bir kampanyalar birliği inşa etmek.

2-Küresel anti kapitalist savaş karşıtı hareketle ilişkilerin çok daha organik hale getirilmesi.

3-"Örgütsüzleri" harekete geçirmek.

Küresel BAK, kendisini bir kampanyalar birliği olarak tarif etmektedir. Hareket, kampanyalar etrafında örgütlenmekte, düzenlediği tüm etkinliklerde, izlediği yöntemlerde ve kullandığı araçlarda kampanyaların kitleselleşmesi için çaba harcamaktadır.

Küresel BAK kampanyaları tek bir ana slogan ve amaç

altında birleşmektedir: Irak'ta savaşı durdurmak. Küresel BAK eski sekreteri Arife Köse, faaliyet alanlarının Irak'taki savaşı durdurmak, ABD'nin dünyaya egemen olma politikalarına karşı çıkmak ve demokratik bir dünya yaratmanın alternatiflerini geliştirmek olduğunu belirtmektedir. Köse, hareketin hedefini Irak'ta savaşı durdurmakla sınırlamanın hareketi kitleselleştirdiğini ve meşru kıldığını belirtiyor: "Belki de hiçbir zaman yan yana gelmeyecek farklı görüşteki insanları, bu kampanyayla bir araya getiriyoruz" (Kişisel Görüşme, Mart 2005).

Tahmaz da Küresel BAK'ın farklılığının değişik politik görüşlerinden bireylerin yan yana gelmesi olduğunu vurguluyor: "Siyasi görüşlerin, kurumların ya da herhangi bir siyasi örgütlenme içerisinde yer almayan 'örgütsüz' kesimlerin eşit koşullar altında bir araya gelmesini amaçlıyoruz. Örgütler arasında bir ittifak değil, bireyleri bir araya getiren ve farklılığı içeren bir hareketiz" (Kişisel Görüşme, Mart 2005).

Küresel BAK, uluslararası savaş karşıtı kampanyalarla da işbirliği içerisindedir. Küresel BAK aktivistleri, 2003'te Paris'te, 2004'te Londra'da ve 2006'da Atina'da düzenlenen Avrupa Sosyal Forumu'na, 2003'te Kahire'de gerçekleştirilen Dünya Savaş Karşıtları Konferansı'na, 2004'te Beyrut'ta yapılan Dünya Savaş Karşıtları Buluşmasına katıldılar.

Örgütlenme Biçimleri ve Kampanyalar

Küresel BAK, yeni toplumsal hareketlerin esnek, merkezsiz, ağa dayalı yapısına uygun bir örgütlenme sergilemektedir. Çeşitli kurumlardan temsilcilerin yanı sıra hiçbir siyasi örgütlenmede yer almayan bireyleri de içeren Küresel BAK, aktivislerden oluşan bir genel meclisin yanı sıra 11 kişilik bir Yürütme Kurulu'na sahip. Küresel BAK'ın yürütme kurulunda şu isimler yer alıyor: Şenol Karakaş (DSİP), Mehmet Demir (HABER-SEN), Tayfun Mater (TMMOB), Yıldız Önen (DSİP), Selahattin Güven (MAZLUM-DER), Bülent Aydın (ÖDP), Nuri Ödemiş (Bağımsız), Faruk Sevim, Kudret Köksal (TÜKODER), Erol Kızılelma (SODEV), Mustafa Turgut (KESK). Genel Meclis 2-3 ayda bir toplantılar düzenlerken Yürütme Kurulu, TMMOB'un Beyoğlu bürosunda düzenli olarak her hafta toplantı düzenliyor. Yürütme Kurulu, karar yetkisine sahip olmamakla birlikte Genel Meclis'in verdiği kararların hızlı biçimde uygulanmasını sağlıyor.

Küresel BAK İstanbul içinde ve Anadolu'nun diğer kentlerinde yerel düzeyde örgütlenmeler olarak varlığını sürdürüyor. 33 ilde üyesi var. Adana, Ankara, İzmir, Bursa ve Trabzon'da da Yürütme Kurulu var. Kendi kampanyalarını örgütlemekte serbestler. Yıldız Önen özellikle vurguluyor: "Biz kendimizi Merkezi Yürütme olarak tanımlamıyoruz." Fakat ana kampanyalarda Küresel BAK onlara bilgilendirme toplantıları düzenliyor. Yereller kendi içinde toplantılar düzenlemektedir. Adana, Adapazarı, Akhisar, Aliağa, Ankara, Aksaray, Aydın, Bartın, Bursa, Kütahya, Çorum, Denizli, Edirne, Gaziantep, Hopa, İzmir, Kırklareli, Muğla, Ordu, Samsun, Sivas, Tekirdağ, Trabzon'da yerel BAK'lar bulunmaktadır. İstanbul içerisinde ise Beyoğlu, Çerkezköy, Gebze, Esenler, Gaziosmanpaşa, Kadıköy, Kuzguncuk, Bakırköy BAK'lar bulunmaktadır. Kadıköy ve Beyoğlu BAK'lar düzenli olarak her hafta toplanmaktadır. Kuzguncuk, Gaziosmanpaşa, Bakırköy, Zeytinburnu'nda, Avcılar, var. Ancak bunlar kampanya bazında bir araya geliyorlar. Yerel BAK'lar kendi kampanyalarını üretme, etkinlikler düzenleme konusunda serbestler.

BAK toplantılarında çoğunluk değil, uzlaşma esas alınıyor. Oylama yerine, ikna yöntemi kullanılıyor. Yıldız Önen uzlaşma sağlanmadan karar almadıklarını belirtiyor. "Bazen beş hafta aynı konuyu tartıştığımız oluyor. Beşinci haftada herkes ikna oluyor. Bazen herkesin ikna olduğu, bir kişinin karşı çıktığı şeye sonra hepimiz karşı çıkıyoruz. Yürütmede konsensüs sağlanmayan bir konuyu dışarıda tartışmamaya dikkat ediyoruz. Yürütmeden geçmeden çıkalım yapalım demiyoruz. Yürütme bir konuda karar aldı ama Kadıköy'den ya da Bursa'dan itiraz geldi diyelim, bunu da yüzde yüz dikkate alıyoruz. Bazen değiştiriyoruz, bazen iptal ediyoruz" (Kişisel görüşme, Haziran 2005).

Küresel BAK'ta üyelik yok; hareket gönüllülük esasına dayanıyor. Kuruluş metnine imza atan herkes aktivist olabiliyor. Küresel BAK, yaptıkları işi tanımlarken eski terimler yerine yenilerini kullanmayı tercih ediyorlar: "Eylemci" yerine "aktivist"i, hatta kendilerini "BAKtivist" olarak adlandırıyorlar, "temsilci", "başkan" sıfatları yerine "sözcü", "moderatör", "gönüllü"yü kullanıyorlar. Aktivist Ayşegül Önen (Kişisel Görüşme, Mayıs 2005), eski tür hareketlerde merkez komiteleri gibi kavramlar yaratılarak insanların katı kurallar ve hiyerarşik yapılar içinde hareketten soğuduğunu belirterek, Küresel BAK'ın bireysel inisiyatife olanak tanıdığını söylüyor.

Küresel BAK, bugüne kadar 10 kampanya düzenledi: Coca-Cola'nın düzenlediği Rock'n Coke'a alternatif Barışarock 2003, Irak'ta işgale son, Filistin'e özgürlük 27 Eylül 2003, 20 Mart 2004 Eylemi, Gelme Bush kampanyası (Haziran 2004), Barışarock 2004 (27-28 Ağustos 2004), Bush'a hayır (27 Eylül 2004), 19 Mart 2005 Eylemi, Bush yargılansın (4 Nisan 2005), 24 Eylül 2005 eylemi, "İncirlik kapatılsın" (18 Mart 2006).

Küresel BAK aktivistlerinin sayısını tespit etmek zor; çünkü sayı eylemin türüne göre kampanyadan kampanyaya farklılık gösteriyor.

Küresel BAK, eylemlerinde "neşeli", herkesin dikkatini çekecek ve "katılımcı" olmaya özen gösteriyor. Bu nedenle çok çeşitli bir yelpazede eylem düzenliyor: Sokak gösterileri, standlar, üniversite toplantıları, trampetlerle bildiri dağıtımı, "afişleme", bisiklet turu, basın açıklamaları, aktivist toplantıları, rock festivali, barış panayırı, imza kampanyaları, barış ormanı, resim sergileri, mektup gönderme eylemi, insan zinciri vb. eylemlerin dikkat çekici, neşeli olmasını aktivistlerin karakterine bağlayan

Oya Demirel, kendileri gibi hareket ettiklerini vurguluyor (Kişisel Görüşme, Haziran 2006).

Mali açıdan, hareket düzenli bir finansal kaynağa sahip değil. Düzenlenen kampanyalar ve etkinlikler çerçevesinde hareketin içinde yer alan kuruluşların imkanları seferber ediliyor. Bunun dışında gönüllülerden bağış toplanıyor, rozet satışlarından sınırlı bir bütçe sağlanıyor. Yıldız Önen (Kişisel görüşme, Haziran 2005),"imece" usulü bir dayanışma içinde olduklarını belirtiyor.

Hareketin İletişim Yöntemleri ve Araçları

Küresel BAK hem kendi aktivisleriyle hem de kamuoyuyla iletişimde her tür iletişim aracını seferber ediyor. Küresel BAK, birçok iletişim tekniğini ve aracını bir arada kullanıyor: Yüz yüze iletişim (sokakta imza kampanyaları, üniversitelerde aktivist kazanmak için toplantılar, mahallelerde etkinlikler düzenliyor), kitle iletişim araçları (kampanyalarını duyurmak ve kamuoyunun dikkatini Irak'ta savaşa çekmek için ünlü kişilerin öncülüğünde basın açıklamaları düzenliyor, ayrıca basında Küresel BAK etkinliklerinin duyurulması için gazetecilerle iletişim halindeler), yeni bilgi ve iletişim araçları (İnternet üzerinden yahoogroups haberleşmek için kullandıkları en düşük maliyetli ve etkin araç, ancak imza kampanyalarında imzacıların cep telefonlarını da alarak kampanya ve etkinlikleri SMS yoluyla duyuruyorlar). Kampanyaların sloganları, aktivist toplantılarında, internet üzerindeki haberleşme grubundaki tartışmalarda ve fikir alışverişlerinde belirleniyor.

Yüz yüze iletişim Küresel BAK için öncelik taşıyor. Arife Köse (Kişisel Görüşme, Mart 2005), yeni aktivistler kazanmak için yüz yüze ilişkinin gerekli olduğunu söylüyor. Sokaklarda kurulan standlar, imza kampanyaları, aktivist toplantıları, üniversitelerde, sendikalarda, işyerlerinde ve yerel BAK'larda düzenlenen toplantılar, bisiklet turları, piknikler, müzik festivalleri, konserler, barış panayırı gibi etkinliklerle yeni aktivistlerle yüz yüze ilişki kuruluyor, "örgütsüzler" savaşa karşı "örgütlenmeye çağrılıyor.

Küresel BAK aynı zamanda kitle iletişim araçlarını da kampanyalarını daha geniş kitlelere duyurmak amacıyla seferber ediyor. Basın toplantıları, ünlü kişilerin basın mensupları karşısında okuduğu metinler, basın bültenleri, basında yer alan aktivist yazıları, gazetecilerle kişisel ilişkiler hareketin kullandığı yöntemler arasında. Basın açıklamaları ve bültenleri genellikle Şenol Karakaş, Bülent Aydın ve Arife Köse tarafından kaleme alınıyor. Yıldız Önen, basın açıklamalarında Mehmet Ali Alabora, Zeynep Tanbay, Mor ve Ötesi, Mehmet Güleryüz gibi sanatçıları tercih etmelerini şöyle açıklıyor: "Bütün bu hikayedeki amacımız, kamuoyuyla irtibat kurabilmek. Kamuoyunu daha çok etkileyebileceğini düşündüğümüz, daha tarafsız duran insanları seçtik" (Kişisel görüşme, Haziran 2005).

Tahmaz (Kişisel Görüşme, Mart 2005), medyanın dikkatini çekmek için Greenpeacevari eylemler düzenlemediklerini, daha katılımcı bir eylem tarzı benimsediklerini belirtiyor. Geniş kesimleri hareket geçirmek için gösterileri kitleselleştirmeyi hedefliyorlar.

Küresel BAK tüm etkinliklerinde reklam ve halkla ilişkiler tekniklerini de seferber ediyor. Grafiker Bülent Erkmen ana kampanyaların poster, afiş, broşürlerinde yer alan görsellerin tasarımını gönüllü olarak üstleniyor. Tasarım programlarına hakim genç aktivistler de kampanyalarda kullanılan malzemelerin üretimine katkıda bulunuyorlar. Küresel BAK ayrıca sokağa yönelik ücretsiz bir bülten yayınlıyor.

Küresel BAK'ın İnterneti Kullanımı:

İnternet Sitesi:

İnternet, Küresel BAK hareketinin kurulmasında ve işleyişinde önemli bir yere sahip. İnternet üzerinden gelen uluslararası bir metin aracılığıyla kurulan hareket, kurulduğu ay içerisinde http://www.kureselbarisveadalet.org/bak/ adresinden yayına başladı. Sitenin teknik altyapısı, tasarımı ve içeriği gönüllü aktivistler tarafından hazırlanıyor. 3 Temmuz 2006 itibariyle Küresel BAK'ın internet sitesinde 354.119 ziyaretçi, 600 tane haber ve 633 üye bulunuyor.

Bülent Aydın (Kişisel Görüşme, Haziran 2005), Küresel BAK'ın internet sitesini hareketin "kartviziti" olarak tanımlayarak sitenin amacının hareketle ilgili bilgi vermek ve arşiv oluşturmak olduğunu söylüyor. Oya Demirel de internet sitesinin başlıca iki temel işlevi bulunduğunu söz ediyor: "Sitenin savaş karşıtı harekete destek olmak gibi bir amacı var. Öncelikle, insanların bizim hareketimizi görmesi gibi bir kaygımız var. Bunun dışında, ulaşabilecekleri çeşitli kitap tanıtımları, makaleler vb. sunuyoruz. Savaşla ilgili insanın aklına birşey geldiğinde savaşın yüzünü ve buna karşı birşeylerin de yapıldığını görmelerini istiyoruz" (Kişisel Görüşme, Haziran 2006).

Sitenin içeriğinde Küresel BAK'a ilişkin genel bilgiler, yerel BAK'ların sözcüleri ve irtibat numaraları, tüm kampanyalara ilişkin yapılmış olan etkinlik, basın açıklaması vb. duyuru metinleri, kampanya fotoğrafları, aktivist olmak isteyenler için üyelik seçenekleri, imza metinleri yer alıyor. Oya Demirel, internet sitesinde en son düzenlenen ya da düzenlenmekte olan kampanyanın duyurusunun en üstte yer aldığını, eyleme gelemeyenler için ise eyleme ve etkinliklere ilişkin raporları düzenli olarak yayınladıklarını belirtiyor: "Internet sitesi sayesinde insanlar, eylemlerin yapıldığını ve nasıl bir eylem olduğun görme fırsatına sahip oluyorlar. Aktivistlerin izlenimlerini koyuyoruz. Sıcak, neşeli eylemler yapıyoruz. Bunlardan haberdar oluyorlar" (Kişisel Görüşme, Haziran 2006).

İnternet sitesine konulan görsel malzemeler (etiket, afiş, animasyon vb.) ve fotoğraflar gönüllü aktivistler tarafından üretiliyor. Siteye konulan fotoğrafların seçiminde eylemleri ve etkinlikleri birebir yansıtmanın önemli olduğuna dikkat çeken Oya Demirel (Kişisel Görüşme, Haziran 2006), canlı renkler ve farklı görüntüler kullanarak siteyi daha dikkat çekici hale getirmeye çalıştıklarını belirtiyor.

Internet sitesi reklam ya da başka bir finansal gelire sahip değil. Internet sitesinde ücretsiz üyelik seçeneği yer alıyor. Siteye üye olan aktivistler aynı zamanda haberleşme grubuna da üye olmuş oluyorlar.

Küresel BAK, internet sitesini duyurmak için basılı materyeller ile interneti kullanıyorlar. Aydın (Kişisel Görüşme, Haziran 2005), Küresel BAK'ın adresi olarak tüm yazılı materyallerin altına www.kureselbarisveadalet.com adresini eklediklerini belirtiyor. Oya Demirel de diğer sitelerin Küresel BAK'a link verdiğini, bazı sanal forumlara ve haberleşme gruplarına Küresel BAK'ı tanıtıcı ve etkinlikleri duyurucu e-postalar attıklarını ekliyor (Kişisel Görüşme, Haziran 2006).

İnternet sitesinde forum olmamasını forumla ilgilenecek moderatörün bulunmamasına bağlayan Oya Demirel, forumu ciddi bir ihtiyaç olarak görmediklerini belirtiyor: "Küresel BAK, kampanyalar platformu. Ancak bir gönüllü çıkıp forum yapalım derse yapabiliriz. Amacımız savaşa karşı durmak ve başka bir konunun yer almasını da pek tercih etmiyoruz aslında. Biz Küresel BAK'ın sadece savaş karşıtlığı üzerinden kendisini ifade etmesini istiyoruz" (Kişisel Görüşme, Haziran 2006).

Yıldız Önen'e göre internet sitesine ilişkin en önemli sorun güncelleme: "Çok az kadroyla çalışmaktan kaynaklanıyor. Büronun dışında birisinin bu siteyi yapma şansı yok. Çünkü buradaki bilgileri bilmesi gerekiyor. İstanbul'dan birkaç gönüllü arkadaş oldu. Siz bize bilgileri gönderin, güncelleyelim dediler. Olmadı. Çünkü bilgiler burada merkezileşiyor ve günlük olarak değişiyor esasında. E-mail grubu bu açıdan çok daha kullanışlı. Yanlış yazıyorsun, aaa yanlış yazdım diyorsun ve bir daha gönderiyorsun. Biri cevap yazıyor. Bir etkileşim var. Web sitesinde bu yok" (Kişisel görüşme, Haziran 2005).

Aydın'a göre ise sitenin avantajı, özellikle İstanbul dışında olan ve BAK'ın ne olduğunu öğrenmek isteyenlere bilgi sağlaması (Kişisel Görüşme, Haziran 2005).

Arife Köse (Kişisel Görüşme, Mart 2005), istatistiklere göre, ziyaretçilerin siteye Google'dan Küresel BAK yazıp girenlerin birinci sırada olduğunu, ikinci sırada ise Mor ve Ötesi grubunun sitesinden geldiklerini girenler olduğunu söylüyor.

Genel bir değerlendirme yapılacak olursa hareketin İnternet sitesi, harekete ilişkin temel bilgileri içeren sayfalardan oluşuyor ve İnternet'in diğer iletişim araçlarından farklı olarak sağladığı çeşitli avantajlardan yararlanmıyor (güncellik, etkileşim, multimedia kullanımı, dil) Hareket, örgütlenmek, birey ve kurumlarla iletişim kurmak, etkinliklerini duyurmak için e-mail gruplarını tercih ediyor.

Haberleşme Grubu:

Küresel BAK'ın haberleşme grubu, Haziran 2003'te Yahoo! üzerinde barisveadalet@yahoogroups.com olarak kuruldu. 12 Haziran 2006 tarihi itibariyle kurulan grupta 2886 üye bulunuyor. Grubun moderatörlüğünü Bülent Aydın, Yıldız Önen, Şenol Karakaş, Arife Köse üstleniyorlar.

İstanbul içinde yalnızca Kadıköy BAK'ın haberleşme grubu bulunurken İstanbul dışındaki yerel BAK'ların internet üzerinde bir haberleşme grubu bulunmuyor. Oya Demirel, yerellerle haberleşirken internetin her zaman etkin olmadığını belirtiyor: "Örneğin, Adana BAK'a internet üzerinden bazen e-posta gönderiyorum. Sonra telefon açıp soruyorum e-posta size ulaştı mı diye, genellikle görmemiş oluyorlar. Yerellerde yaş ortalaması da yüksek. Yereller bizim kadar teknolojiyi yoğun biçimde kullanmıyorlar" (Kişisel Görüşme, Haziran 2006).

Küresel BAK'ı duyup da internette üye olmak isteyen yeni aktivistleri gruba kabul ettikleri gibi sokakta açılan standlarda, düzenlenen imza kampanyalarında imzacıların e-posta adreslerini onları gruba üye yapıyorlar.

Yalnızca üyelere açık olan haberleşme grubunda enformasyon, moderatörün denetiminden geçtikten sonra gruba gönderiliyor. Hangi enformasyonun gönderilip hangisinin gönderilmeyeceğine karar veren moderatörlerin kriteri ise konunun Küresel BAK'ı ilgilendirip ilgilendirmemesi. Yıldız Önen elemede tek kriter olduğunu söylüyor: "Eleme sadece BAK'la ilgili olup olmaması noktasında devreye giriyor. Onun dışında bir eleme yok. Yani bazen çok sert eleştiriler geliyor, onları da yayınlıyoruz. Her şeyin duyurusunu yapan bir e-mail grubu olmamasına çok dikkat ediyoruz" (Kişisel görüşme, Haziran 2005).

Haberleşme grubunda yer alan e-postaları konularına göre sınıflandırıldığında toplantı duyuruları, toplantı raporları, toplantıya ya da eyleme çağrı, etkinlik izlenimleri, uluslararası etkinliklere ilişkin bilgi, savaşla ve savaş karşıtlığıyla ilgili diğer haberler, basında çıkmış konuyla ilgili haberler vb. Haberleşme grubu aynı zamanda savaş karşıtlığına ilişkin "alternatif" bir gündem oluşturuyor. Savaş karşıtlığına ilişkin uluslararası metinler Türkçe'ye çevrilerek aktivistlerle paylaşılıyor. Yıldız Önen günlük olarak basın takibi yaparak Irak'ta savaşla ilgili haberleri gruba iletiyor, Küresel BAK'la ilgili basında çıkan haberleri Bülent Aydın, Arife Köse ve Yıldız Önen derleyerek gruba aktarıyorlar.

Küresel BAK'ın haberleşme grubunda, tartışmaya sınırlı olarak yer veriliyor. Moderatörler bunun nedenini ideolojik tartışmaların hareketi parçalayabilmesi, polemiğe dayalı enformasyonun haber akışını yavaşlatması olduğunu belirtiyorlar. Tartışma, daha ziyade eylemlerin örgütlenmesinde ve türünün belirlenmesinde ortaya çıkıyor. Arife Köse de katılımcılar hangi ideolojiden olursa olsun, asıl amacın Irak'taki savaşı durdurmak olduğunu söylüyor: "Karşınıza büyük bir güç var. Bu gücü durdurmanız için sizin de güç olmanız gerekiyor. Bu da küçük gruplarla mümkün değil. Birleşmeniz gerekiyor. Birleşmek içinse en asgari ortak noktayı bulmak zorundasınız. Bugün Küresel BAK içindeki unsurlar oturup ideolojik tartışmalar yapmaya başlasalar hepimiz ayrılabiliriz" (Kişisel Görüşme, Mart 2005). Oya Demirel de iki yıl öncesine kadar Küresel BAK'ın haberleşme grubunda daha fazla sayıda e-postanın yer aldığını, ancak bu konuda eleştirildiklerini söyleyerek yalnızca savaş karşıtlığına ilişkin konularla sınırladıklarını vurguluyor (Kişisel Görüşme, Haziran 2006).

Bülent Aydın (Kişisel Görüşme, Haziran 2005) haberleşme grubunun etkin işlemesinin önündeki sıkıntıları şöyle özetliyor: Öncelikle gruba katılım İstanbul merkezli bir yapı sergiliyor ve taşraya doğru gittikçe katılım düşüyor. Aydın ikinci olarak, insanların ilgi alanlarına göre birden fazla haberleşme grubuna üye olduğuna dikkat çekerek aynı mesajın gün içerisinde gruba beş kez yollanabildiği durumlardan söz ederek bilgi kirliliğine yol açtığını söylüyor. Bunun yanı sıra grup içinde söz alanların sayısı da sınırlı. Bülent Aydın haberleşme grubundaki aktivistleri şöyle sınıflandırıyor: 1-Aktif olarak izleyen ve yazışanlar var. 2- İzleyen ve çok gerekli gördüğünde yazanlar var (yarı-aktif). 3- Hiç yazmayan, ama her mesajı izleyen okurlar var. 4- Sadece dikkatini çekenlere bakan pasif izleyici. Bunların yanı sıra Aydın, teknolojik engellerin ve kısıtlamalarında grup içi iletişimi zorlaştırdığını belirtiyor. E-postalara getirilen "bouncing" uygulamasının da gruptaki üyeleri pasif kıldığını belirtiyor. "2500 üye varsa bunların 500'ü bouncing alıyor" (Kişisel Görüşme, Haziran 2005). Aydın, Yahoo! içerisindeki gruplarda yine Yahoo! e-posta adresine sahip olan üyelerin daha kolay kabul gördüğünü, Hotmail gibi rakip firmalardan e-posta adresi alanların ise haberleşmede zorlandıklarını açıklıyor. Virüslü e-postaların da kimi zaman sorun çıkardığını söyleyen Aydın, programın İngilizce olmasından ötürü Türkçe'nin kullanımında da sorun yaşabildiklerini ekliyor.

Aydın'a göre cinsiyet de haberleşme grubunu kullanımda önemli bir etkendir: "Kadın üyeler kimi zaman erkeklerin ve erkek dilinin egemen olduğu gruplarda rahatsız olarak kendi ayrı gruplarını kuruyorlar" (Kişisel Görüşme, Haziran 2005). Bülent Aydın (Kişisel Görüşme, Haziran 2005) internette kurulan ilişkilerin yüz yüze kurulan ilişkilerin yerine geçmemesi gerektiğini belirtiyor: "E-postaları başka gruplara ya da kişilere iletmek, "görevi yapmışım" hissi yaratıyor "Yarın Taksim'de basın açıklaması yapacağız" metnini, 5 grup üzerinden 10 bin kişiye yaymakla görev tamamlanmıyor. Önemli olan eyleme katılmak." Arife Köse (Kişisel Görüşme, Mart 2005) de yeni aktivistlerle önce standta tanışıp, sonra onları internetteki haberleşme grubuna dahil ettiklerini söylüyor. Köse'ye göre İnternet "sürekli aktivistler", İstanbul'da 250-300 kişilik gruptan oluşan ve her gün etkinliğe katılan aktivistler için çok da işlevsel değil: "Onlarla telefon ve cep mesajlarıyla haberleşiyoruz. internet yavaş kalıyor. İnternet, çalışıp da sadece toplantılara gelen, biraz daha geri planda duran aktivistlerle iletişim de işe yarıyor" (Kişisel Görüşme, Mart 2005).

Araştırmacının yaptığı yerinde gözlemler de internet sitesinin ve haberleşme grubunun hareketin düzenlediği kampanya ve eylemlere katılım üzerindeki etkisinin sınırlılığını ortaya koyuyor. Haberleşme grubundaki enformasyon akışında ise ağırlıklı olarak moderatörlerden üyelere doğru bilgilendirme amaçlı bir akış söz konusu. Grupta genellikle aynı üyeler söz alıyor, Küresel BAK'a ilişkin üretilen enformasyon aynı aktivistlerin kaleminden çıkıyor.

Bülent Aydın, İnternetin yeni toplumsal hareketler için en önemli bir lojistiği oluşturduğunu ama asla sokakta yüz yüze kurulan ilişkinin yerini tutmayacağını belirtiyor: "İnternetteki gücümüzü ve etkimiz artırmak için uğraşmıyoruz internetteki haberleşmeyi kullanarak sokaktaki gücümüzü ve etkimizi arttırmaya alışıyoruz" (Kişisel Görüşme, Haziran 2005).

Küresel BAK Aktivistlerinin İnterneti Kullanımı: Anket Sonuçları

Küresel BAK aktivistlerinin interneti kullanımını belirlemek üzere **www.freeonlinesurvey.com** adresi üzerinde on-line anket hazırlanarak 8 Haziran 2006'da anket formu link adresi olarak Küresel BAK'ın haberleşme grubuna gönderilmiş ve 12 Haziran 2006 itibarıyla toplam 70 aktivist ankete yanıt vermiştir.(Bkz. Ek1: Anket formu) Anket sonuçlarına göre aktivistlerin büyük çoğunluğu gençlerden oluşmaktadır: 18-25 yaş arası % 41. 4, 26-35 yaş arası % 32.9, 36-51 yaş arası % 21.4'tür. 17 yaş ve altında aktivist bulunmamaktadır.

Grafik 1: Küresel BAK aktivistlerinin yaşa göre dağılımı.

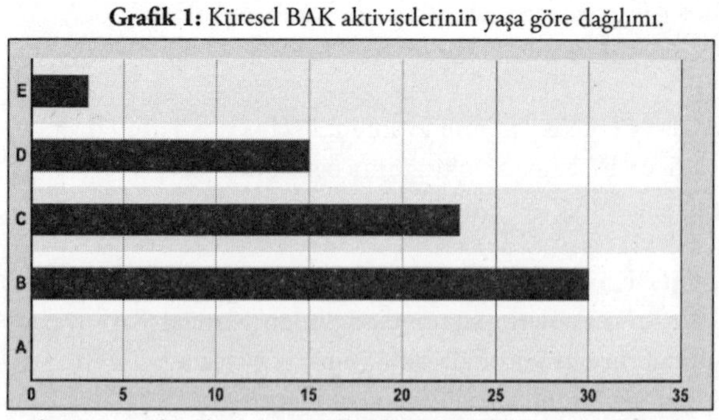

A) 17 yaş ve altı B) 18- 25 yaş C) 26- 35 yaş D) 36-50 yaş E) 50 yaş ve üstü

Aktivistlerin büyük çoğunluğu İstanbul ve büyük kentlerde yaşamaktadır. Aktivistler yaşadıkları kentlere göre sınıflandırıldığında sıralama şöyledir: İstanbul (44 aktivist), Ankara (14), İzmir (4), Mersin (1), Brüksel (1), Bursa (1), Tekirdağ (1), Aksaray (1), Çanakkale (1), Edirne(1),

Burdur (1). Aktivislerin eğitim durumu yüksektir. Aktivistlerin % 45.7'si halen öğrencidir. Aktivistlerin % 1.4'ü ilkokul, %40'ı lise, % 5.7'si yüksekokul, % 38.6'sı üniversite mezunudur. Aktivistlerin %14.3'ü lisans üstü eğitim yapmıştır.

Grafik 2: Küresel BAK aktivistlerinin eğitim durumu.

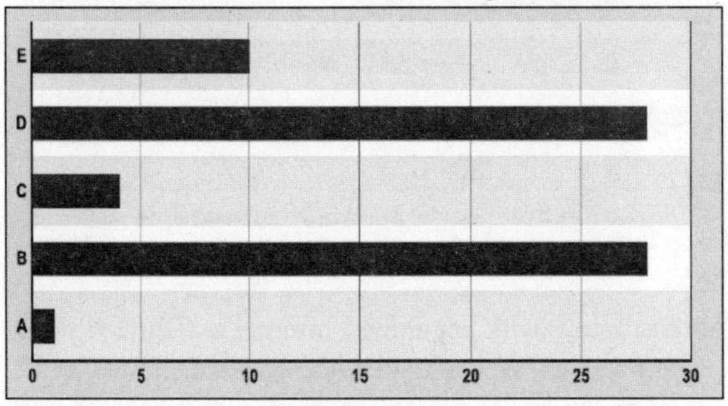

A) İlkokul B) Lise C) Yüksekokul D) Üniversite E) Yüksek Lisans-Doktora

Aktivistlerin % 61.4'ü çalışmaktadır. Aktivistlerin meslekleri şöyledir: Gazeteci (4), çevirmen (4), öğretim üyesi (4), sosyal hizmet uzmanı (1), müşteri temsilcisi (1), kitabevi yöneticisi (1), yayıncı (1), işçi (2), doktor (2), mühendis (1), mimar (1), bankacı (1), tasarımcı ve grafiker (3), muhasebeci (1), avukat (1), model (2), sendika uzmanı (1), danışman (2), işsiz (1), emlak komisyoncusu (1), bilgi işlem personeli (1). Bazı aktivistler mesleklerini belirtmemiş, çalıştıkları sektörleri belirtmişlerdir: Otomotiv (1), oyuncak imalatı (1), elektronik (1), sivil toplum (1), ticaret (1). Aktivistlerin büyük çoğunluğu İngilizce bilmektedir. Aktivistlerin bildikleri dil dağılımı şöyledir: İngilizce (% 58), Almanca (% 4.3), Fransızca (% 4.3), İspanyolca (% 1.4). Aktivistlerin bildikleri diğer yabancı diller ise şöyledir: Hollandaca (1), Osmanlıca (1), Kürtçe (1), Latince (1). Aktivistlerin % 17.4'ü hiçbir yabancı dili konuşamamaktadır.

Grafik 3: Küresel BAK aktivistlerinin bildiği yabancı diller.

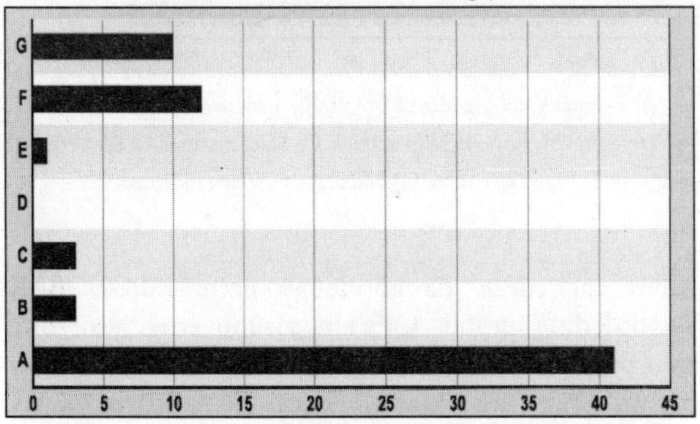

A) İngilizce B) Almanca C) Fransızca D) İtalyanca E) İspanyolca E) Hiçbiri F) Diğer

Aktivistlerin aylık ortalama kazacına ilişkin dağılım ise şöyledir: Aktivistlerin % 28.4'ü 500 milyon YTL. ve altında, % 29.9'u 500 milyon – 1 milyar YTL. arasında, % 31.3'ü 1 -2 milyar YTL., % 10.4'ü ise 2 milyar YTL'den fazla bir gelire sahiptir. Aktivistlerin büyük çoğunluğu Küresel BAK'ın kurulduğu yıldan beri faaliyetin içindedir: Aktivistlerin % 47.8'i 2003'te, % 7.2'si 2004'te, % 20.3'ü 2005'te, % 24.6'sı ise 2006'da harekete katılmıştır.

Grafik 4: Aktivistlerin Küresel BAK'la ilişkisi.

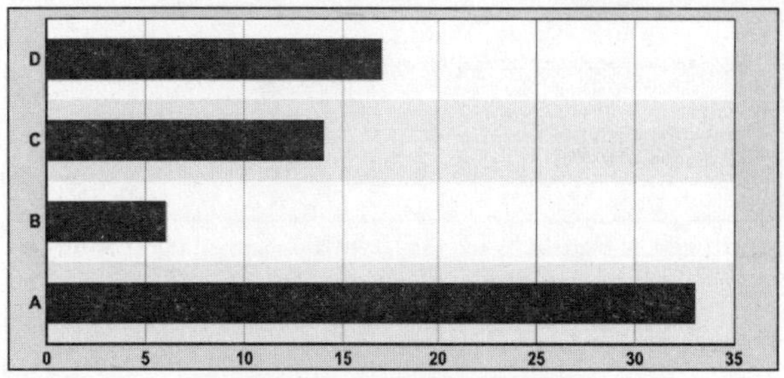

A) 2003 B) 2004 C) 2005 D) 2006

Aktivistlerin büyük bölümü Küresel BAK'tan önce de siyasi faaliyetlerde bulunmuşlardır. Aktivistlerin büyük bir bölümü (% 40) 10 yıldan fazla zamandır siyasi faaliyetlerin içerisinde yer almaktadır. Aktivistlerin % 35.7'si 0-5 yıldır, % 24.3'ü ise 5-10 yıldır siyasi faaliyetlere katılmaktadır.

Grafik 5: Aktivistlerin siyasi faaliyetlerle ilişkisi.

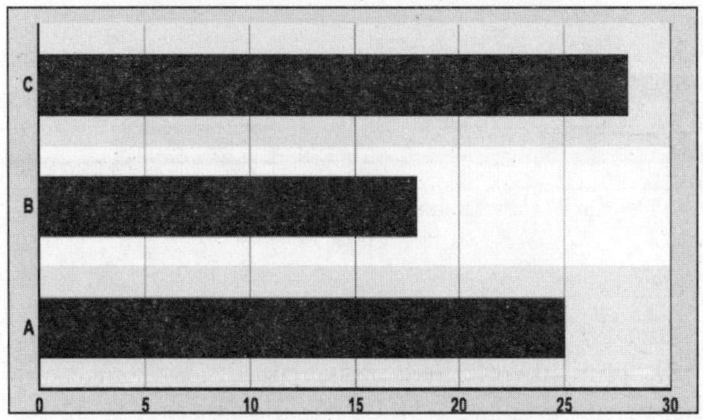

A) 0-5 yıl B) 5-10 yıl C) 10 yıldan fazla

Aktivistlerin "Küresel BAK'ı nereden duydunuz?" sorusuna verdikleri yanıtlar ise şöyledir: Arkadaşlarımdan (%13), ailemden (%2.9), İnternetten (% 11), sokaktaki imza kampanyasından (% 8.7), gazete haberlerinden (% 10.1), televizyon haberlerinden (% 1.4), sokak gösterilerinden (%11.6). 19 aktivist ise hareketi kimseden duymadıklarını, zaten kuruluşunda yer aldıklarını ifade etmiştir. 2 aktivist okulda düzenlenen panelde, 2 aktivist Barışarock etkinliği sırasında Küresel BAK'ı tanıdıklarını belirtmiştir. Aktivistlerin Küresel BAK'ın etkinliklerine katılım oranı düşüktür: % 11.4'ü her gün katılırken, % 30'u haftada birkaç gün, % 11.4'ü ayda birkaç kez, % 34.3'ü ise yılda birkaç gün etkinliklere katıldıklarını dile getirmişlerdir.

Grafik 6: Aktivistlerin Küresel BAK etkinliklerine ayırdıkları zaman.

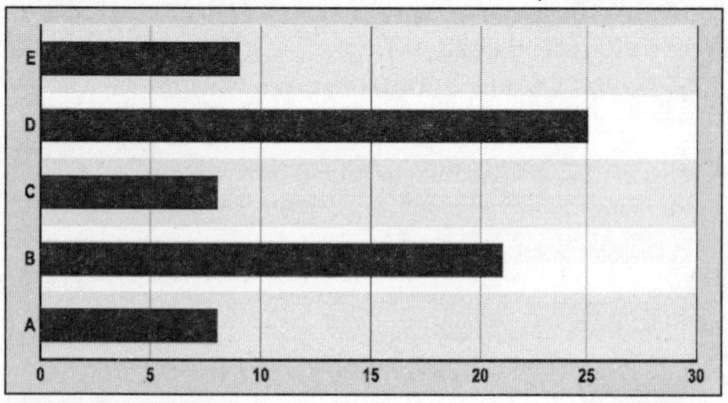

A) Her gün B) Haftada birkaç gün C) Ayda birkaç gün D) Yılda bir-iki defa E) Diğer

Aktivistlerin büyük çoğunluğu haberleşme grubundan gelen e-postaları her gün okumaktadır: Küresel BAK e-postalarını % 75'i her gün okumakta, % 17.1'i haftada birkaç kez okumakta, % 1.4'ü ayda birkaç kez okumaktadır. Aktivistlerin % 5.7'si nadiren okumaktadır.

Grafik 7: Aktivistlerin Küresel BAK e-maillerini okuma sıklığı.

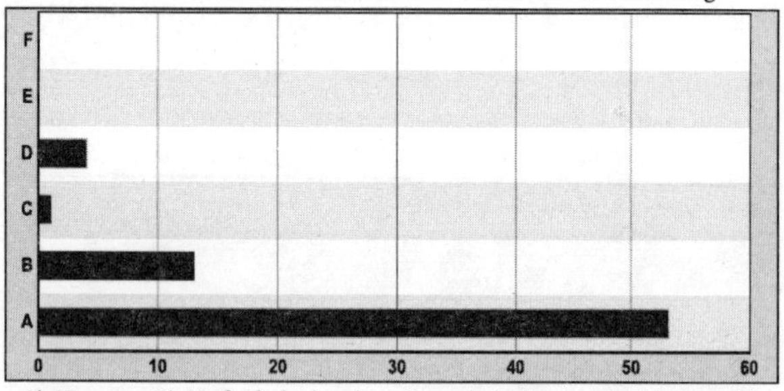

A) Her gün B) Haftada birkaç kez C) Ayda birkaç kez D) Nadiren E) Hiç

Aktivistler Küresel BAK'tan kendilerine genel e-postaları başka gruplarla ve kişilerle paylaşmaktadır: % 40.6'sı başka haberleşme gruplarına, % 1.6'sı iş arkadaşlarına, % 42.2'si yakın arkadaşlarına göndermektedir. Aktivistlerin Küresel BAK'ın internet sitesini ziyaret etme sıklığı ise şöyledir: % 5.9'u her gün, % 36.8'i haftada birkaç gün, % 29.4'ü ayda birkaç kez, % 25'i nadiren, % 2.9'u ise hiç ziyaret etmediğini bildirmiştir. Aktivistler 10 yıldır İnternet kullanıcısıdır: % 19.1'i 0-5 yıldır, % 20.6'sı 3-5 yıldır, % 47.1'i 5-10 yıldır, % 13.7'si 10 yıldan fazla bir zamandır İnternet kullanıcısıdır.

Grafik 8: Küresel BAK aktivistlerinin internet geçmişi.

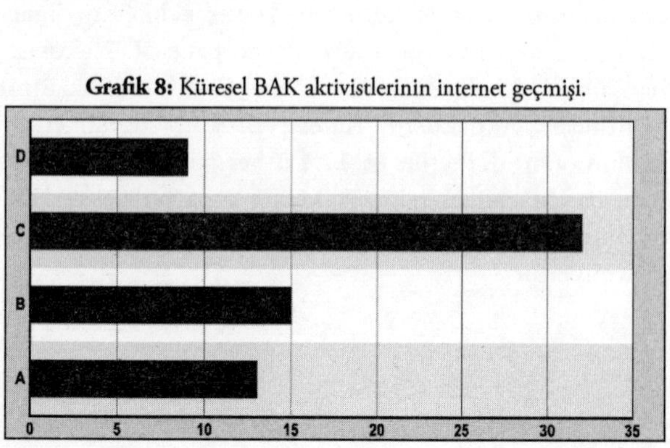

A) 0-3 yıl B) 3-5 yıl C) 5-10 yıl D) 10 yıldan fazla

Grafik 9: Küresel BAK aktivistlerinin günlük ortalama internet kullanımı.

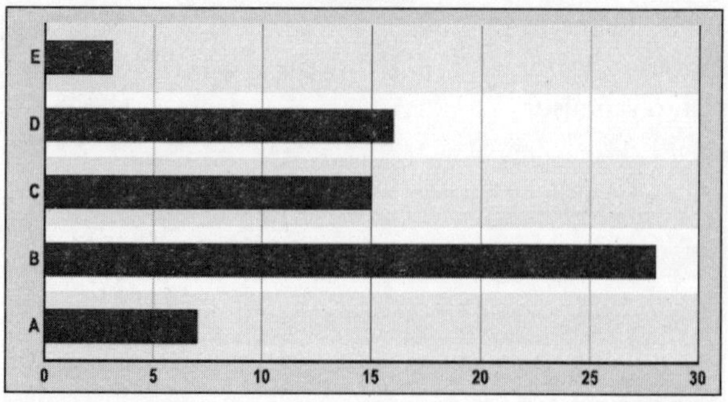

A) 1 saatten az B) 1-3 saat C) 3-5 saat D) 5-10 saat E) 10 saatten az

Aktivistlerin büyük çoğunluğu internet kullanmayı yakın çervesinden ya da kendi kendine öğrenmiştir: % 34.8'i arkadaşlarından, % 15.9'u işyerinde, % 14.5'i okulda, % 7.2'si ailesinden, % 1.4'ü kursta İnternet kullanmayı öğrenmiştir. 16 aktivist İnterneti kendi kendine öğrendiklerini dile getirmiştir. Aktivistlerin büyük çoğunluğunun evinde İnternet bağlantısı mevcuttur: % 49.3'ü evden, % 40.6'sı işyerinden, % 2.9'u okuldan İnternete bağlanmaktadır. Aktivistler İnterneti en çok e-posta gönderip almak amacıyla kullanmaktadır. Aktivistlerin İnternet kullanım amacı şöyledir: E-posta gönderip almak (% 47.8), günlük haberleri takip etmek (%13), herhangi bir konuda bilgi aramak (%15.9), sohbet etmek (% 2.9).

Grafik 10: Küresel BAK aktivistlerinin interneti kullanım amaçları.

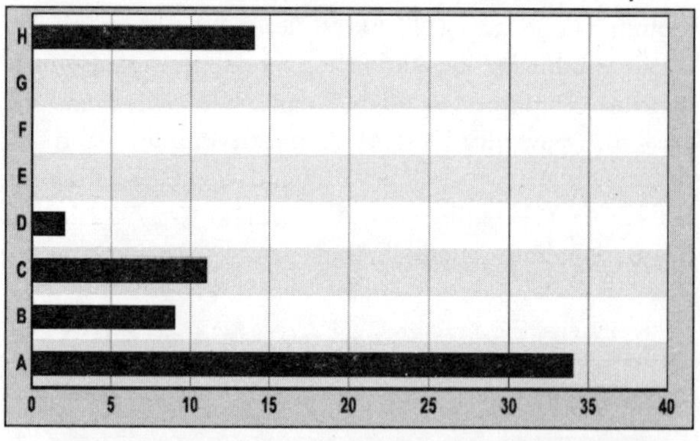

A) E-posta gönderip almak B) Günlük haberleri takip etmek C) Herhangi bir konuda bilgi aramak D) Sohbet etmek E) Alışveriş yapmak F) Oyun oynamak G) Müzik, film, video indirmek H) Diğer

Anket sonucunda da görüldüğü üzere Küresel BAK aktivistlerinin profili, Offe'nin sözünü ettiği yeni orta sınıf profiline uygun gözükmektedir. Hareket; genç (18-35 yaş grubu ağırlıktadır), kentli (aktivistlerin büyük çoğunluğu üç büyük kentte, İstanbul, Ankara ve İzmir'de yaşamaktadır), yüksek düzeyde eğitime sahip, hizmet sektöründe çalışan, İngilizce bilen, aylık kazancı ortalama olan, interneti uzun zamandır kullanan aktivistlerden oluşmaktadır.

Aktivistlerin büyük çoğunluğunun Küresel BAK'tan

önce de uzunca bir zaman siyasi faaliyetlerin içerisinde bulunması hareketin eski hareketlerin unsurlarını da barındırmasına ve toplumsal hareketin sürekliliğine bir işarettir.

Küresel BAK'ın kitleselleşmesinde internetin rolü olmakla birlikte aktivistler hareketten ağırlıklı olarak yakın çevrelerinden, diğer kitle iletişim araçların ve sokak gösterilerinden duyarak haberdar olmuşlardır. Bu da internetin sınırlı etkiye sahip olduğunu göstermektedir.

Haberleşme grubu aktivistlerin en sık kullandığı araçtır. Kendilerine gelen haberleri sıklıkla takip etmekte ve yakın çevreleriyle paylaşmaktadırlar. İnternet sitesini ise daha az kullanmaktadırlar. Ancak haberleşme grubundaki hareketliliğe karşın aktivistlerin Küresel BAK'ın eylemlerine ayırdığı zaman sınırlıdır. İnternet kullanımı ile eyleme katılım paralellik göstermemektedir.

Sonuç

Teknolojinin kamusal alanı canlandırma tezi internetin yeni toplumsal hareketler tarafından kullanımıyla birlikte ele alındığında sınırlılıklar göstermektedir. Küresel BAK örneğinde de görüldüğü gibi internetin birinci sınırı toplumsal kullanımından kaynaklanmaktadır. Fiziksel ortamda alt-orta-üst olmak üzere çeşitli sınıfları biraraya getiren, farklı ideolojileri buluşturan, bireysel ve kollektif katılımlara olanak tanıyan, çeşitliliğe ve farklılığa vurgu yapan bir hareket olan Küresel BAK'ın internet üzerindeki kullanımı ve görünümü anket çalışmasının sonucunda da görüldüğü gibi belirli bir kesimle sınırlanmakta, sayısal uçurum olgusunun bu alanda da geçerli olduğu doğrulanmaktadır. Kentli, eğitimli, genç, İngilizce bilen aktivistler internete daha kolay erişirken yerel BAK'ların interneti etkin olarak kullanamadığı ortaya çıkmıştır.

İkinci olarak, hareketin kamusal alan yaratma yeteneği enformasyonun üretimi ve denetimi tarafından sınırlanmaktadır. Küresel BAK, internet sitesi ve haberleşme grubunda savaş karşıtı harekete ilişkin haberlere, etkinliklere, toplantılara, görüşlere, izlenimlere vb. yer vererek internet kullanıcıları için savaş karşıtı bir kamuoyu, bir "alternatif medya" yaratma işlevini yerine getirmektedir. Ancak, internete erişim sınırlı olduğu gibi, internet üzerinde yer alan harekete ilişkin enformasyonun üretimi ve akışında da merkezileşme gözlenmiştir. öncelikle harekete ilişkin enformasyonun üretimi ve akışı hareketin başından bu yana içinde yer alan "kurucu aktivistler" tarafından sağlanmaktadır. Küresel BAK'ın haberleşme grubunda ve internet sitesinde bireysel, kollektif ya da kurumsal enformasyonlara yer verilmekle birlikte kampanyalara, etkinliklere, toplantılara ilişkin notların, metinlerin ve görüntülerin üretiminin ağırlıklı olarak Beyoğlu ve Kadıköy Bürosu aktivistleri tarafından sağlandığı tespit edilmiştir. Ayrıca anakampanyalara ilişkin materyeller İstanbul'da hazırlanmakta ve buradan yerel BAK'lara ve diğer bileşenlere dağıtılmaktadır. Yine, Yürütme Kurulu toplantıları ve Genel Aktivist toplantıları Beyoğlu BAK bürosunda gerçekleştirilmekte ve kararlar burada alınmaktadır. Bu açıdan Internet, mekansal engelleri sınırlı olarak aşmakta, siyasi katılım coğrafi konumla bağlı kalmaktadır.

Hareketin küreselleşmesinde internet önemli rol oynamaktadır. Yurtdışındaki hareketlerle internet aracılığıyla haberleşilmekte, savaş karşıtı hareketlere ilişkin duyuru, eylem, etkinlik bildirileri Türkçe'ye çevrilerek haberleşme grubu üzerinden aktivistlere gönderilmektedir. Ancak, internet sitesinin İngilizce versiyonunun yetersiz kalması hareketin yurtdışındaki aktivistler tarafıdnan takibini zorlaştırmaktadır.

Diğer yandan kamusal alanın bir diğer özelliği olan rasyonel müzakere sürecinin internette sınırlı kaldığı ortaya çıkmıştır. Kampanyalara ilişkin karar alma ve harekete katılımda internetten ziyade yüz yüze iletişim ve diyalog yoluyla ikna gibi yöntemler tercih edilmektedir.

Kaynakça:

Çayır, K. (Der.). (1999). *Yeni sosyal hareketler*. İstanbul: Kaktüs.

Guedes, O. (2002). New technologies, democracy and social movement. *Globalism and Pluralism Conference* (24 April 2002), Montreal: GRICIS.

Habermas, J. (1997). *Kamusallığın yapısal dönüşümü*. T. Bora ve M.Sancar (Çev.). İstanbul: İletişim.

Johnston, H., Larana, E. ve Gusfield, J. R. (1994). Identities, grievances, and new social movements. *New social movements*. Philadelphia: Temple University.

Leon, O., Burch, S. ve Tamayo, E. (2001). Social movements on the Net. *ALAI*, http://alainet.org/publicamsred/en/chapter2.html (son erişim 30 Haziran 2004).

Langman, L. ve Morris, D. Internet mediation: A theory of alternative globalization movements. http://www.csudh.edu/dearhabermas/langmanbk01.htm (Son erişim 25 Aralık 2005).

12 Eylül Filmlerini Yeniden Düşünmek: Toplumsal Travmadan Toplumsal Hicve

Hakan Erkılıç
Radyo Sinema ve Televizyon Bölümü
İletişim Fakültesi
Mersin Üniversitesi
ehakan@mersin.edu.tr

Giriş

12 Eylül 1980 üzerinden 27 yıl geçmiş. 12 Eylül yeniden ve farklı bakış açıları ele alınmayı hak ediyor; çünkü bugünkü siyasal ve toplumsal sorunlarımızı konuşurken hala 12 Eylül'e göndermede bulunuyoruz. Benim açımdan, bu bildiri, 1997 yılında tamamladığım "Sinema ve İdeoloji: 12 Eylül Filmlerinin Toplumsal Çözümlemesi" adlı yüksek lisans tezime yeniden bakma olanağı veriyor. Bu bildirinin temel zeminini de bu tez oluşturuyor. 1997 yılı itibariyle 25 film saptamışım. Bugün 12 Eylül'le ilgili olarak 34 filme ulaşmışız. Filmlerde görülen dramdan komediye/hicve geçiş bildirinin tartışma konusu. Belki de sonuçta söylenebilecek olan saptamayı şimdi söyleyebilirim: Türk sinemasının 12 Eylül üzerine yaptığı filmler, ister beğenilsin isterse eleştirilsin, dönem itibari ile 12 Eylül'e ilk yüzleşmenin sinema üzerinden gerçekleştirildiğini söylemek çok iddialı olmasa gerek. Diğer kültürel temsiller ve bilimsel çalışmalar göz önüne alındığında bu saptama açıkça görünecektir. Bir diğer önemli değişimde 12 Eylül'le ilgili olarak yapılan akademik ve bilimsel çalışmalarda "yakın tarih üzerine yazmanın" zorluklarını belirtilerek, çoğunlukla siyaset bilimi çerçevesinde toplanırken; 25 yıl sonraki değerlendirmelerde psikiyatriden hareketle değerlendirmelerin arttığı ileri sürülebilir. Bu bildiride de "seçilmiş travma" kavramından hareketle 12 Eylül değerlendirilecek ve toplumsal bir yüzleşmenin yapılmadığı, dönemle ilgili olarak gündelik hayatta yüzleşmekten kaçtığımız şeyi, bir kültürel temsil olarak sinema yapabilir mi? yaptı mı? sorularının yanıtı aranacaktır.

1.Pretoryenizm: 12 Eylül 1980, Askeri Darbe

12 Eylül 1980, ülkenin iç savaşa sürüklendiği ortamda, Türk Silahlı Kuvvetleri'nin kendi iç hizmet kanuna dayanarak emir-komuta zinciri içinde "Türkiye Cumhuriyeti'ni koruma ve kollama" adı altında sivil demokratik yönetime el koymasıdır. Bu askeri darbe, Türkiye tarihinde yeni bir dönemin başlangıcıdır. Siyasal bilimlerde, "askerlerin toplumumda güç kullanımı veya tehdidi ile bağımsız bir siyasal güç haline gelmeleri" pretoryenizm olarak adlandırılır (Örs, 1996, s. 7). 12 Eylül 1980 darbesi, askerlerin üçüncü kez yönetime müdahalesi olarak görülür.

On yıllık darbelerin meşrulaştığı Türkiye'de 70'lı yıllar, düşünce akımlarının hem entelektüel düzeyde hem de sokakta şiddet/terör düzeyinde çarpıştığı bir arenaya sahne olur. İki kutuplu dünyanın soğuk savaş çatışmasını Türkiye terör bağlamında yaşar. Hale (1996, s. 200), özellikle 78-79 yıllarını değerlendirirken teröre dikkat çekerek, "terörün akıttığı kan sürekli artmaya devam ederken, devlet iktidarı yok olmanın eşiğinde gibiydi" saptamasında bulunur. Bu durum darbeyi meşru kılmak için uygun bir zemin oluşturur.12 Eylül öncesi Türkiye'deki durum şu ana başlıklar altında toplanabilir: siyasal kutuplaşma; parlamentoda uzlaşmaz tavır; sokakta terör olaylarının hakimiyeti; can ve mal güvenliğinin yitimi; yanlı MC hükümetleri; ekonomik dar boğaz, petrol krizi;yokluklar, kuyruklar, karaborsa; mezhep çatışmaları; demokratik yapıda iktidarsızlık ve tıkanma; iç savaş görüntüsü; 1979-1980 yılları içinde 5241 kişi terörün kurbanı olarak öldürülürken, 14512 kişi de yaralanmıştır (Kongar, 1995; Hale, 1996; Zürcher, 1995). 12 Eylül darbesini etkileyen dış dinamikler de vardır. NATO'nun yeşil kuşak projesi, 24 Ocak karaları ile Türkiye'nin dünya liberal ekonomisine eklemlenmesi, Yunanistan'ın NATO'ya yeniden kabulü gibi (Parla, 1995).

12 Eylül'ün diğer iki askeri darbeden farkı nedir? 27 Mayıs ve 12 Mart ile 12 Eylül darbesini karşılaştıran Hale (1996), "12 Eylül'ün daha muhafazakar amaçları"

olduğunu belirtir (s. 201). 1960'larda ve 1970'lerde gelişen toplumsal dinamiğe karşın kendini geliştiremeyen devlet, 12 Eylül darbesi ile demokratikleşmeye ket vurur. Batıcılık geleneğini yalnızca ekonomik ve teknolojik ilerleme olarak alan 12 Eylül, Atatürkçülük adı altında militarist, milliyetçi, tek tip toplumu kendine özgü otoriter bir yapı ile gerçekleştirmeye çalışır (Belge, 1992; Kentel, 1990). Toplumsal değişme kuramları açısından 12 Eylül'ü değerlendiren Kongar (1993, 1995), "değişme olayını simgelediğini ve bunun büyük değişme döneminin ikinci aşaması olan iktidarı ele geçirmeye" karşılık geldiğini belirtir. Belge (1992), "12 Eylül neydi?" diye sorar ve şöyle yanıtlar: "her şeyden önce genel bir baskı dönemiydi.1950'den, yani tek parti döneminin kapanmasından bu yana, askeri müdahale zamanları da dahil olmak üzere bu toplumun karşılaştığı en ağır baskı dönemiydi" (s. 9).

12 Eylül döneminin bilançosunu çıkartmak, darbeyi özetlemek için bir çıkış yolu olabilir: "650 bin kişi gözaltına alındı.1 milyon kişi fişlendi. 230 bin kişi yargılandı. 76 bin kişi için idam cezası istendi. 49 kişi asıldı. 98 bin 404 kişi örgüt üyesi olmak suçundan yargılandı. 14 bin kişi vatandaşlıktan çıkartıldı. 388 bin kişiye pasaport verilmedi. 644 cezaevindeki tutuklu sayısı 52 bin. 14 kişi açlık grevinde öldü. Gözaltında ve hapishanede toplam ölü sayısı 229. İHD verilerine göre işkence sonucu öldürülenler 171. İşkence yaptıkları gerekçesiyle yargılanan güvenlik görevlilerinin sayısı 962. Basına, sinemaya, üniversiteye yasaklar getirildi (Teztel ve Topçu, 1991; Yaşa, 1990).

12 Eylül işkence, yasaklar ve baskının oluşturduğu bir karabasan dönemidir. Bu baskı ve yasak ortamı hazırlanan 1982 Anayasası ile de pekiştirilince, ortaya darbe sonrası sivil yönetimlerce de uygulanan, 12 Eylül'ün temel kalıtı olan de-politizaasyon çıkıyor. Depolitizasyon, toplumsalla ilgili her şeyin reddi üzerine yapılanarak 12 Eylül'ün temel amaçlarını "yurttaşın edilginleştirilmesi, düzen ve uyum içinde kalma tercihini önde tutması, başkalarının sorunlarına fazla ilgi göstermemesi, sendika gibi örgütlerin etkisizleştirilmesini" (Belge, 1996, s. 830) gerçekleştirir. 12 Eylül'ü yalnızca 80-83 arası askeri yönetim zamanıyla sınırlı tutulamaz. 80 yıllar, 12 Eylül ile özdeşleşti.

Depolitizasyonla birlikte toplumsalın reddi, küresel bir eğilim olarak bireycilikle örtüşür. Türkiye demokratikleşme, insan hakları gibi temel konularda dünyadan uzaklaşırken; bireyselleşme, ekonomik liberalizm bağlamında dünyayla bütünleşmeye çalışır. Darbe öncesi, Türkiye iki kutuplu dünyanın yansıması olarak ideolojik çarpışmalara sahne olurken; darbe sonrası dünyanın tek kutuplu çekiminde "yeni zamanlar"la tanışır. Yeni zamanların dünyadaki aktörü Thatcher oldu. Thatcherizmi, yeni dünyayı kendisi için ideolojik (sosyalizm öldü, piyasa her şeyi belirler), maddi (politika ve uygulamalarla dünyaya Thatcher'cı bir yön, şekil verme) ve kültürel (yeni bir girişimci kültürü yürürlüğe koyma çabası) olarak değerlendirmek mümkündür (Hall ve Jacques, 1995, s. 20). Darbelerin yeni zamanlara ihtiyaç duyduğu, Şilili yönetmen Miguel Littin'in serüveninde de açıkça görülür. Pinochet darbesinden sonra, adı ülkeye girmesi yasaklananlar listesinde olan Littin, kimlik ve kılık değiştirerek gizlice ülkesine döner.Gizlice Pinochet darbesinin toplumdaki izlerinin filmini yapmaya başlar.Ama geldiğinde her şeyi değişmiş bulur.havaalanı, yollar, kent merkezi, alış-veriş yerleri..Yaratılan bu albenili dünyanın özelliğini Littin şöyle vurgular: *"kentin merkezine yaklaşırken, öldürülen ya da ortadan yok olan onbinlerce kişiyle sürgüne gönderilen yüzbinlerce kişinin kanlarını bu maddi görkemle silmek isteyen diktatörlük rejiminin yapıtlarına hayranlıkla bakmaktan vazgeçtim"* (Marguez, 1996, s. 32). Türkiye'deki darbe süreçleri ile Güney Amerika'daki darbeler arasında benzerlikler gözlenir (Keyder, 1995).

Yeni zamanların Türkiye'deki aktörü Özal oldu. Askeri yönetimin iktidara gelmesini istemediği fakat 24 Ocak ekonomik kararlarını uyguluttığı Özal, darbenin devamı gibi depolitizasyon ortamını sürdürerek, tıpkı Littin'in vurguladığı gibi "yaratılan maddi görkemle", askeri darbenin izlerini unutturmaya çalışır. Türkiye iki ayrı dünyayı aynı anda yaşamaya başlar: içerdekiler ve dışarıdakiler; unutturulmak istenen geçmiş ve yeni bir yaşam vaat eden bu an. Türkiye dünya ekonomisine eklemlenirken bu anı ve vaad ettiklerini tercih etti. Böylece tüketim toplumunu "cilalı imaj devri" (Kozanoğlu, 1993) olarak "vitrinde yaşama"ya (Gürbilek, 1993) başladı. Bu süreç, 12 Eylül'ü bütün 80'li yıllara taşır. 12 Eylül, bir toplumsal ve tarihsel travma olarak tarihimizdeki yerini alır.

2.Seçilmiş Travma: Yas Tut/ama/ma ve Yüzleş/eme/me

Darbeden demokratik sivil ortama geçiş dönemi, sivil yönetimlerin askeri yönetimle örtüşen siyasaları ile süreklilik aldı. Türkiye sanki sonlanmayan bir geçiş sürecine girdi. Can güvenliği ile darbeye sahip çıkan toplum, 1983 seçimlerinde askeri yönetimin istemediği ANAP'ı iktidara taşıyarak değişim isteği gösterdiyse de, 12 Eylül ile hesaplaşmakta istemsiz, çekinik kaldı. *"12 Eylül son analizde, toplumu yüzleşmeye (conformation) çağırdı. Sakin bir yüzleşme, karşılaşma olamazdı bu. Sert geçmesi kaçınılmazdı. Biz toplum olarak, bu çağrıyı işitmezlikten geldik... 12 Eylül oldu ve uzun süreli etkileri yaşıyor, öyleyse bu toplumda böyle bir olayı mümkün kılan bir potansiyel var"* (Belge, 1992, ss. 15-25). Belge'nin saptaması iki olgu hakkında düşünmemizi sağlıyor: yüzleşme ve potansiyel. Bu toplumunda böyle bir olayı mümkün kılan potansiyeli nerede aramalıyız? Otoriteye bağlı, sadık toplum yapımımızda mı? yoksa bu yapıyı oluşturan kamu bilincinde mi? Potansiyeli oluşturan dinamikleri çözümlediğimiz noktada yüzleşmeye dair yanıtlar da bulabiliriz. Bu bildiri çerçevesinde yukarıdaki soruları, bütün yönleriyle çözümlemek olası değildir. Ancak bildiri çerçevesi içinde bize yol gösterebilecek bazı noktalara değinebiliriz. Farklı bir bağlamda Türk bireyini tartışan Ergun'un (1991), Türk toplum yapısına yönelik saptamaları bize ipuçları verebilir.

Ergun (1991), her şeyi devletten bekleyen bir toplum ile toplumun kendiliğinden bir şey yapmasına izin vermeyen devlet ilişkisine dikkat çekerek ailelerdeki çocuk sevgisinin aynı zamanda fazla denetim, engellemeye neden olduğunu belirterek bireyin gelişememesine açıklamaktadır (s. 174). Toplumun bu genel yapısı, siyaset biliminde, zayıf siyasal kültür düzeyi, siyasal kurumlara bağlılık düzeyinin düşük olması, sivil toplumun gelişmemiş olması, örgütlenmenin yasak olması ya da böyle bir geleneğin gelişmemiş olması ile açıklanmaktadır (Örs, 1996, s. 48). Böyle bir yapı, devletin kurucu unsuru olarak kendini konumlandıran ordunun, siyasal bunalımları, işlemez hale gelen siyasal sistemi ve can güvenliğini sağlamak amacıyla müdahalede bulunmasını olanaklı kıldı.

25 yıl sonra 12 Eylül'ü, yeniden değerlendiren Gürbilek, 80'li yılları, 12 Eylül'le sınırlamadan, birbirinden farklı durumların bir arada yaşandığı, yaşayanlar için de yaşamayanlar için de ağır bir dönem, travma olarak değerlendiriyor (Evren ve Usta, 2005, s. 26). Laçiner ise "ben artık ergenim" diyen, annesini ve özellikle babasını dinlemeyen çocuğun cezalandırılması biçiminde, 12 Eylül'ün de toplumu cezalandırdığını ileri sürüyor: *"Bu sefer onun eskiden sahip olduğu hakları, mesela evinin avlusunda oynayabilmesini bile yasakladı. Ve suçluluk hali içinde olan, başaramamış ve bütün bu eylemin sonucunda kendine karşı güvenini önemli ölçüde yitirmiş bir topluma karşı ceza vermek isteyen bir babanın sevgisizliği ve hırsıyla yaklaştı... Ayrıca bütün bu özgüvenini yitirmiş, olumsuz ve kendisiyle iftihar edemediği için bir deney yaşamış olmanın utancı ve baş ezikliği içinde olan topluma da bu durumu kalıcı ve sürekli kılabilecek olan bir toplumsal düzenleme modeli ve anlayışı getirdi"* (Kızıltuğ, 2005, s. 17). Benzer şekilde Kaptanoğlu da (2005), 12 Eylül'ü travma olarak açıklarken (ss. 71-77), darbeden en çok etkilenen Türkiye solu için, anlamını şöyle açıklıyor. *"Türkiye solu için 12 Eylül darbesini travmatik kılan temel etken, balkona kilitlenirken, yan odadaki toplumun, halkın, 'büyük insanlığın', 'sınıfın' koynundan çıkıp gelen devletin verdiği cezayı, sessizce onaylamasıdır"*(s. 73).

Travma olgusu, toplumsal travma ya da tarihsel travma olarak darbeden 25 yıl sonraki değerlendirmelerde yerini aldı. Bu açıdan kavramı açıklamak olgunun anlaşılmasını kolaylaştıracaktır. *"Travma kavramının sosyal teorideki kullanılmasında dikkat çeken ilk husus, kavramın tıp ve psikiyatride karşılık geldiği zedelenmenin, örselenmenin, yırtılmanın aynen korunmasıdır. Tıpta, sözgelimi bir kasın kasılmasının maruz kaldığı bu duruma, psikiyatride bireyin zihinsel tasavvurları, bellek içeriği vb. maruz kalmaktadır. Sosyoloji de ise travmaya kalan kollektivitenin mensuplarının paylaştıkları, ellerinin altında olduğunu düşündükleri, gündelik rutinlerini ve hatta geleceğe ilişkin umut ve beklentileri üzerine dayandıkları, onlar için 'elde var bir' olan hayat dünyasıdır"* (Çelebi, 2002, s. 345). Bu tanımsal çerçeve içerisinde, 12 Eylül'ü bir travma olarak değerlendirebiliriz. Türkiye toplumu için tarihsel, toplumsal ve kültürel bir travmadır.

Bu travma ile yüzleşme nasıl olacaktır? Ya da neden olamamaktadır? Bu soruların siyasal, kültürel, ideolojik açıklamaları olmakla birlikte, psikiyatriden ödünç bir kavramla da açıklamalar geliştirilebilir; seçilmiş travma. Seçilmiş travma, *"bir grubun üyelerinde başka bir grubun üyeleri tarafından aşağılanmışlık ve mağdur edilmişlik şeklinde yoğun duygular uyandıran bir olay"* anlamında kullanılıyor (Volkan ve Itzkowitz, 2002, s. 20). Volkan ve Itzkowitz'e göre (2002) *"bir grup mağdur edilmeyi ve buna bağlı olarak benlik değerini yitirmeyi 'seçmez', ne var ki olayı psikolojize ve mitolojize etmeyi -sürekli bu konuda kafa yormayı- seçer* (s. 20). Seçilmiş travma, *"basit bir anıdan fazlasını anlatır; felaket olayın paylaşılan bir zihinsel tasarımıdır; gerçekçi bilgi, fantezi beklentiler, yoğun duygular ve kabul edilemez düşüncelere karşı savunmaları içerir"* (Volkan, 1999, s. 63). Volkan'a (1999) göre bireyler gibi toplumlarda yas tutmaktadır (s. 51). Seçilmiş travma kavramı, toplum için önemli travmatik bir olayın yasını tutma durumunu ifade etmektedir. Önemli bir travmatik, örseleyici olay, toplumun bir grubunu etkilediği zaman, bütün grupta yas kolektif bir süreç olur. Böyle bir grup, tam olarak yas tutamazsa, travmatik yaşantıyı sürdürürse, küçük düşme hislerini, utancı, mağduriyeti uzlaştırmada başarılı olamazsa, olayın yası tutuluncaya kadar seçilmiş travma varlığını sürdürür. Yas tutma önlenmişse, yas tutma bir tür ruhsal çöküntüye neden olur; yas tutma sürekli hale gelebilir. Kişi, toplum yasını tuttuğu olayı sürekli yaşamaya devam eder (Volkan, 1999, ss. 49-64). Seçilmiş travmadan kurtulmanın yolu, olayın yasını tutma, yası tamamlama ile mümkün görünmektedir. Freud, yası, kayıp veya değişikliğin başladığı zorunlu bir insan tepkisi olarak tanımlamaktadır. Olayın etkisine bağımlı olarak, toplum ortak bir yas görevini yerine getirmek (yeni törenler, yasal işlemler, sanat ve şarkılarda olayın anısını yeniden canlandırmak) için yollar bulacaktır (Volkan ve Itzkowitz, 2002, s. 219). *"Yas tutma işini bitirdiğimizde, yeni projeler yapmamız ya da yeni arkadaşlıklar geliştirme olarak ifade edilebilen yeni bir enerji kaynağı ve uyum sağlayıcı bir serbestiyet buluruz"* (Pollock, aktaran Volkan, 1999, s. 49). Travmanın etkilerini, şaka ve uzaklaşma yöntemleri ile ele almak mümkündür (Volkan, 1999, ss. 52-59). Psikolojik açıdan şakalar, grup yasının başlangıcını ifade etmektedir. Şaka, gülme yoluyla üzüntüyü hafifletir ve bu yolla olayın gerçeğini kabul edilmesini sağlar. Volkan, Challenger felaketi ve Meksika depremi sonrası yapılan şakaları grup yasının başlangıcı olarak değerlendirir. Doğanın yol açtıklarının aksine, politik ve askeri açıdan küçük düşürücü felaketlerin yasını tutmak daha güçtür (Volkan ve Itzkowitz, 2002, s. 21). Travmanın etkilerini ele almanın diğer bir yöntemi kendini ondan uzaklaştırmaktır: Bazen bir gruptaki travmadan doğrudan etkilenmeyenler, onu yaşayanlardan kaçarlar (Volkan, 1999, s. 59). Seçilmiş bir travma için yas tutamamak o grubun toplumsal ve politik ideolojilerini etkiler (Volkan ve Itzkowitz, 2002, s. 22).

Bu teorik çerçeveyi, 12 Eylül'e uyguladığımız da ne görüyoruz? 12 Eylül, Türkiye toplumu için seçilmiş travmadır. Toplumun bütününü etkilediği gibi toplum içindeki farklı siyasal grupları da (özellikle solu) derinden etkilemiştir. Öncelikle zor, güç bir yastır 12 Eylül ve tutul/a/mamıştır. Toplumun büyük çoğunluğu ondan kaçmıştır. 12 Eylül süresince dışarıdakilerin, içerdekileri görmemezlikten gelmelerini, uzaklaşma yaklaşımına bağlamak mümkündür. Buna yaratılan albenili dünyanın vaat ettikleri ve değişen dünya konjüktürü de yardımcı olmuştur. Toplum 12 Eylül'ün izlerini silebilecek anayasal değişiklikleri dahi 27 yıl geçmesine rağmen yapamamıştır. En çok etkilenen grubun (solun) yas tutamaması, ideolojik olarak toplanamamasına neden olmuştur. Bunda iç dinamikler kadar değişen dünya koşularının da (soğuk savaşın sonu, sosyalizmin çökmesi, tek kutuplu dünya düzeni gibi) etkisi vardır. Türkiye toplumunun 12 Eylül'ün yasını tutamamasının, Türkiye'nin demokratikleşme sürecine ket vurduğu ileri sürülebilir. Toplumun ortak bir yas görevini yerine getirmek için yeni törenler, yasal işlemler, sanat ve şarkılarda olayın anısını yeniden canlandırmak gibi yollar bulması, 12 Eylül için gerçekleşmiş midir? Ya da toplum yasını tutamadığı için yüzleşemediği seçilmiş travması ile kültürel temsiller ve özellikle de sinema üzerinden mi bir yol bulmaya çalışmıştır?

3. 12 Eylül Filmleri

Sanat ve kültür ürünleri, var olduğu toplumun, sistemin yapılanmasının bir sonucu olarak oluşurlar. 12 Eylül'ün baskı, yasak ve depolitizasyondan oluşan karakteristik özellikleri, kültürel-sanatsal alanı da etkiler, belirler. 12 Eylül'ün baskı ortamında Gürbilek'in (1993), "sözün bastırılması/söz patlaması" (s. 16) karşıtlığını saptaması anlamlıdır: *"baskının karşıtıyla birlikte, kültürel alanda bir özgürlük vaadiyle birlikte var olması... bu güne değin bütünsel ideolojiler içinde hapis kalmış kültürel kimliklerin serbest bırakılmasını da beraberinde getirdi"* (Gürbilek, 1993, s. 139). Bu durum, iktidardaki gücün tercihlerinin biçimlendirdiği ve yönlendirdiği kültürel hayatta, söylem değişikliklerine neden olur. Kültür ve sanat eserleri toplumsallıktan uzaklaşırken daha kişisel daha öznel konulara yönelirler. Yabancılaşma, yalnızlık başat tema olur, marjinal alanlar ilgi nesnesine dönüşür. Kültür ve sanat eserleri, toplumsallıktan uzaklaştıkça gerçeklikten kopar; daha kişisel, özel konulara yönelirler. Şiir, toplumsallığı mahpushanede yakalarken; müzik özgün olma iddiası ile arabeskleşmeyi birlikte yaşar.

Sinemada bu kültürel ortamdan etkilenir. Sinema toplum ilişkileri, önceleri yansıtma bağlamında ele alınmışsa da günümüzde dolayımlama ve temsil kuramları çerçevesinde değerlendirilmektedir. Filmlerde dünya, "temsil edilecek öğelerin seçilmesi ve bileşimlerinin yapılması aracılığıyla gösterilmektedir" (Ryan ve Kellner, 1990, s. 1). Böylece filmlerin temsil etmek üzere kurulmuş inşalar olduğu kabul edilmektedir (Abisel, 1994, s. 39). Çünkü sinemacı, toplumda varolan her şeyi alamaz; seçme yaparak filmini inşa eder. Bu yaklaşım filmleri, sektör yapılanması, sansür gibi dinamiklerle birlikte değerlendirme olanağı verir. Ekonomik krizler, sansür gibi sektörel dinamiklerin yanında sinema, siyasal ve kültürel ortama rağmen toplumsal olgulara verili koşulların izin verdiği ölçüde değinmiştir: kadın filmleri, göç filmleri, sinemaya bakış ve yaratı sorunları, bireyi sorunsallaştıran filmler, toplumsal güldürüler bu dönemin ürünleridir. Bildiri açısından önemli olan nokta, 12 Eylül'ün sanattaki en önemli temsillerinin sinema alanında verilmiş olmasıdır. Öyle ki 1984 yılından itibaren yapılan filmler kısa süre içerisinde 12 Eylül Filmleri olarak adlandırılmıştır: 12 Eylül 1980 darbesi öncesi ya da sonrası dönemi konu edinen; hapisten çıkan kişinin konumu, dışarıda değişen toplumsal ilişkileri anlatan filmler 12 Eylül filmleri başlığı altında toplanmıştır (Erkılıç, 1997, s. 46). İlginç olan bu filmlerin, yapıldığı dönemde değil de, 90'lı yıllarda 12 Eylül filmi olarak değerlendirilmiş olmalarıdır. Belirlenen filmler şunlardır: *Öç* (Mesut Uçakan,1984), *Sen Türkülerini Söyle* (Şerif Gören,1986), *Ses* (Zeki Ökten, 1986), *Dikenli Yol* (Zeki Alaysa, 1986), *Prenses* (Sinan Çetin, 1986), *Yağmur Kaçakları* (Yavuz Özkan, 1987), *Sende Yüreğinde Sevgiye Yer Aç* (Şerif Gören, 1987), *Su da Yanar* (Ali Özgentürk, 1987), *Kimlik* (Melih Gülgen, 1988), *Av Zamanı* (Erden Kıral, 1988), *Bütün Kapılar Kapalıydı* (Memduh Ün, 1989), *Kara Sevdalı Bulut* (Muammer Özer, 1989), *Uçurtmayı Vurmasınlar* (Tunç Başaran, 1989), *Sis* (Zülfü Livaneli, 1989), *Darbe* (Ümit Efekan, 1990), *İkili Oyunlar* (İrfan Tözüm, 1990), *Suyun Öte Yanı* (Tomris Giritlioğlu, 1991), *Uzlaşma* (Oğuzhan Tercan, 1991), *Bekle Dedim Gölgeye* (Atıf Yılmaz, 1991), *Hoşçakal Umut* (Candan Evcimen İçöz, 1993), *Bir Sonbahar Hikayesi* (Yavuz Özkan, 1993), *Çözülmeler* (Yusuf Kurçenli, 1994), *Bir Yanımız Bahar Bahçe* (Bilge Olgaç, 1994), *80.Adım* (Tomris Giritlioğlu, 1995), *Babam Askerde* (Handan İpekçi, 1994), *Gerilla* (Osman Sınav, 1995), *Gülün Bittiği Yer* (İsmail Güneş, 1999), *Eylül Fırtınası* (Atıf Yılmaz, 2000), *Vizontele Tuuba* (Yılmaz Erdoğan, 2004), *Babam ve Oğlum* (Çağan Irmak, 2006), *Eve Dönüş* (Ömer Uğur, 2006), *Beynelmilel* (Sırrı Süreyya Önder-Muammer Gülmez, 2006), *Zincirbozan* (Atıl İnanç, 2007).

Bu filmlerin yanı sıra Şerif Gören-Yılmaz Güney'in darbe öncesi dönemi 5 izinli mahkum üzerinden anlattığı *Yol* (1980), Yılmaz Güney'in kendi öyküsünden senaryolaştırdığı ve 1976 yılında çocuk koğuşunda geçen olayları oldukça sert ve gerçekçi bir üslupla anlattığı *Duvar,* (1983) doğrudan 12 Eylül filmleri kategorisine girmeseler de dönemin ruhunu anlatma da birçok filmden daha başarılı bulunmuştur. Ömer Kavur'un *Gece Yolculuğu*'nda (1987) 12 Eylüle dair değinmeler, filmin kahramanı olan yönetmenin yaratım sorunları, politik nedenlerle yitirdiği kardeşinin sıkıntısı üzerine kurgulanır. Filmde, dönem belirsizlikler içerir. Tevfik Başer'in *Elveda Yabancı* (1991), filminde, yurt dışında siyasal sığınma isteminin kabul edilmemesi üzerine Türkiye'ye gönderilmek üzere sınır dışı edilen politik göçmenin öyküsü anlatılırken, Türk ceza ve cezaevi sistemine eleştiriler getirilir. Serdar Akar'ın *Dar Alanda Kısa Paslaşmalar* (2000) darbe ile açılır. Küçük bir kasabada ki futbol takımı üzerinden değişen yaşantı öykülenir. Filmin, 12 Eylül'le hiç ilişkilendirilmemiş olması ilginçtir. Darbe, bir cemse dolusu askerle verilir; döneme ait başka bir göstergeye rastlanılmaz.

12 Eylül filmlerinin ilki olan *Öç* filminde, sol görüşlü üniversiteli gencin, örgüt ve arkadaş çevresinden koparak değişen siyasal düşünceleri Milli Sinemaya uygun olarak ele alınır. *Prenses*'te, dönemin sol görüşünü eleştirir. 12 Eylül filmlerinden sıkça işlenen, hapishaneden çıkan kişinin toplumdaki değişimlere uyum çabası, ailesi ve veya çevresi ile ilişkileri *Sen Türkülerini Söyle, Ses, Dikenli Yol, Bütün kapılar Kapalıydı, Hoşçakal Umut* filmlerinde işlenir. 12 Eylül sonrası değişime uyum sağlayamayan 68 kuşağının yenik öyküsü *Bekle Dedim Gölgeye, İkili Oyunlar, Su da Yanar, Çözülmeler* filmlerine konu olur. 12 Eylül öncesi şiddet ve terör ortamı belirsizlikler içinde de olsa *Sis* (kardeşin kardeşi vurduğu günlerde bir savcının değişimi), *Uzlaşma* (İpekçi cinayeti), *Av Zamanı* (terörden kaçarak adaya sığınmış bir yazarın terörle yüzleşmesi) filmlerinde ele alınır. *Bir Yanımız Bahar Bahçe*, cezaevinden çıkarak kendisine yeni bir hayat kurmaya çalışan kişi, tesadüfler sonucu aşık olduğu kişinin kardeşi olduğunu öğrenir. *Suyun Öte Yanı*, hapishaneye girmemek için yurt dışına kaçmaya çalışan kişinin karasızlığı, Yunanistan'da cuntadan kaçarak Cunda adasına sığınan sığınmacı ile benzerlikler kurularak anlatılır. *Yağmur Kaçakları'nda* yurt dışında siyasal sığınma isteği red edilen hükümlünün ülkeye geri dönmesi ve yalnızlığı, Fransız sevgiliyle kurduğu ilişki ile öykülenir. *80.Adım*, 12 Eylül'de yurt dışına kaçan hükümlünün, 83 seçimleri sırasında yurda dönerek, arkadaşları ve kendisiyle hesaplaşmasını anlatır. 12 Eylül'ün baskı ve işkence ortamı *Kara Sevdalı Bulut'ta* masala dönüştürülerek verilir. İşkencenin travmatik etkileri, *Ses* ve *Bütün Kapılar Kapalıydı ve Gülün Bittiği Yer* filmlerinde gösterilir. *Gülün Bittiği Yer*, işkenceyi, gündelik hayattan, tarihten, eğitim sistemindeki dayaktan hareketle sorgular. *Darbe*'de, pişmanlık yasasından yaralanarak yeni bir kimlik ve yüz edinen tutuklunun, özgürlüğüne rağmen ailesinden uzak kalışının bunalımı işlenir. *Sen de Yüreğinde Sevgiye Yer Aç*, 12 Eylül sonrası girdiği mahkemelerde başarılı olan avukatın özel yaşamı ve dönemin siyasal olayları birlikte işlenir. *Kimlik*'te polis tarafından kimliklerine zımba basılarak sakıncalı bulunan çiftin kıstırılmış yaşamı gösterilir. *Gerilla*'da, terör olayları sırasında silah kaçakçılığına karışmış bir iş adamının evinin gerillalar tarafından basılması konu edinir. *Bir Sonbahar Hikayesi*, 70'li yılların sonunda evlenen bir çiftin, 80 sonrası değişimle birlikte evliliklerindeki sancılar üzerinden anlatılır. Filmde, darbe sırasında tanklar sokakta geçerken kadının karşı koyma isteği ve kocasının engellemesi, daha sonraki değişimlerde aldıkları konumları da belirlemektedir. *Babam Askerde'de*, babaları hapishanede olan üç farklı ailenin çocuklarının gözüyle dönem anlatılır. *Uçurtmayı Vurmasınlar'da*, kadınlar koğuşunda annesi ile birlikte kalan çocuğun, siyasal suçlu kızlarla kurduğu ilişki sıkışmışlık ve sevgi kavramları üzerinden anlatılır. *Eylül Fırtınası'nda*, 12 Eylül ile dağılan bir aile, çocuğun gözünden işlenir. Vizontele Tuuba'da, Ankara'da eğitimini sürdüren çocuğun yaz anıları, 12 Eylül'e giden sürecin küçük bir kasabada nasıl yaşandığı komedi unsurları üzerinden anlatılır. *Beynelmilel*, küçük bir şehirde müzisyenlikle hayatını kazanan insanların, darbe günlerinde darbe liderinin ziyareti sırasında bando görevini üstlenmeleri sonucu oluşan traji-komik olaylarla, dönemi anlatır. *Babam ve Oğlum*, 12 Eylül gecesi doğum yapan eşini kaybeden, yıllarca hapishanede kalarak hastalanan bir gazetecinin, hayatının son günlerinde yıllardır küs olduğu babasına, ailesine oğlunu teslim etmek üzere geri dönüşünü ve hesaplaşmasını öyküler. *Eve Dönüş*, 12 Eylül'ün sıradan insanlar üzerindeki etkisini, baskı ve işkence ortamını yeniden gündeme getirir. *Zincirbozan*, 12 Eylül darbesinin oluşum sürecini, dönemin siyasal aktörleri üzerinden anlatır. Bu yönüyle diğer tüm filmlerden farklılık gösterir. Film ayrıca, 12 Eylül'ü oluşturan koşulların CIA işi olduğu savı üzerinden dönemi belgesel bir tavır ile anlatmaktadır.

Seçilmiş travmayı anlatan filmlerden Ses, Bütün kapılar Kapalıydı, Eve Dönüş, Babam ve Oğlum, Vizontele Tuuba ve Beynelmilel'le yakından bakalım. Bu filmlerden ilk üçü dram; son ikisi komedi ve Babam ve Oğlum ise her iki türü de başarıyla harmanlamış bir yapım. Son dönem sinemamızda, 12 Eylül'ü işleyen filmlerde dramdan komediye bir yöneliş var. Bu yönelişi, toplumsal dramdan toplumsal hicve olarak yorumladık.

Ses

Hapishanede işkence görmüş ve sol kolu sakatlanmış genç bir adam, sahil kasabasına gelir. Sahil kasabası 12 Eylül'ü yaşamamış gibidir: insanlar eğlenmekte, yemekte, oyundadırlar... Genç adam bir yabancı gibidir. Bir ses. Rüyalarına giren işkenceleri yapan adamın sesi; tatil kasabasında genç adamı bulur. Bu kişi, karısına, çocuklarına kötü davranan, çevresine sürekli bağıran bir adamdır. Genç adam, işkenceci sandığı kişiyi, yakında bulunan bir kiliseye götürür. Gözleri bağlı ve çıplak olarak tutar: gençliğini istiyordur. Gözleri bağlı adam işkenceci olmadığını söyler. Tatil kasabasında tek iletişim kurduğu genç kız da emin olup, olmadığını sorar. Genç adam emin değildir ve hesaplaşma gerçekleşmez. Film öç alma-bağışlama, gitmek-kalmak, karşıtlıkları içerisinde genç adamın çaresizliği ile biter.

Ses gibi Ariel Dorfman'nın *Genç Kız ve Ölüm* (1991) oyunundan Polanski'nin uyarladığı *Ölüm ve Kız* (1994) filminde de işkencecisini sesinden tanıyan kadın karakter hesaplaşmak ister. Öykü bir Latin Amerika ülkesinde geçmektedir. Darbelerin coğrafya, kültür tanımayan benzerlikleri, sanat üretimlerinde benzer konular oluşturabilmektedir.

Ses'in, dönemin sansür mekanizmasına ve olayın yakın tarihine karşın yapılmış olması bir başarıdır. Filmde doğrudan darbe ile ilgili bir enformasyona ya da genç adamın darbe sonrası işkence gördüğüne dair somut bir yönlendirme olmamasına rağmen, izleyici olayın sıcaklığı ile filmi 12 Eylül'le ilişkilendirebilmektedir.

Bütün Kapılar Kapalıydı

Hapishanede işkence görmüş tecavüze uğramış olan Nil, bilinçaltında yarattığı düşsel çocuğuna sarılarak bu duruma dayanmaya çalışır. Dışarıya çıktığında uyum sorunu yaşar. Kendisi gibi topluma uyum sağlayamamış, yurt dışından yeni dönmüş olan Ateş'in yardımı da sonuçsuz kalır. İkisi içinde toplum mekan ve ilişkiler açısından çok değişmiştir. Film karanlık koridorda Nil'in görüntüsü başlar. Kapı açılınca aydınlık içeri süzülür. Hapishane zaman zaman işkence sahneleri ile verilir. "Birbiri ardına tükeniyor düşlerimiz, nasıl tutunacağız yaşama", derken Nil, değişen toplumsal yapıda kendine yer bulamadığını belirtmektedir. Çalıştığı iş yerinden eskiden onu tanıyan birinin ihbarı ile kovulur. Eski kocasından, kızının hiçbir zaman olmadığını öğrendikten sonra bunalıma girer ve intihar eder. Nil karakteri de yine birçok 12 Eylül filminde olduğu gibi boşluklarla, belirsizliklerle doludur. Neden içeriye girdiği belli değildir. Solcu olduğunu düşünmemizi sağlayan birkaç kitaptan başka gösterge yoktur.

Vizontele Tuuba

1980 yazında, Hakkari'de, darbe öncesi yaşanan fraksiyon kavgalarının yanında sürgün olarak gelen kütüphanecinin, şehre kütüphane kazandırması ekseninde gelişen olaylar, komedi türünde anlatılır. İzleyici olarak öyküyü, Belediye başkanının Ankara'da okuyan oğlunun yaz anılarından öğreniriz. Film, yıllar sonra 12 Eylül üzerine yapılan ilk film olması ve komedi üzerinden döneme yaklaşması ile dikkat çeker.

Eve Dönüş

Filmin kahramanı olan Mustafa apolitik bir işçidir. Ev sahibi ile anlaşmazlığa düşünce, ev sahibi onu ihbar eder ve aranan bir solcuya benzediği için tutuklanır. Ağır bir işkenceden geçirilir. Dışarıya çıktığında işini kaybetmiştir. Arkadaşlarından destek görmemektedir. Ailesi kayınpederinin yanında yaşamaktadır. Kendine güveni kalmamıştır. İşkencecisinden onu ihbar edenin ev sahibi olduğunu öğrenir. Seyirci olarak, hesaplaşmasını bekleriz. Tıpkı Mustafa'da toplum gibi hesaplaşmaz. Film, ağırlıklı olarak, işkence sahneleri ile dönemin ruhunu temsil eder. Bu açıdan son dönem yapılan 12 Eylül filmleri içerisinde ön plana çıkmaktadır. Filmin başarısı aynı zamanda sıradan, apolitik bir kişinin bile darbe dönemlerinde yaşayabileceği yıkımlarla izleyiciyi yüzleştirebilmiş olmasıdır.

Babam ve Oğlum

12 Eylül darbesinin yapıldığı gece, doğum yapan karısını kan kaybından kaybeden ve uzun yıllar hapis yatan Sadık'ın sağlık sorunları vardır ve oğluna kalacak bir yer bulmalıdır. Kavgalı olduğu baba evi, gideceği son yerdir. Sadık, oğlu Deniz için, istediği zaman çekip gidebileceği ve dönebileceği bir yer ararken, babasıyla ve geçmişiyle de hesaplaşacaktır. Film, doğrudan 12 Eylül'le ilgili olarak bir şey söylemezken, dolaylı olarak da dönemin insanlar üzerinde yarattığı tahribat, değişimi gösterirken yüzleşmeye de kapı açtı. Melodramatik yapıdan yararlanmanın yanında, yoğun duygusal sahneler ile güldürü öğeleri içeren sahnelerin iyi bir şekilde yapılandırıldığı film, baba Hüseyin Efendi'nin pişmanlıkları, küçük Deniz'in yurtsuzluğu gibi dokunaklı meseleleri ile izleyiciyle iyi bir bağ kurdu. Ağlamak ve gülmek arasında gidip-gelen seyirci, hapishanede ağır şiddete, işkenceye maruz kalmış Sadık'ın acısından çok dışarıda kalanların sıkıştırılmışların durumu ile özdeşleşti. Film, Sadık tiplemesinin devrimci açılımı açısından da eleştiriler alır. Çarpık bir devrimci/eylemci tipi çizdiği ileri sürülür. Ayrıca melodramatik anlatımın,12 Eylülü bir fon olarak kullandığı belirtiliyor.

Beynelmilel

1982 yılında, sıkıyönetim altında Adıyaman'da, çalışmaları engellenen gevendeler (düğünlerde şarkı söyleyip, çalan müzisyenler), Güvenlik Konseyi üyelerinin şehri ziyareti üzerine bando olarak görevlendirilirler. Üstelik temsili kurtuluş günü etkiliklerinde kullanılan düşman kıyafeti ile. Marş çalmayı beceremez gevendeler. Abuzer'in, Gülendam'ın kayıt yaparken duyduğu ve bahar şarkısı olarak öğrendiği Enternasyonal Marşı'nı, Konsey için hazırlarlar. Bu arada Gülendam'ın aşık olduğu devrimci Haydar ve arkadaşları eylem yapmak için hazırlık içerisindedirler. Konsey üyeleri geldiğinde gevendeler Enternasyonal Marşı'nı çalarlar. Çıkan çatışmada Haydar ölür. Gevendeler tutuklanır. Yıllar sonra televizyonda Kızıl Ordu korosu, Enternasyonal'i söylemektedir. Film, öykü akışını tesadüfler üzerinden yaparak, diğer filmlerle aynı yapıyı kullanıyor görünse de güldürü öğesini, taşlama boyutunda kullanarak diğer filmlerden ayrılır. Toplumsal travmaya, hiciv ile yanıt verir. Ayrıca filmde çizilen halk, yoksul, bilinçsiz, ihbarcı, günü kurtarmaya çalışan, resmi üniformadan korkan, bir kısmı zorla yaptırılsa da pankartlar, posterler asıp sıkıyönetime yağ çeken insanlardan oluşuyor; tıpkı Eve Dönüş'ün ihbarcı ev sahibi gibi.

Sonuç: Filmler Aracılığıyla Yas Tutmak

Filmlerin genel bir değerlendirmesi yapıldığında şu sonuçlara ulaşıyoruz: Filmler, içeride ya da dışarıda olanları anlatsın, öyküye bir savruluş hakimdir. Bir tutunamayanlar dramı sergilenmektedir. Yaşanan travmayı, filmler, beyazperdeye taşımaya çalışmıştır. İçeride, işkence gören ya da yurt dışında kaçak yaşayanlar/kaçmaya çalışanlar (çoğunlukla solcular) olumlu tip olarak çizilmiş fakat ideolojik arka planları ve seçim nedenleri belirgin olmadığı için tip düzeyinden öteye gidememiştir. Dışarıdakiler ise ya yeni düzene uyum sağladıkları için ya da içerdekileri, işkenceyi, baskıları umursamadıkları için olumsuz tipler olarak gösterilmektedir. Karakterler çoğunlukla erkektir. Az sayıdaki kadın kahramanlar ise ya sonunda intihar ederler ya da depresyondadırlar. Filmlerin ağırlıklı olarak dram türünde olmalarına karşılık, melodramın öğelerinden de yararlanırlar. Komedi, ancak 2000'lerde gündeme gelmiştir. Melodramın kadın-erkek kurgusu, tesadüfi yapısı, tip düzeyinde kişileştirme gibi özelliklerine filmlerde çokça rastlanmaktadır. Bu durum melodramın sinemamızdaki kipsel özelliğinden kaynaklanmaktadır. Genel olarak filmlere yöneltilen temel eleştiri, karakterlerin yaratılamaması, "insanların ve dönemin birbirlerini açıklayamadıkları gibi aralarında bir nedenselliğin de kurulamaması" (Belge, 1990) olarak saptanabilir. Bunun senaryo, yönetim gibi sinema sanatına ait teknik ve estetik yetersizliklerden kaynaklandığı ileri sürülebilir. Ayrıca dönemin toplumsal ve tarihsel durumundan soyutlanarak temsilinde oto-sansürün (sinemacıların kafasında oluşan kurumların sansürü ve korkusu) egemen olduğu ileri sürülebilir. "12 Eylül filmi henüz yapılmadı" yargısının genel bir paylaşım oluşturmasının nedeni, bu filmlerin sorunlarla yüzleşme, hesaplaşma ve daha ötesine gidip sorgulayabilme özelliğinden yoksun olmalarına bağlanabilir. Sorunlarla yüzleşme ve sorgulayabilme geleneğinin olmadığı bir kültürde, sinemacılar da aynı genel uylaşımların içerisinde kalmaktadırlar. Ayrıca Türk sinemasında çok uzun bir süre etkin olan sansürün (ekonomik ve siyasal), zamanla sinemacılarda otosansürü (ideolojik) geliştirdiği açıktır. Bu nedenle, 12 Eylül döneminin filmlerdeki temsili inşalarında, dönemle ilgili "büyük suskunluklara", "eksikliklere" rastlanılmakta ve böylece egemen değerler yeniden üretilmektedir. Temsil edilen döneme karşı gözüken filmlerin varolan değerleri (şiddet, kader, değişime karşı olma, ahlaki tutuculuk, ataerkil yapı....) yeniden ürettikleri ve egemen ideoloji içinde kaldıkları ileri sürülebilir.

Son dönem 12 Eylül filmlerinde gözlenen güldürü öğesinin, 12 Eylül'e dair yasın tutulmaya başladığı anlamında yorumlanabilir. Yönetmen Ömer Uğur'un "ben filmde seyirci gülmek istesin, tam gülecekken de 'yok ya gülmemek lazım' desin isterim" açıklaması, bizim tam da seçilmiş travma kavramını açıklamaya çalıştığımız şeyi ifade ediyor. Komedi öğesinin yalnızca eğlence ihtiyacını karşılayan bir unsur olarak değerlendirmemek gerekir. Bu bakış açısı, komediyi yalnızca kitleleri uyumcu hale getiren, konformizmin bir hizmet aracı olarak görmeye götürür. Oysa komedi sineması, eleştirinin en yoğun kullanıldığı bir tür olarak değerlendirilir. Bu nedenle filmlerde görülen komedi unsurlarını hiciv olarak değerlendirdik.12 Eylül filmlerinde görülen komediyi, bu şekilde yorumlamak daha doğru olacaktır. Ayrıca bu filmler, hem travmadan kaçan geniş kitleyi hem de o dönemi bilmeyen yeni kuşakları dönemle yüzleştirmektedir. Son dönem filmlerinin izleyici sayılarına bakıldığında bu durum açıkça görülmektedir. Eve Dönüş 217.983, Babam ve Oğlum 3.813.437, Vizontele Tuuba 2.894.802, Beynelmilel 360.568. İzleyicinin komedi filmini her zaman tercih ettiği bilinen bir gerçektir. 12 Eylül gibi büyük bir travmanın, seçilmiş travmanın, filmlerdeki temsilinde, güldürü öğelerini bu çerçevede değerlendirmemek gerekir. Güldürüyü, dönemi hafife almaktan öte dönemle yüzleşebilmenin, yasın tutulmaya başladığının bir belirtisi olarak yorumlamak gerekir.

" *Hatırlama, insan yapımı felaketlere doğrudan maruz kalmış olanlar için, çoğu zaman, geçmişin travmatik etkilerinden kurtulmanın ve özgürleşmenin yegane yolu olarak görülür... zulüm ve haksızlık pratiklerinin cezasız kalmamasını sağlayacak bir geçmişle hesaplaşma sürecine, başkalarının acısına bakma ve yasını paylaşma kültürünü inşa çalışmasına ihtiyacımız var*" (Sancar, 2006). Toplum olarak yüzleşmekten kaçtığımız, yasını tutamadığımız 12 Eylül, filmler aracılığıyla hatırlanmaya, hesaplaşmaya çalışılmıştır. 12 Eylül, diğer kültürel temsillerden daha çok Türk sinemasında temsil edilmiştir.

Kaynakça

Abisel, N. (1995). *Popüler Sinema ve Türler.* İstanbul: Alan Yayıncılık.

Ahmad, F. (2006). *Bir Kimlik Peşinde Türkiye* (Çev. S.C.Karadeli). İstanbul: Bilgi Üniversitesi Yayınları.

Belge, M. (1990). 12 Eylül Filmleri Henüz Yapılmadı. *Beyazperde,* Dosya: 12 Eylül Filmleri, 7-8.

Belge, M. (1992). *12 Eylül'den 12 Yıl Sonra.* İstanbul: Birikim Yayınları.

Belge, M. (1996). Yeni Toplum Yeni İnsan. *Cumhuriyet Dönemi Türkiye Ansiklopedisi,* Cilt 14. İstanbul: İletişim Yayınları.

Bostan, E., Atam, Z. (2007). Melodramdan Yansıyan 12 Eylül Üzerine Provokatif Düşünceler. *Yeni İnsan Yeni Sinema, 16,* 132-141.

Çelebi, N. (2002). Kültürel Travma Üzerine. *Toplum ve Bilim,* 91/ Kış.

Ergun, D. (1991). *Türk Bireyi Kuramına Giriş.* İstanbul: Gerçek Yayınevi.

Erkılıç, H. (1997). *Sinema ve İdeoloji 12 Eylül filmlerinin Toplumsal Çözümlemesi.* (yayınlanmamış yüksek lisans tezi.) Eskişehir: Anadolu Üniversitesi Sosyal Bilimler Enstitüsü.

Evren,S., Usta, B. (2005). 12 Eylül Üzerine Nurdan Gürbilek ile Söyleşi. *Siyahi, 5,* 26-29.

Görücü, B. (2007). 12 Eylül'ü Anlatmak. *Yeni Film, 13,* 27-35.

Gürbilek, N. (1999). *Vitrinde Yaşamak.* İstanbul: Metis yayınları.

Hale, W. (1995). *Ordu ve Siyaset* (Çev. A. Fethi). İstanbul: Hil Yayın.

Hall, S., Jacques, M. (Der.) (1996). *Yeni Zamanlar* (Çev. A.Yılmaz). İstanbul: Ayrıntı Yayınları.

Kaptanoğlu, C. (2005). Yapısal Travmadan Toplumsal Travmaya Türkiye Solu ve Kafka. *Birikim, 198,* 71-78.

Kavas, V. (2007). Hayallerimiz Küçükse Biz Hiç Büyük Olabilir miyiz Baba? *Yeni İnsan Yeni Sinema, 18-19,* 126-131.

Kentel, F. (1990). 90'lı Yıllara Girerken Merhaba Toplum. *Varlık, 994.*

Keyder, Ç. (1995). *Türkiye'de Devlet ve Sınıflar.* İstanbul: İletişim Yayınları.

Kızıltuğ, K. (2005). 25.Yılında 12 Eylül ve Siyaset, Ömer Laçiner ile Söyleşi. *Siyahi, 5,* 16-25.

Kocabıyık, İ. (2007). 12 Eylül Filmlerinde "Mazi Kalbimde Yaradır". *Yeni Film, 13*, 36-42.

Kongar, E. (1993). *12 Eylül Kültürü*. İstanbul: Remzi Kitapevi.

Kongar, E. (1995). *Toplumsal Değişme Kuramları ve Türkiye Gerçeği*. İstanbul: Remzi Kitapevi

Kozanoğlu, C. (1992). *Cilalı İmaj Devri*. İstanbul: İletişim Yayınları.

Maktav, H. (2000). Türk Sinemasında 12 Eylül. *Birikim, 138*, 79-84.

Marguez, G. G. (1996). *Şili'de Gizlice* (Çev. Ü. İnce). İstanbul: Can Yayınları.

Örs, B. (1996). *Türkiye'de Askeri Müdahaleler*. İstanbul: Der yayınları.

Parla, T. (1995). *Türkiye'nin Siyasal Rejimi*. İstanbul: İletişim.

Ryan, M., Kellner, D. (1997). *Kamera Politika* (Çev. E. Özsayar). İstanbul: Ayrıntı Yayınları.

Sancar, M. (2006). *Geçmişle Hesaplaşma Sorunları*. www.boelltr.org/docs/ gecmisle_ hesaplasma.pdf (Son erişim 15 Eylül 2006).

Teztel, D. ve Topçu, H. (1994). 12 Eylül Dosyası. *Cumhuriyet Gazetesi*, 11-16 Eylül 1994.

Vamık, V. (1999). *Kanbağı Etnik Gururdan Etnik Teröre*. İstanbul: Bağlam Yayınları.

Vamık, V., Itzkowitz, N. (2002). *Türkler ve Yunanlılar*. çev: B. Büyükkal, İstanbul: Bağlam Yayınları.

Yaşa, E. (Haz.) (1990). Hayattan Kopuşun 10 Yılı. *Nokta, 8*, 38.

Zürcher, E. J. (1995). *Modernleşen Türkiye'nin Tarihi*. İstanbul: İletişim Yayınları.

Feminist Challenges to Violence: Differences of the Two Feminist Magazines, *Pazartesi* and *Amargi*

Hanife Aliefendioğlu
Faculty of Communication and Media Studies
Eastern Mediterranean University
hanife.aliefendioglu@emu.edu.tr

Introduction

The contemporary feminist movement and media in Turkey are quite young and goes back only to the first half of 1980s. Although the junta regime was intolerant to any kind of social opposition and protest in the 1980s it did not see any threat in the feminist movements. Obviously the movement was not seen as a political project. By the end of 1980s feminist movement tended to form sustainable and long lasting organizations. The 1990s marked as "period of institutionalizing" and "project based feminism" in the movement (Bora & Gunal 2002, p. 8).

In this paper I aim to show that there is a parallel perspective between women's movement and the content of the feminist magazines. Keeping this in mind, I would like to move on to the transformation of media's view on "culture of violence" including domestic violence.

Violence against women covered in the feminist media is portrayed differently than in most mainstream Turkish media. As in most of the countries it is observed that violence against women is portrayed by the Turkish mainstream media with the victim blaming discourse. Recently they are more careful in representing of the honor killings.

The Feminist Media Discourse

There are two kinds of agencies in the media: media owner/producer and active audience. In the discourse theory it is argued that the discourse of the media is highly driven by existing discourses; producers/decision makers are mostly using already constructed cultural imprint and thus are not independent in their interpretations (Macdonald, 2001, p. 23). Although the feminist media claim uniqueness in their perspectives within this cultural imprint even they are not completely free of these existing discourses.

Donna Allen (1991) defines some of the differences of media in terms of journalistic practice. According to her "the mainstream journalism of male-owned media reports news in the third person"; secondly "men tend to define 'news' as conflict and violence", and lastly "male-owned media claim a journalistic goal of 'objectivity' ". Allen argues that the characteristic analysis of the mass media is that they are hostile to women. She also describes five essential categories of women's news which are "healthy and safe", "economic", "political", "global" and "media" information.

A general view of feminist media argues that news reports tend to be masculine narratives in which women do not play a role as active subjects. Ironically women are over-represented in reports of personal violence like rape, murder or physical assault (Boom and Michielsens 1996, p. 190). In short women are newsworthy only as the victims of violence (Boom and Michielsens 1996, p. 195). Jermyn (2001) notes that violence against women is routinely legitimized by the media by concentrating on the positions of victims in terms of familial relationships, domesticity, and gender norms.

As Boom and Michielsens (1996) mention women are generally clean victims in the violence or disaster news portrayed covered, healthy or even not injured (p. 192). Women personify our sufferings from narrator's point of view. Women as our women, when addressing both sides, represent human suffering visually while their men are portrayed more brutally (p. 194).

In the light of critical paradigm, in feminist studies there is a shift from the traditional understanding of patriarchy and a move towards a wider definition of violence in the alternative media. Recent feminist work moved away from seeing women as "oppressed group" and "victims under male domination" (Mills, 1997, p. 78). Both men and women are affected by being represented within certain stereotypes. Whereas in feminist media, different identities of men and women are represented (von Zoonen, 1994, p. 31). It cannot be claimed that the content of news and article on violence are fully articulated by feminist theory but feminist media is getting more and more eager to analyze other violence related issues such as militarism, colonialism and imperialism. Herewith the perception of violence is changing as well. Violence against women is not taken as a private issue in women's lives anymore. On the contrary domestic violence tends to be connected to the culture of violence.

In the political agenda of Turkey there are many political issues that the feminist media cannot ignore. There are ongoing issues in Turkey's political agenda in which feminists take more and more place. From the 1990s onwards the women took active part in political movements like Kurdish nationalism and Islamist extremism (Altinay, 2000, p. 26; Arat 2001).

In the late 1990s Turkish feminism has become more engaged in anti-militarism and ethnic war in south east of the country. The priority of the movement was raising awareness among women about gendered violence culture which includes domestic violence. Although the feminist media was not completely unaware of militaristic violence before, both the feminist movement and the media became more involved in these issues in the 1990s. There are couple of reasons for that: Firstly, feminists have discovered their differences in terms of ethnicity, political or religious standing. Secondly the feminist movement (so the media) recognized more sensitively that women from different backgrounds may have a common platform to act together for gender equality or against patriarchal male coalition. Thirdly feminist movement in Turkey has more international and global contacts with governmental and non governmental organizations to create new agendas since the 1980s.

Journalists in the feminist media are also active in the feminist movement. As a result of it the waves in feminist movement can be followed in the content in feminist media as well. The feminist media have succeeded in serving "as a political platform of women maintained by a feminist perspective" (Arat 2004, p. 287). Especially second half of the 1990s feminist media have dealt with themes such as militarism, Islamic fundamentalism and Kurdish nationalism politicized which were seemingly not women's issues.

Looking through the agenda in the feminist media, we follow the traces that feminism in Turkey is not only Turkish but also Kurdish and Armenian, not only secular but also Islamist. Kurdish and Islamist women raised their feminist demands within their movement. As Bora and Gunal note Kurdish women questioned patriarchal structure of nationalism as well as Turkishness of feminist movement in Turkey (2002, p. 8). The sensitivity developed in the 1990s towards diversity in the feminist media serves expanding the issues related to women, and gender and feminism. Marginal women were left with their double burden as a result of ethnic awareness within "global/glocal identity construction movements", and also the effects of deregulations, privatization and liberalization. Gender awareness under the effects of Beijing and post Beijing process both united and divided women within feminist movement; It united because of the common ground existing among women to act against domestic violence. It divided because feminist women developed different perspective towards ethnic tension/ conflict and raising nationalism and militarism. There is, for example, a gap between different feminist voices like Kemalist/secular and more importantly nationalist feminists. Kurdish nationalism and Islamic movement put a line between women who act mostly together in many other women's issues in the past. For instance a Turkish Kemalist feminist, Necla Arat, made an official complaint against Eren Keskin's statements from the Human Rights Association about the soldiers' sexual abuse towards Kurdish women. Arat has been thanked later by a high level officer because of her sensitivity and respect to the Turkish Army (Karakus, 2007, p. 84).

Two Feminist Magazines: *Pazartesi* and *Amargi*

Pazartesi first came out in March 1995 as a publication of Women Culture and Communication Foundation. It has been published for the longest period of time for the largest constituency (Arat, 2004, p. 283). Since January 2006, after 106 issues it started to be published as special issues like motherhood, sexuality, labour.[1] *Pazartesi* continues its updated reports in online format[2]. In its 100th issue, the editorial of *Pazartesi* states that readers expect to find the answer to the question of "let's see what the feminists have said," on its pages. Pazartesi, by its radical feminist critique brings two important things together: conservative and liberal policies and popular culture. This brings a different dimension to the reporting, in contrast with the attitudes displayed in mainstream media.

Yesim Arat emphases for *Pazartesi*, feminist media in Turkey "challenged the borders of the political not merely by articulating problems women could not voice as political concerns in public discourse, but also by politicizing popular culture with feminist criticism (p. 282). Arat adds that *Pazartesi* raised a feminist voice in Kurdish problem and Islamic problems not just simply by making news about them but also by giving them a

1 It was funded by a German organization Frauen-Antiftung first, and then Heinrich Böll Foundation and Global Fund for Women located in USA respectively. *Pazartesi* is run by a group of women who have published two important but short lived publications called *Feminist* and *Socialist Feminist Kaktüs* between 1988 and 1990.

2 See www.pazartesi.org

chance to voice their own problems (2004, p. 283). Arat notes that *Pazartesi* 'was the only secular publication that allowed Islamist women to express themselves the way they understood themselves. Pazartesi defended headscarf issue of "women's self-expression, if not freedom of religious practice" (2004, p. 288).

Pazartesi claims militancy towards women's activities rather than professional journalistic objectivity as Donna Allen notes (Seçkin 2005, p. 4). *Pazartesi* is a "political intervention" (Arat, 2004, p. 290) for women making popular culture subject of politics in Turkey. As Arat argues and according to my own experience as volunteer in Ankara *Pazartesi* Group between 1995-1998, the readers enjoyed the popular culture as pictured by *Pazartesi* "because it gave them a sense of freedom from patriarchal norms and empowerment (2004, p. 290). On the other hand bringing feminist interpretation to popular culture is not a priority in *Amargi*. The motivation of *Amargi* comes from its feminist interpretation of hard news or political agenda.

Amargi is a women's academic group established recently, and which publishes the magazine with the same title. It is a non hierarchical women's group and discusses male reason or patriarchy in philosophy, political life and daily practices. Its activities run with issue based committees and workshops[3]. The magazine *Amargi* is quite young and its 6 issue appeared recently.

Amargi, in its first issue, relates the headscarf problem to body politics and the modernism project of "othering" in Turkey. *Amargi*, in its second issue's editorial, notes that militarism and violence mark the politics among oppressed people too. The ones who are militarist, masculine and powerful stand in front of us as "real." the "truth". Peaceful attitudes are seen elitist, liberal and white or as cowardice and as such peaceful standing is feminized and pacified so that it looses the sense of reality (*Amargi* 2nd issue editorial).

Both *Pazartesi* and *Amargi* see themselves as part of the feminist movement rather than a competitive media market. They are extremely generous in giving place to reviewing newly published women and feminist journals such as *Roza, Jujin* (Kurdish feminist publications) *Feminist Yaklaşımlar* (electronic journal). *Pazartesi* also publishes Kurdish version of a news article in each issue.

Analysis

The unique success of *Pazartesi* and *Amargi* -lies in their extreme sensitivity and prioritising of the gendered nature of violence and sexuality; their decisive attitude to bring those issues to public attention by criticizing public morality, and societal honour codes. They are genuinely wise seeing the gendered nature of all types of violence.

Pazartesi is extremely spirited in reporting crimes against women and has been so from its first issue on, even sometimes with an aggressive and angry tone. The front and back covers of *Pazartesi* are allocated almost always to news or messages against violence. Here are some examples from the back cover: "Who is going to calm us down!", "We won't forget, we won't let it be forgotten, we won't forgive!", "Let's stop it [Violence Against Women]!." Almost 40 per cent of the magazine's issues have examined crime and violence against women on the front or back cover pages (Aliefendioglu, 2004). Range of violence related issues are available in those magazines. I will describe some interrelated violence patterns that came out more insistently and decisively in the feminist media from the 1990s onwards.

Pazartesi reveals extensively the violence applied by authorities and the security forces. *Pazartesi* reported widely when women from leftist backgrounds in various organisations or political parties have been kidnapped and harassed by unknown people. In the news entitled "Before and After Rape" Oğuz and Yılmaz noted that Gülbahar was kidnapped and raped by unknown people while she was the head of the women's branch of a leftist Kurdish Party. Gülbahar narrates how she has met the women's movement after this tragic experience (Oğuz & Yılmaz, 2003, p. 4).

Asiye Zeybek Güzel was taken under custody for two weeks in February 1997 and has been raped. *Pazartesi* published this case in different issues. Upon the suggestion of her friends, she wrote a book which was awarded the Swedish Pen Tucholsky prize. (Alkaya, 2003, p. 7).

Pazartesi chases after violence cases. Şükran Aydın was raped and bitten under custody in Derik in the region in 1997. Şükran Aydın took the case to The European Court of Human Rights and won.

Pazartesi and *Amargi* recognize the double burden of Kurdish women. Violence in the case of armed conflict is directed to everyone perceived as the enemy; however, sexual violence targets women particularly. Both attacker and attacked construct their narratives over the bodies of women (Saigol, 2000, p. 237-238). Women are changeable signifiers. Women in ethnic conflict can easily become "their women" in other words, the target of attack (Saigol, p. 241).

In mainstream media, one rarely finds women narratives of physical and sexual violence due to armed conflict. *Pazartesi* regularly reports women's victimization in the south east region. For the 100th issue it commented on the armed conflict in the South-East: "This magazine tried to take sides against the war that has been taking place just in front of us. Women became the victims of this war by becoming widows, losing their sons and daughters, being killed and raped. Besides fighting against gender blindness this magazine tried to increase awareness against

3 See www://amargi.org.tr.

otherization of the oppressed nation's women" (Seçkin, 2005, p. 4).

Dealing with honour killings, both magazines are very careful and critical towards the attitude of the mainstream media which tend to portray honour killings as an ethnic issue, namely Kurdish[4]. Ertugrul Ozkok in his column in Hurriyet writes that honour killings is not Turkey's issue but Kurdish people's issue (cited in Calayan 2007, p. 52). According to Elcik another male journalist, Gunduz Aktan, claims that finally Western media understood that honour killings have ethnic (Kurdish) origin (p. 55).

Feminist media do not see violence against women as a culture or country specific problem but as a part of systematic patriarchal oppression. Modernist discourse of the mainstream media tend to see these issues as third world's issues. Therefore, *Pazartesi* publishes news entitled "Murders of Women in EU" in which legal and practical situation of the issue in EU countries are given (Öztürk, 2004, p. 20). Feminist Media underline the global and regional nature of violence against women throughout the Middle East.

> At the houses, streets, wars, prisons and offices... the means might be different but the violence against women are the same. Besides the hegemony of traditions especially with the spread of liberal culture where gender discrimination is at its height, war and militarism have infiltrated all parts of life and the growing poverty with the colonialism, we, Middle Eastern women, are facing violence even more: beatings, harassment, pressure, rape, imprisonment at homes, psychological violence, poverty and many others (Editorial, 2004, p. 86).

Amargi did not use domestic violence as a team so far. Filiz Karakus in *Amargi* writes on the history of feminist movement in Turkey. Karakus (2007) looking back at the first feminist activism in the 1980s, reminds the missing points in the campaign such as "no stress on patriarchy except masculinity", "no mention of militarism and sexual abuse", "no mention of sexual abuse and rapes under custody and in prisons, sexual abuse in war and ethnic conflict", "power relations between ethnic groups which legitimises sexual abuse" (p. 8)[5]. In other words early contemporary feminism in Turkey did not point out militarism and armed conflict and most importantly ethnic aspects of feminist needs and expectations. Nowadays, feminist point of view in the 1980s and 1990s seems urban, middle class women's movement till other women's voices appeared in with their own agenda.

Pazartesi and *Amargi* are not always a platform of every feminist. Karakus (2007b) in her article entitled in *Amargi*, "A Feminism Bargains with Official Ideology" notes the differences among feminists. Feminists who act together for legal amendments in Civil Code and Penal Code oppose each other as far as the headscarf or Kurdish issue are concerned. They defend secularism against headscarf or Turkish nationalism against Kurdish problem (p. 84). *Pazartesi* argues secularism is necessary to create a less patriarchal state but not enough.

Feminism, Militarism and Masculinity

One of the latest items in women's movement agenda is militarism. Second issue of *Amargi* expands the border of anti militarism from army service to reproduction of masculinity (Selek, 2007, p. 27).

Selek, in *Amargi*, underlines that feminist anti war standing is not limited to policy making for oppressed people, women should discuss the way they walk in rallies, flags, banners and clothing (p. 29). Cynthia Enloe (1990) mentions something the similar in *Bananas, Bases and Patriarchy* and notes that militarization is a gendered process in which certain forms of masculinities and femininities work: Military prostitution is the most common outcome; but there are some others like rape, military recruitment, ideology of national security. Militarism can work harmoniously with other form of oppressive project like nationalism and racism. Militarization is deeply gendered. Militarized pieces of land separate the lands and minds by barbed wire/mines or ideologies as Enloe mentions (1990, p. 200).

Militarism in mainstream news media is equated with masculinity while non violent passive resistance is seen as feminine according to Merrill and Quirk (1994, p. 179). Colleen Burkes' article, from WILPF,[6] notes the necessity of the feminists' challenge to militarism which naturalises oppression over women (2007, p. 45). Women are victims of poverty since all budgets are allocated by military expanditures. Walby takes our attention to the different relation of men and women with militarism in order to understand nationalism. Walby also notes that women are not interested in policy making and nationalism because they have nothing to lose and changes in nationalism do not make any difference in women's lives (Walby, 2000, p. 48).

Feminist media have a transnational perspective: Women's peace camp at Greenham Common is an international feminist classic in antimilitarist feminist movement indicating that the "private is not political but also international" (Walby 2000, p. 49). This camp was the symbol of anti militarism, anti nuclear energy and anti war (49). Second example is the Greens who have always connected with a feminist component. Greens are the platform where anti militarism, environmentalism and

4 Feminist media also blame Kurdish alternative media because of remaining silent about honour killings.

5 "Our Body belong to us! No to Sexual Abuse" campaing was the first event organised by feminists in November 1989 and women provided purple needles to stick men abusers.

6 Women's International League Peace Forum.

internationalism meet (see Ergun, 2004, p. 30-31). Aung San Suu Kyi, Burma's political leader's imprisonment is also an international agenda item of *Pazartesi* (500 bin Askere Karsi Bir Kadin, 2007, 19). Again Women in Black Movement established in Israel becomes news in *Pazartesi* with their Istanbul, Diyarbakır and Mardin visits (Yılmaz, 2007, p. 6).

Enloe offers a persuasive argument on militarism saying that it does not only affect the productions of planes, mines and missiles but also the production of toys, cloths and food (2006, p. 28). As Saigol (2000) puts it, within militarized cultures, the words like "strategy", "action plan" and "target" become regular concepts within the civil institutions as well. Eventually violence remains invisible since it is deeply internalized by societal daily practices (p. 217). Although militarization needs both genders' approval it privileges men against women. Militarized maneuvers without getting women's approval cannot be successful (Enloe, 2006, p. 45)[7].

Second half of 1990s witnessed the raising of another voice in the feminist movement: Female conscientious objectors. In the news entitled "Yes women object too" antimilitarist women talk in *Pazartesi* (Yurdalan, 2005). A female conscientious objector Nazan Askeran says "I object to all kinds of violence... I do not want to kill or die in wars. I do not want to be a threat for any living creatures who will inhabit to the planet in the future... I object to this militarist mentality which surrounds our lives". Another conscientious objector İnci Ağlagül sees military service as women's problem as well and says, "if I remain silent I will be part of the guilt". Two years later *Amargi* made an interview with Ferda Ülker who is a conscientious objector. She explains their ultimate aim as total demilitarization which includes to be against army service. Gedik (2007) connects anti militarism to masculinized nationalism which both interplays with gender (p. 38). Militarism creates enemy from the difference(s) and builds its existence on the existence of an enemy.

Amargi publishes a document in its second issue which is taken from The Naval Academy Command course notes of leadership. In this course notes, there are some instructions about choosing a wife, family's role in gaining leadership, main characteristic of leadership/command and officer's family relation. For example expectations of officer's from his wife are listed as "... coolness, patience and understanding, skilfullness, cheerfullness. She can also have some expectations from him like, understanding, a little appreciation, seeing hints of a caring husband, awareness of family responsibilities" (p. 49). Altough the notes underline the value of women in job market, they still attract the officers' attention to the problem of having a working wife. The document concludes that "according to Turkish tradition woman's place in society is primarily by her husband's side". It is suggested that wife and children should stay in the shadow in order not to harm the leader/officer's prestige (p. 49)" This one page course notes is given without any comment.

Amargi differs from *Pazartesi* in bringing more analytical articles to its pages rather than news stories. Dilsa Deniz (2007) writes about the similarities between the idioms in sexuality and militarism (p. 58). She puts sexuality and militarism as two mutualy overlapping and interdependent concepts. It is ironic that militarism creates dangers for women in order to protect them (2007, p. 58). Militarist success is based on courage and provocation. They (men) can easily get provoked by powerless people (women). Rape in both sexual and militaristic meaning, is commonly used in the army to literally and symbollically refer to penis.

In her responses, Savran (2007) notes in the third issue that "in order for feminism to keep a critical position toward every masculine organization, it can only be against patriarchy rather than seeing anti militarist as an abstract concept (p. 35). Savran sees patriarchy as a dichotomous concept which contains oppressors and oppressed and adds that militarism cannot form sexism but only feed it(p. 35). However militarism without sexism is hardly imaginable. Enloe in the interview published in *Pazartesi* reminds us that patriarchy is a smaller power system than capitalism and shares her concern about how men do not think that feminism makes the main arguments in the public (see Spengler, 2003, p. 21).

Conclusion

As Gallager notes media professionals may change their voice "with a little reflection and effort" (2001, p. 53). Feminist media with their unique voice within the alternative media have been conducting this role since the late 80s in Turkey. Feminist media are not just magazines but also feminist policy project.

Unlike mainstream media, women are represented as individuals in the news related to violence in the feminist media. They strategically turn the news into women's narratives which make women subjects rather than just objects of violence. They chase after violence cases.

Feminist media see themselves as a platform for victims of violence whose voice is generally not heard in the tabloid media. They have a better access to the victims of violence basically because of their approach. *Pazartesi* reporters succeed in interviewing victims of violence or members of their immediate families.

7 Kozanoglu summarizes the militarization in Turkey: In a society who values physical power it had not been difficult to empower police organization starting from 1980s given more authority. Special team were sent to the East and South East of Anatolia replaced the image police against burglar to police against terrorists (Kozanoglu, 2001, p. 142-43). Kozanoglu sees continuity between this sense of "more security" with bodyguards and special guarding in public and private place that hire both men and women. This image and job replace military uniform for those who wish to be a soldier (2001, p. 157).

Amargi's pages are open to more theoretical and analytical commentaries or references to feminist theory, which makes *Amargi* diverge from the popular path in the feminist media taken by *Pazartesi*.

Both *Pazartesi* and *Amargi* recognize the differences among feminists and feminisms and thus also appreciate the conditions of acting together or being in opposition to each other. Both emphasize the immediacy of constructing feminist politics outside the limits of the women's rights movement.

References

Allen, D. (1991). Women News. *The Quill, May*, 36-37.

Aliefendioğlu, H. (2005). *Differences that Matter: Approach of Pazartesi, A Feminist Magazine, on the Issue of Violence Against Women.* Paper Presented 18th Annual Conference 9-11 September 2005 King's College, University of Aberdeen, Scotland.

Alkaya, G. (2004). Nihayet Hesap Verecekler. *Pazartesi, 92*, 4.

Altınay, A. G. (Ed) (2000). *Vatan, Millet Kadınlar*. Istanbul: İletişim.

Anthias, F.; N. Yuval-Davis (1989). *Women Nation State*. London: Macmillan.

Arat, Y. (2004). Rethinking the Political: A Feminist Journal in Turkey: Pazartesi. *Women's Studies International Forum, 27*, 281-292.

Boom ten, A.; M. Michielsens (1996). Illustrating Human Suffering: Women As Victims on the News. In N. Dokovic, D. Derman, K. Ross (Eds.), *Gender and Media* (pp. 188-199). Ankara: Med Campus Project.

Bora, A. & Günal, A. (2002). Önsöz. In Bora, A. & A. Günal (Eds.) *90'larda Türkiye'de Feminizm*, (pp. 7-11). Ankara: İletişim.

Burkes, C. (2007). Kadınlar ve Militarizm: Niçin Toplumsal Cinsiyet Perspektifli Bir Analize İhtiyacımız Var? *Amargi, 2*, 44-46.

Çaglayan, H. (2007). Kadın Katliamına Milliyetçi Prizmadan Bakmak. *Amargi, 3*, 52-54.

Deniz, D. (2007). Penis Ideolojisi: Militarizm. *Amargi, 2*, 58-59.

Elçik, G. (2007). Kadın Sana Söylüyorum Kürt Sen Anla. *Amargi, 3*, 55-56.

Enloe, C. (1990). Bananas, Bases and Patriarchy in Women Militarism and War. In Elshtain, J. B. ; S. Tobias (Eds.), *Essays in History Politics and Social Theory* (pp. 189-206). Maryland: Rawman Littlefield.

Enloe, C. (2006). *Manevralar: Kadın Yaşamının Militarize Edilmesine Yönelik Uluslararası Politikalar* (S. Çağlayan, Trans.). İstanbul: İletişim.

Ergun, E. (2004). Greenham Unutulmamalı. *Pazartesi, 86*, 31-32.

Gallager, M. (2001) *Gender Setting New Agendas for Media Monitoring and Advocacy*. London, NY: Zed Books.

Gedik, E. (2007). Kadınlık ve Vicdani Red Üzerine Notlar. *Amargi, 2*, 38-39.

Jermyn, D. (2001). Death of the Girl Next door: Celebrity, femininity, and tragedy in the murder of Jill Dando, *Feminist Media Studies, 1*(3), 343-359.

Kancı, T. (2007). 1920lerden Bugüne Türkiye'de İlkokul Ders Kitapları. *Amargi, 2*, 65-67.

Karakuş, F. (2007a). Resmi İdeolojiyle Hesaplaşan bir Feminizm İçin. *Amargi, 2*, 84-85.

Karakuş, F. (2007b). Mor İğnenin İzi Silinmez. *Amargi, 4*, 8-9.

Kozanoğlu, C. (2001). *Yeni Şehir Notları*. Istanbul: İletişim Yayınları.

Merrill, L & D. Quirk (1994). Gender, Media and Militarism. In Turner L. H.; H. M. Sterk (Eds), *Differences That Make a Difference. Examining the Assumptions in Gender Research* (pp. 179- 186). Westport, London: Bergin and Garvey..

Macdonald, M. (2003). *Exploring Media Discourse*, London: Arnold.

Mills, S. (1997). *Discourse, The Critical Idiom*. New York: Routledge.

Oğuz, A. and M. Yılmaz (2004). Tecavüzün Öncesi ve Sonrası. *Pazartesi, 84*, 4-5.

Öztürk, Ç. (2004). AB'de Kadın Cinayetleri. *Pazartesi, 92*, 20.

Saigol, R (2000). Militarizasyon, Ulus ve Toplumsal Cinsiyet: Şiddetli Çatışma Alanları Olarak Kadın Bedenleri. In Altinay A. (ed). *Vatan, Millet Kadınlar* (pp. 213-245). Istanbul: İletişim.

Savran, G. (2007). Cinsiyetçilik her Zaman Militarist mi? *Amargi, 3*, 34-35.

Selek. P. (2007). Feminizme ve Anti-Militarizme İhtiyacımız Var. *Amargi, 2*, 27-29.
Seçkin, B. (2005). 100 Sayı Yine Düştük Yollara. *Pazartesi, 100*, 4-5.

Spengler, A. (2003). Asıl Meseleleri Erkekler Belirliyor. *Pazartesi, 84*, 19-21.

Walby, S. (2000). Kadın ve Ulus. In Altınay A. (Ed.). *Vatan, Millet Kadınlar* (pp. 29-57). Istanbul: İletişim.

Ülker, F. (2007). Yine Kadınlar Yine Vicdani Red. *Amargi, 3*, 36.

Von Zoonen, L. (1994). *Feminist Media Studies*. London: Sage.

Yılmaz, M. (2005). Siyah Sessiz Caydırıcı. *Pazartesi*, 6-7.

Yurdalan, N. (2007). Kadınlar da Reddeder. *Pazartesi, 103*, 26-27.

Yuval-Davis N. & F. Anthias. (1989). "Introduction." In Yuval-Davis N., F. Anthias (Eds.), *Women, Nation State* (pp. 1-15). London: Macmillan.

Reklam Mesajlarının Algılanmasında İletişimsizlik: Kültürel Yanlış Anlamalar

Işıl Karpat Aktuğlu
İletişim Fakültesi, Halkla İlişkiler ve Tanıtım Bölümü
Ege Üniversitesi
isil.karpat@ege.edu.tt

Nihan Aytekin
Ege Meslek Yüksekokulu, Kariyer Koordinatörlüğü
Ege Üniversitesi
nihanaytekin@yahoo.com

İnsanlığın varoluşundan itibaren devam eden, karşılıklı olarak birbirini besleyen iki evrendir iletişim ve kültür. Sadece kişilerarası iletişimde değil kitle iletişiminde de duyuş, düşünüş ve davranış tarzlarına belirli bir yol çizen kültür, ticari amaçla gerçekleştirilen bir iletişim çabası olarak tarif edilebilecek reklam için de, aynı belirleyici özelliğe sahiptir. Bu yönlendiricilik, ulusal veya uluslararası hedef kitleye yönelik gerçekleştirilen reklam ürünlerinde, hedef kitlenin bakış açısını olumlayıcı biçimde kendini göstermektedir. Kimi zaman da reklam faaliyeti ile hedef kitlesine ulaşmak isteyen kurumun, kültürel kodları reklam mesajına doğru biçimde yerleştirememesi veya yanlış kodları yerleştirmesi nedeniyle iletişim çabası iletişimsizliğe dönüşebilmektedir. Reklam mesajının yanlış kodlanması yanlış algılanmasına, bu da reklamın yayından kalkmasından reklamı hazırlayan kuruma veya o kurumun menşei olarak görülen ülkeye yönelik toplumsal tepkiye kadar değişik sonuçları beraberinde getirebilmektedir.

Reklam mesajlarının kurmaya çalıştığı iletişimin, kültürden kaynaklanan farklı bakış açıları nedeniyle yanlış anlama ile sonuçlanmasına ilişkin bu çalışmada, öncelikle kültür ve iletişim kavramları kısaca tanıtılacak, kültürün bir iletişim formu olarak reklam için öneminden ve kültürel öğelerin reklamda kullanımından bahsedilecektir. Daha sonra reklamı kültürel yanlış anlamalara götüren sebeplere ve dil, din, cinsiyet, etnik köken, adet, gelenek, görenekler gibi kültürel öğeler üzerinden bu tür iletişimsizlik örneklerine yer verilecektir. Son olarak da, bu iletişimsizliği daha oluşmadan önlemede veya oluştuktan sonra giderilmesinde dikkat edilmesi gerekenler unsurlara değinilecektir.

a) Kültür ve İletişim

Latince'de *toprağa bir şeyler ekip ürün almak, üretmek* anlamına gelen **cultura** kelimesinden doğan ve dilimize de Fransızca'dan giren (http://www.historicalsense.com/Archive/Fener64_1.htm 15.04.2007) kültür kavramını tanımlama çabası pozitif anlamda ilk kez 1871'de antropolog Tylor ile başlamış, daha sonraları 1952'de Kroeber ve Kluckhohn'un kültürün 164 farklı tanımını ortaya koymaları ile devam etmiştir (Ana Britannica, Cilt 20, 120). Voltaire'den Marx'a pek çok düşünür tarafından tanımlanmaya çalışılmış olan ve üstelik farklı bilimsel sahalarda farklı anlamlar kazanan kültür kavramına ilişkin olarak şöyle bir tanım ortaya koyabiliriz:

Kültür;

–İnsanların topluluk oluşturarak yaşamaları ile ortaya çıkan,

–Sosyalleşme süreci içerisinde öğrenilen ve paylaşılan,

–Nesilden nesile aktarılan,

–Bireyde kimliğin oluşumuna zemin sağlayan,

–Bir topluluğu, bir örgütü, bir ülkeyi eşsiz kılan ve onu diğer topluluklardan, örgütlerden, ülkelerden ayıran,

–Topluluğun üyeleri arasında birliği sağlayan,

–Varlığı inkâr edilemez,

–Hem geçmişten bugüne ve geleceğe taşınan sağlam temeller üzerinde yükselen, hem de zaman içinde değişebilen,

–İnsanın hayatta kalmasına ve çoğu zaman karşısına çıkan problemlere geçmiş deneyimlerden elde edilmiş çözümleri kolayca bulmasına yardım eden,

somut varlıklar ve örf, âdet, gelenek, alışkanlıklar, fikirler, sanat, inançlar, değer yargıları, roller bütünüdür. Davranış, duyuş ve düşünüş kalıpları kısaca bir yaşam biçimidir.

Her kültürün, üzerinde yükseldiği bazı temeller bulunmaktadır. Bunlar; ekonomik sistemler, aile, eğitim sistemi ve sosyal kontrol sistemleridir (kanunlar, ahlak kuralları, gelenekler vs.) (Ferraro, 1998, s. 23-24). Kültürde yaşanan değişimin, bu temellerden kaynaklandığı ve yine bu ekonomik, politik, sosyal unsurları etkilediği söylenebilir.

Dünyadaki tüm kültürler, kültürel evrenseller olarak tanımlanabilecek bir takım ortak özellikleri paylaşırlar. Bununla birlikte, farklı toplumlar evrensel sosyal ihtiyaçları karşılamak için farklı yöntemler geliştirmişlerdir (Ferraro, 1998, s. 22-23).

Kültürün yukarıda yer verdiğimiz tanımına dikkatli bakıldığında, insanların kültürel öğeleri oluşturmalarını ve nesilden nesile aktarmalarını sağlayan anahtarın aslında iletişim olduğunu görürüz.

İletişimi, teknik açıdan kaynaktan hedefe doğru mesajın kodlanarak iletimi ve hedefin bu kodları çözerek mesajı alması, bunun sonucunda da mesaja ilişkin hedefe bir geri bildirimde bulunması olarak tanımlayabiliriz. Bu çabayı özünde "iletişim" yapan ise, karşılıklı mesaj alışverişi ile ortaya çıkan duygu, düşünce veya bilgidir (Mora, 2006) .

Birey, içinde yaşadığı toplulukla ilişkisini iletişim sayesinde devam ettirir. İletişimde bulunan iki taraf arasındaki ortak anlam paydasında buluşma sonucunda kültür ortaya çıkar. Bununla birlikte, hangi ortak anlam paydasında hangi kavramlarla buluşulacağını iletişimin kültürel boyutu belirler. İletişim kültürü taşırken, kültür de iletişimi mümkün kılar. Kültürel unsurları bir arada tutan iletişim, kültürün devamlılığını sağlarken diğer yandan, içinde doğup büyüdüğümüz kültür de bizim neyi nasıl söyleyeceğimizi ve yapacağımızı belirleyen unsur olmaktadır. Bu doğrultuda, belirli nesneler, olaylar, durumlar hakkında kültürün bilincimize yerleştirdiği ve bu dış uyaranları algılamamızda etkili olan, olumlu veya olumsuz kalıplara da sahip oluruz. Ayrıca, gazete, TV, internet, radyo, sinema gibi kitle iletişim araçlarının bize aktardığı, haber, dizi film, reklam gibi ürünler aracılığıyla da dünyayı algılayışımızı şekillendiren bu kalıplara yenilerini katarız veya mevcut bakış açımızı değiştiririz.

b) Kültürün Reklam İçin Önemi ve Kültürel Öğelerin Reklamlarda Kullanımı

İçinde yaşadığımız topluma genel olarak baktığımızda, aile, arkadaş çevresi gibi birey olarak içinde bulunduğumuz küçük toplulukların varlığını fark ederiz. Bu grupların üzerinde, içinde yaşadığımız ülkenin bir vatandaşıyızdır. Ülkelerin de üzerinde evrensel olarak insan türü içinde yer alırız. Kendi kimliğimizi, ailemiz, üye olduğumuz sivil toplum kuruluşu, yaşadığımız ülke gibi topluluklara göre ifade ederiz. Bununla birlikte kimliğimizi belirleyen dilimiz, dinimiz ya da dini inanca sahip olmayışımız, etnik kökenlerimiz, yaşama biçimimiz bir diğer deyişle kültürümüz de olabilmektedir. Bu doğrultuda bir tanımlama çabasına sadece birey olarak bizler yönelmeyiz. Ticari alanda faaliyet gösteren ve temel amacı ürün veya hizmetini satarak kâr etmek olan kurumlar da potansiyel veya mevcut müşterilerini belirli kriterlere göre tanımlama çabası içindedirler. Rekabet ortamında ayakta kalma çabası içinde olan kurumlar stratejik düşünebilmek için iç ve dış çevreyi analiz ederken, misyon ve vizyonlarını ortaya koyarken, faaliyetlerinin sonuçlarının artı ve eksilerini değerlendirken kısaca her adımda kültürü dikkate almak zorunda kalmaktadırlar.

Kültüre pazarlama ve pazarlama iletişimi alanlarındaki belirleyiciliği açısından baktığımızda şu sonuçlar karşımıza çıkar (Onkvisit ve Shaw, 1989, s. 219-221).

–Kültür, toplum tarafından kabul edilmiş davranış kalıplarını içeren bir perspektif olduğundan, müşterinin karar verme sürecinde onu, toplum tarafından kabul edilebilir ürün seçimleri yapmayla sınırlandırarak kendini gösterir. Kültür, insanlar arasında ortak duygu ve düşünce biçimleri oluşturarak iletişimi kolaylaştıracağı gibi, farklı gruplar arasında ortak kültürel değerlerin olmaması sebebiyle iletişimi zorlaştırabilir. İşte bu, pek çok değişik ülkede yayınlanmak üzere hazırlanmış standart bir reklamın başarısız olmasının sebebidir.

–Kültürün öğrenilebilir oluşu, bireyin yeni kültürel eğilimleri öğrenmesinde kolaylık sağlar.

–Kültür özneldir, bu nedenle de farklı kültürlerden insanlar aynı obje hakkında farklı düşüncelere sahip olabilirler, farklı kültürlerde ortaya çıkan aynı fenomen, farklı anlamlara gelebilir.

–Kültürün kalıcılık özelliği nedeniyle, hedef pazara bir ürünü yerleştirmek için kültürü değiştirmeye çalışmak yerine, o kültüre uygun ürünler üretmek kurum için daha kolay olacaktır.

–Kültür dinamik ve yeni durumlara, yeni bilgi kaynaklarına kendini adapte edebilmesi özelliği, yeni satın alma alışkanlıklarının da oluşmasında kolaylık sağlar. Bunula birlikte değerler ve fikirler zaman içinde değiştiğinden, pazarlamacılar da yeni kültürel değerlere ayak uydurmalılardır.

Bireyin kimliği, algıları, değer yargıları, ihtiyaç ve beklentileri, tüketim alışkanlıkları, tercihleri ve alışkanlıkları, hayattaki kısa ve uzun vadedeki hedeflerinin hepsi, kültürden etkilenerek şekillenmektedir. Kültür, insanların ihtiyaçlarını nasıl tatmin edeceklerini, neyin tüketilip neyin tüketilmeyeceğini belirler. Örneğin Müslümanlar domuz etinin, Hindular da dana etinin tüketiminden kaçınırlar. Günümüz serbest pazar koşullarında rekabete rağmen ayakta kalabilen uluslararası veya ulusal kurumlara baktığımızda, müşterilerinin kültürünü tanıyan ve planlamadan tasarıma, üretimden dağıtıma, satış sonrası hizmetlere kadar bu kültürel öğeleri dikkate alan kurumlar olduğunu görürüz. Kültürel farklılıklara özen gösterilerek gerçekleştirilen reklamlara örnek olarak Drakkar Noir isimli erkek parfümünün reklamı (Milovanovic, 1997, s. 71-78) verilebilir. Arap ülkeleri için hazırlanan reklamda bir kadın elinin, bir erkeğin parfümü tutan elini okşadığı görülürken, ABD'de aynı bayan elinin erkeğin bileğini sıkıca kavradığı görülmektedir. Bu tür farklılıkların bilincinde oluşturulan reklam kampanyaları, kültürel olarak bu konuda duyarlı toplumların bireylerinin olumsuz tepkisinin önüne geçebilmektedir.

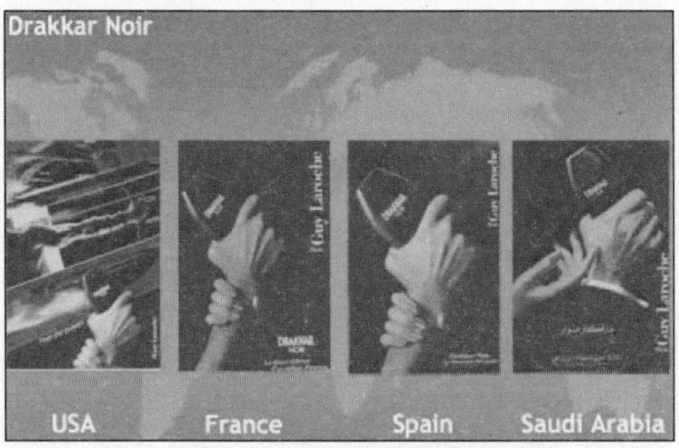

Resim 1: Drakkar Noir Reklamı

Kaynak: "I Am A Netizen" Rumuzlu Kullanıcı, http://myvocalchords.blogspot.com/2006_05_01_myvocalchords_archive.html, 30.03.2007

Pazarlama iletişimi, özelde de reklam çabalarında hedef kitlenin kültürel "hassasiyetlerine" duyarlı olunması, reklamın stratejik olarak planlanması aşamasında başlayan bir süreçtir. İster ulusal ister uluslararası pazar olsun, hedef kitlenin kültürel anlamda kabul edebileceği sınırlar içinde yer alan bir reklam mesajı, bu mesajı düşünüş biçimiyle ortaya koyabilecek bir ajans tarafından yaratıldığı ve yine bu düşünceye olumlu yaklaşan bir medya kanalında yayınlandığı takdirde hedefe ulaşması kolaylaşır. Bu açıdan, uluslararası reklam çabaları için yerel kültürlerin "kırmızı çizgileri"nin bilincinde olan uluslararası bir reklam ajansı veya o kültür içinde faaliyet gösteren yerel bir reklam ajansından da yardım alınabilir.

Reklam mesajı açısından konuya yaklaştığımızda, mesajın içeriği yani metin, başlık, görsel gibi bileşenler konusunda da farklı ulusal kültürlerin farklı tercihlere sahip olduğunu söylemek mümkündür. Kültürlerin yüksek bağlam ve düşük bağlam kültürleri olarak sınıflandırılması, reklam mesajını da şekillendirebilmektedir (Onkvisit ve Shaw, 1989, ss. 223-224). Düşük bağlam kültürlerinde iletişim, sözlü iletişim üzerine yoğunlaşmış, mesajlar, açık ve anlaşılır, mesajın içeriği, mesajın verilme biçiminden daha önemli iken yüksek bağlam kültürlerinde iletişimin odak noktası sözsüz iletişim, mesajların yan anlamları, ilk anlamlarından nispeten daha önemli, mesajın aktarılış biçimi içeriğinden daha önemlidir. Mesajın kaynağı ve hedefinin fiziksel, ruhsal, kültürel özellikleri, mesajın arka planı daha dikkat çekici unsurlar olabilmektedir.

Düşük bağlam kültürleri açısından reklam mesajı içinde de metnin görsel öğelere nazaran biraz daha dikkatle inceleneceğini söylemek mümkündür. Yüksek bağlam kültürlerinde de reklam mesajında görsel öğelere, reklamda kullanılan renklere, fotoğraftaki kadının veya erkeğin duruşu, bakışına, radyo, TV'de yayınlanıyorsa, reklamdaki sesin tonuna, açıkhava ürünüyse reklamın hangi ortamda sergilendiğine ve bu ortamın uygun olup olmadığına vb. bağlam ile ilgili noktalara biraz daha fazla dikkat edecektir. Bu açıdan hedeflenen kültüre göre reklam mesajının bileşenlerini şekillendirmek doğru olacaktır.

Reklamlar ve İletişimsizlik - Kültürel Yanlış Anlamalar

Kültür ve iletişim arasındaki dengenin hassaslığı, ulusal ve yerel kültürlerin değişime uğradığı, uluslararasılaşan bir popüler kültürün ve tabii ki tüketim kültürünün etkisine açıldığı günümüzde, kurumlar hedef pazarlarını olabildiğince genişletme çabası içindeyken, beraberinde kültürel anlamda iletişimsizlik problemini de getirmektedir. İletişimsizliği genel olarak tanımlamak istersek, açık biçimde iletişim kurma çabasının başarısızlığa uğramasıdır diyebiliriz (Traum, 1996). İletişim sürecini düşünürsek, kaynaktan hedefe mesajın iletilmesi ile birlikte hedefin mesajı doğru biçimde anlamaması veya kaynağın mesajı yanlış biçimde aktarmasıdır. İletişimi kaynak ve hedef arasındaki sözlü veya sözsüz mesaj alışverişi olarak düşünürsek, kaynak ve hedef alanlarının kesişmesinden oluşan ortak deneyim alanında buluşmanın gerçekleşmemesi iletişimsizlik olarak değerlendirilebilir. Ayrıca iletişim sürecindeki kırılma olarak da değerlendirilebilecek iletişimsizlik, gönderilen mesajın karşı tarafın aldığı mesaj olmamasıdır da diyebiliriz (Beckham ve King, 2007).

İletişim problemlerinin nedenlerine baktığımızda (Erdoğan, 2005, s. 99),

–Mesajda uygun olmayan sözcüklerin seçilmesi,

–Mesajın uygun olmayan bir kanalla aktarılması,

–Mesajın uygun olmayan bir biçimde şekillendirilmesi (içerik sorunları doğurur),

–Alıcının mesaja dikkat etmemesi, ilgisizliği,

–Sözlü ve sözsüz iletişim arasında tutarsızlık,

–Kaynak ve hedef arasında farklı kültürel geçmiş (dil, dünya görüşleri, ideoloji, inanç, beklenti, alışkanlık, bilinç farklılığı, cinsiyet, ırk),

–Kötü veya yetersiz tasarım ve sunum,

–Uygun olmayan zamanlama (strateji sorunlarını beraberinde getirir),

–Yetersiz geri besleme (talep azlığı, hedefin amaca uygun olarak davranışta bulunmaması gibi şekillerde kendini gösterir) gibi unsurlar karşımıza çıkmaktadır.

Kültürlerarası iletişim boyutundan baktığımızda üzerinde durulan ve çözümlenmeye çalışılan sorunlar ise şunlardır (Erdoğan, 2005, s. 155):

–İnsanları belli kalıplara yerleştirme,

–Diğerleri hakkında önyargılara sahip olma,

–Cinsiyet, yaş, ırk, din gibi farklılıkların getirdiği yanlış anlamalar,

–Hoşgörüden yoksun olma,

–Kültürün dışa kapalı, dışa karşı şüpheci olması,

–Kendini beğenmişlik ve diğer kültürlere saygı eksikliği,

–Kültürel empati yokluğu,

–Geleneksel kültürel değerlere sahip olma.

"İletişimsizlik" ve "Yanlış Anlama" arasındaki bağlantıya baktığımızda, McRoy ve Hirst, İngilizce'de "Misunderstanding" kelimesi ile ifade edilen "Yanlış Anlama"yı, iletişimsizliğin bir türü olarak kabul ederek şu şekilde tanımlamışlardır (Traum, 2007): Yanlış anlama, iletişimdeki iki taraftan birinin mesajı tüm ve doğru bir biçimde yorumladığını düşünmesine rağmen diğer tarafın, mesajı bu biçimde aktarmamış olmasıdır.

Konuya ticari iletişimin bir kolu olarak reklam açısından baktığımızda, *"İletişim süreci bazı aşamalardan oluşur. Öncelikle reklamcı hedef kitle için uygun olan mesajı belirler. İkinci olarak mesaj, farklı kültürel bağlamlarda anlaşılabilecek şekilde kodlanır. Mesaj daha sonra medya kanalları vasıtasıyla hedef kitleye aktarılır, hedef kitle mesajın kodunu çözer ve mesaja bir tepki verir. Sürecin her aşamasında kültürel engeller mesajın etkin bir biçimde iletimini engelleyebilir* (Douglas ve Craig, 2007)." Reklamda mesajın hedefe yöneltilmesinin ardından hedeften beklenen geribildirimin dışında kimi zaman olumsuz bir tepki almak, o reklam çalışmasının iletişim amacını gerçekleştiremediğinin kanıtıdır. Bu iletişimsizliğin arkasında, kültürel yanlış anlamaların önemli bir rolü vardır.

Reklamın kültürel olarak yanlış anlaşılmasının sebeplerine baktığımızda ise;

–Uluslararası pazara reklam üreten bir reklamcının, kendi kültürüne yoğunlaşarak bilinçli veya bilinçsiz olarak diğer kültürleri objektif bir biçimde değerlendirememesi, farklılıkların sebeplerini bilmeden bu farklılıkları "kendi kültürüne nazaran" doğru veya yanlış olarak değerlendirmesidir.

–Gerek ulusal gerekse uluslararası reklam çabalarında, farklı kültürler için standart bir reklam çalışması oluşturma, bir başka deyişle aynı reklam metni, görseli ile farklı ülke pazarlarına kimi zaman aynı ülke içinde farklı yörelerde hedefe yönelme çabası, farklı kültürlerden insanların aynı reklam metni veya görseline benzer tepkiler vermemesi ile sonuçlanabilir.

–Reklamı hazırlayan kişi ya da kurumun zihninde, ırk, din, cinsiyet, dil gibi unsurlara ilişkin basmakalıp düşünceler, iletişimsizliği, kültürel anlamda yanlış anlamaları doğurabilmektedir. Bir başka deyişle, reklam yazarının veya reklam stratejisini ortaya koyan kişi ya da kurumun zihnindeki, o bölgeye, pazara veya ulusa dair imaj, yaratılan çalışmayı da etkilemektedir. Örneğin milliyet açısından bakınca, Türk deyince akla, fes giymiş, bıyıklı, pis erkekler, çarşaflı ya da başı kapalı kadınlar, katı sosyal kurallar gelebilmektedir.

–Sadece reklamın belirli bir kültürel öğeyle uyumsuzluğundan bahsetmek kimi zaman yeterli değildir çünkü kültür de sabit bir ürün değildir, değişkendir. Dolayısıyla kültürel değerler de zaman içinde değişikliğe uğramaktadır. Bunda medyanın da etkisi olmaktadır. Örneğin, kültür için önemli bir unsur olan toplumsal roller açısından baktığımızda, bir zamanların Şanzımanlı Arçelik'i için bayan oyuncuların çitileyerek çamaşır yıkadıkları, fakat çamaşır makinasının onları elde çamaşır yıkamaktan kurtaracağını düşünerek "hayat bu işte" diye haykırdıkları reklamın yerini bugün "Çocuk da yaparım, kariyer de" diyen Orkit reklamı almıştır.

Ekonomik ve sosyal şartların değişikliğe uğramasının yanısıra medya da reklamlardaki bu dönüşümü desteklemektedir. Ancak kimi zaman da reklam, toplumdaki sosyo-kültürel pratiklerin bir adım ilerisinde yer aldığında, bir başka deyişle, daha toplumda bir dönüşüm gerçekleşmeden toplumun önünde giderek bu dönüşümü adeta bir itiş gücüyle gerçekleştirmeye çalıştığında da ters tepki alabilmektedir. Bu tepkiden çekinildiğinden reklam daha yayındayken reklam içeriğinde değişikliğe gidilebilmektedir. Genç Rozi reklamında genç kızın isteklerini sıraladığı cümlede yer alan "anlayışlı bir sevgili" ibaresinin daha sonra "anlayışlı bir nişanlı"ya dönüştürülmesi bir örnektir (http://www.halklailiskiler.com.tr/detay.asp?id=131, 28.04.2007) .

–Genel anlamda doğru bir stratejik plan hazırlanmaması ve bu doğrultuda da reklamın yayınlanacağı pazarın, hedef kitle analizlerinin doğru yapılmaması, ulusal veya uluslararası reklamın istenen etkiyi gösterememesine neden olabilir. Anahtar sözcük, hedef kitleyi doğru analiz etmektir. Hedef pazar veya pazarların demografik, ekonomik, politik özelliklerinden de bir bakıma etkilenen kültürel özelliklerini doğru analiz etmek, bu analiz üzerinden doğru bir yol haritası ortaya koymak, reklam kampanyasının başarı şansını arttıracaktır.

–Reklam ortaya yeni bir fikir koyuyorsa, kişinin ve toplumun kültürel anlamda değişikliğe direnme, eskiyi devam ettirme arzusu da bu yeni fikri benimsemesinde engel olabilmektedir.

–Reklam mesajı, yaratıcı çabaların satış hedefini göz ardı ederek "farklı" olma amacına odaklanması, bunu yaparken de reklam mesajını hedefin anlayamayacağı bir biçimde kodlaması nedeniyle de yanlış anlaşılabilmektedir. Örneğin Boyner'e ait T-box markası, "Uyuyan müşteri kitlesini uyandırmak" amacıyla gerçekleştirdiğini iddia ettiği *"Prezentabl maymun aranıyor"* başlıklı reklam kampanyasında mizahı, sıra dışı ve düşündürücü bir biçimde kullanmıştır. T-box reklamları iş arayan insanları "maymun" olarak tarif ettiği şeklinde görüşlerin de doğmasına sebep olmuştur (Gözler, 2005).

–Reklamın hedef aldığı kitlenin ekonomik gelişme çizgisi üzerinde hangi noktada durduğu da iletişim kurma çabasını etkileyebilmektedir. Sanayileşmiş ve bilgi çağı olarak tabir edilen dönemi yaşayan toplumlar için bir tek ebeveynli aileler, evlilik dışı birlikte yaşamak vb. olağan iken, sanayileşmekte olan üçüncü dünya ülkeleri olarak ifade edilen toplumlar için bu tür kültürel unsurlar ahlaki açıdan doğru kabul edilmeyebilir. Örnek olarak, Yataş'ın ürünlerinin "trendy and friendly" sloganıyla sunulduğu reklam filminde, gencin evlenmeden ayrı eve çıkması (http://haydisohbet.com/sozluk/trendy_and_friendly.html 01.04.2007) verilebilir.

Reklamdaki kültürel yanlış anlamalar ve yanlış anlaşılmalar, kültürün değişik öğelerinde karşımıza çıkmaktadır. Bu öğelerden **dil, din, cinsiyet, etnik köken/milliyetçilik, âdet, gelenek, görenekler** ve kültürü taşıyan toplumsal bir olgu olarak **şiddet** aşağıda örnekler ile açıklanmaya çalışılmıştır.

-Dil

Dil, insan topluluklarını eşsiz kılan ve insanların kimliklerinin temelindeki önemli bir öğedir. Türkiye'de yaşayışımız, Türkçe konuşmamız ile de şekillenir. Dolayısıyla o ülkenin veya bölgenin insanlarına yönelik bir reklam çalışması, o bölgenin dilinin ve dile özgü ayrıntılarının da bilincinde olunarak hazırlanabilir. Başka bir kültürü, o kültürün içinde filizlendiği dili bilmeden anlamaya başladığımızı söylemek mümkün değildir.
Dil konusunda uluslararası reklamcıların yaşadığı en büyük sorun, standart bir mesajın başka bir dile çevirimi aşamasındadır. Bu konuda en bilindik örnek, General Motors'un Chevy Nova adlı ürününü Latin Amerika'da satamamasının sebebinin "NO VA" kelimesinin İspanyolca'da "gitmez" anlamına gelmesi oluşudur (http://faculty.css.edu/dswenson/web/335ARTIC/CULTCOMM.HTM, 10-8-01) .

Toplumda dilin, yabancı sözcüklerin etkisinden korunması, milletin özgürlük ve bağımsızlığın korunması olarak algılanabilmektedir. Türkiye'den güncel bir örnek vermek gerekirse, Kinder Chocolate reklamında çocuklarına Kinder çikolata veren annenin, çikolataya "çaklıt" demesi, Türkçe yerine aynı kelimenin İngilizce karşılığının tercih edilmesi nedeniyle tepki çekmiştir (Aytuğ, 2007).

Dünyaca ünlü piyanist Fazıl Say'ın, 2006 Mart ayında İsrail'de vereceği bir dizi konser için hazırlanan ve Hareetz Gazetesi'in hafta sonu sayısında yer alan reklamlarda ***"Fazıl. Say no more"*** ifadesine yer verilmiştir. Bu ifade; ***"Fazıl, başka söze gerek yok"*** ve İngilizce'deki "say" kelimesi, Türkçe'de "söz" demek olduğundan ***"Sadece Fazıl Say"*** anlamına gelmektedir. Fakat "Fazıl Say no more" aynı zamanda ***"Artık Fazıl Say yok, istenmiyor"*** anlamına gelip olumsuz bir anlatıma da yol açmaktadır (http://www.halklailiskiler.com.tr/detay.asp?id=1616, 09.03.2006) .

-Din

Din, kültürün önemli bir öğesidir. Dine özgü anlatılar, kültür ile iç içe geçmiştir. İnsanların nesilden nesile anlattıkları ve birer öyküye dönüşen kültürün diğer öğeleri de dine özgü imiş gibi algılanabilmektedir. Dine özgü anlatılar kimi zaman o kadar içselleştirilir ki, insanların toplumsal yaşamında ortaya çıkan başka anlatılar da dinsel anlatılar ile bir araya getirilerek yeni formlar oluşturulabilir.
Örneğin, Nisan 1997'de Nike tarafından basketbol ayakkabısı olarak dizayn edilip piyasaya sürülen ayakkabıların arka yüzünde ve tabanındaki "Air" yazısının Arapça "Allah" kelimesinin yazılışına benzerliği ("yldrm.exe" Rumuzlu Kullanıcı, http://www.webhatti.com/genel-sohbet/24395-nike-firmasi-ve-allah-in-ismi.html 28.04.2007), müslüman çevrelerce tepki ile karşılanmış, Amerikan İslami İlişkiler Konseyi Nike'ı uluslararası boykot ile tehdit etmiştir. Nike bu geniş çaplı tepkiye karşılık, 38.000 çift ayakkabıyı geri almak zorunda kalmıştır (http://web.cba.neu.edu/~hlane/footwear.html, 28.04.2007 ve http://www.cnn.com/US/9811/21/nike.islamic/ 21.11.1998).

Türkiye'den örnek verirsek, 2005 İzmir Universiad Oyunları için Türkiye`ye gelen Budist sporcular, Garanti Bankası`nın Shop&Miles kredi kartı için hazırlanmış, Türk Hava Yolları (THY) ikram kutuları üzerinde bulunan, THY uçağına yan bakan Buda reklamına tepki göstermişlerdir. Buda'nın her zaman yan değil ileri baktığı ve reklamda kullanılamayacağı gerekçesiyle Dışişleri Bakanlığı, THY ve Garanti Bankası'na iletilen tepkiler üzerine banka, reklamın derhal durdurulmasına karar vermiştir. Garanti Bankası Reklam ve Halkla İlişkiler Müdürü Naciye Günal, *"Reklam kampanyalarımızın öncesinde çok detaylı çalışarak araştırmalar yaparız. İlgili kurum ve kişilerin görüşlerine başvuruyoruz. Sanırım burada akla gelmeyen bir unsurun üzerinde durulmamış. Aslında Buda`nın ağlayan gülen fotoğrafları var. Fakat Buda`nın yan bakamayacağı konusunda bir fikrimiz yoktu. Ancak olay bize iletildiğinde reklamı hemen durdurttuk."* ifadesini kullanmıştır (http://www.halklailiskiler.com.tr/detay.asp?id=1070, 01.09.2005) . Bu da reklamın üretim sürecinde, mesajın içeriği olarak kullanılacak kültürel özellikle de dini kodların reklam yayınlanmadan önce doğru analizinin gerekliliğini karşımıza çıkarmaktadır.

Resim 2: Garanti Bankası Shop & Miles Reklamı,
Kaynak: Kadife Şahin, **Buda'nın Gözü Kayınca Garanti'nin Canı Sıkıldı**, http://www.milliyet.com.tr/2005/08/31/ekonomi/axeko02.html, 31.08.2005

Kültürün yaşadığı değişimi, "dini unsurlara yönelik hassasiyetin artması" noktasında ele aldığımızda, medyanın bu değişime etkisini şu şekilde örnekleyebiliriz: Efes Pilsen, 1978 yılında Dünya Kupası için üretilen bardak attıklarını, 2006 Dünya Kupası için nostalji amacıyla piyasaya promosyon olarak yeniden dağıtmıştır. Bu bardak altlıklarında Birayevski, Biraienne, Biraviç, Biraçek, Biramann ve "Biraullah" gibi hayali isimler Rus, Fransız, Yugoslav, Çek, Alman ve Arap futbolcu adlarını simgelemekteydi. Bunlardan "Biraullah" yazısı, Türkiye'nin 78'lerde içinde bulunduğu sosyolojik çerçeve içinde kimsenin dikkatini çekmediğinden Efes Pilsen olumsuz bir geribildirim almamış ancak aradan geçen 28 yıl Türkiye'de değer yapısında önemli değişimlere yol açtığından, 2006'da onlarca sivil toplum kuruluşu Efes Pilsen'e karşı tavır almış, Tüketiciler Birliği ise konuya ilişkin savcılığa suç duyurusunda bulunmuştur. Bu olumsuz tepkiye karşılık Efes Pilsen yaptığı yazılı açıklamada özür dileyerek bardak altlıklarını bütünüyle yok ettiğini duyurmak zorunda kalmıştır (Can, 2006).

– Toplumsal Cinsiyet

Kültürü nasıl anladığımız cinsiyetimiz ile de ilgilidir. Kadın veya erkek olmak, doğumumuzdan itibaren birey olarak bize yüklenen toplumsal roller olarak tezahür eder. Ancak cinsellik, muhafazakâr toplumlarda hâlâ bir tabu olarak yer almaktadır. Bu da reklamcıyı dikkatli olmaya, tabulara fazla yaklaşmamaya yöneltmektedir. Alper Menteşoğlu'na göre *"İletişim sanatı, var olan tabuları yıkmak demek değildir. Tam tersine var olan tabuları beceriyle kullanarak kitleleri yönlendirme sanatıdır. Tabulara aykırı reklamlar sadece toplumsal gruplar tabuları yıkmaya başladığında ya da tabular yıkıldıktan sonra kullanılabilir. Çünkü, sadece bu dönemlerde ürünün pazarlanabileceği bir kitle var olacaktır"* (Menteşoğlu, 2006) .

Reklamlarda cinselliğin kullanımı kimi zaman olumsuz tepkilere neden olabilmektedir. İtalyan tekstil firması Armani'nin reklamlarında Uzakdoğu'daki çocuklara yönelik seks turizmini hatırlatan görüntüler kullanılması üzerine, Madrid Çocuk Hakları Koruyucusu Ombudsman, reklamlar hakkında savcılığa ve uluslararası kuruluşlara şikayette bulunacağını açıklamıştır (Hürriyet, 11.03.2007, 15) .

Türkiye'de de benzer bir örnek verilebilir: Eczacıbaşı Topluluğu'na ait prezervatif markası Okey'in (OK) reklamlarından biri ile ilgili olarak Vakit Gazetesi, fuhuşu teşvik ettiği iddiasında bulunmuştur. Eleştirilen reklamın spotları şöyleydi: "Baba, kız arkadaşım hamile", "Doktor... Yoksa ben H.I.V. pozitif miyim ?", "İyi günler, bir kutu OK alabilir miyim ?", "Hangisini söylemek daha zor". Bülent Eczacıbaşı, eleştiri ile ilgili olarak şunları söylemiştir: *"Aslında reklamlarımızı biz de yayına girmeden önce dikkatle inceleriz. İşin bu yönü benim de dikkatimden kaçmış. Baktım, eleştri haklıydı. Çünkü, 'Baba, kız arkadaşım hamile' gibi bir reklam spotu, Türkiye'de örf ve adetlerimize, geleneklerimize uymaz".* Sonuç olarak Bülent Eczacıbaşı Okey'in o reklamını hemen yayından kaldırtmıştır (Hürriyet, 11.03.2007, 22) .

– Etnik Köken/Milliyetçilik

Reklamın hedef kitlesini oluşturan ülke ya da bölgelerde, reklamı yayınlanan kurumun menşei olan ülke ya da topluluğa yönelik resmi kararlar, yaygın toplumsal politik düşünceler, bu firmaların ürün/hizmetlerinin ve reklam çalışmalarının olumsuz biçimde algılanmasına sebep olabilmektedir. Örnek vermek gerekirse, alkolsüz bir içecek, Arap ülkelerine, üzerinde altı noktası olan yıldızları taşıyan çekici bir etiket ile tanıtılmıştır. Araplar bunu, İsrail yanlısı olarak kabul edip bu ürünü satın almayı reddetmişlerdir (http://faculty.css.edu/dswenson/

web/335ARTIC/CULTCOMM.HTM, 10-8-01).

Reklamda tarih ile ilgili unsurların kullanımında da, toplumun belleğinde yerleşmiş kabuller ve değerleri zedelememeye dikkat edilmelidir. Örnek vermek gerekirse, McDonalds'ın ürünü Dolgun Kanatlar'ın tanıtım kampanyasında Tavukçuzade Niyazi Efendi karakterinin kullanılması ile ilgili olarak, Alo RTÜK 178 Hattı'na şikayetler gelmiştir. Habertürk'te yer alan habere göre, McDonald's'ın mizahi tavuk menü reklamının Hezarfen Ahmet Çelebi'yle alay ettiğini düşünen izleyiciler "Tavukçuzade" karakterini eleştirerek, "Tarihimizle, Ahmet Çelebi'yle bu kadar alay etmelerini kınıyoruz" yorumunu yapmışlardır (http://www.marketingturkiye.com/Haberler/Detay/?no=4908, 16.03.2007).

Reklamlarda milliyetçi duyguların kullanılması büyük bir cesaret gerektirmekte ve milliyetçilik duygusunun yoğun olarak işlendiği bir reklam her zaman riskler de taşıyabilmektedir.

Unilever'in ürettiği "Sure" markalı vücut spreyi ile ilgili 2002 yılında İngiltere'deki bazı dergilerde yayınlanan reklamda, *"Bir Türk havaalanında güvenlik gerekçesi ile iç çamaşırıma kadar soyuldum. Hem küçük hem büyük tuvaletim geldi ama koca yerde bir tane bile tuvalet yoktu. Yanımda sevgilimin babası vardı"* ifadelerine yer verilmiş ve sadece "Sure" markalı vücut spreyinin bu durumun üstesinden geldiği belirtilmişti. Reklam ile ilgili olarak Unilever Türkiye yönetim kurulu Üyesi Hakan Behlil, ilgili reklam için İngiltere'ye başvurduklarını, İngiltere'den reklamın dergilerde yayınlanmış olsa da bir daha kullanılmayacağı, ***bir değerlendirme hatası olduğu*** cevabını aldıklarını belirtmiştir (Milliyet, 12.10.2002).

Akbank'a ait bir reklamda ise bir Amerikalı, bir Japon ve bir Türk hızlı trende seyahat etmektedirler. Amerikalı, cep telefonunu icat ettiği ile, Japon, Amerikalının icat ettiği cep telefonunu geliştirdiği ile, Türk ise cep telefonu aracılığıyla 20 dakikada kredi çekmekle övünmektedir. Bu reklam filmi, icat ettiği ile övünen ABD`li, icat edileni geliştirmekle övünen Japon ve başkasının teknolojisi ile en hızlı borcu almakla övünen Türk olarak algılanmıştır (Oflu, 2006). İletişim uzmanlarına göre Akbank reklamı mesajını çok net anlatmakla beraber milliyetçi bir ruh yakalamaya çalışırken reklamın temasında çarpıklık oluşmaktadır. Ayrıca, Türkiye'nin sadece bir tüketim toplumu olarak gösterildiğine ilişkin eleştiriler de yöneltilmiştir. Metin Can'a göre *"Akbank reklamındaki sorun, dünyayı fethetmeye alıştığımız reklamlardaki duyguyu vermemesi ve kafalarda birçok soru işareti uyandırmasıdır,"*(Can, 2006).

– Adet, Gelenek ve Görenekler

Toplumun bilinçaltına işlemiş kurallar, yasalardan bile güçlü olabilen, değiştirilmesi güç ve değişimi zaman alan adet, gelenek ve görenekler, toplumu bir arada tutan kültürün en önemli öğelerindendir.

Procter & Gamble'ın, Avrupa'da yayınladığı ve karısı banyo yaparken içeri girip ona dokunan bir adamı gösteren TV reklamı, Japonya'da, mahremiyetin bozulması, uygunsuz davranış ve zevksizlik olarak kabul edilmiş ve tepki almıştır. Mountain Bell firmasının, telefon ve hizmetlerini Suudilere tanıtmak istediği bir diğer reklamda yönetici, telefonda konuşurken aynı zamanda tabanları gözükecek biçimde ayaklarını masaya çıkartmıştır ki bu Arapların hiçbir zaman yapmayacakları bir şeydir. (http://faculty.css.edu/dswenson/web/335ARTIC/CULTCOMM.HTM 10.08.2001) .

Türkiye'den örnekler vermek gerekirse, Kadir İnanır'ın rol aldığı, bir çarşaf firmasının reklam filminde çamaşır yıkaması, İnanır'ın "Kadirizm"i yerle bir ettiği şeklinde eleştirilere neden olmuştur (http://www.stargazete.com/index.asp?haberID=77193 04.09.2005). Reklam filminin, markaya değer katmada ve satışları arttırmada ne derece başarılı olduğu şüphelidir.

Bir başka örnek, 2002 tarihli Sütaş Ayran reklamında, meşrubatın negatif etkileri, geğiren genç kızla vurgulanmaktaydı. Film, "geğirme" unsurunun kullanılmasıyla tartışma yaratmış, filmin yeni versiyonunda geğirme sesi "bip"lenmişti. Sütaş ve reklam ajansı yetkilileri eleştirilere karşı reklamı savunarak "insana dair gerçekleri" kullandıklarını vurgulamışlar, Benetton, İkea, Smarthbeep, gibi dünyaca ünlü bir çok markanın bu tarz iletişimi kullanmaktan çekinmediğini ifade etmişlerdir (http://www.marketingturkiye.com/Haberler/Detay/?no=47 01.08.2002) . Türk kültüründe, topluluk içindeyken geğirme, gaz çıkarma gibi davranışların ayıp olarak kabul edilmesi, reklamın beğeni yaratarak hoşa gitme amacını zedelemiştir.

Kültürün dil, din, cinsiyet, etnik köken/milliyetçilik, âdet, gelenek ve görenekler gibi öğelerinin yanısıra, kültürden etkilenen ve zaman zaman kültürü etkileyebilen **Şiddet** olgusuna dair reklamlar da yanlış anlamalara sebep olacak mesajlar iletebilmektedirler.

– Şiddet

Şiddet, kültür içindeki pek çok unsurdan kaynağını alarak zaman zaman su yüzüne çıkan zaman zaman da toplumsal bilincin derinliklerinde yaşamına devam eden bir öğedir. Şiddetin reklamlarda kullanımı, her ne kadar ilgi çekici olabilmekte ise de, çoğu zaman eleştirilmiştir. Bununla birlikte şiddet unsurları içeren reklamlar, her ne kadar toplumdan eleştiri alsalar da, bir tür ağızdan ağıza pazarlama fırsatı doğurmaya çalışmakta, böylece reklam medyadan silininceye kadar markadan ve reklamdan bahsedilmeye devam edildiği görülmektedir.

İngiltere'de Dolce & Gabbana'nın bıçaklar ve yaralar taşıyan modellerin yeraldığı kampanyası reklam denetim kurumlarınca sorumsuz ve şiddeti yücelten nitelikte bulunarak eleştirilmiş, Times ve Daily Telegraph'ın eklerinde yayımlanan iki reklama ilişkin Reklam Standartları Kurumu'na (ASA) 166 şikayet gelmiştir.

Cinayet ve Saldırıya Karşı Anneler Derneği'nin de dahil olduğu şikayetçiler ilanların şiddeti destekleyip yücelttiğini ve silahsızlanma çalışmalarını baltaladığını belirtmişlerdir. D&G ilanların ABD ve Çin gibi başka ülkelerde de yayımlandığını ve şikayet alınmadığını, ilanların fazlasıyla stilize ve teatral olduğunu, bu yüzden şiddet veya zarar verme eylemini sergilemediklerini açıklamıştır (Bali, 2007) .

Türkiye'de de, tokat sesinin duyulduğu ve saldırgan bir tavır içeren Regal beyaz eşya markasının reklamlarına benzer Eti Wanted'ın "Farklı Olmak Suç mu?" başlıklı reklamında Komiser ve Polis Memuru, Eti Wanted'ı bir insan gibi sorguya çekmekte ve şu ifadeleri kullanmaktadırlar: *"Utanmıyor musun bütün gençleri baştan çıkarmaya ? Konuş !!", "Bak Wanted, konuşmadığın her saniye içerde bir adamını yiyorlar", "Sorguya devam. Konuşana kadar ısırın".* Eti Wanted'ın bu reklamına ilişkin Barış Girişiminin, "savaş, şiddet ve silahı çağrıştırdığı" gerekçesiyle yaptığı şikayet başvurusunu değerlendiren Reklam Özdenetim Yürütme Kurulu, reklamın söz konusu haliyle yayınlanmamasını istemiştir. Konuyla ilgili açıklamada, reklamda yer alan mesajların hedef kitlesinin gençler olduğunun dikkate alındığı belirtilerek, *"**Parça tesirli pirinç patlakları, uzun menzilli karamel** ve **kamufle edici sütlü çikolata** mesajları, günümüzde dünyanın ve toplumumuzun bir numaralı sorunu olduğunda kuşku bulunmayan şiddeti simgeleyen unsurları taşımaktadır"* denilmiştir (http://www.halklailiskiler.com.tr/detay.asp?id=2165, 07.10.2006) .

c)Reklamlarda İletişimsizlik/Kültürel Yanlış Anlamaların Sonuçları

Kişilerarası iletişimde *"bazı yanlış anlamaların negatif sonuçları ve etkileri olabilmekte, kızgınlık veya hayal kırıklığı gibi duygulara neden olabilmektedir. Bu tür yanlış anlamalar her türde ilişkide ve sosyal alanda gerçekleşse de farklı kültürlerden insanlar, toplumlar, örgütler, gruplar arasında gerçekleştiğinde probleme dönüşmesi kolaylaşmaktadır. Etnik önyargılar, etnik azınlıklara karşı farklı davranmaya sebep olabilmektedir"* (Tzanne, 2007).

Kitle iletişimi açısından baktığımızda da iletişimi gerektiği gibi kuramayan ve dolayısıyla yanlış anlaşılan reklamların olumsuz sonucu genelde, hem yasal hem sosyal anlamda yoğun bir şikayet ve ötesinde ürünlerin boykot edilmesi olmaktadır. Kimi zaman da başarısız bir reklam kampanyası, firmanın kötü bir imaj ile pazardan tamamen çekilmesine sebep olabilmektedir. Kültürün nesilden nesile aktarımı unsurunu dikkate alırsak, bu firmaya yönelik olumsuz düşünceler o toplumda nesilden nesile aktarılarak o marka için olumsuz bir kurumsal ünün doğmasına kadar gidebilir.

Reklam mesajının esas amacı, kârı arttırmak, marka bilinirliğini arttırmaktır. İletişim kurmada başarısız bir reklam, tüketici tercihlerini etkiler. İmaj kaybına neden olur. Satış oranları düşer, bu nedenle de reklam esas hedefine yani kârı arttırma amacına ulaşamaz. Ürün yaşam eğrisi açısından konuya baktığımızda, eğer ürün pazara yeni sunulacaksa, daha baştan pazara girişte engelle karşılaşma, olgunluk aşamasında ise, ürünün kötü imajı nedeniyle müşteri tarafından tercih edilmemesi, daha az talep görmesi ve dolayısıyla rekabette geri kalma, şirket için gelecekte yine aynı pazara başka ürünler sunmaya çalışırken de, geçmişteki imaj kaybının tekrar hatırlanması ile yeni ürünlerin daha başlamadan olumsuz biçimde değerlendirilmesi gibi sonuçlar doğurmaktadır.

d) Yanlış Anlamayı Önlemek İçin Yapılabilecekler

Reklam içeriğinin kültürel öğeler açısından yanlış değerlendirilmesini önleyebilmek için firma, reklamı varolan veya potansiyel müşterisine sunmadan önce;

- Reklam mesajlarının içeriğinin (hem sözel hem de görsel anlamda), reklam mecralarının, mesajın tasarım ve sunumunun, mesajın sunulduğu anın, günün, dönemin, hedef kitlenin din, dil, kadın ve erkeğin toplumsal rolleri, etnik köken, adet, gelenek ve görenekler gibi kültürel öğelerine uygunluğuna dikkat etmelidir.

- Düşük bağlam kültürlerine yönelik bir reklam hazırlanıyorsa bilginin sözlü mesajla taşınması ve içerik ihtiyacını karşılamak için ürün veya hizmet ile ilgili doyurucu bilgi vermek, yüksek bağlam kültürleri için ise görsel öğeleri ön planda tutmak fakat mesajın iletildiği bağlamı da gözden kaçırmamak gerekir.

- Hedeflediğimiz pazarın kültürünün zaman içinde değişime uğrayabileceği de göz önünde bulundurulmalıdır. Türkiye açısından düşündüğümüzde günümüz insanı artık 40 yıl öncesinin Türkçe'si ile konuşmamakta, bu nedenle de 70'lerin Türkçe'sinden reklamlara giren bazı kelimeler bugün artık kullanılmaz olmuştur. İnternetin hayatımızdaki rolünün artmasıyla da artık teknolojik terimler yavaş yavaş kullanım içine girmektedir. Türk adet ve geleneklerinden bazılarının artık yaşamadığını, yeni adetlerin oluştuğunu, bazılarının da değişikliğe uğradığını söylemek de mümkündür.

- Öteki'ni anlayabilmek de, kültürel unsurların iletişim sürecindeki kullanımı açısından kolaylık sağlar. Toplumda din, ırk, cinsiyet, adet ve görenek olarak farklı olan insanların farklılıklarının bilincinde olunarak ve toplumdaki hoşgörü ortamını zedelemeden iletişim kurma çabası, özellikle farklılıkların kimileri tarafından problem olarak gösterilmeye çalışıldığı günümüzde, önem taşımaktadır.

Eğer ki hedef kitlede reklamı yanlış anlama şeklinde bir sonuç ile karşılaşıldı ise, olayı örtbas etmek veya yanlış yapıldığını kabul edilmeyip yanlışın savunulması yerine, yanlış derhal kabul edilmeli ve bu doğrultuda bilgi verici, firmanın asıl iletişim amacının ne olduğunu ortaya koyan yeni bir iletişim haritası çizilerek, problem olabildiğince ortadan kaldırılmaya çalışılmalıdır. Kısaca bu durumu bir kriz olarak kabul edip, kriz dönemi iletişim politikalarını devreye sokmak, yapılabilecek en doğru şey olacaktır.

Yanlış anlamanın reklam sonucunda ortaya çıkmasını önlemek için yapılması gerekenleri kısaca özetlemek için, Roger Fisher ve William Ury'nin bu amaçla ortaya koydukları önerileri (Burgess, 2003), reklama uyarlayabiliriz:

1. **Aktif dinleme:** Karşımızdaki kitlenin bizi yanlış anlamasında bizim de kendimizi yanlış ifade etmemiz sebep olabilir. Onların gözünde şirketimizin imajı nedir ? Bunu bilmeden gerçekleştirilecek iletişim çabası, başarısız olabilir. Reklam yayınlanmadan önce tüketicinin reklam hakkındaki görüşlerini isim çağrışım, cümle tamamlama gibi pretestler ile ölçmek genelde reklamın etkinliğini kültür ile etkileşiminin izleyici/dinleyici tarafından nasıl algılandığını görmeyi sağlar.

2. **Karşınızdaki ile doğrudan konuşmak:** İletişimi, hedef kitle ile işletmenin ortak tecrübe alanında, açık ve net mesajlar yönelterek gerçekleştirmektir.

3. **Belirli bir amaç için konuşmak:** Reklamın stratejik açıdan çerçevesini çizerken hedef kitleyi, politik, ekonomik, sosyal ve kültürel olmak üzere tüm yönleriyle iyi analiz etmek, özellikle de reklamda kültürel öğelere yer verilecekse, bu öğelerin hedef kitle için anlamının farkında olmak önemlidir. Doğru hedef kitleye, doğru reklam ajansı ve yaratıcı ekip, doğru bakış açısı ile doğru reklam mesajını yönlendirmek işletmeyi, reklamın temel amacı olan "kâr elde etme"ye yaklaştıracaktır.

e) Sonuç

Kültürel öğeler, iletişimin her alanında olduğu gibi pazarlama iletişiminin önemli bir kolu olan reklam için de, sunulmak istenen mesajın anlam kazanmasına yardım eden öğelerdir. Bu öğeleri reklamda doğru kullanmak gerek ulusal gerekse uluslararası reklam çabaları için hedefe giden yolda başarıyı beraberinde getirirken, bu öğeleri yeterince analiz etmeden, basmakalıp düşünceler dışında o kültürü tüm yönleriyle tanımadan, o kültürün yaşadığı dönüşümü bilmeden, stratejik bir planlamaya gitmeden kimi zaman da bilinçsiz bir biçimde reklamda kullanmak, hedef kitlede olumsuz tepkilere sebep olabilmektedir. Bunların yanısıra, "farklı" olma çabası uğruna reklamın, reklam mesajının içeriği, tasarımı, mecrası vb. ile kültür ile uyuşmayan yapay bir yeniliği sunması da reklamın yanlış anlaşılması sonucunu doğurabilmektedir.

Reklamı gerek firma için satışı arttırmada öncü güç olarak, gerekse popüler kültür ve tüketim kültürünün önemli bir kaynağı olarak, toplumun duygu, düşünce ve anlayışı üzerinde etkili bir iletişim yolu olarak alırsak, iletişimsizlik ve özellikle de kültürel yanlış anlamaların olumsuz sonuçlarının boyutlarını daha kolay kavrayabiliriz. Dil, din, etnik köken, toplumsal cinsiyet, adet, gelenek ve görenekler gibi kültürel öğelerin reklam mesajı olarak doğru biçimde kodlanmaması ve doğru bir biçimde aktarılmaması sebebiyle reklamın, *"hedef aldığı tüketici kitlesi üzerinde belirli bir etki yaratmak ve bu kitlenin düşünme ve alışkanlıklarını etkilemek yoluyla satın almaya yöneltmek* (Kocabaş ve Elden, 1997, s. 18)" amacını gerçekleştirmesi zorlaşmaktadır. Bu durumda da yapılması gereken öncelikle reklam daha yayına sunulmadan önce bu noktaların farkına varmak, eğer reklam yayında ise derhal hedef kitlenin görüşleri doğrultusunda reklam mesajının sebep olduğu yanlış anlamayı düzeltmektir.

Kaynakça

*Kültür (*1994), Ana Brittannica Cilt 20, s. 120. İstanbul: Ana Yayıncılık ve Sanat Ürünlerini Pazarlama San. ve Tic. A.Ş.

Armani'ye Suçlama—Afişi çocuklarla seks turizmini çağrıştırıyor, Hürriyet, 11 Mart 2007, s. 15.

Aytuğ, Y., *Reyting Canavarı Bu Kez "İnci" Yuttu!* http://www.sabah.com.tr/gny/haber,C5059F5AB351425294886 5F7A4E9AEF6.html (Son erişim 10.04.2007).

Bali, S., *Dolce&Gabbana'nın bıçaklı ilanları eleştirildi.* http://www.marketingturkiye.com/Haberler/Detay/?no=7034 (Son erişim 12.01.2007).

Beckham, K., King, J., *Communication in Coalitions.* http://ohioline.osu.edu/bc-fact/0006.html (Son erişim 28.04.2007).

Burgess, H., *Misunderstandings.* http://www.beyondintractability.org/essay/misunderstandings/ (Son erişim 09.09.2007).

Can, M., *1978'de Sorun Olmayan "Biraullah" Sözü 2006'da Efes Pilsen'in Başını Ağrıttı.* http://www.halklailiskiler.com.tr/detay.asp?id=1509 (Son erişim 24.01.2006).

Can, M., *Reklamlardaki Türk Bir Dünyaya Bedeldir.* http://www.milliyet.com.tr/2006/02/19/son/soneko11.asp (Son erişim 19.02.2006).

Cultural Misunderstandings. http://faculty.css.edu/dswenson/web/335ARTIC/CULTCOMM.HTM (Son erişim 10.08.2001).

Çarşaf yıkadı arabayı kaptı. http://www.stargazete.com/index.asp?haberID=77193 (Son erişim 04.09.2005).

DouglaS S, P. , Craic C. S., *International Advertising. ht*tp://pages.stern.nyu.edu/~sdouglas/rpubs/intad.html (Son erişim 14.04.2007).

Erdoğan, İ. (2005). *İletişimi Anlamak.* Erk Yayınları, Ankara.

Eti'nin Çikolatası Savaşa Takıldı. http://www.halklailiskiler.com.tr/detay.asp?id=2165 (Son erişim 07.10.2006).

Fazıl Say'ın İlginç Reklamı. http://www.halklailiskiler.com.tr/detay.asp?id=1616 (Son erişim 09.03.2006).

Ferraro, G.P. (1998). *The Cultural Dimension of International Business* (Third Edition). Prentice Hall, Inc.

Footwear International. http://web.cba.neu.edu/~hlane/footwear.html (Son erişim 28.04.2007).

Genç Rozi Kızımız Nişanlanmış. http://www.halklailiskiler.com.tr/detay.asp?id=131 (Son erişim 28.04.2007).

Gözler, Ö., *T-box, Prezentabl Maymun Arıyor*. http://www.halklailiskiler.com.tr/detay.asp?id=1236 (Son erişim 18.10.2005).

I Am A Netizen Rumuzlu Kullanıcı. http://myvocalchords.blogspot.com/2006_05_01_myvocalchords_archive.html (Son erişim 30.03.2007).

Kocabaş, F., Elden, M. (1997). *Reklamcılık: Kavramlar, Kararlar, Kurumlar*. İstanbul: İletişim Yayınları.

Menteşoğlu, A., *Reklamcılıkta Yaratıcılığı Yanlış Anlamak*. http://www.halklailiskiler.com.tr/detay.asp?id=1794 (Son erişim 06.05.2006).

Milovanovic, G. (1997). Marketing Dimensions Of Global Advertising. *The scientific journal FACTA UNIVERSITATIS*, Series: Economics and Organization, *1(5)*, 71 – 78, http://facta.junis.ni.ac.yu/facta/eao/eao97/eao97-08.pdf (Son erişim 28.04.2007).

Miscommunication.http://discover.edventures.com/functions/termlib.php?action=&termid=3360&alpha=m&searchString= (Son erişim 28.04.2007).

Mora, N., *Çağımızın Hastalığı İletişimsizlik Sorunu*. http://www.bianet.org/2006/01/26/73847.htm (Son erişim 26.01.2006).

Munyar, V., *Bir "t" harfi için üç ülkede anket yaptılar*. Hürriyet, 11 Mart 2007, s. 22.

Nike And Islamic Group End Logo Logjam. http://www.cnn.com/US/9811/21/nike.islamic/ (Son erişim 21.11.1998).

Oflu E. A., *Fıkra Misali*. http://www.halklailiskiler.com.tr/detay.asp?id=1709 (Son erişim 07.04.2006).

Onkvisit, S., Shaw, J.J. (1989), *International Marketing: Analysis and Strategy*. Merrill Publishing Company.

Sütaş artık geğirtmiyor. http://www.marketingturkiye.com/Haberler/Detay/?no=47 (Son erişim 01.08.2002).

Tavukçuzade'yi RTÜK'e şikayet ettiler. http://www.marketingturkiye.com/Haberler/Detay/?no=4908 (Son erişim 16.03.2007).

Traum, D., *Miscommunication: the Good, the Bad, and the Ugly", Symposium on Miscommunication*. http://www.psych.unito.it/csc/cogsci05/frame/symposia/sp11-healey.pdf (Son erişim 28.04.2007).

Traum, D., *What is Miscommunication?* http://tecfa.unige.ch/tecfa/research/cscps/Papers/Aaai96m3ws/node2.html (Son erişim 23.03.1996).

Trendy and Friendly. http://haydisohbet.com/sozluk/trendy_and_friendly.html (Son erişim 01.04.2007).

Tzanne, A., *Talking at Cross-Purposes: The Dynamics of Miscommunication*. http://www.informatik.uni-bremen.de/~tenbrink/TzanneChap1_talkBartnik.pdf (Son erişim 14.04.2007).

Unilever'den reklam özürü. Milliyet, 12.10.2002

Uygarlık, Kültür ve İnsanlık. http://www.historicalsense.com/Archive/Fener64_1.htm (Son erişim 15.04.2007).

Yan Bakan Buda Reklamı Durduruldu. http://www.halklailiskiler.com.tr/detay.asp?id=1070 (Son erişim 01.09.2005).

yldrm.exe Rumuzlu Kullanıcı, *Nike Firması ve Allah'ın İsmi*. http://www.webhatti.com/genel-sohbet/24395-nike-firmasi-ve-allah-in-ismi.html (Son erişim 28.04.2007).

Nasıl Bir Medya: Uzlaşan mı Çatışan mı? Orhan Pamuk ve Nobel Ödülü Üzerine Bir Değerlendirme

İzlem Vural
İletişim Bilimleri Fakültesi, Basın Yayın Bölümü
Anadolu Universitesi
ikvural@anadolu.edu.tr

Son yıllarda Türkiye'de giderek artan Milliyetçilik akımının medyada da çeşitli boyutlarda görüldüğü; özellikle televizyon kanallarında, izlenme oranları ve popüleritenin arttırılması adına "popüler milliyetçilik" olarak tanımlanabilecek içerikteki yayınlara zaman zaman yoğunlukla yer verildiği gözlenmektedir. Ermeni ve Kürtlerle ilgili gerek Türk gerekse yabancı medya'ya demeçler veren 2006 Nobel Edebiyat Ödülü sahibi Orhan Pamuk'un 12 Ekim 2006 tarihinde Ödül'ü almasıyla birlikte, özellikle Türk medyasında birçok farklı görüş dile getirilmiştir.

Pamuk'un ödül almasının açıklandığı tarihte, Fransız Parlamentosu'nun "Sözde Ermeni Soykırımı Yasa Tasarısı"nın Alt Meclis'te kabul edilmesinin ardından, eş zamanlı olarak Pamuk'la ilgili olumsuz görüşlerin özellikle Türk medyasında çarpıcı ve yoğun bir şekilde yer bulduğu; Pamuk'un Ödül'ü almasıyla birlikte ise, Türk kamuoyunda var olan mevcut yaygın görüşün, Pamuk tarafından zaman zaman yapılmış olan Türkiye ve sözde Ermeni Soykırımı'na ilişkin açıklamalarla dönemsel olarak eş düştüğü görülmektedir. Bu bağlamda Türk televizyon kanallarında "haber programları" çerçevesinde Pamuk'a ilişkin ne tür yorumlarda bulunulduğu ve yaygın medya olarak kabul edilebilecek olan televizyonun konuya ilişkin ne tür bir tutum ve tavır geliştirildiği incelenmiştir; diğer bir deyişle, entelektüel düzeyi yüksek olan programlarda (izler kitlenin sosyo- kültürel ve eğitim düzeyi açısından yüksek olduğu varsayılan) popüler milliyetçilik kavramının Orhan Pamuk ve Nobel Ödülü üzerinden nasıl ele alındığı, çerçevelendirildiği; pompalandığı mı, uzlaştırmacı bir üslup ile mi, yansız mı değerlendirildiği incelenmeye çalışılmıştır.

Çalışma kapsamında izlenme oranları en yüksek olan haber programları karşılaştırılmak üzere seçilmiştir. Haber bültenlerinde haberciliğin etik ve mesleki ilkeleri çerçevesinde yorumdan uzak, objektif habercilik anlayışının var olduğu ön kabulüyle, sözü edilen konuya ilişkin, yoruma ya da kişisel perspektife dayalı olarak görüşlerin daha açık olarak ortaya koyulabildiği "haber/tartışma programları"na yoğunlaşılması gerektiği düşünülmüştür. Bu nedenle çalışmada 2006 Nobel Edebiyat Ödülü'nü alan Pamuk'la ilgili Türk Ulusal televizyon kanallarında yayınlanan "entelektüel düzeyi" yüksek olarak kabul edilen/ varsayılan "haber programlarının" 12 Ekim – 19 Ekim 2006 tarihlerini kapsayan 7 günlük periyot içerisindeki içerikleri incelenerek, Türk televizyonlarındaki haber/ tartışma programlarında sözü edilen spesifik olaya ilişkin söylem ve yaklaşım ortaya konulmaya çalışılmıştır.

Kültürlerin, yaşam biçimlerinin, tüketim alışkanlıklarının evrenselleştiği ve tek tipleşme yolunda hızlı bir ivme ile yol almasına karşın bugün "milliyetçilik" kavramı halen birçok platformda tartışılan ve görüş bildirilen konu olmaktan çıkamamıştır. Bu nedenle, çalışmanın temel çerçevesini oluşturan "milliyetçilik" ve milliyetçiliğin "popüler" bir söylem olarak yer bulmasını açıklamak üzere öncelikle "milliyetçilik" kavramı üzerine geliştirilmiş olan tanımlamalara değinmenin yerinde olacağı düşünülmektedir.

Guibernau'ya göre "milliyetçiliğin gücü her şeyden önce bir kimlik duygusu yaratma yeteneğinden kaynaklanmaktadır ve kuşku ile dolu bir dünyada parçalanmışlık içinde ve bireyler için yaşamı anlamlı kılacak ideolojilerin yokluğunda ulusalcılık en etkin güç haline gelir". Hroch'un ise "çözülen bir toplumda ulusalcılık bütünleştirici faktörleri içermektedir" (Aktaran Guibernau, 1997, s. 221) ifadesinde bireyin toplumsal bir kimliğe sahip olma ihtiyacının da etkili olduğunu söylemek mümkündür; diğer yandan, Hroch'un milliyetçiliğe ilişkin "çözülen toplumlar" yaklaşımı da farklı bir bakış açısı olarak değerlendirilebilir; ancak, tarihsel süreçlere bakıldığında milliyetçiliğin her zaman çözülme halinde olan toplumlarda ortaya çıktığını ya da ivme kazandığını söylemek mümkün değildir.

Milliyetçiliğin üç tarihsel süreç içerisinde incelenmesi gerektiğine değinen Hobsbawm, kavramın başlangıçta kültürel, edebi ve folklorik bir içeriğe sahip olduğunu, bu çerçevede dernek ve cemiyetler gibi tam siyasi kimliği olmayan yapıların ortaya çıkmaya başladığını, daha çoğunlukla geçmiş tarihsel süreç ve gelişmeler çerçevesinde şekillendiğini ve bu bağlamda da tarihsel bir yorumlama yapıldığını ifade etmektedir. Bu yarı siyasi oluşumların sonrasında millet kavramının ön plana çıkartıldığı ve savunucularının farklı ölçeklerde siyasi yapılanmalar içerisine girdiğini ve böylelikle toplumsal bir görüş ve sınıf yaratmak adına ortak hedefler yaratılması mücadelesinin yer aldığına dikkat çekmektedir; diğer bir deyişle, toplumsal ait olma duygu ve davranışını siyasi bir çerçeve içinde yeniden düzenleme sürecinin başladığını vurgulamaktadır. Yarı siyasi ve ardından gelen siyasi yapılanma çabaları sonucunda kitlesel boyutta hareket başlamış ve iktidarlar açısından dikkate alınan bir akım ortaya çıkmıştır (Hobsbawm, 1993, ss. 26-28). Yaklaşımından da anlaşılacağı üzere tarihsel gelişme aşamasından da bakıldığında, milliyetçilik kavramının temelinde "ortaklık ve ait olma" hissinin ve aynı zamanda bu ortaklığın belli bir siyasi tabanda birleştirilme isteğinin ön plana çıkmakta olduğu görülmektedir.

Milliyetçiliğin bugünün toplumsal düzeninde birçok siyasi ideolojiden baskın bir birleştirici güç kaynağı olduğunu savunan Yeniçeri'ye göre ise milliyetçilik, birey olmanın, yabancı ölçütleri kaldırmanın, onurlu olmanın ve kendine saygı duymanın doğal sonucudur. "Milliyetçi hareketler, milletlere kendi kaderini belirleme, millî karakterini koruma ve özel vasfını insanlığın ortak mirasına katma noktasında tarih boyunca katkı sağlamışlardır. Kendi kendini yönetmek, kendi geleceğine egemen olmak düşüncesinin bir toplumda fonksiyonel hâle gelebilmesi, bireylerin kendilerinin ne olduğunu farkına varmaları ile mümkündür. Ortak kimlik, ortak heyecan, ortak kader ve bir topluma âidiyet duyma, özgürlüğün ilk şartıdır. Milliyetçiliğin, ortak değerleri bu yöndeki geliştirme yeteneğinin, her türlü duygunun önünde olduğu görülmektedir. Hatta milliyetçilik bu değerleri tutum, davranış, töre ve gelenek hâline sokarak kurumsallaştırmaktadır" (Yeniçeri, 2007).

Maksudyan (2005) Türk milliyetçiliğinin vatandaşlığa dayalı milliyetçiliklerden biri olduğunu, dolayısıyla üstünde yaşanan toprak parçasını temel aldığını ve bireylerin din, dil, ırk gibi farklılıklarını göz ardı eden ortak bir vatandaşlık bağıyla bir arada tutulduklarını savunmaktadır (s. 7).

Kent yaşamına geçişle birlikte değişen toplumsal yapılar, ahlak anlayışının yeni bir form alması gibi sosyo-kültürel değerlerdeki değişim ve bu yeni ortamın yarattığı etkiyle artan sosyal ve ekonomik sorunlara bir tepki olarak, toplumsal kimlik arayışı kolayca ulusal kimliğin kurulmasını sağlayabilmektedir. Beraberinde bu oluşum diğer tüm kimlikleri bastıracak tutucu milliyetçilik duygu ve iddiasına da dönüşebilmektedir. Grupların arkada kalan ya da üstü örtük biçimde ifade edilmeye çalışan ortak sorunlarının etkisiyle bir araya gelme isteği aynı şekilde diğerlerinden güç alma refleksiyle birleşince kitlesel hareketlere dönüşmede kolaylık sağlamaktadır. Ulusal kimliğin oluşturulması için—bütün bu sorunlar dışında—birey ve grupların arasındaki ortaklığı vurgulayan simge ve inanç kümelerinin tekrar tekrar üretilmesi, etkili bir şekilde dolaşımı ve tüketimiyle mümkün olabilmektedir (Mutlu, 2005, s. 345).

Tılıç'a (2001) göre milliyetçilik, son derece insani ortaklık duygularını iktidarlar adına manupile ettiğine, iktidarlara kalkan olduğu ve yabancı düşmanlığı beslediği için insanlığın kuşkuyla bakması gereken bir ideolojidir. Milliyetçiliğin ve öteki söyleminin temelinde bir siyasal elitin kendi iktidarını meşrulaştırma çabaları vardır. Aslında, bütün siyasal iktidarlar kendi yönetimlerini meşrulaştırmak için değişik düzeylerde milliyetçiliğe ve "öteki" söylemine sarılmaktadırlar (s. 198).

Hobsbawm'ın ortaya koymuş olduğu tarihsel gelişim sürecine göre Türk milliyetçiliğine bakılacak olursa, Cumhuriyet dönemi boyunca Türkiye'de milliyetçilik ilk iki aşamayı tamamlamış ve günümüzde siyasal ve toplumsal sahnenin ayrılmaz bir unsuru olarak, üçüncü aşamasını yaşamaktadır. Türk milliyetçiliğine özgü bir durum olarak bu aşama, ***siyaset ötesi* ve *ideolojiler üstü*** bir durum olarak yaşanmaktadır. Milliyetçilik bir refleks olarak ve toplumdaki bireylerin ilksel aidiyet bağı olarak anlaşılmakta ve yaygın olarak bu şekilde kabul görmektedir. Söz konusu kabul görmede ulusal basın kuruluşları, sadece olağanüstü dönemlerde değil olaysız dönemlerde de, belirlediği gündemler, milli sembollerin kullanımı, üslubundaki milliyetçilik vurgusuyla bu işlevi yerine getirmekte önemli bir araçtır. Ulusal basın kuruluşları kolaylıkla özel hayatlara müdahil olabilmeleri dolayısıyla da milliyetçi ideolojilerin yaygınlaştırılmasında ve siyasi propagandada kullanılmaktadır (Bostancı, 1999, s. 78).

Türkiye'de ise Ulus'u kuran ve topluma sunulan milliyetçilik ideolojisi, Cumhuriyet söyleminde ilk bakışta, toplumda var olan kültürel, etnik, dinsel aidiyetlerden bağımsız bir üst kimliğe gönderme yapsa da, süreklilik sağlayamamış ve Ulus'u oluşturan unsurlardan biri zaman içinde farklı vurgularla araçsallaştırılmıştır. Buna bağlı olarak, ulus ve milliyetçilik konusunda tek bir Cumhuriyet söyleminden bahsetmek de mümkün görünmemektedir. Dolayısıyla, Ulus'a ait olma duygusunu sağlaması beklenen milliyetçilik, toplumu oluşturan bireyler arasında benzer bir algılama oluşturamamış ve gerilimli bir alan olmuştur. Buna ek olarak, zaman içinde ulusal ve uluslararası ölçekte yaşanan sorunlar karşısında, çeşitli devlet kademelerinde alınan tepkisel ve sadece o güne uygun geçici önlemler, sürekli yeniden gözden geçirilen tarih okumaları, din konusunda farklı zamanlarda alınan farklı tavırlar Türk milliyetçiliğinin sorunlu bir alan olma özelliğini pekiştirmiştir. Türk milliyetçiliği doğallaşarak, "kendiliğinden" paylaşılan bir ideoloji olmak yerine, çatışmaya yatkın bir alan olmuş,parçalanma ve kutuplaşmaları önleyememiştir.

Türkiye'de milliyetçilik dalgasının giderek artması ve hemen hemen tüm toplumsal kesimleri etkisi altına almasının birçok nedeni olmakla birlikte, özellikle 1993 yılında yoğunlaşan ve giderek artan terör olayları başta gelmektedir. Devamında yaşanan olayları DSP, MHP ve ANAP'ı iktidara taşımış ve terör örgütünün başı Abdullah Öcalan'ın yakalanmasıyla Milliyetçi dalga giderek büyümüş ve aynı partiler oyları artırarak yeniden iktidara gelmişlerdir. Bu olayların ardından 1999 yılında Helsinki'de yapılan Avrupa Birliği devlet ve hükümet başkanları zirvesinde Türkiye'ye tam üyelik kapısın açılmasına ilişkin ilk işaretin verilmesiyle milliyetçi dalga giderek artmış, Avrupa Birliği uyum sürecinin ulusal egemenliğimizi bazı yönlerden etkileyeceği düşünülmeye başlanmıştır. Özellikle Avrupa İnsan Hakları Mahkemesi'nden Abdullah Öcalan'ın yeniden yargılanmasına ilişkin yeni bir kararın çıkma olasılığı, kültürel haklarla ilgili yapılan yasal düzenlemeler, azınlıklarla ilgili kararlar ve Türkiye'de bunun üzerine hazırlanan raporlar, yabancılara gayrimenkul satışıyla ilgili yasal düzenlemeler bütün bu süreçteki en etkili unsurlar arasında ilk sıralarda yer almaktadır.

Bunlara ek olarak Ermeniler ile ilgili AB üyesi ülkelerde Türkiye'nin soykırım yaptığı iddialarının ortaya atılması, ulusal ve bölgesel meclislerinde bu iddiaların görüşülmesi o dönemlerde kamuoyunun yoğun olarak dikkatini çekmiş ve toplumsal tansiyonu kayda değer anlamda yükseltmiştir. Benzer şekilde ABD'nın Irak'a demokrasi getirmek adına başlattığı işgal ve Kuzey Irak'ta ortaya çıkan durum da bu etkenler arasında yer almıştır. 6-7 Eylül Olayları'nın yeniden hatırlanması, Mersin'de iki çocuğun Türk Bayrağı'nı yakması da toplumda hatırı sayılır tepkilerin ortaya çıkmasına neden olmuştur.

Toplumsal değişim açısından bakılacak olduğunda, son 15- 20 yıl içinde nüfusun terör ve ekonomik nedenlerden dolayı Türkiye'nin Doğu'sundan Batı'sındaki kentlere kaymasının ve bunun da beraberinde getirdiği yoksulluk, işsizlik, kentsel gerilim, Türkiye'nin 2001 yılında yaşadığı ekonomik kriz, sorunların aşılmasında tutunacak bir dal olarak Milliyetçiliği popüler hale getiren nedenler arasında bulunduğu söylenebilir. Milliyetçi söylemleriyle egemenliğe ortak olmak veya siyasal iktidarı elde etmek isteyenlerce her daim canlı tutulan popüler milliyetçilik dili, iktidarı kollayanları cazip hale getirirken aynı hislerle yaşayan yoksullara ve dışarıda kalanlara da iktidara dâhil olma hissi vermesi nedeniyle etkisi altına almaktadır. Bunun en canlı örnekleri televizyon kanallarında gösterilen bazı dizilerde görmek mümkün olabilmektedir (Kara, 2007). Popüler milliyetçiliğin izleri "Deli Yürek", "Kurtlar Vadisi" gibi dizilerdeki kurgusal yapıyı kendilerinin gerçek yaşam koşullarına adapte etmeye çalışanların basına yansıyan dramatik öykülerinde de yer almaktadır. Var olmayı diğerinin yok edilmesi üzerine kuran ideoloji azınlıkları, farklılıkları, çeşitliliği, dinsellikleri ulusal güvenliğe karşı bir tehdit olarak algılamaya devam etmektedir. Çok kültürlülüğü devamlı olarak dışlayan katı ve birbirinin aynı, tek tip vatandaş modelini egemenliğin teminatı sayan bürokratik "devletçi" yapının son yüzyıl içinde ürettiği "resmi" milliyetçi söylemin informal bir söyleme dönüşerek Mersin'de bayrak krizini, Trabzon'daki linç girişimlerini, Hırant Dink ve yine Trabzon'daki papaz cinayetlerine sosyal bir zemin hazırladığı söylenebilir.

Türkiye'ye ifade özgürlüğünün sınırlarını genişletin tavsiyesinde bulunan Avrupa Birliği, birlik üyesi Fransa'nın Ermeni soykırımı iddiasının inkârını suç sayan kararını engelleyememiş ve tepki dalgası yine yükselmiştir. Avrupa Birliği ekseninde oluşan milliyetçi tepki, vatan hainliği suçlamalarına varan saflaşmaları beraberinde getirmiş ve gerilimin tırmandığı görülmüştür. Avrupa Birliği süreci, özellikle de Ermeni meselesi, PKK sorunu gibi başlıklarla tırmanan gerilim, toplumsal kıvanç sahasını da daraltmıştır. Birçok uluslararası başarıda kendini gösteren sevinç, Orhan Pamuk'un Nobel'i almasında aynı coşkuyla ortaya çıkmadı. Nobel'e Eurovizyon kadar sevinemedi Türkiye (NTV, 17. 10. 2006)

Ulusal gururu ayakta tutmak için spor, sanat ve politik alanlardaki uluslararası başarıların oldukça etkili olduğu ve yine resmi milliyetçi söylemin yansımalarının bu tür dönemlerde yoğun olarak görüldüğü söylenebilir. Türkiye toplumda giderek artan yabancı düşmanı, farklılıkları hazmedemeyen, bütünleştirici olmayan ve etnosentrik niteliğe sahip vulgar milliyetçi anlayışa sahip basının ciddi etkisi olduğu gözlenmektedir. Özellikle sportif karşılaşmalarda—futbol maçlarında—"Gürültüyü bu adi Fransız çıkarıyor" (05.11.1993, Fotomaç), "Adi satılmış Fransız hakem üçlüsü" (24.08.1994, Fotomaç), "İşte Avrupai kesim Cim Bom İspanyol Boğası Mallorca'yı AB standartlarına uygun şekilde şoklayarak kurban etti" (17.03.2000, Zaman), "Çanakkale'de dedelerimizi geçemeyen İngilizler Kopenhag'da aslanlarımızı geçemedi (18.5.2000, Star), "Al sana soykırım" (14.3.2001, Star), "Binlerce şehit verdiğimiz Kore'de, Koreli bir hakem yüzünden Brezilya'ya boyun eğdik" (4.6.2002, Takvim) şeklinde atılan başlıklar bunun en önemli göstergeleri arasında yer almaktadır (Ulus, Ocak 2007, s. 213). Devamlı olarak "Tarih yazan", "Destan Yazan", "Avrupa'yı sallayan" "Fatih'in torunları" bu toplum istese de alternatifsizlikten bu söylemlere daha fazla dayanamamaktadır. Milliyetçi söylemler popüler, beğenilir hale getirilerek yoksulluğun, sınıfsal çelişkilerin ve buna bağlı baskıcı rejimlerin en yoğun olduğu ülkelerde bilinçli olarak revaçta tutulduğu görülmektedir.

Destan yazılan milli maçlar gazete sayfalarını boy boy

kaplarken, işsizlik, aile içi dramlar, ekonomik sorunlar, enflasyon, terör, trafik kazaları gibi Türkiye'nin önemli sorunları ikinci hatta üçüncü plana itilmekte "üçüncü sayfa" haberi olarak yer bulmaktadır. 12 Eylül'den itibaren her tür siyasi düşünce yasaklanırken milliyetçiliğin tek ve mecburi bir istikamet olarak gösterilmesi toplumda yan etkileri bilinmeyen acı bir ilaç olarak farklı sonuçların ortaya çıkmasına neden olabilecektir. Malı tarlada kalan köylüden, tek geçim yolu elinden alınan dolmuşçuya, devlet arazisi üzerine yaptığı kaçak gecekondusunu belediye ekiplerinin elinden kurtarmaya çalışan bu ve bunun gibi her sorununu İstiklal Marşı söyleyerek bayrak önünde dile getiren, protesto için otoyolları kapatmaya giderek bu yolu "öteki"ne dayatma şekline dönüştüren toplum fertleri aslında sekteye uğrayan adalet anlayışı içinde yine "biz bu ülkenin çocuklarıyız" demeye çalışmakta "devlete" aynı milliyetçi söylemle tepki vermektedirler.

Kitle iletişim araçlarının 21. yüzyılda toplumu ve bireyleri yönlendirme ya da ortak dünya görüşü yaratma gücüne sahip olduğu yapılan birçok bilimsel araştırma ve ölçme sonucunda kuşkusuz yadsınamaz bir gerçek olarak kabul edilmektedir. Bu araçların içerisinde, etkinlik ve yaygınlık açısından bakıldığında, televizyonun toplumsal yapı içerisinde "biz" duygusunu yaratabilmesinde ya da güçlendirmesinde özellikle söz konusu olan milliyetçilik bağlamında popülarite yaratabilmesinde önemli bir aktör olduğunu söylemek de mümkündür.

Milliyetçilik ve milli devletlerin XIX. yüzyılın temel özelliği olduğunu ve buna karşılık kitle iletişim araçlarının egemen müdahil bir faktör olarak toplumsal ve siyasal hayata etkilerinin XX. yüzyıl içinde gözlendiğini ifade eden Bostancı, milliyetçiliği doğuran nedensellikler içinde kitle iletişim araçlarının sayılamayacağı ancak araçların varlıklarıyla, içerikleriyle ve mesajlarıyla sürece katıldıklarını vurgulamaktadır (Bostancı, 1999, s. 77).

Medyayı "yardımcılık" rolünü aşar şekilde ve adeta kişilerin kendilerini bir millete ait olarak hayal edebilmelerine güçlü kanıtlar sunan bir işlevde tanımlayan Deutsch'a göre "iletişim süreçleri toplumların, kültürlerin ve hatta bireylerin kişiliklerinin tutarlılıklarının temelini oluşturur; bir halka mensup olmak, toplumsal iletişimin geniş tamamlayıcılığından ibarettir" (Aktaran: Bostancı, 1999, s. 78). Naven ise, insanların genel olarak çevrelerindeki dünyayı bir kalıp içinde algıladıklarını ve buna model de denilebileceğini ve bu modelin de bir tür harita fonksiyonu gördüğünü ifade etmekte ve karşılaşılan hangi olayların olumlu ya da olumsuz sayılacağını gösterdiğini dile getirmektedir (Aktaran Bostancı, 1999, s. 78).

Modleski'nin (1998) artık "tanıdıklarımız" televizyonda seyrettiklerimiz, "tanımadıklarımız" ise dışarıda kalan diğer dünyadır (s. 32) ifadesine paralel olarak, özellikle televizyon gibi görselliği ön plana çıkartma üstünlüğüne sahip olan bir aracın "biz" ya da "ortaklık" hissi yaratmada kitlelerin kuşkusuz aynı görselliği izliyor olmalarının üstün ikna ediciliği kayda değer bulunmakta ve böylelikle benzer ya da ortak kaygıların, amaçların, yorumların ve yayılmaların ortaya çıkabildiğini söylemek mümkündür.

Canetti kitle iletişim araçlarının milliyetçilik üzerindeki etkilerinin çözümlenmesinde kitlenin özelliklerini/niteliklerini tanımlarken, kitlenin devamlı olarak büyümeyi isteyen (coşkun milliyetçi gösterileri kameranın özel perspektifiyle ekrana sınırsız kalabalıklar olarak yansıtması ve bu sayede kitlenin büyüme arzusuna cevap verdiğini), kitle içinde üyelerin eşit hissetme ihtiyacının baskın olduğu (kolektif biçimde kardeşlik hissi yaratmak ve aynı ortaklık içinde bulunmak), kitlenin yoğunluğu sevdiği (özdeş ve ortak kılan yayınların birleştirici unsur) ve kitlenin belli bir yöne gereksinimi olan (medyanın farklı mekanlarda bulunan ve birbirlerinden farklı sorunlarla uğraşan bireyleri "milli konularda" oluşturduğu ortak gündemin etrafında toplayan) bir takım özellikler taşıdığını ön planda tutmaktadır (Aktaran, Bostancı, 1999, s. 81).

Kitlesel medya, fiili milli sembolleri her bireyin yaşamının bir parçasına haline dönüştürme konusunda çok etkilidir. 1918'den sonra yükselen milliyetçilikte milli kimlik, kendini modern, şehirleşmiş ve yüksek teknolojili toplumlarda ifade etmenin yeni araçlarından biri olarak modern kitlesel medyanın (basın, sinema ve radyonun) yükselişinden söz etmek gerekmektedir. Popüler ideolojiler bu araçlarla hem standartlaşabilir, homojenleşebilir ve dönüştürülebilir hem de açıkça özel çıkar sahipleri ve devletler tarafından maksatlı propaganda amacına yönelik olarak kullanılabilirdi. (Hobsbawm,1995, s. 168).

Milliyetçilik kavramına ilişkin genel tanımlamaların ardından çalışmanın bundan sonraki bölümünde 2006 yılında Edebiyat dalında Nobel Ödülü'nü alan yazar Orhan Pamuk'un Ödül'ü almasının açıklanmasıyla birlikte özellikle Türk medyasında dile getirilen görüş ve yorumlar incelenecektir (incelemenin temel amacı milliyetçiliğin tam da özel bir örnek teşkil ettiği düşünülen dönem, olay ve kişi üzerinden yapılabilmesidir). Aynı gün Ermeni Soykırımı'na ilişkin Yasa Tasarısı'nın Fransız Alt Meclisi'nde onaylandığı da göz önüne alınacak olduğunda Türk kamuoyunun genel tepkisinin özellikle milliyetçilik söyleminde olduğu hatırlanacaktır. Bu çerçevede 12 Ekim- 19 Ekim 2006 tarihleri arasında Türk televizyon kanallarında entellektüel düzeyi yüksek olarak varsayılan haber programlarının Türk kamuoyunda da en çok tartışılan başlıklar çerçevesinde olumlu, olumsuz ve nötr verilişlerine ilişkin içerik ve söylem çözümlemesi yapılarak aşağıdaki sorulara cevaplar aranmaya çalışılmıştır:

–Orhan Pamuk nasıl sunulmuştur,

–Nobel'i Orhan Pamuk'un alması nasıl sunulmuştur,

–Orhan Pamuk'un edebiyatçı kimliği nasıl sunulmuştur,

–Nobel Ödülü nasıl sunulmuştur,

–Orhan Pamuk'un Ermeni Soykırımı'na ve Türkiye'deki Kürt sorununa ilişkin verdiği demeçler nasıl sunulmuştur,

–Milliyetçilik kavramına değinilmiş midir,

–Orhan Pamuk'u haklı bulanlar ve bulmayanlar nasıl sunulmuştur,

–Nobel Ödülü ile Fransız Alt Meclisi'nin kararı ilişkilendiriliyor mu,

–Orhan Pamuk'a Nobel Ödül'ü siyasi gerekçelerle mi verilmiştir.

Yukarıda belirtilen sorular 12 Ekim - 19 Ekim 2006 tarihleri arasında aşağıda isimleri belirtilen haber programlarda ele alınmıştır. Çalışma da bir haftalık zaman diliminin seçilmesindeki neden, tepkisel söylemlerin net olarak görülebilmesine ilişkin olmuştur; diğer bir deyişle soğukkanlılığı dışlayan, ani tepkilerin ölçülmesi temel unsur olarak değerlendirilmek istenmektedir. Belirtilen tarihler arasında aşağıdaki televizyon kanallarının haber programlarının ağırlıklı olara Milliyetçilik, Nobel Ödülü ve Orhan Pamuk üzerinde yoğunlaştığı görülmektedir.

Çalışmanın bir sınırlılığının bazı televizyon kanallarının daha önceden belirlenmiş olan rutin yayın akışlarının değiştirilememesi ve Pamuk ve Ödül'e ilişkin özel yayın gerçekleştiremediklerinden kaynaklandığını söylemek mümkündür.

Çalışmada aşağıda isimleri belirtilen televizyon programları ele alınmıştır:

ATV: *Son Baskı* – Ergun BABAHAN, Yılmaz ÖZDİL

HABER TÜRK: *Nobel Özel Yayını* –Murat ONGUN, Ali ÇAĞATAY (Telefon. Konukları Gazeteci Yazar Güneri CİVAOĞLU, Gazeteci Yazar Oral ÇALIŞLAR)

CNN TÜRK: *5 N 1K*-Cüneyt ÖZDEMİR (Konuk: Prof. Dr. Jale PARLA, Edebiyat Eleştirmeni Ömer TÜRKEŞ)

NTV: *Neden* -Can DÜNDAR (Konuk: Prof. Dr. Orhan KAVUNCU, Gazeteci Yazar Prof. Dr. Mehmet ALTAN, Yazar Alev ALATLI, Gazeteci Ömer LAÇİNER, Öğretim Üyesi Anıl ÇEÇEN, Yazar Tanıl BORA ve İstanbul Teknik Üniversitesi öğrencileri)

TRT 1: *Sınırlar Arasında* -Banu AVAR

KANAL D: *Arena* -Uğur DÜNDAR (Konuk: Başbakan Recep Tayyip ERDOĞAN)

KANAL 7: *Sözün Özü*- Nazlı ILICAK (Konuk: Gazeteci Yazar Hırant DİNK, Gazeteci Yazar Etyen MAHÇUPYAN, Türk Tarih Kurumu Prof. Dr. Kemal ÇİÇEK, Gazeteci Yazar Uluç GÜRKAN, Avukat Belkıs BAYSAL, Gazeteci Yazar Oral ÇALIŞLAR)

Çalışma boyunca yapılan çözümlemelerde Orhan Pamuk'un Nobel Ödülü'nü almasına ilişkin olarak, medyada kişisel yorum ve analizlerin yapılabildiği bir biçim olması nedeniyle haber programları tercih edilmiştir. Bu çerçevede Türk televizyon kanallarında yer alan bu programlarda sözü edilen ana unsurlara ilişkin nasıl ve ne doğrultuda bir tutum ve tavır sergilendiğinin saptanması amaçlanmıştır.

Orhan Pamuk Nasıl Sunulmuş

Genel bir ifadeyle hemen hemen incelenen tüm programlarda Pamuk'un entellektüel, tabu kıran bir fikir adamı, dünyaca ünlü edebiyatçı, muazzam başarı kazanmış bir aydın olarak "olumlu" sunulduğu söylenebilir. Söylemler arasında özellikle HABER TÜRK kanalında yayınlanan Nobel Özel Yayını'nda genel olarak Ongun ve Çağatay'ın Pamuk ve Nobel'i almasına ilişkin olarak abartılı denilebilecek ifadeler kullandıkları dikkati çekmektedir; öyle ki olay ve kişi sürekli olarak "muazzam", "muhteşem" ve "son derece önemli" olarak tanımlanmakta ve aynı zamanda Pamuk'un sadece Nobel'i almasıyla çok değerli bir kişilik haline gelmediği, bundan uzun yıllar önce de Pamuk'un yurt dışında "misafir alim" olarak ders verdiği, 27 yaşından bu yana birçok ödüle layık görüldüğü, Nobel tarihinde en genç yaşta bu Ödül'e layık görülen aday olduğu vurgulanmıştır. Aynı programda bugüne kadar Nobel'i almış kişilerin hemen hemen hepsinin yaşadıkları toplumsal ve siyasal sisteme "muhalif ve aykırı" kişiler olduğunu ve Pamuk'un da böyle bir kişilik özelliği sergileyerek standarda uyan bir kişi olarak sunulduğu, ayrıca Nobel'i alan ilk ve tek Müslüman olduğu ifadeleri göze çarpmaktadır.

KANAL 7'nin programında ise "Pamuk toplumun çok önünde", "bu ülkenin başına düşebildiği kadar Orhan Pamuk düşsün", "Mutluluk ve gurur veren bir yazardır", "Orhan Pamuk'un hamuru Türkiye'dir" şeklindeki ifadeler konuklar tarafından dile getirilmiş ve olumlu söylem üzerinde yoğunlaşılmıştır. Programa kısa telefon mesajları ve elektronik posta soruları aracılığıyla birçok izleyici katılmıştır, ancak bunların içerisinden konuklara sorulacak soruların Ilıcak tarafından özenle seçildiği gözlenmiştir. Sorular arasından yaptığı seçimlerinden dolayı Ilıcak'ın Pamuk kişiliğinde milliyetçilik söylemini yoğunlaştıran ve programda ağırlıklı olarak tartışılmasını ve bir anlamda tansiyonu yükseltip gerilimi arttıracak nitelikteki soruları tercih ettiği dikkati çekmektedir. Bu sorulardan ya da yorumlardan ön plana çıkartılan bazıları: "Orhan Pamuk vatan hainidir", "Orhan Pamuk şehit anaları için ne yapmıştır", "Orhan Pamuk Merve Kavakçı için ne yapmıştır" şeklindedir.

Nobel'i Pamuk'un Alması Nasıl Sunulmuştur

CNN TÜRK kanalında yayınlanan 5N 1K haber programında Özdemir'in, günlerdir medyada Pamuk'un konuşulduğunu ve bu ödülü almasına sevinenler kadar ne yazık ki üzülenlerin de var olduğunu söylemesi ve edebiyatçı kişiliğinin tartışılması gerektiğine dikkat çekmesi; kullanılan "ne yazık ki" ifadesinin gerçekte haksızlık ya da üzüntü alt okumasını çağrıştırabilecek bir gösterge/vurgulama olduğu düşünülmektedir.

NTV deki programa katılan konuk Laçiner, Pamuk'u Türkiye'nin kalburüstü birkaç romancısından biri olarak tanımlamakta ve Ödül'ü de hak ederek aldığını ifade etmektedir. Benzer şekilde HABER TÜRK kanalında da "herkes eline vicdanına koysun ve düşünsün; Dünya, Pamuk sayesinde Türkiye'yi tanıdı, gurur verici ve muhteşem bir öyküdür bu Türkiye için, bugün şölendir, düğündür" ifadesi kullanılarak kamuoyuna olumlu yönde mesaj verilmiştir. Programa telefon konuğu olarak katılan Çalışlar, dünyanın önde gelen yazarlarının genel olarak sisteme karşı kişilikler olduklarını; ancak Nobel'in Pamuk'a verilmesinin Türkiye adına büyük bir zafer olduğunu vurgulamıştır.

KANAL 7'nin program konuklarından Çiçek "Orhan Pamuk'un Nobel almasını içime sindiremiyorum çünkü yabancı basın Nobel Edebiyat Ödülü Orhan Pamuk'a verildi diyor ama arkasından da ekliyor: Kimdir bu Orhan Pamuk, Türkiye'yi kastederek bu topraklarda bir milyon Ermeni 30 bin Kürt öldürüldü diyen yazardır deniyor" ifadesiyle olumsuz olarak görüşünü dile getirmiştir.

NTV'de yayınlanan Neden programında ise öncelikle Türkiye'de son yıllarda yükselen bir değer olarak ortaya çıkan milliyetçilik dalgası üzerinde durulduğu, Pamuk ve Nobel'in de bu dalgalanmalar çerçevesinde yerini bulduğu görülmektedir. Programda sunulan sesli bant görüntülerinde (vtr) kullanılan ifadeler ve görüntüler yükselen milliyetçilik duruşunu destekleyen miting ve gösteri biçimindeki arşiv görüntülerinden oluşmaktadır. VTR'de geçen *"İtalya'ya kaçan Abdullah Öcalan'ın Türkiye'ye iade edilmemesine 1998 yılı sonbaharında ülkenin dört bir yanında tepki yükseliyordu. Aslında sadece protestolarda değil, sevinç gösterilerinde de politik ve milliyetçi mesajlar bolca kullanılmaktaydı. Galatasaray'ın 2000 yılında UEFA kupasını alması sonrasındaki kutlamalar ve tezahüratlarda hedefte Avrupa vardı. Sevinç başka bir alanda yakalanınca da sonuç değişmiyordu. Eurovizyon birinciliği de Türkiye'yi sokağa döktü. Puansız sonunculukların ardından gelen bu başarının mimarı Sertap Erener'i Taksim meydanında on binler karşılayacaktı. Bu başarıdan yaklaşık 1 yıl önce ise aynı kalabalıklar Fransa Parlamentosu'nun Ermeni soykırımı iddiasını tanıyan bir karara imza attığında yine sokaklardaydı. Türkiye'ye ifade özgürlüğünün sınırlarını genişletin tavsiyesinde bulunan Avrupa Birliği, birlik üyesi Fransa'nın Ermeni soykırımı iddiasının inkarını suç sayan kararını engelleyemedi ve tepki dalgası yine yükseldi. Avrupa Birliği ekseninde oluşan milliyetçi tepki, vatan hainliği suçlamalarına varan saflaşmaları beraberinde getirdi, gerilim arttı. Avrupa Birliği süreci, özellikle de Ermeni meselesi, PKK sorunu gibi başlıklarla tırmanan gerilim, toplumsal kıvanç sahasını da daralttı. Pek çok uluslararası başarıda kendini gösteren sevinç, Orhan Pamuk'un Nobel'i almasında aynı coşkuyla ortaya çıkmadı. Nobel'e Eurovizyon kadar sevinemedi Türkiye. Yani özellikle Fransa'nın son kararından sonra bu konu gündeme geldi. Orhan Pamuk'un ödül alması bir başka dalga yarattı. Türkiye'de sevinemediğini gördük insanların Nobel ödülüne"* ifadesiyle Türkiye'nin özellikle son yıllarda yükselen milliyetçilik dalgasıyla Nobel'i alan ancak verdiği demeçleriyle daha ön plana çıkan Pamuk'a ilişkin üstü çok da açık olmayan bir gönderme yapılmaktadır. Bu ifadelerle kamuoyunun Nobel'e sevinememesinin bir nedeni olarak Pamuk isminin etkili olduğu ve Ödül'ün anlam ve içeriğinden çok Pamuk ve açıklamaları çerçevesinde ön plana çıktığı vurgulanmaktadır.

Orhan Pamuk'un Edebiyatçı Kişiliği Nasıl Sunulmuştur

Genel olarak programlarda Pamuk'un başarılı bir edebiyatçı olarak değerlendirildiği ve olumlu yönde edebiyata katkılar sağladığı üzerinde durulmuştur. Ödül'ün gerçek nedeni olarak edebiyatçı kişiliğin ön plana çıkartıldığı 5N 1K programında Pamuk'un tamamen edebi açıdan değerlendirildiği ve konuklarla bu çerçevede görüşüldüğü; romanlarının 40 dile çevrilerek birçok ülkede okunduğu ve Pamuk'un edebi yönünün tanımlanırken "kendi şehrinin melankolik ruhunun arayışında kültürlerin çatışması ve birbirlerine karışması için yeni semboller keşfeden" bir yazar olduğu üzerinde durulmuş ve olumlu bir söylem sergilenmiştir. Konuk Türkeş ise benzer olumlu ifadeler kullanarak Pamuk'u edebi anlamda yeni bir imge yaratan ve yazarlığı yanında zanaatkarlığı da olan bir yazar olarak tanımlamıştır. HABERTÜRK kanalında Pamuk, Türk dilinde yazan dünya devi bir yazar, Nobel'i almasaydı da büyük bir yazar olarak tanımlanırken, ATV'de dile hakim, okuması zor ve usta bir yazar olarak tanımlanmıştır.

KANAL 7'nin programında ise "Orhan Pamuk'un edebiyatçı kimliği sunulurken evrensel bir dil oluşturduğu, Türk kültürünü yeni bir anlatıma kavuşturduğu şeklinde olumlu söylemler gözlenmiştir.

Nobel Ödül'ü Nasıl Sunulmuştur

Nobel Ödülü'ne ilişkin yapılan yorumlarda kimi zaman olumsuz olarak nitelendirilebilecek ifadelerin bulunduğu göze çarpmaktadır. HABER TÜRK kanalında "son derece önemli 105 yıllık bir çınar, rüştünden kuşku duyulmayacak bir Ödül olarak tanımlanırken, ATV'de Ödül'e ilişkin bir takım siyasi ve ideolojik unsurların üzerinde ağırlıklı olarak durulduğu göze çarpmaktadır. ATV'de yayınlanan programda Özdil, edebiyat alanı dışında verilen ödüllerin genellikle Amerika'lı adaylara verildiğini, dolayısıyla Ödül'ün bir ideolojik boyutunun da mutlak surette var olduğunu vurgulamaktadır. Özdil, Uzay'a ilk çıkan ülkenin Rusya olmasına karşın Rus bilim adamlarına Nobel verilmemesini ve soğuk savaş döneminde antikomünistlik duruşunun var olduğunu ifade etmektedir.

NTV'de ise Alatlı Nobel'e ilişkin olarak "Nobel neticede bir dünya görüşünü ittirmek üzere kurulmuş bir kurumdur ve bu dünya görüşü Avrupa'nın dünya görüşüdür ve ne barış tarafı, ne de edebiyat tarafı konjonktürel doğrularda ayrılmaz ve ters düşmez. Yani 1974'de Solijenitsin'e Nobel verirsiniz, Gulak takım adaları için. Edebi eser olduğu için mi? Hayır. Gulak takım adaları olduğu için. Döner ...... verirsiniz vs. vs" şeklindeki açıklamasıyla benzer biçimde siyasi ve ideolojik boyutta Nobel'i değerlendirmektedir.

TRT 1'de yayınlanan programda ise genel olarak Nobel Ödül'ünün siyasal ve ideolojik boyutu, uluslararası siyasi çıkar ve dengeler çerçevesinde tanımlayan söylemlerin ön planda tutulduğu dikkati çekmektedir. *"Oslo bir kuzey ülkesi olan Norveç'in başkenti. Aynı zamanda son 15-20 yılın barış görüşmelerinin yapıldığı yer. Oslo, ABD'nin terörle mücadelede en büyük destekçisi. "Oslo, yüz yıldır silah satıyor aynı zamanda yüz yıldır barış ödülü dağıtıyor. Tüm barış görüşmelerinin başkenti olan Oslo, dünya silah sanayinin en önde gelen ülkesi. Acaba verilen onca barış ödülü neyin bedeli?" Ortadoğu'ya en çok silah satan ülkeler arasında, İsrail ilk nükleer yeteneklerini Norveç'ten alıyor. Irak'ta toplu katliamlar yapılırken barış havarileri ve silah üreticileri Oslo'da bir araya geliyor. 11 Eylül'den sonra Norveç'in silah satışı artıyor. Özellikle Afganistan operasyonları sırasında silah satışında patlama yaşanıyor. "Nobel 85 batılı ülkeye verildi son yıllarda da Batılı ülkelerin çıkarları için çalışanlara veriliyor"* ifadesi kuşkusuz Nobel ödül'üne ilişkin farklı bir noktaya işaret edilen ve olumsuz olarak değerlendirilen bir söylem içeriyor.

Orhan Pamuk'un Ermeni Soykırımı'na ve Türkiye'deki Kürt Sorunu'na İlişkin Verdiği Demeçler Nasıl Sunulmuştur

Yazar Pamuk'un İsviçre'de yayınlanan *Das Magazin* adlı dergide yer alan röportajında "Türkiye'de bir milyon Ermeni, 30 bin Kürt öldürüldü" şeklindeki ifadesinin sözü edilen haber programlarında nasıl sunulduğu çalışmanın ortaya konmasına çalışılan amacı açısından büyük önem taşımaktadır.

HABER TÜRK kanalında Pamuk'un Türkiye ve Ermeni Soykırımı'na ilişkin İsviçre'de verdiği demece ilişkin Çağatay ve Ongun genel olarak olumlu; Pamuk'un yeterince açıklama yaptığını ancak kamuoyunu yine de ikna edemediğini ve Nobel'e sevinemediklerini dile getirmişlerdir. Programa telefon bağlantısı ile konuk olan Civaoğlu, Nobel ile Fransa Meclisi'nin kararının aynı güne denk gelmesini "ilahi" bir rastlantı olarak değerlendirmiş ve Pamuk'un yaptığı açıklamaları "talihsiz" olarak tanımlamıştır. Pamuk'un bundan sonraki tüm açıklamalarında Nobel'i almış bir kişi olarak çok daha dikkatli olması gerektiğini çünkü bundan sonra özellikle soykırımla ilgili söyleyeceklerinin her kelimesinin Ermeniler için referans olacağının altını çizmiştir.

ATV'de yayınlanan programda Babahan ifade özgürlüğünden yana olduğunu ve birilerinin de çıkıp "kral çıplak" diyebilmesi gerektiğini söylemiştir. "Kral çıplak" ifadesinin alt okumasında Pamuk'un vermiş olduğu demeçten dolayı suçlanamayacağını, sorumlu olanın söyleyen değil bu işi yapan kişi olduğunun altının çizilmesi gerekliliği üzerinde durmuştur. Buna karşılık programın diğer yapımcısı ve özellikle karşıt söylemleri ile dikkat çeken Özdil ise, gerçekte Pamuk'un neyi söylemediği ile ilgilenilmesi gerektiğine dikkat çekmektedir. Özdil'e göre Pamuk, Fransa Meclisi'nde görüşülen Ermeni Yasa Tasarısı ile ilgili fikir beyan etmediğini, aydın bir kişi olarak bu Tasarı'nın düşünce özgürlüğüne bir darbe olacağını ifade etmediğini defalarca vurgulamıştır. Özdil ayrıca "Kürt öldü, Ermeni öldü de, peki hiç mi Türk ölmedi, ölen Türkleri neden söylemedi. Ermeni meselesini tartışmanın yolu şu kadar bu kadar Ermeni mi öldürüldü demektir; hiç Türk öldürülmemiş gibi..Cumhuriyetimizi sokakta bulmadık biz. Tüm dünyanın yükünü gariban Türkiye ve halkı mı çekecek..Bu son derece ahlaksız bir demeçtir" söylemiyle milliyetçilik hissini yoğunlaştırmış ve dikkatleri bu yöne, milliyetçilik boyutuna taşımıştır. Özdil'in sözü tamamlamasının ardından Pamuk'un "sözlerimin bütünüyle arkasındayım, söylediğim sözlerin sorumluluğuna sahibim. Türkiye'deki fikir özgürlüğü, kendini ifade etme davasına sonuna kadar bağlıyım" açıklamasının bulunduğu bir VTR ye yer verilmiştir. Programın devamında ise bir Amerika'lı rock grubunun Atatürk görüntülerinin ardında "yalancı, katil, şeytan Türkiye" sözlerinin defalarca tekrarlandığı bir müzik klibine yer verilmiştir. Klip, demece ilişkin olumsuz düşünce ve söylemlerin vurgulanması açısından oldukça anlamlı bulunmuştur.

KANAL 7'de yayınlanan programda Çiçek, "Pamuk, Resmi devlet anlayışını yansıtmasın, yansıtmayabilir ama verdiği demeç yanlışlarla dolu, yanlış bilgi veriyor" ve yine aynı programda Gürkan ise, Pamuk'un sisteme değil kendi ülkesine karşı bir çıkışı olduğunu ifade ederek demece ilişkin düşüncelerini olumsuz bir söylem içerisinde dile getirmişlerdir. Programın bir diğer konuğu olan Çalışlar " Türkiye Pamuk'u 301'den dolayı mahkeme etti. Eğer 301. madde olmasaydı, kaldırılsaydı, Pamuk'un daha önce verdiği demeçler dünya gündemini bu kadar meşgul etmeyecekti! Bugün bana AB işbirlikçisi hain diye bağırıyorlar, neden, çünkü Avrupa Medyası da söylenen bazı sözleri bağlamından kopararak yayınlıyor. Pamuk'un başına gelen de aynı şeydir" ifadesiyle Pamuk'un demecini farklı bir bakış açısıyla değerlendirmiştir. Ilıcak ise Ermeni sözcüğü ile soykırım sözcüğünün bir arada kullanılmasının Türk insanını rencide ettiğini ve gelen elektronik posta ve kısa mesajlarda hep milliyetçi bir tavrın ve söylemin var olduğuna dikkati çekmektedir. Bunun ardından Dink'e izleyicilerden gelen şu soruyu yöneltmektedir: "Acaba siz Ermenistan'a gidip Ermeniler Türkleri öldürdü diyebilir miydiniz". Dink'e yöneltilen bu sorunun, programın izlenirliğini arttırmak ve tansiyonu yükseltmek amaçlı olduğu düşünülmektedir.

KANAL D'de yayınlanan Arena programına konuk olarak katılan Başbakan Erdoğan ise Dündar'ın "ödül sizce Pamuk'un edebiyatçı kişiliğinden mi yoksa medyada yer alan demecinden dolayı mı verilmiştir" sorusuna Erdoğan "verilen demeç ile Nobel'i karıştırmak yanlış olur. Ödül'den hemen sonra Pamuk'un "Fransa Parlamentosu ayıp etmiştir" şeklindeki açıklaması gerçek kimliğini bulduğunu bizlere göstermiştir" diyerek siyasetçi kimliğinin de bir gerekliliği olarak nötr bir yaklaşım sergilemiştir.

Milliyetçilik Kavramına Değinilmiş midir

Genel olarak programların birçoğunda tartışmaların milliyetçilik kavramı üzerinden şekillendiği gözlenmiştir. En yoğun olarak NTV'de yayınlanan Neden programı içerisinde değinilmiştir ki, daha önce de değinildiği üzere program Türkiye'de yükselen bir dalga olarak milliyetçilik ana teması başlığı altında verilmiştir. Burada dikkati çeken, yukarıda da değinildiği üzere, yükselen milliyetçiliğin Türk kamuoyunun Nobel Ödülü'ne sahip çıkmaması, Nobel'in Pamuk'un açıklamalarından dolayı Eurovision şarkı yarışmasında elde edilen birincilik kadar ses getiremeyişi üzerine yoğunlaşıldığıdır. Diğer programlarda da benzer yaklaşımlar üzerinde durularak Türkiye'de milliyetçi akımın ivme kazandığı, Fransız Meclisi'nin kararının Pamuk'a Ödül'ün verilmesiyle ilişkilendirilerek sunulduğu, Türk kamuoyunun milliyetçilik hissi ile Nobel ve Pamuk'a karşı genellikle olumsuz tutum sergilediğine dikkat çekmektedir.

Orhan Pamuk'u Haklı Bulanlar ve Bulmayanlar Nasıl Sunulmuş

HABER TÜRK kanalında açık olarak Pamuk'u haksız bulanlar eleştiriliyor. Büyük Ödül'ün karşısında muhaliflerin gerçekten de çok küçük kaldıkları, demeçle Ödül'ü ilişkilendirenlerin ifadelerinin aşağılandığı ve enteresan kişilikler oldukları ve bu başarıyı karalamaya çalışanlara imkan tanınmaması gerektiği söylemlerde vurgulanıyor; bir anlamda programın sunucu ve yapımcılarının objektiflikten ve taraf olmaktan uzak söylemler geliştirdikleri de göze çarpıyor.

TRT 1 kanalındaki programda ise Pamuk'u haklı bulmayanlar "düzeysiz" ve "art niyetli gözler bu başarıyı görmek istemiyor" söylemi ile dile getirilmiştir.

KANAL 7'nin programında ise net olarak haklı bulanlar ve bulmayanlar özellikle inter aktif olarak programa katılan kişiler tarafından vurgulanıyor. Pamuk'u destekleyenler, bu toplumun Pamuk ve başarısını hazmedemeyecek bir toplum olduğunu, Türkiye'nin Pamuk'u taşımaya hazır olmadığını, bu toplumun bireylerinin kendisi gibi düşünmeyenleri ve marjinalleri reddetme eğiliminde olduğunu ve toplumun Pamuk kadar olamadığını ve bu ülkenin karşı duruşu anlamakta zorlandığını farklı ifadeleriyle dile getirmişlerdir. Pamuk'u desteklemeyenler ise genellikle programa katılan konukları işaret ederek "Bu kadar haini nereden buldunuz", "Neden Türkiye'ye hakaret edenler ödüllendiriliyor", "Türkiye Ermenileri bağrına bastı", "Sırada toprak ve tazminat talebi var", "Soykırım var diyenler ataları gibi haince davranıyorlar", "Her ülkede vatan haini vardır; Pamuk ve onun ödülüne sevinenler haindir" ifadeleri programın popülaritesini ve özellikle de farklı görüşlerin temsilcileri olarak stüdyoda bulunan konukların tansiyonunu yükseltmek ve tartışmanın dozunu arttırmak amaçlı söylemler olarak değerlendirilmektedir.

Nobel Ödülü ile Fransız Alt Meclisi'nin Kararı İlişkilendiriliyor mu

HABER TÜRK kanalında yayınlanan programda Pamuk'un aldığı Ödül'ün pırıltısı altında cılız, yapay Fransız oylarının ezilip kaldığı ifadesi kullanılmış ve olumlu bir söylem geliştirilmiştir. Programın yapımcı ve sunucuları, diğer medyanın daha çok bu demeçle ilgilendiğini, kendilerinin bunu yapmayacaklarını çünkü demeçlerin unutulup, Ödül'ün hatırlanacağını vurgulamışlardır.

KANAL 7'nin programında ise konuk Hırant Dink, Pamuk'un Ödül'ü almasında Fransızların kararının hiçbir etkisi olmadığını, Fransızların yasa tasarısının gayri ciddi olduğunu, ifade özgürlüğünün engellenmesi konusunda ne Türkiye'nin ne de Fransa'nın birbirinden farkı olmadığını ve her iki ülkenin de akıl dışı yöntemlerle yönetildiğini, ifade özgürlüğünün bir insanın temel hakkı olduğunu ve bunun engellenemeyeceğini vurgulayan bir söylem içinde olduğu dikkati çekmektedir. Dink, ayrıca, kendisinin de Ermeni soykırımı vardır diyerek yargılanacağını ama hiç inanmadığı halde Fransa'ya giderek orada da Ermeni soykırımı yoktur diyebileceğini sözlerine ekleyerek konuya ilişkin tarafsız bir tutum içinde olduğu algılamasını ortaya koymaktadır.

Orhan Pamuk'a Nobel Siyasi Gerekçelerle mi Verilmiştir

KANAL 7'de yayınlanan programda konuk olan Dink, Pamuk'un Nobel'i almasındaki tek önemli unsur olarak yazarın edebi yönden yüksek bir seviyede olmasından kaynaklandığını ifade etmiştir. Programın bir diğer konuğu olan CHP eski milletvekili Gürkan ise Ödül'ün siyasi bir gerekçeyle verildiğini, hatta Pamuk'un "ülkemde yaşamak benim için küçük düşürücü" açıklamasıyla Ödül'ü alması arasında doğrudan bir ilişki olduğunu ifade etmiştir. Burada kullanılan "ülke" Pamuk ve Ödül'ü üzerinden yapılan milliyetçilik kavramını program içerisinde daha bir ön plana çıkartmıştır.

Sonuç

Programlara ilişkin genel bir değerlendirme yapılacak olduğunda çalışmanın başında belirlenmiş olan sorulara çoğunlukla hemen her programda değinildiğini ve cevaplandığını söylemek mümkündür. Çoğunlukla denilmesinin nedeni, öncelikle her haber programının farklı format ve içeriklere sahip olmasıdır. Bu farklılık kuşkusuz öncelikle televizyon kanalının ve program yapımcısının bakış açısı ya da vizyonu, kanalın ve programın kimliği, kanalın siyasi, ideolojik duruşu ve bunun bir uzantısı olarak program kişiliğinin duruşu, milliyetçilik kavramını ne tür bir çerçevede ele alıyor oluşu gibi birçok değişkene göre farklık sergileyebilecek olmasından kaynaklanmaktadır.

Bu değişkenler göz önüne alındığında incelenen programlar içinde en yoğun olarak tartışılan ve görüş bildirilen konuların çalışmada da cevaplanması beklenen sorulara paralellik gösterdiği söylenebilir: Pamuk'un sunulma biçimi, Nobel Ödülü'nün sunulma biçimi, Nobel Ödülü'nün Pamuk'a verilmesinin sunulma biçimi, Pamuk'un Ermeni soykırımına ve Türkiye'deki Kürt sorununa ilişkin verdiği demeçlerin Ödül'ü almasıyla ilişkilendirilerek sunulma biçimi, Fransız Alt Meclisi'nin kararına ilişkin düşüncelerin sunuluş biçimini olumlu, olumsuz ya da nötr olması açısından değerlendirilmiştir. Bu noktada programlara ilişkin bir değerlendirmeyi yapmak da yerinde olacaktır. Programlara konuk olara alınan kişiler kuşkusuz sözü edilen ana temayı ya net olarak destekleyen ya da net olarak karşısında olan kişilikler olarak özenle seçilmiştir. Ermeni asıllı Gazeteci yazar Dink, Türk Tarih Kurumu Ermeni Araştırmaları Birimi'nden Öğretim Üyesi Prof. Dr. Çiçek, CHP eski milletvekili Gürkan, yazar Mahçupyan, yazar Çalışlar, yazar Altan, ve diğerleri Türk medyasında milliyetçilik hakkında görüş bildiren, düşünce ortaya koyan ve araştırmalar yapan kişiler olarak kamuoyu tarafından tanınmakta ve takip edilmektedirler; diğer bir deyişle, popüler denilebilecek mesleki kişiliklerdir. Bu seçimin temelinde elbette farklı nedenler olduğunu söylemek de mümkündür: Programın izlenme oranını popüler konu ve konuşmacılarla arttırmak, kanalın yayın politikasına ilişkin siyasi duruşu temsil yeteneklerinin yeterli görülmesi, ana temanın karşısında ya da destekleyicileri olması gibi.

İncelenen programlar çerçevesinde Türk medyasının ya da daha spesifik olması açısından televizyon kanallarının entelektüel izleyici düzeyinin yüksek olduğu var sayılan programlarına ilişkin genel olarak "uzlaştırıcı" bir tavır sergilemediğini söylemek mümkündür. Programlarda söz alan konukların ya da kendi düşüncelerini ortaya koyan yapımcı ve sunucuların "öteki" söylemlere karşı ılımlı bir tavır içinde olmadığı, orta yol bulmaktan uzak ve "ötekini" çürütmeye yönelik söylemler içerisinde olduklarını ifade etmek mümkündür. Muhafazakâr yayıncılığın ön planda tutulduğu bir kanal olarak, KANAL 7'de Ilıcak tarafından konuklara sorulan sorular, izleyicilerden gelen soruların içinden daha çok program konuklarının tansiyonlarını yükseltecek, provoke edebilecek ve tartışmalara neden olacak olanlarının seçilmesi bu öngörüye örnek olarak gösterilebilir. Bunun çatışma ve polemik ortamı yaratarak gündem oluşturmak, yüksek izlenme oranına sahip olarak ticari girdiyi yükseltmek amaçlarını da içinde barındıran bir yaklaşım olduğunu söylemek mümkündür.

Genel olarak haber izleyicisinin ve gündemi takip eden izleyicilerin tercihi olan CNN TÜRK ve NTV'de ise çoğunlukla ana temanın, ortalama çatışma ortamı yaratmadan verilmeye çalışıldığı gözlemlenmiştir. TRT 1'de ise ağırlıklı olarak ana tema olan Nobel'e karşı bir söylem ve duruşun var olduğunu söylemek mümkündür. ATV'de izlenen durum iki program sunucusu açısından oldukça farklı özellikler sergilemektedir; bir sunucu Pamuk ve Nobel hakkında son derece ılımlı ve olumlu ifadeler kullanırken, diğeri ise Nobel'i, ancak, özellikle Pamuk'u ve demeçlerini eleştiren olumsuz ifadeler kullanmaktadır. KANAL TÜRK'ün ise tamamen Pamuk ve Ödül'ü, genel olarak koşulsuzca, savunan ve destekleyen bir söylem içinde milliyetçilik kavramıyla bütünleştirmeden ele aldığı gözlenmiştir.

Genel bir değerlendirme yapılacak olduğunda, daha önce de değinildiği üzere, programların içeriklerinde ve dile getirilen söylemlerde uzlaşmadan uzak, çatışma ve polemik yaratmaya daha yakın ve yatkın bir yaklaşımın olduğu söylenebilir. Orhan Pamuk'un yanında ya da karşısında olan tarafların uzlaşmadan uzak ve "öteki" ni çürütmeye ya da yok saymaya yönelik uzlaşma ötesi, hatta zaman zaman çatışma denebilecek yönde kamuoyunun karşısında yer almış oldukları göze çarpmaktadır. Özellikle programlara katılan konuşmacıların geçmiş dönemlerde ya da halen gazetecilik mesleğinin içinde aktif olarak var olan profesyoneller olduğu düşünülecek olursa, yaygın anlamda haberci kişiliklerin en az ana tema kadar dikkate değer oldukları ve gerçekte birer aktör olarak sürecin içinde yer aldıklarını söylemek yerinde olacaktır. Kendi içlerinde çatışan ve uzlaşma kültürüne sahip olamayan, gazetecilik/habercilik mesleğinin profesyonel kişiliklerinin, Türkiye'nin gerek siyasi gerek ekonomik gerekse toplumsal boyutta önemli dönemeçlerden geçtiği şu son yıllarda temel misyonlarını yerine getiremediği, bütünleştirme sürecinde ciddi sıkıntılar yaşadığını ve yarattığını söylemek mümkündür.

Kaynakça

Bostancı, N. M. (1999). *Bir Kolektif Bilinç Olarak Milliyetçilik.* İstanbul: Doğan Kitap.

Guibernau, M. (1997). *Milliyetçilikler: 20. Yüzyılda Ulusal Devlet ve Milliyetçilikler.* (N. N. Domaniç, Çev.). İstanbul: Sarmal Yayınevi.

Hobsbawm, E.J. (1993). *1780'den Günümüze Milletler ve Milliyetçilik Program, Mit, Gerçeklik.* (O. Akınhay, Çev.). İstanbul: Ayrıntı Yayınları.

Maksudyan, N. (2005). *Türklüğü Ölçmek, Bilimkurgusal Antropoloji ve Türk Milliyetçiliğinin Irkçı Cephesi 1925- 1939.* İstanbul: Metis Yayınları.

Modleski, T. (1998). *Eğlence İncelemeleri Kitle Kültürüne Eleştirel Yaklaşımlar.* (N. Gürbilek, Çev.). İstanbul: Metis Yayınları.

Mutlu, E. (2005). *Globalleşme, Popüler Kültür ve Medya.* Ankara: Ütopya Yayınevi.

Tılıç, D. L. (2001). *2000'ler Türkiye'sinde Gazetecilik ve Medyayı Anlamak.* İstanbul: Su Yayınları.

Ulus, S. (2007). Sporda/Futbolda Şiddet ve Kışkırtılan Milliyetçilik. *Marmara İletişim Dergisi*, Sayı 12, Ocak

2007, İstanbul: Marmara Üniv. Yay.

Yeniçeri, Ö. (2007). *Milletlerin Orta Direği: Milliyetçilik.* http://www.ulkuocaklari.org.tr/arastr/ozcanyeniceri1.htm (Son erişim 10.03.2007).

Kara, A. (2007). *İktidara Ulaşma Aracı Olarak Stratejik ve Taktik Milliyetçilik.* http://www.yenisafak.com.tr/yorum/?t=11.04.2007&q=1&c=12&i=38503&İktidara/ulaşma/aracı/olarak/stratejik/ve/taktik/milliyetçilik (Son erişim 11.04.2007).

ATV. *Son Baskı,* 18. 10. 2006.

CNN TÜRK. *5N 1K,* 18.10. 2006.

HABER TÜRK. *Nobel Özel Yayını,* 12. 10. 2006.

KANAL D. *Arena,* 16. 10. 2006.

KANAL 7. *Sözün Özü,* 19. 10. 2006.

NTV. *Neden,* 17. 10. 2006.

TRT 1. *Sınırlar Arasında,* 16. 10. 2006.

Peace Work With Communities: Peace Work With Thai Muslim and Buddhist Communities in Conflict

Kathryn L. Norsworthy,
Ahimsa International: Projects for Peace, Justice, and Mindful Living &
Graduate Studies in Counselling
Rollins College
knorswor@rollins.edu

Introduction

Since 2004, I have been collaborating with local Thai partners in preparing peace-building teams comprised of community leaders who are addressing issues of violence and conflict in the southern three provinces of Thailand. In this paper, I describe our efforts at building capacity within Buddhist and Muslim communities in an area of the country where ongoing ethno-political conflict between Muslims and Buddhists has escalated and led to tragic community ruptures.

The paper will begin by briefly describing the historical, social and political context of the violence in the southern three provinces of Thailand. Next, I discuss how relevant concepts and practices drawn from feminist psychology, counseling psychology, critical theory, liberation psychology, and participant action methodologies inform the model that my Thai colleagues and I utilize in our work with the Buddhist-Muslim groups. This discussion will illuminate the ways in which indigenous wisdom and spirituality, participant-centered approaches, and processes that capitalize on already-existing knowledge and skills of local partners contribute to an empowering, culturally grounded process. This paper includes sections in which I describe the process by which participants analyze their experiences (at the structural, cultural, and community levels) with the ethno-political conflict of south Thailand; the effects of the ongoing violence on communities and families; action plans for community peace work; and the healing that takes place in these processes of collaboration. Also, I will discuss our efforts to disrupt psychological colonization and neocolonialism through a mutual commitment by my local partners and me to a critical, culture-centered, liberatory process of research and practice, particularly given the power structures in Thailand and my positionality as a white, U.S. professional psychologist. Finally, I will discuss my own challenges as a white, U.S. counseling psychologist to effectively engage in these collaborative projects, particularly given the U.S. location globally.

A Brief History and Context of Violence in Southern Thailand

The northern part of the Malay Peninsula was annexed by the Buddhist Kingdom of Siam in the early twentieth century. Seven years later the British colonial government of Malaysia forced the King of Siam give up sovereignty over all of this area except what is now the southern three provinces of Thailand; Narathiwat, Pattani, and Yala. The people of these provinces, predominantly Muslim, were pressured to take Thai names, speak Thai, and convert to Buddhism. However, today, in this predominantly agricultural region, over 80% of the population of the three provinces remain Muslim and speak dialects of Malay as their primary language. Since the 1930's there have been various separatist and autonomy movements, mostly suppressed until the liberalization of the Thai government in the 1980's. Within the past three years, the violence has escalated, with much criticism launched against the heavy-handed, violent responses by the government led by the recently ousted Thai prime minister, Thaksin Shinawatra.

Though there was some hope that the 2006 coup removing Thaksin from office would be a turning point for peaceful resolution to the ethno-political violence, in fact, just the opposite has happened. Today, there are daily attacks on soldiers, police officers, government officials, and civilians. The targets are predominantly Buddhists or Muslims who are viewed as disloyal to the insurgent groups, though many are simply in the wrong place at the wrong time. Schools and other buildings symbolizing government authority have also been bombed, burned, and vandalized. It has come to light that this area of Thailand is home to high levels of poverty and illiteracy. Sadly, due to the escalation of the violence and targeting of teachers, many of the schools in the south are now closed. According to February, 2007, articles in the Bangkok Post, during Chinese New Year weekend, February 18 to 19, "insurgents executed 38 bombing attacks, 26 cases of arson, and seven ambushes. The bombings targeted hotels, karaoke bars, power grids and commercial sites. Two public schools were torched." Yet, there is a small, but active peace movement in the south. Even in the face of their fears, community members make efforts to talk with their neighbors, understand one another, and care for each other in the aftermath of terrorist attacks or other violence.

Current Projects

For the past three years, I have been traveling to the south of Thailand to collaborate with mixed Muslim and Buddhist groups in peace-building workshops and participant action research. The participants' main goals are to analyze the social and political context of the ongoing ethno-political violence, to explore the impact of the violence at the community, family, and individual levels, to increase their knowledge and skills in peace work in preparation for engagement in peace-building efforts in their home communities, and to develop action plans for their return home.

Participants typically travel to locations outside of the three provinces to attend the workshops facilitated by my Thai colleagues and me. The three to six day workshops of approximately 15 to 20 individuals take place in remote or secure locations that allow participants to relax from the day-to-day anxiety associated with the ongoing violence in their communities. They are a range of ages and education levels, men and women, Muslims and Buddhists, teachers, nurses, lawyers, students, community leaders and volunteers, law enforcement officers, mental health professionals, and others, from all walks of life. Because the stakes are so high, workshop members are deeply committed to increasing their knowledge and skills in peace building and healing from trauma so that they can continue their own work and train others in their home communities. They bring their own trauma as well as their tremendous strengths and resources to the experience. The workshops are called "counseling and building communities of peace" and the lead process is supporting participants in developing basic non-violent communication and counseling knowledge and skills. There is strong emphasis on "deep listening", "mindfulness" (non-reactively paying attention from moment to moment), and "inner peace work" as foundations for all other work. Participants also learn a basic version of our transformative training methodology that they can use at home to work with others.

The Methodology

Our workshops are informed by overlapping principles and practices from the disciplines of multicultural counseling psychology (Sue & Sue, 2003); liberation theory (Freire, 1972; Ivey, 1995; Martin-Baro, 1994), feminist theory (Brown, 1994; hooks, 1994; Landrine, Klonoff, & Brown-Collins, 1995; Worell & Johnson, 1997), critical theory (Agger, 1998; Matsuda, 1995; Kincheloe & McLaren, 2000; Schor, 1996; West, 1993), and participant action research methodologies (Herr, 1995; Kemmis & McTaggart, 2000). Multicultural counseling psychology (Sue & Sue, 2003) brings together traditional western counseling psychological theories and practices with local and indigenous worldview, wisdom and healing paradigms in order to offer culturally grounded approaches in counseling, psycho-education, and advocacy. Liberation theory, as discussed by Paulo Freire (1972) and Ignacio Martin-Baro (1994), challenges conventional perspectives in education and psychology by taking the position that those most subordinated in society are capable of defining and analyzing their own situations and in engaging in social transformation aimed at their own liberation. Liberation theory encourages a structural analysis of social and community systems from the perspective of those in the affected positions; thus, the voices of the least empowered are centered as the authorities of their own lived experience. Further, there is recognition that everyone is caught in the "systemic web" and that everyone has a stake in addressing the issues if we are all going to be truly free. In group work, practices of liberation theory involve beginning with the experiences of group members and supporting them in articulating the issues or concerns based on their cultural and socio-political contexts. Facilitators utilize a problem-posing, dialogic approach to support this process, and work collaboratively, offering frameworks within which the wisdom of the group can emerge as participants attempt to find solutions and directions for social change. Through this kind of process, group members cultivate a critical consciousness (Freire, 1972), whereby they can reflect on their lived experiences, analyze them, and then take appropriate action to address the systems that are contributing to their current condition.

Contemporary feminist psychology, as articulated in the groundbreaking edited volume, *Shaping the Future of Feminist Psychology* (Worell & Johnson, 1997), brings in the importance of gender and its interactions with other aspects of identity, such as race, ethnicity, class, sexual orientation, age, ability/disability, and spiritual tradition, as a central organizing principle in human lives. The implication here is that experience must be contextualized to truly understand its complexities and meanings, and that, like liberation theory, the individual holds authority in defining his or her experiences and the meanings of them. There is an emphasis in feminist theory on analyzing power in relationships and in contexts as an essential part of meaning making and in developing solutions to problems. Laura Brown (1994) poses two core values, diversity and anti-domination, in guiding feminist theory and practice. Valuing diversity means recognizing multiple perspectives and multiple standpoints as important and necessary to fully represent the complexity of a situation or an issue. Anti-domination values call for active efforts to oppose, interrupt, and change situations and systems based in domination and subordination.

Like feminist theory, as an emancipatory discipline, critical theory (Agger, 1998; Matsuda, 1995; Kincheloe & McLaren, 2000; Schor, 1996; West, 1993), an amalgamation of the agreements and disagreements of a multitude of scholars, also analyzes the ways power operates within a society, particularly in terms of who gains and who loses, from an individual and group perspective. Thus, there is an interest in the study of privileged groups, those who benefit from the social and political power arrangements, as well as the ways in which those who seek emancipation journey through this process (Kincheloe & Mclaren, 2000). Because these systems of inequality tend to be naturalized within a society and at the global level, critical theory is useful because it calls for an interrogation and questioning of these structures of "normality" in terms of the human costs. With a strong emphasis on reflexivity, criticalists make explicit their values and assumptions as they enter into research and praxis, recognizing that there is no "objective" stance. Thus, a critical theorist/practitioner makes no apologies for grounding their work principles of justice, liberation, and transformation of violent social and political systems. Simultaneously, she or he will also recognize that other variables, such as social locations and identities, cultural background, social and political context, influence perception and must be consistently reflected upon in terms of how one is influenced and influencing others.

Participant action research methodologies share common ground with liberatory, feminist, and critical theory in the commitment to a participant centered approach that strives to facilitate local actors in (1) defining their own questions, (2) engaging in discourse and activities aimed at examining the questions more deeply, (3) generating and acquiring the knowledge and skills to address their needs and/or the needs of the community or society, and (4) implementing the plans generated by local actors to address the questions and concerns coming out of the research process. Brinton Lykes (2001), based on her work with grassroots women from the highlands of Guatemala, stresses the importance of recognizing the activist researcher as "other" – an outsider – and that this positionality has an impact on the research process. In the Freirian spirit, she reminds us that our work needs to be done in solidarity with the research community rather than on behalf of the local actors and that the research process needs to offer something of value to the community of participants. Michelle Fine and colleagues (2000) describe an emphasis on drawing knowledge and meaning from indigenous customs and practices and incorporating this wisdom into the meaning-making and action phases of a project. Fine et.al. (2000) and Smith (1999) also stress that the research project should equip local collaborators to carry on after the activist researcher has concluded the "official" project – the passing of the torch.

All of these theoretical and practice frameworks describe various ways in which participants in a project are centralized, that their knowledge and wisdom is privileged, that they define their own predicaments and solutions in collaboration with facilitators or researchers, and that the work leads to action and social change. Further, through the praxis of this decolonizing methodology, everyone is humanized and transformed by the process.

The Work

Based on the previously described theoretical contributions, we are developing a methodology with the goals of 1) facilitating analysis and problem-solving based on participants' cultural and community contexts, 2) collaboratively developing culturally relevant solutions and action plans for social change and 3) preparing participants to take the liberatory workshop methodology back to their home communities (see Norsworthy & Khuankaew, 2004, for a more detailed description of the workshop theory and methodology and examples of its implementation with women from the refugee communities of Burma).

In working in the south of Thailand, as a white western counseling psychologist I have found that it is very important to collaborate with Thai partners, preferably from the areas in which I am working, in order to increase the likelihood that the work will be culturally relevant, will center the needs of the local people and will mitigate against my tendency to overemphasize western methods and ideas in the work. Local partners are familiar with indigenous wisdom that can contribute to dealing with local issues. I work to embody the paradox of my position. On one hand I need to recognize that, as an outsider with knowledge and experience in counseling and peace work, I have things to offer. Yet having grown up in a different part of the world, in a society with worldviews that are different than those of the people with whom I am working, and having been enculturated into a society that prides itself on being the "best", the "global standard", and therefore, entitled to define the needs and directions of other societies, particularly those outside the west, I have much to learn and unlearn. Thus, my work is never done – the work of unlearning and changing any ways that I hold privileged ideas and engage in the attendant behaviors and learning to take a decolonizing, partnership, "solidarity-oriented" stance in my work with my Southeast and South Asian colleagues.

The workshops include numerous components. For the purposes of this paper, I will discuss a few examples of the kinds of activities and analyses we undertake with a group. At the outset a project, the important work of building community and relationships among participants is vital. It is only within the context of a solid, well-tended "container" that the more difficult and challenging issues, ideas, and emotions can arise. For example, at the outset, my Thai workshop facilitators and I might ask group members to engage in an exercise called a "mingle." In this exercise, participants first independently draw symbols on four quandrants of a sheet of paper that represent themselves, their families, their work, and a hope or dream for the future. Then, within a specified period of time, they move around the room and introduce themselves to other participants by sharing their drawings and the meaning of the symbols in each quandrant. Participants are guided to begin practicing "deep listening" immediately by really paying attention with respect and appreciation for what their fellow participants are sharing during the mingle. Other trust and community building exercises are interspersed throughout the workshops to continue cultivating an atmosphere that supports open, authentic exchange and understanding.

A structured series of listening exercises take place early on in each workshop process. Deep listening, which involves listening without needing to respond, ask questions, or make comments while the other person is sharing, is heavily emphasized during the first hours. This sets the frame for the listener to focus efforts on "witnessing"; offering undivided attention, seeking to understand what is being said while conveying sincere respect and appreciation. Deep listening circumvents the tendency to become preoccupied with what we want to say in response to the speakers' communication and also challenges the listener to remain non-reactive and present. Systematically, basic counseling skills such as reflection, empathy, use of open questions, and encouraging body language are introduced. The "counselor" of the pair is strongly discouraged from advice-giving and personal commentary. They are reminded that their efforts are to be devoted to centering the friend who is sharing, supporting him or her in sharing, and using deep listening and the other skills to demonstrate empathy and understanding.

Each time group members practice skills, they are guided to choose a new partner or small group of participants with whom they have not yet worked and whom they don't know as well until they have had the opportunity to work with everyone. At various points, members are asked to deliberately work with participants who do not share the same religious or spiritual tradition. The listening and basic counseling exercises offer a chance for participants to explore meaningful material that can potentially build greater connection and understanding among group members, particularly between Muslims and Buddhists. For example, when the container of the group is sufficiently strong, Muslim-Buddhist dyads are asked to share about a recent situation in which each of them was afraid because of the violence in their communities and a way that someone from the other religious tradition could be an ally or advocate for them in their home community.

At some point in a workshop, group members may divide into two groups; one group, Muslim, the other, Buddhist. They then engage in an exercise in which each religious group shares with the other, using a fishbowl approach, what they would like for their friends to know about their faith tradition. Included is a discussion of what their faith means to them, the ways it offers sources of strength and healing in traumatic or difficult times, and what it has to contribute to the process of peace work in their home communities. One group is in the center of the circle, discussing these questions among themselves, while the other group is in the outer circle, listening intently. When the inner circle concludes their discussion, outer circle members are asked to talk about what stood out for them and what was important for them to hear that they did not know already. This is a time when questions can be answered. Finally, after both groups share and listen, the participants are requested to find a partner who is from the other faith tradition, and to sit together and talk about the values they are discovering that they share that support a common vision of peace in their communities.

Another important element of the workshops is the social and political analysis of the violence and conflict within the communities of the southern provinces. The group members are asked to draw on their deep listening practices and the other inner work practices that support non-reactivity and steadiness of mind so that they can hear one another during this part of the workshop. The process of analysis involves having participants divide into mixed groups of Buddhists and Muslims and to use an approach called "the tip of the island model." In this model, I draw a diagram in the shape of a mountain or island, with a wavy horizontal line across the middle of the "island". Participants comment that they see the diagram as an island with water covering the bottom half so we discuss the idea that, in the case of an island, we can see the upper part of the land mass, but there is much "below the surface" that requires deeper and closer investigation in order to understand its qualities and composition. The island model represents the violence in the south, with the top (the visible part of the island) representing what we can actually see and witness on a daily basis. The lower part of the island represents the "root causes" or what is supporting, maintaining, or contributing to the violence and conflict.

In the large group, members are asked to identify the visible aspects of the violence and conflict, and they shout

out "Bombings, nails on the roads, shootings, burning buildings, etc." They also say that the targets of the violence are Buddhists as well as some Muslims who are either in the area or targeted because they don't agree with the tactics of those committing the violence. Next the small groups meet to discuss how they see what is under the water, what holds up, supports, causes, and maintains the violence. This is a challenging part of the discussion, where facilitators stay tuned in to the "temperature" of the discussions and periodically invite everyone to stop, notice what they are feeling and thinking, take a couple of deep breaths, and then continue. Participants are encouraged to engage with a primary goal of deeply hearing what others are saying and sharing their perspectives in a way that others can hear (non-violent communication). After this discussion is concluded, group members report back to the larger group and we record the findings of the groups. Many factors are generated: history of occupation of the region by Thai government, Thai government forcing Muslims to take Buddhist names, language, and religion; heavy handed policies of Thaksin government to suppress dissonance, exploitation of the situation by more extremist terrorist or separatist groups, each side's lack of understanding of the other, and other variables.

This part of the workshop elicits many difficult emotions; thus, after the analysis we spend time in an emotional check-in with participants. Group members report feeling anger, sadness, fear, a sense of injustice, and in some cases, deeper empathy for members of the other group. There is usually a period of discussing the fact that people on all sides are suffering and that everyone is interested in reducing or ending the suffering. Many of the Thai participants struggle with the ways in which they hold a privilege position in the larger society, particularly since they too are suffering as the minority in the south.

Following this analysis, workshop participants spend time examining the effects of the violence on individuals, families, and communities. The concepts of individual and collective post-traumatic stress are introduced and group members explore how the violence and conflicts in their own communities and country are impacting them personally as well as their families and communities. Again, there is much emotion, but the sharing of this material between Buddhists and Muslims humanizes each side and promotes deeper understanding of one another. Most participants arrive at a common perspective that violence is not the pathway to solving the problems in their provinces.

The question is how to stop it and address the deeper issues that create and maintain the conditions for violence and conflict. Also, group members frequently express a desire to explore how to offer support and healing for the victims of violence and their families.

One of the final tasks in this workshop is to determine action plans based on the work that has been done in the group. Group members spend the final period of a workshop discussing ways to address the violence in their provinces at the individual, family, community, organizational, and societal levels. They also identify what else they would like to know or learn in order to implement their plans. This part of the workshop leads to much discussion about how to change the systems and practices that suppress Muslim culture in institutions such as schools, government, and communities. Also, group members recognize the importance of learning non-violent methods of social change and ways of dealing with differences and conflict. They identify that more work in deep listening, non-violent communication, and social-justice based counseling are needed. Also, because participants experience the transformative effects of the workshop methodology, they express a desire to develop the knowledge and skills to facilitate workshops using the transformative workshop methodology. The group members organize and make plans for series of workshops addressing several important areas such as conflict transformation, non-violent communication, peace-building, and training of social action trainers.

A workshop ends in a large circle with expressions of deep appreciation for fellow participants and their willingness to take the risks to really engage and connect, particularly across the differences. Tears fall and there is some trepidation connected with the dangerous journeys home as people remember what they are facing back in their communities. We all hope to see one another again soon.

Thai-U.S. Collaboration

When a white westerner works in a community in the Global South, it is highly desirable to collaborate with partners from the region. My Thai collaborators and I explicitly define our positions in the groups as co-learners and co-constructors of the knowledge to be generated and view our primary function as one of designing questions and experiences that encourage the wisdom of the group members to emerge through the group process. We attempt to address the tension of centralizing the values of anti-domination and diversity by inviting and valuing multiple perspectives while challenging our collaborators to deconstruct any of their ideas that appeared to be rooted in oppression and domination. We also encourage and support group participants in challenging our ideas, techniques, and practices of facilitating the groups. Critically important to me, as a white westerner, is to engage in a power-sharing partnership with my Thai partners and with group members. To accomplish this goal, my Thai colleagues and I engaged in continuous reflection in order to mediate the power dynamics within our relationships and to address those dynamics that might undermine mutuality and collaboration. We are committed to processing our experiences honestly within our partnership, even when the feedback involved difficult dialogues. Additionally, we regularly engaged in similar reflexive processes with the groups with whom we worked in order to encourage power sharing. We find that the use of this methodology acknowledges all of our contributions, strengths and resources, as facilitators and group members, and minimizes power-over dynamics. To us, this is particularly important since the home community issues involve abuses of power and use of violence and control to solve problems or make changes. We believe that when workshop participants experience power-sharing facilitation and reflect on their experience in a workshop that utilizes a power-sharing, liberatory methodology, they are more likely to replicate these dynamics in their own work back home.

Closing

This paper represents a small snapshot of the peace and justice projects in which my Thai colleagues and I have been engaged for the past three years. The projects we undertake demonstrate that culturally competent western counselors and counseling psychologists partnering with local colleagues from the global south can serve as agents of empowerment and social change. Rather than confining our work to the counseling office or university classroom, we can use the multicultural counseling knowledge and skills we have acquired to work in solidarity with friends and colleagues from grassroots, non-governmental, and governmental settings toward the goal of social justice, undoing oppressive social systems and replacing them with structures and institutions of peace and justice (Arredondo & Perez, 2003).

References

Agger, B. (1998). *Critical social theories: An introduction.* Boulder, CO: Westview.

Brown, L. S. (1994). *Subversive dialogues: Theory in feminist therapy*. New York: Basic Books.

Fine, M., Weis, L., Weseen, S. & Wong, L. (2000). For whom? Qualitiative research, representations, and social responsibilities. In N.K. Denzin & Y.S. Lincoln (Eds.). *Handbook of qualitative research* (2nd Ed., pp. 107-131). Thousand Oaks, CA: Sage.

Freire, P. (1972). *Pedagogy of the oppressed.* New York: Herder & Herder.

Herr, K. (1995). Action research as empowering practice. *Journal of Progressive Human Services, 6*(2), 45-58.

hooks, B. (1994). *Teaching to transgress: Education as the practice of freedom.* New York: Routledge.

Ivey, A. (1995). Psychotherapy as liberation: Toward specific skills and strategies in Multicultural counseling and therapy. In J.G. Ponterotto, J.M Casas, L.A. Suzuki, & C.M. Alexander (Eds.), *Handbook of multicultural counseling* (pp. 53-72). Thousand Oaks, CA: Sage.

Kemmis, S. & McTaggart, R. (2000). Participatory action research. In N.K. Denzin & Y.S. Lincoln (Eds.). *Handbook of qualitative research* (2nd Ed., pp. 567-605). Thousand Oaks, CA: Sage.

Kincheloe, J.L. & McLaren, P. (2000). Rethinking critical theory and qualitative research. In N. K. Lincoln & Y. S. Lincoln (Eds.). *Handbook of qualitative research* (2nd Ed., pp. 279-313). Thousand Oaks, CA: Sage.

Landrine, H., Klonoff, E.A., & Brown-Collins, A. (1995). Cultural diversity and methodology in feminist psychology: Critique, proposal, empirical example. In

H. Landrine (Ed.), *Bringing cultural diversity to feminist psychology: Theory, research, and practice* (pp. 55-75). Washington D.C.: American Psychological Association.

Lykes, M. B. (2001). Activist participatory research and the arts with rural Maya women: Interculturality and situated meaning making. In D. L. Tolman & M.

Brydon-Miller (Eds.), *From subjects to subjectivities: A handbook of interpretive and participatory methods* (pp. 183-100). New York: NYU Press.

Martin-Baro, I. (1994). *Writings for a liberation psychology.* Cambridge, MA: Harvard University Press.

Matsuda, M. (1995). Looking to the bottom: Critical legal studies and reparations. In K.

Crenshaw, N. Gotanda, G. Peller, & K. Thomas (Eds.), *Critical race theory: The key writings that formed the movement* (pp. 63-79). New York: New Press.

Norsworthy, K.L. & Khuankaew, O. (2004). Women of Burma speak out: Workshops to deconstruct gender-based violence and build systems of peace and justice. *Journal for Specialists in Group Work, 29*(3), 259-283.

Schor, I. (1996). *When students have power: Negotiating authority in a critical pedagogy.* Chicago: University of Chicago Press.

Smith, L. T. (1999). *Decolonizing methodologies: Research and indigenous peoples.* London: Zed Books.

Sue, D.W. & Sue, D. (2003). *Counseling the culturally diverse: Theory and practice* (4th Ed.). New York: John Wiley & Sons.

West, C. (1993). *Race matters.* Boston: Beacon.

Worell, J. & Johnson, N.G. (1997). *Shaping the future of feminist psychology: Education, research, and practice.* Washington, D.C.: American Psychological Association.

Conflict Resolution: Film as The Third Party/ Mediator

Müberra Yüksel
Department of Advertising
Faculty of Communication
Kadir Has University,
mubberray@khas.edu.tr

I. Introduction:

The Cyprus conflict has been on the agenda for a long time and the two communities are victims of each other, each other's motherlands with different perspectives on the island's history. The dividing line and the buffer zone, which has kept the two communities apart over thirty years, have made Cyprus an odd case of conflict prevention and transformation. The framework in relation to Cyprus might help us explain, if not understand conflicts that stem from "in-group/out-group feelings" at the intra group level (Cockburn, 2004).

When recounting the recent history of the island, members of each group tend to mention only their own glories and sufferings, and blame the other side and to refer to the other group only as victimizer. Both sides have suffered injustices and massive deaths in their past which have become a living part of the present problem. The two sides have been divided both politically and economically. The Turkish Cypriots have isolated from the rest of the world for about four decades. Any durable solution should accommodate to the needs of both communities and their respective motherlands and regard the widely agreed upon norms of the international law.

The United Nation Mediation has released several reports and prepared plans to promote peace—the final draft plan was the Annan Plan. Conciliation and prevention seemed to have paved the way for later stages of the mediation process. Having kept peace for years, now it was the time to go further: making peace and later building peace so that once disputed issues were resolved, then relations would be easier to develop. With the opening of the buffer zone and simultaneous referenda scheduled for each side of the island of Cyprus on April 24, the UN-sponsored Cyprus peace process had seemingly entered a new phase. At that time, goals and political aspirations with sharp differences had seemed to converge. It was seen as a hope for peaceful reunification, then. However, with the Greek Cypriots rejecting the "Annan Plan" proposal, another stalemate period started and increasing contact between the two communities has not created reconciliation.

II. Conflict Resolution Theories

I have employed the theories of Vamık Volkan and John Burton, which aimed at "an optimum degree of generality" linking theory and practical tools. Both Burton and Volkan use the term "conflict resolution" to incorporate "transformative" processes. Regarding intergroup conflict as pathological; they use prevention in the sense of preventive care. Burton uses the term "prevention" to imply taking steps to remove root sources of conflict and to promote contexts where collaborative civil initiatives influence behavior patterns (Burton, 1990).

My brief overview of large group comparisons is largely guided by Vamık Volkan's theory on the psychology of neighbors. Volkan states that when neighboring large groups are in conflict, most of their political, social, economic and "real-world" issues are distorted with psychological emotions. He focuses on context and poses such questions:

- How are individual and large-group identity intertwined?
- What is the role of massive shared trauma in modifying a large-group identity?
- Do large-groups relate to one another in a ritualistic fashion?

He explains the determinants of large group regression and analyzes the inhibiting role of guilt and/or victimization along with ways to overcome them (Volkan, 1999). Each community sees itself as "the mirror image" of the other. One can infer, therefore, that each group must be in some sense quite similar to the other. But, there appears to be another psychological factor, besides the substantial cultural differences and important similarities that influence intergroup relations: "The rituals or the narcissism of minor differences" (Volkan, 1993). These differences are observed in cases of intergroup conflict where the two opposing groups may seem alike but they have minor differences. According to Volkan, these rituals are for maintaining these differences; thus, keeping a psychological gulf between the opposing groups. They absorb the flow of aggression and keep them from killing each other. Violence occasionally may erupt "when playful ritualization of the preoccupation with minor differences is no longer maintained." (1988, pp. 103-107).

According to Volkan (2000), when neighboring communities are in protracted conflict, most of their "real world" concerns are contaminated with psychological issues of their inner world and they are ill framed by distortions and misperceptions. People have a deep-rooted psychological need to have a "core identity" through which they simplify and establish enemies and allies after their "chosen glories and traumas" This phenomenon happens on individual and group levels. This is an unconscious need, which feeds conscious relationships in our group lives. This often plays an important role in forming ethnic or national self and group identities.

Vamık Volkan's therapeutic approach is especially based on the concept of "Chosen Trauma and Chosen Glories", i.e. on the subjective perception of participants' own (collective) identity. These ideas play a major role in ethno-political conflicts as they often block constructive approaches to conflict transformation. The purpose of Volkan's workshop methodology is to explore these patterns of perception consciously and thus open them up to discussion. His psychodynamic approach also rests in part on the application of psychoanalytic defense mechanisms such as externalization, projection, and identification that individuals use to protect themselves from perceived psychological threat along with social identity theory (Volkan, 1990).

Victimized groups do not see beyond their own pain and anguish without their own wounds being healed. These groups do not take responsibility for victims created by their own actions out of revenge or feel guilt about the violence committed in the past. The egoism of victimization" is "the incapacity of an ethno-national group, as a direct result of its own traumas of war history, to empathize with the suffering of another group" The last psychological mechanism is the inability to mourn according to Volkan. He describes mourning as the reaction to real or threatened loss or change (Volkan, 1990).

John Burton, however, focuses on the generic root causes of conflict and fundamental human rights. For Burton, conflict avoidance is not resolution. He uses the term "provention" to imply taking steps to remove sources of conflict and to promote contexts where collaborative relations, cooperative training and civil initiatives and mediations control behavior patterns. He explains that there are fundamental universal values or human needs that must be met if societies are to be stable. Then, a non-ideological basis for the establishment of institutions and policies can be argued. Unless prospects for the pursuit of all societal developmental needs are possible, conflict is inevitable regardless of context (Burton & Dukes, 1990).

The first theory examines the source and motivational factors through the individual subconscious. The purpose is to reflect long-held feelings of alienation as a result of individual's worldview and sense of identity in terms of his/her relations with the other. That way, by facing the personal and interpersonal reality and coping with it or adapting, one can focus on common grounds for a shared future rather than dwelling upon the bitter past. The latter theory suggests that there is a need for a paradigm shift away from hegemonic power politics towards the social and psychological reality of individuals. Burton has suggested that the rights for security, identity, and recognition underlie most deep-rooted and protracted ethnic conflicts. Besides, such conflicts are not interest-based conflicts and hence core issues can neither be managed nor negotiated. Therefore, only by restructuring and transforming the society so that all groups' fundamental needs are met, conflicts can be resolved (Burton & Dukes, 1990).

In protracted conflicts, borders are not solely the objects of conflict. The dividing line often has a higher symbolic meaning for the recognition of group identity. Social identity refers to the way people see themselves--the groups they feel a part of, the significant aspects of themselves that they use to describe themselves to others. Burton emphasizes personal identity over collective or social identity of the community and emphasizes universal human rights of individuals (1990, pp. 1-13).

"How do you help people overcome their version of the past and work toward a future they can share now?" Volkan asks. "They must create a vision of the future that takes into account the needs of both communities" is the answer. He opts for reconciliation programs that allow a society to face its tragedies openly, healing the psychological wounds of the conflict rather than denying it through various defense mechanisms.

By and large, the two theories are mainly used in practice by "track two diplomacy" with a "pluralist discourse" on issues concerning civil society of both sides and they are complementary. The processes of "problem-solving conflict resolution workshops" or "therapeutic diagnostic dialogues" of both theories have been applied at various settings including Cyprus (Cunningham, 1998).

The way one frames a conflict is based on many factors beyond what "actually" happened.

"Framing" of the problem is often the starting point for making both parties see the bigger picture and realize it does not have to end in a zero sum game. It is used to mean the process of describing and interpreting an event to focus attention in conflict resolution just like framing in a film or a painting. It is used by both theories since it is a cognitive road map that enables us to process information in patterns. It helps the parties understand and interpret what the conflict is about--what is going on and what they should do about it.

III. Method: Selected Films as the Third Party

The films have added value in terms of breaking the "spiral of silence" about such a deep-rooted conflict in Turkey. They have made the audiences question the accepted norms of the old paradigm, which were taken for granted. Rather than acting as an agent that reinforces the status quo and mainstream, they have both acted partially as change agents and have given momentum for promoting peace-building activities.

A Turkish-Cypriot Dervis Zaim and a Greek-Cypriot Panicos Chrysanthou as both directors and producers have joined forces to make a shocking documentary called **Parallel Trips** about their divided island. It was the first joint Turkish-Cypriot movie ever made which reveal similar experiences and emotions of Turkish and Greek Cypriots. By engraving a common perspective, the film reveals a shocking map of sentiments and pains of the Island's residents of both sides. It enhances self-reflexivity along with empathy since fairness is possible if it entails the willingness and ability to imagine what it is to be someone other than you.

Zaim and Chrysanthou have formed a partnership that defied the "frozen politics" of the island. The documentary is shot with two parallel perspectives within the framework of same structural format. The plan was to weave the two narratives into a feature length documentary called **Parallel Trips**. "Our film is about trying to find why - why we did this to one another. The border opening did not change that," says Zaim. He continues: "Because for so long, despite what 'politicians' and nationalist 'historians' who say there were always problems, and the divisions the British created, we did live together well. Put two Cypriots together and they will eat, drink and dance" (Zaim, 2004).

Parallel Trips' objective is to represent the human drama of the island in a balanced oral history format and a parallel narrative structure whereby respective Cypriot narrators reveal similar tragic experiences of both sides. Experiences of villagers who had been subject to massacre, and have their family in collective graves, dislocated women and children who had waited for their lost husbands or fathers in refugee camps, stories of missing people and looting, crippled soldiers who have not lost their hope and attachment to life after having suffered so much are some examples from the documentary. The most significant role of such a film is in making the audience become aware of the similar feelings and emotions as people from either side. Even the melding of music that of Byzantine Church Chorus with the voice of the Imam, in **Parallel Trips**, superimposes the reciprocal sentiments of each other.

There are numerous contemporary concerns, but it is clear that the past traumas live on. "Young people are fed a lot of propaganda about the other community in schools and media. That keeps bitterness alive," says an academician. "How much longer are we going to make these young people suffer due to a past they are not responsible for?" Hence, de-institutionalization of socialization might enhance frame-breaking.

Zaim concentrated on the notorious slaughter of the Turkish-Cypriot men, women and children of three villages on the central Cypriot plain; while Chrysanthou focused on the killings of Greek Cypriots by their neighbors in Palykythio. "I wanted to drag their stories back from the hands of the nationalists, from those who have used these people for propaganda," says Zaim. "We know we can live together, but we still have to ask why we did this to each other. If you leave things unsaid they will become the bad dreams that haunt us and will again be exploited by the nationalists." (Zaim, personal communication, April 2004).

The whole problem is with the paradigm of revenge instead of forgiving says a widow narrator. Both sides state we will not and cannot forget our sufferings and pain. Yet, one of the biggest problems is that people tend to forget what the others suffered and remember only their own sufferings. Overall, voice over is used seldom and commentary or the directors' voice are heard rarely since quoting as many voices as possible has been at the heart of the film.

Towards the end of the film, both Greek Cypriots and Turkish Cypriots cross over the border to go to the "other side". They quickly overcome the remnants of bitterness when meeting people from the other side and become strong proponents of reconciliation" in spite of criticism and attacks from extremist elements. Some have realized once more the Turkish and Greek Cypriots are in the same boat and they have decided voluntarily to sail against the tide together. Finally, we see Hüseyin and Patros- residents from different sides that we were introduced in the beginning of the film- together with families rejoicing food and dancing together as Zaim had said in his interview.

Parallel Trips is a thought-provoking film that is funded by "bi-communal development program". The documentary demonstrates that both Greek and Turkish Cypriots are rediscovering that they share many common features after so many years of stressing their differences in the documentary. Lay people along with scholars and journalists in the film have all expressed that forgiveness is not forgetting, but is rather an acknowledgment of the shared past and a willingness to move on in a new way for the benefit of both sides. This is claimed to be superior to revenge since revenge only continues the pain, prolongs the conflict and enhances the divide instead of recovery.

Hope and long-term reconciliation efforts have to be born form the tragedies of the past so that we can move on, civilians and unofficial people say in the film. In Cyprus, freedom for one group has often been purchased at the expense of the other's freedom as depicted in the documentary. As Isaiah Berlin has stated: "If the liberty of myself or my class or nation depends on the misery of a number of other human beings, the system which promotes this is unjust and immoral."(Bryant, 2004, s. 244). The documentary employs a multi-perspective approach. Portraying the convergent and divergent worldviews by recounting of daily events, the directors have aimed at changing both the frame (reframing) and the script of conflict resolution. In understanding intractable conflicts, as Allan King (2006) has suggested about his film *The Dragon's Egg* that was released in 1999:

> "You don't expect to change people, you hope that people will hear something or recognize something that will allow them to change or modify their behavior, to have a broader capacity for feeling, to feel for others."

Zaim has made the feature film that uses film images metaphorically, while the documentaries revealed multiple viewpoints about Cyprus. His film is a fiction film and it has won the Unesco Award last September. Zaim as the director and Mark Müller as the producer have worked together on **Çamur (Mud),** a powerful surrealist allegorical tale about a conscript soldier's search for a cure, which was shown at the Venice film festival in 2003 and at Istanbul film festival this April just before the referenda in Cyprus.

The plot revolves around the subconscious or unconscious trauma, malady and the recovery process. It is rather complex because of the chain of coincidental and chaotic events have symbolic meanings. Ali, a late conscript soldier, Ayşe, his sister who is a gynecologist, her lover Halil, along with their close friend Temel who are all over the age of forty, are haunted by the violent past of the divided Cyprus. Temel wants desperately to confront his past and to confess about the bodies buried in the mud of a dried up salt lake. Yet, his fear keeps him from even going near the mud. Halil would rather keep the past buried so he is indifferent to his friends' anguish.

Zaim has critically distanced himself from the particulars of the issue and highlighted the universal human side. Instead he has emphasized the psychological aspects of human nature by using the conflict within and between his fictive characters in a rather abstract setting that is set apart from social dynamics. Zaim's film seems to be in line with Volkan's theory about coping with trauma such as the need for mourning and along with numerous examples of positive and negative defense mechanisms.

Both principles relate to the fact that people in one large group have a tendency to "externalize, project, and displace" certain unwanted elements onto the other. As described earlier, "mud" is thrown onto the "other's" canvas, and it sometimes leaves a "stain." There is, however, also anxiety and fear that the "mud" could be hurled right back at the sender. The two principles exist to prevent the "mud" from coming back, thus, following Volkan, helping each projectors' identity remain cohesive (2002).

Finally, the name of the film—Mud—was a metaphor both about hope and suffering; it suggests creation of new forms and rebirth on one hand, and covering up, burying and forgetting on the other. The sight of people with mud for healing their wounds is a visual display of collective pain and despair. The films may be solely analyzed as the reflections of the " social, political and cultural context" and the work of art might be viewed mainly as an ideological phenomenon, on one hand. On the contrary, an ahistorical and romantic approach with an all-embracing humanistic assumption may overlook the particular yet profound issues, on the other hand. A balance between two simplifications and extremes is essential, yet not easy.

Zaim's Mud, for instance has been criticized for his disregarding ethnic or class basis of conflict and the political history of Cyprus. Indeed, he has focused on the workings of the subconscious due to the psychoanalytical framing of his film. He has also narrowed down his emphasis on the soul searching and in-betweenness of the characters.

As in other deep-rooted conflicts, awareness, apology and forgiveness of both parties are found to be essential for conflict resolution. As long as both sides blame each other for their problems and avoid looking at their own crimes, healing the wounds cannot occur. Hence, relationships based on mutual acceptance and trust cannot be formed. Apology is often difficult, as it requires acknowledging guilt. National pride and discourse usually block it. However, lack of apology suggests to each side what had happened in their past was appropriate and fair. This creates the fear that the opponent's unjust or violent behavior will continue for the other side. An apology is a signal that mutually both sides regret the past actions and want to rebuild a new relationship on a stronger foundation

(Papadakis, 2005).

Forgiveness is also critical for reconciliation. Many people refuse to forgive, feeling that forgiveness is essentially acceptance and forgetting the past. Or rather, they think that it will mean giving up or letting the enemy get away with their actions. The assumption is that justice is achieved by revenge or punishment. Yet, the need for revenge or punishment can prohibit the resolution of a conflict as fear of retaliation can keep opponents from accepting guilt and apologizing. For this reason, it is often superior to forgive opponents' past deeds to stop further atrocities from happening (Angeliki, 2003).

The two films are all conflict sensitive witnesses as "the mirror of our times" that lay out the efforts of building peace through recovery or relations between two communities. The documentaries have helped in changing the frame and the script of conflict resolution of the audience. Films can be used as a metaphor that helps to clarify general considerations of processes and reframe our vision. They seem to illustrate Michéle Lagny's (1997) observation:

> History resembles an image, as it requires as in photography or the moving picture the selection of framing and lighting options. As with film, it requires an editing and reflecting process (p. 221).

Concluding Remarks:

As the evidence depicted in the films along with the theories have indicated prolonged border conflicts cannot be resolved without a paradigm shift or a corrective lens. In this vein, transformation is accomplished by viewing and grasping the world from an entirely different frame and organizing it accordingly. The aim is to move away from the "the freeze" that encourages calling each side "alleged" or "pseudo" in order to widen the communication gap toward a vision of transformation and dialogue.

Reflective processes either through the impact of media or direct experiences are necessary to broaden one's perspective or to integrate one's practical experiences with theoretical knowledge of conflicts. What role do media as the third party and films in particular play in sensitizing public to enhance mutual understanding? Can they enable or enhance a process for sharing and learning about another group's beliefs, feelings, interests, and/or needs in a non-adversarial, open way as third party? The answer from our query is yes. Although multi-perspective films cannot play the role of a mediator to reach a resolution, they can help us improve interpersonal understanding and trust. In short, although films may not provide us solutions or answers, they can assist us in asking the right questions and in searching for alternative frames. Films as third parties are themselves frames and they either act as "alternative social accounts" or help maintain a civil dialogue when mediation is not an accepted option, according to Gray (2005).

On the whole, we need cooperative studies with multi-perspectives against double standards and distortions that probe into cultural values and socially shared ideas about what is desirable in communities, i.e. social norms and perceptions about both themselves and the other. In our efforts at short-term management or resolution of complex conflicts, we may continue to respond to intractable conflicts in simple and often "technologically-neat-and-smart" systematic manner and forget about the people concerns and their human needs. Otherwise, if we only focus on the humanitarians issues and forget about the political equality in partnership or security issues that are serious and sensitive, we may not comprehend the conditions and the consequent climate.

An entire generation on each side has grown up on the divided island and extremist elements constantly stir up trouble and increase divergence between the particularistic cultures. Both sides have much ground to cover and many years of hatred to overcome, still they might see how cooperation could benefit them for a more secure future, once they stop looking back in anger. In this vein, the transformation is possible only if conscientious and informative media instead of advocacy and propaganda that verifies "the other as the historical enemy" backs up the rapprochement by the motherlands along with civil initiatives. Independent and/or collaborative films, be it documentary or fiction, may pave the way for us as the audience to understand the "whole" picture.

Cypriots having been deprived of their mobility and communication by the line have bridged the "hostility gap" by shared values and increasing trust-building endeavors after April 23rd of 2003. Probing into the nature of citizenship within the framework of universal discourse of human rights and identity, i.e., "personhood and membership" and "post-national" models, pluralist discourses and a socio-political theory of neighborliness are possible areas to be studied in near future (Soysal, 1994).

What we should seek is freedom that starts with the responsibility to others rather than the security of ourselves and ends with an effective universal discourse of human rights. In that regard, the quality of leadership at all levels will determine the state of the world that future generations will inherit. Peace journalism for building dialogue is not always about being right or presenting accurately events and developments. It is also about matching the opposite narratives of the two sides. Often mainstream approaches and orthodox methodologies strengthen adversarial confrontation and heighten the existing tensions as a consequence of which making the situation more difficult to resolve.

There are no absolute norms or points of reference from

which to comprehend or judge the "others" existence: there is no neutral or absolute ground. However, the standards are relative to each other and they are connected. Obviously, there are simultaneous commonalities as well as differences between and among us. When we cannot see similarities we believe that our position is the sole truth. Yet, truth must always be understood in terms of how it is made as a process, for whom it is made, and for whom and at what time it is "true".

References

Burton, J. W. (1990). *Conflict: Resolution and prevention* (vol. 1 of the Conflict Series). New York: St Martin's Press.

Bryant, R. (2004). *Imagining the modern: The cultures of nationalism in Cyprus.* London: I.B. Tauris.

Burton, J. W. and F. Dukes, eds. (1990a). *Conflict: Human needs theory.* (vol. 2 of the Conflict Series), New York: St Martin's Press.

Burton, J. W. and F. Dukes, eds. (1990b). *Conflict: Readings in management and resolution.* (vol. 3 of the Conflict Series). London: Macmillan.

Burton, J. W. and F. Dukes, eds. (1990c). *Conflict: Practices in management, settlement and resolution.* (vol. 4 of the Conflict Series). London: Macmillan.

Cockburn, C. (2004). *The line: Women, partition and the gender order in Cyprus.* London: Zed Books.

Cunningham Jr. W. G. (1998). *Conflict theory and the conflict in Northern Ireland.* An unpublished MA Thesis: The University of Auckland.

Deutsch M. and P. T. Coleman, eds. (2000). *The handbook of conflict resolution: Theory and practice.* CA: Jossey-Bass.

Fisher, R. J. (1990). *The social psychology of intergroup and international conflict resolution.* New York: Springer-Verlag.

Galtung, J. and C. G. Jacobsen (2000). *Searching for peace, a road to TRANSCEND.* London-Sterling: Pluto Press in association with TRANSCEND.

Galtung, J. et al.(2002). *Peace by Peaceful Means: Peace and Conflict, Development and Civilization.* London, New Delhi Thousand Oaks: SAGE.

Giannakaki, A. (2003). *The Cyprus problem: Obstacles and chances for the implementation of Kofi Annan's plan.* University of Vienna, an unpublished Master's Thesis.

Gray, B. (2005). Mediation as framing and framing within mediation. Paper presented at the IACM 18th Annual Conference, Seville June.

Istanbul Foundation for Culture and Arts (2004). *23rd International Film Festival.* April 10-25, Istanbul, Mas Pub.

King, A. (1999). http://www.healthsystem.virginia.edu/internet/csmhi/estonia.cfm and http://www.allankingfilms.com/index2.html (Accessed March 5th, 2006).

Lagny, M. (1997). L'histoire contre l'image contre la mémoire. *De l'histoire du Cinéma: Méthode Historique et Histoire du Cinéma.* Paris, 1997.

Papadakis, Y. (2005). *Echoes from the Dead Zone: Across the Cyprus divide.* London: I. B. Tauris.

Soysal, N. Y. (1994). *Limits of Citizenship: Migrants and postnational membership in Europe.* Chicago: University of Chicago Press.

Volkan, V. (1979). *Cyprus – war and adaptation: A psychoanalytic history of two ethnic groups in conflict.* Charlottesville. VA: Univ. Press of Virginia.

Volkan, V. (1990). An overview of psychological roots of ethnic and sectarian terrorism. In Vamik Volkan, et al. (Eds.), *The Psychodynamics' of International Relationships.* Volume 1: Concepts and Theories. Lexington, MA: Lexington Books.

Volkan, V. (1992). *Ethno nationalistic rituals: An introduction.* Mind and Human Interaction, *4*, 3-19.

Volkan, V. (1997). *Bloodlines. from ethnic pride to ethnic terrorism.* Boulder: Westview Press.

Volkan, V. (1998). The tree model: Psychopolitical dialogues and the promotion of coexistence. In Eugene Weiner, (Ed.), *The Handbook of Interethnic Coexistence* (pp. 343-358). New York, NY: The Continuum Publishing Company.

Volkan, V. (1999). Psychoanalysis and Diplomacy Part II: Large-Group Rituals. *Journal of Applied Psychoanalytic Studies, 1*(3), 223-247.

Volkan, V. (2000). *A psychopolitical approach for the reduction of ethnic and other large group regression.* Bonn: ZEF.

Volkan, V. (2004). *Blind Trust: Large Groups and Their Leaders in Times of Crisis and Terror.* Charlottesville, Virginia: Pitchstone Publishing.

Volkan, V. (2006). What some monuments tell us about mourning and forgiveness. In Elazar Barkan and Alexander Karn (Eds.), *Taking wrongs seriously: Apologies and reconciliation* (pp. 115-131). Stanford, CA: Stanford University Press.

Zaim, D. (2004). An interview with the director at Bilgi University on April, 2004.

The Challenges Posed to Critical Pedagogy by the Transformation(s) of the University

Müge Orun
Faculty of Communication and Media Studies
Eastern Mediterranean University
muge.orun@emu.edu.tr

An Introductory Remark

Cyprus is experiencing significant political and economic transformations. These transformations have recently accelerated and are informed by discourses that take the European Union as a reference point, as well as the (re)solution (or lack thereof) of the Cyprus problem. Universities in our society are affected by these transformations as well. In my university we have been going through a series of reforms for two and half years.

Here in North Cyprus, universities have been on the agenda of public discussion and debate for a long time. I think that this is because of their enormous economic importance for North Cyprus. Additionally, however, universities were seen to be important institutions for carrying out the task of the political legitimation of the Turkish Republic of Northern Cyprus. Thus, the establishment of universities in North Cyprus was also shaped by political concerns, and not exclusively economic ones. The ongoing changes and transformations in the "globalizing" world and in North Cyprus are forcing all the political and economical institutions to change as well. Universities are required to redefine themselves in terms of the new and changing understanding of "the university."

It is no longer apparent what role the University plays in society. The structure of the contemporary University is transforming quickly in most places, and we need to understand what in particular these changes will mean. Is a new age beginning for the University? Is the regeneration of higher education in progress? Or is the University in the twilight of its social function and the ruin of higher education fast impending? We can answer such questions only if we look carefully at the different roles the University has played historically.

Yet, as important as the role of education has been in society, this role is having an unparalleled attack from promoters of market ideology who effectively support the expansion of corporate culture. As Bill Readings (1996) argues in *The University in Ruins*, as we move towards the millennium, the university came to an end to create cultured subjects for a nation state, and to a greater extent is setting out to train subjects for the transnational world (p. 3).

In this paper, I focus on the transformation of the universities nowadays. I also attempt to question what kind of opportunities is being created or would be created through these transformations of the university, which includes the concept of "the university" and institutional changes. I also question concepts like "globalization/ internationalization", "quality" and "excellence" in this regard.

Concept of "University"

The word university passed from the Latin word **universitas** (total, all, entire) to Western languages, then with the establishment of the Republic, from the French word **universitè** (the institution which is open to the whole society and where all knowledges are being taught) to Turkish language. In Latin, universitas is derived from the words *universum* (the whole, the universe, total), *universal* (general), *universus* (all together, whole, entire). In the middle ages, where the first universities established the word, *universitas* was used to mean "a community formed by people who have an independent legal personality forwarding common interests" (Eyüboğlu, 1991, p. 698). Nowadays the word university generally refers to an institution where faculties, institutes of higher education are held in its structure and more advanced education and research takes place with conferral of degrees to accomplished practitioners.

If social institutions were ranked in an order of importance in various countries, the university would, most likely, take one of the first places in the rank. It is not hard to understand this general belief, if we think the university is known as the place of searching for the realities and where knowledges of such realities are produced. The contribution of the universities to scientific research and findings can not be denied throughout the history. But, examining historically, we cannot say that universities have been dominant in this field until recent times. History of science and philosophy shows that most of the creativity in this field came from outside the university (Timur, 2000).

At the beginning, universities did not have the function of presenting realities, developing science and disseminating it. In the first place, in that period when the universities were established, there were neither independent/free philosophy nor an understanding of science as it means today. Taner Timur, in his book *Social Change and Universities* (2000), examines this phenomenon:

> Like it was in the Middle Ages, and in its modern meaning, science and philosophy were born as a result of the progress of the communities and with the growth of the division of labor. And in this development, universities, under the domination of churches, mosques, and every kind of temple, were far from being creative. Universities, after the development of the division of labor, emerged as an extension of "school"...Schools and universities, throughout the centuries, were in the hands of dominant classes, they were used as tools to, in Nietzsche's words, *domesticate*, and aimed to educate the public (p. 14).

In North Cyprus the universities are accepted as an important indicator of the well being of a democratic society. Universities are accepted (or said) to be places where values are passed to young people consecutively to make them think critically; to contribute to policy decisions that concern their lives; and to transform every kind of (racial, social, and economic) inequities that threaten democratic social relations. I grew up in a community where the idea of having a university diploma is one indicator of being an adult and what is considered to be adult is to have a university education which ends with a graduation ceremony. As Samuel Weber (n.d.) says "The university is thus characterized as a kind of womb in which the embryo of the social being is brought to fruition before being expelled i.e., born(e) – into the world. This is reinforced by the fundamental task of the university, which however it is defined, involves the acquisition of knowledge" (para. 21).

There is a long list of well-known books on "the idea of the university," the most famous of which is indisputably the book of John Henry Cardinal Newman first published approximately a century and a half ago. John Henry Newman (1996) in *The Idea of a University* discusses that universities are places where one can gain universal knowledge. Newman argues that university education is almost by its meaning different from training for a vocation or a profession. As a human institution, as Newman argues, a university should produce a person of "broad knowledge", "critical intelligence", "moral decency" and "social sensitivity", however its function should not be an institution with the intention of fundamentally transforming morally wrong human beings.

The Transformations of the University

Here, I want to acknowledge Bill Readings and his book *The University in Ruins*, which I find to be very important for any serious discussion of the university today, whether of its idea, its mission or its future.

Bill Readings (1996) in his book *University In Ruins* "performs a structural diagnosis of contemporary shifts in the university's function as an institution, in order to argue that the wider social role of the University as an institution is now up for grabs" (p. 2). Readings argues that the University's role has shifted, and this shift is revealed by the decline of the national cultural mission that has up to now endowed the university with its underlying principle. While the University used to be the producer, protector, and inculcator of the national culture by its virtue, now it is becoming a different kind of institution, one that is not anymore connected to the destiny of the nation-state. The role of the university has transformed at the same time as the forces of globalization have turned out to be more obvious:

> The University is becoming a different institution, one that is no longer linked to the destiny of the nation-state by virtue of its role as producer, protector, and inculcator of an idea of national culture. The process of economic globalization brings with it the relative decline of the state as the prime instance of the reproduction of capital around the world. For its part, the University is becoming a transnational bureaucratic corporation, either tied to transnational instances of government such as European Union or functioning independently, by analogy with a transnational corporation (1996, p. 3).

The process of economic globalization leads to the relative decline of the nation-state as the prime instance of the reproduction of capital around the world. Here, in considerable ways, Readings argues that the modern university is like a multinational corporation, and its links with big business may well increase as administrators search for sources of funding to replace diminishing governmental allocations.

Readings writes of the university by referring to the German model of the university that Humboldt established at the University of Berlin in 1812. For him, the notion of culture as the main idea of the modern university has moved towards the end of its convenience. General character of the university has turned out to be corporate more willingly than cultural. The university's mission is now defined in terms of "excellence" rather than "culture" (Peters, 2004). Readings (1996) argues that "what gets taught or researched is less important than the fact that it be excellently taught or researched" (p. 13).

Michael Peters (2004) in his article "Higher Education, Globalization and the Knowledge Economy," outlines his claims, drawing from Readings' arguments, that three ideas of the university dominate in the modern era: "the Kantian idea of reason"; "the Humboldtian idea of culture"; and "the techno-bureaucratic idea of excellence". He cites Bill Readings (1996) to summarize the modern history of the university in terms of three overarching ideas:

> The history of the modern university can be crudely summarized by saying that the modern University has had three Ideas, the Kantian idea of reason, the Humboldtian notion of culture, and now the technological idea of excellence. The distinguishing feature of the last... is that it lacks all referentiality—it is the simulacrum of the Idea of a University...in the Kantian University (the president's) function is the purely disciplinary one of making decisive judgments in inter-faculty conflicts on the reason alone. In the University founded on culture, the president incarnates a pandisciplinary ideal of a general cultural orientation...In the contemporary University, however, a president is a bureaucratic administrator...From judge to synthesizer to executive (p. 163).

What these arguments suggest is that it is no longer feasible to have a discussion on the idea of the modern university or of an institution unified through the force of a single idea, as of the pressures of globalization, managerialism and marketization. The idea of the modern university based on Kant, Humboldt or Newman has become historical in the sense that the techno-bureaucratic idea of excellence has instituted an historical break or rupture with the modern. As a result, the university has become nearly identical with the transnational corporations that serve as a kind of surrogate state. Since universities have become corporate in their structure plus in their curriculum, they develop the imprecise goal of "excellence" to which the transnational corporations are promised. According to Peters (2004), "universities now function as more bureaucratic subsystem among others harnessed in the service of national competitiveness in the global economy. In the age of global capitalism universities have been reduced to a technical ideal of performance within a contemporary discourse of 'excellence'" (p. 71).

Accordingly, globalization is seen as having eradicated the recognized idea of the university which is centered on the cultural production of a liberal, reasoning, citizen subject. Readings (1996) asserts that "the University...no longer participates in the historical project for humanity that was the legacy of the Enlightenment: the historical project of culture" (p. 5). The University of Excellence takes the place of the University of Culture. As Readings (1996) argues:

> "The economics of globalization mean that the University is no longer called upon to train citizen subjects, while the politics of the end of the cold war mean that the university is no longer called upon to hold national prestige by producing and legitimating national culture" (p. 14).

According to Carmen Luke (1998):

> The university has long been characterized as an international enterprise in terms of research and the international, indeed global, dissemination of scholarship (and scholars) through publication systems and conference circuits. Globalization, some argue, has accelerated the pace of information and people flows enabled by electronic communication and post-jet-age travel. Academic business in the age of globalization is much about increased pressure for more research output as it is about electronic content delivery, marketing, and strategic research alliances with business and industry. The ivory tower has become a marketing machine, and the armchair academic is being pried out of old comfort zones and pushed into public debates and accountability. Some label this new class of academic-cultural workers as cosmopolitan intellectuals. These globally mobile intellectuals and cultural "translators" are as likely to be on university recruitment jaunts..." (p. xx-xxi).

Since the university is equally the place of work and educational organization, the global formation of a fundamentally European model of university, together with a flow in the direction of increasing homogeneity of educational content, delivery, and credentialing shaped by educational globalization, puts forward a more and more standardized and universal institutional constitution.

Excellence thus intersects with "integration and standardization" and Luke (1998) continues to say that "normalization" gives a strong sense of what is at stake in "standardization". Readings' (1996) arguments work to tie the University into a similar net of bureaucratic institutions through the notion of excellence. It makes the University to be understood as the structure of a corporate administration. He refers to Alfonso Borrero Cabal's report to UNESCO which is called *The University as an Institution Today,* as an administrative approach to University that shows the need of the University "to become part of the international scene" (cited in Readings,

1996, p. 30). And that is the requirement of globalization where greater attention is given to administration with the purpose of authorizing the integration of the market in knowledge that Alfonso Borrero Cabal relates with the need for "development" (cited in Readings, 1996, p. 30). Borrero Cabal structures the university by using the language of economic management. That's why as he argues "planning, execution, evaluation: natural actions of responsible persons and institutions. They make up the three important stages that complete the cycle of the administrative process. In logical order, planning precedes execution and evaluation, but all planning has to start with evaluation" (cited in Readings, 1996, p. 30)

Stanley Aronowitz in his book, *The Knowledge Factory* (2000) similarly argues that the academic system as a whole is wedged in a market logic that demands students to be job-ready after graduation. He argues that colleges and universities are unable to implement an educational program that prepares students for a world of great complexity. Instead, he says, "academic leaders chant the mantra of 'excellence,' the new horizon of university administration, as corporate slogans corresponding to bottom-line corporate practices drive higher education's goals" (p. 158). For Aronowitz (2000), excellence means "that all of the parts of the university 'perform' and are judged according to how well they deliver knowledge and qualified labor to the corporate economy and how well the administration fulfills the recruitment and funding goals needed to maintain the institution" (p. 158).

According to Readings (1996), when university administrators talk about excellence, they inadvertently situate the issue of value in accord with measurement and accounting solutions for questions of accountability (p. 119). As an incorporating principle, excellence has the benefit of completely bureaucratizing the university. Similarly Michael Peters (2004) argues that universities have turned out to be locations for the development of "human resources" (p. 71). He states that guided by mission statements and strategic plans, performance output is measured and total quality management (TQM) assures quality outcomes.

To explain it shortly, total quality management is an organization philosophy that focuses on the consumer satisfaction and perceives quality as "excellence." It is "a particularly influential comprehensive approach to quality management that places emphasis on factors such as continuous improvement, customer focus, strategic management, need for explicit systems to assure quality of higher education, and a view of leadership and supervision that stresses employee empowerment and delegation" (Vlăsceanu, L., Grünberg, L. & Pârlea, D. , 2004, p. 50). Quality is either assumed to require that one orient oneself to the demands of the consumer or satisfying the consumer by meeting his/her demands. Philip Crosby, who uses terms like "quality" and "quality management," defines quality as "conformance to requirements, not as 'goodness' or elegance" (cited in Hand,1992, p. 26). In the *Quality Assurance and Accreditation: Glossary of Basic Terms and Definitions* (2004), which is prepared by Lazăr Vlăsceanu, Laura Grünberg, and Dan Pârlea for UNESCO, they state that quality may have different meanings depending on various conditions, such as the insights of various interests of different constituencies or stakeholders in higher education, or according to its inputs, processes, outputs, missions, objectives, etc.; *or* the attributes or characteristics of the academic world which are worth evaluating. They thus point out an extensive range of definitions of quality in academia:

> ***Quality as excellence***: a traditional, élitist academic view, according to which only the best standards of excellence (usually meaning a high level of difficulty and of complexity of a programme, the seriousness of the student)... ***Quality as fitness for purpose***: a concept that stresses the need to meet or conform to generally accepted standards such as those defined by an accreditation or quality assurance body, the focus being on the efficiency of the processes at work in the institution or programme in fulfilling the stated, given objectives and mission... **Quality as fitness of purpose:** a concept that focuses on the defined objectives and mission of the institution or programme with no check of the fitness of the processes themselves in regard to any external objectives or expectations... **Quality as enhancement or improvement:** focusing on the continuous search for permanent improvement, stressing the responsibility of the higher education institution to make the best use of its institutional autonomy and freedom...

When we look at the definitions of this approach we can see that the overriding concern is the consumer or consumer satisfaction

The case of Turkish Cypriot Universities

I mentioned that the concept of quality is widely used in the realm of education. In these days there are frequent references to quality which shows us that the concept broadened its meaning and its incidence from its starting point of administrative/managerial sciences. Evaluating this phenomenon in another ways is to say that education increasingly started to be bureaucratized. In this part of my paper I examine how the quality concept entered into the discourses of universities in Northern Cyprus.

Administrative staff of the universities often discuss the need to develop academic and administrative evaluation systems in order to provide quality and efficiency in administration. Another concern mentioned is that when universities are working on their duties like education, research and service to society, they have to do this without conceding quality. This view is embraced for the sake of being a "good university". I have to say that as the word "quality"is polysemic there are many benefits to comprise quality in education. I think everyone wants to work in an institution that has quality standards. And "high quality standards" can not be denied in an institution when looked from the perspectives of administration, students and academic staff. However, we have to consider the concept of "quality" in its relation to the concept of "excellence." And the most important question here is to ask what is "quality," "excellence" and "good" things that Cyprus needs and with what this can be compared?

Faced with these dilemmas, the present EMU administration, for instance, has tried to adopt corporate thinking and language. It has embraced quality assurance, and the logics and practices of excellence. There happened numerous meetings where issues of quality, excellence, management, assessment and accountability were presented as being the major issues in order to carry the EMU to "the peak of quality." The discourse of excellence is on the way. Here I want again to cite Readings' (1996) words where he says:

> University mission statements, like their publicity brochures, share two distinctive features nowadays. On the one hand, they all claim that there is a unique educational institution. On the other hand, they all go on to describe this uniqueness in exactly the same way. The preeminent signs under which this transformation is taking place are the appeals to the notion of "excellence" that now drop from the lips of University. Administrators at every turn. To understand the contemporary University, we must ask what excellence means (or does not mean) (p. 12).

The following is from our Rector Halil Güven's welcoming message put on the university web site:

> EMU, with a very proud past of 25 years in the service of higher education, is on its way to becoming an EU University in the very near future, and with a brand new vision and dynamism has launched a university-wide initiative to «Aim for the Peak of Quality." The new EMU is the perfect candidate to be the «leading shining star» of the region with its new administrative staff and the new programs it is implementing to achieve quality and accreditation (http://www.emu.edu.tr/e/welcomemasseage.html, para. 2).

The words like "quality" and "accreditation" are very important issues for university administrators. The sentences of the administrators which includes "total quality management," "brand new vision and mission," "learning outcomes," "accountability" always refer to the discourse of excellence. These concepts are seen in every realm of daily life inside the universities. The whole idea of the university is established on these concepts. These concepts of quality and total quality management were introduced recently in North Cyprus and to the discourse of the university. In view of the fact that quality assurance in universities has gained importance both at an international level in general, and in frame of the Bologna Process for the last five years, the attention of our university's discourse to quality assurance has significantly increased. We can see the notion of excellence as an extension of the "quality" concept which is developed by the bureaucratic organization of global capitalism. Here, I again want to cite another example to show how the top university administrators attach importance to the concept of quality:

> We will be continuing our work at a rapid pace towards modernizing and developing our university, and "aiming for the peak of quality" in student support, facilities, teaching, research, and administration. Developing the mission and the vision that will carry our university to the pinnacle of quality (personal trasncription of a speech given by the Rector during his visit to the Faculty of Communication and Media Studies).

The administrators think that "an already excellent university" is exhorted to create a working environment devoted to excellence.

On a leaflet of EMU's EUA campaign in 2007, which the administration distributed throughout the university, we read the following questions:

> Do you wish…
> Your university to accomplish change for the better?
> Your university to be the one that offers a competitive transnational education?
> Your university to have autonomy and accountability?
> To improve the capacity for change through improvement of Quality culture?
> To have systems monitoring quality improvement and to use them to achieve excellence?
> Your university to be a competitive European partner in higher education?

The language where global debates are to be carried out is not that of cultural conflict but of economic management. And this also shows us the importance of three terms for the university: Being international, European and global. These three terms are explained by Ulrich Teichler (2004) as:

> -internationalization is often discussed in relation to physical mobility, academic cooperation and academic knowledge transfer as well as international education
>
> -Europeanization is addresses frequently when referring the cooperation and mobility…it also covers such issues as integration, convergence of contexts, structures and substance ("European dimension", European culture", "European citizen").

-Globalization is often associated with competition and market-steering, trans-national education and finally commercial knowledge transfer (p. 7).

It is very obvious here that EMU has a mission to be a part of ERASMUS (horizontal mobility and cooperation between institutions) and The Bologna Process (the process of integration of European higher education and standardization of study programmes and degrees).

References

Aronowitz, S (2000). *The knowledge factory: Dismantling the corporate university and creating true higher learning.* Boston: Beacon.

Cabal, B. Cabal, B. (1993*). The university as an institution today*. Paris: UNESCO.

Eyüboğlu, İ. Z. (1991). *Türk Dilinin Etimoloji Sözlüğü*. Sosyal Yayınlar.

Hand, M. (1992). Total quality management—One God but many prophets. In M. Hand & B. Plowman (Eds.), *Quality management handbook* (pp. 26-46). Oxford: Butterworth Heinemann

Luke, C. (2001). *Globalization and women in academia: north/west south/east.* London: Lawrence Erlbaum Associates.

Newman, J. H. (1996). *The idea of a university: Rethinking the western tradition*, F.M.Turner, (Ed.). New Haven & London: Yale University.

Peters, M. (2004). Higher education, globalization and the knowledge economy. In M. Walker & J. Nixon (Eds.), *Reclaiming universities from a runaway world* (pp. 67-82). Berkshire: London University Press.

Readings, B. (1996). *University in ruins*. Cambridge: Massachusetts

Teichler, U. (2004). The changing debate on internationalization of higher education. *Higher Education, 48*, 5-26.

Timur, T. (2002). *Toplumsal değişim ve üniversiteler*. Ankara: İmge Kitabevi.

Weber, S. (n.d). The future campus: Destiny in the virtual world. Retrieved January, 29 2007 from http://culturemachine.tees.co.uk

Vlăsceanu, L. Grünberg, L. & Pârlea, D., (2004). Papers on higher education: *Assurance and Accreditation: Glossary of Basic Terms and Definitions*. Retrieved on February, 20 2007 from http://www.bologna-bergen2005.no/Docs/02-UNESCO-CEPES/04_UNESCO_CEPES_Glossary.pdf

Okullarda Yaşanan Şiddet Olaylarını Azaltmaya Yönelik "Tüm Okulu Kapsayan Arabuluculuk Modeli"nin Uygulanmasına İlişkin bir Çalışma

Nermin Koruklu
Eğitim Fakültesi
Adnan Menderes Üniversitesi
nonerkoruklu@hotmail.com

Okulların temel işlevlerinden biri, öğrencilere istenmeyen davranışlardan arındırılmış bir atmosfer sunarak barışçı bir toplumun temellerini atmaktır. Fakat, son yıllarda öğrenciler arasında şiddet içerikli davranışların görülme sıklığının arttığı kaygıyla izlenmektedir. Söz konusu artış eğitim kurumlarında yeni düzenlemeler yapılmasının gerekliliğini ortaya koymaktadır. Bu çalışmada uygulanmaya çalışılan "Tüm Okulu Kapsayan Arabuluculuk Modeli" nin en temel hedefi öğrencileri kendi sorunlarının çözümüne ortak kılmaktır. Bilindiği gibi, okullarımızda yaşanan şiddet olayları geleneksel dış denetime dayalı ceza-ödül disiplin anlayışı ile çözülmeye çalışılmaktadı (Öner, 1996). Öğrenciler kendi yaşadıkları sorunların çözümünde yer almamaktadırlar. Yaşadıkları en küçük anlaşmazlığı bile öğretmene yansıtma ihtiyacı hissetmektedirler.

Varolan okul disiplin anlayışı yerine öğrencilerin katılımını temel alan bir anlayışa geçilmesi gerekmektedir. Yapılan araştırmalar öğrencilere fırsat verilirse kendi kendilerine sorunlarını çözeceklerini ve okullarda yaşanan disiplin olaylarında azalmaların yaşanacağını ortaya koymuştur (Maxwel, 1989). Okulda öğrencilerin yaşadığı çatışmaları öğretmenlerinin çözmesi, öğrencilerin iç denetimlerini kurmalarına engel olmaktadır bunun yanı sıra öğrencilerin okula karşı olumsuz tutum geliştirmelerine neden olmaktadır. Bu nedenle, okullarda öğrencilerle işbirliği yapılırsa daha nitelikli okul ortamlarının oluşturulabileceğini saptanmıştır (Glasser, 1990).

Bu çerçevede okullarımızda çatışma çözme programlarının uygulanmaya konması konusunda yetkili kişilerin acil önlemler almaları gerekmektedir. Okul programlarında çatışma çözme programlarına yer verilmesi ile aşağıdaki konularda fayda sağlayacağı araştırmalarla saptanmıştır (Öner, 1999). a) Çatışma çözme eğitimi içersinde yer alan problem çözme sürecinin ve iletişim becerilerinin öğretilmesiyle okul ortamı geliştirilebilir. b) Çatışma çözme yollarının öğretilmesi ile okullarda yaşanan şiddet olaylarında, okuldan kaçma ve sürekli devamsızlıklarda azalma sağlanabilir. c) Çatışma çözme eğitimi, öğrencilerin ve öğretmenlerin kendi kendilerini ve çevrelerindeki diğer kişileri daha iyi anlayabilme güçlerini geliştirerek onlara önemli yaşam becerileri kazandırır. d) Çatışma çözme alanında eğitim almak bireylerin iyi bir vatandaş olma düzeylerini artırır. e) Çatışmalarını çözme sorumluluğu öğrencilere verildiğinde öğretmenler zamanlarının çoğunu disiplin sorunlarıyla uğraşmak yerine öğretme etkinliklerine verirler. f) Çatışma çözme eğitimi bireyin kendi kendisini yönetebilmeyi öğrenmesi, iç-denetimini kazanmasında tüm diğer disiplin yaklaşımlarından daha etkilidir. g) Çatışma çözme eğitimi, tüm öğrenme ortamları için temel oluşturan dinleme, eleştirel düşünme ve problem çözme becerilerinin gelişmesini sağlar. h) Çatışma çözme eğitimi, öğrencilere farklılıkları barışcıl yollarla kabul edebilmek için sorunları bir de karşıdaki kişinin bakış açısından görebilme becerisi kazandırır. Bu beceriyi kazanmak farklı kültürlerde yaşayabilmeyi kolaylaştırır. ı) Gençler, çatışma çözme yollarını öğrenince, karşılaştıkları problemleri yetişkin yardımına başvurmadan kendi kendilerini çözebilme gücünü kazanırlar. i) Çatışma çözme eğitiminden kazanılan problem çözme ve iletişim becerileri, okul dışı yaşantılarda da etkili bir biçimde kullanılarak eğitimi alan bireylerin yaşam kalitelerinde gelişmelere neden olabilmektedir.

Görüldüğü gibi okullarda çatışma çözme programının uygulamaya konulması ile hem öğretmenlerimiz hem de öğrencilerimiz farklı alanlarda kazanımlar elde edeceklerdir. Öğrencilerin bireysel gelişimlerinin yanı sıra arkadaşlık ilişkilerinin niteliğinde de artışlar olacaktır. Öğretmenler ise ders saatlarinde etkin olarak ders işleyebilecektir.

Horowitz ve Boardman (1994), okullarda çatışma çözme programının gelişimsel bir süreç içersinde okul öncesinden başlanarak yüksekokula kadar sürdürülmesinin bir zorunluluk olduğunu ortaya koymuşlardır. Bu programların farklı yaş gruplarının dönemlerinin gerektirdiği gereksinimlere, yeteneklere göre ayarlanması gerektiğini söylemişler ve çatışma çözme programlarının okullarda yaşlara göre uygulanma içeriğini şu şekilde ifade etmişlerdir (akt. Sweeney ve Carruthers, 1996): Okul öncesinde kişilerarası ilişkiler konusunda eğitilmeye başlanmalıdır. Bu yaş grubunun öğretmenleri, zamanlarının çoğunu kişilerarası ilişkiler konusuna ayırmalıdırlar. Yüksekokula doğru gidildiğinde ise konu içeriği daha derinleşerek şiddetin doğası ve kuramsal açıklamalar üzerinde durulması gerekmektedir.

Bodine ve Crawford (1998) çatışma çözmenin diğer ders konularından farklı bir program olarak algılanmaması gerektiğini söylemişlerdir ve gelişimsel bir süreç içersinde öğrencilere çatışma çözme becerileri ile problem çözme sürecinin öğretilebileceğini ortaya koymuşlardır. Aşağıda bu süreç özetlenmiştir: 1) Okulöncesinden ilkokul ikinci sınıfa kadar olan çocuklara; hikayelerle, rol yaparak, işbirliğini gösteren oyunlarla, sınıf projeleri, etkinlik kartları, posterler, büyük çocukların da yer aldığı etkinlikler ile çatışma çözme öğretilebilir. 2) İlkokul üçüncü sınıftan başlanarak beşinci sınıfa kadar öğrencilere, problem çözme analizi varolan okul programı içersine alınarak, rol yapma, sınıf projeleri, toplantılar, akran arabuluculuğu programları, video, oyunlar, sınıf gösterileri ve öğrencilerin ailelerine ve halka hazırladığı gösteriler yoluyla öğretilebilir. 3) Altıncı sınıftan sekizinci sınıfa kadar olan öğrencilere, yukarıda verilen öğrenme ve uygulama etkinliklerine ek olarak; eğitici öğrencilerin çatışma çözmenin problem çözme stratejilerini öğretebileceği, ayrıca okul programı içersine alınarak öğretilebileceği, öğrencilerin kendi rol yapma etkinlikleri oluşturmalarına izin vererek, sosyal organizasyonlar için seminerler hazırlayıp sunmaları sağlanarak öğretilebileceği ortaya konmuştur. 4) Yüksekokul öğrencilerinin çatışma çözme programlarını öğrenme ve uygulama etkinlikleri: akran arabuluculuğunun uygulanması, öğrencilerin diğer öğrencileri arabulucu olarak eğitmesi için eğitilmesi, okul toplantılarının ve gösterilerinin düzenlenmesi, rol yapma etkinliklerinin oluşturulması, videoların kullanılması, daha büyük topluluklara çatışma çözme hizmetinin verilmesi, büyük öğrencilerin küçük öğrencilere çatışma çözme programlarını oluştururken yardım etmelerine izin verilmesi, okul içersinde arabulucu olarak çalışmalarının sağlanması, öğrencilere farklı okullardaki çatışmaların çözümünde görev almalarının desteklenmesi, olarak sıralanabilir (Bodine ve Crawford, 1998).

Bu çalışmada Bodine ve Crawford'un da önerdiği gibi, akran arabuluculuk yönteminin, ilköğretimin ilk yıllarından başlanarak sekizinci sınıfa kadar öğretilmesi anlayışı benimsenmiştir. Arabuluculuk, iki ya da daha fazla bireyler arasında yaşanan çatışmaların giderilmesinde üçüncü kişilerin çatışma çözme ve iletişim becerilerini kullanarak yardımcı olmaları sürecidir (Smith ve Sidwell, 1990). Bu süreç içerisinde tarafsız kalarak ve çatışma çözme-iletişim becerilerini kullanarak çatışması olan taraflara yardımcı olan üçüncü bireylere de arabulucular denir.

Okulda arabuluculuk sürecinin uygulanması kademelere göre farklılık göstermektedir. Bu nedenle aşağıda farklı kademelerde uygulanmasının daha etkili olacağı göz önünde bulundurularak bazı arabuluculuk uygulamaları ve bu çalışmada yararlanılan model kısaca açıklanmıştır (akt. Lupton-Smith ve diğerleri, 1996):

1-*Tüm okulu kapsayan arabuluculuk modeli*: Tüm okulu kapsayan arabuluculuk sürecinin, ilköğretim kademesinde uygulama kolaylığı nedeniyle daha etkili olacağı düşünülmektedir. Tüm öğrencilere arabuluculuk ve çatışma çözme eğitimi verilerek, temel eğitimden itibaren olumlu çatışma çözme ve iletişim becerilerini kazandırılmış olacaktır. Johnson ve Johnson (1994)'a göre tüm okulu kapsayan arabuluculuğun en belirgin avantajı, bütün öğrencilerin arabuluculuk eğitimini alması ve hepsinin de arabulucu olarak çalışabilme şanslarının olmasıdır. Böylece öğrencilerin hepsi çatışmalarını yapıcı yollarla çözmeyi öğrenmektedir ve arabulucu olarak çalıştıkları için de çatışma yönetimi ve iletişim becerileri konusunda yeterlilik kazanmaktadırlar. Sonuçta, okul ortamındaki şiddet olaylarında ve disiplin olaylarının sayısında azalmalar yaşanmaktadır. Bu modelin dezavantajı ise; bu programı uygulamanın zaman alması ve tüm yönetimin katılımının zorunlu olmasıdır. Bu durum, maliyetlerin artmasına neden olmaktadır

2-*Kulüp çalışmasını kapsayan arabuluculuk modeli*: Bu modelde okulun tüm birimlerinden gönüllü olarak katılan öğrencilerle okul ders programı dışında bir araya gelinerek eğitim yapılır. Genellikle de tercih edilen ders bitişi ya da hafta sonları toplantılarıdır. Bazı durumlarda çalışmalar öğle aralarında ya da yoğunlaştırılmış iki günlük programlarla uygulanabilir. Bu model içersinde arabuluculuk; okuldan önce, öğle arası, okul çıkışı planlanır. Bu modelin en önemli avantajı arabulucu olarak seçilen öğrencilerin tüm okul evrenini temsil etme düzeyinin yüksek olmasıdır. Modele özgü bir diğer avantaj, okul içersinde dışlanmış, grup arkadaşlığı yapamayan, okulun sosyal faaliyetlerine katılamayan öğrencilere bir fırsat yaratmasıdır. Klüp modelinin dezavantajı ise, arabuluculuk eğitiminin istenilen ölçüde derinleştirilememesidir (Lupton-Smith ve diğerleri, 1996). Bu model ortaöğretim ve yükseköğretim için önerilmektedir. Öğrencilerin hem boş zamanlarını değerlendirme ve hem de farklı arkadaş gruplarıyla etkileşimde bulunma olanağı sağlaması anlamlı bir kazanç olarak görülmektedir.

3-*Seçmeli ders kapsamında arabuluculuk modeli*: Graham ve Cline (1989)'a göre arabuluculuk için kısa süreli kurslar ya da dersler düzenlenebilir. Bazı Amerikan okullarında arabuluculuk eğitimi seçmeli ders olarak okutulmaktadır. Bu dersler "Akran Buluşu" adı altında verilebilmektedir. Bu dersleri veren öğretim elemanları koordinatör olarak uygulamalarda görev almaktadırlar. Derse katılan öğrencilerden de arabulucu olarak görev yapması istenmektedir. Bu model yüksekokullar için en etkin olanıdır (akt. Lupton–Smith ve diğerleri, 1996). Bu modelin bazı avantajları vardır. Bunlar; dersler öğrencilerin arabulucu olarak eğitilmesine olanak sağlar ve arabuluculuğun uygulanmasına ortam hazırlar. Ayrıca bireylerin birbiriyle iletişimleri ders aracılığı ile kolay olduğundan arabuluculuk için yapılacak zaman planlamasında sorun yaşanmaz. Arabulucuların yaptığı uygulamalar sürekli değerlendirildiği için modelin etkililiği artmaktadır. Bu modelin dezavantajları ise, arabulucu olarak görevlendirilecek bireylerin sadece dersi alan bireylerden seçilme zorunluluğudur. Bu da ders alan öğrencilerin genel öğrenci kitlesini tam olarak temsil etme düzeyini düşürmektedir. Diğer bir zayıf yönü ise arabuluculuk zamanı dersin olduğu saatlerle sınırlı olmasıdır (Lupton-Smith ve diğerleri, 1996). Araştırmacı, 2003 yılından beri Aydın Adnan Menderes Üniversitesi Eğitim Fakültesi Sınıf Öğretmenliği Bölüm öğrencilerine arabuluculuk sürecini seçmeli ders olarak vermektedir.

Yöntem

Bu çalışma Aydın ilinde bulunan bir özel ilköğretim okulunda yürütülmüştür. Çalışmanın temel amacı "Tüm Okulu Kapsayan Arabuluculuk Modeli"nin uygulanması olduğu için, çalışmanın örneklemi aynı zamanda evrenidir. Okulun öğrenci sayısı toplam 426'dır. Bunların 196'sı kız, 230'u erkek öğrencidir.

Veri Toplama Aracı

Çalışmada, öğrencilerin yaşadıkları çatışma durumları ve bu çatışmalara verdikleri tepkiler araştırmacı tarafından hazırlanan açık uçlu sorular kullanılarak saptanmaya çalışılmıştır. Ayrıca belirli çatışma durumları verilerek böyle bir durumda nasıl davranırsınız şeklinde açıklamalı örnek olaylardan da yararlanılmıştır. Araştırmacı, hazırlanan örnek durumları daha önce başka bir ilköğretim okulu öğrencilerinde uygulamış ve yüzeysel geçerliliğine bakmıştır. Anlaşılmayan ya da yanlış anlaşılan durumlar çıkartılmış ve yeniden düzenlenmiştir. Öğrencilere; "Teneffüste arkadaşlarınızla oyun oynarken bir grup öğrenci gelip oyununuzu bozsa ne yaparsın" şeklinde örnek durum verilip onun kendi tepkisi öğrenilmeye çalışılmıştır. Formlar doldurulurken sınıf öğretmenliği bölümünden "İlköğretimde Arabuluculuk ve İletişim Becerileri" seçmeli dersini alan öğrencilerden yardım alınmıştır. Özellikle anasınıfı, 1. ve 2. sınıflarla birebir görüşmeler yapılarak formlar doldurulmuştur.

İşlem

Tüm Okulu Kapsayan Arabuluculuk Modeli'nin uygulamasına ilişkin işlem basamakları şu şekilde sıralanmaktadır: 1) Okuldaki tüm öğrencilerin, hazırlanan soru formalarını doldurması: Öğretmen adaylarının yardımıyla tüm öğrenciler okullarında arkadaşlarıyla ya da öğretmenleriyle yaşadıkları çatışma durumlarını ve bu durumlara verdikleri tepkileri yazmışlardır. Ayrıca araştırmacı tarafından hazırlanan örnek çatışma durumlarında nasıl davrandıkları konusunda cevaplar vermişlerdir. 2) Arabuluculuk sürecini, tüm okulu tanıtma toplantıları: Arabuluculuk ülkemizde yeni yeni duyulmaya başlayan bir yöntemdir. Bu bağlamda konu hakkında öğrenci ve öğretmenlerin bilgisi yoktur. Söz konusu durum göz önüne alındığında modelin etkin uygulanabilmesi için tüm öğrencilere ve öğretmenlere tanıtım toplantıları yapılmıştır. Model, öğrencilere drama ve projeksiyonlu sunumlar eşliğinde tanıtılmıştır. Öğretmenler ile küçük grup toplantıları yapılarak model anlatılmıştır. 3) Arabuluculuk ve İletişim Becerileri Eğitimi: Tanıtım toplantılarının arkasından her sınıfta 4'er kişilik eğitmen ile eğitimler yapılmıştır. Eğitimler haftada 1 saat olmak üzere 5 hafta sürdürülmüştür. 4) Arabuluculuk süreci uygulamaya konmuştur: Tüm öğrenciler, eğitim aldıkları için sınıflarda nöbetçi öğrenci gibi sırayla arabulucu olarak görev yapmaya başlamışlardır.

Verilerin Analizi

Elde edilen veriler nitel özellik taşımaktadır. Bu nedenle çocukların verdikleri cevaplardan yararlanılarak okullarında yaşanan çatışma durumları ve sıklığı listelenmiştir. Arkasında çatışma durumlarında gösterdikleri tepkiler ve yüzdelik değerleri saptanmıştır. Bu çalışma temelde bir modelin uygulanmasına ilişkin veriler elde etmek amacıyla yapıldığı için elde edilen veriler üzerinde değil modelin uygulanmasında yaşanan sorunlar ve çözüm önerileri üzerinde odaklanılmıştır. Bu çerçevede araştırmacı, model uygulanmaya başlandıktan 1 ay sonra ve 3 ay sonra okula geri bildirim alma amaçlı ziyaretler yapmıştır. Bu ziyaretlerde öğretmenlerle ve arabulucu olarak çalışan öğrencilerle görüşmeler yaparak, sürecin uygulanmasına ilişkin problemleri saptamaya çalışmıştır.

Bulgular ve Tartışma

Tüm Okulu Kapsayan Arabuluculuk Modeli'nin uygulama aşamasında ve uygulama sonucunda elde edilen bulgular aşağıda tartışılmıştır.

Model uygulanmadan önce öğrencilerle yapılan görüşmelerden ve açık uçlu sorulara verilen cevaplardan

elde edilen veriler aşağıdaki gibidir:
1) Okul bahçesinde ve sınıf içinde arkadaşlarınızla yaşadığınız çatışmalar nelerdir sorusuna tablo 1'deki cevaplar verilmiştir:

Çatışma Nedenleri	f	%
Bir şeyi paylaşamadığımızda	5	0.94
Oyunumuzu bozduğunda	**92**	**17.36**
İzinsiz eşyamı aldığında	**67**	**12.64**
Beni oyuna almadıkları zaman	12	2.26
Ödev yüzünden	13	2.45
Oyunda liderlik tartışmasından dolayı	8	1.51
Gruplaşmalar yüzünden	19	3.58
Oyunda mızıkçılık yapıldığında	4	0.75
Benimle dalga geçildiğinde	25	4.72
Bana zarar verdikleri zaman	**57**	**10.75**
Çatışma yaşamıyorum	20	3.77
Eşyalarıma zarar verdiklerinde	14	2.26
Derste birbirimize şaka yaptığımız zaman	12	2.26
Büyük abilerin bize sataşmasından dolayı	14	2.64
Nöbetçiyken tahtayı karaladıkları zaman	5	0.94
Ad taktıkları için	**81**	**15.28**
Kıskançlık nedeniyle	42	7.92
Kötü söz söyledikleri için	6	1.13
Farklı görüşlerden dolayı	5	0.94
Yemek sırasında sorun oluyor	5	0.94
Kız-erkek karşılaşmasından	24	4.53
Toplam	**530**	**100**

Tablo 1. Öğrencilerin Arkadaşları ile Yaşadığı Çatışma Nedenleri ve Yaşanma Sıklığı

Tablo 1'de görüldüğü gibi öğrencilerin birbirleriyle yaşadıkları sorunların yoğunluğu oyun esnasında oyun bozma % 17.36 ile ilk sırada, ikinci sırada % 15.28 ile ad takma, % 12.64 ile izinsiz eşya alma üçüncü sırada yer almaktadır. Bunun yanında önemli bir çatışma nedeni olanı "bana zarar verdikleri zaman" maddesi % 10.75 ile dördüncü sırada yer almakta ve öğrenciler arası saldırgan davranışların sıklığını da ifade etmektedir.
2) Arkadaşınızla yaşadığınız çatışmaları nasıl çözüyorsunuz sorusuna verilen cevaplar tablo 2'de listelenmiştir:

Çatışma Çözme Biçimleri	F	%
Öğretmenime söylerim	**58**	**13.39**
Özür dileyerek barışırım	**71**	**16.39**
Konuşarak çözüyorum	51	11.78
Kızarım, kavga ederim, döverim	**86**	**19.86**
Öğretmenimiz bizi uyarıyor	12	2.77
Bağırıyorum	43	9.93
Küserim	46	10.62
Arkadaşlarımın aracılığıyla çözüyoruz	3	0.69
Olay yerinden uzaklaşıyorum ve 10'a kadar sayıyorum	8	1.85
Önce uyarırım, devam ederse ben de ona aynısını yaparım	27	6.24
Alttan almaya çalışırım	12	2.77
Müdüre şikayet ederim	7	1.62
Karşımdakinin fikrini kabul ederim	9	2.08
Toplam	**433**	**100**

Tablo 2. Öğrenciler Arkadaşlarıyla Yaşadıkları Çatışmaları Çözme Biçimleri

Öğrencilerin genellikle yıkıcı stratejiler kullandıkları tablo 2'de görülmektedir. "Kızarım, kavga ederim, döverim"% 19.86, "öğretmene söylerim" % 13.39, "bağırıyorum" % 9.93, "küserim" % 10.69, "müdüre şikayet ederim" % 1.62 olmak üzere yıkıcı stratejilerin toplam kullanılma sıklığı % 55.49'dur. Okuldaki öğrencilerin büyük bir çoğunluğu, çatışmalarını şiddet içerikli davranışlarla çözmeyi tercih etmektedirler. % 15.01'i öğretmenlerine ya da müdüre şikayet ederek çözüm aramaktadır. Bu bulgu, öğrencilerin disiplin anlayışının hala dış denetim odaklı olduğunu göstermektedir. Öğrenci kendi sorununun çözümünde yer alabileceğinin farkında değildir. % 11.78 öğrencinin "konuşarak çözüyorum" seçeneğini tercih etmeleri sevindiricidir. Türnüklü ve Şahin (2004)'nin 13-14 yaş grubu öğrencilerin çatışma çözme startejilerinin incelenmesi konulu çalışmadan elde ettikleri verilere göre de öğrenciler yaşadıkları çatışmaların çözümünde yıkıcı davranışları daha sıklıkla başvurmaktadırlar.

Tüm Okulu Kapsayan Arabuluculuk Modeli'nin uygulanmaya başlandıktan sonra öğretmenlerle yapılan değerlendirme toplantılarından elde edilen verilere göre; 1) Öğrencilerin, eğitim aldıktan sonra öğretmenlere yansıttıkları şikayet sayılarında azalmalar görülmüştür. 2) Öğrenciler, bir sorun yaşadıkları zaman öğretmene değil, sınıflarındaki akran arabulucusuna giderek çözüm bulma yoluna gitmeye başlamışlardır. 3) Özellikle arabuluculuk yapmaya başlayan öğrencilerde kendine güven duygusunda artışların gözlendiği ifade edilmiştir. 4) Öğrenciler arası iletişimde olumlu gelişmelerin olduğunu ve sınıf içersinde görülen çatışmalarda azalmaların görüldüğü ifade edilmiştir. Elde edilen bulgular yurtdışında yapılan çalışmalarla da desteklenmektedir. Amerika'nın kırsal kesimlerindeki okullarda yapılan bir araştırmada, akran arabuluculuğunun etkisi incelenmiştir. Öğrencilerin arabuluculuk sürecini başarıyla tamamladıkları ve öğrendikleri becerileri gerçek çatışma ortamlarında kullanabildikleri gözlenmiştir. Ayrıca bu eğitimi alan öğrencilerin çatışmalarını daha olumlu davranışlarla çözme eğiliminde oldukları ve bunların sınıflarındaki şiddet olaylarında azalmaların görüldüğü saptanmıştır (Sweeney ve Carruthers, 1996). Bir başka araştırma: Bu konuda yapılan pek çok çalışma vardır. Bunlardan birisi Brown (1991) tarafından yapılmıştır. Bu çalışmada bir grup öğretmen ve öğrenciye arabuluculuk eğitimi verilmiştir ve eğitiminin okuldaki disiplin olaylarında azalıp azalmayacağını saptamaktır. Sonuçlara göre, okul içersinde şiddete bağlı disiplin problemlerinin yüzdesinde önemli düzeyde düşmenin olduğu görülmüştür.

Arabulucu öğrencilerle yapılan görüşmeler sonucunda ise: 1) Arabulucu olarak çalışan her öğrenci rolünü çok sevdiğini ve bu sürecin devam etmesini istediğini ifade etmişlerdir. 2) Öğrenciler arkadaşlarının sorununun çözümüne yardımcı oldukları için memnun olduklarını söylemişlerdir. 3) Arabuluculuk eğitiminden sonra, arkadaşlarının, çatışmalarının çözümünde öğretmene şikayet etmek yerine kendilerinin çözüm ürettiğini söylemişlerdir. 4) Bazı sınıflarda sınıf öğretmeninin "Arabuluculuk Saati" uygulamaya başlamasıyla öğrencilerin hafta içinde yaşadıkları çatışmaları o derse kadar ertelediklerini ve bu süre içersinde de pek çok sorunun derse gelmeden çözüldüğünü ifade etmişlerdir. 5) Arabulucu olarak görev yapan öğrencilerin arkadaşlarıyla ilişkilerinin olumlu yönde geliştiğini söylemeleri aldıkları eğitimin onların sosyal ve iletişim becerileri yönünden gelişmelerine yardımcı olduğunu göstermektedir. Öner Koruklu (1998), bir grup ilköğretim 5,6,7,8. sınıf öğrencilere arabuluculuk ve çatışma çözme becerileri eğitimi vermiş ve eğitim alan öğrencilerin saldırgan davranışlarında bir değişmenin olup olmayacağını incelemiştir. Eğitimden sonra öğrencilerin saldırgan davranışlarında azalmaların görüldüğü saptanmıştır. Johnson (1988)'ın ortaokul 6. sınıf öğrencileri ile yaptığı çalışmada da arabuluculuk eğitim programına katılan öğrencilerin iletişim becerileri ve sosyal problem çözme becerileri kazandıkları görülmüştür. Başka bir araştırmada deney grubu öğrencilerine arabuluculuk eğitimi çerçevesinde iletişim ve problem çözme becerileri verilmiştir. Çalışmada temel amaç, okulda yaşanan şiddet olaylarında ve antisosyal davranışlarda azalma sağlayabilmektir. Veriler; arabulucuların gözlemlerinden, öğretmenlerden, öğrenci arabuluculardan, anlaşmazlık yaşayanlardan ve ailelerden elde edilmiştir. Sonuç olarak, öğrencilerin kendi arkadaşlarının çatışmalarının çözümünde yardımcı olabildikleri ve ayrıca okul ortamında da olumlu yönde değişme sağladıkları saptanmıştır (Emerson, 1990).

.Elde edilen bu bulgular yanında uygulama açısından önemli olabilecek eleştiriler de elde edilmiştir. Bu çerçevede: 1) Modelin daha etkili olabilmesi için İlköğretim 1. ve 2. sınıflarda öğrenci arabulucuların çok etkili olamadığı bunun yerine öğretmenlerin arabuluculuk rolünü üstlenmelerinin daha etkili olacağı söylenmiştir. 2) Öğretmenler kendilerinin de aynı eğitimi almalarının daha etkili olacağını söylemişlerdir. 3) Öğretmenler 6 ile 8. sınıflarda kulüp modelinin daha etkili olabileceği görüşünde olduklarını ifade etmişlerdir.

Sonuç ve Öneriler

Bu çalışmada, bir özel ilköğretim okulunda uygulanan "Tüm Okulu Kapsayan Arabuluculuk Modeli" nin uygulama süreci ve sonrası incenlenmiştir. Uygulama öncesi öğrencilerden alınan bilgilere göre okullarında en sık yaşanan çatışma durumları; oyun sırasında oyunu bozma, birbirine zarar verme, izinsiz eşya alma, dalga geçme olarak sıralanabilir. Öğrencilerin çatışma çözme davranışları değerlendirildiğinde, en sık başvurulan seçenek "kavga etme, dövme ve kızma" % 19.86 ile ilk sırada yer almaktadır. Okullarımızda şiddet içerikli davranışların sorunların çözümünde ilk sırada yer alması, medyaya yansıyan şiddet olaylarını da açıklayıcı niteliktedir.

Modelin uygulanmasına ilişkin öğrenci ve öğretmen değerlendirmelerine göre, akran arabuluculuğu süreci uygulanmaya başlandıktan sonra öğrenciler arasında yaşanan çatışmaların sayısında azalmaların görüldüğü söylenmiştir. Öğretmenler, derse başlamadan önce yaşadıkları şikayet süresinin hemen hemen hiç kalmadığını ifade etmişlerdir. Öğrenciler ise, arkadaşları ile yaşadıkları çatışma durumlarının hepsini öğretmene götürmek yerine kendi kendilerine çözmekden dolayı memnun olduklarını söylemişlerdir.

Bu çalışmanın sonuçlarından yola çıkılarak okullarımızda ilköğretim okullarından başlanarak çatışma çözme ve iletişim becerilerini kapsayan akran arabuluculuğu yönteminin uygulanmaya konması önerilmektedir. Ayrıca alanda çalışan uzmanlara konuya ilişkin araştırmalara yönelmeleri önerilmektedir. Özelllikle, yurt dışında yıllardır uygulanan çatışma çözme programlarının bizim kültürümüze uyarlanarak, ülke çapında yaygınlaştırılması önerilmektedir.

Kaynakça

Bodine, R. J., ve Crawford, D. K. (1998). *The handbook of conflict resolution education: A guide to building quality Programs in schools.* National Institute for Dispute Resolution, California: Jossey-Bass Publishers.

Brown, R.B. (1991). Conflict Resolution: A Strategy For Reducing Physical Confrantation In Public Schools (Doctoral dissertation,). *Dissertation Abstracts International, 53*, 995-A.

Emerson, J.M. (1990). Conflict Resolution For Students: A Study Of Problem Solving And Peer Conflict Management (Doctoral dissertation,). *Dissertation Abstracts International. 53*, 995-A.

Glasser, W. (1990). *The Qality School.* New York: Haeper & Row Publishers.

Johson, K.K. (1988). The Impact Of Conflict Management Training On Behavior And Self-Esteem Of Middle School Students (Doctoral dissertation,) *Dissertation Abstracts International 50*, 2432-2433-A.

Lupton-Smith,H. S., Carruthers, W.L., Flyte, R., Goettee, E. & Modest, K., H. (1996). Conflict resolution as peer mediation: Programs for elementary, middle, and high school students. *School Counselor, 43*(5) 374-392.

Maxwell, J.P. (1989). Mediation in the schools: Self regulation, self esteem, and self discipline. *Mediation Quarterly, 7*(2), 149-155.

Öner K. N. (1998). Arabuluculuk eğitiminin bir grup ilköğretim düzeyindeki öğrencinin çatışma çözme davranışına etkisinin incelenmesi (Yüksek Lisans Tezi, Ankara Üniversitesi, 2001).

Öner, U. (1996). *Farklı okullarda görev yapan öğretmenlerin çocuk istismarı potansiyelinin incelenmesi.* Ankara: 72 Tasarım Dizgi Fotokopi Ofset Bilgisayar Yayıncılık.

Öner, U. (1999). *İlköğretimde rehberlik.* (Y. Kuzgun, Ed.). Ankara: Nobel Yayın Dağıtım.

Smith, M. ve Sidwell, J. (1990). *Trainning and implemantation guide for student mediation in secondary schools.* New Mexico Center For Dispute Resolution.

Sweeney, B. ve Carruthers, W. L. (1996). Conflict resolution: History, philosophy, theory, and educational applications. *The School Counselor, 43*, 327.

Türnüklü, A.ve Şahin, İ. (2004). 13-14 Yaş grubu öğrencilerin çatışma çözme stratejilerinin incelenmesi. *Türk Psikoloji Yazıları, 7*(13), 45-61.

Savaş Filmlerinde Kadın Temsilleri

Nesrin Kula Demir
Güzel Sanatlar Fakültesi, Sinema ve Televizyon Bölümü
Afyon Kocatepe Üniversitesi
dknesrin@aku.edu.tr

Giriş

Sinema temsiller üzerine kurulmuştur. Dönemsel olarak toplumda ve akademik kuramlarda üstünlük kazanan temsiller ve konuların, sinema filmlerinde de arttığı görülmektedir. Örneğin; 1980'lerden sonra feminist hareketin hız kazanması, sinemada kadın, zenci, gay ve lezbiyen temsillerinin de artmasına neden olmuştur. Aynı şekilde, I. ve II. Dünya Savaşları ve Soğuk Savaş, XX. yy.a damgasını vurduğundan; savaş, militarizm ve barış konularını ele alan pek çok film çekilmiştir.

Milliyetçiliği, militarizmi ve savaşları anlamlandırabilmek için feminist bir bakış açısı geliştirmek gerekmektedir. Çünkü toplumsal cinsiyet kimliği bir inşa süreci olarak ele alındığında, militarizm ve savaş erkek kimliğinin inşasında önemli bir yer tutmaktadır. Ulus-devlet kimliğinin inşasında erkekler askerlik yaparak vatana hizmet ederken, kadınlara düşen görev askerleri doğurmaktır. Barışın olabilmesi için militarizmin var olması gerektiği görüşü, erkek kimliğini sert, acımasız, duygusuz olarak biçimlendirdikçe, kadın erkeğin negatif ötekisi olarak zayıf, güçsüz ve duygusal olarak kodlanacaktır. Dolayısıyla, militarizm ve savaşları anlayabilmek için toplusal cinsiyet ilişkilerine; kadınlığı ve erkekliği anlayabilmek için militarizm ve milliyetçiliğe bakmak gerekmektedir.

Savaş erkek işi olarak görülmekte ve savaş filmlerinde erkeklerarası dostluk ve bağlılık ilişkilerine yer verilmektedir, dolayısıyla bu tür filmlerindeki kadın temsilleri daha az olduğundan feminist bakış açısından önem kazanmaktadır. Hollywood Sineması, iki dünya savaşı ve Vietnam savaşını tema olarak ele alan pek çok filme yer vermektedir. Bir kısmında neden yenildiklerini anlamaya çalışan, bir kısmında ise yenilgiye rağmen izleyenlerdeki milliyetçi duyguları önplana çıkaran ve bazen de Amerikan ordusu için gönüllü askerlik başvurularını teşvik etmeyi amaçlayan filmler çekilmektedir. Savaş filmleri her zaman için izleyici bulmuş, en azından izlenmeyi garantilemiş filmler olarak görülmektedir.

Çalışmada seçilen on film üzerinden feminist bir çözümleme ile kadın temsilleri ortaya konmaya çalışılacaktır. Militarizm, savaş ve feminizm arasındaki ilişki tanımlandıktan sonra, savaş filmlerinin toplumsal cinsiyet ekseninde okuması yapılacaktır. Savaşların ve askerliğin, kadınlık ve erkeklik tanımlamalarını nasıl etkilediği ve kadınların savaş filmlerinde nasıl temsil edildiği araştırılacaktır.

Militarizm ve Feminizm İlişkisi

Feminist kuram, tarihin, savaşlar tarihi ve erkeğin tarihi olduğunu ortaya koyarak, militarizm ve milliyetçiliğin; toplumsal cinsiyet kimliklerini belirlediğine erkek egemen tahakküm biçimini, cinsiyetçi söylem ve değer yargılarını yeniden ürettiğine işaret etmektedir. Bu nedenle savaşların, militarizmin ve milliyetçiliğin anlaşılabilmesi için feminist bir bakış açısına ihtiyaç duyulmaktadır. Militarizasyon erkekliğin yeniden üretimi açısından önem taşımaktadır, erkeklik üretilirken, kadın öteki olarak görülüp ikincil konuma itildiğinden, militarizm feministler tarafından çalışılması, anlaşılması ve üzerinde düşünülmesi gereken bir konu haline gelmektedir. Bu yüzden militarizmin toplumsal cinsiyet perspektifli bir analizini yapmak gerekmektedir.

Militarizm, genel olarak "askeri kültüre ait değer"lerin, toplumun geneline, gündelik yaşam pratiklerine kadar yayılması olarak tanımlanabilmektedir. "Militarizm; ordunun devlete eklemlenmesi, askerin halkın kendini yönetmesinin doğal bir parçası haline gelmesi, barışın ancak savaşla tesis edileceği fikri, kamusal alanın daralması, seslerin kısılması, tek söylemcilik, temel özgürlüklerin kısıtlanması, kayıtsız şartsız silah bırakarak barış yapmak yerine intikam almanın tercih edilmesi, savaş ekonomisinin sürdürülmesi, ölümlerin döngüsünün spiral biçiminde uzayıp gitmesi ..." olarak tanımlanmaktadır (Direk, 2006, s. 24). Tanımdan da anlaşılacağı üzere militarizm konusu "kadınların savaş mağduriyeti" ile sınırlandırılamayacağından, feminist çalışmaların anti-militarizme ihtiyacı bulunmaktadır.

Feminist çalışmalar, "ulus-devletlerin inşasında kadınlığın görünmez kılındığı" önermesinden yola çıkarak, kadın deneyimlerine eğilmekte ve kadınları tarih içinde görünür kılmaya çalışmaktadır. Oysa toplumsal cinsiyet çalışmalarının sadece kadınlar üzerinden yürümesi, erkekliğin de bir inşa süreci olduğunun gözardı edilmesine neden olmaktadır. "Hangi süreçlerden geçerek erkek olunduğu, erkekliğin ne şekilde tanımlandığı ve farklı erkeklik kurgularını anlamak, kadınlığı ve toplumsal cinsiyetin işleyişini anlamak açısından gereklidir" (Altınay, 2000, ss. 15-16). Militarizm erkekliğin güçlü bir şekilde örgütlendiği bir iktidar yapısı olduğundan, feminist kuram erkekliğin üretim mekanizmalarını sorgularken anti-militarist bir perspektif geliştirmektedir.

Militarizm erkekliği yücelterek; güçlü, sert, dayanıklı, dinamik, kadın gibi zayıf olmayan erkek prototipi çizmektedir. "Militarist düşünce sadece 'askeriye'nin sınırları içinde kalmayıp günlük hayatın içine de yedirilen 'militer' bir dünya kurgular, ki bu kurguda kadın aşağılanır, kadınlar genellikle görmezden gelinir, yok sayılır ..." (Altınay, 2006, s. 26). Erkeklerin askerlik yapmak için kışlalara toplanması, dış dünyadan ve kadınlardan izole edilmesine ve "erkek dünyası"nın ortaya çıkmasına neden olmaktadır. Bu durum, bir taraftan askerlik yapmadıkları için kadının toplumdaki vatandaşlık konumunu ikincilleştirirken, diğer yandan oluşturulan bu "erkek dünyası"nda sürekli kadınların ve kadın gibi olmanın aşağılanmasıyla, erkeklerin zihninde kadına ilişkin olumsuz temsiller oluşturulmasına neden olmaktadır.

Militarist söylemler erkekliği yüceltirken, erkekleri her daim vatanı korumaya hazır "bekçiler" olarak kodlamaktadır. Kadın ise savunulacak vatanla özdeşleştirilmekte, böylelikle pasif bir konuma itilmektedir. Kadınların toplumla bir tutulması, onların "fedakar anne-sadık eş" rolünü desteklemektedir, bu görüşün sonucu olarak da kadının savunulan, uğruna savaşılan ve ölünen durumuna gelmesi kolaylaşmaktadır. Annelik kutsal olarak görüldüğünde kadınların vatanı koruyacak yeni askerler doğurmaları gerektiği ve onları yetiştirmekle görevli oldukları savı doğallaştırılmaktadır. Böylece "Erkeklerin vatanı koruyan eyleyici özneler, kadınların da vatanla özdeşleştirilmiş savunulması gereken pasif nesneler olarak kurgulanmasına neden olur" (Gedik, 2006, s. 39). Yani, erkek kimliğinin kurgulanması için askerlik önem taşımakta, askerlik yapmak çocukları "erkek" yapmaktadır. Bu nedenle ülkemizde "askerliğini yapmamış olanlara, kız verilmemektedir". Ancak asıl sorunun erkeğin çocuktan değil, kadından ayrılması olduğu düşünülmektedir.

Genç erkeklerin, çocukluklarını geçirdikleri evden ayrılıp askerlik yapmaya gitmeleri, aralarında daha önce hiçbir ilişki bulunmayan insanların aynı yerde toplanarak "kardeşlik" fikrinin oluşturulması, evin kadına ait özel alanı ile, erkeğe ait kamusal alan arasındaki uçurumun giderek artmasına neden olmaktadır. "Militarizmin, en temel özelliklerinden biri 'öteki üzerinden iktidar'dır ve erkekliğin yüceltilmesi, kadınlığın küçümsenmesi aracılığıyla kadınlar açıkça 'öteki'leştirilir" (Burke, 2006, s. 46). Toplumsal cinsiyet ilişkileri, modernizmin de etkisiyle genellikle ikili karşıtlıklar şeklinde düşünülmekte ve kadını erkeğin "ötekisi" olarak görmektedir. "Etkin/edilgen, aydınlık/karanlık, mantıksal/sezgisel, sağ/sol, olumlu/olumsuz ... gibi" ikili karşıtlıklardan, dikotomik (ikili karşıtlıklardan birine üstünlük veren) bir bakış açısıyla birinciler erkeğe ait olarak kodlanırken, ikinciler yani daha olumsuz olduğu düşünülen özellikler ise kadına ait özellikler olarak görülmektedir. Bu düşünme biçimi toplumdaki ataerkil doktrinler tarafından da desteklenmektedir. Örneğin; çok bilinen çocuk şarkısında "küçük Ayşe, bebeğine mama verirken, küçük asker tüfeğini silmektedir." Militarizmin toplumsal cinsiyet kimliğinin düalist inşasına ihtiyacı bulunmaktadır.

Savaş "erkek işi" olarak görüldükçe, kadınların savaşta yaşadıkları ve barış çabaları görünmez kılınacaktır. Militarizm, vatanla özdeşleştirdiği "kadınların namusunun korunması" tezi üzerinden yürümektedir. Dolayısıyla, savaşlar sırasında "benim kadınım", "düşmanın kadını" ayrımı askerlerin zihininde oluşmakta, savaş sırasında toplu tecavüzler karşı tarafın moralini bozmak, nesli bozmak gibi nedenlerle yapılabilecek doğal eylemler olarak görülmektedir. Tecavüz, erkeğin karşısındaki kadın (veya erkeğe) kendi üstünlüğünü kanıtlayabileceği, ötekinin rızası dışında güç kullanarak onun bedenine, kişiliğine, kimliğine ve tüm ilişkileri üzerine yapılmış fiziksel, sosyal ve psikolojik bir eylem haline gelmektedir. Kadınlar, milliyetçi hareketlerde ya yüceltilip korunacak ikonlar ya da ele geçirilip aşağılanacak savaş ganimetleri olarak görülmektedir.

Savaşlar sadece erkekleri değil, kadınları da ilgilendirmektedir, çünkü; cephe gerisinde, bazen de cephe önünde kadınlar da erkekler kadar çalışmak zorunda kalmaktadırlar. Askerlerin üniforma, çorap ve çamaşır gibi ihtiyaçlarını karşılamak üzere fabrikalarda genellikle kadınlar çalışmaktadır. Mermi yapımı ve cepheye taşınması gibi işler yine kadının görevi haline gelmektedir. Kurulan ilk yardım ünitelerinde gönüllü hemşirelik görevi yine kadınlara düşmektedir. Askerlerin cinsel ihtiyaçlarını karşılayan fahişeler ise yine kadınlardır.

Savaş Filmleri ve Feminist Okunması

Feminist film eleştirisi, filmlerde kadının temsil edilişinin erkek bakış ile gerçekleştiğini belirtirken, ataerkil normları ortaya koymak için feminist edebiyat eleştirisinden etkilenmiştir. "Feminist eleştirmenler sinema perdesine yansıyan kadın imgelerinin gerçek kadınlara ait olarak değil, erkeğin kadına yönelik bilinçaltı duygu ve düşüncelerinin, arzu ve korkularının temsil edilmesi işlevi içinde yansıma bulduklarını, kadının erkek için temsil ettiği şey olarak sunulmasına aracılık ettiğini kabul etmektedirler" (Özden, 2000, s. 164). Feminist eleştiriden önce, kadının sinemada ataerkil kodlarla temsili eleştirel bir ilgi alanı olarak görülmemektedir. Hem kadın, hem de erkek izleyiciler tarafından, kadınların sinemada ataerkil ideoloji çerçevesinde temsil edilmesi doğal karşılanmaktaydı. Feminist film kuramları ve eleştirisinin hızla gelişmesi ve üniversitelerde filmle ilgili bölümlerin açılmasıyla birlikte yönetmenler, ne tür kadın temsillerine yer vereceklerini bilemediklerinden, God Father (Baba), Star Wars (Yıldız Savaşları) ve diğer savaş filmleri gibi aksiyonun fazla olduğu, erkeklerarası ilişkilerin gösterildiği ve kadın karakterlerin ise neredeyse hiç temsil edilmediği filmleri çekmeye yönelmişlerdir.

Savaş filmleri de ataerkil mantıkla çekildiğinden, çoğunlukla erkeklerarası dostluk ve kardeşlik teması işlenmekte, kadınların özdeşleşebileceği kahramanlar ise bu tür filmlerde yer almamaktadır. "Birçok savaş filminde kadınlar oldukça rizikolu serüvenlerde yatıştırıcı, sakin anlar sağlayan, erkeklerin peşinden koşan nesneler olarak vardır. Kadınlar erkeklerin cinsel gereksinimlerini karşılayabilir ama ilişki doruğa çıkamaz" (Suid, 1978, s. 8). Çünkü filmi izleyen erkeklerin duygusal sağaltımı (katharsis) savaş sahneleri ve zaferle sağlanmaktadır. Kadınlar ise her an erişilebilecek olan nesneler olarak gösterilmektedir. Savaş filmleri kadınların amacının "asker tavlamak" olduğunu çünkü; "askerin daha erkek" olarak görüldüğünü, dolayısıyla askerlerin ilişki kurulabilecek kadınlara daha kolay ulaşabileceğini sürekli vurgulamaktadır.

Savaş filmlerinde kadınlar edilgen rollerde temsil edilmektedirler. "Kadınlar, erkeklerini savaşa hazırlayan ve onların dönüşünü sebatla bekleyen eş yada sevgili rolünü üstlenerek .... ya da bazen subay gibi görevlerde ama yine cephe gerisi işlerde, çoğu zaman hemşirelik gibi geri hizmetlerde 'yara sarıcı' (hem fiilen hem de moral açısından) görevini üstlenirler." (Yılmaz, 1993a, s. 68). Ordu ve askerler savaş filmlerinde, militarist düşüncenin devamı olarak güç, cesaret, erkeklik, irade... vb. temelinde sürekli yüceltilmektedir. Toplumsal cinsiyet ayrımını pekiştiren ataerkil ve militarist bakış açısı savaş filmlerinde açıkça görülebilmektedir.

Savaş filmleri, kadına ilişkin militarist bakış açısının devamı olarak; onları savaş için yeni askerleri doğuran rahimler olarak görmektedir. "Militer değerler babadan oğla aktarılırken, kadınlara düşen tek görev çocuk doğurmaktır. Ailenin orduyu meşrulaştırıcı bir metaforik analoji modeli olmanın ötesinde militer değerlerin gerçek döl yatağı olduğu göz önüne alınırsa, bu iş bölümünün tesadüfi olmadığı anlaşılır" (Ryan ve Kellner, 1997, s. 323). Birbirinden ayrı iki kurum gibi görünen (aile ve ordu), savaş filmlerinde toplumsal cinsiyet kalıplarını yeniden üretme konusunda birbirine eklemlenmektedir. Oysaki "ailenin çocuk yetiştirdiği, ordunun ise öldürdüğüne" ilişkin zıtlık görmezden gelinmekte, yoksayılmaktadır.

Savaş filmleri özellikle de Hollywood yapımı olanlar gerçeğe yakın savaş ve çatışma sahneleri çekmek için oldukça büyük bütçeler harcamaktadır. Şiddet görüntülerinin fazla olduğu, adam öldürmenin doğallaştırıldığı bu savaş sahneleri, "Amerika'nın savaşma nedenlerini doğrulamak ve bu konularda halkı bilgilendirmek amacıyla" Pentagon'da kurulun Sinema Dairesi (Bureau of Motion Picture) (Yılmaz, 1993b, s. 42) tarafından desteklenmektedir. Sinema Dairesi maddi ve silah-tank ...vb. teçhizat açısından desteklediği filmlerde, askerlik başvurularının arttırılması amacıyla, savaşın, "erkekleri özgürleştiren" bir ortam olarak betimlenmesini sağlamaktadır.

Sıradan ve monoton bir yaşam süren izleyiciler, filmdeki erkek karakterlerin, savaş sırasında kahramana dönüşmesini ve gündelik yaşamda kurulmayan dostluklar kuruşunu izleyerek, adeta savaş ortamına özenmekte, savaşa katılmak için istekli hale gelmektedirler. "İzleyici, bu filmler aracılığıyla realitesinden kaçma olanağı bulurken bu arada askeri yaşamın sunduğu serüven, başka ve güzel kadınlarla ilişki, değişik yerlere gitme gibi olayları izlemekte ve bundan haz almaktadır" (Yılmaz, 1993b, s. 42). Böylelikle savaş filmleri, ordunun halkla ilişkilerini düzenleme ve orduya gönüllü çekme görevini de üstlenmektedir.

Savaş karşıtı filmler dahi, heyecanı doruğa yükselten ve şiddet içeren savaş sahnelerine yer vermekte, filmin olay örgüsünü geleneksel kalıplar içinde kurmakta, savaş karşıtı mesajları ise satır aralarında vermektedir. İnsan öldürme ve şiddet savaş filmleri yoluyla doğallaştırılırken, izleyici olaylar karşısında acı yerine heyecan duyar hale gelmektedir. Savaş filmlerinde, vatan, millet, milliyetçilik, militarizm ve özgürlük gibi ideolojilerle desteklenerek, savaşın acı veren, yıkıcı yönleri estetize edilmekte, hatta savaş çekici hale getirilmektedir.

Araştırmanın Yöntem ve Tekniği

Savaş filmleri, sadece erkekler değil, kadınlar tarafından da erkek kahramanlarla özdeşleşilerek izlenen ve sinema salonlarına azımsanmayacak ölçüde izleyici çeken bir tür olarak ortaya çıkmaktadır. Bu nedenle savaş filmlerinde temsil edilen "erkeklik" ve "kadınlık" kavramları önem kazanmaktadır. Temsil kavramı, gerçekle düşünce arasındaki ilişkinin kavramsallaştırılmasında anlamlandırma, simgeleme, dolayımlama ve imgelem/tahayyül (imagination) rolü oynadığından; göstergebilim, dilbilim, Marksizm ve Feminizm için vazgeçilmez bir kavram haline gelmektedir. "Feministler temsilin stereotipik toplumsal cinsiyet kimliği fikirlerini sürekli olarak yeniden yarattığını ve onayladığını ileri sürmektedirler" (Marshall, 1999, s. 725). Tüm medya imgeleri -özellikle reklam ve sinema- ataerkil bakış açısı ile kurulup "gerçek" olarak kabul edilip mite benzer zihinsel şemalar haline gelmektedir. Birisi tarafından, belirli bir izleyici kitlesi göz önünde tutularak kurulan bu imgelerin, ne anlama geldiklerini ve anlamı nasıl inşa ettiklerini kavrayabilmek için, bu imgeleri "kim, nerede, ne zaman, hangi özel izleyicinin bakış açısına göre inşa ediyor?" sorularının cevaplarının araştırılması gerekmektedir.

Temsil günlük hayatın yapısını ve biçimini belirleyen söylemlerden oluştuğundan, filmler toplumsal yaşamdaki temsilleri, söylemleri şifreleyerek aktaran anlatı türleri olarak görülmektedir. Temsiller, bireylerin içinde yaşadıkları toplumun kültürel hayatına ilişkin algılamalarını şekillendirdiği ve sınırlandırdığı için önem taşımaktadır. Yani, sinemada hangi tip kadınların daha baskın olarak temsil edildiği, o toplumun bireylerinin zihnindeki kadına ilişkin algılamaları klişeleştirebilmektedir. "Filmler, muhtelif temsil biçimlerinin, toplumsal gerçekliğin nasıl kavranacağını, daha da fazlası ne olacağını belirlemek için birbiriyle yarıştığı bir kapışma zeminidir" (Ryan ve Kellner, 1997, ss. 37-38). Örneğin; 1960'lardan sonra feminist hareketin yükselişine tepki olarak, Hollywood Sineması filmlerde geleneksel kadın temsillerine daha çok yer vermektedir.

Araştırmanın Örneklemi

Sinemanın temsiller üzerine kurulduğu göz önüne alınarak, Dünya Sinema Tarihi'nde önemli yer tutan savaş filmlerinde kadın temsilleri incelenecektir. Millitarizmi ve savaşı daha iyi anlayabilmek için, toplumsal cinsiyet ilişkilerine, kadınlık ve erkeklik tanımlamalarına bakmak gerektiği önermesinden yola çıkılarak, ulaşılabilirlik ölçütü ile belirlenen 10 savaş filmi; militarizm, toplumsal cinsiyet, feminizm, savaş ve barış kavramları temelinde çözümlenecektir. Seçilen 10 savaş filminden oluşan örneklemden yola çıkılarak, toplumsal cinsiyet, milliyetçilik ve militarizm arasındaki ilişkinin nasıl şekillendiği, feminist kuram çerçevesinde incelenecektir. Savaşların, orduların ve askerliğin, kadınlık ve erkeklik tanımlamalarını ve deneyimlerini nasıl etkilediği, kadınların savaş filmlerinde nasıl temsil edildiği ortaya konmaya çalışılacaktır.

Kwai Köprüsü (The Bridge On The River Kwai) -1957- David Lean

Zafer Yolları (Paths of Glory) -1957- Stanley Kubrick

Arabistan'lı Lawrance (Lawrance of Arabia) -1962- David Lean

Kıyamet (Apocalypse Now) -1979- Francis Ford Coppola

Müfreze (Platoon) -1986- Oliver Stone

Full Metal Jacket -1987- Stenley Kubrick

Er Ryan'ı Kurtarmak (Saving Private Ryan) -1998- Steven Spielberg

İnce Kırmızı Hat (The Thin Red Line) -1998- Terrence Malick

Pearl Harbor -2001- Michael Bay

Tarafsız Bölge (No Man's Land) -2001- Danis Tanovic

On savaş filmini içeren örneklemdeki filmlerin 1957 - 2001 yılları arasında yer aldığı ve yaklaşık yarım yüzyılı içeren savaş filmleri göz önüne alındığında, savaş filmlerinin genellikle erkek yönetmenler tarafından, dolayısıyla erkek bakış açısıyla erkek izleyici için çekildiği söylenebilmektedir. Tarafsız Bölge ve Full Metal Jacket bu filmler arasında ilk bakışta savaş karşıtı söylem üretme açısından, diğer filmlerden ayrılmaktadır. Filmleri hepsi izlendiğinde şiddet içeren uzun savaş sahneleri ve savaşın getirdiği yıkım ve acıları göstermeleri ile izleyiciye "Savaşa Hayır" dedirtmektedir.

Araştırmanın Verileri ve Örneklemde Yer Alan Filmlerin Çözümlenmesi

Kwai Köprüsü (1957) Film 2. Dünya Savaşı sırasında Burma'da Japonlar tarafından esir edilen bir grup İngiliz askerinin köprü yapımında görevlendirilmesini anlatmaktadır. Japon Albay Saito'nun amacı bu köprüyü kullanarak birliklere cephane taşıma konusunda avantaj sağlamaktır. Albay Nicholson başkanlığındaki esirler, köprünün düşmanına avantaj sağlayacağını unutarak, onu mükemmelleştirmek için elinden geleni yapmaktadırlar. Nicholson, düşmanın esiri konumunda olsa da, Saito ve adamlarının yapabileceğinden daha iyi bir köprü inşa ederek, onun ve adamlarının moralini bozmayı düşünmektedir. Bu arada İngilizler, yapımı devam eden köprünün imha edilmesi için bir komando birliği görevlendirir. Filmdeki kadın karakterler komandolara yardımcı olan Şilili kızlardır. Bu kızlar askeri eğitim almışçasına tüfek doldurma gibi işlerde komandolara yardım etmektedir. Komandolar ise kızlar nehire girmiş eğlenirken, onlara yaklaşan Japon askerlerini öldürerek onların "namuslarını" korumaktadırlar. Kızlar, filmde daha çok erkek izleyicilere nefes alma eğlenme olanağı sağlamaktadır. Kwai Köprüsü, 1957'de sekiz dalda Oscar'a aday olmuş ve En İyi Film, En İyi Yönetmen, En İyi Erkek Oyuncu, En İyi Senaryo, En İyi Görüntü, En İyi Kurgu ve En İyi Müzik dallarında Oscar almıştır.

Zafer Yolları (1957) Film savaş karşıtı duruşu ile öne çıkmaktadır, çekildiği yıllarda gösterim şansı bulamasa da, Vietnam savaşı sırasında tekrar gündeme gelmiştir. I. Dünya Savaşı'nda Fransız general Broulard, Almanların son derece güçlü birliklerle savundukları Ant tepesini ele geçirmeyi aklına koyarak, birliklerine taarruz emri vermektedir. General Mireau ise bu kararın intiharla eşanlamlı olduğunu bilmesine rağmen, kendi itibarını yükseltmek için adamlarını ölüme gönderecektir. Albay Dax'in komutasındaki Fransız güçlerinin ilk saldırıları başarısız olunca, bir grup asker siperleri terk etmeyi reddederler. Yenilgi karşısında çaresiz kalan, fakat kararının hatalı olduğunu kendisine itiraf edemeyen Mireau, topçu birliklerine kendi askerlerine ateş açmasını emretmeyi düşünecek kadar ileri gitmekte, ardından isyankar askerlere ibret olması için üç askeri idam ettirmeye karar vermektedir. Albay Dax adamlarının hayatlarını kurtarmak için onları savunsa da, ölümlerine engel olamamaktadır.

Filmin son sahnesinde görülen kadın karakter, Alman bir şarkıcı kız'dır. İzlemeye gelen erkekler önce ona "striptizci kız" muamelesi yapmakta, sahneye çıktığında cinsellik içerikli laflar atmaktadır. Ancak kızın sesini duyduktan sonra, salon sessizliğe bürünmekte ve "erkek" askerler birbirinden sakladıkları göz yaşlarını silerek, duygusal şarkıyı dinlemektedirler. Yani, kadın önce "cinselliği" sonra "duygusallığı" ile önplana çıkmaktadır. Olanları kapının dışından izleyen Dax, askerlerin dinlenme süresinin "birkaç dakika daha" uzamasına izin verdiğini belirtir ve film sona ermektedir. Bu kısa süren duygusallık anı ordunun zayıf düşmesine işaret etmektedir.

Arabistan'lı Lawrence (1962) Film, İngiliz ordusunda görevli genç teğmen, T. E. Lawrence'ın biyografisini çizmektedir. Arap yarımadasında görevli olan Lawrence, Arabistan ordusunun lideri Prens Faysal'ın gözcülüğünü yapmak istemektedir. Lawrence, burada kalıp Arap ordusunun içine sızmakta ve onların Osmanlı'ya karşı kışkırtılmasını da kapsayan geniş bir casusluk hareketi başlatmaktadır. Bir gazeteci olan Jackson Bentley, Lawrence'ın yaşadığı maceraları kaleme almaktadır. Filmde kadın karakter bulunmamaktadır, Prens ve Lawrence'a çölde hizmet edenler dahi erkektir, çöl egzotizminin Arap kadınlarla verilmesi beklenirken, fonda dekor olarak kullanılan ve arka planda görülen birkaç kadın dışında kadın karakter bulunmamaktadır.

Kıyamet (1979) Kaptan Williard, Vietnam Savaşı yıllarında Kamboçya'nın ormanlık alanlarında kendini yerli halka tanrı olarak tanıtan ve burada nüfusunu genişleterek küçük bir ordu kuran Albay Kurtz'u ele geçirmekle görevlendirilmektedir. Williard'ın askerleri ilaçlara yenik düşmeye başlamakta ve bir bir öldürülmektedir. Yolculuk ilerledikçe Williard'ın Albay Kurtz'la ilgili fikirleri değişmeye başlamaktadır. "Operasyona engel olmaya çalışan yaralı bir köylü kadını öldürdüğünde ise kendini Kutz'a daha yakın hisseder" (Ryan ve Kellner, 1997, s. 368). Filmdeki kadın karakterler ise askerlere gösteri yapmak üzere helikopterle getirilen üç tane show-girl'dür. Kızların showu sırasında çığırından çıkan askerlerin sahneye atlayıp kızların üzerlerindekileri çıkarmaya çalışması nedeniyle, kızlar apar-topar helikoptere bindirilmekte ve show yarım bırakılarak götürülmektedir. Bu filmde de kadınların cinsel obje olarak görüldüğü ve askerler için eğlence amaçlı olarak kullanıldığı bir temsil biçimiyle karşılaşılmaktadır.

Müfreze (1986) "En İyi Film" dahil dört dalda Oscar ödülü alan film, Vietnam Savaşı'nda masumiyetini yitiren tüm askerler için bir ağıt niteliği taşımaktadır. Genç ve idealist bir Amerikalı Chris Taylor, üniversitede okumasına rağmen, ailesinin karşı çıkmasını dinlemeyerek, gönüllü olarak savaşa gelir. Ancak, çok geçmeden Vietnam'da sadece Viet Cong'larda değil, aynı zamanda içinde büyüyen korku, fiziksel bitkinlik ve gitgide artan kızgınlığıyla da savaşmak zorunda olduğunu anlamaktadır. Çelişkiler, kaos ve nefret Taylor'ın inançlarını boğmakta ve duyularını hayata karşı giderek hissizleşmektedir. Birbiriyle zıtlaşan, biri daha hümanist, diğeri daha acımasız olan iki çavuşun zıtlaşması filmdeki ana temayı da vermektedir. Askerler girdikleri bir köyde köylülere çeşitli eziyetler yapmaktadır. Dayak, adam öldürme, tecavüz gibi, Taylor ve İleyas'ın bunları önleme çabaları filme konu olmaktadır. Filmin ilgi çekici sonu kaba ve vahşi olan çavuş, daha insancıl olanı yaralar ve ölüme terk eder. "Takımın son saldırısı sırasında hareketli gölgelere benzeyen Viet-Konglu askerler zorlukla fark edilir ve gerçek savaş vahşi adamla idealist genci karşı karşıya getirir" (Valantin, 2006, s. 58). Taylor, geri dönüp İleyas'ı aramak ve savaş alanından gitmek arasında seçim yapmak zorunda kalır ve helikopterle giderken yukarıdan onu görür. Filmde iyi asker, kötü asker ikilemini vurgulayan bir başka sahne köyü yakılan köylülerle birlikte yürüyen ve çocukları kucaklarında, sırtlarında taşıyan askerlerdir. Filmdeki kadın karakterler Viet Cong'lu köylü kadın ve çocuklardır. Bunlar arasından oğlunu korumaya çalışan yaşlı kadın, Şefin öldürülen karısı, kızı ve tecavüz kurbanı kız öne çıkanlardır. Filmde gösterilen kadınlar "öteki"nin kadınlarıdır, dolayısıyla aşağılanmaktadırlar. Askerlerin genç kızlara tecavüzü, düşmanı "kadınını koruyamayacak kadar zayıf erkek" konumuna düşürmektedir. Dolayısıyla, savaş sırasındaki toplu tecavüzlerde, cinsel tatminden çok düşmanı aşağılama ve küçük düşürme önem taşımaktadır. Bu sahnede Taylor'a diğer askerler "sana ne oluyor, burası senin ülken değil ki" demektedirler. Yani, "senin ülkenin kadınları değil" vurgusu yapılmaktadır. Taylor "onlar insan" diyerek, millet kavramındansa insanlık kavramını önplana çıkarmaktadır.

Full Metal Jacket (1987) Karakterlerin çözümlendiği ve tanıtıldığı askeri eğitimi anlatan ilk bölüm, genel bir çerçeve ile Vietnam savaşının anlamsızlığının altını çizen ikinci bölüm olmak üzere film ikiye ayırılmaktadır. Yani film, ilk bölümde özelden genele ikinci bölümde ise genelden özele inerek seyirciyi etkisi altına almaktadır. Filmde askeri eğitim acımasızlığı ve askerlerin psikolojilerinin bozularak birer "ölüm makinesi" haline getirilme sürecinin anlatıldığı ilk bölüm de, erkekliğin yüceltilmesi için kadınlık sürekli olarak aşağılanmaktadır. Eğitim çavuşu erlere sürekli "kızlar" (ladies) olarak hitap etmekte, cinselliğin cezalandırma olarak kullanıldığı çok sayıda küfür bu bölümde yer almaktadır.

"This is my rifle, this is my gun. This is for fighting, and this is for fun.","this is my rifle, there are many rifles, but this one is mine..." gibi yaratıcı repliklerde, silahla erkek cinsel organı arasında bağlantı kuran ve militarizmin erkekliği yüceltmesi, savaşın erkek işi olması ve cinsel birleşmenin yok etme anlamına geldiği bir bağlantı kurulmaktadır. Eğitim çavuşu Hartman (ismi de sertliği çağrıştırmaktadır) erlere silahlarına birer kadın ismi vermelerini ve geceleri onunla yatmalarını istemektedir. Erkek erkeğe bu eğitim ortamında kadın gibi veya homoseksüel olmak aşağılamak için kullanılan sıfatlar arasında yer almaktadır.

Filmin 2. bölümünde Private Joker, Vietnam'da ordu gazetesinde çalışmaktadır. Haberlerin nasıl çarpıtılarak verildiği vurgulanır, gittiği görev sırasında gördükleri onun gözü ile izlenmektedir. Çektiği görüntülerde erler kamera karşında konuşmakta ve hemen hepsi "Vietnam'da ne işleri olduğunu" anlamadıklarını vurgulamaktadırlar. "Özgür olacaklarına, hayatta kalsalardı daha iyiydi." veya "ölülerin bildiği tek bir şey vardır, o da yaşamanın güzel olduğu" gibi sözlerle yönetmen askerlerin ağzından savaşın anlamsızlığını ve insan hayatının önemini vurgulamaktadır. Filmde ikisi fahişe, biri sniper (keskin nişancı) olmak üzere üç kadın karakter bulunmaktadır. Filmdeki fahişeler, askerlerin kadına fahişe/madonna ikilemi ile baktığının göstergesini taşımaktadır. Üç arkadaşlarını öldüren kişinin kadın olması karşısında askerler şaşkındır, kadınları aşağılayan sert bir eğitimden geçtikten sonra askerlerin kadın sniper tarafından vurulmaları ayrı bir ironi içermektedir. Kadın bozuk bir aksanla "shoot me" diyerek kendisini vurmalarını istemektedir. Joker yaralı da olsa kadını vurarak "erkekliğini" ispatlamaktadır. Diğer askerlerin ise yüzlerinde ya şaşkın ya da gülen bir ifade bulunmaktadır. "Arkadaşları onu kutlar. Biri ona 'sıkı herifsin' der. Joker Kendisinden hoşnuttur" (Kolker, 1999, s. 120). Joker'in silahı sniper kızı ilk gördüğü anda tutuluk yapar ve onu başka bir asker yaralar. Savaşa fiilen katılmayan gazetecilik yapan Joker'in yaralı bir kadını öldürmesi ile rüştünü ispatlaması, diğerleri tarafından erkekliğinin onaylanması anlamına gelmektedir.

Er Ryan'ı Kurtarmak (1998) Film II. Dünya Savaşı yıllarında 3 oğlunun birden ölüm haberini alan annenin, 4. ve son oğlunun yaşadığını duymak istemesi üzerine kurulmaktadır. Artık tüm Amerikan ordusunun hedefi annenin son oğlu olan James Ryan'ı ne pahasına olursa olsun kurtarmaktır. Askerler, her yerde, ona ait bir iz aramaya başlamakta ve kayıp Amerikalı eri bulmaya çalışan bir grup oluşturulmaktadır. Bu grubun Er Ryan'ı ararken yaşadıkları ve kendileriyle olan çatışmaları filmin temelini oluşturmaktadır. Gruptaki askerler, bir kişiyi kurtarmak için, sekiz kişinin hayatını tehlikeye atan ve onları düşman hattına yollayan zihniyeti sorgulamaktadır. "Özellikle filmin bir bölümü değişimi gözler önüne serer: askerler gülüp eğlenerek üzerinde ölü askerlerin isimlerinin yazılı olduğu plakalarla oyun oynarlarken, yeni askerler çarpışarak yanlarından geçer" (Valantin, 2006, s. 129). Savaşın acımasız gerçekleri, filmdeki çok kanlı savaş sahneleri ile anlatılmaktadır. Filmde Ryan'ın annesi, taziye mektuplarını yazan daktilograf kızlar ve düşman hatlarında gördükleri kız çocuğu ve onu kurtarmaya çalışan anne, ayrıca filmin başında Ryan'ın karısı, kız ve erkek çocukları olmak üzere daha çok anne-kadın karakter bulunmaktadır. Filmde anneliğin daha çok vurgulandığı, daktilograf kızlar dışında diğer kadınların anne veya kız çocuğu olarak aile içinde konumlandırıldığı görülmektedir.

İnce Kırmızı Hat (1998) Film, 2. Dünya Savaşı sırasında Guadalcanal'da savaşan bir grup Amerikalı erkeğin değişmelerinin, acı çekmelerinin ve kendileriyle ilgili önemli keşifler yapmalarının öyküsünü anlatmaktadır. Filmde Pasifik Adaları'nda Japonların ilerlemelerini durduracak olan, savaşta anahtar görevi görmüş çatışmalardan biri arka planda anlatılmaktadır. Ama öykü, bunun ötesinde, hayatta kalmak için savaşan, korkunç stres altındaki insanların aralarında gelişen güçlü bağları, savaşın "brotherhood" (erkeklerarası kardeşlik içeren geleneği üzerinde durmaktadır. Film, Pasifik Okyanus'unda yerli kadın ve çocukların okyanus kenarında yüzmeleri ile başlamaktadır. Kadınlar kucaklarında çocuklarını taşımaktadırlar. Ottan yapılmış etekler bile giyseler, kadınların öncelikle anne oldukları vurgulanmaktadır. Kadınlar bu ortamda doğa ile özdeşleştirilmektedir, savaş ise doğayı bozan bir unsur olarak kurgulanmaktadır. Filmdeki diğer kadın karakterler askerlerin hayalinde yer almaktadır, bu nedenle görüntüler soft-filtreler ve romantik müzik eşliğinde verilmektedir. Bunlardan ikisi bir askerin annesinin ölüm anını hatırladığı sırada görülen annesi ve kız kardeşi, diğeri ise başka bir askerin anıları sırasında görülen uzaklarda kalan eşidir. Bunun dışındaki sahnelerde hep erkek erkeğe ilişkiler ve savaş ortamı yer almaktadır. Kadınlar hayal aleminde, cennette, başka bir yerde yaşamaktayken, erkekler ise acımasız ve gerçek olan savaş ortamında yaşamak zorundadırlar, şeklinde bir ikilem yaratılmaktadır. Savaşların erkek işi olduğu vurgulanmaktadır.

Pearl Harbor (2001) Rafe Mc Cawley ile Danny Walker, çocukluk yaşlarından itibaren, çok iyi dost olarak birlikte büyüyen cesur iki genç pilot olarak filmin temel karakterleri arasında yer almaktadırlar. Okuldan mezun olduktan sonra Amerikan Hava Kuvvetlerine yazılmışlardır. Rafe, Birleşik Amerika Donanmasında görev yapan güzel ve cesur hemşire Evelyn Stewart'a aşık olmuştur. Ama onun savaş tutkusu bu iki sevgiliyi ayırmaktadır. İdealist bir genç olan Rafe, 2. Dünya Savaşı'nın giderek kızışması karşısında Avrupa kıtasında Nazilere karşı mücadele eden Eagle Squadron birliğine gönüllü olarak katılmaya karar vermektedir. Gönüllülerden oluşan, bu birlikte Amerikalı, Kanadalı, Avustralyalı, İsveçli ve diğer tarafsız ülkelerden gelen pilotlar bulunmaktadır. Döneceğine söz vererek sevgilisinden ve en yakın arkadaşından ayrılarak Manş Denizinin yolunu tutmaktadır. Aynı sıralarda Evelyn ile Danny'nin tayini Pasifik Cenneti olarak bilinen Hawaii'deki Pearl Harbor'a çıkar. Rafe'in uçağının düştüğü haberi gelmesinin üzerine, en yakın arkadaşı olan Danny ve sevgilisi Evelyn çok acı çekmekte ve üzülmektedir. Ortak üzüntülerinin onları yakınlaştırması sonucunda birlikte olurlar, ancak Rafe ölmemiş kurtulmuştur. Evelyn'nin Danny'den hamile olduğunu anladığı dönemde Rafe geri döner. Rafe, durumu öğrendiğinde önce Danny ile kavga etse de, arkadaşlıkları ağır basar. Aşk üçgeni aslında Hollywood sinemasında çok kullanılan bir öğedir. Kadınlar erkekler arası bağı sağlamlaştırma aracı olarak kullanılmaktadır. "Diğer erkeğin aynı kadına duyduğu arzu, kadının iki erkek arasında bağlantısal işlev görmesini sağlar. İlk erkek, kendi gücünün ve statüsünün doğrulanması için diğer erkeğin arzusunu biraz da arzular. Bu, duyduğu arzunun bir başka erkeğin arzusu üzerinden onaylanması yoluyla erkek kimliğinin pekişmesini sağlar; aracı konumundaki kadının her ikisinin de eril cinsel kimliğini güvenceye alması sayesinde, erkeklerin eşcinsellik korkusu olmadan bağlanmalarına izin verir" (Ryan ve Kellner, 1997, ss. 237-238). Bu sırada Pearl Harboor baskınında iki arkadaş üstün başarı gösterirler. Japonya'ya yapılacak saldırı için iki pilot da görevlendirilir. Danny mecburi iniş yapmak zorunda kaldıkları Japonya'da çatışmada öldürülür. Rafe ve Evelyn, Danny'nin adını verdikleri oğlunu birlikte büyütürken film bitmektedir. Film daha çok kadın karakter bulunması ve bir aşk hikayesinin filmdeki varlığı ile diğer filmlerden ayrılmaktadır. Dört önemli kadın karakterin hepsi hemşiredir ve filmde askerlerle birlikte olmak için can atan kişiler olarak temsil edilmektedirler. Asker olmalarına rağmen, görevleri savaş sırasındaki klasik kadın görevlerinden olan hemşireliktir.

Tarafsız Bölge (2001) Filmde 1993 tarihteki Sırp-Boşnak çatışması sırasında kendilerini düşman hatları arasındaki Tarafsız Bölge'de terk edilmiş bir siperin içinde bulan üç asker'in (Bosnalı Ciki ve Çera ile Sırp Nino) hikayesi anlatılmaktadır.Bir yandan birbirlerini yok etmek için fırsat kollarlarken, bir yandan da içinde bulundukları kötü durumdan kurtulmak için zorunlu olarak işbirliği yapmak zorunda kalmaktadırlar. Birleşmiş Milletler Barış Gücü'nde görevli bir çavuş, üstlerinin emirlerini hiçe sayarak yardımlarına koşmaktadır. Bu savaşta pek çok tarafın yer almasından ve uluslararası basın kuruluşlarının muhabirlerinin baskısından kaynaklanan gerginlik sürerken Ciki, Çera ve Nino savaşın çılgınlığı içinde hayatta kalabilmek için mücadele etmektedirler. Gerçekten kötü bir talihe sahip bir Bosnalı asker Ciki ve başka askerler cephedeki Bosnalı yoldaşlarına katılmak istediklerinde sisin içinde kaybolurlar ve Sırp askerlerinin silah sesleri arasında sabah olur sis aralanır. Tüm arkadaşları ortadan kaybolmuşsa da Ciki bir şekilde kurtulmanın yolunu bulmaktadır. Sonra, bir Sırp askeri olan Nino, saklanan Ciki'yi bulmaktadır ve böylece ikisi de silahlı ve "tehlikeli" olan bu iki "düşman" arasında savaşın anlamsızlığına ve trajikomikliğine dair ilginç bir ilişki başlamaktadır. En çarpıcı yönü ise, yaşanan katliamı, tüm dünyanın gözleri önünde akan kanı, dökülen gözyaşını özgür dünyanın inanılmaz bir umarsızlıkla izlemesidir. Film, beyazperdenin eleştirel anlamda nasıl kullanılabileceğine dair güzel bir örnekleme sunarken, barış için kargaşanın ortasına düşen güçlerin adalet kavramını nasıl tek yanlı kullanabileceklerini; medyanın gözü önünde cereyan eden vahşete nasıl ruhsuz yaklaşabileceğini de gözler önüne sermektedir. Film, Birleşmiş Milletler Temsilcilerinin ve Medya mensuplarının bu savaş karşısındaki tutumunu eleştirmektedir. Birleşmiş Milletler Barış Gücü'nden olan bir kadın asker ve kadın muhabir filmin kadın karakterlerini oluşturmaktadır. Ancak ikisi de komutanın sözlerini eleştirmeden kabul etmekte ve doğruluğundan şüphe etmeden söylenilenlere inanmaktadırlar. Dolayısıyla edilgen konumda temsil edilmektedirler.

Değerlendirme ve Sonuç

Savaş erkek işi olarak görüldüğünden, savaş filmlerinde temsil edilen kadın karakterler niceliksel anlamda azdır. Ama temsil edilen karakterlerin niteliksel olarak, tam da ataerkil bakış açısının istediği kadın tipleri olduğu görülmektedir. *Müfreze, Kıyamet* ve *Full Metal Jacket* filmlerinde düşman kadınlar görülmektedir. Üç filmde de düşman kadınının öldürüldüğü sahneler yer alırken, *Müfreze* filminde ek olarak düşman kadınlara dayak, tartaklama ve tecavüz ... gibi şiddet uygulandığı görülmektedir. *Zafer Yolları* ve *Kıyamet* filmlerinde askerleri eğlendirmek için şarkı söyleyen ve dans eden kadın temsillerine rastlanmaktadır. *Zafer Yolları* filminde askerler önce farklı davransalar da, sonra kızın sesinin güzelliği karşısında saygı ile dinlemektedirler, *Kıyamet* filminde ise askerlerin sahneye fırlaması üzerine kızlar zorla kaçırılarak helikoptere bindirilmekte ve uzaklaştırılmaktadır. *Full Metal Jacket* filminde iki sahnede Vietnam'da fahişelerle pazarlık yapan askerler görülmektedir. Fahişeler yine Amerikalı değil, "ötekinin kadını" olarak temsil edilmektedir. *Kwai Köprüsü* filminde kızlar komandolara yardım etse de, onların göründüğü sahneler eğlenme-nefes alma sahneleri gibi verilmektedir, ayrıca kızlar askerler tarafından korunmaktadır. *Arabistanlı Lawrance* filminde öne çıkan kadın karaktere rastlanmazken kadınlar figüran olarak veya dekor malzemesi olarak yer almaktadırlar, *Er Ryan'ı Kurtarmak* filminde kadın karakterler anne olma özellikleriyle önplana çıkmaktadırlar. *İnce Kırmızı Hat* filminde ise, anne ve sevgili olan karakterler önplanda yer almaktadırlar. *Pearl Harbour* filminde ise sevgili olarak temsil edilen kadın karakterin mesleği hemşireliktir. Son olarak Tarafsız Bölge filmde ise kadın karakterlerin meslek grupları Birleşmiş Milletler Barış Gücü askeri ve savaş muhabiridir.

Sonuç olarak savaş filmlerinde kadın karakterlerin temsilinde ataerkil toplumsal düzenin kadına atfettiği bakire/vamp kadın ikileminin dışına çıkılmadığı gerçekçi kadınlar yerine show-girl, şarkıcı, fahişe veya anne, sevgili, eş, kız kardeş olarak kadın karakterlerin temsil edildiği görülmektedir. Bir üçüncü temsil "düşmanın kadını" temsilidir, bu kadın tipi ise öldürülmeyi veya tecavüze uğramayı hak etmektedir. Bir filmde dekor malzemesi olan kadınların yanısıra meslekleri, daktilograf, hemşire, gazeteci ve asker olan kadınlar görüntülenmektedir. Ancak meslek sahibi olsalar dahi kadın karakterler erkeklerden aşağı konumdadırlar ve onlara tabi durumda, dediklerini sorgulamayan karakterlerdir.

Kaynakça

Altınay, A. G. (2000). *Vatan, millet, kadınlar*. İstanbul: İletişim Yayınları.

Altınay, A. G. (2006). Asker Türkleri ve onların asker kardeşlerini kim doğuruyor? *Amargi, 2*, 25-26.

Burke, C. (2006). Kadınlar ve militarizm: Niçin toplumsal cinsiyet perspektifli bir analize ihtiyacımız var? (Çev. E. Çoşkun). *Amargi, 2*, 44-46.

Direk, Z. (2006). İmkansızdan da imkansız. *Amargi, 2*, 23-24.

Gedik, E. (2006). Kadınlık ve vicdani red üzerine notlar. *Amargi, 2*, 38-41.

Kolker, R. P. (1999). *Yalnızlık sineması*. (Çev. E. Yılmaz). Ankara: Öteki Matbaası.

Maschall, G. (1999). *Sosyoloji sözlüğü*. (Çev. O. Akınhay ve D. Kömürcü). Ankara: Bilim ve Sanat/Ark Yayınları.

Özden, Z. (2000). *Film eleştirisi*. İstanbul: Afa Yayınları.

Ryan, M. ve Kellner D. (1997). *Politik kamera*. (Çev. E. Özsayar). İstanbul: Ayrıntı Yayınları.

Suid, L. H. (1978). *Guns and glory*. USA: Addison-Wesley Publishing.

Valantin, J. M. (2006). *Hollywood, Pentagon ve Washington*. (Çev. Ö. F. Turan). İstanbul: Babıali Kültür Yayıncılığı.

Yılmaz, E. (1993a). Hollywood savaş filmlerinin semantiğine bakış. *Edebiyat Eleştiri, 6*, 63-72.

Yılmaz, E. (1993b). Hollywood savaş filmlerinin semantiğine bakış III. *Edebiyat Eleştiri, 4*, 39-51.

Power-sharing Arrangements, Right-based Theory and Deliberative Democracy for Peace versus Conflict, and Stability versus Deadlock

Nur Uluşahin
Department of Constitutional Law
Başkent University, School of Law
nurulusahin@hotmail.com

The challenge of globalization and its effects on nation-states confront us with the question whether the classical liberal democracy can be accepted as the only legitimate form of government. There is no doubt that democracy is much more than free and fair elections or majority rule. But this does not mean that a variety of forms regarding different arrangements on minority and majority relationships can not be recognized under the name of democracy. It should be noted that these different concepts of democracy provide us different opportunities for modes of conflict resolution. Especially the developments after the end of Cold war showed that the constitutional protection of human rights does not necessarily safeguard minority interests (Kymclika, 1995, p. 1). The demise of Communism, the liberation of Eastern Europe from Soviet tutelage has paved the way to ethnic struggles within a State in place of wars between nation-states. It is an undeniable fact that the fear of the majority of losing its preferred status, especially the fear of the secession and self-determination pushed by geographically concentrated minority groups often result harsh repression which is thought to be likely to maintain the territorial integrity. The more condense is the fear, the more condense would be the repression and the more condense is the repression, the more condense would be the fear and this vicious circle so goes on. Though it's not hard to realize such responses cost too much for minority groups and destroy peace which can not be sacrificed at any cost, sometimes the price to pay may not seem as perilous as we think to some others. Unfortunately that circle is not only offensive to rational interests of the majority group but are also detriment to democratic pluralism and the notion of democracy itself (DiSarro, 2005, p. 1)

Then the question is whether there are any options which will prevent both secessionist movements in the name of peace; at the same time protecting minority rights adamant to the fundamental principles of democracy. In other words, is there a reasonable option for conflict resolution even in the difficult combination, especially in countries which are deeply divided along religious, ideological, linguistic, cultural, ethnic or racial lines?

In this paper, taking Ronald Dworkin's rights thesis (1977, pp. 171-177) as a starting point, my principal argument will be that the approach treating men as less than a man or treating men as less worthy of other men cannot be in agreement with the idea of law. Classical liberal democratic theory which basis democracy for citizens on the idea of nation-state by creating a "super society" neglects that every citizen also belongs to a particular community (a cultural, linguistic, or ethnic group that provides a sense of belonging, identity, meaning and purpose) and so it is obliged to confront with the attacks of multiculturalism (Smooha, 2001, p. 13). Now the main problematic is who the law-maker will be in a state bounded with law. Should the groups relying their rights on cultural diversities be recognized as the subject of law? This paper suggests reorganizing liberal democracy under the light of Ronald Dworkin's right-based approach as a solution of the paradox of national minorities and nation-state. The new consensual base which liberal democracy should be constituted on will necessarily demonstrate a new minority-majority relation which will encompass a set of institutional devices like proportionality, grand coalition and mutual veto to protect the rights of minorities. Especially in segmented societies these consociational arrangements and the government of power sharing will effect related cooperative attitudes of political elites and lead them to transcend the borders of their own groups, to be receptive to the claims of others and to accommodate the divergent interest and claims of the segments (Lijphart, 1969, p. 216). In this context, I will try to discuss main arguments of "deliberative" democracy which can roughly be classified under two main schools, one broadly influenced by John Rawls and the other by Jürgen Habermas. Lastly, I will try to show that in current democratic systems consociational democracies are more prone to producing deliberative politics. Therefore, especially in deeply-divided countries where the flexibility necessary for majoritarian democracy is likely to be absent, liberal democracy should abandon the prevailing majoritarian model shaped generations ago (Riggs, 2002, p. 35) and organize itself on a new minority-majority relations basis giving chance to consociational arrangements and deliberative politics for peace versus conflict and stability versus deadlock.

Right-based Theory

Human rights, animal rights, moral and political rights have got an important place in contemporary political and legal theory. A modern trilogy of legal and moral theories which are *right-based, duty-based* and *goal-based* has been introduced by Professor Ronald Dworkin. Any moral theory may allow for the existence of rights if it regards the interests of individuals to be sufficient for holding others to be subject to duties. R. M. Dworkin has suggested that rights are the foundation of political morality. Professor Dworkin (1977) asserts that,

> Political theories differ from one another ... not simply in the particular goals, rights, and duties each sets out, but also in the way each connects the goals, rights, and duties it employs. It seems reasonable to suppose that any particular theory will give ultimate pride of place to just one of these concepts; it will take some overriding goal, or some set of fundamental rights, or some set of transcendent duties, as fundamental, and show other goals, rights, and duties as subordinate and derivative (p. 171).[1]

In order to illuminate this distinction we may give the prohibition of torture. Of course we all oppose to torture. If our opposition is based on the suffering of the victim, our approach is *right-based.* If our opposition to torture is based on conviction that torture debases the torturer, our concern is *duty-based.* If we think the torture is unacceptable only when it affects the interests of those other than the parties involved, then our approach is *goal-based.* Professor Dworkin's "rights thesis" argues for the primacy of rights over considerations of the general welfare. A political right arises only when the reasons for giving *me* what I want are stronger than some *collective* justification which normally provides a political justification for a decision (Wacks, 2005, pp. 273-275).

1 Professor Ronald Dworkin (2001) says that "liberty consists in being able to do what one wishes, short of violating the rights of others, with the resources assigned by a reasonably just distribution of resources." (p. 256.)

In Dworkin's words (1977),

> The institution of rights against the Government is not a gift of God, or an ancient ritual, or a national sport. ... Anyone who professes, to take rights seriously, and who praises our Government for respecting them, must have some sense of what that point is. He must accept, at the minimum, one or both of two important ideas. The first is the vague but powerful idea of human dignity. This idea, associated with Kant, but defended by philosophers of different schools, supposes that there are ways of treating a man that are inconsistent with recognizing him as a full member of the human community, and holds that such treatment is profoundly unjust. The second is the more familiar idea of political equality. This supposes that the weaker members of a political community are entitled to the same concern and respect of their government as the more powerful members have secured for themselves, so that if some men have freedom of decision whatever the effect on the general good, then all men must have the same freedom" (pp. 198-199).

He points out that, "... if rights make sense at all, then the invasion of a relatively important right must be a very serious matter. It means treating a man as less than a man, or as less worthy of concern than other men. The institution of rights rests on the conviction that this is a grave injustice, and that it is worth paying the incremental cost in social policy or efficiency that is necessary to prevent it" (p. 199).

The importance of this approach arises out of the fact that the need for peace and democracy contradicts any kind of thought and action treating a man as less than a man, or as less worthy of concern than other men. Then what I want to emphasize that if our real and sincere desire is overcoming the obstacles which hinder us to reach the ultimate goal of peace versus conflict and stability versus deadlock, we should not forget that any kind of difference which distinguishes us do not have the capability to make any of us more or less a man and a woman.

Power-Sharing Arrangements

In 1861 John Stuart Mill (1958) wrote that democracy is "next to impossible in a country made up of different nationalities"—that is, in a multi-ethnic society—and completely impossible in linguistically divided countries, where the people "read and speak different languages" (p. 230). Though it's a bit inflexible argument, most experts on divided societies still agree that deep ethnic and other societal influences pose a grave problem for democracy and it is more difficult to establish and maintain democracy in divided than in homogenous societies. They also agree that the problem of ethnic and other deep divisions is greater in countries that are not yet democratic or not fully democratic than in well-established democracies (Lijphart, 1999b, p. 2). Then we can conclude that such deep divisions present a major obstacle to further democratization in future.

In the West, along with the dominant form of liberal democratic nation-state, there is another noteworthy form known as consociational democracy found in only several countries like Switzerland, Belgium and Canada. These democracies do not only recognize group differences and collective rights but provide the minority with maximal recognition. Consociational democracy operates through the mechanisms of group autonomy, proportional representation, politics of compromise and consensus, coalition government and veto power on decisions vital to group interests (Smooha, 2002a, p. 424).

The theory of consociationalism was originally developed in the late 1960s and early 1970s by several writers including Gerhard Lehmbruch, Jorg Steiner and Hans Daalder.[2] However the name most closely associated with this theory is Arend Lijphart who has developed and advocated the concept throughout his life time.[3] In his early work, Lijphart identified four characteristics of *"consociational"* constitutions as an ideal type: *executive power-sharing* among a "grand coalition" of political leaders drawn from all significant segments of society; a *minority veto* in government decision-making, requiring mutual agreement among all parties in the executive; *proportional representation* of major groups in elected and appointed office; and a high degree of *cultural autonomy* for groups (Lijphart, 1968 & 1977). According to Lijphart, the sharing of executive power and group autonomy are the two "primary characteristics" of consociational democracy. Power-sharing means the participation of the representatives of all significant groups in political decision-making, especially at the executive level; whereas group autonomy means that these groups have authority to run their own internal affairs, especially in the areas of education and culture (Lijphart, 1995, pp. 853-865).[4] On the other hand, for Lijphart, the other characteristics of proportionality and mutual veto can be qualified as secondary which strengthen executive power-sharing and autonomy (Lijphart, 1999a).

Lijphart maintains that consociational democracy is appropriate to societies with moderate ethnic differences and conflicts. He also argues that these power-sharing arrangements are likely to have several benefits over majority rule, generating "kinder, gentler" governance with more inclusive processes of decision-making, more egalitarian policy outcomes and better economic performance (Liphart, 1999a, pp. 293-300). Lijphart admits that the potential advantages of power-sharing institutions are nowhere more important than in segmented societies with cross-cutting cleavages. Especially in plural societies with deep religious, ideological, linguistic, cultural, ethnic or racial cleavages as the flexibility for majoritarian democracy is likely to be absent, "under these conditions, majority rule is not only undemocratic but also dangerous, because minorities that are continually denies access to power will feel excluded and discriminated against and may lose their allegiance to the regime " (Lijphart, 1999a, pp. 32-33).

In the most deeply divided societies, it is no doubt that majority rule spells majority dictatorship and civil strife rather than democracy. In Lijphart's words (1999a) "what such societies need is a democratic regime that emphasizes consensus instead of opposition, that includes rather than excludes, and that tries to maximize the size of the ruling majority instead of being satisfied with a bare majority" (p. 33).

Deliberative Democracy

According to political theorists like Jürgen Habermas, Joshua Cohen and Seyla Benhabib, the justification of political authority vested in any particular policy depends partly on the process by which it was created or enacted (see Cohen, 1989; Benhabib, 1994 & Habermas, 1994). And in modern pluralistic societies in which it's hard to find any transcendental point of reference capable telling actors what the right perspective is, reasonable deliberation or discourse ethics is seen as a necessary means to arrive at legitimate decisions (Chambers, 1995, p. 233). Therefore, it is confirmed that on the one hand political and societal actors should listen to each other and show mutual respect and on the other hand while reasonably justifying their policy positions, they should be ready to re-evaluate and revise their initial preferences in a reasonable deliberation or discourse (Gutman & Thompson, 1996). As a result, in modern pluralistic societies it is required that a reasonable deliberation should take place for arriving rational and legitimate decisions.

2 For the development of this concept, see Lehmbruch, G. (1967). *Proporzdemokratie. Politisches System und politische Kultur in der Schweiz und Osterreich.* Tubingen: Mohr; Steiner, J. (1974). *Amicable Agreement versus Majority Rule: Conflict Resolution in Switzerland.* Chapel Hill: University of North Carolina Press; Daalder, H. (1974). The Consociational Democracy Theme, *World Politics,* 26, 604-21; McRae, K. (1974). *Consociational Democracy: Conflict Accommodation in Segmented Societies.* Toronto: McClelland and Stewart.

3 Lijphart, A. (1969). Consociational democracy, *World Politics,* (21), 207-225; Lijphart, A. (1975). *The Politics of Accommodation: Pluralism and Democracy in the Netherlands.* Berkeley: University of California Press; Lijphart, A. (1977). *Democracy in Plural Societies: A Comparative Exploration.* New Haven: Yale University Press; Lijphart, A. & Grofman, B. (Eds.). (1984). *Choosing an Electoral System: Issues and Alternatives.* New York: Praeger; Lijphart, A. (1984). *Democracies.* New Haven: Yale University Press; Lijphart, A. (1986). Degrees of Proportionality of Proportional Representation Formulas. In B.Grofman & A. Lijphart (Eds.), *Electoral Laws and Their Political Consequences.* New York: Agathon Press; Lijphart, A. (1991). Constitutional Choices for New Democracies, *Journal of Democracy,* 2, 72-84; Lijphart, A. (1991). Proportional Representation: Double Checking the Evidence, *Journal of Democracy* 2, 42-48; Lijphart, A. (1994). *Electoral Systems and Party Systems: A Study of Twenty-Seven Democracies, 1945-1990.* New York: Oxford University Press; Lijphart, A. (1995). Electoral Systems. In S. M. Lipset (Ed.), *The Encyclopaedia of Democracy.* Washington D.C.: Congressional Quarterly Press; Lijphart, A. (1999). *Patterns of Democracy: Government Forms and Performance in 36 Countries.* New Haven: Yale University Press; Lijphart, A. (2004). Constitutional design for divided societies. *Journal of Democracy,* 15 (2), 96-109.

4 Lijphart asserts that agreement on the central role of these two characteristics extend far beyond the consociational school. Ted Robert Gurr who is a good example with his book "Minorities at Risk: A Global View of Ethnopolitical Conflicts," has not insp0
ired by consociational theory but mentions the arguments alike (1999, p. 3; Gurr, 1993).

In this context, consociational democracy can be seen as a model which maximizes the chance of deliberative politics with the institutional setting in which it survives (see Bächtiger, Spőrndli & Steiner, 2002). The institutional mechanisms like proportional representation, grand coalition, minority veto which consociational model requires are also likely to serve to deliberative political process by maximizing the size of the ruling majority more than any other form of liberal democracy seen in plural societies. As the deep divisions and disputes can not be eliminated and should be taken as given according to the main premise of consociational democracy (Smooha & Hanf, 1992, p. 32); consociationalism is likely to be close interaction with the deliberative concept of democracy. Avoiding majority rule, consociational model may antagonize the smaller or weaker groups and run on the basis of *compromise* and *power-sharing* (Smooha & Hanf, 1992, p. 33)

It is no doubt that in deeply divided societies, as the constituent ethnic or racial groups are different in culture, separate in institutions, unequal in power and privilege and most of the time disagreeing on fundamental issues, the potentiality for *conflict* among them is high and *violence* are quite common. Therefore, deliberative democracy which requires an ideal of "talk-centric" style of decision making instead of a "voting-centric" style is appropriate for such societies. As the ultimate goal of arriving rational and legitimate decisions needs to determine the outcomes by "reasons" rather than "numbers" (Chambers, 1999, p. 1) and the outcomes should be "qualitative" rather than "quantitative" (Perczynski 2000, pp. 1-2); the possibilities which deliberative concept of democracy present are more likely to solve the problems generated from the polarization of different cultures and groups within a deeply divided society.

In fact, any deliberation in real world politics may fall short of the ideal discourse envisioned by Jürgen Habermas. Although he defends what he claims to be a strictly proceduralist approach in which no limits are put on the scope and content of the deliberation, it is hard to assume a constraint-free communicative environment in politics. Therefore it would not be wrong to accept the Habermasian ideal discourse merely conceived as a regulative idea . It should be underlined that though Habermas shares with communitarians the vision of an active, talk-centric participation of possibly all citizens; he rejects the communitarian premise of a citizenry united and actively motivated by a shared conception of the good life as being unrealistic (Bächtiger, Spőrndli, & Steiner, 2002). He shares this criticism with liberalism and promotes liberal neutrality: "The state should not act in ways intended to promote a particular conception of the good life since that would constitute a failure to show each citizen *equal concern* and *respect*." (Baynes, 1995, p. 223). However, Habermas does not accept liberalism's interpretation of the political process as being primarily the competition among private and fixed preferences. In deliberative political process, the preferences are not only fixed or exogenous to political process but are adaptive to a wide range of societal influences as well (See Sunstein, 1991). Different from liberal democracy, one of the most essential features of deliberative democracy is the possibility of transformation of the initial preferences of participants (Manin, 1987; Chambers, 1999).

The principles of Habermas's ideal deliberative procedure are as follows: First of all, deliberation is held argumentatively. "The parties are required to state their reasons for advancing proposals, supporting them or criticizing them" (Cohen, 1989, p. 22). Ideal deliberation is inclusive and public as well as it is free from external and internal coercion. Participation in such a deliberation is governed by the norms of equality and symmetry. Each participant has an equal chance to put issues on the agenda, propose solutions and criticisms and each has an equal voice in the decision. Lastly, ideal deliberation "aims to arrive at a rationally motivated consensus" (Cohen, 1989, p. 23). Cohen (1989) after stating that democratic legitimacy arises from collective decisions among equal members, declares: "According to deliberative conception, a decision is collective just in case it emerges from arrangements of binding collective choices that establish conditions of public reasoning among equals who are governed by the decisions" (p. 25).

As a consequence, deliberative democracy is a participatory model of democracy as opposed to the inherent elitism of most existing political systems. For the deliberative conception of democracy which is basically input-oriented, the most important issue is the legitimacy of a decision process. "In such a view, it is not enough for a democratic process to take account of the interests of all and to reach compromise that will establish a modus-vivendi. The aim is to generate *communicative power* and this requires establishing the conditions for a freely given assent of all concerned, hence the importance of finding procedures that would guarantee moral impartiality. Only then, one can be sure that the consensus that is obtained is *a rational one* and not a mere agreement" (Mouffe, 2000, p. 5).[5]

Result

What has happened in the 1990s is that ethnic divisions have replaced the Cold War as the world's most serious source of violent conflict. Lijphart justifiably demonstrates the clash of this phenomenon with the third wave of democratization which has started with the democratic revolution in 1974 (Huntington, 1991) culminated in

5 As Mouffe excerpts from Benhabib, "According to deliberative model of democracy, it is a necessary condition for attaining legitimacy and ratinonality with regard to collective decision making processes in a polity, that the institutions of this polity are so arranged that what is considered in the common interest of all results from processes of collective deliberation conducted rationally and fairly among free and equal individuals." (Benhabib, 1996, p. 69).

the early 1990s with the collapse of Soviet Union and run into trouble by the mid-1990s. As Larry Diamond (1996) demonstrates that the continued growth of electoral democracy takes place at the same time with the stagnation of liberal democracy in the latter part of the third wave and in his words "electoral" or "illiberal" democracy is not really a democratic form of government at all" (p. 28).

Advocates of power sharing as a means for improving democracy suggest that government by many is more legitimate than mere majority rule. That is indicated in the premise of "as many as possible". The consensus rule also admits that majority rule is better than minority rule but it accepts majority rule only as a *minimum* requirement; "*instead of being satisfied with narrow decision-making majorities, it seeks to maximize the size of these majorities*" (Lijphart, 1999a, p. 2).

It is no doubt that what we need is a democracy which is much more than free and fair elections or majority rule. Democracy requires more robust modes of participation than just voting or majority rule such as free discussion, and the give and take of opposing arguments. In democracy there should be "widespread actual participation, including the most disadvantaged" (Drèze & Sen, 2002, p. 24) and an "equitable distribution of power" (Drèze & Sen, 2002, p. 347). Popular decisions should enable people to exercise their agency and make a difference in the world (Drèze & Sen, 2002).

Democracy is not only instrumentally valuable but it also has intrinsic value. It enables citizens to shape their own lives and communities which means to have human dignity. If one is prevented from political involvement, she would not have control over decisions which affects her own life. The freedom to determine one's own destiny is "one of the elementary freedoms that people have reason to value, even among people who lead very deprived lives in material terms" (Drèze and Sen, 2002). On the other hand, democracy values all adult members of the group equally in worth and dignity. Therefore, a right-based approach as emphasized in Dworkin's rights thesis may simply be created only if a democracy tries to maximize the size of the ruling majority instead of being satisfied with a bare majority. Though this simple approach may not solve all the problems related to governing many; it may be taken as a starting point which demonstrates the right direction just as Habermas's ideal discourse.

References:

Bächtiger, A., Spörndli M. & Steiner, J. (2002). The consociational theory and deliberative politics. A conceptual framework for cross-national analysis. In S. Brooks (Ed.), *The Challenge of Cultural Pluralism* (pp. 77-95). Westport, Connecticut: Praeger.

Baynes, K. (1995). Democracy and the *Rechtsstaat:* Habermas's *Faktizität und Geltung.* In S. White (Ed.), *The Cambridge Companion to Habermas* (pp. 201-233). Cambridge: Cambridge University Press.

Benhabib, S. (1994). Deliberative rationality and models of democratic legitimacy. *Constellations, 1*(1), 26-52.

Chambers, S. (1995). Discourse and democratic practices. In S. white (Ed.), *The Cambridge companion to Habermas* (pp. 233-263). Cambridge: Cambridge University Press.

Cohen, J. (1989). Deliberation and democratic legitimacy. In A. Hamlin & P. Pettit (Eds.), *The good polity: Normative analysis of the state* (pp. 17-34). New York: Blackwell Publishers.

Diamond, L. (1996, July). Is the third wave over?. *Journal of Democracy, 7*(3), 20-37.

DiSarro, B. (2005). *The theory of democracy and permanent minorities in Southeastern Europe.* Retrieved March 23, 2007, from http://www.politicsandgovernment.ilstu.edu/downloads/icsps_papers/2005/Desario2005.pdf

Drèze, J. & Sen, A. (2002). *India: Development and participation.* Oxford: Oxford University Press.

Dworkin, R. (1977). *Taking rights seriously* .Cambridge: Harvard University Press.

Gutman, A. & Thompson D. (1996). *Democracy and disagreement.* Cambridge, MA: Belknap Harvard.

Habermas, J. (1994). Three normative models of democracy. *Constellations 1*(1), 1-10.

Huntington, S. P. (1991). *The third wave: Democratization in the late Twentieth Century.* Norman, Oklahoma: University of Oklahoma Press.

Kymclika, W. (1995). *Multicultural citizenship.* Oxford: Oxford University Press.

Lijphart, A. (1968). *The politics of accommodation: Pluralism and democracy in the* Netherlands. Berkeley: University of California Press.

Lijphart, A. (1969). Consociational democracy. *World Politics* (2), 207-225.

Lijphart, A. (1977). *Democracy in plural societies: A comparative exploration.* New Haven: Yale University Press.

Lijphart, A. (1995). Multiethnic democracy. In S. M. Lipset, et al., (Eds.), *The* encyclopedia *of democracy.* Washington D.C.: Congressional Quarterly, 853-865.

Lijphart, A. (1999a) *Patterns of democracy: Government forms and performance in 36 countries.* New Haven: Yale University Press.

Lijphart, A. (1999b, December 9-11). Power-sharing and group autonomy in the 1990s and the 21st century. *Constitutional Design 2000,* University of California, San Diego. Retrieved March 23, 2007, from http://www.tamilnation.org/conflictresolution/consociationalism/Lijphart.pdf

Mill, J. S. (1958). *Considerations on representative government.* New York: Liberal Arts Press.

Mouffe, C. (2000, December). Deliberative democracy or agonistic pluralism. *Political Science Series,* Institute for Advanced Studies, Vienna. Retrieved February 2, 2007, from http://users.unimi.it/dikeius/pw_72.pdf

Riggs, F. W. (2002, May). Globalization, ethnic diversity, and nationalism: The challenge for democracies. *The Annals of The American Academy* (581), 35- 47.

Smooha, S. & Hanf, T. (1992). The diverse modes of conflict-regulation in deeply divided societies. *International Journal of Comparative Sociology, XXXIII* (1-2), 26-47.

Smooha, S. (2001). The model of ethnic democracy. ECMI Working Paper no. 13, *European Centre for Minority Issues,* October. Retrieved March 22, 2007, from http://www.ecmi.de/download/working_paper_13.pdf

Smooha, S. (2002a). Types of democracy and modes of conflict management in ethnically divided societies. *Nations and Nationalism, 8*(4), 423-431.

Smooha, S. (2002b) The model of ethnic democracy: Israel as a Jewish and democratic state. *Nations and Nationalism, 8*(4), 475-503.

Steiner, J. (1974). *Amicable agreement versus majority rule: Conflict resolution in Switzerland.* Chapel Hill: University of North Carolina Press.

Wacks, R. (2005). Understanding jurisprudence: An introduction to legal theory. Oxford: Oxford University Press.

Medyanın Barış ve Savaşa Etkisi (Irak)

Nural İmik
İletişim Fakültesi
Fırat Üniversitesi
nimik@firat.edu.tr

1. Giriş

Her gün yeni bir teknolojik gelişmenin yaşandığı, dünyanın haberleşmenin kolaylaştığı küçük bir köy haline geldiği günümüzde, medyanın topluma olan etkisini önemsememek mümkün görünmemektedir. Çünkü medya toplumun haber ihtiyacını gidermekte, eğlendirmekte, eğitmekte ve kamuoyu adına denetim ve eleştiride bulunmaktadır. Bu bağlamda medya; kültürel değerlerimizi, davranışlarımızı, insanlarla olan ilişkilerimizi etkilemektedir.

Toplumsal bir varlık olan birey, gün içerisinde çok geniş bir iletişim ağı ortamında yaşamaktadır. Toplumsallaşma sürecinde birey medyadan yararlanmaktadır. Gazeteden televizyona, sinemadan bilgisayara, uydudan fiber optik ve lazerli iletişim sistemine kadar çok geniş bir alanı içinde barındıran medya, önemli bir güç kaynağıdır (Can, 2000, s. 150). Bu güç kaynağının doğru olarak kullanılması gerekmektedir. Medyada yer alan görüntülü haberler ve diğer programlar, çocuklar başta olmak üzere toplum üzerinde olumsuz etkilere neden olabilmektedir. Bu olumsuz etkilerden biri de Irak eski lideri Saddam Hüseyin'in infaz görüntülerinin medyada yer almasının ardından yaşanmıştır. Bu çalışma ile medyada yer alan görüntülerin ve haberlerin, ülkelerin savaş ve barış ortamlarına etkisi açıklanmaya çalışılmıştır.

Çalışmanın kuramsal kısmında, medya kavramı, medyanın topluma etkileri ve işlevleri tanımlanmıştır. Ayrıca şiddet içerikli görüntülerin medyada yer alması ve bireye etkileri doğrultusunda, Saddam Hüseyin'in infaz görüntüleri ele alınmış ve bu görüntüler sonucunda dünyanın çeşitli yerlerinde yaşanan olumsuz olaylar, gazete ve haber sitelerinden alınan haber örnekleri ile açıklanmaya çalışılmıştır. Savaş halinde bulunan ülkelerin barış sürecine kısa zamanda ulaşmalarında ve barış içinde bulunan ülkelerinde bu huzurlu ve güvenli ortamı korumalarında medyanın rolü ifade edilmeye çalışılmıştır.

Araştırmanın son kısmında ise Irak eski lideri Saddam Hüseyin'in infaz görüntülerinin medyada yer almadan önceki üç ay boyunca Irak'ta çıkan olaylar ile Saddam Hüseyin'in infaz görüntülerinden sonraki üç ayda Irak'ta meydana gelen olaylar, yaralı ve ölü sayıları verilerek tablolar halinde sunulmuştur. Bu veriler doğrultusunda medyada yer alan bu görüntülerin insan psikolojisine ve Irak'ta oluşturulmak istenen barış sürecine olumlu ve olumsuz etkileri ortaya konulmaya çalışılmıştır.

2. Medya Kavramı

İnsanlık tarihine bakıldığında iletişim olgusunun, insanla birlikte doğup zaman içerisinde geliştiği görülmektedir. İlk zamanlarda çeşitli bedensel hareketler ve ilkel yöntemlerle sağlanan iletişim zaman içerisinde toplumsal gelişmeye paralel olarak değişiklik göstermeye başlamıştır.

15. yüzyılın ikinci yarısında matbaanın bulunması, 19. yüzyıldan itibaren başlayan Sanayi Devrimi, kitle iletişim araçlarının ortaya çıkmasına zemin hazırlamıştır. Teknolojik gelişmelerle birlikte kitle iletişim araçlarının yani medyanın işlevi ve gücü artmıştır. Medya sözcüğü Latince "medius" sözcüğünün çoğuludur. Araç, orta, ortam, aracı anlamlarına gelmektedir. Medya kavramı en geniş anlamı ile kullanıldığında, çok kişiye ulaşabilen her türden yazılı, sözlü, basılı, görsel metin ve imgeleri(kitaplar, gazeteler, dergiler, broşürler, billboardlar, radyo, film, televizyon, internet gibi) kapsamaktadır (Nalçaoğlu, 2003, ss. 43-45).

Williams Raymond 1976 yılında yazdığı *A Vocabulary Of Culture And Society* adlı eserinde medya kavramının üç ayrı anlamı ve bunlar arasındaki yakınlaşmaya dikkat çekmiştir. Bunlar: 1. Medya eski genel anlamında aracılık eden ya da arada bulunan bir aktör ya da kurumdur.

2. Teknik anlamda, yazılı basın ile sesli ve görüntülü basın arasında bir ayrım yapılmaktadır.

3. Kapitalist anlamda; halihazırda var olan ya da planlanan; bir gazete veya yayın hizmeti, reklamcılık gibi başka bir şeyin aracı olarak görülür (İrvan, 2002, s. 11).

Medyanın insan yaşamına girişi her alanda köklü değişikliklere yol açmıştır. İnsanların yaşam tarzlarını bile etkilemektedir. Medya ile insan geleneksel yaşamdan uzaklaşmaya başlamıştır. Geleneksel toplumlardaki bilgi kaynağı durumunda olan yaşlılar ve din adamları gibi kişiler yavaş yavaş terk edilmeye başlanmıştır. Bunun yerini medyada gösterilenler ve sunulanlar almıştır (Gönenç, 2005, s. 59). İnsanların kıyafetlerini seçerken, konuşurken, evlerini dizerken ve yaşamlarının birçok alanında karar verirken medyadan etkilendiklerini söylemek mümkündür.

Modern demokrasilerin en önemli özelliği sosyal, siyasal ve ekonomik katmanların hepsine seslerini duyurma imkanı sağlamalarıdır (Avşar, 2004, s. 88). Son dönemlerde medyaya 4. güç denilmektedir. Medyaya 4. güç denmesi, onun; yasama, yürütme ve yargı güçlerini kamu adına denetleme, izleme görevinden kaynaklanmaktadır. Medyanın gerçekten güçlü olması, gerçek anlamda denetim yapabilmesi diğer üç gücünde daha iyi işlemesini sağlamaktadır (Tılıç, 2001, s. 119). Medyanın tam anlamıyla işlevlerini yerine getirdiği ülkelerde, ülkenin siyasi ve hukuksal kurumlarının daha iyi işlediğini ve insanlarının haklarını aramakta güçlük çekmediklerini ifade etmek mümkündür.

3. Medyanın Topluma Etkileri

Medya toplumsal bir iletişim kurumudur ve içinde bulunduğu topluma yeni ufuklar açmaktadır. Toplumun kültürel düzeyini yükseltmede ya da bunun aksi yönünde rol oynamaktadır. Medyaya içinde bulunduğu toplumun önemli toplumsal dinamiklerinden biridir demek doğru olacaktır (Vural, 2000, s. 105). Çünkü kişiler dünyayı ve çevrelerinde olup bitenleri medya sayesinde öğrenmektedir. Medya olay ve olguları kişiye nasıl iletirse, kişi de o yönde algılamaktadır. Dolayısı ile medyanın etki alanları ve gücünün boyutu da zaman içerisinde değişmektedir. İlk dönemlerinde medyanın düşünce, tutum ve davranışları değiştirme gücü üzerinde odaklanan ve sınırlı bir etkisi olabileceğine dikkat çeken araştırmalar, daha da kapsamlı hale getirilmiştir. Artık medyanın bildirme ve farkına varma gücü üzerinde de durulmaktadır (Gezgin, 2005, s. 11).

Toplumlar tarihin ilk zamanlarında yüz yüze iletişimi kullanmaktadır. Zaman içerisinde teknolojik gelişmelere paralel olarak kitle iletişim araçları ortaya çıkmıştır. Kitle iletişim araçlarındaki gelişme de bilginin toplumdan topluma aktarılmasını sağlamıştır. Böylece toplumlar kendi yaşam tarzlarını, geleneklerini başka toplumlara aktarmaya başlamışlardır. Özellikle batıdan gelen bu yaşam tarzı, diğer toplumlara da empoze edilmektedir (Gönenç, 2005, ss. 58-59). 1980'lerden sonra iletişimin küreselleşmesinden bahsedilebilir. Artık medya da küreselleşmiştir. Büyük şirket guruplarının, ulus aşırı örgütlerin ve dünyanın dört bir yanından aynı televizyon kanallarının izlenebildiği, internetin var olduğu bir iletişim ortamı ortaya çıkmıştır (Kejanlıoğlu, 2003, ss. 83-86). Medyada ki bu küreselleşmenin toplumsal küreselleşmeyi hızlandırdığını söylemek mümkündür. Bu bağlamda toplumlardaki geleneksel ve kültürel yapının yavaşça yok olduğu ifade edilebilir.

Toplum üzerinde son derece büyük etkilere sahip olan medyanın, demokratik toplumlarda önemli toplumsal işlevleri vardır. Bunlar:

- Haber verme,
- Kamuoyu adına denetim ve eleştiride bulunma,
- Kamuoyunu aydınlatma ve kamuoyunun serbest oluşumunu sağlama,
- Eğitme ve eğlendirme işlevleridir (Vural, 2000, ss. 105-106).

Toplum üzerinde son derece önemli etkileri olan medya işlevlerinin içinde haber verme, kamuoyunu aydınlatma ve denetim-eleştiri işlevleri daha farklı bir öneme sahiptir. Özellikle haber verme işlevi, medyanın en temel işlevidir. Medyanın varlık nedenini oluşturmaktadır. Basın tarihine bakıldığında, haber verme işlevi geçmişte tek işlev olarak karşımıza çıkmaktadır (Can, 2000, s. 152). Denetim-eleştiri işlevi de demokrasinin gerçek anlamda uygulanmasını sağlamaktadır.

Medyanın işlevlerinin her biri farklı bir öneme sahiptir. Birçok program eğlendirici ögeler taşımaktadır. Eğlendirme işlevi ile bireyler günlük hayatın sorunlarından kurtularak, boş zamanlarını doldurmaktadırlar (Severin, Tankart & James, 1994, s. 85). Eğlence programları ile toplumun sıkıntılardan biraz olsun uzaklaştığını söylemek mümkündür.

4. Şiddet İçerikli Görüntülerin Medyada Yer Alması ve Bireye Etkileri (Saddam Hüseyin'in İnfaz Görüntüleri)

İnsanlık tarihi ile var olduğu söylenebilen şiddet olgusu, kendisini farklı şekillerde göstermektedir. Geniş anlamda şiddet, bireylerin yaralanmasına, sindirilmesine, öfkelendirilmesine veya duygusal olarak baskı altına alınmasına yol açan fiziki veya herhangi bir şekildeki davranış veya muameleleri ifade etmek için kullanılmaktadır. Şiddet dövme, yaralama, öldürme, tecavüz şeklinde olabildiği gibi, sözlü, duygusal veya zihinsel olarak da görülebilmektedir (Akşit, 2004, ss. 17-18).

Şiddet' in farklı tanımları bulunmaktadır. Sosyal antropolog David Richs şiddetin kullanıldığı yere göre alttan alta değişiklik gösterdiğini savunmaktadır (İşcan & Demirergi,

1994, s. 90). "Parkin'e göre şiddet bir yandan fiziksel zor yoluyla sınırlama ve tahrip, diğer yandan da bu fiziksel zorun hukuk ötesi olarak değerlendirilmesi anlamlarını taşımaktadır. Şiddetin anlamı açıkça kurumlaştırılmış meşruluk sorunlarını gerekli kılar; diyelim görevlerini sergileyen gardiyanlar tarafından uygulanan fiziksel kural, yasa önünde şiddet olarak adlandırılmaz. Fakat eğer gardiyanlar, bir şekilde belirli idare standartlarının ötesine geçmiş bulunursa, şiddet haline gelir" (İşcan & Demirergi, 1994, s. 91).

Şiddeti çeşitlendirmek mümkündür. Kadına yönelik şiddet, çocuklara yönelik şiddet, aile içi şiddet bunlara birer örnek teşkil edebilmektedir. Bu şiddet olayları medyada da yer almaktadır. Burada önemli olan nokta bu haberlerin medyada yer alması değil, bu haberlerin medya tarafından nasıl ele alındığıdır.

Medyanın zaman içerisinde ticari açıdan büyük kar ve zararların olduğu şirketler haline gelmesi ile bazı etik değerlerin göz ardı edildiğini söylemek mümkündür. Gazetelerde ve dergilerde okuyucunun tüketici-müşteri olarak görülmesi, televizyonların toplumu bir pazar ya da piyasa olarak algılaması etik değer ve ilkelerin bazen dikkate alınmamasına yol açmıştır (Oktay, 1996, s. 4). Günümüzde özellikle gelişmiş ülkelerden gelişmekte olan ülkelere doğru yaşanan tek yönlü akış, medyanın içeriğini de etkilemiştir. Dolayısı ile şiddetin tüm programlarda sıkça yer bulduğu, haber programlarının magazinleştiği, cinselliğin ön plana çıktığı, yasal düzenlemelerin yetersiz, regülasyonun gevşek, rekabetin yoğun yaşandığı, kalabalık ve oldukça hareketli bir medya endüstrisinin doğuşu hız kazanmıştır (Öksüz, 2003, s. 182).

Televizyon kitle iletişim araçlarının en önemlisi olarak kabul edilmektedir. Kamuoyunun oluşumunda önemli görevler üstlenmektedir. Göze ve kulağa hitap ettiği için birçok açıdan halka ulaşmak için televizyon kullanılmaktadır (Gönenç, 2002, s. 155). Bu bağlamda televizyonda yer alan haberlerin içeriğine de dikkat etmek gerekmektedir.

Şiddeti üç odaklı değerlendirmek mümkündür. Bunlar: şiddeti bireysel yönden tanımaya yarayan, şiddet davranışını doğuştan gelen bir güdü olarak temellendiren psikolojik yaklaşım, şiddetin toplumsal çevre sonucu kazanıldığını söyleyen toplumsal yaklaşım ve yansıttığı şiddet odağı nedeniyle medya'dır (Şirin, 2002, s. 35). İnsan davranışı üzerinde olumlu ve olumsuz etkileri bulunan medyanın, şiddet içerikli görüntülere yer vermesi özellikle gençleri ve çocukları olumsuz yönde etkilemektedir. Medyanın insan davranışları üzerinde olumsuz etkisinin neden olduğu davranış bozuklukları ile ilgili olarak Amerikalı medya etikçisi Luis Day, birkaç örnekle bunu açıklamaya çalışmıştır. Bunlar: NBC'de Eylül 1974'de "Born Innocent" isimli film televizyonda yayınlandıktan sonra, California'da dört genç tarafından dokuz yaşında bir kız çocuğuna saldırılmıştır. Saldırganlar suçu işlemeden önce televizyonda bu filmi izlediklerini ve tecavüz sahnesini mahkemede tartıştıklarını kabul etmişlerdir. Bir diğer örnek ise 1980 yılında yirmi sekiz yaşındaki David Rdmis'in televizyonda gösterilen "Deer Hunter" filmindeki Rus Ruleti sahnesini taklit etmesi sonucu yaralanmasıdır. Bu filmden etkilenerek kendini yaralayan en az yirmi dokuz kişiden daha söz edilmektedir (Özkaya, 2002, s. 415). Bu örneklerden de anlaşılacağı üzere, izleyiciler televizyonlardaki programları örnek alıp, onları taklit etme yoluna gitmektedirler.

Televizyon ile şiddet arasındaki ilişkiyi inceleyen çok sayıda araştırma bulunmaktadır. Nabi Avcı televizyonda yayınlanan ve şiddet öğesi içeren programların, izleyiciyi özellikle çocukları şiddete özendirdiğini gösteren araştırmaların sonuçları olduğu gibi, tam tersine, bu programların bir tür arınmaya yol açarak, olumlu etkiler yaptığını gösteren araştırmaların olduğunu ifade etmektedir (Şirin, 2002, s. 41). Televizyonun insan üzerinde olumlu etkileri de bulunmaktadır. Televizyonda yer olan şiddet içerikli programları gören izleyicilerin, bu davranışların kişiye ve topluma ne kadar zararlı olduğu bilincine ulaşıp, bu olumsuz davranışı yapmama eğilimi içerisine girebileceğini söylemekte mümkünüdür. Fakat özellikle çocuklar için bu durum söz konusu değildir.

1960'lı yıllarda geliştirilmiş bazı tekniklerden "öğrenme ve taklit etme" konusunda araştırmalar yapılmıştır. İki gurup çocuğa, dört hafta boyunca farklı içerikte programlar izletilmiştir. Şiddet içeren programları izleyen ilk guruptaki çocukların, bir süre sonra oyuncakları parçaladıkları, kaba bir dil kullandıkları ve daha agresif oldukları gözlemlenmiştir. İkinci gruptaki çocukların ise daha hoşgörülü ve işbirlikçi olduğu tespit edilmiştir (Çelenk, 2004, s. 88). Bu bağlamda medyanın doğru kullanıldığında bireyi olumlu yönde eğittiği yanlış kullanıldığında ise olumsuz etkileri olduğunu söylemek mümkündür.

Medya da yer alan şiddet içerikli görüntülerin bireylere etkilerini gözler önüne seren en önemli örneklerinden biri de, 30 Aralık 2006 tarihinde infaz edilen Irak eski lideri Saddam Hüseyin'in medyada yer alan infaz görüntüleridir. İnfaz anında cep telefonu ile çekilen görüntüler kısa sürede medyanın eline ulaşmıştır. Televizyonlarda defalarca gösterilen infaz anı, bu görüntüleri izleyen bireyleri farklı şekillerde etkilemiştir. Bunu görüntülerin ardından yaşanan olaylar ve yapılan eleştirilerle ifade etmek mümkündür.

Sabah Gazetesinin 06.01.2007 tarihli haberinde "Saddam'ın İdam Oyunu: 2 Ölü" manşeti kullanılmış ve Saddam Hüseyin'in televizyonlarda defalarca gösterilen idam cezasını infaz görüntülerinin, çocukları derinden etkilediği. İdamı "oyun zanneden" Pakistan ve ABD'deki iki çocuğun, infaz sahnelerini taklit edince canlarından olduğu, Hindistan'da ise bir genç kızın, Saddam'ın idamına tepki için kendini ipe çektiği, ABD'nin Teksas eyaletinde 10 yaşındaki Sergio Pelico'nun, boynuna ip bağlayarak kendisini ranzasından aşağı bırakınca öldüğü haberleri yer almıştır. Yine aynı tarihli gazetedeki haberde; Pakistan'da "Saddam asmaca" oynayan 9 yaşındaki Mubaşer Ali'nin hayatını kaybettiği, Saddam'ın idamını canlandırmak isteyen Ali'nin haberlerdeki görüntüyü izlediği, ablasıyla oyun oynarken idamı taklit ettiği, Hindistan'da da 15 yaşındaki genç kızın Saddam'ın ölümüne tepki için kendini astığı belirtilmiştir. Bu haberleri aynı tarihli daha birçok gazetede görmek mümkündür. Ayrıca bazı medya kuruluşları özeleştiri yaparak, sorumsuz davrandıklarını belirtmişlerdir. Haber7.com adlı internetteki haber sitesinde 05.01.2007 tarihinde yer alan yazıda, Saddam'ın idamının defalarca televizyonlarda gösterilmesinin intihar vakalarını tetiklediği üzerinde durulmuş ve meydana gelen intihar vakaları belirtilmiştir.

BİA haber merkezinin 09.01.2007 tarihli haberinde "Medya Çocuklar İçin İdamı Olağanlaştırdı" başlığı kullanarak, Prof. Dr. Tüzün ve Yard. Doç. Dr. Çelenk'in medyayı duyarlı olmaya çağırarak, medyanın Saddam Hüseyin'in görüntülerini sürekli yayınlayarak çocukların gözünde ölümü ve ölüm cezasını normalleştirdiği görüşüne yer verilmiştir.

Sabah Gazetesi'nin 06.01.2007 tarihli "Çocuklar Oyun Konusu Yapabilir" manşetli yazısında Yeditepe Üniversitesi Tıp Fakültesi Öğretim Üyesi Prof. Dr. Arif Verimli'nin görüşlerine yer verilmiştir. Verimli, Saddam Hüseyin'in idam görüntülerinin medya organlarında yer almasının büyükler ve küçükler üzerinde ayrı etkiler oluşturacağını ifade etmiştir. "10 yaşın altındaki çocuklar, sosyal yargıları gelişmediği için bu görüntüleri somut olarak algılayıp oyunlarına konu edebilirler. 10 yaşından büyükler de sosyal yargıları biraz geliştiği için, politika ve siyaset konusunda olumsuz fikirler edinecekler" demiştir. Verimli vahşice bir sahnenin hazırlanmış olmasının da adalet kavramının sarsılmasına yol açacağını belirtmiştir.

Çeşitli gazete ve haber sitelerinden alınan ve bu çalışmada yer verilen haberlerde de görüldüğü üzere, Saddam Hüseyin'in infaz görüntülerinin, dünyanın her yerindeki bireyleri özellikle çocukları olumsuz yönde etkilediğini söylemek mümkündür.

5. Medyanın Savaş ve Barışa Etkisi

Demokratik toplumlarda halkın temel bilgi kaynaklarından biri medyadır. Yerel, ulusal ve uluslar arası boyutta meydana gelen olay ve olgularla ilgili olarak topluma haber sunan medya, söz konusu olay ve olguların algılama ve tepki biçimlerinde de etkili olmaktadır (Işık, 2005, s. 116). Medya bireylerin ve dolayısı ile toplumların kanaatlerinin oluşmasında rol oynamaktadır. Bu bağlamda medyada yer alan haberler ve bunların sunum şekilleri önem kazanmaktadır. Çünkü medya bireylerin bilgi, kanaat, tutum, duygu ve davranışları üzerinde büyük oranda bir etkileme gücüne sahiptir. Medyanın siyasal, ekonomik ve sosyal yapı ile ilişkileri bulunmaktadır. Medyanın özellikle de televizyonun, vatandaşlara gönderilecek olan verilerin tirajını yapmada üstlendiği rol, medyayı kamuoyunu yönlendirme de birinci sıraya koymaktadır. Bu durumda televizyon siyasal sistem ile vatandaşların tümü arasında sürekli bir arabuluculuk görevi yapmaktadır (Gönenç, 2005, s. 60). Bu bağlamda özellikle farklı kültürlerden gelen azınlıklardan oluşmuş toplumlarda ya da savaş ortamından yeni sıyrılmış olan ülkelerde, medyada yer alan siyasi haberlerin toplumu yönlendirmede çok daha etkili olduğunu söylemek mümkündür. Bu ülkelerde medyada yer alan haberler ya da görüntülerin tam da sağlanamamış sükûnet ortamını tekrar bozabileceği ifade edilebilir.

Savaş çelişkinin en belirgin, en açık ve en çarpıcı biçimde yaşanan şeklidir. Bu nedenle birçok sorun savaş dönemlerinde daha açık bir şekilde, gizlenmeden yaşanmaktadır (Tılıç, 2001, s. 176). Bu dönemlerde yaşanan şiddet haberleri ve intihar saldırılarının sunumu önem kazanmaktadır. Çünkü şiddeti besleyen en önemli gıda propagandadır ve şiddetten, savaştan yana olanlar bu propaganda unsurunu büyük ölçüde kullanmaktadır (Bengi, 2003, s. 16). Medyanın bu dönemlerde daha duyarlı olması ve haberleri sunarken ve gösterirken şiddet yanlılarının aleyhine olacak tarzda görüntülere yer vermemesi gerekmektedir. Şiddeti özendirmek, insanları birbirine düşürücü, düşmanlık duygularını besleyen yayınlar yapmak, kan dökülmesine çağrılar çıkarmak, gazeteciliğinin ve dolayısı ile medyanın en temel ilkeleri ile çelişmektedir (Tılıç, 2001, s. 177).

Daha öncede değinildiği gibi medyanın en önemli işlevlerinde biri de kamuoyunu aydınlatmak ve kamuoyunun serbest oluşumunu sağlamaktır. Medya da yer alan görüntüler de bu süreci etkilemektedir. Medyada yer alan haberlerde bireyleri psikolojik olarak etkileyecek ve toplumsal uzlaşmayı yok edebilecek haberlere ve görüntülere yer vermemek gerekmektedir. Savaş halinde bulunan ülkelerin barış sürecine kısa zamanda ulaşmalarında ve barış içinde bulunan ülkelerinde bu huzurlu ve güvenli ortamı korumalarında medyanın rolünün oldukça yüksek olduğunu söylemek mümkündür.

6. Araştırmanın Genel Çerçevesi

6.1. Araştırmanın Amacı

Medyada yer alan haberler kamuoyunu yönlendirerek, bireylerin davranışlarında etkili olmaktadır. Özellikle televizyonlarda yer alan görüntülerin insanları daha çok etkilediğini söylemek mümkündür.

Irak eski lideri Saddam Hüseyin'in idam görüntülerinden yola çıkarak, medyada yer alan görüntülerin insan psikolojisine ve Irak'ta oluşturulmak istenen barış sürecine olumlu ve olumsuz etkilerini ortaya koymak çalışmanın amacını oluşturmaktadır.

6.2. Araştırmanın Hipotezi

Medyada yer alan görüntülerin ülkelerin savaş ve barış ortamlarına etkilerinin ele alındığı çalışmada;

- Irak eski lideri Saddam Hüseyin'in idam görüntülerinin çocuklar başta olmak üzere insanlar üzerinde olumsuz etkilerde bulunduğu,
- Bu görüntülerin Irak'ta sağlanmak istenen barış ve huzur ortamına ters yönde etki yaptığı,
- Medyada yer alan siyasi haberlerin savaş dönemlerinde veya siyasi iktidarın tam olarak sağlanmadığı farklı kültürlerden gelen azınlıklardan oluşmuş ülkelerde toplumu yönlendirmede daha çok etkili olduğu hipotezlerinden hareket edilmiştir.

6.3. Araştırmanın Evreni ve Örneklemi

Araştırmanın evrenini, savaş sonrası yeni bir hükümetin kurulduğu ve buna rağmen şiddet olaylarının bir türlü sona ermediği, farklı kimliklerin bir arada yaşadığı Irak'taki olaylar oluşturmaktadır.

30 Aralık 2006 tarihinde idam edilen Irak eski lideri Saddam Hüseyin'in idam görüntülerinin medyada yer almadan üç ay önce ve üç ay sonra Irak'ta gelişen sivil halka yönelik medyada yer alan intihar saldırıları ve bombalı saldırılar ile bu saldırılarda yaralanan ve ölen insan sayıları ise araştırmanın örnek olayı seçilmiştir. Araştırmanın örneklemini ise 30 Aralık 2006 tarihinden üç ay önceki ve üç ay sonraki Irak haberlerinin manşetlerde yer aldığı Hürriyet gazetesi oluşturmaktadır.

6.4. Araştırmanın Yöntemi

Niteliksel türdeki bu alan araştırmasında, belgesel kaynak derlemesi yapılmıştır. Konuyla ilgili kaynaklar taranarak elde edilen veriler çalışmanın kuramsal kısmında kullanılmıştır. Ayrıca çalışma için Hürriyet Gazetesi'nden elde edilen veriler kullanılmıştır. Bu gazetede yer alan konuyla ilgili haberler belirlenmiş ve manşetler olduğu gibi tablolarda belirtilmiştir. Yaralı ve ölü sayıları gazeteden aynen alınmış ve tablolarda gösterilmiştir.

6.5. Araştırmanın Sınırlılıkları

Araştırmada zaman nedeniyle sadece Saddam Hüseyin'in idam görüntülerinde önceki ilk üç ve son üç ayda meydana gelen olaylar ele alınmıştır. Bu olayların tespitinde gazeteye başvurulmuştur. Bu doğrultuda haberleri elde etmek için Hürriyet Gazetesi kaynak olarak seçilmiştir. Bu gazetenin seçilmesindeki amaç ise; Türkiye'nin tirajı en yüksek gazetesi olmasıdır.

Ayrıca olaylar seçilirken sadece sivil halka yönelik olan ve medyada geniş yer bulmuş saldırılar ele alınmıştır. Diğer olayların ele alınmamansın nedeni; Irak'ta her gün yazılı kaynaklara geçmeyen ve nedeni tespit edilemeyen çok fazla ölüm olayının gerçekleşmesidir. Bu nedenlerle çalışma sivil halka yönelik yapılan intihar saldırıları ve patlamalar ile bunlar sonucunda yaralanmış ve hayatını kaybetmiş insan sayıları ile sınırlı tutulmuştur.

7. Gazeteden Elde Edilen Veriler

Çalışmanın bu kısmında verileri elde etmek için Hürriyet Gazetesi'ndeki konuyla ilgili haberler incelenmiştir. Hürriyet Gazetesi'nin seçilmesinin nedeni Türkiye'nin en yüksek tirajlı gazetesi olmasıdır. Irak eski lideri Saddam Hüseyin'in idamından önceki ilk üç ayda meydana gelen olaylar ve idam edildikten sonraki ilk üç ayda meydana gelen olayların ele alındığı çalışmada elde edilen veriler şöyledir:

Tablo 1: 1–31 Ekim Tarihleri Arasında Hürriyet Gazetesinde Çıkan Haberlerden Elde Edilen Veriler

TARİHLER	MANŞET	YARALI SAYISI	ÖLÜ SAYISI
13.10.2006	MUSUL VE KERKÜKTE ÇATIŞMA	22	12
14.10.2006	IRAKTA İNTİHAR SALDIRISI	-	8
16.10.2006	IRAKTA MEZHEP ÇATIŞMALARINDA ÖLÜ SAYISI 91'E YÜKSELDİ	-	91
17.10.2006	BAĞDATTA ROKET SALDIRISI	7	3
22.10.2006	BAĞDATTA PAZARYERİNDE PATLAMA	5	2
30.10.2006	IRAKTA GÜNÜN KANLI BİLÂNÇOSU	59	69

Saddam Hüseyin'in idamından önceki dönemde Ekim ayında Irak'ta sivil halk yönelik gerçekleşen intihar ve bombalı saldırı eylemleri tabloda belirtilmiştir. Toplam yarılı sayısı 93, ölü sayısı 185'dir.

Tablo 2: 1 – 30 Kasım Tarihleri Arasında Hürriyet Gazetesinde Çıkan Haberlerden Elde Edilen Veriler

TARİHLER	MANŞET	YARALI SAYISI	ÖLÜ SAYISI
1.11.2006	BAĞDATTA ÇOCUK KATLİAMI	19	23
9.11.2006	BAĞDATTA PAZARYERİNDE BOMBALI SALDIRI	27	16
13.11.2006	BAĞDATTA İNTİHAR SALDIRISI	20	16
19.11.2006	BAĞDATTA TERMİNALE SALDIRI	30	6
19.11.2006	IRAKTAKİ SALDIRILARDA ÖLÜ SAYISI 22 YE ÇIKTI	44	22
23.11.2006	BAĞDATTAKİ SALDIRILARDA 150 KİŞİ ÖLDÜ	238	150
24.11.2006	IRAKTA BOMBA YÜKLÜ ARAÇ HAVAYA UÇTU	26	22

Kasım ayında Irak'ta sivil halka yönelik gerçekleşen intihar ve bombalı saldırı eylemlerin belirtildiği tablodan elde edilen verilere göre toplam yaralı sayısı 404, ölü sayısı 255'dir. Bu ayda gerçekleşen olaylar, yaralı ve ölü sayıları ekim ayından daha fazladır.

Tablo 3: 1–29 Aralık Tarihleri Arasında Hürriyet Gazetesinde Çıkan Haberlerden

TARİHLER	MANŞET	YARALI SAYISI	ÖLÜ SAYISI
2.12.2006	BAĞDATTA KANLI GÜN	91	51
5.12.2006	BAĞDATTA BOMBA YÜKLÜ ARAÇLA SALDIRI	25	16
8.12.2006	IRAKTA HAVAN TOPU SALDIRSI	22	25
9.12.2006	BAĞDATIN GÜNEYİNDE SALDIRI	16	8
10.12.2006	BAĞGATTA Şİİ EVLERİNE BASKIN	-	9
12.12.2006	BAĞDATTA İNTİHAR SALDIRISI	151	71
23.12.2006	IRAKTA ÇATIŞMALAR	17	5
25.12.2006	IRAKTA SALDIRILAR	11	12

Irak'ta aralık ayında meydana gelen şiddet olayları, yaralı ve ölü sayılarının belirtildiği tabloda yaralı sayısı 333, ölü sayısı ise 197'dir. Kasım ayına oranla yaralı ve ölü sayısının daha düşük olduğu görülmektedir.

Tablo 4: 30 Aralık – 31 Ocak Tarihleri Arasında Hürriyet Gazetesinde Çıkan Haberlerden Elde Edilen Veriler

TARİHLER	MANŞET	YARALI SAYISI	ÖLÜ SAYISI
30.12.2006	SADDAM'IN İDAMININ ARDINDA İLK SALDIRILAR	58	75
14.01.2007	IRAKTA ŞİDDET	9	15
16.01.2007	BAĞDATTA ÜNİVERSİTE YAKININDA SALDIRI	60	110
18.01.2007	BAĞDATTA SALDIRILAR	10	25
30.01.2007	BAĞDATTA HAVAN TOPU SALDIRISI	5	20

Saddam Hüseyin'in ölümünden sonraki 30–31 Aralık tarihlerini ve Ocak ayını içine alan bu tabloda ise yaralı sayısı 142, ölü sayısı ise 245'dir. Aralık ayına oranla çıkan olaylarda ölü sayısının arttığı görülmektedir.

Tablo 5: 1 – 28 Şubat Tarihleri Arasında Hürriyet Gazetesinde Çıkan Haberlerden Elde Edilen Veriler

TARİHLER	MANŞET	YARALI SAYISI	ÖLÜ SAYISI
3.02.2007	BAĞDATTA PATLAMA	305	130
3.02.2007	IRAKTA BOMBALI SALDIRI	8	1
12.02.2007	BAĞDATTA KANLI SALDIRI	150	71
13.02.2007	BAĞDATTA İNTİHAR SALDIRISI	30	15
17.02.2007	KERKÜKTE BOMBALI ARAÇLA SALDIRI	60	10
18.02.2007	BAĞDATTA ŞİİLERE SALDIRI	127	56
19.02.2007	BAĞDATTA YİNE BATLAMA	127	60
25.02.2007	EL KAİDEYİ KINAYAN İMAMIN CAMİSİNE SALDIRI	65	37
28.02.2007	18 ÇOCUK NEREDE NE ZAMAN ÖLDÜ	30	18

Saddam Hüseyin'in idamından sonraki ikinci ayda meydana gelen olaylarda yaralı ve ölü sayısının diğer aylara oranla büyük ölçüde arttığı görülmektedir. Bu ayda meydana gelen saldırılarda 902 kişi yaralanmış, 398 kişi ölmüştür. Rakamlar idam görüntülerinin medyada yer almadan önceki 3 ayın nerdeyse iki katı oranındadır.

Tablo 6: 1 – 31 Mart Tarihleri Arasında Hürriyet Gazetesinde Çıkan Haberlerden Elde Edilen Veriler

TARİHLER	MANŞET	YARALI SAYISI	ÖLÜ SAYISI
6.03.2007	IRAKTAKİ SALDIRILARDA ÖLÜ SAYISI 90'A YÜKSELDİ	100	90
7.03.2007	KERBELA YOLUNDA 118 KİŞİ ÖLDÜ	200	118
10.03.2007	BAĞDATTA PATLAMA	-	-
11.03.2007	BAĞDATTA SALDIRI	23	41
17.03.2007	FELLUCE'DE SALDIRI	75	6
19.03.2007	IRAKTA NAMAZDA SALDIRI	32	6
27.03.2007	TÜRKMEN KENTİ TELAFERDE İNTİHAR SALDIRISI	150	63
31.03.2007	BAĞDATTA BOMBALI SALDIRI	24	2

Bu ayda meydana gelen saldırılarda 604 kişi yaralanmış, 326 kişi ölmüştür. Bu rakamlarda idam görüntülerinin medyada yer almadan önceki ayladaki rakamlardan çok daha fazladır.

Aşağıdaki tablolarda idamdan önceki üç ay ve sonraki üç ay boyunca Irak'ta, sivil halka yönelik düzenlenen intihar saldırılarının ve bombalı saldırıların sayısı ve bu saldırılarda yaralanan ve ölen kişi sayıları toplu halde verilmiştir. Bu veriler aylar arasındaki farkı açıklamada daha da yardımcı olacaktır.

Tablo 7: İdamdan Önceki 3 Ay Süresindeki Ölü ve Yaralı Sayıları

AYLAR	OLAY SAYISI	YARALI SAYISI	ÖLÜ SAYISI
EKİM	6	93	185
KASIM	7	404	255
ARALIK	8	333	197
TOPLAM	21	830	637

Tablo 8: İdamdan Sonraki 3 Ay Süresindeki Ölü ve Yaralı Sayıları

AYLAR	OLAY SAYISI	YARALI SAYISI	ÖLÜ SAYISI
OCAK	5	142	245
ŞUBAT	9	902	398
MART	8	604	326
TOPLAM	22	1648	969

8. SONUÇ

Diğer bir adı da kitle iletişim araçları olan medya, var olduğu günden beri bilinçli ya da bilinçsiz olarak toplumu etkilemektedir. İnsan yaşamı üzerinde geniş bir yere sahip olan medya, insanların yaşam tarzlarından, kıyafetlerine, siyasi tercihlerinden, konuşma tarzlarına kadar hayatlarının her köşesinde karşısına çıkmaktadır.

Toplumları yönlendirmede çok fazla bir güce sahip olan medya da yer alan şiddet içerikli görüntüler ve haberler bireyleri olumsuz yönde etkilemektedir. Şiddet olayları medyada yer almalıdır. Fakat burada önemli olan nokta bu haberlerin medyada yer alması değil, bu haberlerin medya tarafından nasıl ele alındığıdır. Ticari açıdan büyük kar ve zararların olduğu şirketler haline dönüşen medya sektöründe, bazen haberde uyulması gereken etik ilkeler ihlal edilerek şiddet içerikli görüntü ve haberlere yer verilmektedir. Özellikle göze ve kulağa hitap eden bir kitle iletişim aracı olan televizyonda yer alan programlara, bu açıdan daha çok dikkat edilmelidir.

Medya demokratik toplumlarda halkın temel bilgi kaynağıdır. Kamuoyu adına denetim ve eleştiride bulunma, kamuoyunu aydınlatma ve kamuoyunun serbest oluşumunu sağlama görevlerini de üstlenen medyanın, bir anlamda ülkelerin siyasi yapısı ve huzur ortamları açısından da etkili olduğunu söylemek mümkündür. Özellikle savaş dönemlerinde ya da iç savaşın yaşandığı, siyasi iktidarın tam olarak sağlanmadığı farklı kültürlerden gelen azınlıklardan oluşmuş ülkelerde, medyada yer alan siyasi haberlerin, toplumu yönlendirmede daha çok etkili olduğunu ifade etmek mümkündür.

Irak eski lideri Saddam Hüseyin'in infaz görüntülerinin medyada yer almasından yola çıkarak, medyada yer alan görüntülerin ülkelerin savaş ve barış ortamlarına etkilerinin ele alındığı çalışmada;

- Irak eski lideri Saddam Hüseyin'in idam görüntülerinin çocuklar başta olmak üzere insanlar üzerinde olumsuz etkilerde bulunduğunu söylemek mümkündür. Gazetelerden elde edilen veriler doğrultusunda bu görüntüleri izleyen dünyanın farklı yerlerindeki çocukların taklit yolu ile kendilerini öldürdükleri, bu durumu en iyi şekilde ifade etmektedir.

- Bu görüntülerin Irak'ta sağlanmak istenen barış ve huzur ortamına ters yönde etki yaptığı tablolardaki olay, ölü ve yaralı sayılarının, idam görüntülerinin medyada yer almasından sonra daha çok arttığı ile ispat edilmeye çalışılmıştır. Olay sayısında çok fazla artış yoktur. Fakat olayların boyutlarının ve sivil halka verdiği zararların bu görüntülerin yayınlanmasından sonra daha da arttığını söylemek mümkündür.

- Medyada yer alan siyasi haberlerin savaş dönemlerinde veya siyasi iktidarın tam olarak sağlanmadığı farklı kültürlerden gelen azınlıklardan oluşmuş ülkelerde toplumu yönlendirmede daha çok etkili olduğunu, Saddam Hüseyin'in idam haberlerinden sonra gelişen olaylar ve boyutlarına bakarak ifade etmek mümkündür. Çünkü bu görüntülerin medyada yer alması ile ülkede bulunan farklı etnik kökendeki vatandaşlar arasındaki çatışmaların daha farklı boyutlar kazandığı, tablolarla gösterilen idam haberlerinden sonraki üç aydaki manşetlerin içeriğinden de anlaşılabilmektedir.

Kaynakça:

Akşit, G. (2004). Açılış konuşmaları. RTÜK (Der.), *Medyada şiddete duyarlılık paneli kitabı* (ss. 17-25). Ankara: RTÜK Yayınları.

Avşar, Z. (2003). Terör haberleri ve medya. RTÜK (Der.), *Medya ve polis paneli kitabı* (ss. 13-15). Ankara: Gökçe Ofset.

Avşar, Z. (2004). Medyada yoğunlaşma ve şeffaflaşma: Yasal düzenlemeler, beklentiler, sorun alanları. *İletişim Araştırmaları Dergisi, 2*, 88-113.

Bengi, H. (2003). Terör haberleri ve medya. RTÜK (Der.), *Medya ve polis paneli kitabı* (ss. 15-17). Ankara: Gökçe Ofset.

Can, A. (2001). Demokrasi ve medya ilişkisi. *Maltepe Üniversitesi İletişim Fakültesi Dergisi, 1*, 149-165.

Çelenk, S. (2004). Medyada şiddet ve kadın. RTÜK (Der.), *Medyada şiddete duyarlılık paneli kitabı* (ss. 83-92). Ankara: RTÜK Yayınları.

Gezgin, S. (2005). Küreselleşmenin medya ve toplum üzerine etkileri. *İstanbul Üniversitesi İletişim Fakültesi Dergisi, 22*, 9-13.

Gönenç, Ö. (2005). Medyanın toplum üzerine etkileri. *İstanbul Üniversitesi İletişim Fakültesi Dergisi, XXI*, 57-63.

Gönenç, Ö. (2002). Medyanın kamuoyu oluşturmadaki etkisi. *İstanbul Üniversitesi İletişim Fakültesi Dergisi, XIV*, 151-157.

Haber7com. (2007, 19 Ekim). Biz de dahil sorumsuz yayıncılığın sonu. http://www.haber7.com/haber.php?haber_id=209419 (Son erişim 10.03.2007).

Işık, M. (2005). Medya ve demokrasi paradoksu: Medya yoluyla demokrasinin tehdit edilmesi. *Selçuk İletişim Dergisi, 4*, 115-121.

İrvan, S. (2002). *Medya, kültür, siyaset.* Ankara: Alp Yayınevi.

Nalçaoğlu, H. (2003). Medya ve toplum ilişkisini anlamak üzerine bir çerçeve. Alankuş, S. (Der.), *Medya ve toplum* (ss. 42-56). İstanbul: İletişim Vakfı Yayınları.

Oktay, E. (1996). Medya neden yeniden yapılanmalı? *Gazi Üniversitesi İletişim Fakültesi Dergisi, 3*, 1-7.

Özmen, K. (2006). Medya çocuklar için idamı olağanlaştırdı. http://www.bianet.org/2006/11/01_c/90044.htm (Son erişim 02.03.2007).

Öksüz, S. (2003). *Küreselleşmede nasıl bir dünya düzeni.* Ankara: Star Ajans Matbaacılık.

Özkaya, I. (2002). Medya ve toplum: Anti sosyal davranışlar ve medya ilişkisi. *İstanbul Üniversitesi İletişim Fakültesi Dergisi, XIII*, 411-428.

Sabah. (2007, 6 Ocak). Çocuklar oyun konusu yapabilir. http://www.sabah.com.tr/2007/01/06/gnd107.html (Son erişim 12.03.2007).

Sabah. (2007, 6 Ocak). İdam oyunu: 2 ölü. http://www.sabah.com.tr/2007/01/06/gnd104.html (Son erişim 12.03.2007).

Severin, W., Tankard, J. Wr. & James W. (1994). *İletişim kuramları: Kökenleri, yöntemleri ve kitle iletişim araçlarında kullanımları.* A. A. Bir & S. Sever, (Çev.). Eskişehir: Anadolu Üniversitesi Yayınları.

Şirin, R. M. (2002). Televizyon, şiddet içerikli haber öyküleri ve çocuk. *Radyo ve televizyonlarda şiddet içerikli haberlerin sunumunun toplum üzerine etkileri sempozyumu*, Ankara, 35-46.

Tılıç, L. D.(2001). *2000'ler Türkiye'sinde gazetecilik ve medyayı anlamak*. İstanbul: Su Yayınları.

Vural, M. (2000). Medyanın kültürel kalkınmayı sağlama ve eğitim işlevi. *İstanbul Üniversitesi İletişim Fakültesi Dergisi, X*, 105-113.

"Near And Far": The Iraq War on North Cyprus Press

Nurten Kara
Faculty of Communication and Media Studies,
Eastern Mediterranean University
nurten.kara@emu.edu.tr

Melek Atabey
Faculty of Communication and Media Studies,
Eastern Mediterranean University
melek.atabey@emu.edu.tr

Cyprus represents one of the most problematic areas in the world. Today, there exist two *de facto* mini-states in Cyprus: Republic of Cyprus, which is recognized internationally and recently became the full member of the EU, and Turkish Republic of Northern Cyprus (TRNC), which is not recognized by any state other than Turkey. Cyprus's relations with the outside world have been shaped profoundly by the chronic dilemma of the island's political identity. Both communities are very much politicized about, and immersed in the conflict. The Cypriot people's preoccupation with the problem can be explained mainly with the unresolved and complex nature of the problem. On the other hand, there appears to be little public debate, if any, in both communities on the way in which the problems of Cyprus are related to the international power relations, other international matters and conflicts.

The central concern of this study is to examine the ways in which the North Cyprus press reported the Iraq War between 20 March 2003 and 1 May 2003, the period which starts with the invasion of Iraq by the American-led multinational forces, and stops with the announcement of the US president that ends major military operations in Iraq. Our research questions are as follows: How does one of the main international crisis areas' national media see and represent the Iraq war? What are the ways in which major global crises are made "meaningful" and "relevant" to the local reader? To what extent does the foreign reporting on North Cyprus news media generate information about the world that would enable the North Cyprus community to operate in the newly defined world of increasing political and economic globalization and to make sense of their own problem within the context of international developments? The news coverage of the Iraq War by the Turkish Cypriot newspapers was overshadowed by the debates on the UN Annan Plan on Cyprus, the entry of Cyprus Republic to the EU without finding a solution for both communities on the island, and the opening of the gates between Greek and Turkish parts. Due to the intensity of the above mentioned local developments, the attention that the war received by the North Cyprus press faded away after the early days of the bombings.

This study revolves around the argument that although much of the foreign news coverage depends heavily on news agencies for copy, the newspapers connect their readers to these events by inserting local perspectives and angles to the story. The coverage, orientation and framing of news by the mass media of a specific society, when dealing with international subject material, are predisposed by the circumstances that are prevalent within that society. As a country that has historically suffered from colonialism, imperialism, war and conflicts, the North Cyprus reads and interprets distant conflicts and wars through its own experience.

Foreign News on North Cyprus Media

There are 10 daily and 3 weekly newspapers in Turkish, 1 in three languages (Turkish, Greek and English) and 2 daily newspapers in English aimed mainly at ex-patriots.

Almost all foreign news in North Cyprus media is received

from Turkish Cypriot news agency TAK, which receives international news items from Anatolian Agency in Turkey. The news taken from AA is subject to another selection and editorial process by TAK's reporters according to the news criteria based on local and regional concerns. In some newspapers there is no separate page or a section called as "Foreign or International News". When one looks at their online pages, there is no subheading called as "Foreign News", and foreign and international news appear in "Home News" sections. Most newspapers in North Cyprus do not even have their own reporters let alone employing foreign correspondents since they receive both their home and foreign news from TAK agency. In this sense Turkish Cypriot press depend on this "borrowed news" coming mainly from Turkey, whose news agencies also depend on big international news agencies.

Kıbrıs with the circulation of 12.500 and *Afrika* with the circulation of 2.500 are chosen for the analysis because they are the first two widely circulated, influential, elite newspapers and agenda-setters for important debates in the North Cyprus public sphere. However, the ownership and the ideological stance of these newspapers are different. *Kıbrıs* belongs to Kıbrıs Media Group, which is owned by Turkish Cypriot businessman, Asil Nadir. The newspaper has a right-wing liberal political perspective and supporting the present governments' policies on Cyprus issue. The owner of *Afrika* is its leading journalist-writer, Şener Levent.[1] It has an alternative, radical and left-wing stance. In terms of the revenues, as being part of the most profitable media company in North Cyprus newspaper the main financial source of *Kıbrıs* come from this group and the advertisements it publishes. *Afrika*, on the other hand, depend mostly on the revenue it gets from its sales and receives very little adverting. *Afrika* has a small team of journalists, composed of 5 compared to that of *Kıbrıs*, which are 26. The differences in the nature of the ownership and in the revenue and human resources of both newspapers influence the selection and the presentation of the news (Eda Hançer, 2006) This together with their different ideological position are reflected also in the style, the content and the discourse of their foreign news coverage.

The Analysis

This study focuses on the initial *official war period* – 20 March 2003–1 May 2003. The main focus of the analysis is the individual news article but editorials related to the war were also evaluated to get deeper insights into the coverage of the event. Hard copies of the newspapers under our investigation were evaluated using the Eastern Mediterranean University Library newspaper archives. Out of 268 news articles in total, 153 news articles were in *Kıbrıs and* 115 news articles in *Afrika*. There were 18 editorials in *Kıbrıs* and 68 editorials in *Afrika* on the Iraq war.

Main frames that the analysis was concerned included[2]:

1. Military conflict (troops, equipment, combats, maneuvers, security)
2. Human interest (stories of individual people, celebrities)
3. Violence of war (losses, death toll, human suffering)
4. Reactions to the war, anti-war and anti-American protests
5. Diplomatic meetings, visits, press conferences of the politicians
6. Causes of the war (who or what caused the war)
7. Consequences of the war (economy, security, health, environment)
8. Humanitarian aid (food, money, health)

These frames were evaluated also according to their global/international or national/local angle. However, the boundaries between international/foreign news and national/home news in Turkish Cypriot newspapers are not clearly defined. This is not only because of the professional reasons we have mentioned earlier. It is related also to the nature of the Turkish part. Although TRNC declares itself as an independent state it is politically and economically dependent on Turkey, so news related to Turkey constitutes both foreign and home. Also, the news related to the Greek part is both foreign and home news because two parts have economic, cultural and political interactions.

Despite the difficulty of defining foreign and home news, the concept of framing was still found to be useful. The concept of framing refers to the "specific properties of . . . [a] narrative that encourages those perceiving and thinking about events to develop particular understandings of them" (Entman, 1991, p. 7). As "mentally stored principles for information processing" (Entman, 1991, p. 7), frames offer ways of explaining, understanding and making sense of events.

After finding out the quantity of these frames we have carried out a detailed analysis by focusing on the headlines and the subheadings of the news articles. As Teun A. van Dijk (1988) points out, headlines are important elements in analyzing the news. They attract the attention and give the main theme, but more than that they form macrostructures which serve as crucial strategic cues in controlling the local understanding of the subsequent text. Despite the fact that all Turkish Cypriot newspapers use the same news which is received from TAK news agency, the headlines reflect different presentation and discourse. We have also looked at the opinion-columns of the newspapers on the war. They enabled us to see the views and opinions about the

1 After the court decision which seized all property and income of Avrupa due to Şener Levent's critics on the then TRNC president Rauf Raif Denktaş, Sener Levent decided to open a new firm in order to continue publishing the newspaper. The name of the newspaper has also changed as Africa since 15 December 2001. Although the real owner of the firm is Sener Levent, Ali Osman Tabak appears as the official owner of the newspaper in order to eliminate any further political and financial pressures on the newspaper (Eda Hançer, 2006).

2 Research on Iraq war use similar frames with variations depending on the case studies. See Alozie, E. C. (2006); Christie, T. (2006); Dimitrova, D. V. and Strömbäck, J. (2005); Lee, S. T. (2006).

relationship of the war and Cyprus, which one cannot find openly in the news articles. It is important to note that there are no editorials in Turkish Cypriot newspapers. It is "obvious that opinions and ideologies also have prominent social, political and cultural functions. Thus, in our case opinions and ideologies are expressed in the socially and culturally relevant genre of newspaper opinion columns. The opinion pieces play a role in the formation and change of public opinion, in setting the political agenda, and in influencing social debate, decision making and other forms of social and political action" as described by van Dijk (1996) The initial analysis of the news coverage of the Iraq war found a number of persistent frames and themes on both newspapers though with varying style, importance and emphasis. The recurrent themes were as follows:

1. The initial shock of the war: the bombings as well as concerns about the future outcomes of the war on Cyprus' economy and politics.
2. The relationship between the war and Cyprus (Turkey and the USA, involvement of Turkish and Greek sides, outcomes of the war for the island etc.), which constituted a large portion of the whole coverage.
3. Anti-war stance, which appears particularly in the content of the opinion columns.

Reporting the First Biggest War of the 21st Century

The 2003 Iraq War, termed "Operation Iraqi Freedom" by the US administration, began on 20 March. The first news in the newspapers about the military operations in Iraq appeared on the 21 March. However, the war and its possible consequences for the island were discussed months before the war started. Although the pre-war news is beyond the scope of the present analysis, we have considered also the news few days before the first day of the war. *Kıbrıs* and *Afrika* put emphasis on the consequences of the war for North Cyprus. The headline of *Kıbrıs* reads *"The strike of the war to the tourism"* (20 March, *Kıbrıs*) while *Afrika* says *"Kıbrıs is tied to Iraq"* (18 March, *Afrika*)

As far as the front pages of the two newspapers are concerned, *Kıbrıs* covers the war with a more global angle than *Afrika* on its front page. The first days of the war appeared on the front pages of *Kıbrıs* with a focus on the bombings, combats and the violence of the war.

On the other hand, *Afrika* put more emphasis on the Iraq war with regard to its outcomes for North Cyprus concerning such issues as the unification, the Annan Plan the referendum, Turkey and the USA, the EU, etc. On the 21 March *Kıbrıs* reads *"Iraq Under Intensive Fire"* on the front page and followed inside by news on the security measures and how the economy was to be influenced by the war. *Afrika* on 21 March reads *"Alarm also in Cyprus: The Iraq war dropped Cyprus from the top ranks of the world agenda"*. In the following pages we read news on the outcomes of the war for North Cyrus tourism sector. *Kıbrıs* on 23 March headline reads *"Bombing continues"* and also reports the reactions of Turkish Cypriots to the war and on 24 March *"The target is Baghdad"*. The second major difference between the newspapers is the variety of the news stories and the use of photographs, which were more in *Kıbrıs* than in *Afrika*. Both newspapers covered similar news stories on the war but their editorial preferences for the front page news stories differed in terms of the global and local news angle on the war. *Kıbrıs* gave more prominence to the war as it was while *Afrika* connected the war to the Cyprus problem especially in the front page news. *Afrika* differs from *Kıbrıs* also in the way it links the war to the Cyprus problem by cynical and humorous comments put above and below the fold. For example, the news headline below the fold reads: *"The Yankee is Coming to us too: Our airfield, airports and ports will be opened to the USA and Britain"* On the same page, *Afrika* makes an interesting analogy between Cyprus and Iraq and between Saddam and the then North Cyprus leader Denktaş. *"North Cyprus opened everything to the American and the English. Are those, who are going to save Iraq from Saddam coming*

21 March 2003

"Alarm also in Cyprus"

"Iraq Under Intensive Fire"

22 March 2003

Fiasco in Cyprus, shock in Iraq"

"The War will be hard and long"

Figure 1: ***Kıbrıs*** **and** ***Afrika*** newspapers on 21 and 22 March 2003

23 March 2003 **24 March 2003**

"The Yankee is coming to us too" " Bombing continues" " Threat by the EU" "The Target is Baghdat"

Figure 2: ***Kıbrıs*** **and** ***Afrika*** newspapers on 23 and 24 March 2003

also here to save us from Denktaş?" (21 March, *Afrika*). Another difference between *Kıbrıs* and *Afrika* was the placement of the war news in their inside pages. *Kıbrıs* had a special page under the title of "foreign news" while Iraq war news appeared on almost every odd page of *Afrika*. The news stories on the destruction, the violence and the suffering of civilians that was caused by the war in Iraq were taken mostly from the news agencies, others were taken either from Turkish newspapers or Greek Cypriot newspapers, but both newspapers showed also their own emotions, reactions and concerns about these events.

While the economic impact of the war on North Cyprus, Turkey and other countries gained a great deal of attention in *Kıbrıs*, *Afrika* was more concerned on the security issues. News and comments dealt with the short and long term economic and political impact of the war on Cyprus. During the first days of the war *Kıbrıs* mentioned the impact of the war on the tourism and economy of North Cyprus through the views of the experts and also *vox populi*. *Kıbrıs* also reports on the donations and loans provided or cancelled by the USA to other countries, the possible investments in restructuring of Iraq after the war, and previous depths of Iraq. Compared to *Afrika*, *Kıbrıs* mentions more the impact of the invasion on the foreign currency and stock exchange rates and oil prices. *Afrika*, however, mentions the impact of the war on the Greek part, which appear on the news items taken from Greek Cypriot newspapers.

Despite these differences in reporting the news on Iraq war, both newspapers adopted a conflict/war news framework when covering the war. The war news/journalism focuses on the conflict, visible effects of war (casualties, dead and wounded, damage to property) and on what the elites say about war. Both newspapers gave extensive coverage on the military operations and the destruction caused by the war. There were 15 news items in *Kıbrıs* and 18 in *Afrika* on the violence of the war, which included news on the bombings, the losses, the death toll and the destruction of the war. The tone of this type of news appears to be on the side of civilian Iraqi people. *Kıbrıs* newspaper covered these stories with more verbal and visual space than *Afrika* did. The economic impact that Iraq faced was also covered. Diplomatic meetings, press conferences and declarations of the politicians and diplomats on the war provided an important source of information. In addition to the news from the war front, the invasion was also reported through the official statements on the relationships between Turkey and the USA, Turkey's possible involvement in the war, and the political and economic outcomes of the war for different ethnic and religious groups.

The Anti-War Stance

Both newspapers expressed their view that the war in Iraq will have dire consequences for Cyprus and the Middle East. Accounts and commentaries dealt with the short- and long-term impact of the war. The anti-war stance and criticism towards the USA and Britain was more visible in the opinion columns. The opinion columns on *Afrika* (68 items) and *Kıbrıs* (18 items) expressed their reactions and feelings about the war in a highly critical manner. Although the opinions on *Afrika* shared similar concerns and opinions with those in *Kıbrıs,* some of them were more blunt and emotive in reacting towards Anglo-American forces and the tragedies of the war. The frames of 86 opinion columns about Iraq War on the *Afrika* and *Kıbrıs* have similar frames with news articles, though they had a much more critical stance towards the war.

One comment which came forward repeatedly in almost all articles of *Kıbrıs* and *Afrika* is that the Iraq war is part of an imperialist game and of power tricks in the Middle East designed mainly by the USA and Britain. It has been argued that the attack would enable the Anglo-American influence on the Middle East and in the region and subjugate the area by controlling its natural resources thereby imposing political and economic implications.

In most opinion columns, Iraq war was defined as part of an imperialist strategy of the USA to gain control over the energy sources in the region. Other countries can get a share from this cake by standing close to America. Some writers were also critical of the parties who consider the war as an opportunity. Another underlying point of these opinion columns was that war cannot be the means of peace and that the USA cannot establish peace. Some columnists also argued that Cypriot people should not be deceived by these tricks and hope anything from the imperialist powers for any kind of solution in Cyprus since it was these countries which paved the way towards the tragedies of Iraqi people. It was argued that the powerful "protectors" cannot protect "Cyprus", considering what has been happening in Iraq.

Speaking from an island that has historically suffered from colonialism, imperialism, war and conflicts, the North Cyprus press remained concerned that those who oppose the USA and the Western role in Cyprus and the Middle East would view the war in Iraq as an instrument of new imperialism and domination.

Cyprus, Turkey and Iraq Connection

Both newspapers gave attention to the relationship between the USA and Turkey with regard to the war. *Kıbrıs* mentioned the voting by the Turkish parliament on the law to permit Turkish soldiers to enter Iraq and the consequences of the rejection of this law for Turkey. News mentions Bush and Blair's messages to the Turkish government on the involvement of Turkey in Iraq and also Turkish government's reply to these messages. On 12 April, *Kıbrıs* mentioned the voting by the Turkish parliment on the memorandum for Turkish soldiers to enter Iraq and the consequences of the rejection of this note on Turkey. On the other hand, *Afrika* is not as distant and neutral about the relatiponship between Turkey and the war. It is highly critical of the way that Turkey managed the crisis. It covers this criticism on two different days as the front page news. On 22 March the headline of *Afrika* says *"Fiasco in Cyprus, Shock in Iraq"*. On 24 March, the headline on the front page reads as *"The threat by the EU"*.

The comments on this issue appear more intensively in the opinion columns, which refer to the weaknesses of Turkey against American urges. Some columnists blame Turkey for not taking action, and for being a passive observer of the developments in Iraq. Another important point made in the editorials is that Turkey lost the political and economic support of the USA since it refused to take part in Iraq war.

Loosing Connection with Iraq

As the Iraq war continued the Turkish Cypriot journalists seemed to loose their attention mainly because there were important developments concerning the Cyprus problem. Iraq war hardly appeared in both newspapers after 15 April. Even the opinions on the issue stopped. The Iraq war news becomes more and more scarce and dissappear completely from both newspapers after the fall of Baghdat (8-9 April). Despite the ongoing operations and violence in the region, the North Cyprus press turned its head to the internal developments such as the process of unification, the opening of the gates etc.

AFRIKA

Irak değil, Kıbrıs!

Esir mi Turist mi Vatandaş mı?

" Cyprus, not Iraq: Hostage, Tourist or Citizen?"

Figure 3: 30 April 2003, ***Afrika***

It was surprising to find out that even on the 2nd of May, a day after the cease of major operations there was no news even on this development. The sensation and the drama of Iraq were replaced by the excitement over the opening of the gates, and the talks over the referendum for unification. The only time the name of Iraq was mentioned was on 30 April 2003, the day after the gates opened. The front page news on *Afrika* reads *"Cyprus, not Iraq"*, asking if the people queuing in front of the gates are hostages, tourists or citizens. This news story makes an analogy between the situation in Iraq and Cyprus though both cases have their unique characteristics. The reason behind using Iraq may be the psychology of victimizing oneself in a deadlock situation. Here Iraq is used only as a metaphor to explain the suffering and misery of the Cypriots.

Conclusion

The starting point of this study was to explore the ways in which the North Cyprus press connected their readers to the global events- the war in Iraq. Despite the fact that almost all foreign news about the war came from news agencies, journalists used local angles and concerns in framing the war. The study aimed at assessing the ways in which North Cyprus media related news on the war to local and global concerns, in order to provide a better understanding of the reasons and consequences of the war. To achieve this goal, the positions of and the dominant frames used by *Kıbrıs* and *Afrika* in relation to the initial period of the war in Iraq were analyzed. The study found that the destruction, sufferings of the war, and the possible impact of the war on Cyprus dominated the coverage of both newspapers. *Kıbrıs* tended to provide more straight news than commentaries. On the other hand, *Afrika* portrayed the war with a more local angle rather than a global one, providing more analysis in the opinion columns.

We can say that the attention that the Iraq war received from both newspapers faded away after the initial war operations and bombings. Our analysis showed also that the news coverage of Iraqi war was shadowed by local news. The local frames in the Iraq war news reflected the historical, political, economic and cultural sensitivities of Cyprus, which has been one of the unresolved "crisis" and "conflict" places in the world. Despite the differences in style, content and ideology, *Kıbrıs* and *Afrika,* the newspapers under our investigation shared similar frames and words when referring to Iraq war. The differences between two newspapers were led by their different political ideologies, which became more evident in the news articles and opinion columns about the involvement of the island in the war, and about the possible outcomes of the war for North Cyprus in particular, and for Cyprus and the world in general.

References

Alozie, E. C. (2006). International diplomacy and the prelude to the 2003 invasion of Iraq: African news coverage and assessment, *International Gazette, 68*, 449-472.

Christie, T. (2006). Framing rationale for the Iraq War, *International Gazette, 68*, 519-532

Dimitrova, D. V. and Strömbäck, J., (2005). Mission accomplished? Framing of the Iraq War in the elite newspapers in Sweden and the United States, *International Gazette, 5*, 399–417.

Entman, R. (1991). Framing U. S. coverage of international news: Contrasts in narratives of the KAL and Iran Air incidents. *Journal of Communication, 41*(4), 6-26.

Hançer, E., (2006). Kıbrıs Türk basınında sahiplik yapısı ve haber üzerindeki etkileri. *Küresel İletişim Dergisi, 1.* Retrieved 20 September 2007 from http://globalmedia-tr.emu.edu.tr/bahar2006/Lisansustu_Calismalari/index.htm

Hovit, B., (2006). International news agencies and the war debate of 2003, *International Gazette, 68*, 427-447.

Lee, S. T., Maslog C. C., and Kim H. S. (2006). Asian conflicts and the Iraq War: A comparative framing analysis. *International Communication Gazette 68*, 499-518.

Van Dijk T. A. (1988). *News as discourse.* Hillsdale, NJ: Erlbaum, 1988.

Van Dijk, T. A. (1996) Opinions and ideologies in editorials. *Paper for the 4th International Symposium of Critical Discourse Analysis, Language, Social Life and Critical Thought, Athens, 14-16 December, 1995.* Second Draft, March 1996. Retrieved 26 September 2007 from http://www.discourses.org/UnpublishedArticles/Opinions%20and%20ideologies%20in%20editorials.htm

Uzlaşma mı, Kışkırtma mı?

Nükhet Güz
Safiye Kırlar Barokas,
İstanbul Kültür Üniversitesi
n.guz@iku.edu.tr

Safiye Kırlar Barokas,
İstanbul Kültür Üniversitesi
s.kirlar@iku.edu.tr

Giriş

Kadın programları, halkın sesini dinleme ve o sesi kitlelere ulaştırıp genel bir çerçeve içinde halkın sorunlarına ya da özele indirgeyecek olursak kadınların sorunlarına çözüm getirmek amacıyla ortaya çıkmıştır. Bu tür programlar; Yasemin Bozkurt'un "Kadının Sesi" ile gündeme geldi ve tek kanalda gösterime başlayan program, kısa bir süre sonra mantar gibi bir çok kanalda yayınlanmaya başladı. Bu tür programlar; Ayşenur Yazıcı'nın "Yalnız Değiliz" ve Serap Ezgü'nün "Serap Ezgü ile Biz Bize" adı altında en çok izlenen ve tartışılan programlar olarak gündem oluşturdular. Bu programlar, kadınların sorunlarına çözüm bulmak amacından yola çıkar ve bu sorunları masaya yatırır. Zaman zaman bir şenlik içinde süren program, zaman zaman da drama dönüşür. Programlar canlı yayına konuk ve katılımcı izleyicilerden oluşur. Sorunlarını anlatan konuklara izleyiciler doğrudan katılıp görüşlerini bildirirler. Konuklar, aynı bir savcı ya da hakim gibi onları sorgular, zaman zaman haklı bulup onlarla ağlar, zaman zaman da suçlar. Mağdur durumda olan konuk için gözyaşı döküp onu savunurken, birbirleriyle görüş ayrılığına düşüp çatışırlar. Ayrıca; programlarda canlı yayına anında telefonla katılıp görüş bildiren izleyiciler de yer alır.

Bu tür programlar, aile yapısındaki gizlere girdiğinden ve bütün gizler ortaya çıktığından bazı istenmeyen durumlara neden olmuştur. Programlar, birçok soruna çözüm getirmesine karşın, bazılarında istenmeyen olaylar sergiledi. Bunların en önemlilerinden biri, belkide en önemlisi, Yasemin Bozkurt'un "Kadının Sesi" programında yaşandı. Kadının sesi programına koca dayağından bıkan dört çocuk annesi Elazığ'lı bir kadının derdini anlatmasından sonra programda derdini anlatan kadın Elazığ'a döner dönmez kocasının oğluna verdiği bir silahla otobüsten iner inmez öldürüldü. Bunun üzerine program yayından kaldırıldı (www.habervitrini.com/haber.asp?id=174357). Özgür basının rolü, yalnız bilgi sağlamak değil, aynı zamanda bilinç ve en önemlisi genel çerçeveye ulaşma yolunu benimseyerek halkın gözü ve kulağı olmaktır" (www.zmag.org/turkey/291204.html). Halkın sesi kulağı olmak iyi de, halkın sesini toplumlara duyururken ve halkın sorunlarına çözüm getirirken dikkatli davranmak gerekir. Başka bir deyişle kışkırtıcı olmamak gerektiği söylenebilir. Programı yöneten kişinin konukların gizlerini açığa çıkarırken sonucunun nereye varacağını önceden düşünmesi gerektiği kanısındayız. "Kadının sesi" programı yayından kalktıktan sonra Yasemin Bozkurt yeni bir program yapmadı.

Çalışmamızda, Kanal D televizyonunda Esra Ceyhan'ın hazırlayıp sunduğu "Esra Ceyhan'la" programı incelenecektir. Program hafta içi hergün 15.00-17.00 arasında yayınlanmaktadır. Çözümlemesi yapılan bölümde 23 Mart 2007 Cuma ve 26 Mart 2007 Pazartesi günü Müşerref Akay, Yıldız Tezcan'ın iddialarını yanıtladı. Anlatı biçimi içeren program, kişi, zaman ve uzam üçlemesini içerir. Belli zaman dilimleri ve uzamlarında gerçekleşen (Yücel, 1979, s. 13) olayların en önemli kişileri Esra Ceyhan (Sunucu), Yıldız Tezcan (Aktrist-Şarkıcı, Mahmut Tezcan'ın ilk eşi), Müşerref Akay (Aktrist-Şarkıcı, Mahmut Tezcan'ın ikinci eşi) ve programa canlı yayına telefon bağlantısıyla katılanlar oluşturmaktadır. Şu an ayrılmış olsalar da aynı kişiyle ayrı zaman dilimlerinde evlenen iki kadının birbirlerini kışkırtmalarıyla ve medyada gündem oluşturmuşlardır. Bu program, "Dobra Dobra" programında söylenenlere yanıt verip bir sonuca ulaşma amacıyla yapılmıştır. Programda kışkırtmanın mı, uzlaşmanın mı? Ön plana çıktığı çözümlemenin sonunda ortaya çıkacaktır. İncelemeye başlamadan önce programın kısa bir özetini vermekte yarar görüyoruz.

Programın Konusu

Esra Ceyhan'la programında olay, Yıldız Tezcan'ın Orhan Gencebay'la aşk yaşadığı iddiasıyla başladı. Cuma günü Müşerref Akay, katıldığı programda Yıldız Tezcan'ın iddialarını görüntülü dinledi. Olaylar, Yıldız Tezcan, Kanal D'de yayınlanan "Dobra Dobra" programında bir izleyicinin canlı yayına bağlanıp *"sizin evliliğiniz Müşerref Akay yüzünden mi yıkıldı"* sorusuna *"bilmiyorum"* yanıtı vermesiyle gelişti. Müşerref Akay ikinci kez "Esra Ceyhan'la" programına konuk oldu ve sorulara yanıt verdi. Soruları yanıtlarken zaman zaman kızdı, zaman zaman da (çoğu zaman) güldü. Telefonla canlı yayına bağlantılar oldu. İki hafta boyunca magazin dünyasının gündemini oluşturdu.

Esra Ceyhan'la Programının İncelemesi

Telefonla Katılım: Programın Pazartesi günkü bölümüne telefonla altısı kadın, biri erkek yedi kişi katıldı. Erkek konuk, Müşerref Akay'ın üvey oğlu, iki kadından biri Müşerref Akay'ın gelini, diğeri de yeğeniydi. Bunlardan yalnız dört kadın izleyici konuk olarak programa katıldılar. Cuma gününün en önemli telefon konukları da Müşerref Akay'ın üvey oğullarıydı.

Cuma günkü program:	Ömer Tezcan: Yıldız Tezcan'ın büyük oğlu.
Birinci Gün:	Önder Tezcan: Yıldız Tezcan'ın küçük oğlu.

Ömer Tezcan; *"Müşerref hanımın bize bilerek ya da bilmeyerek iyilikleri ve kötülükleri oldu"* sözü üzerine Müşerref Akay çok öfkelendi ve *"Ömer Antalya'ya düğününe geldiğimde havuz başında anlattıklarını sakın unutma...Ben asil bir kadınım bunu unuttum"* diye yanıtladı.

Önder'in canlı yayın telefon bağlantısında daha konuşmasına başlamadan

Müşerref Akay; *"Benim ağzımı sakın açtırmayın, anan da sen de..."*

Önder Tezcan ; *"Ben bilmiyorum, açarsan aç, ama..."* sözünü bitiremez.

Müşerref Akay; *"Açarım, açarsam kaçacak delik ararsın sonra"*

Dışardan kışkırtma; burada dışardan telefonla gelen bir kışkırtma söz konusu. Müşerref Akay, soğukkanlılığını kaybedip, tepkisini kızgınlık ve hiç de yumuşak görüntüsüne uymayan yanıtlarla gösterildi.

Cuma Günkü Program:

Müşerref Akay kışkırtmadan önce → Güler yüzlü, neşeli

Müşerref Akay kışkırtmadan sonra → Öfkeli, gergin

Pazartesi Günkü Program

İkinci gün:

1. Konuk: Beyhan Özgen; Müşerref Akay'ı haklı buldu, geçmiş bir olaydan örnek verdi.

Müşerref hanım, çok mutlu ve neşeli.

2. Konuk: Nurdan Saner; Müşerref Akay'ı haklı buludu. 16 yaşında üvey çocuklarına annelik yaptığı için takdir etti.

Müşerref hanım, çok mutlu ve neşeli.

3. Konuk: Naime Aras; Ne söylediği belli olmadı. Açık değildi, olumsuz konuştu.

Müşerref Akay; kızgın *"Defol pis kadın, beni konuşturmayın"* dedi.

4. Konuk: Zeynep Öztürk; Müşerref Akay'ı hem yaşından, hem de gülmesinden dolayı eleştirdi.

Müşerref Akay kızdı, yanıt vermek istemedi.

5. Konuk: Ömer Tezcan; *"Cuma'dan bu yana Müşerref hanımın yüzde yüz haklı olduğu bir konu var. Babam annemle Müşerref yüzünden ayrılmadı. Babam ayrıldıktan sonra Nazan Ş adında bir hanımla on ay kadar beraber oldu, sonra Müşerref hanımla evlendiler."*

Müşerref hanım mutlu, neşeli sevecen.

6. Konuk: Pınar Saran; *"Müşerref hanımın gelininin annesiyle bir piknikte tanıştık. Benim yeğenimle sizin torununuz Bakırköy'de aynı okula gidiyorlar. Gelininizin annesi; Müşerref hanım torununu söylediği kadar sık görmez dedi. Bunların doğru olup olmadığını sormak istiyorum"*

Konuk çok anlaşılır ve düzgün konuşmasına karşın, Esra Ceyhan ve Müşerref Akay tarafından yanlış anlaşıldı ve konuğu şaşırtarak olay gelinin annesinden çıkarılıp gelinine yönlendirildi. Yanlış anlamanın bilinçli mi yoksa bilinçsiz mi yapıldığı anlaşılamadı.

Müşerref hanım çok kızdı ve öfkelendi.

7. Konuk: Bahar hanım; Müşerref hanımın eski gelini; 6. konuğun sözleri üzerine aradı. Çok üzüldüğünü söyledi. *"Bizi rahat bıraksınlar"* dedi. Müşerref hanım için iyi şeyler söyledi.

Müşerref hanım mutlu.

8. Konuk: Şenay Akyüz; Müşerref hanımın yeğeni, halası için övgü dolu sözler söyledi.

Müşerref hanım, çok mutlu ve neşeli.

	Kışkırtma	Uzlaşma
1. Konuk	yok	övgü dolu/haklı
2. Konuk	yok	övgü dolu/haklı
3. Konuk	kışkırtıcı	yergi dolu/haksız
4. Konuk	kışkırtıcı	yergi dolu/haksız
5. Konuk	yok	övgü dolu/haklı
6. Konuk	kışkırtıcı	yergi dolu/haksız
7. Konuk	yok	övgü dolu/haklı
8. Konuk	yok	övgü dolu/haklı

Müşerref Akay telefondaki konuklar tarafından övüldüğünde mutlu, rahat, sevecen davranış biçimi sergilerken, konukların haksız bulduğu durumlar karşısında öfkelendi ve hırçınlaştı. Televizyonda milyonlarca kişinin karşısında olduğunu unuttu, öfkesine yenik düştü. Müşerref Akay, çok kuvvetli ve mutlu gibi gözükmesine karşın öfkelendiğinde herşeyin altüst olduğu görülür. Gücünü kaybeder, hiddetlenerek yanıtlarında kavgaya dönüşen bir davranış biçimi sergiler. Öfkesini bastıramaz ve ağzından sonradan üzüleceği sözcükler dökülür. Övgü dolu sözler duyduğundaysa anında kimlik değişimi gösterir ve başka bir kişilik sergiler. Bu değişim saniyeler içinde gerçekleşir.

Mutluluk, sevgi, rahatlık, tutku ⇄ Öfke, keder, hırçınlık, tutku

Programdaki davranış biçiminden ve sözcüklerinden, Müşerref Akay, kendini çok beğeniyor. Çok genç ve çok güzel görüyor, çok mükemmel olduğuna inanıyor. Tersi söylendiğinde de kaplan gibi kükrüyor. Eleştiriye açık değil. Richard Sonett'in; Narkisos söyleminden (mitosundan) esinlenilerek; narsizmin içine düşen toplamsal insanı yorumladığı gibi, Müşerref Akay, kendine hayran ve mükemmel olduğuna inanıyor, yaptığı herşey doğru gözüküyor. En küçük bir eleştiriye, büyük tepki gösteriyor (aktaran Tekinalp, 2003, s. 346). Aynı, sudaki kendi görüntüsüne aşık olup onu okşamak isterken düşüp boğulan Narkisos gibi hep kendinin doğru, iyi ve haklı olduğuna inanıyor. Buradan yola çıkılarak televizyonun bir ayna ya da su yansıması olduğu varsayılırsa; televizyon-toplum ilişkisi bağlamında toplumsal gerçekliğin yansıtılma biçimini ya da gerçekliğin saptırılma biçiminin yansıtıldığı görülür. (aktaran Bulck, 1993)

Müşerref Akay → *"Ben bu kadar işi nasıl başarıyorum, ben cimcimemiyim neyim."*

Müşerref Akayın yukarıdaki tümcesinden de anlaşılacağı gibi kendini ne denli sevdiği ve hayran olduğu ortadadır.

Gerçeklik

Gerçekliğin; topluma yansıması, özellikle kadın programlarında göz önüne seriliyor. Gerçekleri giz'leri topluma açılan bireyin, daha sonra toplumun içinde yaşamını önceki gibi sürdürüp sürdüremeyeceği belirsizdir ve ne gibi zorluklar yaşadığını bilmek de pek olası değildir. Gerçekliğin bilinen üç türü vardır. Bunlar nesnel, öznel ve simgesel sosyal gerçekliktir. Nesnel gerçeklik; gerçek dünyayı içerir. Nesnel gerçekliğin biçimlendiği öznel gerçeklik ve simgesel sosyal gerçeklik de insanın ürettiği herşey biçiminde açıklanır (Aktaran Bulck, 1993) Bunların edebiyat, resim, grafik ve televizyon içeriğini kapsadığı düşünülürse televizyon bir simgesel gerçekliği; ünlü kişilerin, sanatçıların imajlarını, onların gizlerini sunmaktadır. Bu gerçekliği aktarırken de yeniden kurgulayarak, özel yaşamı bir kez daha değiştirmektedir.

Müşerref Akay
→ *Konuşursam kaçacak delik ararsın sonra!*
→ *Ömer, Antalya'ya düğününe geldiğimde havuz kenarında bana söylediklerini sakın unutma!*

Gerçeklik ve Belirsizlik

Müşerref hanım, ne biliyor? Söylemediği zaman giz'ler daha çok etkili ve daha çok ilgi uyandırıyor. İnsanları o konu üzerine çekip düşündürüyor. Müşerref hanım konuşursa bir felaket mi yaşanır? İnsanlar kendi kendilerine sorar nedir bu giz? Belki de duysalar söylenmeyen giz, düşündüklerinden çok daha az etkili olabilir. Böyle sonuca ulaşmayan, açıkta bırakılan durumlarda belirsizlikten sözedilir. "Bu boyut bir topluluğun, bilginin yetersiz olduğu veya açık olmadığı, karmaşıklığın varolduğu, değişmezlerin hızlı ve kestirilmez bir biçimde geliştiği durumlar" (Pira, 2004, s. 172) dır. Konuklar açık değiller, yeterli bilgi yok, korkutma ve tehdit var. Ancak sunucu bu durumda Ömer'in Cuma günkü telefon konuşmasında Nazan "Ş" kimdir? Açıklayın diye zorlamasına karşın, Müşerref Akay'ı konuşması için zorlamıyor. Bu da programda hangi olaylara değinilip hangilerine değinilmeyeceğinin önceden kurgulandığını gösteriyor. Programda belirsizlikler başından beri sürüyor.

Yıldız Tezcan: *"Benimle uğraşmasın"*
"Çocuklarımı göstermediler"
"Bana Aliye filmini yaşattılar"
"Müşerref hanım yalan söylüyor"
"Ömer onlarda, Önder bende kaldı"
"Çikolataları, salatalıkları çocuklarımdan sakladı"

Müşerref Akay: *"Çocuklarını görmedi, torunlarını görmedi"*
"Antlaya'ya Ömer'in düğününe gelmedi"
"Onları ben büyüttüm"
"Ona acıyorum, hafızasını kaybetmiş"

Müşerref Akay, kendi aktarmak istediği konuları yanıtlayıp, istemediklerini yanıtlamıyor. Çok sıkışırsa da ona acıdığını söyleyip, hafızasını kaybettiğini iddia ediyor. Hangisi doğru, hangisi yalan söylüyor. Birtürlü çözülemiyor, belirsizlik söz konusu, açıklık yok.

Gerçek mi / Yalan mı → Belirsiz

Olayların oluş biçimi, yaşanmışlığı, toplum için ***giz,*** bunların doğruluğunu ya da yanlışlığını saptamak kolay değil. Anlatı biçimi içinde kişilerin anlattıkları doğrultusunda gerçek olup olmadığı saptanır. Anlatılanların doğruluğu kanıtlanamaz, ancak bize sunulan modellerle değerlendirilir. Norveçli Sosyolog Stein Braten'in öne sürdüğü modeller üzerinde durularak, çözümlemeye bu modellerin de katkısı olacağı görüşündeyiz. Bu modellerle daha önce değinilen karşıtlıklar özdeşleştirilerek kurgulanmaya çalışılacaktır. Modeller; ***"Model güç"*** ve ***"Model zayıf"*** kavramlarını içerir. Belli bir düşüncesi ve kavramları olan aktörler "Model güç"ü simgeler. Bu güçler; "Model zayıf"ların üstünde bir güç kazanıp onları denetimleri altına alırlar. Aynı 5. Konuk Ömer'in *"Bilerek ya da bilmeyerek kötülük yaptı"* tümcesi üstüne Müşerref Akay'ın baskın ve tehditkar tutumundan sonra Ömer'in telefonla katıldığı Pazartesi günkü programda yumuşayıp Müşerref Akay'ı yüzde yüz haklı görmesini Müşerref'i "Model güç" Ömer'i de "Model zayıf" olarak belirler. "Model zayıf"lar gerçeği başkalarının gözüyle algılar ve bunun "Model güç"lülerin görüşlerinin olduğu bilincine varamazlar (Johnson & Mathiesen, 1992, s. 12). Güç mesafesi, bir toplumun bireyleri ve örgütlerinde gücün eşit olmayan bir biçimde dağılımı ile ilgilidir. Güçlüler zayıfların üzerinde baskı oluşturur. Programda, kışkırtmaya neden olduğu bilinen bu "giz" Ekonomik mi? Toplumsal mı? Duyulmaması gereken bir giz'mi? (Pina, 2004, s. 173). Bunların hiçbiri programın sonunda belirlenmedi ve açıklanmadı.

Model Güç	**Model Zayıf**
↓	↓
Müşerref Akay	Ömer Tezcan

Gerçeklik ve Ritüelleşme

Müşerref Akay; bazı yerlerde model güc'ü simgeliyor. Ömer'e telefonda çıkışıp, tehdit ettikten sonra Ömer'in tutum ve davranışları değişir. Başka bir deyişle sözlerinin arkasında duramadan geri çekilir. Ömer'de burada model zayıf'ı simgeliyor. Bunların yanısıra programda gerçeklikle birlikte ritüelleşme de sözkonusudur. Ritüelleştirme toplumsal olay olmaktan çıkarılıp cisimlendirilerek sunma biçimidir (Becker, 1995, s. 629). Televizyon, belirli toplumsal olayları, ya da ünlülerin yaşamlarını yeniden biçimlendirir. Önce bir olaya dikkat çekilir ve olay bir ritüel biçiminde göz önüne serilir. Programda, Yıldız Tezcan'ın evliliğini Müşerref Akay'ın yıkıp yıkmadığını söylemesiyle örgü yumağı açılır, karışır ve olayların içine girildikçe yumak daha da karışır, bir türlü düzeltilemez.

Gerçeklik ve Gündem Oluşturma

Televizyonun toplum üzerinde yoğun bir biçimde etkili olduğu bilinmektedir. Güncel sorunların gündeme gelmesi ve bu sorunların tartışılması aşamasında, toplumdaki bireyler de aktif ya da pasif katılımcı olarak programlardan etkilenmektedir. "İlginç olan medya aracılığıyla elde edilen çözümlerin daha sonraki olaylara örnek teşkil etmediğidir"(Kazancı, 2002, s. 218). Çözüm getiriliyor. Ancak, getirilen böyle çözümlerin ne denli doğru olduğu bilinmiyor. Ayrıca, getirilen çözüm bir uzman kişi tarafından gerçekleşmediğinden, geçerliliğinin ne denli doğru olup olmadığı da tartışılacak bir konudur.

Programlardan etkilenen toplumun tutum ve davranışları değişerek onları yönlendirir. Kitle iletişim araçlarının öneminden yola çıkılarak, araçların etkilerinden oluşan bir kuram, gündem oluşturma kuramından halkın çeşitli güncel sorunların görece önemini algılamasının kökenini açıklamaya çalışan bir iletişim kuramıdır (Mutlu, 1998, s. 148). Programın, kabaca iki hafta kadar sürmesi, yukarda sözü edilen bu olayların iki hafta gündemde kalması, başka bir deyişle gündem oluşturması, ya da gündemi tutması istenilen amaçtı ve bu amaç gerçekleştirildi. Televizyonda sürekli tekrarlanan, üzerinde yorum yapılan olay ve olgular, toplumun gündemi durumuna gelmektedir (aktaran Tekinalp, 2003, s. 355). Kurgulanmış sanal olay yaratarak gündeme gelenler ya da gelmek isteyen ünlüler her an yüzünü her olayla gündeme gelmek isteyen kişiler televizyon için bazı sanal öyküler üretip izleyici kitlenin odak noktası durumuna gelmek isterker (Bulck, 1993, s. 12). Bu sanal öyküler yalnız medya için kurgulanmış öykülerdir. Bunlar ya gündemden düşmek istemeyen ünlüler ya da unutulmuş, ama bir türlü gündeme gelmek için Yıldız Tezcan gibi yaklaşık kırk yıl sonra olmuş olaylardan bir öykü kurgulayıp gündeme gelmeyi başardı. Televizyonculara da yeni bir malzeme çıktığından gündem oluşur. Nazan Şoray ve Orhan Gencebay için de gündem oluşturulmak istendi. Ancak onlardan yanıt gelmeyince gündem oluşturulamadı. Bu öykü kurgulanıp gündem oluşurken, olayların çoğu ya eski zaman diliminde gerçekleştiğinden ya da bir bölümü gerçek olmadığından sözler arasında çelişki yaşanır. "İnsanlar çelişkinin etkisini geniş bir dizi durumunda yaşarken tipik bir çelişki durumu, kişinin tutumuna ters düşen bir davranışta bulunmasını içerir; böylece, kişinin tutumu ile tutarsız davranışı arasında çelişki için bir gizli güç oluşur (Milburn, 1998, s. 169).

Eğlence:

Böylesi kadın programlarının gün içinde ve çoğunluğunu ev kadınlarının oluşturduğu hedef kitlenin daha çok orta ve alt gelir gurubunu gösterir. Bu gurubun eğitimlerinin yüksek olmadığı düşünüldüğünde, izleyiciyi televizyonun başına bağlaması için eğlence ağırlıklı olması gerekir.

Böylece çok reyting alan programda yayında kalma süresini uzatır. TRT'nin yapmış olduğu bir araştırmadan 12:00-18:00 saatleri arasında televizyon izleyenlerin sayısı ilkokul mezunlarının, ünüversite mezunlarının izleme sayısının iki katı olduğu düşünülürse (TRT, s. 122) kadın programlarının hedef kitlesini, orta ve alt gelir düzeyinde, eğitimi yüksek olmayan kadınların oluşturduğunu söylemek olasıdır. Buradan yola çıkarak, böylesi programların da eğlence ağırlıklı olması kaçınılmazdır. Show programları genelde eğlence türü içerikli programlardır. Bunlar, stüdyoda katılımlı gösteri programları olarak bilinir (Aziz, 2006, s. 88). Medyada olup bitenler; bilgi, eğitim ve eğlence arasındaki değişen ilişkilerdir. Eğlence her zaman dayanak noktası gibi görülmüştür (Briggs & Burke, 2004, s. 339). Program, sunucusundan konuklarına kadar ciddi iddialara yanıt vermek üzere kurgulanmış. Ciddi ve üzücü konular açığa çıkarılmak istenmiştir. Ancak, program başlarken müzik ve şarkıyla açılır. Özellikle de hakkında iddialar olan ve onlara yanıt vermek için programa katılan Müşerref Akay, programın başında ve ortasında iddialara yanıt veren zaman zaman gülerken zaman zaman öfkelenen ve ağlayan kimliğinden çıkıp şarkıcı kimliğine bürünüp eğlendi ve eğlendirdi."Sorun televizyonun bize eğlendirici temalar sunması değil, bütün temaların eğlence olarak sunulmasıdır (Postman, s. 99). Buradan, üzücü de olsa, düşündürücü de olsa, eğitici de olsa her temada oynatan ve oynayan bir tutum sergilendiğinin örneklerini de televizyonun temel amaçlarından birinin eğlence olduğu da ortaya çıkmaktadır.

Eğlencesiz / Eğlenceli

Keder / Neşe

Ciddi / Hafif

Programda eğlence-üzüntü, neşe-keder ve hafif-ciddi karşıtlıkları yaşanır. Böylece son yıllarda insanın temel gereksinimini televizyon giderir. Televizyonla her alana girilmiştir. Özellikle evde oturan ev hanımları, işini ve alışverişini televizyon programlarına göre yapmaktadır. Sorulduğunda televizyon izlemekten başka eğlenceleri olmadığını söyleyenler, televizyonu bir eğlence aracı gibi görürler. Yapılan bir araştırma, eğlence programlarının izleyiciler üstünde olumlu etkileri olduğunu gösterir. Eğlence programlarını izleyen kadınların günlük yaşam stresinden, yarışma programları izleyen kadınlara göre daha çabuk kurtuldukları vurgulanmıştır (Anderson, 1996). Eğlendirmek için müzik yapılsa da, kadın programlarında, programa katılan kadınların sorunları çekişmeleri, karşıt düşüncelerden birbirleriyle atışmaları ve konukların üzüntüleri izleyiciler üzerinde hiç de olumlu etki yapmadığı, başka bir deyişle onların çekişmelerinden depresyon yaşadıklarını söylemek yanlış olmayacaktır. Programın yapım biçiminde de uzlaşma içermediğini söyleyebiliriz. Programdaki konuklar ve sunucu, önemli sayılan konular işlenirken birdenbire konulara ara verip şarkı türküyle eğlence başlar, eğlence bittiğinde de hemen önemli konulara dönülür. Bu da yukarıda saptadığımız karşıtlıklarla örtüşmektedir.

Sonuç:

Televizyonda yapılan kadın programları, vatandaşın sesini yansıtan "sorun dinleyen", "sorunlara çare bulan" ve bu "sorunları" toplumun görüşlerine sunan ve onların da görüşlerini alan programlardır. Böylesi programlarda, toplamsal olaylar gündeme getirir. Kadın programları da toplumsal açıdan ilginç olaylarla ilgilenir. Toplum, ünlü kişilerin de sorunlarıyla yakından ilgilidir. Programda, zaman zaman izleyiciler, zaman zaman da programı sunan kişi tarafından olaylara kendilerine göre çözüm getirirler.

Çözümlemesi yapılan "Esra Ceyhan'la" programının konukları telefonla katıldılar. Pazartesi günü sekiz konuğun katıldığı program kadın ağırlıklıydı. Konuklardan yalnız biri, Yıldız Tezcan'ın büyük oğlu Ömer erkek konuk olarak kadınların arasında yer aldı. Ömer'in açığa çıkardığı bir konu; annesiyle babasının boşanmasına Müşerref Akay'ın neden olmadığıydı. Bunun dışında bir çok iddia öne sürüldü, hepsinin de ucu açık kaldı.

Programda yalnız bir uzlaşma görüldü. Yıllardır birbirini görmeyen ve konuşmayan iki kardeş Ömer ve Önder'in telefonla konuşmalarıyla iyi bir ortam oluşturuldu. Belki de bundan böyle kardeşler arasındaki kırgınlık geçip, görüşme olanağını program onlara sunmuş oldu.

Canlı yayındaki telefon bağlantılarında eleştirel yaklaşan kimi konuklar Müşerref Akay'ın kızmasına, öfkelenmesine neden oldular. Başka bir söyleyişle, kışkırttılar. Öfkelenen ses sanatçısı, tam bir kimlik değiştirme modeli oluşturdu. Övgülü sözlerle neşelenirken, sözcükler az da yergi içerdiğinde öfkelendi. Bu da Müşerref Akay'ın kendi içinde saklamaya çalışsa da karşıtlıklar içinde olduğunu gösterdi.

Program sunucusu Esra Ceyhan, istediği olayların üzerine gidip, olayların kesinlikle açığa çıkmasını isterken, Ömer'den "Nazan Ş" nin kim olduğunun açıklamasını isterken, Müşerref Akay'ın "konoşursam kaçacak delik ararsın sonra" tümcesini açıklaması için hiçbir tepki göstermedi. Nazire Dedeman'ın, 15 Temmuz 1994, Umut Vakfı Ortadoğu Etkinlikleri, konulu konferansta "...haber medyasının ise belli bir tarafı savunan bir rol oynadığına sıklıkla tanık oluyoruz"[1]. Medyanın görevinin ateşe körükle gidip onu daha yakıcı yapma ve uyuşmazlığı daha da içinden çıkılmaz bir duruma getirme yerine uzlaştırıcı rol olması beklenir. Söylenmeyen ya da açıklanmayan olaylar, izleyici daha uç düşüncelere yönlendirir.

Programda eski iki ünlü ses sanatçısının arasında olaşan anlaşmazlığa çözüm getiriemedi. Programda az da olsa uzlaşma ve kışkırtma görülmesine karşın, çok büyük olaylara yol açacak kışkırtmalarla karşılanmadı., yeni bir program için başka bir gündem oluşturmak isteyen

1 www.umut.org.tr/etkinlikler/ortadogu_html

sunucu başarılı olamadı. Kanımızca; bunun en önemli nedenlerinden biri ani bir gündem oluşturacak kişilerin gündeme girmek istenmediklerinde kaynaklandığıdır. Uzlaştırıcılık görünen ve üzerinde durulan bir simge biçiminde ortaya çıkarken, gerçekte kışkırtıcılık yokmuş gibi kurgulanmaktadır.

Kaynakça:

Anderson, D. Vd. (1996). Stresfull life events and television viewing. *Communication Research, 23*(3), 243-261.

Aziz, A. (2006). *Televizyon ve radyo yayıncılığı*. Ankara: Turhan Kitapevi.

Becker, K. (1995). Media and the ritual process. *Media Culture and Society, 17*(4), 629-647.

Briggs, A & Burke, P. (2004). *Medyanın toplumsal tarihi.* (Çev. İ. Şener). İstanbul: İzdüşüm Yayınları.

Johnson, J. & Mathiesen, T. (1992). A war in the name of freedom, The Nordicom. In *Review of Nordic Mass Communication Research, 2.*

Kazancı, M., (2002). *Kamuda ve özel kesimde halkla ilişkiler.* Ankara: Turhan Yayınları.

Milburn, M. A. (1998). *Sosyal psikolojik açıdan kamuoyu ve siyaset* (Çev. A. Dönmez & V. Duyan). Ankara: İmge Yayıncılık.

Mutlu, E. (1998). *İletişim sözlüğü* (3. ed.). Ankara: Ark Yayınları.

Pina, A. (2004). *Etkinlik yönetimi*. Ankara: Media Cats.

Televizyon yayınları, kamuoyu araştırması (2003). Ankara: TRT Ofset Tesisleri Basımı.

Tekinalp, Ş. (2003). *Radyo ve televizyon: Camera Obscura'dan Synopticon'a*. İstanbul: Der Yayınları.

Yücel, T. (1979). *Anlatı yerlemleri*. İstanbul: Y.K.Y. www.habervitrini.com/haber.asp?id=174357 (Son erişim, 24.01.2007).

www.umut.org.tr/etkinlikler/ortadogu_html (Son erişim, 2.01.2007).

www.zmag.org/turkey/291204.html (Son erişim, 25.01.2007).

Toplum, Töre Ve "Öteki"

Rengin Küçükerdoğan
Sanat ve Tasarım Fakültesi
İstanbul Kültür Üniversitesi
r.kucukerdogan@iku.edu.tr

Işıl Zeybek
Sanat ve Tasarım Fakültesi
İstanbul Kültür Üniversitesi
i.zeybek@iku.edu.tr

Ölüler Büyük Değişim Yaşasalar Bile 100 Yıl, Dirileri Ayaklarından Çeker.

Karl Marx

Giriş

Bireyler, dünyaya gözlerini açtıkları anda, attıkları ilk çığlıklarıyla başlayan ve ölümlerine kadar geçen süreç içerisinde gerek kişilik özellikleri gerek önyargıları gerekse toplumsal ölçütleri çerçevesinde edindikleri inançları, tutumları ve yaşam biçimleri doğrultusunda diğer bireylerle etkileşim içine girmektedirler. Ancak sözüne ettiğimiz bu etkileşim, her zaman olumlu, uzlaşmaya dayalı, karşılıklı sevgi, saygı ve hoşgörü anlayışını gözeten bir etkileşim değildir. Bireyler her ne kadar aynı toplum içinde yaşasalar da, becerilerini, yeteneklerini, bilgilerini aktarma biçimleri, birbirlerini doğru anlamaları ve algılamaları çok farklıdır. Bu farklılaşma, "ben mi anlatamıyorum, başkalarımı beni anlamıyor", "duygularımı, düşüncelerimi anlatabilmem için ne yapmam gerekiyor", "neden kimse benim düşüncelerimi önemsemiyor", "kendimi doğru anlatabilmem için ne yapmam gerekir" gibi söylemlerin oluşmasına ve gerek kullandığımız yöntemleri gerekse kullandığımız araçları sorgulamamıza neden olmaktadır. Hemen Hemen herkes, başkarıyla etkili iletişim kurduğu, iletişim kurmada başarılı olduğu, diğer bireylerle rahat anlaştığı düşüncesi taşımasına karşın herkesin birbirine karşı sabırsız, anlayışsız, sinirli, saldırgan, dinlemeyen, kendi düşüncesini körü körüne savunan, sorgulamayan, irdelemeyen tutum ve tavır sergilediği gözlemlenmektedir. Amerikan Perdue Üniversitesinin başarısızlığın nedenleri üzerine yaptığı bir araştırma bu gözlemi doğrular niteliktedir. Duygusal yaşam, iş yaşamı ya da toplumsal yaşam söz konusu olduğunda başarısızlığa uğramış insanların yüzde 80'ninin başkarıyla iyi, nitelikli ilişkiler kuramadığı, iletişim kurma konusunda yetersizlikleri bulunduğu ortaya çıkmıştır (Guilane-Nanchez, 2003, s. 7).Böylesi bir durumda iletişim kurma konusunda yetersiz kaldığımız, bilinçli olmadığımız, bilinçli davranmadığımız açıkça gözler önüne sergilenmektedir. Dolayısıyla, neden-sonuç ilişkisini kurmayan, anlaşmazlıklar, hoşgörüsüzlükler ve savunucu iletişim üzerine yapılandırılmış bir etkileşimin varlığı söz konusudur çoğu zaman. Kimileyin bu etkileşim sonucunda ortaya konan, üretilen her türlü tinsel ve tensel dışavurumların ölümle sonuçlanabilen iletişim kazalarına yol açtığı da sıkça görülmektedir. İletişim kazalarına neden olan başlıca etmenler arasında ekinsel-toplumsal gürültü, kalıplaşmış düşünceler, alıcı-verici karşıtlığı, eşduyumsal (empatik) iletişimin kurulamaması, rol ve konum (statü) farklılığı gibi birçok etmeni saymak olasıdır. Bu iletişim kazalarının yaşanmasının temelindeki etmenlerin en önemlilerinden biri de, hergün, her saat kitle iletişim araçlarından duyarak, işiterek ve okuyarak neredeyse kanıksadığımız, sıradanlaştırdığımız haberleri çevreleyen "töre" olgusudur. Uygulayımda yıllardır varolan ancak son dönemlerde gerçekliğini yeni yeni kabul ettiğimiz, duyumsadığımız, tepki verdiğimiz töre cinayetine göz göre göre töreye kurban giden Güldünya aracılığıyla törelerin acımasızlığıyla toplumca yüzleştik. Oyun çağındaki çocukların berdel karşılığında evlendirilmeleri, berdel bozulduğunda öldürülmeleri, küçük yaştaki erkek çocukların cinayet işlemeleri, zorla evlendirilmek istenen kız çocuklarının evden kaçmaları ya da intihar etmeleri... gibi olaylar zinciri bu yüzleşmeyi sağlayan yalnızca bir kaç örnek olay. Bu örnek olaylar bir başka anlatımla töresel etkileşim yaşamımızı o denli çevrelemiş durumdadır ki, TBMM'de bir "Töre Komisyonu" kurulmuştur ve başta TÜBİTAK desteğiyle Dicle Üniversitesi Araştırma Komisyonu olmak üzere birçok komisyonun töresel etkileşim üzerine araştırmalar yapmaya başladığını görmekteyiz. Diyarbakır Dicle Üniversitesinden Doç.Dr. Mazhar Bağlı, çeşitli üniversitelerde psikolog, sosyolog ve antropolog olarak görev yapan 8 kişilik ekibiyle Güneydoğu'daki göç, eşi ölenin kayın-baldızla evlendirilmesi ve intiharla ilgili araştırmalar gerçekleştirilmiştir. Günümüze dek bu konuyla ilgili herhangi bir araştırma yapılmamış olması şaşırtıcıdır hiç kuşkusuz. Cinayet işleyen suçlu ve zanlıların toplumsal değer yapıları, aile ilişkileri ve kişilik özellikleri ile bunların toplumsal-ekonomik çözümlemesini içeren proje Diyarbakır, Mardin, Şanlıurfa, Siirt, Gaziantep ve Batman'daki 43 cezaevindeki tutuklu ve hükümlülerle görüşülmesini kapsamaktadır. Bugüne kadar görüşülen 51 hükümlüden yalnızca 3 kişinin pişmanlık duyduğunu dile getirmesi, konunun ne denli önemli ve ne denli aşılması güç olduğunun göstergesidir. Bu araştırma, bireylerin töreden ne anladıklarının, aile ilişkilerinin türü, toplumsal ölçütlerin niteliklerinin bilinmesi açısından yol gösterici, aydınlatıcı, bireylerin bilinçlendirilmesi açısından belirlenecek stratejilerin oluşturulması ve alınacak önlemler bağlamında son derece işlevsel bir araştırmadır (www.hurriyet.com.tr). Türk Dil Kurumu töre kavramını "*Bir toplulukta benimsenmiş, yerleşmiş davranış ve yaşama biçimlerinin kuralların, görenek ve geleneklerin ortaklaşa alışkanlıkların, tutulan yolların tümü, adet*" (www. tkd.gov. tr) biçiminde açımlarken, töre kavramı sosyoloji sözlüğünde, "*bir toplumun üyelerinin çoğunun inandığı, terbiye standartlarını sağlamada esas olan ahlaki kurallar ve davranış biçimleri (...) etkin bir biçimde uygulanır ve ihlalleri ya grup kınaması ve yaptırımıyla ya da ahlaki tutumların yasa haline geldiği durumlarda hukuki yollarla*" (Marshall, 1999, ss. 763-764) cezalandırılması olarak tanımlanmaktadır. Kavrama ilişkin bir başka tanım, *toplumdaki etik, gelenek, görenek ve ortaklaşa uzlaşımlarla belirlenmiş, kabul gören tutum ve davranışlar, kuşaktan kuşağa aktarılan toplumsal kurallar biçiminde yapılmaktadır* (Püsküllüoğlu, 2004, s. 1347). Prof. Dr. Ünsal Oskay'ın ise töreye ilişkin ortaya koyduğu tanım şöyledir: "*Denenmiş belli bir hayat biçiminin işleyişini sağlamak için geleneğin geçerli olduğu anlaşılmış kurallarını haklaştıran bir türü*" (www.turkforumuzbizshow). Yapılan tanımlara bakıldığında töre olgusunun yapıcı, kucaklayıcı, bütünleştirici, bireyleri birarada tutmayı amaçlayan, paylaşımcı etken bir bağlama ilişkin ortak gönderge çerçevesinde konumlandırıldığı, anlam evreni oluşturulduğu görülmektedir. Oysa töre dendiğinde bireylerin kavrama yükledikleri ilk anlam ikinci tanımda vurgulanan "grup kınaması ve yaptırımı" sonucu cezalandırmadır. Bu bağlamda kavramın içi, namus cinayetleri, şiddet, ölüm gibi olumsuz düşüncelerle doldurulmaktadır. Bir başka deyişle, çağdaş yaşama göre kendini yenileyen, devingen bir yapı içermeyen, bireyleri bütünleştirici, birleştirici özelliği olmayan, koruyucu olmayan tam tersine, hak, hukuk, kanun tanımayan, bireylerin özgürlüklerini ellerinden alıp onları tutsak eden, kapana sıkıştıran, bireylerin belleklerini uyuşturarak, iç benliklerinde önüne geçilemez öfke ve şiddet yaratarak, kişilerarası iletişimi koparan, kişilerarası çatışmalara yol açan düşünce ve eylem bütünü olarak belleklerimize yer ettiğini söylersek yanlış olmaz sanırız. Her toplum, kendi düzenekleri, kendi sistemleri, kendi kültürleri, kendi değerleri içerisinde bir bütündür. Her sistemin, her ekinin oluşturucuları birbirinden değişiktir. Bu değişkenlik içerisinde yer alan "farklı kültürel ortamlarda bireylerin sözlü olmayan davranışları" (Odabaş ve Ağırbaş, 2002, s. 317) olarak tanımlanan gelenekler, yazılı kurallar ya da yazılı bilgiler içermemesine karşın, kuşaktan kuşağa aktarılan olaylar, eylemler, alışkanlıklar, öğretiler çizgiselliğinde bireylerin davranışlarını etkiler nitelikte manevi bir yaptırım gücü taşımaktadır. Manevi yaptırım gücü taşıyan bir diğer olgu da "değer" kavramıdır. Kimi davranış ve amaçları diğer davranış ve amaçlara göre ya bireysel ya da toplumsal biçimde yeğlenebilen, sürekliliği olan inanışlar (Odabaş ve Ağırbaş, 2002, s. 212) biçiminde dile getirilen değer kavramı, her toplumun içinde değişik dizgelerden, değişik göstergelerden oluşarak bireylerin davranışlarını biçimlendiren, yaşam biçimlerini oluşturan toplumsal ve ruhsal etkileşimli bir olgudur. Bu etkileşimlilik kimi zaman kimi yerlerde kendini yerel hareket etme, birliktelik, tek yürek olma, özdeşleşme eylemine iten, yerel değer biçiminde kendini göstermektedir. Değer kavramı aynı zamanda iyi/kötü, olumlu/olumsuz, doğru/yanlış, namus/namussuzluk gibi karşıtlıkları ortaya koyan, sözcüklere, kavramlara anlam yükleyen ve toplumun kimi ölçütlerinin oluşmasını sağlayan taşıyıcı nitelikte bir olgudur. Değer kavramı törensel uygulayımları da beraberinde getirmektedir. Aynı ekinden gelen, birbirleriyle ilişki içindeki, aynı grubun paydaşları bireyler değerlerini, kültürlerini törensellik çerçevesinde yaşatmakta, sürdürmektedirler. Ekinsel değerlere ilişkin Hofstede'in Türkiyede dahil olmak üzere 53 ülkeyi kapsayan araştırması (Küçükerdoğan, 2005) kültür ölçütlerini açıkça ortaya koymaktadır.

- Güç aralığı (gücün konumdan kaynaklanıp kaynaklanmadığının sorgulanması, otoriterlik): Toplum içinde bireylerin doğal saydıkları emir-kumanda zincirinin birer halkaları olarak kabullenmeleri bir başka anlatımla eşit olmayan güç dağılımına boyun eğmeleri. Aşağılanma, bayağılık, başkaldırmama vb. göstergeler güç aralığını simgelemektedir.

- Belirsizlikten kaçınma: Grup üyeleri olarak risk alıp alamamanın değerlendirilmesi, geçmişte ve gelecekte varolmak, güven duygusu verip vermemekle ilintili göstergeler. Canının güvende olmaması, baskı, korku, endişe vb. göstergeler.

- Bireycilik: Bireyin içinde bulunduğu gruptan ayrılarak, kendi başına yaşaması ve gurup baskısından uzak özgür yaşamasıyla ilintili göstergeler. Birliktelik, özgürlük, farklılık aktaran göstergeler.

- Erkeksilik: Kültüre uygun biçimde her cinsiyete belli toplumsal işlevlerin verilmesi. Saldırgan kişiliklere toplumun bakış-görüş açısı, başarı, cesaret, kendine ve çevreye saygılı olmak, üretkenlik göstergeleri.

- Zaman kullanımı: Belirlenen hedeflere ulaşmak için kişilerin kendilerine haz veren, günlük zevklerden uzaklaşarak, geleneksellik, gelenekselliğe ve çağdaşlığın birleşimi gibi olgular, eylemler, davranışlar, olgunluk aktaran göstergeler.

Bu ana başlıklar doğrultusunda, ekin öğeleri oluşmakta ve sözcüklere, davranışlara, simgelere anlamlar yüklenmektedir. Bu anlam evrenini sorgulayan araştırma, gerçekte bireylerin tutumlarını, ilgi odaklarını, düşüncelerinin sınırlarının çizilmesini, ekinsel değerlerin saptanmasını, kişilerin toplumsal konumlarının belirlenmesini de açığa çıkartmaktadır. Kısacası bireylerin yaşam biçimlerinin nasıl, hangi ölçütlere göre oluştuğunun, yaşamlarının, alışkanlıklarının, duyarlılıklarının, yaşam biçimlerinin hangi çizgisellik doğrultusunda geliştiğinin ve ilerlediğinin dolayısıyla toplumsal biçemlerin oluşum özelliklerinin somut nedenlerini öğrenmek adına yararcıl bir işlev yüklenmektedir. Örneğin Türk toplumu erkekegemen bir toplum özelliği yansıtması nedeniyle, güç aralığı, erkeksilik, zaman kullanımı türk kültürü için vazgeçilmez bir önem taşımaktadır. Hofstede'in güç aralığı ölçütü, ülkemizdeki töre kavramıyla birebir örtüşmektedir. Çünkü töre denildiğinde "boyun eğme", "aşağılanma", "büyüklerin ya da söz sahibi olanların baskıları" akla gelmektedir ki bunlar doğrudan "töre" kavramına gönderme yapmaktadır. Ülkemizde toplumun belirleyicisi niteliğindeki "ataerkillik" doğrudan Hofstede'nin "bireycilik" ölçütüne bağlanabilir. Çünkü ataerkil toplumumuzda "evden ayrılma", "birey olarak yanlız yaşama" gibi olguların kabul edilmesi söz konusu değildir ve bu yine gücü elinde tutanlar tarafından "saygısızlık", "töreye aykırılık" biçiminde görülmektedir. Ayrıca türk toplumu erkek egemen bir toplumdur ve kadın ikinci sıradadır. Erkeğin kadına baskı yaptığı, sindirdiği bir ortamdır kimi zaman söz konusu olan. Yine Türk toplumunda töre olduğu değerlendirildiğinde, Hofstede'nin zamansallık, zaman kullanım ölçütüne göre Türkler geleneklerine ve geçmişlerine bağlı toplumlardır denilebilir.

Ancak değerlerin, kültürlerin değişkenlik gösterdiği gibi törenler de, törensel göstergeler de farklı inanışlar doğrultusunda biçimlenerek, oluşarak değişkenlik göstermektedir. Toplum kimliğini kazandıran, toplumu toplum yapan en önemli ögelerden biridir töreler. Ancak, manevi yaptırım gücünün tersine, törelere uymama, sürdürmeme durumunda cezayla sonlanan bir yaptırım söz konusudur. Bu törelerin devamlılığını, sürekliliğini sağlayan, özellikle kimi bölgelerde, kimi yörelerde bireylerin yazgılarını belirleyen, yaşamlarının sınırlarını çizen, siyasal ve toplumsal güç olarak karşımıza çıkan aşiret, ağa, şeyh gibi soy birliğine dayalı toplumsal örgütlenmeler, varlıklarının, işlevlerinin ötesinde, tek bir kültüre bağlı yaşamanın savaşını verirken aynı zamanda ekin değişiminin, alışkanlıkların, tutum ve davranış değişikliklerinin de yaşanılmasına karşı savaşmaktadırlar. "Aşiretler mozaiği olan bölgelerde, bu bağlılık, bütünleştirici olmaktan çok, ayırıcı bir etken olarak rol oynamaktadır" (Faraç, 2006, s. 161). Böylesi bir durumda da, töre olgusunun yüzeysel yapıda karmaşık, bulanık ancak derin yapıda kavramsal olarak açık ve anlaşılır olduğunu söylemek olasıdır. Törelerin değişimi açısından ekinsel değişime açık olmanın ne denli önemli olduğunun altının önemle çizilmesi gerekmektedir. Bu konuyla ilgili düşüncelerini bir sınıflandırmayla ortaya koyan Clark Wizmed, töre şemsiyesi altında yer alan manevi kültüre ilişkin bir sınıflandırma yapmaktadır:

- İletişim (Dil ve yazı sistemler)
- Maddi özellikler (Yeme-içme adetleri, uzam, nakil, ulaşım, giyim-kuşam...)
- Sanat (Müzik, tiyatro, resim, plastik sanatlar...)
- Söylenbilim ve Bilim
- Dini şekiller
- Mülkiyet biçimleri
- Savaş
- Yönetim (Devlet şekilleri, hukuk sistemleri...)
- Aile ve toplumsallaşma sistemleri (Evlenme, nikahlanma biçimleri, akrabalık sistemleri toplumsal denetim...) (Yirmibeşoğlu, 2007, ss. 25-26).

Yukarıdaki sınıflandırmada da görüldüğü gibi, manevi kültürün oluşturucuları arasında birçok etmen yer almaktadır. Tıpkı törelerin oluşturucuları arasında yer alan etmenler gibi. Ataerkillikle ilgili töreler, yönetimle ilgili töreler, dinsel töreler, sanatsal töreler...vb. olmasına karşın töre dendiğinde toplumun dikkate aldığı en önemli etmen namus, cinsellik, aile ve toplumsallaşma sistemleridir. 2003 yılında, Güneydoğu Anadolu'da 320 erkek ve 240 kadınla yüzyüze yapılan bir araştırmanın sonucu bu anlayışı doğrulamaktdır. Töre ile cinayeti birleştirmek, bütünleştirmek, bağdaştırmak son derece yanlış ve yanılsatıcıdır. Ancak, filmlerde, dizilerde izlediğimiz, gördüğümüz kurgusal bir senaryonun, sanal bir metnin ötesinde, "gerçekliğin", toplumsallaşma sürecinde gözlemlenerek, öğrenilerek kazanılan "somut bir eylemin" ta kendisidir. Her ne kadar iletişim çağında, çağdaş bir dünyada yaşadığımızı savunsak da, her toplumun kendine özgü, gerçekliği yadsınamaz ve insan yaşamını hiçe sayan kimi törelerinin varlığı "öteki" kavramını da beraberinde getirerek ne denli toplumsal ve ekinsel bir çemberin içinde birarada, birlikte varolduğumuzun, yaşam alanı bulduğumuzun göstergesidir. Varolan ekin göstergeleri, kültür biçimleri bir taraftan kendine diğer taraftan da başka kişilere karşı kendini temsil etmek amacıyla bir takım araçlar kullanmak durumundadır. Bir kültürün ögelerinin, değer ve inançlarını görünür kılma yöntemlerinden en önemlilerinden bir tanesi görsel araçlardır (Barnard, 1998, s. 138). Toplumbilimci-Yazar Prof. Dr. Emre Kongar, kitle iletişim araçlarının toplum üzerinde yönlendirici, etkileyici bir işlevi bulunduğunun altını çizerek, kimileyin rayting ve tiraj kaygısı nedeniyle haber metinlerinde yer alan sözcüklerin, söylemlerin, başlıkların ya da simgelerin toplum üzerinde olumsuz etkiler yarattığını, farkındalık yaratmak yerine sıradanlık yarattığını şu tümceleriyle ortaya koymaktadır: "Kitle iletişim araçlarının doğrudan sorumlu oldukları konuların başında, ilkel cinayetlere, "aşk cinayeti", "töre cinayeti" ya da "namus cinayeti" gibi isimler vermek gelmektedir. Gazeteler ve televizyon kanalları, bu tür başlıklarla, bu ilkel cinayetleri sadece aklamakla kalmamakta, bunları yüceltetek, toplumda bu yönde özendirirci bir etki de yapmaktadırlar" (Barnard, 1998, s. 176).

Bu bağlamda, çalışmamızın ana konusu iletişim çatışmalarına neden olan "töre" kavramını temel almakta ve bireylerin yaşamlarını tutsak eden, insanların toplumsal ve ruhsal özelliklerini gözetmeksizin onları robotlaştıran ve önüne geçilemez bir duruma gelen "kültür" ve "öteki bağımlılığını" göstergebilimsel açıdan çözümlenmesi oluşturmaktadır. Televizyonda yayınlanan dizilerin izlenme oranlarına ilişkin yapılan araştırmaların birçoğunda "Sıla" dizisinin beğeniyle izlenilen diziler arasında ilk sırayı aldığı belirtilmektedir. Töre konusu üzerine kurgulanması ve en fazla izlenme oranına sahip olması nedeniyle "Sıla" dizisinin seçmeci bir yöntemle ilk üç bölümünün ve son üç bölümünün anlam evreni ve tutum, davranış açısından göstergebilimsel çözümlemesi yapılacaktır.

Dizinin Konusu:

İstanbul'da köklü bir ailede evlatlık olarak büyüyen Sıla bir gün öldü sandığı ailesiyle ve onların karşı konulmaz töreleriyle yüzyüze gelir. Kökleri doğu'da, batı dünyasına ait Sıla, hiç tanımadığı ağabeysinin öldürülmesini engellemek için o güne kadar hiç duymadığı berdel uygulamasıyla yaşamının seyri değişmiştir. Töreler gereği berdel verildiği Genco Aşiretinin ağası Boran'la zorla evlendirilir. Çünkü Sıla'nın abisi Azad, ağanın kızkardeşi Narin'i kaçırmıştır ve kan dökülmemesi için aşiret berdele karar vermiştir. Sıla artık kanunların yok sayıldığı, törelerin kabul edildiği bir yerde, öz ailesi tarafından töreye kurban edilmesinin acısını yaşarken, zorla evlendiği ancak daha sonra aşık olduğu Boran ağayla birlikte bir taraftan berdeli bozmaları nedeniyle kendileri için çıkan ölüm kararını durdurmanın savaşını verirken diğer taraftan o yörede yaşayan bireyleri bilinçlendirmenin ve özgürlüklerini nasıl kazandıracaklarının savaşını vermektedirler.

Sıla Filminde üstdil olarak "Töre" olgusuna ilişkin töre yaptırımı "çatışma" içeren ve töre karşıtı "barış" içeren anlam öbekleriyle birlikte bağlama göre hem "çatışma" hem de "barış" içeren aşağıdaki belirtilen kimi sözcüklerle belirlenmiştir.

Töre Yaptırımı Çatışma Ve Töre Karşıtı Barış

Töre Yaptırımı Çatışma İçeren Sözcükler

"kılına dokunmak", "razı olmak", "aşiret", "başı bağlı olmak", "son söz", "zaptırap altına almak", "yakalamak", "öldürmek", "ağa", "kıymak", "erkek adam", "tir tir titremek", "kan dökmek", "evlat acısı", "kararı tez elden vermek", "boynun kıldan ince olması", "kefen giymek", "kurban etmek", "toprağa girmek", "merhamet", "yüreğin yaşdan büyük olması", "kız almak-kız vermek", "rahmetli", "yüreği yakmak", "insafı olmamak", "buyurmak", "çile", "hanım ağa", "kara gün", "ilkellik", "ceset", "rezillik", "can borcu", "yasal hak", "kan istemek", "can almak", "hüküm vermek", "kıymak", "soy", "korkmak", "canının yarısını götürmek", "karşı durmak", "toprağa vermek", "can vermek", "ağlamak", "yas tutmak", "kızgın olmak", "dövünmek", "engel olmak", "vebal", "kan", "ölüm döşeği", "dert", "candan can koparmak", "hasretten yanıp tutuşmak", "berdel", "yürek üşümesi", "göze batmak", "yargılamak", "perişan olmak", "savaşmak", "kabalık", "korktuğu başına gelmek", "kan davası", "hortlamak", "devralmak", "davanın kapanması", "töreyi saymamak", "töre kanunu", "cezalandırmak", "korku", "tutsaklık", "öfke", "kendini yok etmek", "yıkmak", "kabüllenmek", "yok etmek", "kavga", "suçlu bulmak", "susturmak", "tezgahlamak", "silah", "katil", "düşmanlık", "kahretmek", "şansını kaybetmek", "komplo", "suçlu çıkartmak", "işleri çıkmaza sokmak", "hayatı zindan etmek", "kabus", "cahillik", "mahkeme", "delil", "suç aleti", "ispat etmek", "boğmak", "ceza çekmek","maşa olmak", "azmettirmek", "itiraf etmek", "mücadele", "hükmü geçmek", "esirgemek", "aşmak", "dönüşü olmamak", "yemin etmek", "boyun eğmek", "vurmak", "hayatın mahvolması", "bedel ödemek", "dönüş olmamak", "canı burnunda olmak", "içinin parçalanması", "emir vermek", "ölüm emri", "belaya bulaşmak", "cezasını vermek", "töreyi ensesinde hissetmek", "aşiret meclisi", "hakimiyet", "yetki", "kabahatli olmak", "itiş-kakış", "tokat", "cezaevi", "ibreti alem için", "eliniş sürmek", "kazanın mübarek olması", "emri olmak", "icabına bakmak", "elini sürmek", "hicazet almak", "alna düşen lekenin temizlenmesi", "haddini aşmak", "ayağına çağırmak","kanına susamak", yüreğini sökmek", "dirliğe kastetmek", "son nefesini almak", "yalan", "hile", "dünyası kararmak", "aşirettekilerin selasını vermek", "içi korkmak", "yaralanmak", "şişlemek".

Töre Karşıtı Barış İçeren Sözcükler

"kılına dokunmamak", "kız kaçırmak", "kurtarmak", "kaçmak", "çaresiz kalmak", "içine korku düşmek", "yalvarmak", "yol aramak", "kalbi dayanmak", "içi yanmak", "acı yaşamak", "allahtan korkmak", "hakkı olmak", "huzur", "affetmek", "özgür", "medet ummak", "güçlü kılmak", "antlaşma", "sahip çıkmak", "bağışlama", "göze almak", "başkaldırmak", "sır saklamak","vicdan azabı", "kalp kırıklığı", "hüzün", "kavuşmak", yüreğinin izin vermesi", "vicdan sesi", "yaraları sarmak", "kendini bağışlatmak", "güven kazanmak", "yufka yürekli olmak", "acıları paylaşmak", "çabalamak", "endişelenmek", "korumak", "sorumluluk", "sabır vermek", "içtenlik", "inanmak", "dim dik ayakta durmak", "tasalanmak", "zorluklara direnmek", "rahat nefes almak", "yanında olmak", "üstesinden gelmek", "kötülüklerden korumak", "hak", "düzen", "hayata tutunmak".

Töre ve Barış İçeren Sözcükler

"karar kılmak", "kaldır kapak etmek", "sevmek", "birbirine katmak", "yüreklilik", "sevda", "cesaret", "birarada tutmak", "kırmızı kuşak", "bacı", "düğün", "acele karar almak", "reşit olmak", "hır çıkarmak", "kandırmak", "deli deli konuşmak", "adet", "şahit olmak", "düğün", "el öpmek", "cennet", "nikahına almak", "namus", "söz vermek", "nazar", "hayır olmak", "kıymetli", "beklenti", "derdi olmak", "kanıt", "bütünlüğün bozulması", "tutuklamak", "inkar etmek", "dirayet", "deliğe girmek", "müşkül durumda olmak", "eli böğründe beklemek".

Daha önce de öneminden ve etkisinden söz ettiğimiz değer kavramı burada da karşımıza çıkmaktadır. İyi/kötü, olumlu/olumsuz, doğru/yanlış, namus/namussuzluk, hüzün/mutluluk, karşı çıkma/affetme, korku/güven, boyun eğmek/başkaldırmak, tutsaklık/özgürlük, kabullenmek/reddetmek, çaresiz kalmak/medet ummak, çatışma/barış gibi karşıtlıkların, karşıt görüşlerin oluşturucu öğelerinden biridir. Tutum ve davranışlar da bu karşıtlığın altını sıkça çizmektedir. Yalnızca sözcüklerle çatışma ve barış karşıtlığı aktarılmamaktadır Sıla dizisinde. Ayrıca dizinin kimi sahnelerinde yer alan kimi davranışların töre gereği aşağıdaki biçimde sergilenmesi gerçekle ne denli ilintili olduğunun göstergesidir.

Tutum ve davranışlar

-Ağaların, aşiret reislerinin yanında ayak ayak üstüne atmamak

-Ağaların, aşiret reislerinin önünde el-pençe durmak

-Ağaların, aşiret reislerinin yanında düşüncelerini açıklayamamak, her söylenene sorgusuz boyun eğmek, istenileni yapmak

-Ağaların, aşiret reislerinin şiddet içeren tutum ve davranışlarına tepki vermemek

-Aşiret Meclisinin belirlediği kurallara aykırı davranışlarda bulananlara ölüm emrinin çıkması

-Aşiret Meclisinin aldığı kararların dışına asla çıkılmaması

-Bir çeşit evlilik türü olan karşılıklı kız alıp verme, berdelin uygulanması (berdel töresi gereği 11-12 yaşlarındaki çocukların evlendirilmesi)

-Yeni evlenmiş gelinin ilk gününde aile büyüklerine kahve yapması

-Evlenecek kişinin gelinliğini evlenmeden önce giymemesi

-Öldürülmesine karar verilmiş bir kadının hamile olması durumunda ölüm emrinin doğuma kadar durdurulması

Sonuç

Dizinin yayınlanan bölümlerinin bütününe baktığımızda, ana karakterlerden Sıla kentli, eğitimli, toplumsal ve bireysel haklarına sahip çıkan, toplumsal sorumluluk çerçevesinde çevreye duyarlı ve töre söz konusu olduğunda yaşamını, canını ortaya koyarak başkalarının, öteki insanların varolan düzene karşı durmalarına, savaşmalarına ve insanca yaşamalarına örnek model oluşturan bir kimlikle karşımıza çıkmaktadır. Boran ağa karakteri ise, bir aşiret reisini canlandırmakta ve içinde büyüdüğü, yoğrulduğu toplumun gerçeklerini görerek, kan dökülmeden iletişim ve ikna aracılığıyla yüzyıllardır uygulanan sistemin değişimi konusunda uğraş veren bir karakteri canlandırmaktadır. Ancak tüm yetke ve yetki ağa olarak elinde olmasına karşın bu değişimin yaşanmasının hiç de kolay olmadığını, uzun bir zaman sürecinde kimi anlayışların değişebileceğini gerek sözcüklerle, gerek davranışlarla göstermektedir hedef kitlesine. Sıla ve Boran ağa karakterleri birbirine karşıt iki kültürü, iki toplumu, iki yaşam biçimini, iki anlayışı simgelemelerine karşın gerçekte namus üzerine yapılandırılmış töre olgusu bağlamında yerleşen yanlış düşüncelerin ve yanlış davranışların düzeltilmesine ilişkin topluma verdikleri yapıcı, olumlu iletilerle ayrıcalıklı bir dizi konumunda karşımıza çıkmaktadır. Bir anlamda ben (Sıla- Boran Ağa) ve öteki (Boran Ağa'nın Babası, Amcası, Amcasının oğlu, Celil Karakterleri) kavramının simgesi konumundaki iki kişinin töre kavramına ilişkin birbirleriyle tartıştırılması, konuşturulması söz konusudur. Tartıştırılan, konuşturulan bu iki kişilik, insan hakları açısından toplumun kanayan yarası olan töre cinayetlerine ilişkin bilinmeyenlerin görülmesi, öğrenilmesi, gerçeklerin yansıtılması, gerekli duyarlılığın ve tavrın gösterilmesi bağlamında etkin rol oynamaktadır.

Yıllardır töreyle ilgili yaşanan sorunların temeline baktığımızda, öncelikle kavramın, olgunun kimi soyut kavramlar gibi doğru tanımlanamadığını, içeriğinin somut bir biçimde ortaya konmadığını görmekteyiz. Kısacası bir anlam karmaşası söz konusudur ve bu anlam karmaşasını yok etmenin birincil koşulu yazılı ve sözlü dili etkin ve etkili bir biçimde kullanmaktır. Bu tür kavramlara, olgulara açıklık getirilmesi bireylerin değişimi gerçekleştirmeleri, bilinçlenmeleri açısından ön koşuldur. Bilinçlenme ise öncelikle eğitimle sağlanmalıdır. Dizinin izleksel düzlemi çerçevesinde yapılandırılan ana örgü, töre gereği çocukların erken yaşta evlendirilmeleridir. 12-13 yaşında evlendirilen çocuklardan öğrencilik rolü üstlenmeleri gerekirken, eş rolünü sergilemeleri beklenilmektedir. Ancak bilinmelidir ki, töre cinayetlerinin ya da kadına yönelik şiddetin görüldüğü tek ülke Türkiye değildir. 2004 yılında Avrupa'da % 25-50 arası kadının şiddete maruz kaldığı istatistiklerle, bilimsel araştırmalarla kanıtlanmıştır. Toplulumumuzda yaşanan en belirgin çatışmalardan biri budur. Toplumun bilinçlenmesi en temel toplumsal katman olan aileden başlamalıdır. Ancak toplumumuz "öteki" korkusu, "öteki" baskısı nedeniyle ya da "öteki" tarafından dışlanma, aşağılanma kaygısıyla bu tür açılımları kabul edememektedir. Bu doğrultuda, söz konusu bilinçlenmenin kitle iletişim araçlarında, özellikle televizyon ve ilköğretim okullarında yerleştirilmesi son derece önemlidir. Dikkat edilmesi gereken bir diğer önemli noktada, ikna edici iletişim sürecinde, belirlenen hedef kitleye yönelik oluşturulan iletilerle kaynağa karşı güven ortamı yaratılması, doğru, uygun sözcüklerle bireylerin ikna edilmeye çalışılmasıdır. Hedef kitleye yönelik, hedef kitleye uygun doğru düzgülemenin doğru araçlarla yapılmaması durumunda bir başka deyişle hedef kitle deneyim ve yaşadıklarına ters iletiler alımladığında rahatsızlık duyacak ve aktarılanları reddecektir. Bireylerin, kimileyin dinsel inanışlarına, kimileyin manevi inanışlarına, kimileyin yaşamlarını sürdürdükleri yerlerin gizemli, kutsal sayma anlayışına körü körüne bağlanmaları, kimileyin başka kişileri tabulaştırma, kutsallaştırma, kahramanlaştırma gibi büyülü inanışları ikna edilmelerini, tutum ve davranışlarında değişiklik göstermelerini zorlaştırıcı etmenlerdir. Dolayısıyla iletişimi etkin ve etkili kılacak olan aktarılan iletilerin nasıl ve ne biçimde aktarıldığının ne denli önemli olduğunun ayırdına varmaktır. Törelerin, olumsuz / kötücül / ölümcül / cezalandırıcı / ürkütücü / boyun eğdirici nitelik içeren yanlarını biran önce terketmek ve "barış" / karşılıklı sevgi ve saygı / iyilik kavramlarının "mutluluğun" egemen olduğu tutum ve davranışları benimsemek ülkelerin, toplumların gelişim ve ilerlemeleri açısından birincil derece önemlidir.

Kaynaklar

Barnard, M., (1998). *Sanat, tasarım ve görsel kültür* (Çev. G. Korkmaz). Ankara: Ütopya Yayınevi.

Faraç, M., (2006). *Töre kıskacında kadın*. İstanbul: Günizi Yayıncılık.

Guilane-Nanchez, E., (2003). *İletişim mi? Kolay!* (Çev. G. Ercenk). İstanbul: Sistem Yayıncılık.

Küçükerdoğan, R., (2005). *İletişimde ikna ders notları*. İstanbul Kültür Üniversitesi Sanat ve Tasarım Fakültesi.

Marshall, G., (1999). *Sosyoloji sözlüğü* (Çev. O. Akınhay & D. Kömürcü). Ankara: Bilim ve Sanat Yayınları.

Odabaş, Y., & Ağırbaş, G., (2002). *Tüketici davranışı*. İstanbul: Mediacat Yayınları.

Püsküllüoğlu, A., (2004). *Türkçe sözlük*. Ankara: Arkadaş Yayınevi.

Türk Dil Kurumu, "Töre Maddesi", www. tkd.gov.tr (Son erişim 10.02.2007).

www.hurriyet.com.tr/pazar/6244871.asp?gid=159 (Son erişim 01.04.2007).

www.turkforumuzbizshowthread.php?t=206551 "Töre Üzerine" (Son erişim 18.03.2007).

Yirmibeşoğlu, V., (2007). *Toprağa düşen sevdalar*, İstanbul: Hürriyet Yayınları.

Public Discussions on Turkish Citizenship: 1993-1995

Seçil Deren van het Hof
Communication Faculty
Akdeniz University
secilderen@akdeniz.edu.tr

Introduction

In Turkey, the 1990s will be remembered as the decade in which all contradictions became more open and acute. The Kurdish problem transformed from a regional "low-intensity war" to a "civil war" as it spread to the metropolitan areas. Along with this, a number of unforgettable events took place: two left-inclined academics, Çetin Emeç and Bahriye Üçok, were murdered in 1990, the prominent left-inclined journalist Uğur Mumcu was murdered in January 1992, 37 Alevite intellectuals were killed at the arson of Madımak Hotel in Sivas in July 1993, and in March 1995, riots took place in the Gazi district, an Alevite neighbourhood of Istanbul. These events stimulated the public discussions around, laicism and Islamism, Kemalism and Second Republicanism, Turkish nationalism and democratisation of Turkey. Through these discussions, the pre-1980 political groupings were shuffled: the basic political fronts, left and right, became more complex as they became dispersed along new political positions, based on their attitude in the above mentioned events.

Among all these significant events, the Kurdish problem left its mark in the mid-1990s. Most passionate public discussions flourished out of this problem in a vocabulary of identity politics. The ethnicist/racist tone of the new identity constructions became a source of political and social tension culminating especially after the 1990s. To resolve this tension, politicians, intellectuals and publicists began talking about "making peace with our own past/ Ottoman past", "revival of the multi-cultural Ottoman order" and "constitutional citizenship". Obviously, such talk attracted the resentment of Kemalist circles, in whose minds Islamic reactionism and Ottomanist nostalgia meant almost the same thing.

The public discussions of 1993-1995 mainly polarized on the concept of "constitutional citizenship". In a reshuffled but still polarized political environment, discussions on constitutional citizenship also brought up the questioning of Kemalist nationalism and the official ideology: was the Kemalist definition of the "Turk" already constitutional in origin, or did Turkey need a redefinition of Turkishness as "being from Turkey" to resolve ethnic identity claims? Within the limits of this paper, I will not delve into the theoretical origins of the constitutional citizenship conceptualization or into the origins of ethnic problems in the Turkish Republic.

This paper focuses on the public discussions that took place after the replacement of Turgut Özal as the president by Süleyman Demirel in June 1993. Roughly, both Özal and Demirel are known as leaders of the Turkish center-right; but more meticulously, they represent different ideological currents. While Demirel was attending the Assembly of Turkness in Antalya on the same day as Newruz, Özal was chairing a congress organized by a neo-Ottomanist group in March 1993.

Public discussions after 1993 are also important because the cease-fire between the TAF and PKK ended by the end of May same year, when the PKK kidnapped 33 soldiers and 30 civilians on the Bingöl-Elazığ road and killed 40 of them on the next day (Toprak, 2005, p. 396). This event darkened the mood in Turkish public opinion: the hopes for peace died away.

In this mood, the Turkish public opinion was actually divided into an opposition of concepts: Turk versus citizen of Turkey, military solution versus political solution, Kemalism versus Second Republicanism, Republicanism versus neo-Ottomanism. Some of these concepts were brought up and were actively pursued by publicists who acted as opinion leaders through their editorials in daily papers. This paper tries to illustrate the expressions of polarization by looking at the editorials of five newspapers, *Milliyet*, *Hürriyet*, *Sabah*, *Cumhuriyet* and *Türkiye*, which were seen worth of digitilization by the library of Turkish Parliament due to their influence, not because of their circulation.

Political Background of Public Discussions

The origin of the contemporary public discussions on Turkish citizenship can be traced back to the late 1980s, when the Kurdish problem entered the agenda. The Kurdish ethnic and cultural claims - arisen under the non-democratic rule following a military coup - were represented by PKK. Supposedly based upon Marxist-Leninist principles, PKK was a separatist movement aiming at achieving an "independent Kurdistan". The vicious struggles of the PKK against all perceived agents of the Turkish state from the mid-1980 on have been handled by Turkish governments with extensive military fortifications and measures in the eastern and south-eastern provinces. Extraordinary powers given to the government for the solution of this problem brought up limitations on the freedom of thought in general, which in turn became a basic obstacle against the liberalization of Turkey and paved the way to violations of human rights. The military solution for the Kurdish problem entailed further strengthening of the position of the Turkish army in the political life of the country, alongside the militarization of the society and the popularization of Turkish nationalism.

In this atmosphere, the first attempts at a civil solution were brought up by Turgut Özal, the ex-leader of the Motherland Party (MP), the first civilian Prime Minister after 1980 and then the President. After he became the President, he supported democratic solutions through public discussion and the recognition of the Kurdish ethnic identity. This radical chance of position by Özal in Turkey's major conflict was criticized by the publicists. For instance, Rüştü Şardağ pointed to Özal's silence while he was the prime minister and to his declarations "I have partial Kurdish blood" and "let's declare amnesty to PKK" (*Milliyet* 22.07.1993).

Özal's basic proposal to public discussion was some form of Ottomanism, which allowed for the existence of ethnic and/or religious communities so long as they do not threaten the authority of the central state. Thus, Özal supported a conference on neo-Ottomanism, second Republicanism and similar topics in Ankara in January 1993 (*Nokta* 7-13 Februaury 1993, 28 March-3 April 1993). However, after Özal's death in April 1993, the National Security Council gained the upper hand on the Kurdish problem again. Süleyman Demirel, the new President, declared that cultural issues could not be discussed before a final solution in terror was achieved (*Turkish Daily News,* 15.7.1993). As a result, the attention of the public opinion diverted from democratic solution through public discussion back to military advances in the south eastern Turkey.

In the mean time, the radical right, that is, Erbakan's *Milli Görüş* (National View) and Alparslan Türkeş's Nationalist Action Party (NAP), was on the rise, sweeping out the centre-right parties in Turkish politics, while soon centre-right also assumed a more military and nationalist tone with Tansu Çiller's accession to power in the True Parth Party (TPP).

The 1994 elections once again triggered the public discussions around ethnic/civic national identity. The positions of the political parties at that crucial moment were as follows. Erbakan held that Islam as the main bond of society still had a resonance strong enough to transgress ethnic differences (Çalmuk, 2001) while the Welfare Party (WP) secured an impressive increase in its votes in the regions with a Kurdish majority. The discourse of Erbakan brought NAP and WP in direct conflict, although the electoral base of the two parties were pretty close (*Nokta,* 24-30 April 1994). To counter Erbakan's successful campaign, the discussion on political freedoms initiated by Turgut Özal was this time taken over by Tansu Çiller and the present leader of MP, Mesut Yılmaz. Çiller began to talk of the possibility of education, publication and broadcasting in Kurdish. However, Çiller and Yılmaz now clashed with President Demirel.

Demirel maintained that such discussions would encourage separatist tendencies and threaten the integrity of the Turkish state. Moreover, he was convinced that any democratic or cultural solution would be a compromise to PKK terror. In the wake of increasing pressure from the Western countries for a compromise and for the recognition of minority rights of the Kurds, Demirel stressed that the Turkish people did not want a democracy which would lead to the division of their territory. These minority rights could not be granted to Kurds. Demirel's position was similar to that of Ecevit, who was now representing the traditional Kemalist nationalism with his Democratic Left Party (DLP).

The wordings of Ecevit and Demirel were only slightly different. The main reason behind the terror was seen as a conspiracy of the Western powers aiming at the partitioning of Turkey, as had been the case in Sevres. DLP remained loyal to the traditional nationalist and centralist or "left of centre" position of the pre-1980 Republican Peoples Party (RPP). In this perspective, Ecevit and DLP cadres saw the problem as socio-economic, not ethnic. Terror was the outcome of unemployment and poverty prevailing in the region, stipulated by the interference of imperialist western powers having interests in an independent Kurdish state. Ecevit suggested land reform to break down the feudal structure and the increase in investments for the industrialization of the region as solutions to the problem. He rejected both the village guardians system and the education in Kurdish. But most strikingly, he rejected the discourse based on the Muslim brotherhood of Turks and Kurds as part of his RPP secularism, constantly suspicious of abuse of religion for political aims. Thus, Ecevit accused the Welfare Party for being far more separatist than PKK by abusing religion.

Among the Turkish political parties, NAP, DLP and the dominant militant cadres of TPP pointed only to the problem of terror, rejecting any ethnic claim. Particularly Alparslan Türkeş harshly criticized those who talked of Kurdish reality and who supported political solution, on the ground that they were aiming at the division of Turkey. According to Türkeş, Kurds were of Turkish race (*Yeni Yüzyıl*, 26.12.1995). In similar vein, on the occasion of the admission of seven Turkish tribes to NAP, the leader of the Alan tribe, Hemo Meral, proudly declared that they were pure Oguz Turks (*Hürriyet* 24.9.1994, *Aktüel* 12-18.10.1995, Kirişçi &Winrow, 2000, p. 147). NAP was also supported by the Kurdish groups which favoured the preservation of the village guards (*köy koruculuğu*) system. Moreover, the dominance of the militant sections in TPP, after the 1991 elections represented by Coşkun Kırca, İsmail Köse, Yaşar Topçu and Baki Tuğ, put a stop to Çiller's liberal discourse. As a result of this dominance, Aldülmelik Fırat, grandson of Sheikh Said and Demirel's colleague for 37 years, resigned from the party in February 1994. Simultaneously, MP distanced itself gradually from Özal's position, getting closer to the dominant militant perspective prevailing in TPP, although the leader of that party, Mesut Yılmaz, continued expressing that his party recognized the Kurdish problem with its social and cultural aspects and the need for free public discussion of the matters (*Cumhuriyet*, 20.8.1994).

This brief portrayal on their positions demonstrated that political parties did not have a stable attitude. As in the case of TPP, there could be disagreement between the leader and the leading cadres, or as exemplified by Süleyman Demirel, politicians could change their attitudes from one end to the other. Despite the instability of the discourse of political parties, publicists who carried on parallel discussions held considerably more stable attitudes.

Polarizations and their Advocates

The topic of Turkish national identity was so sensitive that it had to be discussed under the protection of an influential political figure. However, the positions of the political leaders and the major parties were reflected and became more diversified in the hands of newspaper editors, opinion leaders and influential civil society organizations. This brought up a lively public discussion environment. As I mentioned above, the public discussions on citizenship originated from the Kurdish problem, which highlighted the ethnic aspect in the definition of Turkish national identity on the one hand, and stimulated the awakening of other ethnic identities on the other. The increasing migration from east to west, and the public debates around the Kurdish problem awakened the ethnic consciousness of other minorities such as Pomak, Laz, Bulgarian immigrants, Circassian, etc. Although they did not necessarily align themselves with the Kurdish cause, they began to assert the recognition, protection and survival of their ethnic cultures and languages, and pursued publication and organization activities. The poem below appeared in *Ogni*, a journal published by Laz people in March 1994:

My father is Laz
My mother, Circassian
Me, hybrid.
I am hybrid,
My wife, Turk,
My children, sheared.
Bloodline
Schmoodline
Nationality boiling,
T.R. registered trade mark
Pot.[1]

Together with ethic identities, the mix of them in Anatolia for centuries was brought up. Although this "mixing" sounded very romantic to some, it was dreadful for others like Türkeş, who rejected the comparison of Turkish society with a mozaic and certified that it was a marble!

Consequently, the public discussions on citizenship nourished a polarization in the public opinion. The Turkish-Kurdish conflict determined the public discussions on citizenship. İlhan Selçuk noted: "Today, our political discourse rests on Turkish-Kurdish conflict instead of on the capital-labour conflict (*Cumhuriyet*, 16.06.1992). Hasan Cemal was expressing a common concern on how to handle pluralism in identities when he wrote "Long live unity in differences! Long live the harmony of differences!" (*Sabah*, 10.11.1992).

In a way, Mehmet Altan "started" the public discussions on Turkish citizenship in 1992, when he brought up the concept of the *Second Republic*. Depending on its definition in the Constitution, Altan argued that Turkish citizenship required neither ethnic Turkishness nor Islam, nor the Sunni sect membership as a prerequisite. In fact, contrary to certain European practices, like in Germany, the Turkish Constitution did not stipulate the full comprehension of the Turkish language for the admittance of Turkish citizenship. Moreover, even the Constitution of 1982, which is infamous for its non-democratic character, mentions in Article 10 that there is no discrimination based on language, race, colour, sex, political ideas, philosophical belief, religion, sect and any such reason among Turkish citizens. Then what was the problem with Turkish citizenship?

1 Babam Laz / Anam Çerkez / Ben kırma. Ben kırma / Karım Türk / Çocuklarım kırpılma. Şecere / Mecere / Milliyet kaynatan / T.C. markalı / Tencere. Cited in *Nokta* 10-16 April 1994.

According to Mehmet Altan, Article 10 was not practiced in daily life in terms of cultural rights. For example, private Kurdish language courses were banned by a decision of the National Security Council. According to Mehmet Altan, the legal rights that came along with citizenship, and citizenship culture was drown out in Turkey by the official view, official history, official ideology and official culture, which was disseminated for years (*Sabah*, 13.03.1992, 23.08.1992). All the "official"s as adjective in the above sentence can actually be replaced by "Kemalism".

In opposition to Mehmet Altan, Mümtaz Soysal, who was Member of Parliament, of RPP at various periods and was known for his "left Kemalist nationalism", argued that ethnic identity claims are fashionable excuses to conceal the real target of imperialist Western powers: the breaking down or weakening of developing nation states in accordance with the interests of Western capitalism. Thus, Soysal confronts Altan by saying that the understanding of citizenship peculiar to nation states refuses to acknowledge minorities. When nobody is different from another, when the religious, cultural, ethnic privileges were abolished, there was no need to protect a minority against a religious, cultural, ethnic majority (*Hürriyet,* 26.09.1992).

In similar vein, a famous theoretician of Kemalism, Toktamış Ateş argued that despite the Turkism of the late Ottoman period, which was based on race and language in accordance with the ideological trends of the age, "being a Turk" was a concept that developed with the Republic. In the Republican framework, a modern perspective was adopted and all citizens of the Turkish Republic, irrespective of their race, native language, religious sect, culture were accepted as Turks (*Milliyet,* 10.03.1993).

In May 1994, this time President Süleyman Demirel brought up "constitutional citizenship". This concept reopened fervent public debate. This debate accelerated in January 1995, when the Turkish media discovered an interview of Tansu Çiller with French journalist Josette Alia, in which Çiller said:

> I am ready to recognize more rights for all our citizens, but not specifically to Kurds. Turkey is a mosaic. We have 24 different ethnic groups. Greeks got mixed with us. We cannot even know our ancestors. I cannot say to some of our citizens that they have more rights and freedoms, that they are first class citizens. (*Nokta,* 8-14 January 1995)

Later, Çiller also implied that it could be better to replace "how happy who says I am a Turk" with "how happy who says I am a Turkish citizen". MP leader Mesut Yılmaz reacted to Çiller by saying "there have been people saying that the Turkish nation is stupid, but no one has claimed that our linage is unclear". Yılmaz's wording had double meaning when he said *nesebi gayri sahih*: it both means unclear linage and to be born out of wedlock. Demirel tried to end the discussion by saying "our linage is clearer than that of any other nation".

But now the topic was difficult to wipe out from the public discussion (*Nokta,* 8-14 January 1995). TOBB (Türkiye Odalar ve Borsalar Birliği / Turkish Federation of Chambers and Stocks) contributed with a Report in the same year, with which, the Turkish business circles offered the replacement of the expression "Turkish people (Türk halkı)" by "the people of Turkey (Türkiye halkı)". This proposal was a reformulation of Turkish national identity and the reshaping of Turkish nationalism.

Replacement of "Turkish people" by "the people of Turkey" and "Turk" by "citizen of Turkey" was indeed hinting at a civic conception of Turkish identity (Uyanık, 2003, İçduygu, A., & Keyman F. 1998, İçduygu, A., & Çolak Y., & Soyarık N., 1999). This appeared in the public discussions as *Türkiyelilik.* This concept rises on similar notions to Ottoman identity as a unifying bond in the Second Constitutional Period, which in fact delineated a loose relation between the state and the citizenry and left identities to the private sphere. Consequently, the concept of "neo-Ottomanism", together with *Türkiyelilik,* entered the vocabulary of public discussions.

During his presidency, Özal commented that the Ottoman Empire had been a conglomerate of nations and that it was nationalism that had caused its disintegration. Neo-Ottomanism was radically criticized by Kemalist intellectuals and the military-bureaucratic establishment. This criticism was partly directed to the Islamic elements, partly to the irredentism inherent in neo-Ottomanist visions. İlhan Selçuk described neo-Ottomanists as enemies of Kemalism (*Cumhuriyet,* 30.01.1993). Back in 1992, he criticized Ottomanism in a bitter irony: "Let's light a Marlboro, blow its smoke up, we are roasted by Turkish-Islamic synthesis well enough, let us turn back to the Ottoman system totally. Leave aside nation-state, unitary state!" (*Cumhuriyet,* 29.04.1992). In contrast, Ege Cansen was celebrating Ottomanism in 1995: "No one needs to deny their ethnic roots. Maintaining such ethnic features also gives the country a cosmopolitan beauty. And this is very appropriate to our Ottoman tradition. Being multi cultured is indeed in our social genes." He concludes by saying that sub-identities should not overwrite the national identity which he equated with citizenship (*Hürriyet,* 18.03.1995). On the other hand, İsmet Miroğlu stressed that cosmopolitantism was the rejection of nationalism (*Türkiye,* 06.02.1995).

Constitutional Citizenship

In 1994, the ethnic tension was so acute that many people believed Turkey was at the edge of a genuine civil war. Popular nationalism was visible at every aspect of social life. Rauf Tamer witnessed to the rise of popular nationalism in most of his articles. He wrote that he had never seen so many Turkish flags hanging around before. He asks "are we suffering from homesickness in our own country?" (*Hürriyet*, 16.03.1994). Ertuğrul Özkök applauded Türkeş for not encouraging civil war (*Hürriyet*, 15.05.1994).

Free-lance columnists of *Cumhuriyet* emphasized the dangers of ethnic identity chauvinism and micro-nationalism (Şevket Çobanoğlu "Dünya Vatandaşlığı ya da Küresel Bütünlük" 26.08.1992; Mustafa Bozoğlu "Mikromilliyetçilik Kışkırtması" 20.10.1992). *Cumhuriyet* reprinted an article by Uğur Mumcu (originally dating 16.05.1977): "These are the colors of nationalism in the hands of the dominant classes. "We will turn back and feel proud with our ancestors; we will turn inside and kill our citizens" (13.05.1993). Moreover, regular columnists of *Cumhuriyet* like Ergun Balcı stressed the need for alternative solutions other than miliary: "Would not it be a one-sided approach to the problem to focus on military measures only, without producing any political solution in a democratic perspective?" (*Cumhuriyet*, 05.11.1993).

At the same time, as the public interest in the Turkic Republics acquired a new impetus with the Convention for Friendship, Brotherhood and Cooperation among the Turkish States and Societies in March 21-23, 1993, Kirghizstan declared Newruz a national holiday associating it with the mythical Turkish exit from Ergenekon. This declaration became an interesting opportunity to turkify Newruz which was known in Turkish public opinion as a Kurdish folk celebration. Thus, Nevruz was ascribed an "official" history by being associated with Ergenekon, one of the most popular symbols of Turkish nationalism (Özdoğan, 1993, p. 74). Yalçın Doğan criticized the official policy of pumping Turkish nationalism against Kurdish nationalism by pointing to the disgrace of beating iron on the day of the Kurdish festival (*Milliyet*, 23.03.1993). On the other hand, Mim Kemal Öke, a conservative nationalist[2], is one of the publicists who wrote on Mustafa Kemal's "hidden" desire for Turan. Öke argued that Kemal believed in the union of Turks. He ordered the return of the Balkan Turks home, that is, Anatolia; but when the population import from the East, from Turkistan and Iran was suggested, he rejected it by saying "we will meet them in China one day" (*Türkiye*, 02.02.1994).

At this crucial point, Demirel opened the public discussions on constitutional citizenship. In March 1994, he commented that equality should be built on constitutional citizenship denying any racial basis. Fatih Çekirge found the concept of constitutional citizenship an opportunity to open Turkey's way to supremacy against international pressures (*Sabah*, 27.03.1994). Ömer Öztürkmen applauded Demirel's comments as an invitation to a full-fledged democratization (*Türkiye*, 25.05.1994). In similar vein, Hadi Uluengin found Demirel's comments very important. Uluengin wrote that "How happy he who says I am a Turk!" implied a main perspective of Republican ideology. But for him, the contemporary problems required going beyond the slogans of "How happy he who says I am a Turk!" or "How happy he who says I am a Kurd!" thus, President's constitutional citizenship concept focuses on the common and willing declaration of both Turks and Kurds as "How happy he who says I am a citizen of Turkish Republic!" (*Hürriyet*, 24.05.1994)

In opposition, for Toktamış Ateş, being a Turk in Turkey did not mean "being of Turkish race". Instead it meant being attached to Turkey by bonds of citizenship. Consequently, Kemal Atatürk's "How happy he who says I am a Turk!" has the emphasis on "who says": it is a matter of free personal choice, not a matter of racial origin. Thus, when President Demirel brought up constitutional citizenship, it implied that there has been racial inequality. Ateş invited Demirel to be more careful on what he says (*Cumhuriyet*, 26.05.1994). Oktay Ekşi maintained that Demirel "invented" the concept of constitutional citizenship. But, the relation between a man and a state cannot be reduced to a constitutional article. He emphasized that attempts at replacing Turkish nationalism by nationalism of Turkey are just as absurd as the invention of constitutional citizenship (*Hürriyet*, 01.11.1994). Yet, Yılmaz Aktuğ emphasized that nationalism was the unity in ethic origin, religion, culture and tradition" (*Türkiye*, 21.11.1994).

In 1995, Deniz Baykal, the leader of RPP, aimed at the revival of the 1920's mission in the 1990s, and initiate a second nationalization process in Turkey. In opposition to this aim, Zülfü Livaneli wrote that Turkey needed to perceive a multi-lingual and multi-cultural structure as richness and allow for the expression of all identities within democracy. In this manner, he contributed to the discussions on citizenship. Livaneli wrote that modern understanding of democracy, which respects every language, every belief, every culture but that gives the upper hand to Turkish citizenship is the only way to establish the currently most needed brotherhood to overcome Turk-Kurd, Alevite-Sunni, laicist versus anti-laicist separations (*Milliyet*, 13-14.09.1995). These comments attest that Livaneli, who was not a Second Republican, also supported the discussions in favour of constitutional citizenship.

The interference by the European governments for the recognition of minority rights and the talks of Kurdish autonomy in south-eastern Turkey, which was brought up among possible solutions to the problem, attracted strong negative reactions in the Turkish public opinion. Suggestions of cultural or political autonomy were immediately associated with the Treaty of Sevres, which anticipated the establishment of Armenia and Kurdistan, confining Turks to central Anatolia. Thus, the "Sevres syndrome" entered the Turkish political agenda in the spring of 1995. The Serves syndrome was a very good means to legitimize at least a defensive Turkish nationalism. Against that, Ali Rıza Kardüz questioned: "Is it that

2 Öke wrote that he is a Turkish nationalist, but his nationalism was bounded by the approval of Islam [*Türkiye* 29.10.1994].

difficult to embrace all people who accept this land as their patria and feel proud to live under this flag irrespective of their language, religion, race? What shall we be left with if we fall into pieces due to religious and ethnic differences?" (*Sabah*, 09.03.1995). Doğan Heper maintained "Simple citizens do not pursue any discrimination" but they are indoctrinated into Turkish and Kurdish nationalism each day (*Milliyet*, 25.12.1995)

The immediate effects of the syndrome can be observed on Demirel's change of position: one year after his remark on "constitutional citizenship", Demirel was in the opposite position. In the face of the increasing pressure from the Western countries for a compromise and recognition of minority rights of Kurds, Demirel, in a television interview in May 1995, spoke of a Western conspiracy against Turkey targeting a far worse situation than anticipated in Sevres (Kirişçi & Winrow, 2000, p. 197). Demirel stressed that the Turkish people did not want a democracy that would lead to the division of their territory. Thus, minority rights could not be granted to Kurds.

Conclusion

In the public discussions on Turkish citizenship, we can discern two main parties: the advocates of Kemalism and the proponents of the revision of Turkish national identity. This new polarization replaced the left-right politics in Turkey. The new political camps that emerged out of this replacement brought up surprising alliances. Political polarization based on the attitudes on the Kurdish problem and possible solutions to it, was also reflected in the Turkish press. Contributions of the press were realized in a not so properly democratic environment. Thus, all perspectives had to be expressed in relation to the leadership of high level politicians and still in a manner of political correctness.

As the Kurdish problem continued, measures taken against it bred an undemocratic environment. The parties to the discussion of citizenship faced a polarization through mutual accusations, further hindering the freedom of expression in Turkish society. By the end of 1995, business circles and civil society organizations became more active in engendering democratic solutions and the recognition of a Kurdish identity. The Kurdish problem began to be discussed in relation to minority rights, while the consensus in the public sphere on the indivisible integrity of Turkey was firm. Any compromise on minority rights, such as education and broadcasting in a mother tongue should not threaten the unitary character of the Turkish Republic. Thus, the Serves syndrome became one of the historical icons in the definition of Turkish national identity in the 1990s.

Despite the limits on the freedom of expression, the press in Turkey played an important role to mediate between parties in this controversial environment. Editors not only elaborated on existing ethnic problems but also contributed for the explanation of certain perspectives. However, the Turkish press was not completely free in every respect while playing the role of a mediator in public discussions. Pressures from the governments defined the boundaries of the discussions. Still, in the example of the five newspapers, we can discern that the Turkish press was successful in creating the medium for discussing radically different ideas in a peaceful language. Although in a language of political correctnes.

References

Akşin, S. et al. (Eds.). (2000). Türkiye tarihi (Cilt 5). *Bugünkü Türkiye: 1980-1995.* İstanbul: Cem Yayınevi.

Argun, B. E. (1999).Universal citizenship rights and Turkey's Kurdish question. *Journal of Muslim Minority Affairs, 19* (1), 85-101.

Ayaz, B. (1997). *Türk basını: Türkiye'de insan hakları ve Kürt sorunu örneğinde.* İstanbul: Belge.

Belge, M. (1996). *Türkler ve Kürtler: Nereden nereye.* İstanbul: Birikim Yayınları.

Bora, T., & Can, K. (2004). *Devlet ve kuzgun: 1990'lardan 2000'lere MHP.* İstanbul: İletişim.

Budak, N. (1994). *Varlığımızı hedef alan tehdit: Bölücü terör.* İstanbul: Boğaziçi.

Bulut, F. (1998). *Kürt sorununa çözüm arayışları.* İstanbul: Ozan Yayıncılık.

Çalmuk, F. (2001). *Erbakan'ın Kürtleri. Milli Görüş'ün Güneydoğu politikası.* İstanbul: Metis Yayınları.

Ergil, D. (1999). A synopsis of the Kurdish problem. *International Spectator, 34* (1), 19-22.

Ergil, D. (2000). The Kurdish question in Turkey. *Journal of Democracy, 11*, 122-135.

İçduygu, A., & Keyman F. (1998). Globalleşme, anayasallık ve Türkiye'de vatandaşlık tartışması. *Doğu Batı, 2*, 143-155.

İçduygu, A., & Çolak Y., & Soyarık N. (1999). What is the matter with citizenship? A Turkish debate. *Middle Eastern Studies, 35*, 187-208.

Kirişçi, K., & Winrow, G. M. (1997).*The Kurdish question and Turkey: An example of a trans-ethnic conflict.* London: Frank Cass Publishers.

Öke, M. K. (2005). *Derviş ve komutan: Özgürlük-güvenlik sarkacındaki Türkiye'nin kimlik sorunsalı.* İstanbul: Alfa.

Özdoğan, G. G. (1993). Türk ulusçuluğu ve Türki cumhuriyetler: Kuramsal ve tarihsel bir yaklaşım," *Toplum ve Bilim, 62*, 57-75.

Poulton, H. (1997). *Top hat, grey wolf and crescent.* London: Hurst & Company.

Saatçi, M. (2002). Nation-states and ethnic boundaries:

Modern Turkish identity and Turkish-Kurdish conflict. *Nations and Nationalism, 8*, 549-564.

Salt, J. (1995). Nationalism and the rise of Muslim sentiment in Turkey. *Middle Eastern Studies, 31* (1), 13-27.

Uyanık, M. (2003). *Üç tarz- siyaset. bir üst kimlik tasarımı olarak Türkiyelilik*. İstanbul: Metropol.

Watts, N. F. (1999). Allies and enemies: Pro-Kurdish parties in Turkish politics, 1990-1994. *International Journal of Middle East Studies, 31*, 631-656.

Yavuz, M. H. (1996). Turkey's "imagined enemies": Kurds and Islamists. *The World Today, 52*(4), 99-101.

Yeğen, M. (1999) The Kurdish question in Turkish state discourse. *Journal of Contemporary History, 34*(4), 555-568.

Newspapers and Periodicals

Milliyet (1992-1995)

Hürriyet (1992-1995)

Cumhuriyet (1992-1995)

Sabah (1992-1995)

Türkiye (1992-1995)

Nokta (1993-1995)

Küreselleşmenin Yarattığı Gerilime Sinemanın Yanıtı: Belgesel Sinema

Senem A. Duruel Erkılıç
Mersin Üniversitesi
saduruel@mersin.edu.tr

Giriş

Küreselleşme kavramının sıklıkla telaffuz edildiği 1990'lı yılların başından itibaren, belgesel sinema ürünleri de dikkat çekmeye başlamıştır. Dijital teknolojinin de sunduğu yapım, dağıtım ve gösterim olanakları ile belgesel film yapımında belirgin bir canlılık görülmüştür. 2004 yılında sadece Fransa'da 51 belgesel film, sinemada gösterim ağına girmiştir. (Marie, 2005, s. 89) Hollywood'un yarattığı fantastik dünyanın karşısında belgeseller, Amerika'da büyük gişe başarıları elde etmeye başlamış, Michael Moore eleştirel tavrını göstermekten sakınmadığı *Benim Cici Silahım (Bowling for Columbine, 2002) Fahrenheit 9/11 (2004)* gibi filmlerle türe büyük bir popülarite kazandırmıştır. Daha önceleri televizyon ekranlarına sıkışmış olan belgesel sinema, *Kuşlar Kanatlı Uygarlık (Le Peuple Migrateur 2001) Şirket (Corporation, 2003), 100 Yılın İtirafları (The Fog of War, 2003), Şişir Beni (Super Size Me, 2004)* gibi filmlerle beyaz perdeye taşınmıştır. Bu belgesellerin arasından sıyrılarak ele aldığı sosyal konularla dikkat çeken Agnes Varda'nın *Les Glaneurs et la Glaneuse* (2000) sadece Fransa'da değil, dünyada ses getiren bir yapım olmuştur (Marie, 2005, s. 89). Kısaca belgesel sinema sert bir biçimde eleştirdiği sistem içinde, kendine zor da olsa bir yer açmıştır. 1996'dan 2002'ye kadar yaklaşık olarak 15 belgesel film Amerikan iç pazarında gösterim ağına girmiştir. 2003'te bu rakam neredeyse 3 katına çıkmış, 2004 yılında 50 film olmuştur. 50 belgesel yapım, Amerika'da gösterim ağına giren sinema filmlerinin toplamının %10'unu oluşturmaktadır (Arthur, 2005, s. 18). Michael Moore'un *Fehrenheit 9/11* adlı filminin Amerika'da aynı anda 868 sinema salonunda gösterime girmiş olması, buna karşılık 10 yıl önce 1994 yılında Oscar ödülü alan *Brother's Keeper* filminin videobantlarının dağıtımcı bile bulamamış olması, belgesele duyulan ilginin nereden nereye geldiğini daha da net ortaya koymaktadır. Tabii ki kurmaca filmlerin baskın var oluşuna karşın, sinemalarda gösterim ağına girmeyi başaran belgesel filmlerin, çoğunlukla ya Amerika yapımı ya da belli merkezlerde üretilen filmler olduğu gözden kaçmamalıdır. Dolayısıyla bu çalışmada ele alınan yapımlar da, genellikle sinemalarda yaygın olarak gösterim şansı bulan belgesellerdir.

Belgeselin yükselişe geçtiği bu süreçte, yanlılığı ve tarafsızlığı da tartışmaya açılmıştır. Michael Moore'un ve ardıllarının etkisiyle, belgesel sinemanın dili ve söylemi değişmeye başlamıştır. Gerek dijital teknolojinin sağladığı olanak ve kolaylıklardan dolayı, gerekse taraflılık veya tarafsızlık gibi politik ve etik nedenlerle, belgesel sinemada gerçek ve gerçeklik sorunu irdelenmeye başlanmıştır.

Bu çalışmada, 2000'li yıllarda küreselleşme rüzgarının yarattığı ortamda Rönesansını yaşayan belgesel sinemanın köklerinin 1960'lı yılların militan sinema, cinéma vérité, direct cinéma akımlarına uzandığı belirtilecek, buna karşılık, "yeni tarz belgesel", "radikal belgesel" olarak tanımlanan bu dönemin belgeselleri ile 1960'ların politik sinema örnekleri arasında farklılıklar olduğu dile getirilecektir. İkinci olarak küreselleşmenin etkisiyle oluşan "gerçeklik kaybı"nın belgesel yapımlara yansıması üzerinde durulacaktır. Belgeselin, gerçeklik arzusunu ve ihtiyacını karşılayan bir tür olarak öne çıkmasına rağmen, kurmacaya eğilim gösteren anlayışın yaygınlaşması; belgeselle kurmacanın iç içe geçişli hale gelmesi, bununla bağlantılı olarak "mocumentary" (sahte belgesel) veya "pseudo-documentary" (sözde belgesel) gibi alttürlerin varlığı tartışılacaktır. Üçüncü olarak ise belgeselin anlatım yapısının ve biçiminin dramatik yapımlara kaydığı, belgesel dilinin kurmacayı da etkilediği görüşü üzerinde durulacaktır. Bu çerçevede Michael Moore'un *Benim Cici Silahım, Fahrenheit 9/11* belgeselleri ile Metin Yeğin'in *Patronsuzlar* serisi üzerinde durulacak; belgesel ve kurmacanın iç içe geçmesi *Bir Başkanın Ölümü* ile *Guantanamo Yolu* filmleri üzerinden tartışılmaya çalışılacaktır.

Belgesel sinema, toplumsal çatışmaların irdelendiği, küreselleşme sürecinde barış ve savaş konularının özgün yapımlarla tartışıldığı bir platform olarak ele alınacaktır. Son yıllarda yaşanan kültürel ve toplumsal farklılıkları ve bunların oluşturduğu çatışmayı anlamanın ve anlatmanın bir yolu olarak belgesel sinema ön plana çıkmaktadır. Belgeselin yükselişine ilişkin bu dönüşüm nasıl olmuştur? Hollywood'un ürettiği fantastik dünya ile bağımsız yapımların yansıttığı gerçek (tartışmalı olsa da "gerçek"), nasıl eş zamanlı olarak bir arada var olabilmektedir? Bu soruların yanıtlarını arayabilmek için belgeselin yükselişinde küreselleşmenin etkilerini ve küreselleşmeye dair yaklaşımları incelemek faydalı olacaktır.

Küreselleşme ve Belgesel

Küreselleşme kavramı, 80'li yıllardan itibaren farklı disiplinler tarafından, sosyal, politik, ekonomik, teknolojik ve kültürel perspektiflerden sıklıkla değerlendirilmiştir. Bir görüşe göre küreselleşme, daha önceden başlayan bir sürecin devamıdır (Robertson,1991, Thompson ve Hirst, 2003). Bir başka görüşe göre ise, geçmiştekinden farklı, özellikle son 20 yılda, bilgi ve iletişim teknolojileriyle öne çıkan bir süreçtir. Robertson'a (1999) göre "bir kavram olarak küreselleşme, hem dünyanın küçülmesine, hem de bir bütün olarak dünya bilincinin güçlenmesine" gönderme yapar (s. 21). Küreselleşmeyle birlikte enformasyon ve sermayenin hızla yer değiştirebildiği, ulusal sınırların çözüldüğü, etnik ve dinsel kimliklerin öne çıktığı, çok uluslu şirketlerin yaygınlaştığı bir döneme girilmiştir. Küreselleşme sürecinde, serbestleşme-özelleştirme, yerel-küresel, evrensel-tikel, homojenleşme- farklılık, melezlik-çeşitlilik gibi birbirine zıt ilkeleri ve eğilimleri diyalektik açıdan bir arada görmek olanaklıdır (Tomlinson, 2004, s. 31). Bir bakıma küreselleşme, karmaşık süreçlerin bir arada olması anlamını içermektedir.

Bu süreçte, ulus devletlerin sonunun geldiği iddia edilirken milliyetçiliğin bir karşı tepki olarak dünyada yaygınlaştığı görülmektedir. Aynı zamanda küreselleşmenin yerelleşmeye yaptığı vurgu, etnik kimliklerin yeniden yapılanmasını sağlamaktadır. Böylece milliyetçilik hem etnik kimliklere bağlı olarak, hem de etnik kimliklerin karşısında durarak yükselmektedir. Küreselleşme sürecinde çok uluslu şirketlerin ve sermayenin sınır tanımaz biçimde gelişmesi, çevresel/iklimsel felaketlere neden olabilmektedir. Benzer biçimde, küreselleşen sermayenin etkisiyle zengin-fakir ayrımı katlanarak artmaktadır.

Morley ve Robins, (1997) küreselleşme süreçlerinin yarattığı korku ve endişenin "Amerikanlaşma" tehdidi ile ilişkilendirildiğini belirtir (s. 39). Bu düşünceye göre, kültür endüstrisinin önemli bir parçası olan sinema, "globalization=americanization" (küreselleşme= Amerikanlaşma) formülü çerçevesinde yer almaktadır (Morley ve Robins, 1997).

Belgesel sinema küreselleşmenin doğurduğu gerilimleri yansıtan ve sonuçlarını tartışan, kendi içinde küreselleşme=amerikanlaşma denkleminin dışına çıkmaya çalışan bir üretim ortamı olarak görünmektedir.

Neden Belgesel Sinema?

Belgesel yapımların artmasında küreselleşmenin doğrudan ve dolaylı birçok etkisi vardır. Öncelikli olarak küreselleşmenin yarattığı toplumsal gerilimler söz konusudur. Karmaşık süreçleri içeren küreselleşme, değerlerin sarsıldığı, ön kabullerin yerinden oynadığı bir dönemi de işaret etmektedir. Belgesel sinema, arayışın, araştırmanın, anlamaya ve çözüm bulmaya çalışmanın bir yöntemi olarak karşımıza çıkmaktadır. Joris Ivens, bir belgesel filmin amacının, genellikle toplumsal, ekonomik, teknik, siyasal, kültürel bir sorunu; topluma tüm düşünceleri iletmeye ve bilgileri öğretmeye yardımcı olacak veya ona toplumsal bir çözüm bulduracak şekilde anlatmak olduğunu ifade etmiştir (aktaran Cereci, 1997, s. 25). Bu açıdan baktığımızda, belgesel sinema ürünlerinin, genellikle toplumsal krizlerin yaşandığı dönemlerde artması anlaşılır olmaktadır. Günümüzde belgesel sinema, yeni sistem arayışının doğurduğu toplumsal açmazların dile getirilebileceği ve tartışılabileceği bir mecra olarak karşımıza çıkmaktadır.

Belgeselin yükselişinin arkasındaki bir diğer neden ise dijital teknolojidir. Belgesel film yapım pratikleri, yapım içeriği ve film dağıtım mekanizmaları üzerinde, küreselleşmenin ve onun kardeş kavramı dijitalleşmenin etkileri belirleyicidir. Hızla gelişen dijital teknoloji, sinema gibi belgesel yapımına da belirgin olanak ve kolaylıklar getirmiştir. "Gözün demokratikleşmesi" dijital teknolojinin varlığı ve sunduğu olanaklarla gerçekleşmektedir. 1980'lerden itibaren enformasyon teknolojilerinin (iletişim teknolojileri-bilgisayarlar, uydu ve internet) yaygınlık kazanması, uluslararası değişim/etkileşimi hızlandırmakta ve küresel dönüşüm sürecini etkilemektedir. Bu açıdan dijital çağda kolaylıklar sadece yapım olanakları ile sınırlı kalmamakta, ana akım medyanın dışında kalan yapımlar da, oluşturulan dijital dağıtım ağlarından kısıtlı da olsa yararlanabilmektedir.

Belgesel Sinema Küreselleşmeye Nasıl Bakıyor?

Küreselleşmeyi olumlu açıdan değerlendiren bakış açısına göre temel olarak belgesel sinema, küreselleşmenin getirdiği ekonomik, politik, kültürel boyutta toplumlararası bütünleşmeyi destekleyen veya amaçlayan yapımlar ortaya koyarken bir yandan da varolan farklılıkların tanınmasına, bu farklılıkların ortaya çıkarılmasına hizmet etmektedir. Belgeseller dünyanın farklı uçlarındaki insanların, kültürlerin, yaşantıların paylaşımını ve birbirleriyle etkileşimini sağlamaktadır. Aynı şekilde belgesel sinema, yağmur ormanları ile ilgili bir çevre sorunu, nesli tükenmiş bir kuş, mülteciler, dünyanın herhangi bir bölgesindeki etnik çatışma gibi pek çok olayın, sorunun, faaliyetin, gerçekleştiği sınırları aşarak küresel ölçekte ses getirmesinde önemli bir kanala dönüşmektedir.

Küreselleşme ile Amerikanlaşmayı eşanlamlı olarak

değerlendiren bakış açısına göre ise belgesel, tek tipleşmenin önüne geçecek, küreselleşme dediğimiz olguya panzehir olacak potansiyeli taşımaktadır. Bu bakış açısına göre, Hollywood'un önerdiği tek tipleşmenin karşısında belgesel sinema, yerel ve özgün olanı aktaran ve dolayısıyla insanı özgürleştiren bir yapıya sahiptir. Büyük oranda tüm dünyayı kuşatan benzeri durumlardan, yaşama biçimlerinden, görsel formlardan ya da zihinsel döngülerden, yani bir aynılaşma sürecinden başka bir düzleme seyircisini taşıma gayretindedir. Bu açıdan küreselleşmenin temel araçlarından biri olan anaakım medyanın karşısında belgesel, alternatif bilgilenme kaynaklarını oluşturmakta ve içinde bulunduğumuz gerçekliğe ilişkin farklı yorumlar geliştirilebilmesinin yolunu açmaktadır.

Bununla bağlantılı olarak belgesel filmlerde, iktidarın meşruiyetini küresel ölçekte sorgulama potansiyeli mevcuttur. Bu sorgulamayı yapan belgesel sinema, bir bakıma alternatif küresel hareket gibi yeni siyasal paradigmanın içinde yer almakta ve özerk, parlamento dışı bir mücadele biçiminin, günümüzdeki sözcülüğünü yapmaktadır. Örneğin çeşitli eleştiriler aldığı kadar, övgülerle de adından söz edilen Michael Moore'un belgesel filmleri, küresel ölçekteki bu sorgulamayı gerçekleştirmekte, Bush yönetimini ve uygulamalarının iç yüzünü yorumlayarak tartışmaktadır. Birleşmiş Milletlerin Irak ambargosu ve Irak savaşı üzerine Tom Jackson ve Kathy Keller'in gerçekleştirdikleri *Greetings From Missile Street/ Füze Sokağından Selamlar (2001)* ile Avusturalyalı gazeteci ve yönetmen John Pilger'ın *Paying the Price: Killing the Children of Iraq /Bedel Ödemek: Iraklı Çocukları Öldürmek (2000)* adlı belgeselleri de küresel ölçekte egemen olanı sorgulayan yapımlardır.

Belgeselin bir ifade mecrası olarak, giderek daha fazla tercih edilmesinin temel nedenlerinden biri, insanlık dramlarının yaşandığı, yoksulluk, evsizlik, savaş, işkence gibi sosyo-ekonomik ya da politik meselelerin görselleştirerek tartışıldığı zemini oluşturması olarak değerlendirilebilir. Ryan ve Kellner'a göre (1997) sinema, günümüzde politik mücadelelerin yürütülmesi açısından özel önem taşıyan bir kültürel temsil arenasıdır (s. 38). Filmler, toplumsal gerçekliğin nasıl kavranacağını, daha da fazlası ne olacağını belirlemek için muhalif temsil biçimlerinin birbirleriyle yarıştıkları bir zemindir. Kurmacanın egemenliği karşısında muhalif anlatımını geliştiren belgesel sinema, bir bakıma günümüzde politik aktivizmin sürdürüldüğü etkili bir platformdur. Parlamento dışı bir mücadele alanı ve neoliberal düzenin muhalifi olarak özellikle 2000'li yıllarda sesini geniş kitlelere duyuran belgesel sinema, 11 Eylül sonrasında muhalif olma özelliğini daha da keskinleştirmiştir. Günümüzde farklı görüşlerdeki toplum kesimlerinin kamusal ve politik alanda seslerini ve taleplerini duyurmalarında belgesel sinema önemli bir kanala dönüşmüştür.

Metin Yeğin'in yönettiği *Patronsuzlar* (2006) serisi küreselleşmenin farklı yüzleri üzerine düşündürür. Bu belgesel serisi küreselleşmeye karşı bir eleştiri ve başkaldırı niteliğindedir. Neoliberal politikaların sonuçlarını, Galler'den Arjantin ve Uruguay'a, oradan da Bolivya ve Venezüella'ya kadar uzanan bir dizge içinde ele almaktadır. Galler'de işsiz bırakılan madencilerin oluşturduğu kentlerin yok olması, işçilerin Tower Madeni'ni ele geçirerek direnişe geçmeleri, neoliberal politikalar sonucu krize sürüklenen Arjantin ve Uruguay'daki işçilerin direnişleri, Chavez'in Bolivar devrimi, doğalgaz satışını durduran Bolivya'lı işçiler, Bolivya ve Venezülla'daki altın ve gümüş madenlerindeki özelleştirmelere direnişlerin öyküsü anlatılmaktadır. *Patronsuzlar* serisinin ilk filmi Galler Tower Madeni, kürselleşmenin sonucunda "devletin küçüldüğü söyleminin aksine, devletin büyük sermayeye hizmet eder duruma getirilmiş olduğu, büyümeye devam edenin devlet olduğu; aslında devletin küçülmesi söyleminin, emekçi ve mütevazi kesimlerle ilgili işlevler budanırken, başka yanlarının büyümesini ifade ettiği" düşüncelerini (Başkaya, aktaran Uluç, 2003, s. 183) kanıtlar niteliktedir. *Patronsuzlar* serisi aynı zamanda, küreselleşmenin bir başka sonucunu hatırlatmaktadır: O da dünyanın uzak noktalarındaki insanların birbirlerinin problemlerine duyarlı hale gelmeleridir. Yeğin'in bu belgesel film serisi, küreselleşmenin ortaya çıkardığı sorunlara eğilirken, Türkiye'den İngiltere'ye, oradan da Güney Amerika'nın çeşitli ülkelerine uzanarak sorunun küresel ölçekte olduğunu dile getirmektedir.

Belgeselin kamusal alanda sesini duyurmak için bir kanal olarak kullanılması yeni değildir. İngiliz Belge Okulu'nun önde gelen yönetmen ve kuramcılarından Basil Wright'a göre, "belgesel film, şöyle ya da böyle bir film değil, yalın olarak kamuoyuna yaklaşım yöntemidir." (Wright, aktaran Adalı, 1989, s. 15). Paul Rotha'ya (2000) göre, "belgeseller, zamanın keskin bir eleştirisini yapmak zorundadır. Belgeseller toplumsal amaca sahiptir. Onun ereği, yalnızca bugünün yapısını ortaya koymak değil, aynı zamanda geçmişin ürünlerinin değerlendirmesini yapabilmektir. (...) Bu nedenle belgesel filmlerin işlevleri ve gelişiminin, eğlence sinemasından uzak tutulması gerekmektedir" (s. 18). Bu düşünceye göre belgesel sinemaya, en temelinde toplumsal bir amaca hizmet etme işlevini yüklenmiştir.

Paul Rotha (1968) belgeselin toplumsal işlevlerine dair bugünle de bağdaştırabileceğimiz şu düşüncesini dile getirir: "Benim inancıma göre, belgeselcinin en başta gelen görevi, halkı ve onun sorunlarını, işlerini ve hizmetlerini yine halkın gözleri önüne sermek için, kitleyi inandırma sanatındaki ustalığını gösterebileceği durumlar bulmaktır. Onun işi, halkın bir yarısını öbür yarısına tanıtmak, çağdaş toplumun bütün karşıt yanlarını kapsayan daha derin ve daha anlayışlı bir toplumsal çözümleme getirmek, güçsüzlüklerini araştırmak, olayları bildirmek, deneylerini dramatize etmek ve toplumun egemen sınıfı arasında daha geniş ve daha içten bir anlayış yaymaktır" (s. 343). Rotha'nın bu sözleri, uzun bir aradan sonra belgeselin bugün geldiği durumu tanımlamaktadır. Doğa ve tarih belgeselleri ile televizyona sıkışmış olan bu sinema türü, bir bakıma küreselleşme rüzgarıyla başlangıç noktasındaki işlev ve amaçlarına geri dönmüştür. Kendi içinde farklı açılımlar sağlamıştır. Daha önceki yıllarda teorileri oluşturulmuş, gerilla sineması, cinema vérité, cinéma direct gibi akımlara dayanan alt türlerinden yeniden söz edilmeye başlanmıştır. Bu kapsamda küreselleşme karşıtı hareketin sözcüsü olan belgesel yapımlar da, belgeselin temel işlev ve amaçlarına geri dönüşünün işareti olarak görülebilir.

Belgesel sinema ile II. Dünya Savaşı sonrası kaynaklarını Üçüncü Dünya ülkelerinden alan Üçüncü Sinema arasında benzerlikler vardır. Üçüncü Sinemacılar, pasif izleyiciyi eğlendirmeye yaslanan Hollywood sinemasıyla, Avrupa'nın birey odaklı sinemasını, içinde bulundukları toplumsal mücadelede işlevsiz, hatta zararlı görmüş, bunun yerine militan ve politik bir sinemayı savunmuşlardır. (Buchsbaum, 2007, s. 51) Bu çalışmada söz konusu edilen son dönem belgesel filmler de, tıpkı Üçüncü Sinema örnekleri gibi küreselleşme sürecinde oluşan sorunlara karşı mücadelelerini, 1960'lı yılların muhalif hareketlerine benzer biçimde yürütmektedirler.

Laurent Marie (2005) , "Counterglobalization Documentary" olarak tanımladığı küreselleşme karşıtı belgesel film yapımını, militan sinemanın genetik bir devamı niteliğinde değerlendirmektedir (s. 90). Fakat küreselleşme karşıtı belgesellerin, 1968 yılında ve Berlin Duvarının yıkıldığı yıllarda yükselen militan sinemadan farkları vardır. Laurent'e göre (2005) militan sinema, 60'ların sonunda – özellikle de Fransa'da – işçi sınıfını, baskılanmış kitleleri, solunun reformist yaklaşımlarını anlatmaktadır (s. 91). Bugün gerçekleştirilen küreselleşme karşıtı belgeseller ise, işçi hareketlerine karşın kapanan fabrikaları, finans sektörü tarafından konulan kuralları, eşitsizliğin yükselişini, çalışma koşullarının küresel düzlemde bozulmasını ele almaktadır. Bir diğer deyişle, küreselleşme karşıtı belgeseller, militan sinemanın savunduğu devrimci ve ilerici ideallerin çöküşünü resmetmektedirler. Geçmiş yıllardaki militan sinemanın izleyicilerine umut vaat eden ruhundan farklı olarak karamsarlık yaratan bir dünya gerçeğinden söz etmektedirler.

İdeallerin deforme olduğu ve en temel insani değerlerin tekrar tartışılır hale geldiği bir dünyayı Michael Moore'un filmlerinde görürüz. Propaganda sineması, gerilla sineması, militan belgesel, yeni radikal belgesel gibi farklı sözcük ve kavramlarla tanımlanmaya çalışılan filmleriyle Moore, Amerikan sistemine derinlikli ve sert eleştirilerini getirmekte, anti-Bush tavrıyla dikkat çekmektedir. Bir bakıma ilerici ideallerin çoktan çökmüş olduğunu Amerika sistemi üzerinden anlatmaktadır. Ahmet İnsel (Radikal, 2004), egemen medyanın karşısında Moore'un sinemasının açıktan ve haklı bir propaganda olduğunu belirtir. Gösteri toplumunu can alıcı yerinden vurduğunu ve bu yeni radikalizmin en büyük silahının gerçek olarak sunulanın gizli yüzüne ışık tutmak olduğunu dile getirir.

Yönetmen *Roger and Me*'de, Flint kasabasındaki General Motors otomobil şirketinin fabrikalarının bazı bölümlerini kapatmaları üzerine otuz bin kişinin işsiz kalmasını anlatır. *Benim Cici Silahım/Bowling for Columbine*'de 1999'da Colorado'da iki çocuğun bir okula saldırarak 12 öğrenci ile bir öğretmeni öldürmesi olayından yola çıkarak Amerikan toplumunun silahla ilişkisine eğilir. Bireysel silahlanma ile Amerikanın silahlı müdahalelerinin artması arasında paralellik kurar. *Fahrenheit 9/11*'de ise Amerika'daki 2000 yılının şaibeli başkanlık seçimlerinden yola çıkarak zaafları olan Bush yönetiminin iç ve dış politikadaki tavırlarına odaklanır. Barnouw (1993), Moore'un *Roger and Me* (1989) adlı filmini bir "makale film" olarak niteler ve cinéma vérité'den gerilla belgesele dönüştüğünü ifade eder (s. 338). Moore, *Benim Cici Silahım* ile "En İyi Belgesel Oscar"ını alırken görüşlerini ve genel tutumunu şu sözlerle açıklar: "*Biz (belgeselciler/halk) kurmaca olmayanı seviyoruz ama kurmaca zamanlarda yaşıyoruz. Kurmaca seçim sonuçlarına dayanılarak seçilen kurmaca bir başkanın seçildiği zamanlarda yaşıyoruz*" (aktaran Genco, 2003, s. 61). Bu sözleri ile Moore, anti-Bush tavrını göstermenin ötesinde, 2000'li yıllar dünyası için giderek sorunsallaşan bir konuya parmak basmaktadır: O da şiddetli gerçeklik arzusuna karşın, gerçeğin yerini alan kurmacadır.

Belgesel Sinema ve Gerçeklik

Bonitzer'e göre (2006) görüntüye en çok inanan Hollywood sinemacıları aynı zamanda görüntünün gerçekliğine de en çok inanan, hiç değilse arzulayan sinemacılardır (s. 114). Bütünüyle görüntüye dönüştürülmüş gerçeklik, gerçekliğe dönüştürülmüş görüntü, bir Amerikan rüyasıdır. Hiperrealizm bu rüyanın bir ürünüdür.

Gerçek dünyada referansı bulunmayan nesnelerin bilgisayar ortamında yaratılabildiği, fiziksel gerçekliğinden bağımsız olarak varlığını sanal ortamda sürdürebilen yaratıkların oluşturulabildiği dijital çağda, "gerçek" kavramı doğrudan sinemanın tartıştığı ana meselelerinden biri olmuştur. Lev Manovich'in (1996) belirttiği gibi dijital verinin değişebilirliği, sinemanın doküman olarak gerçeklik değerini de değiştirmiştir. Özellikle belgesel sinemada ve tarihsel filmlerde etik kavramının sıklıkla ele alınması ihtiyacı doğmuştur. Görüntü bir taraftan belge olarak değerlendiril(e)meyecek bir düzleme taşınırken diğer taraftan güvenlik kameralarına kaydedilen görüntülerin yansıttığı gerçek, her zamankinden daha fazla önem taşımaya başlamıştır.

Dijital teknoloji, görüntünün gerçeklikle olan ilişkisinin bir kez daha sorgulanmasına zemin hazırlarken, belgeselin gerçeklikle kurduğu ilişki onu sinemanın bir alt türü konumundan çıkarmaktadır. Politik belgesel, haber-belgesel ve gerilla belgesel gibi alt türlere, "küreselleşme karşıtı belgesel"in (counterglobalisation documentary) yanı sıra, sözde belgesel (pseudo-documentary), bir başka deyişle sahte belgesel (mockumentary) gibi alt türler de eklenmeye başlamıştır.

Belgesel sinemanın, bugün kitlelere daha fazla seslenebilmesindeki temel nedenlerden biri gerçeğe ve gerçekliğe yaklaşımı olarak görünmektedir. Çağdaş sorunlarla ilgilenmek, Hollywood'un yarattığı kaçış psikolojisinden arınmak, toplum olarak silkelenerek gerçeklerle daha dolaysız ilişki kurmak, özellikle Batı dünyasında, 11 Eylül sonrasında gelişen önemli bir paradigma olarak göze çarpmaktadır. Belgesel sinema çıkışı ve tarihsel gelişimi açısından ele alındığında toplumsalla bağı olan ve "gerçek" olana kanal açan bir sinemadır. Hatta bu nedenle, Armes, geçmişteki baskıcı ortamlardan dolayı, politik sinemanın belgeselden çok kurmaca yönünde geliştiğini vurgular (Armes, aktaran, Çetin-Erus, 2007, s. 41).

İngiliz Belge Film Okulunun kurucusu John Grierson, belgesel sinemayı "gerçeğin yaratıcı bir şekilde yorumu" olarak tanımlamaktadır. L Herman'a göre, "belgesel film, öyküsü gerçeğin içinden çıkan bir çalışmadır. Bu nedenle de gerçekçi bir konum içinde, öykünün geçtiği gerçek yerde ve öyküyle ilgili kişilerle uygulanır" (aktaran Adalı, 1986, s. 14). Belgesel, modern toplumların yaşadığı gerçeklerin bir kritiğidir (Talbot, aktaran Cereci, 1997, s. 25). Sinclair Road, İngiliz Belge Okulu'nun İngiltere'deki "günlük yaşamı, çalışma ortamını, emekçi insanı konu alarak ve etkinliğini koruyan konut, beslenme gibi sorunlara eğilerek çağdaş sorunlardan (Hollywood'un yaptığı gibi) kaçma değil, bunlarla savaşma istemini ortaya koyan" yapıtlar sergilediğini belirtmiştir. (aktaran Adalı,1986, s. 9). Belgesel sinemanın gerçeklikle olan kuvvetli ilişkisi, onun amacından kaynaklanmaktadır. Roy Levin'e göre (aktaran Cereci, s. 25), belgesel film hiçbir zaman popüler bir nitelik taşımamıştır. Çünkü o popüler, avantür yapımların, eğlence dünyasının standartlarına boyun eğmemiştir.

Weiss'den yola çıkarak Adalı şunları ifade eder: "Toplumsallık açısından ele alındığında, gerçekçi sinemadan daha da etkin bir yaklaşım biçimi olarak karşımıza belgesel sinema çıkmaktadır. Gerçeği bir öykünün yörüngesinde değil, gerçekliğin kendi dramatik gerilimi içinde aktararak seyircinin gerçek dünyaya yeni bir gözle bakmasını sağlamaya çalışan belgesel sinemanın en önemli niteliği, seyirciden olaylar ve kişilerle kendini özdeşleştirmek yerine, bunları tartıp yorumlamasını beklemesidir" (Weiss, aktaran Adalı, 1986, s. 8).

Belgesel sinema çoğunlukla gerçeğin kanıtı olarak değerlendirilmiştir. Belki de hiçbir zaman bugün olduğu oranda taraflılığı veya tarafsızlığı tartışılmamış, gerçekliği ve nesnelliği sorgulanmamıştır. Belki de hiçbir zaman bu oranda kurgusal olmamıştır. Gösterilenin seçilmiş bir gerçeklik olduğu konusu sıklıkla dile getirilse bile, belgeselin gerçekle kuvvetli bir bağı olduğu düşüncesi kabul görmüştür. Bonitzer (2006), "belgeselin tuzaklarla dolu, iğrenç dalaverelere, en göz boyayıcı hilelere elverişli bir tür olduğu"nun bilindiğini belirtir (s. 121). Bunun "tam da gerçek adına ve aygıtın görünürdeki nesnelliğinden" kaynaklandığını söyler.

Sözde-belgesel (pseudo-documentary), hayali belgesel, kurgusal belgesel /kurmaca belgesel (mockumentary) gibi kavramlarla tanımlanan yapımlar, belgeselin oluşturduğu bu nesnellik yanılgısını kullanmaktadır. İlk denemeleri 1950'li yıllara, dayanan—hatta Orson Welles'in *Dünyalar Savaşı* adlı ünlü radyo oyununa göz kırpan—bu belgesel türü, gerçekte olmamış olay veya durumların gerçekmiş gibi anlatıldığı, ele alındığı bir yapıya sahiptir.

Söz konusu belgesel tarzının en çok tartışılan son örneklerinden biri, *Bir Başkanın Ölümü*'dür. *(Yön: Garbriel Range, 2007)* Film, George Bush'un 2007 yılında bir suikast sonucu ölümünü ve bu olayı takip eden soruşturma sürecini konu alan almaktadır. Belgesel anlatım yöntem ve biçemiyle ilerleyen filmde, yönetmen gerçek olayların görüntülerini farklı şekillerde bir araya getirerek, efektlerle müdahalelerde bulunarak kurmaca sahneler oluşturmaktadır. (Bush'un vurulduğu sahnede CGI efekleri ve dublör kullanılmıştır). Filme yönelik eleştirilerden biri, Bush karşıtlarına bir Bush suikastı fantezisi yaşatıldığıdır. Bir diğeri ise Bush'un masum bir kurban gibi gösterilmesidir. *Bir Başkanın Ölümü*'nde olası suikastçının Suriye asıllı bir Müslüman olması, toplumsal önyargılara ilişkin önemli ipuçları içerir. Bush'un ölümünden sonra Başkanlık koltuğuna oturan Cheney, suikastın ardında Suriye'yle Başkan Esad'ın olduğunu öne sürerek, Amerikan filolarını Suriye üzerine yollar. Gabriel Range bugün için geçerli olan toplumsal gerilim noktalarını gayet net bir biçimde tanımlar. Günümüz Amerika'sında süregelen ırkçılığı, vatandaşlık haklarının çiğnenmesini ve en önemlisi her geçen gün yeni komplo teorileri üreterek dünyayı kontrolü altına almaya çalışan zihniyeti sorgular. Bu sorgulamayı yaparken belgesele yüklenen gerçeklik yanılsamasını altüst eder. Gerçeklik zemini, artık yapısal olarak gerçeğe yaslanan belgesel türü dolayımıyla ayaklarımızın altından kaymaktadır.

Bu filmle birlikte, gerçek ve kurmaca arasındaki ayrımların günümüzdeki geçişliliğine bir kez daha dikkat çekilmektedir. Zizek'in (2002) deyimiyle, bilgisayarlarla yaratılan sanal gerçeklikte değil de daha temel bir düzeyde medyanın bizi bombardımana tabi tuttuğu imgelerin artan hipergerçekliğinde meydana gelen "gerçeklik kaybı"nı yaşadığımız bir dönemde, belgesel gibi gerçeklikle ilişkisi doğrudan olan bir anlatım türünün, "gerçeklik kaybını" somutlayan alt türlere yönelmesi yadırganmayabilir (s. 168).

Belgeselin Kurmacayı Dönüştürmesi

Bir yandan belgeseller kurmacaya kayarken, diğer yandan da belgesel sinemanın dili ve estetiği, kurmaca filmler üzerinde etkili olmaktadır. Belgeselin anlatım dilinin, kurmaca filmlere nüfuz ettiğini söylemek yanlış olmayacaktır. Artık kurmaca filmde gerçeklik duygusunu pekiştirecek biçimde hareketli kamera görüntüleriyle, bir haber röportajını anımsatacak biçimde kameraya bakarak konuşan oyuncularla, gerçek olayların nerdeyse birebir anlatımlarıyla, kurmaca görüntülerin içinde yer alan gerçek belge görüntüleriyle karşılaşırız. Hollywood'un kurduğu fantastik dünyalara, gerçek dışı yaratıklara, olaylara, anlara karşın, gerçek; belki fantastik olandan çok daha ilgi çekici olduğu için kurmacanın yerini almaktadır. Küreselleşme ile başlayan süreçte gerçekle olan bağlarımız öncesinden farklı bir biçimde oluştuğu için kurmaca, belgesele öykünmektedir.

Gerçek bir olayı aktaran, ama kurmaca bir yapım olan *Guantanamo Yolu (2006)*, kumaca ile belgeselin iç içe geçtiği melez bir örnektir. Alan Rosenthal'ın (1995) tanımlamasından yola çıkarsak iyi bir docu-drama örneğidir (s. 15). *Guantanama Yolu*'nun anlatım dili, "haber gerçekliği" üzerine kurulmuştur. 10 Eylül 2001'de İngiltere'deki evlerinden ayrılan Pakistan asıllı İngiliz vatandaşı üç Müslüman gencin öyküsünü aktarmaktadır. Bu gençlerin tek amacı, arkadaşları Asıf'ın düğününe katılmaktır. Pakistan'da namaz kıldıkları camideki vaazdan etkilenip insani yardımda bulunmak üzere Afganistan'a geçerler. Bu tam da Amerika'nın Afganistan'ı işgaline denk gelir ve kendilerini savaşın ortasında buluverirler. El-Kaide militanı sanılan bu gençler, ABD askerleri tarafından esir alınır. Bundan sonra Pakistan asıllı Müslüman İngiliz gençlerin, Guantanamo'da yaşadıkları esaret ve işkence aktarılır. Gençlerin kameraya bakarak başlarından geçenleri anlattıkları sahneler, gerçek bir belgesel izlenimi yaratmaktadır. Ayrıca filmde ara ara izlediğimiz Amerikan medyası tarafından çekilmiş haber görüntüleriyle, yaşanan gerçeklerin arasındaki derin uçurum, medyanın yönlendirici etkisi üzerine bir kez daha dikkat çekmektedir.

Guantanamo Yolu'nun tıpkı bir belgesel gibi karakterlerle özdeşleşmeyi önleyecek yapıda olması, izleyicilerin dikkatini, sadece karakterlerin dramına değil, olayların nesnel bir sorgulama zemininin bulunmayışına da çekmektedir. Film, Michael Moore'un *Benim Cici Silahım* belgeselindeki gibi, kendisine düşman arayan bir sistemin yarattığı korkuların vardığı boyutları ve bunların insanlar üzerindeki etkilerini tartışmaktadır. Kürselleşmenin sonucunda etnik ve dini kökenlerin daha da belirleyici hale geldiğini bu bakımdan ırkçılığın ve milliyetçiliğin giderek yükseldiğini hatırlatmaktadır.

Küreselleşmenin Yan Etkisi: Korku ve Dehşet

Benim Cici Silahım ile dikkatleri üzerine çeken ve son yıllarda arka arkaya gerçekleştirilen *Uygunsuz Gerçek/An Inconvenient Truth(Yön: Davis Guggenheim, 2006), The Fog Of War/Yüzyılın İtirafları (Yön: Eroll Morris, 2003)* gibi Amerikan belgesellerinin yarattığı ortak bir duyguya ve düşünceye değinmekte fayda var. Gerek Al Gore'un küresel ısınmanın sonuçları üzerine alınacak tedbirleri dile getirdiği *Uygunsuz Gerçek*; gerekse Kennedy ve Johnson dönemlerinde ABD Savunma Bakanı olarak görev yapan Robert McNamara'nın, Küba krizine, Vietnam savaşına ilişkin gizli kalmış gerçekleri anlattığı *Yüzyılın İtirafları*, izleyicilere verdikleri anlamlı mesajların ötesinde bir şey daha söylemektedirler: O da "gerçek" vurgusudur. Daha önce Hollywood tarafından üretilen kurmaca filmlerde izlediğimiz gibi, Amerikanın parçası olduğu veya sorumlu olduğu, dünyayı ilgilendiren pek çok olayda, bilinenlerin ötesinde bir "gerçek" vardır. *Yüzyılın İtirafları*'nda, Kennedy ve Johnson'ın oval ofisteki görüşmelerinin bant kayıtlarını dinleriz. *Uygunsuz Gerçek*'te ise küresel ısınma gerçeğinin uzun zamandan beri farkında olunduğuna dair kanıtları izleriz. Bu filmlerdeki "gerçek" vurgusuyla, şimdiye kadar açıklan(a)mayanları artık öğrenmenin vakti geldiği söylemekte, fantasmaya doymuş izleyicilere, gerçeğin acı verici ve şiddetli yüzü gösterilmektedir. Bu filmlerdeki ortak motif ise, Amerika'da 11 Eylül sonrasında oluşan korku ve dehşet duygusundan kaynaklanan, "itiraflar" gibi görünmektedir. Amerika alternatif belgesel yapımlarıyla adeta günah çıkartmakta ve "uygun olmayan gerçekler"i açıklayarak arınmaktadır. *Benim Cici Silahım*, -belki de fark etmeden- bu arınma sürecinin başlangıcında katalizör görevini üstlenmiştir.

Benim Cici Silahım, Amerikanın kapıldığı "korku hastalığını", bu nedenle Ulusal Silah Birliği'nin kuruluşunu, 1980'lerden itibaren korku hastalığının sonucu olarak sağ politik görüşe meyil edilmesini mizahi bir dille anlatmaktadır. Moore, Amerikan insanında korku yaratan ögeleri birer birer ele alır: Afrika'dan gelen katil arıları, 2000 yılında hayatı durduracağı söylenen bilgisayar virüslerini, Çin'in atomik casuslarını... Korku ve dehşet öyle bir noktaya varmıştır ki, herhangi bir uluslararası olası tehlikeye karşı tedbir olarak, başka bir ülkenin toprakları işgal edilmektedir. Zizek, bu derin dehşet duygusunu Spielberg'in *Azınlık Raporu* filmiyle bağlantılandırarak şöyle aktarır: "Azınlık Raporunda canavarca bilimsel deneylere maruz bırakılarak geleceği görme kapasitesi ile donatılan üç insan sayesinde, suçlular henüz suçlarını işlemeden tutuklanıyorlar. Bu fikri uluslararası ilişkilere uyarlarsak kamuya resmi Birleşmiş Devletler uluslararası politika felsefesi olarak ilan edilmiş Bush'un (ya da Cheney'nin) yeni doktrinini elde etmez miyiz? Bu doktrin ABD'ye, kendisine karşı açık bir tehdit oluşturmayan ama ileride bu türden bir tehdit oluşturabilecek ülkelere saldırma hakkı tanıyor" (aktaran Yücel, 2004, s. 40). Bir bakıma korku ve dehşet, işgalin, şiddetin meşrulaştırılmasında kullanılan silahlardan birine dönüşmektedir.

Sonuç

Son dönem belgesel sinema, küreselleşme rüzgarından beslenmiştir. Küreselleşme ile bağlantılı olarak ortaya çıkan toplumsal, ekonomik, kültürel, politik, ekolojik vb. sorunların dile getirilmesinde önemli bir kanala dönüşmüştür. Küreselleşme sürecinde aynılaşan medya seçenekleri arasından sıyrılarak, özgün ve farklı olanın sesini duyurmuş, politik aktivizmin yeni biçimini oluşturmuştur. Bu açıdan belgesel sinema, çıkış noktasındaki temel işlevlerine kavuşmuştur. Küreselleşmeyi eleştiren belgesel sinema, diğer taraftan da küreselleşmenin önemli bir taşıyıcısı olan yeni iletişim teknolojileri dolayısıyla sesini geniş kitlelere duyurma imkanı bulmuştur. Dijital teknolojinin gerek film yapımına getirdiği kolaylıklardan, gerekse büyük dağıtım ağları dışında filmin gösterimini sağlayan internet gibi olanaklardan yararlanmıştır.

Yapısı gereği popüler kültür endüstrisine mesafeli duran belgesel sinema, 2000'li yıllarda, sıkıştığı televizyon ekranlarının dışına taşmış, "belgesel sinema"dan sadece "doğa belgeseli"ni çıkarsayan anlayışı kırmıştır. Kurmaca filmleri aşarak genel gösterim ağı içinde gişede ilk kez bu oranda başarılı olmuştur. Düşük maliyetle üretilmesine karşın büyük gişe başarıları elde eden bu türe yönelimin gerek ticari gerekse sosyo- kültürel nedenleri vardır. Bu filmlerin çoğunlukla Amerikan yapımı olması ise dikkat çekicidir. İroniktir; baskın ve egemen olan artık sadece Hollywood sineması değil, aynı zamanda ona muhalefet eden Amerikan bağımsız sinemasıdır.

2000'li yıllarda Amerika Birleşik Devletleri tarafından işgal edilen ülkelerde temel yaşam koşullarının, uluslararası hukuk, insan hakları gibi küreselleşme söyleminin sahiplendiği kavramların yerle bir olduğu bir dönemde, belgesel sinema bunlara karşılık ortak değerleri savunmak adına oluşan safın sözcüsü olmuştur. Bir bakıma Amerikan anaakım medyası, karşıtı olan El-Cezire'yi nasıl yarattı ise, 80 sonrasının muhafazakar Hollywood'u, militan Amerikan sinemasını ve muhalif dünya sinemasını ortaya çıkarmıştır. Masalsı, fantastik, dijital efekt harikası kurmaca yapımlar; politik, gerçekçi, haber gerçek mantığını taşıyan belgeselleri görünür kılmıştır.

Kurmaca ve belgesel eş zamanlı olarak var olmuş, gerçeğe duyulan ihtiyaç ile kurmacaya duyulan ilgi her ikisini de eş zamanlı olarak var etmiştir. Melez sinema türleri oluşmaya başlamıştır. Sahte belgesel, sözde belgesel gibi türler bu ihtiyaç veya arayışın sonucunda başkalaşarak ortaya çıkmıştır.

Belgesel sinema, "kuşku çağı" söylemini kamçılamadığı, komplo teorilerinin gişe yapmadığı, genel gösterim ağı içinde farklı ve özgün olanın sesini duyurabildiği, küreselleşme=amerikanlaşma denklemini kendi sınırlı alanı içinde de olsa aştığı noktada küreselleşmenin yarattığı gerilimlere yanıt oluşturabilecektir.

Kaynakça

Adalı, B. (1986). *Belgesel sinema.* İstanbul: Hil Yayınları.

Arthur, P. (2005). Extreme makeover: The changing face of documentary. *Cineaste*, s. 18-23.

Barnouw, E. (1993). *Documentary, a history of non-fiction film.* New York: Oxford University Press

Bonitzer, P. (2006). *Kör alan ve dekadrajlar* (Çev. İ. Yasar). İstanbul: Metis Yayınları.

Buchsbaum, J. (2007). Üçüncü sinemaya yakından bir bakış (Çev. E. Kaya). E. Biryıldız, & Z. Erus (Eds.), *Üçüncü sinema ve üçüncü dünya sineması* içinde (s. 51-72). İstanbul: Es Yayınları.

Cereci, S. (1997). *Belgesel film.* İstanbul: Şule Yayınları.

Çetin-Erus, Z. (2007). Manifestolardan günümüze üçüncü sinema tartışmaları. E. Biryıldız, & Z.Erus (Der.), *Üçüncü Sinema ve Üçüncü Dünya Sineması* içinde (s. 19-50), İstanbul: Es Yayınları.

Genco, E. (2003). 11 Eylül'ün ardından ABD'ye bakmak. *Yeni Film, 2*, 47-64.

Hirst, P., & Thompson, G. (2003). *Küreselleşme sorgulanıyor* (Çev. Ç. Çiğdem & E.Yücel). Ankara: Dost Yayınları

İnsel, A. (Ağustos, 2004). Moore vesilesiyle yeni gerçekçilik. *Radikal İKİ.*

Manovich, L. (1996). *What is digital cinema?*

http://jupiter.ucsd.edu/~manovich/text/digital- cinema.html (Son erişim 8 Haziran 2006).

Marie, L. (2005) French documentary and globalization. *French Politics, Culture and Society, 23*(3), 89-105.

Morley, D & Robins K.(1997). *Kimlik mekanları* (Çev. E. Zeybekoğlu). İstanbul: Ayrıntı Yayınları.

Robertson, R. (1999). *Küreselleşme -toplum kuramı ve küresel kültür* (Çev. Ü. H. Yolsal). Ankara: Bilim ve Sanat Yayınları.

Rosenthal, A. (1995). *Writing docudrama/dramatizing reality for film and TV.* Newton: Focal Press.

Rotha, P. (2000). *Belgesel sinema* (Çev. İ. Şener). İstanbul: İzdüşüm Yayınları.

Ryan, M., & Kellner, D. (1997). *Politik kamera* (Çev. E. Özsayar). İstanbul: Ayrıntı Yayınları.

Tomlison, J. (2004). *Küreselleşme ve kültür* (Çev. A. Eker). İstanbul: Ayrıntı Yayınları.

Uluç, G. (2003). *Küreselleşen medya: İktidar ve mücadele alanı.* İstanbul: Anahtar Kitaplar.

Yücel, F. (2004). Moore'u anlamak. *Altyazı Dergisi, 32*, 35-40.

Zizek, S. (2002). *Kırılgan temas* (Çev. T. Birkan). İstanbul: Metis Yayınları.

Ethical Media, Creating Shared Symbols Toward Intercultural Communication

Seyyed Hassan Hosseini
Sharif University of Technology
hoseinih@sharif.edu

Introduction

Issues concerning religion and media studies which in recent years more than ever before have sparked the interest of scholars including theologians and media researchers could be discussed from various perspectives. This studies range from the mere theoretical to the radical applied studies of religion, ethics and media.

In this article, while touching upon some of theoretical issues of religion and media, a new theory on this subject is to be presented along with some of its outcomes. I contend that in this new theory, the essence of religious and Ethical teachings could be compatible with the framework of media, especially when the main objective is related to the intercultural communication and peace.

It is worth mentioning here that although I don't agree with the idea upon which religion and religious tenets and teachings are reduced to the norms of Ethical values, in this paper we are not entering the very complicated debates and discussions about the religions and their correlation with Ethics, whether the religion is the consequence of Ethics or visa-versa. However, with the recognition of the two different and separate domains of religion and Ethics, in this paper the core concepts of Ethics and morality are to be considered as equivalent to the common religious teachings, if one focuses on the common foundations, the main objectives of religions, and the outcomes and consequences.

As it was said, the essence of media can be classified into three following branches, Functionalist, Essentialist and Interactive approaches which will be discussed very briefly.

1-Functionalist Approaches

Outlooks which generally could be termed as functionalist, consider the media as a mere tool and instrument which can be unproblematically employed by religious and ethical concepts and notions as well as other concepts which might even be contradictory to religion and ethics. However, this perception that the functionalist theories consider the media as an absolute container and carrier of different messages, seems to be inaccurate and shallow. Those who through philosophical approaches consider the technology as a tool for certain objectives or regard it as a human activity, are among those who regard the modern technology including the media as having the functionalistic nature. Heidegger is one of the philosophers who have strongly criticized the neutral approach to technology (Krell, 1977, p. 40).

From the functionalist viewpoint, the media in itself has no independent cultural identity and as a tool could be utilized and employed for dissemination of various and different messages. Undoubtedly, those who believe that the media are just the carrier and container and disseminator of messages and such a characteristic is the essential nature of the media, belong to the functionalist school. They even believe that commitment of the media to existing values is in fact turning the means into the goal, while the tool should not interfere in the outcome.

2- Essentialist Approaches

Essentialist approaches claim that the media essentially and intrinsically have an independent cultural and historical identity. Therefore in their interaction with other aspects of human life, the compatibility or incompatibility of this nature and essence with the other entities should be fully taken into consideration (Postman, 1993). These approaches are mainly supported by two different philosophical and media studies bases.

On one side, we should mention Heidegger's analysis in

this respect which is regarded as a philosophical aspect, and on the other side, Postman is very important from the media studies angle. Heidegger, by evaluation and analysis of the ontological basis of technology, strongly rejects the functionalist paradigm. In contrast to traditional interpretation, Heidegger considers the Technology as an ontological phenomenon (Krell, 1977). From Heidegger's perspective, the outlook based on functionalism should be rejected and cannot be reformed. Thus, technology is not a mere tool but is a kind of emergence and revelation (Heidegger, 1977). Based on this, Heidegger gives a strong warning to mankind about technology.

Heidegger points to the intrinsic danger of technology. He believes that the threat posed by technology against mankind is the secondary danger and the real and fundamental peril is aimed at the essence of the human being (Hoover, 1997, pp. 73-80).

> The threat to man does not come in the first instance from the potentially lethal machines and apparatus of technology. The actual threat has already afflicted man in his essence (Heidegger, 1966).

Based on his hypothesis, since the essence of technology (including the media), by conquering the nature, history and culture of human beings, has shaped man's cosmology and ideology, and such a domination and hegemony can never be oriented by any other means or nature, therefore any attempt to religionize the media or turn religion and ethics to media - according to Heidegger - is fruitless, useless and abortive. Similarly, technology could not have any interaction with religion and ethics and there exists a contradictory nature between them. However, he has spoken of a solution known as salvation, but this concept is so ambiguous that no clear or explicit meaning emerges (Heidegger, 1977).

On the other side, usually, in studies dealing with religion and media, references are made to McLuhan and his famous proposition, "The Medium is The Message" and to his disciple Neil Postman and those who believe that media have an independent essence. Here, due to the importance of views expressed by Postman, I briefly touch upon what he has said about opposite relationship between religion, Ethics and media (and television in particular).

By paying tribute to Mcluhan's views, Postman affirms that studying the tools which a culture uses for exchange of ideas and messages is essential for perception of that culture. He emphasizes that any new medium or tool is capable of imposing its essential form and content on public opinion and consequently determines the ideas, ways of thinking and the sentiments of the people. According to Postman, McLuhan means the same when he declares that "The Medium is The Message". Postman believes that in the social systems which pass through technocracy and enter the technopoly stage, culture, ethics and religion is necessarily surrendered to technology. He believes that in technocracy systems, despite the clashes and competitions, two different ideologies, culture and technology, did exist together and both were present. For instance, America in 19th century had technology at one side, and culture and tradition at the other side, both coexisted.

But by emergence of technopoly (monopoly of technology) one of these two ideologies is eliminated from the scene (Postman, 1993, chapter 3). Thus technopoly has a certain characteristics and nature and the most prominent feature of the technology is that it has replaced God.

He has expressed the same view about the media and television in particular, and in his critical view toward the media and specially television, has completely ruled out the possibility of combining media and religion because of their entirely different nature and essence. He says that the most important and fundamental element of a religion and ethics are their spiritual and super-natural sanctity, and because television by its nature is worldly, integration of these two would result in turning a holy concept to a materialistic ritual.

Thus, according to what Postman has said about the nature of the media, the consistency and compatibility of the two categories of religion, Ethics and the media is impossible. To him, it would result in the destruction of religion from holiness to nonsacredness (Postman, 1995, p. 175).

Consequently, any attempt to integrate ethical norms with the media would be fruitless and senseless.

3- Interactive Approaches

Although in studies dealing with two realms of religion and media, no such a term as "interactive approach" has been mentioned, I intend to point to those views which either without considering the theoretical basis or only through applied works, try to find a way to interact and interconnect these two important elements of contemporary man's life (Clark, 1997). I have mentioned many of theses solutions in a paper devoted precisely to the interactive approaches, and here no time and need to enter into that detailed discussion, nevertheless my intention to have a glance at such a topic is to indicate the significance and application of these valuable works in this regard. Generally saying, one can categorize all these efforts to the applied studies of religious use of media or media use of religion (Hoover, 1997).

4- Ethical Media Theory

Here, I will attempt to review what seems to me the ideal model, but before entering this discussion, some basic points should be clarified.

There is no doubt that what the essentialists have said about the nature and essence of the media is precise and accurate. Both the views expressed by Heidegger and his students, McLuhan, Postman and their followers are fundamental. Of course I do not mean to argue that the exclusive essence of the media could not be compatible with other independent entities such as religious or ethical identity, but undoubtedly the media are not mere tools for transmission of messages. However, rejection of functionalism and instrumentalism does not require the acceptance of radical essentialist approach of Heidegger and Postman about the media.

On the other side, an essential distinction should be made between religious doctrines and the ultimate objectives of religion. The strong pessimistic views expressed by Postman towards the possible compliance of media with religion probably originated in the lack of such a distinction. In my opinion, the main problem with Postman's view is that he has not made any distinction between fundamental religious concepts and the ultimate objectives of religion which is equivalent to the common norms of Ethics among the various cultures, which all revolves around the main axis of peace, tolerance and compromise. If by religion one means the exclusive religious doctrines, then postman's reasoning and conclusions might be to some extent acceptable or at least arguable. But as it was said, if we look at religion through its ultimate objective as an ethical, spiritual, or sacred notion, then Religious and Ethical Media which deal with the absolute goals of religion could be consistent with the essential characteristics of the media, including television (which is held by Postman the worst kind of the media in this regard).

Thus, what Postman has said about the essential incompatibility and inconsistency of the media with religious beliefs might be justifiable and relevant, if one means Mediated Religion by this combination. Mediated Religion is in itself the religion and its exclusive teachings and doctrines utilizes the media as a mere tool for transmission of the messages. A conservative media functionalist might believe in Mediated Religion, or precisely should believe, but any essentialist attitude towards the media prevents being a fundamental functionalist.

But by Religious Media, I mean the utilization of media through its unique identity, for achieving the religious objectives, ultimate goals and divine aspirations, rather than monopolistic teachings and beliefs of religions. It is worth mentioning that attaining the ultimate objectives of religions can be provided even through non-religious (but not anti-religious) concepts and perceptions (Hosseini, 2001, pp. 120-140).

Thus, in Religious Media, instead of paying attention to exclusive teachings of religions, their ultimate objectives, goals and meanings have to be taken into consideration. This sort of attention to Religious Media could even take place through non-religious and irreligious programs. For instance, if a fully entertaining program, piece of music or a video clip is aimed to fulfill the main objectives of religion, such as bestowing the meaning and direction to human life, or promoting the moral values among human beings, undoubtedly such programs are able to be included in the general category of Religious Media, even though no explicit religious teaching is distributed.

5- Ethical Media toward Intercultural Communication

What I would like to discuss here is how we can guarantee the freedom to create different cultural identities and at the same time have sufficient consensus at some level of values so that we can not only tolerate each other in peace but actually let the values of all groups inform our vision of the good society to achieve the global peace. My hypothesis is that the best way for achieving the mentioned objective is to focus on common norms and values among different cultures and make them the main core of intercultural communication.

Here, I would like to point briefly the main foundations of intercultural communication within which, tolerance, truthfulness of others, multiculturalism, and peace could be achieved.

1. As it was said, the most common values and norms among the chief cultures and religions could be perceived through moral norms. On the other hand, the main core of all human morality revolves around peace, compromise and truthfulness among all human societies. Thus, the role of ethical communication seems crucial and substantial.

2. Today we are facing a rise of multicultural frame of societies, but not necessarily cross-cultural. But what seems more important in this century is cross-cultural or intercultural communication. Indeed recognizing diversity is not recognizing the multiple mono-cultural models living together, but accepting to share humanity within respecting diversity (White, 1997). Of course intercultural communication not only does not negate exclusive identity of each culture, but also complements it. Thus the intercultural communication based on moral and religious norms are shared by all human communities. We do need a new culture based on believing in diversity. A new interest inside each culture for understanding diversity and considering it an essential element for establishing a common human universal. Such an interpretation of diversity and cultural pluralism which is founded on the commonalities among the diverse cultures, is not contrary to the oneness, but it is complemented by the unity. Based on this religious pluralism theory, the way the media interact with religion is based on acceptance of all cultures as having the same central tenets.

3. An important condition for an intercultural

communication is the respect of others which also could drive easily from the common values of Ethics among all human community. Additionally, it is worth mentioning that a frequent condition for conflict is the perception of the common good as limited. This means that if one group grows and develops, the others automatically lose because the common resources are limited. In an interactive world view, the common good is viewed as continually growing due to the diversity of contributions. If one group flourishes, all are automatically benefited because all view themselves as interdependent (Christians, 2003, pp. 293-304). This is also the other common moral value which human being believe in its significance and influence.

To conclude, I would like to restate the significance of Ethics of intercultural communication. Indeed, the sources of moral behavior are discovered within us, even though religions have come to flourish, activate and develop those values, in the will to live, realize our desires and give ourselves to others. Ethics is practiced in a human relationship of some degree of love, respect, and responsibility. No doubt that the essential and central message of all human values which are understood by common sense and have its validity and truthfulness primordially is peace and love.

Also, a sign of the maturity of the process of cultural communication is when all major cultural groups can affirm that the presence of other groups are important for the cultural richness of all, even while each group strongly defends itself as the bearer of a particular cultural standard.

At the end, I would like to emphasize that any attempt toward intercultural communication should be based on common goods and moral values. These values which are perceived intrinsically by human nature and primordiality, are to be considered by media the main message for attaining peace and compromise.

References:

Christians, C. (2003). Cross cultural ethics and truth. In M. Jalyon, M. Sophia, (Eds.), *Mediating religion: Conversation in media, religion and culture* (pp. 293-304). London: Continum.

Clark, L. S., & H, Stewart. (1997). At the intersection of media, culture and religion. In S. Hoover, K. Lundby (Eds.), *Rethinking media, religion and culture.* London: Sage Publication.

Heidegger, M. (1997). *The question concerning technology and other essays.* New York: Harper and Row.

Heidegger, M.(1966). *Discourse on thinking.* New York: Harper and Row.

Hosseini, S. H. (2001). *Religious pluralism or pluralism in religion.* Tehran: Sorosh press.

Hoover, S., & Lunby, K. (1997). *Rethinking media, religion and culture.* London: Sage Publication.

Hoover, S. (1988). *Mass media religion.* London: Sage Publication.

Postman, N. (1993). *The surrender of culture to technology.* New York: Vintage Book.

Postman, N. (1995). *Amusing ourselves to death.* Penguin Books.

Krell, D. (1997). *Martin heidegger: Basic writings.* New York: Harper and Row.

White, Robert. (1997). Religion and media in the construction of cultures. In S. Hoover, *Rethinking media, religion and culture.* London: Sage Publication.

Savaş/Barış Karşıtlığına Göstergebilimsel Yaklaşım: "Yazı Tura"

Simten Gündeş
Sanat ve Tasarım Fakültesi
İstanbul Kültür Üniversitesi
s.gundes@iku.edu.tr

Melis Oktuğ
Sanat ve Tasarım Fakültesi
İstanbul Kültür Üniversitesi
m.oktug@iku.edu.tr

1. Giriş

Dünyada çıkan tüm savaşların bir ya da birkaç filminin yapıldığı bilinmektedir. Bu filmlerden bazıları, "Kwai Köprüsü" (Davis Lean), "Apocalypse Now" (F.Ford Copolla), "Platoon" (Oliver Stone), "Full Metal Jacket" (Stanley Kubrick), "Saving Private Ryan" (Steven Spielberg),"Thin Red Line" (Terence Malick), "Pearl Harbor"dır (Michael Bay). Dünya Savaşları özellikle II. Dünya Savaşı ve Vietnam Savaşı, sinema da belki de aşk kadar sıklıkla kullanılan bir izlek olmuştur.

Sinema tarihinde, "Life is Beautiful" (Roberto Benigni), "Shindler's List" (Steven Spielberg) adlı filmlerde olduğu gibi soykırımın ya da son yılların en çarpıcı terorist saldırısını perdeye yansıtan "September 11" gibi çeşitli güç odaklarına dayandırabileceğimiz şiddet öykülerinin işlendiği birçok film de bulunmaktadır.

"Dramaturgie de la Guerre" (Lescot, 2001) adlı kitabın yazarı David Lescot'a göre, tiyatro sanatı tarihi, savaşı konu alan yapıtlarla başlamaktadır: "tiyatro savaşla doğmuştur çünkü dramatik yapının özünde olan çatışma, trajedinin kaynağı olan yaşam ve kentin üzerindeki tehdit unsurlarından doğmaktadır" (s. 10). Ancak yazarın altını çizdiği bir başka nokta da, tiyatro tarihinde savaşı konu olan yapıtlarda, savaş sürecinden çok, savaş sonrası yaşanan toplumsal ve ruhsal çöküşün ele alınmasıdır.

Bu çalışmaya konu olan "Yazı Tura" filminde, "düşük yoğunluklu savaş" ortamında, Güneydoğu Bölgesi'nde askerlik görevlerini yaparken gazi olan iki kişinin sivil yaşama uyum sağlama sürecinde yaşadıkları anlatılmaktadır. Bu süreçte ortaya çıkan kişi-içi ve kişilerarası çatışmalar göstergebilimsel çözümleme yöntemi ile ele alınacaktır.

2. Filmin Genel Betimlemesi

Yönetim ve senaryo: Uğur Yücel
Sanat Yönetmeni: Gülay Doğan
Kurgu: Valdis Oskarsdottir
Müzik: Erkan Uğur
Yapım: Türk-Yunan ortak yapımı, 2004
Oyuncular: Kenan İmirzalıoğlu, Olgun Şimşek, Bahri Beyat

Filmin adı, Yazı Tura "kaybetmek ya da kazanmak" üzerine kurulu iki seçenekli bir oyunu anımsatmaktadır. Yönetmen Uğur Yücel'in bir söyleşisinde belirttiği gibi, "*askerde ölmek mi yoksa askerden sağ çıkıp yaşamın içerisinde ölmek mi? Yazı mı tura mı? Bunun hangisi; ne fark ederdi ki hangi yüzü gelse...*" Başka bir deyişle, film kahramanları için madalyonun yalnızca bir yüzü görünmektedir bu filmde.

"Yazı Tura"da, 1999 yılında, aynı yerde askerlik yapan biri Göreme'li diğeri İstanbul'lu iki gencin kötü yazgıları ve askerlik sonrası yaşadıkları düş kırıklıkları dışında film boyunca asla kesişmeyecek yaşam öyküleri birbirinden bağımsız biçimde ele alınmaktadır. Filmin ana kişileri, iyi futbol oynadığı için ve fiziksel benzerliğinden ötürü "Şeytan" diye anılan ve annesiyle oturan Rıdvan; yaşamını çek ve senet mafyası adına para toplayarak kazanan ve babasıyla birlikte yaşayan "Hayalet Cevher"dir. Askerde,

Rıdvan, mayına basarak bir bacağını kaybetmiş; Cevher'in ise, sağ kulağı, patlama sonucu sağır olmuştur.

Rıdvan ve Cevher, ailelerinin yanına hem bedenlerini hem de ruhlarını Güney Doğu'da bırakarak dönmüştür. Rıdvan bacağıyla birlikte geleceğe ilişkin umutlarını da yitirmiştir. Artık futbol oynayamayacaktır. Ayrıca, askere gitmeden önce nişanlanan Rıdvan'ın kayınpederi tek bacaklı olması nedeniyle artık kızıyla evlenmesini istememektedir. Cevher ise, karanlık işler yaparak girdiği bataklıktan kurtulmayı ve "Gazi Büfe"yi açmayı düşlemektedir. Ancak, onun yaşamı da 17 Ağustos depremiyle sarsılacaktır. Depremde amcasının ölümü; deprem sonrası babasının Yunan olan ilk eşinin eşcinsel oğlunu da yanına alarak İstanbul'a gelmesi, Cevher'in yaşamında yeni bir karmaşaya yol açacaktır. Rıdvan, alkolle bu olumsuzluğa karşı koymaya çalışırken Cevher, yaşama duyduğu öfkeyi saldırgan davranışlarla, kimi zaman şiddete yönelerek yansıtmaktadır ve uyuşturucu kullanmaktadır.

Filmdeki ilk sahnelerde iki öykünün kahramanları tanıtılmaktadır. Daha sonra Uğur Yücel kamerasını Şeytan Rıdvan'a çevirecek ve uğruna savaştığı, bacağını verdiği insanlar tarafından nasıl düş kırıklığına uğratıldığını gözler önüne serecektir. "Yazı Tura"nın başlangıç sahnesinde, olayın gerçekleşme nedeni açıklanmadan Rıdvan'ın mayına bastığı an görülmektedir. Bir sonraki sahnede, protez takıldıktan sonra annesiyle eve dönen Rıdvan'ın kaygılı yüzü yansıtılmaktadır. Annenin oğlunun durumu karşısındaki çaresizliği, Rıdvan'ın yeni bedenine alışma güçlüğü ilk karelerden başlayarak öyküye egemen olmaktadır. Hemen ardından askerden dönen Hayalet Cevher'in sivil yaşama uyum çabaları görülmektedir. Kalabalık ortamlardan kaçınma, askeri üniformaya gösterdiği aşırı tepki, terleme, şiddete varan öfke, Cevher'in ruhsal durumunu betimlemektedir. Buna karşın, karanlık işleri bırakarak "Gazi Büfe"yi açma umudunu taşımaktadır. Şiddeti de, büfeyi açmak için son hazırlıklarını yapmakta olan Cevher'e ödenmesi gereken akçayı erteleyen kişiye yönelik olacaktır. Ona olan öfkesi öylesine büyük ve denetlenemez niteliktedir ki, cebinden çıkarttığı bıçağıyla saçını ve kafa derisini yüzer.

Film, bu sahneden sonra Şeytan Rıdvan'ı intihara sürükleyen olayların betimlenmesiyle sürmektedir. Rıdvan'ın öfkesi, Cevherin tersine "ötekine" değil kendisine zarar verecektir ve bu olaylar sırasında Rıdvan hem en sevdiği, güvendiği, anılarını, sırlarını paylaştığı arkadaşı Sencer hem de nişanlısı Şefika tarafından aldatılacaktır. Şefika, ailesinin Rıdvan'la evlenmesine karşı çıktığını bahane ederek onu reddedecektir. Oysa, Sencer'le kaçma hazırlıkları yapmaktadır. Rıdvan ise, her gece alkole sığınarak, onu kaçıracağını düşünmektedir. Bir gece, Sencer ve arkadaşları Firuz'la yine çok fazla alkol aldıktan sonra ayrılırlar. Aynı gece, Rıdvan bacağını kaybettiği günü arkadaşlarına anlatır. Lise aşkı Elif, köylerini terk ederek Bingöl'e yerleşmiştir. Ayrılırken ona okul bahçesinde çekilmiş bir fotoğraflarını bırakır. Mayına bastığı gün, teröristler karakolu basmış ve sabah saatlerine dek çatışma yaşanmıştır. Gün ışıdıktan sonra, gizlendikleri siperden çıkacakları sırada, Rıdvan yerde sürünen yaralı kadın teröristi fark etmiş ve dur uyarısında bulunmuştur. Bu uyarı karşısında silahını ona doğrultan teröristi öldürür. Kadın terörist lise yıllarında aşık olduğu Elif'tir ve göğsünden Rıdvan'da olan fotoğraf çıkmıştır. Bunu fark eden Rıdvan bilinçsizce çevreye ateş etmeye ve koşmaya başlar. Bu sırada da bacağının kopmasına neden olan mayına basmıştır. Öyküyü anlattığı gecenin bitiminde çok sarhoştur ve eve doğru yürürken arkadaşı Sencer'in arabasıyla nişanlısını kaçırdığına tanık olur. Onların ardından koşmaya çabalarken protez bacağı çıkar ve yere düşer. Doğrulur ve silahını ağzına götürerek ateşler. Rıdvan, film boyunca, sanrı (halüsinasyon) görmektedir. Gece ve gündüz Elif'in hayali peşinde dolaşmakta; Rıdvan'ın kabuslarında yer alarak onu ürkütmektedir. Silahı ateşlemeden hemen önce, yine Elif'in sokakta yürüyen düşünü görür ancak, ilk kez, gördüğü düş karşısında irkilmez ve gülümser. Mayına basmasına neden olan bu olayın düş mü yoksa gerçek mi olduğu açık bir biçimde belirtilmemektedir. Arkadaşı Firuz'a göre, Elif hala yaşamaktadır. Rıdvan'ın öyküsündeki son sahnede beliren gülümseme, onun yaşadığı düş kırıklığına karşı bir savunma aracı olarak geçmişe sarılması biçiminde de yorumlanabilmektedir.

Rıdvan'ın öyküsü intiharla sonuçlanırken, İstanbul'da yine kötü sonla bitecek olan Hayalet Cevher'in öyküsü başlamaktadır. Cevher'in babası Kıbrıs Barış Harekatı sırasında, Yunan olan ilk eşi Tasula'yı babası ajan olduğu gerekçesiyle henüz bebek olan oğluyla birlikte evden kovmuştur. Yaşanan depremin ardından Tasula, yanına oğlu Teoman'ı da alarak yıllar sonra ilk kez İstanbul'a gelmiştir. Teoman'ın eşcinsel olması Cevher için büyük bir yıkım olmuştur. Üvey kardeşinin tüm ısrarlarına karşın onunla dostluk kurmak, yakınlaşmak istemez. Tasula ve Teoman'ın Yunanistan'a dönmeden önce İstanbul'daki son gecesinde Teoman Tarlabaşı'na giden Cevheri aramaya çıkar. Cevher'e telefon ederek Beyoğlu'nda kaybolduğunu söyler ve eşcinsellerin buluştuğu bir barda biraraya gelirler. Ancak, tartışırlar ve Cevher barı terk eder. Teoman eve dönmeye çabalarken bir sokak kavgasına karışır ve ölümcül bir biçimde dövülür. Olaya rastlantısal olarak tanık olan Cevher, üvey ağabeyini dövenleri öldürür. Beyoğlu ve Tarlabaşı'ndaki karanlık yaşama çok alışkın olmasına karşın polisten kaçamaz. Onun da, Göremeli arkadaşlarına "ben bacağımı verdim size, sizin için savaştım" diye haykıran Rıdvan gibi polis aracına bindirilirken son sözleri "bana kelepçe takamazsınız, ben bu ülke için savaştım, gazi oldum" olacaktır. Filmin son sahnesinde Rıdvan ve Cevher'in yolda ilerleyen askeri cemse görüntüsü üzerine düşen sözleri vardır. Her ikisinin de kötü yazgılarını hazırlayan düşlerinin aktarılmasıyla film son bulmaktadır.

3. Çözümleme Yöntemi

Her sinema filmi kendi görüntü göstergelerini (ikonografi), kendi düzgülerini (kod), kendi iletilerini izleyiciye öncelikle türe, daha sonra konu ve izleğe özgü bir anlatım dili ile ulaştırmaktadır. *"Çözümlemenin ereği 'konu film'in genörneğini çıkartmaktır öncelikle, tıpkı bir giysinin kalıbını çıkartmak gibi! Yoksa, her türden filme 'kalıp' sayılabilecek bir 'genörnek' olarak değil hiç kuşkusuz... Her film kendi 'kalıbını' içermektedir"* (Gündeş; 2003, 13). Bu erek kapsamında, sinema dilinin teknik özellikleri ve filmsel anlatı yapısı çözümlenmektedir. Çözümleme sürecinde, teknik özellikler açısından; çekim ölçekleri, kamera açıları, kamera devinimleri, ışığın türü ve işlevi, renk kullanımı, konuşma, giysi ve bezem, ses ve görsel etkiler, geçişler ele alınırken; film olgusu, anlatı düzeyinde, kişi, zaman ve uzam bağlamında incelenmektedir.

Çalışmamamıza konu olan "Yazı Tura" filminde, film kişiliklerinin öyküsünü biçimlendiren temel izlekler, "savaş", "askerlik", "deprem", "mafya", "eşcinsellik"tir. Bu izlekler, filme konu olan iki yaşam öyküsünde, ötekiyle kurulan karşıtlık ilişkileri ve bundan doğan çatışmaların taşıyıcısı konumundadır. Öykülerin buluştuğu diğer nokta ise, anlatı kişilerinin yaşadığı travma sonrası oluşan stres bozukluğudur. Filmsel anlatıda, kişi-içi ve kişilerarası çatışma kapsamında ortaya çıkan karşıtlıklar, kişiliklerin askerlik sonrası yaşadıkları travma çerçevesinde yapılandırılmaktadır. Bu bağlamda, travmanın neden olduğu gerek kişi-içi gerekse kişilerarası çatışmalar göstergebilimsel çözümleme yöntemiyle tanımlanacaktır.

3.1. Çözümleme Aracı Kavramlar: Çatışma ve Travma Sonrası Stresin Yol Açtığı Ruhsal Bozukluk

Çatışma, Latince'de, tüm taraf olanların kayıplar verdiği savaş, çarpışma anlamını taşıyan "conflictus" sözcüğünden gelmektedir. Çatışma, geniş anlamıyla, insan topluluklarında ve bireylerde duyguların, güç ve yetkenin çeşitli koşullarda karşıtlaşmasına gönderme yapmaktadır: "1.Bireyler ve toplumlar arasında karşıtlık, düşünce uyuşmazlığı, bağdaşmazlık, savaşım 2. Bireyde karşıt duyguların aynı anda belirmesi, belirginleşmesinden kaynaklanan ruhsal gerginlik durumu, bağdaşamaz, uzlaşmaz içtepi, istek ve eğilimlerin bireyi aynı zamanda ve hemen hemen aynı güçle etkilemesi" (Güz, Küçükerdoğan, Sarı, Küçükerdoğan, Zeybek, 2000, s. 77). Çatışmayla ilgili tanım, uyuşmazlıkların kişi-içi ve kişilerarası düzeyde gerçekleştiğini göstermektedir. Kişinin çevresi ile kuracağı iletişim, kendi içinde başlamaktadır. İnsanın düşünmesini, duygulanmasını, kişisel gereksinimlerinin ayırdına varmasını, iç gözlem yapmasını, rüya görerek kendi içinden ileti almasını ya da kendine sorular sorarak bunlara yanıtlar üretmesini bir iç iletişim sayabiliriz. Kişiler iç iletişimin yanı sıra iç çatışmalar da yaşamaktadırlar. Bilinçaltındaki ya da bilinçlerindeki kimi etkenler iç çatışmalara yol açabilmektedir. Sonuç olarak kişi-içi çatışmalar, kişilerarası çatışmanın da başlangıç noktalarından birini oluşturmaktadır. Özellikle, yaşam koşullarındaki beklenmedik değişimler, bu çatışmaların oluşmasına ortam hazırlayan etkenler arasında yer almaktadır.

Çoğu kez, yaşamımızdaki değişimlere ayak uyduracak yeterli zamanı bulabilmekteyiz. Yaşamın zorlu deneyimleri, ameliyat gibi ağır sağlık sorunları karşısında, değişim sonucu oluşacak koşullara uyum sağlayabilir, yaşamla ilgili beklentilerimizi değiştirebiliriz. Ancak travma, kişinin planlı bir etkinliği sonucu oluşmamaktadır. İnsan eliyle oluşturulan savaş, şiddet gibi felaketler ya da doğa karşısında insanı güçsüz kılan deprem, sel gibi olaylar bu beklenmedik değişimlere örnek olarak gösterilebilmektedir. Bu türden olaylar, aynı ölüm gibi sıradan yaşam süren insanların deneyim alanına girmemektedir. Yaşadığımız dünya, çevremizdeki her nesne ve kavramın anlığımızda bir karşılığı bulunmaktadır. Su göstergesi, bireylerin dünya deneyimlerine göre ayrıksı çağrışımlar yapmakla birlikte, herkes için karşılığı bulunan bir kavramdır. Oysa, "ölüm" göstergesi, insan deneyiminin dışında kalmaktadır. Yaşam süren hiç kimsenin konuyla ilgili deneyimi olmadığından ancak ölüm sonrasıyla ilgili yaşantılar sonucu bazı çağrışımlar oluşmaktadır. Bu bağlamda, "anlamdırma" süreci de, travmatik olaylar oluştuktan sonra gerçekleşecektir hiç kuşkusuz.

Günümüzde, savaşta ölenlerin sayısı, çevrenin dengesinin bozulmasıyla yaşanan doğal afetler, toplumsal yozlaşmanın neden olduğu suç ve şiddet olaylarında görülen artış düşünüldüğü zaman, sıradışı olarak nitelenen bu travmatik durumlar artık insan deneyiminin bir parçasına dönüşmüştür. Şiddetin doğası ve türleri, savaş yöntemleri ve stratejileri öylesine geniş bir kapsama yayılmaktadır ki, çözümleme boyutunda oluşacak karşıtlıklar ve ayrımların belirginliği azalmaktadır.

Sıradan şansızlıkların karşısında travmatik olaylar, "hayat ya da beden bütünlüğüne yönelik tehditlerle ya da şiddet ve ölümle kişisel karşılaşmayı gerektirir. İnsanları terör ve çaresizliğin son haddiyle karşı karşıya bırakır ve felaket karşısında tepkilere neden olur" (Herman, 2007, s. 44). Savaş, doğal afet, cinsel taciz gibi travmalar sonrasında insanlar benzer duygular yaşamaktadır: "yoğun korku, çaresizlik, kontrol kaybı ve yok olma tehdidi" (Andreasen, 1985, s. 920).

İnsan, olumsuz durumlar, tehlikeler karşısında bedensel ve bilişsel tepkiler vermektedir. Ancak travmatik bir durum sözkonusu olduğunda, bu tepkiler anlamını yitirmektedir. Bu da, deneyim alanı dışında bulunan olağanüstü bir güç karşısında bireyin çaresizlik duygusunu ortaya çıkartmaktadır.

Travmatik olaylar, insan ruhunun derinliklerinde, duygu, bilinç ve bellekte kalıcı değişiklikler yaratmaktadır (Bkz. Herbert, 2007). Bu türden bir deneyim yaşamış kişi şimdiki zamandan kopmuş gibi hissetmektedir. Deneyimin ardından ise, tehlikenin her an yeniden ortaya çıkabileceği kaygısıyla sinir sistemi altüst olmakta ve aşırı düzeyde ruhbilimsel uyarılma gözlemlenmektedir. Gürültülere karşı aşırı duyarlılık, uyku bozukluğu, kabus görme, sanrı tüm bu belirtilerin bir göstergesi biçiminde bireyin yaşamını denetim altına almaktadır.

Olayın anımsanması sırasında, travmanın yaşandığı sürede ortaya çıkan duygu, düşünce ve imgeler yeniden canlanmaktadır. Bu canlanma da insanın belleğinde, travmatik olayın kalıcı bir yer edinmesine yol açmaktadır. Böylece, sürekli aynı tehdidin yaşanabileceği kaygısı ortaya çıkmakta ve adrenalin gibi beden kimyasallarının salgılanmasında düzensizlik oluşmaktadır. Travma sonrasında, kişi, her olayı bir tehlike, bedenine ve ruhuna yönelik bir tehdit gibi algılayabilmektedir.

Huzursuzluk ve öfke, travma yaşayanlarda en yüksek sıklıkla görülen tepkilerdir. Bu nedenle, insan duygu ve düşüncelerini denetlemekte güçlük çekmekte; çoğu zaman anlamsız ve gereksiz tartışmalara girmektedir.

Travma sonrası yaşanan stres bozukluklarının en ağır olanlarından biri, fiziksel zarar görme ya da bedenin bir parçasının yitirilmesi sonucunda oluşmaktadır. Çünkü, bu, aynı zamanda, travma öncesi kimliğin de yitirilmesi anlamını taşımaktadır. Birey, yeni bir kimlik edinme ve uyum sağlama süreciyle karşı karşıya kalmaktadır.

Travmatik olaylar, çalışmamıza konu olan "Yazı Tura" filminde olduğu gibi, "temel insan ilişkilerinde sorun yaratır. Aile, arkadaşlık, sevgi ve toplum bağlarını kırar. Başkalarıyla ilişkileri biçimleyen ve destekleyen kendilik yapısını paramparça eder" (Herman, 2007, s. 67). Bu bağlamda, filmsel anlatıda dramın kaynağında bulunan iki gazinin, askerlik sonrası yaşama uyum sürecinde yaşadığı travma sonrası stres bozukluğu kişi-içi ve kişilerarası iletişim çatışmalarının da temelini oluşturmaktadır. Çözümlemede, travma sonrası stres bozukluğunun sinema dili ve göstergeler aracılığıyla nasıl yansıtıldığı irdelenecektir.

4. Çözümleme

4.1. Sinema Dili Çözümlemesi

"Yazı Tura" adlı filmde kullanılan teknik özelliklerden en çarpıcı biçimde öne çıkan öğeler, ses ve görsel etkilerdir (efekt). Özellikle, Hayalet Cevher'in öyküsünün anlatıldığı bölümde, kameranın çok devinimli olması, film kişisinin karmaşık ruh durumunun bir göstergesi olarak kullanılmaktadır. Filmin ritmi kimi zaman, izleyicide baş dönmesi yaratacak kadar yüksektir. Ayrıca, film boyunca, yoğun bir uğultu ve kimi zaman kulakları sağır edecek bir gürültü etkisi duyulmaktadır. Her iki öykünün kahramanı da bir patlama sonucu gazi olmuştur. Bu nedenle, filmin genel akışı içindeki bu gürültü ortamı, kişilerin belleklerinden silinmeyen travmatik olaya gönderme yapmak amacıyla yapılmış bilinçli bir seçimdir.

Hayalet Cevher'in, kalabalık ortamlarda duyduğu kaygı, film kareleri flulaştırılarak yansıtılmıştır. Ayrıca ses efekleri kimi zaman belleklerinde yer eden patlama ve gerçek yaşam arasında geçiş sağlamak için de kullanılmaktadır. Gazi Büfe'nin duvarına askerlik arkadaşı Şeytan Rıdvan'la çekilmiş fotoğraflarını çakarken çekicin çiviye vurulmasıyla çıkan ses, filmde bir patlama gibi duyulmaktadır.

Şeytan Rıdvan'ın ruhsal durumu ise, daha çok dingin kamera devinimleriyle izleyiciye aktarılmıştır. Filmin Hayalet Cevher'in yaşamını konu alan sahnelerinde çeşitli ölçek ve açılar kullanılmıştır. Oysa Rıdvan'ın öyküsünün anlatıldığı bölümde yakın planlar çok az sayıdadır; ağırlıklı olarak orta ve genel ölçekli planlar çekilmiştir. Sinema dili aracılığıyla, Rıdvan'ın içine kapanık ruhsal durumu, Cevher'in öfke patlamaları, şiddetin dışavurumu sergilenmiştir.

Şeytan Rıdvan için kullanılan ses ve görüntü etkileri, lise aşkı Elif'le ilgili sanrılarda ortaya çıkmaktadır. Genellikle, korku filmi türünü andıran ses etkilerinin kullanıldığı gözlemlenmektedir. Bu bağlamda, Yazı Tura adlı filmde, biçim ve içeriğin birbirini tamamladığı söylenebilmektedir.

4.2. Anlatı Çözümlemesi

Filmin içeriğinin anlamlandırılması çözümlemenin bu düzeyinde ele alınmaktadır. Anlamlandırma sürecinde, kişi zaman ve uzam gerek birbiri içine geçmiş gerekse birbirini tamamlayan nitelikte bir yapı sunmaktadır. "Zaman, uzam ve kişi yerlemlerinin bir erdemi de bir anlatıda yeralabilecek bütün öğelerin bu yerlemlerle sıkı bir bağıntı içinde bulunması"dır (Yücel, 1993, s. 19). Kişilerin giydikleri giysiler, örneğin, işleri ve yaşama yönelik beklentileriyle özdeşleşmekte; başka bir deyişle, anlatının yapılandırılmasında yerlemlere eşlik eden bir "tutarlılık" göstergesi işlevini görmektedir. Anlatı kişilerinden Cevher karanlık işleri çağrıştıran kravatsız gömlek ve takım elbise giyerken, Rıdvan, bacağını yitirmesine karşın futbol oynayacağı günü düşleyerek milli futbol takımının ayyıldızlı üniformasıyla görülmektedir.

"Yazı Tura" adlı filmde, ana kişiler, Cevher ve Rıdvan, askerlik sonrası, yaşadıkları kentlere büyük umutlarla dönmelerine karşın bu isteklere ulaşamamaktan kaynaklanan bir düş kırıklığı yaşamaktadırlar. Ayrıca, bu vatan uğruna savaşarak gazi olmaları karşısında hak ettikleri ilgi ve saygıyı çevrelerinden görmediklerini düşünmektedirler.

Filmde yaşanan sarsıcı olaylar iki ana kişiliği farklı biçimlerde etkilemiştir. Travma sonrasında yaşanan ortak belirtilerin yanı sıra, Cevher ve Rıdvan'ın geçmişlerinin ve kişiliklerinin farklı oluşu, travma sonrasında sergiledikleri davranışların da farklılık göstermesine neden olmuştur. Filmde, daha çok askerlik sonrası bu kişiler tarafından yaşananlara ağırlık verilmektedir. Ancak yetiştirilme biçimleri, yetiştikleri çevreler, geçmiş yaşantıları konusunda da ipuçları vardır. Örneğin, kentte büyümüş olan Cevher'i yasadışı olaylara iten çevresel etkenlerin, savaş öncesi yaşamında da var olduğunu görmekteyiz. Cevher'in babası da kendisi gibi gençlik yıllarında uyuşturucu kullanmıştır. Annesi doğumunda kan kaybından öldüğünden babası tarafından büyütülmüştür.

Annesiyle yaşamakta olan Rıdvan'ın ise, savaş sonrasında daha içe dönük bir tutum sergilemesinin, yetiştiği ortamın dış dünyadan soyutlanmış bir çevre olmasıyla ilgili olabileceğini anlamaktayız. Bu temeller üzerinde gelişmiş olan kişilikleri nedeniyle, savaş sonrası yüzleşmek zorunda oldukları gerçekler ve kayıpları ile baş başa kaldıklarında, farklı tutum ve davranışlar göstermişler, acılarla başa çıkma yöntemlerini belirlemek için değişik yollara başvurmuşlardır.

Tüm bireylerde olduğu gibi, anlatı kişileri de, kendilerini çevresel etkenlere ve strese karşı korumaya çalışmışlardır. Ancak "Hiçbir kişilik çok yoğun ve uzun süreli strese dayanacak kadar güçlü değildir. Sonuç hastalığa kadar gidebilen reaktif davranış bozukluğu olabilir. Savaştaki asker bu konuya örnek olarak verilebilir" (Kozacıoğlu ve Gördürür, 1995, ss. 66-67).

Her iki ana kişiliğin de, gazi olmalarından kaynaklanan travmanın yanı sıra sivil yaşamda da yeni travmalar yaşadıkları görülmektedir. Şeytan Rıdvan'ın evlenmeyi düşlediği nişanlısı, askerlik dönüşü acılarını paylaştığı yakın arkadaşı Sencer'le kaçmıştır. Cevher ise, depremde amcasını kaybetmiş ve Yunanistan'dan gelen eşcinsel ağabey gerçeğiyle yüzleşmek zorunda kalmıştır.

Özellikle, Cevher'de travma sonrası stres bozukluğunun göstergelerinden olan, artmış uyarılmışlık belirtileri yoğun bir biçimde gözlemlenmektedir. Olaylar karşısında şiddete varan tepkiler gösterebilmektedir. Her iki kişilikte, film boyunca, travmatik olayı ya da bir yönünü çağrıştıran durumlar karşısında, terleme, huzursuzluk gibi fiziksel ve duygusal davranışlar belirmektedir. Travmanın bir başka fiziksel göstergesi de, bedenin bir bölümünün yitirilmesi sonucu ortaya çıkan ağrılardır. Böylece, film kişileri kendilerini sürekli varolan bir tehlikenin pençesinde gibi hissetmekte, gazi olmalarına yol açan olay, yeniden belleklerinde canlanmaktadır. Cevher ve Rıdvan, deyim yerindeyse kendi cehennemlerini yaşamakta ve insanlardan uzaklaşma, yeni kimliklerine uyum sürecinde bir yabancılaşma sözkonusu olmaktadır.

Bu yabancılaşma, Cevher'in Yunanistan'dan gelen eşcinsel ağabeyiyle tepe noktasına ulaşmıştır. Aynı babadan olmalarına karşın ağabeyin gerek Yunan gerekse eşcinsel olması nedeniyle, ötekiyle yüzleşme, iç hesaplaşma döneminde dönüm noktasını oluşturmaktadır. Cevher, babasının ağabeyini benimsetme çabaları ve yıllardır görmediği oğluna duyduğu özlemle sahip çıkması karşısında ailesinden daha da uzaklaşmıştır.

Kişinin çevreyi ve olayları algılama biçimleri ruhbilimsel koşullara göre değişmektedir. İçinde bulunulan durumun algıları etkilemesi, kişinin kendisiyle olan iletişim biçimini de etkileyebilmektedir. Algılar, ruhbilimsel durumun olduğu kadar, hatta kimileyin daha da fazla, davranışlar üzerinde etkili olmaktadırlar. "Psikolojik durumun algıyı etkilemediği koşullarda bile, kararı etkiler ve dolayısıyla iletişimin tarzını değiştirebilir: Örneğin sevdiğiniz birine herhangi bir nedenle öfkelendiğinizde, hala onu seviyorsunuzdur, yani onunla ilgili algı ve değerlendirmeniz değişmemiştir; fakat öfkenin altında yatan neden veya nedenlere bağlı olarak düşünür, karar alır ve davranırsınız; örneğin, kapıyı çarpıp çıkarsınız" (Erdoğan, 2005, s. 168).

Anlatı kişilerinden Rıdvan'ın algıları, savaş sonrası yaşadığı stresin etkisi ile hastalık derecesinde bozulmuştur. Kendisi de, ruhbilimsel bozukluğun ayırdına varmış ve film boyunca, ailesine, arkadaşlarına "benim kafam sağlam değil, ben sakatım" sözleriyle düşüncelerini aktarmıştır. Gerçek ile ilişki kopmakta, algı sapmaları, sanrılar yaşamaktadır. Yaşadığı iç çatışma onu intihara kadar sürüklemiştir.

Cevher'in işlediği cinayetin bir boyutu da algılarla ilgilidir. Cevher, cinsel sapmaları olan insanlara karşı nefret duygusu beslemekte, bunu da davranışlarına yansıtmaktadır. Üvey kardeşinin eşcinsel olmasını kabul etmekte zorluk çekmektedir. Ancak ona duyduğu tepki, onu "kardeş" olarak algılamasını değiştirmemiştir. Bu nedenle, üvey kardeşine zarar verenleri öldürmüştür. İçinde var olan hastalıklı yıkıcılık eğilimi, kardeşine zarar verene yönelmiştir. Yaşadığı travma sonrası duygularını denetleyememesi onu sağlıklı bir çözüm yolu aramaktan ya da uzlaşmadan alıkoymaktadır. Başa çıkamadığı öfkesi, üvey kardeşine de yönlenmekle birlikte, patlama noktası üvey kardeşiyle değil, ona zarar verenlerle yaşanmıştır. Eşcinsellere duyduğu nefret, zihnindeki "kardeş" kavramını yıkamamış, ancak denetleyemediği öfkesi onun katil olarak cezaevine girmesine neden olmuştur.

Cevher'in içinde yaşattığı kimi öfke ve birikimler, yaşantısında kendini fazlasıyla göstermektedir. Kişiliğinin başa çıkamadığı yoğun öfke duygusunu farklı biçimlerde yaşamış, çevresiyle olan iletişimine yansıtmıştır. Kişilerarası iletişimin sağlıklı olmasındaki temel koşul, kişinin kendiyle olan iletişiminde başarılı olmasıdır. Kişilerarası iletişim karmaşık bir süreçtir. Bireyler öncelikle buna gereksinim duymalıdır. Ancak ruhbilimsel açıdan sağlıklı olmayan bireyler, çevreyle sağlıklı iletişim kurma becerilerinden yoksun kalmaktadırlar. Kimi durumlarda, özellikle travma sonrası stres bozukluğu bulunan bireylerde, iletişim bir güç gösterme aracına dönüşebilmektedir.

Öfke ve düşmanca eğilimler, boyun eğme davranışına veya saldırganlık davranışına neden olmaktadır. Boyun eğen kişilerin düşmanca duygular içinde olmadıkları söylenemez. Ancak, onlar bu duygularını dışarıya değil kendi içlerine yöneltmeyi yeğlemektedirler.

"Yazı Tura" filmi bağlamında, Rıdvan'ın, savaş sonrasında yaşadığı öfkeyi daha çok içe yöneltttiği, Cevher'in ise dışa yöneltiği saptaması yapılabilmektedir. "Uysal tip boyun eğme eğilimi gösterirken, saldırgan tip iyi bir kavgacı olmak için elinden gelen her şeyi yapar. Tartışmalarda uyanık ve zekidir ve haklı olduğunu kanıtlamak için yoğun bir püskürtme savaşına girer. Sırtını duvara dayadığı ve kavga etmekten başka seçeneği kalmadığı zaman ustalığının ve gücünün doruğuna ulaşabilir" (Horney, 1995, s. 53).

Şiddet, herhangi bir kaynaktan geleceği düşünülen zarara karşı canlıların kendini koruma tepkisi olarak da tanımlanabilmektedir. Bu tepkisel bir şiddettir, yani burada amaç yok etmek değil, kendini korumaktır. "Küçük düşürülmeyle sarsılmış olması halinde güçsüzlerin ve sakatların yaralı öz-saygıyı onarmalarının tek yolu vardır: *lex talionis*'e yani 'dişe diş, göze göz' yasasına göre intikam almak. Öte yandan üretken bir yaşamı olan kişi, böyle bir şeye, olsa bile, çok az ihtiyaç duyacaktır. Yaralanmış, kalbi kırılmış küçük düşürülmüş bile olsa, üretken yaşam sürecinin kendisi, ona geçmişin yaralarını unutturmaya yetecektir" (Fromm, 1995, s. 27).

Cevher'in yaşamını niteleyen özellikler, üretkenlikten çok düş kırıklıklarıdır. Yaşadığı travmatik olayları aşamadığı gibi, şiddeti yaşamındaki sorunları çözmek için kullanmıştır. Rıdvan da, aynı nedenlerden ötürü kendi yaşamına son vermiştir. "Yaşamı yaratmak, güçsüz insanın yoksun olduğu nitelikler gerektirir. Yaşamı yok etmek, tek bir nitelik (güç kullanma) gerektirir. Güçsüz insan, elinde tabancası, bir bıçağı ya da güçlü bir kolu varsa, başkalarındaki veya kendindeki yaşamı yok ederek yaşamı aşabilir. Böylece kendini ona olumsuzlayan yaşamdan intikam alır" (Fromm, 1995, s. 31).

Cevher, bir başkasının yaşamını yok ederken, Rıdvan kendi yaşamını yok etmiştir. Geçmiş yaşantılarının ve kişilik özelliklerinin yanı sıra, savaşın olumsuz etkilerinin yaşanan dramdaki büyük payı tartışılmazdır. Yaşadıkları travmalar sonrasında yeterli desteğin sağlanabileceği bir ortamdan yoksun oluşları da onları bu sona sürüklemiştir.

Filmin ana kişilerinden birinin şiddete yönelmesi, diğerinin ise içine kapanması her ikisinin de yaşam öykülerinin geçtiği uzamlara da yansıtılmaktadır. Rıdvan'ın yaşadığı Nevşehir Göreme'nin, karlı ve puslu bir ortamı, ıssızlığı onun zaman zaman cehenneme dönüşen dünyasını çerçeveleyen bir öğe olarak karşımıza çıkmaktadır. Bu ortamın, film boyunca, Kapadokya Bölgesi'nin büyülü ve gizemli ortamına karşıt bir görünüm oluşturduğu söylenebilmektedir. Göreme'nin kalın karla kaplı, yokuş sokaklarının, sanki, Rıdvan'ın protez bacağıyla yürümesine engel oluşturacak bir etken gibi yansıtıldığı görülmektedir.

Filmde Cevher'in öyküsüne geçişte, ilk gösterge, uçan güvercinlerdir. Çerçevede yalnız uçan kuş görüntüleri yer alsa da, İstanbul'un simgesel uzamı, Eminönü'nde cami avlusunda yem atılan güvercinleri çağrıştırmaktadır. Nevşehir'de kameraya yansıyan dingin görüntülerden karmaşaya geçiş de kısa, ancak devinimli planla sağlanmıştır.

Filmsel zaman, iki ayrı mevsimde geçmektedir. Rıdvan'ın öyküsü, içe dönük kişiliğiyle özdeş kış; saldırgan kişilik Cevherin yaşamının anlatıldığı bölüm ise, yaz mevsiminde kurgulanmaktadır. Rıdvan'ın sahneleri genellikle loş ve karanlıkken Cevher'in yeraldığı bölümlerde, çok ışıklı ve aydınlık ortamlar tasarlanmıştır. Olay örgüsü, film kişileri askerden döndükten bir süre sonra başlamakta, birinin intiharı diğerinin ise, suç işlemesiyle sonlanmaktadır. Filmin başlangıcında, geriye dönüş vardır. Rıdvan'ın gazi olmasına yol açan olaydan bir parça görülmektedir. Daha sonra, Rıdvan, annesiyle birlikte protez takılması için ameliyata gitmesinin ardından, eve dönüş yolculuğu sırasında görülmekte; Rıdvan'ın yeni kimliğine alışma konusundaki kaygıları, annesinin duyduğu büyük acı beden dili göstergeleriyle izleyiciye ulaşmaktadır. Bu görüntüleri, Cevher'in geleceğe yönelik büfe açma düşleri ve bu düşü gerçekleştirmek için karanlık işlerle uğraşmasını konu alan sahneler izlemektedir. Kişiliklerin kısa tanıtımından sonra film, Rıdvan'ın öyküsüne odaklanmaktadır ve Rıdvan'ın öyküsü sonuçlandıktan sonra, ikinci bir film başlıyor gibi bir izlenimle Cevher'in öyküsüne geçilmektedir. Filmde, iki kişiliğin yeniden birlikte algılandığı tek sahne, son sahneye yansıyan konuşmalardır. Bu sahnede, izleyiciye ikisinin de aynı yerde aynı zamanda askerlik yaptığını anımsatmak istercesine, yönetmen, ilk tanıştıkları günlerde, Rıdvan ve Cevher'in düşlerini birbirlerine anlattıkları diyalogları yeniden sunmuştur.

5. Sonuç

"Yazı Tura" filmi kapsamında gerçekleştirilen film çözümlemesinde anlatıda kullanılan gerek teknik gerekse anlatısal araçların aşağıdaki karşıtlıkları ortaya koyduğu gözlemlenmektedir:
Sinema dili açından Rıdvan için dingin Cevher için ise, devinimli bir anlatım kullanılmıştır.

Rıdvan		Cevher
Dingin	≠	Devinimli

Anlatı yerlemleri açısından kişi düzleminde içe dönük ve saldırgan karşıtlığı oluşmaktadır.

Rıdvan		Cevher
İçe dönük kişilik	≠	Saldırgan kişilik

Uzam, filmin ana kişilerinin ruhsal durumlarıyla bağdaşan ıssız, dingin/ kalabalık, devingen karşıtlıklarını ortaya koymaktadır.

Rıdvan		Cevher
Issız	≠	Kalabalık
Dingin	≠	Devingen

Zaman, bağlamında ise, kişi ve uzam yerlemlerini tümleyen nitelikte bir karşıtlık ortaya çıkmaktadır.

<u>Rıdvan</u>		<u>Cevher</u>
Karanlık	≠	Aydınlık
Kış	≠	Yaz

"Yazı Tura"yı diğer savaş sonrası filmlerden ayıran özellikleri, iki bireysel **anlatı izlencesi**nin koşut bir biçimde ancak ardışık konumda **kişi/uzam/zaman** yerlemleriyle **mutluluk/mutsuzluk**, **sevi/sevisizlik** ve **ölüm/yaşam** ikilikleri ve karşıtsallıklarının çözümleme sürecinde aktarılan yapıya yerleştirilmesinde aramalıdır.

Kaynaklar

Lescot, D. (2001). *Dramaturgie de la guerre*. Paris: Circé.

Gündeş, S. (2003). *Film olgusu: Kuram ve uygulayım yaklaşımları*. İstanbul: İnkılap.

Güz, N., Küçükerdoğan, R., Sarı, N., Küçükerdoğan, B., & Zeybek, I. (2002). *Etkili iletişim terimleri*. İstanbul: İnkılap.

Herman, J. (2007). *Travma ve iyileşme* (Çev. T. Tosun). İstanbul: Literatür.

Andreasen, N.C. (1985). *Comprehensive texte-book of psychiatry*. Baltimore: Wiliams& Wiliams.

Herbert, C. (2007). *Travma sonrası ortaya çıkan psikolojik tepkileri anlamak* (Çev. M. Z. Sungur, E. Cömert). İstanbul: PsikoNET Yayınları.

Yücel, T. (1993). *Anlatı yerlemleri*. İstanbul: YKY Yayınları.

Kozacıoğlu, G., & Gördürür, H.E. (1995). *Bireyden topluma ruh sağlığı*. İstanbul: Alfa Basım Yayım.

Erdoğan, İ. (2005). *İletişimi anlamak*. Ankara: Erk Yayınları.

Horney, K. (1995). *Ruhsal çatışmalarımız*. (Çev. Selçuk Budak). Ankara: Öteki Yayınevi.

Fromm, E. (1995). *Sevgi ve şiddetin kaynağı*. Ankara: Öteki Yayınevi.

Oral History as a Method for Peace Journalists: Sevgül Uludağ as a Case Study

Süleyman İrvan
Faculty of Communication and Media Studies
Eastern Mediterranean University
suleyman.irvan@gmail.com

Sevgül Uludağ is an internationally renowned Turkish-Cypriot journalist. She describes herself as a peace activist and at the same time a journalist. In recent years, she has begun doing oral history, interviewing people in search of missing persons and mass graves in both sides of Cyprus.

In this paper, I will evaluate her work from the point of peace journalism. Peace journalism, as an alternative to traditional conflict oriented journalism, not only tries to contribute peace initiatives, it also calls journalists to investigate the wrongdoings in both sides. In the famous chart created by Johan Galtung (2006), contrasting peace journalism with war journalism, it is stated that peace journalism humanizes all sides; focuses on invisible effects of violence; exposes untruths of all sides; uncovers all cover-ups; focuses on suffering all over; gives name to all evil-doers.

These are all what Sevgül Uludağ has been doing. She began interviewing the children of the missing persons. She called those children the "Oysters with the Missing Pearls". She then began searching the missing persons in both communities under the title, "In Search of the Missing Persons". She interviewed the children of the victims of nationalisms on both sides under the title of "The Orphans of Nationalism". Recently she has started publishing interviews about missing persons and mass graves in Cyprus. Her work is also a good example of oral history. Oral history can be defined as a method of collecting first hand knowledge on the significant events of the past. As an oral historian, Sevgül Uludağ aims at painting the history of ordinary people as it is never told in the official history.

Sevgül Uludağ: A Short Biography

Sevgül Uludağ was born in 1958 in Nicosia, and graduated from the English College. Her journalism career begun in 1980 in the *Nothern Weekly Mail.* This newspaper, owned by Raif Denktash was an English language weekly. Her job in the paper was to redact the paper. After a while, when the only reporter of the paper, Alan Cavinder, resigned from the paper, she was asked to fill the pages. Her first journalistic product was a series on the beauties and historical values of Cyprus. She then wrote an investigative article on Arabahmet women. Uludağ won her first journalistic awards with these stories from the Turkish Journalists Union. She actually received two awards, one in the investigative journalism, and the other in the reportage.

She moved to *Olay*, a weekly news magazine owned by Ismet Kotak. She was writing on culture and history, and doing interviews for the magazine. Then Ismet Kotak started publishing the first popular newspaper, *Kıbrıs Postası* where she continued publishing her interviews.

From the beginning, she concentrated on doing investigative stories with interviews. One of the first things she did for *Kıbrıs Postası* was an investigative story on "Disappearing Crafts". She says that these series took the interests of the readers, because they were the first stories on the topic (Irvan, 2007).

She was fired from the paper, because of a series called "Gençlik Gençlik Dediğimiz" (What We Call Youth). In the series she was investigating the problems of the youth. She interviewed a drug user, a soldier, an unemployed, an apprentice etc.. The story on the soldier took the reaction of the military. Because the soldier was saying how unreasonable the military service was, how they were beaten etc. The military wanted to know the name of the soldier.

After *Kıbrıs Postası*, she joined the staff of *Yenidüzen* newspaper where she first prepared international news pages. In 1987, she was awarded the Julius Fucik Medal of Honor by the International Organization of Journalists. Unfortunately, this award resulted with her unemployment (Irvan, 2007).

She then established Uludağ News Agency with the help of her husband, Zeki Erkut. She worked as a freelance journalist trying to sell stories to different newspapers.

Sevgül Uludağ returned to *Yenidüzen* in 1998. However, for a long time she was not allowed to write there. With a group of journalists, they established the first internet journal in North Cyprus, *The Cocroaches*, in 2001. The slogan of the journal is, "Cocroaches are not dirty. They live to clean the dirt. The state does not like Cocroaches, because they remind the state how dirty it is."

Oral History as a Method

Oral history can be defined as a method of historical investigation through "interviews with the living survivors of the time being investigated" (http://en.wikipedia.org/wiki/Oral_history, retrieved on April 28, 2007). The method is primarily used by historians to get first-hand knowledge about certain historical events. According to Paul Thompson (2000), existing records of history "reflect the standpoint of authority" (p. 6-7). In contrast, oral history, by way of giving opportunity to the witnesses, "provides a more realistic and fair reconstruction of the past, a challenge to the established account" (p. 7). Since oral history relies on the memories of the witnesses, there are some criticisms on using memories to search the past. Two terms need to be mentioned here: reliability and validity.

In terms of oral history interviews, reliability refers to the consistency of the interviewee "to tell the same story about the same events on a number of occasions" (Hoffman, 1974, p. 25). In other words, reliability is about the trustworthiness of the witnesses. Validity refers to the conformity of the oral testimony to the other records of history (Hoffman, 1974, p. 25). In order to test the validity of oral testimonies, we may use written records or similar testimonies. However, it is better to think that the testimony provided by the informants as being revelatory (Blee, 1993, p. 598). As Alessandro Portelli (1997) argued, "what the informant believes is indeed *a fact* (that is, the *fact* that he or she believes it) just as much as what 'really' happened" (p. 67). Therefore, the credibility problem should be assessed differently. Again, according to Portelli (1997), "the importance of oral testimony may lie not in its adherence to fact, but rather in its departure from it... Therefore, there are no 'false' oral sources" (p. 68).

Peace Journalism

Peace journalism as a concept has become popular in the last decade. According to Jack M. Lynch and Annabel McGoldrick (2005), "peace journalism is when editors and reporters make choices –of what stories to report and about how to report them- that create opportunities for society at large to consider and value non-violent responses to the conflict" (p. 5). The basic premise of peace journalism is that the media can and should play a positive role in promoting peace (Irvan, 2006; Shinar, 2004).

According to Johan Galtung (2006) who coined the term, peace journalism is an ethical alternative to war journalism which is the dominant style in the global media market (p. 1). Galtung's conceptualization of peace journalism as opposed to war journalism sheds light to what I am trying to do here in this article. Peace journalism is not just a better practice for dealing with currrent conflicts, it also asks journalists to look at the historical roots of the current conflicts. In order to better understand what Sevgül Uludağ has been doing, I will use Galtung's (2006) conceptualization:

1. Peace journalism is peace-oriented:
   - It gives voice to all parties; shows empathy and understanding.
   - It humanizes all sides.
   - It focuses on invisible effects.
2. Peace journalism is truth-oriented:
   - It exposes untruths on all sides.
   - It uncovers all cover-ups.
3. Peace journalism is people oriented:
   - It focuses on sufferings on all sides; giving voice to the voiceless.
   - It names all evil-doers.
4. Peace journalism is solution-oriented:
   - It highlights peace initiatives.
   - It focuses on reconciliation.

In a similar vein, some of the suggestions made by Jake Lynch and Annabel McGoldrick (2005, pp. 28-31) to conduct peace journalism also helps us understand the journalistic approach of Sevgül Uludağ. Especially three of their 17 suggestions explain her journalistic attitude very well.

1. Peace journalists should avoid focusing exclusively on the suffering of one side. They should treat as equally the sufferings of all sides.

2. Peace journalists should avoid victimizing language. They should not just ask what people feel; they should also ask how they are coping with and what

they think. Do they have any suggestions?

3. Peace journalists should try to name all wrongdoers, and treat allegations made for all parties equally seriously.

The first series: The Oysters Which Lost Their Pearls

Sevgül Uludağ made her first series of interviews with the children of missing persons. The people she talked were Tijen Gülle, Kutlay Erk, Özel Pinardan, Mehmet Ali Göçer, Semi Bora and Salih Bayraktar. These interviews were first published in *Yenidüzen* (New Order) newspaper in January and February 2002. She later republished all interviews in a book called *İncisini Kaybeden İstiridyeler* (Oysters Which Lost Their Pearls) in 2005. In the introduction she wrote for the book, she says, "everything started with my learning that Kutlay Erk was a child of a missing person" (2006a, p. 13). Because the issue of the missing persons was a taboo subject in the Turkish Cypriot community (2006a, p. 13).

Tijen Gulle was just an eleven months old baby, when her father went missing on 18th of December, 1963. In the interview, Sevgül Uludağ asks questions mostly related to her feelings about being a daughter of a missing father: "What kind of feeling was it to grow up with knowing that your father was missing? What kind of feeling is it that there is no grave? How was your mother affected? In order our children not to live similar pains, what sort of Cyprus do you have in your mind?" etc (Uludağ, 2006a, pp. 23-29).

Kutlay Erk was 11 years old when his father went missing in December, 1963. Since he remembers his father, Sevgül Uludağ's first question was "what do you remember about your father?" She then asks, "what happened in 1963?" We learn from the interview that Kutlay Erk went to the Kyrenia Gate every day when exchange of prisoners of war began. But his father never came (Uludağ, 2006a, p. 30-41).

Özel Pınardan was 6 years old when his father went missing in August 1974 during the second operation of the Turkish army. His family was trying to escape from Greek Cypriot gangs. She asks, "what do you remember from that day?" then, "was it the last time you saw your father?" We learn from the interview that the tractor his father was trying to escape with was found, but there was no sign about his father (Uludağ, 2006a, pp. 42-49).

The brother of Mehmet Ali Göçer disappeared on the 29th of December, 1963 from Aretyu village. Sevgül Uludağ starts the interview with this explanation: "Mehmet Ali bey, your brother Naim Huseyin disappeared on 29th of December in 1963" He replies: "He did not disappear. He was taken from home by the Greek Cypriot police" (Uludağ, 2006a, p. 50). She then asks, "what happened that day?" One further question, "what should be done to stop the pain you have been living with?"

Şemi Bora was 12 years old when his father Şahap Şemi disappeared on 26th of December in 1963. The first question Sevgül Uludağ asked was, "what was the job of your father in 1963?" Then second question, "when did he disappeared?" Then, "what happened that day?" Another question, "what calms you heart? I am sure it must be a terrible feeling. Do you have a grudge against Greek Cypriots?" Another question, "what should be done to make you feel better? What is your solution to the Cyprus problem?" (Uludağ, 2006a, pp. 57-62).

Salih Bayraktars father was shot dead in 1957 by the EOKA underground organization. Salih Bayraktar was 10 years old when he lost his father. He is not in the list of the missing, but the perpetrators are still not known.

The second series: In Search of the Missing Persons

Sevgül Uludağ began conducting her second series of interviews which she named "in search of the missing persons". These interviews were not only conducted with the Turkish Cypriots, she also began interviewing Greek Cypriots who have lived similar pains. The interviews were first published in *Yenidüzen* newspaper in July and August 2004. She republished 9 of these interviews in *İncisini Kaybeden İstiridyeler* (Oysters Which Lost their Pearls) in 2005.

From those tragic stories, we learn that Sevilay Berk lost her father and mother on the 11th of May in 1964. She then was 17 years old. Her family was living in the village of Bahçeler close to Famagusta. That day her father and mother did not return from Famagusta (Uludağ, 2006a, pp. 91-112).

Ülgen Gülnihal was 11 years old when her father Hasan Halil Bulli disappeared on the same day of Sevilay Berk's parents, on the 11th of May in 1964 (Uludağ, 2006a, pp. 114-132).

From these two interviews we learn that the bones of both Sevilay Berk's parents and Ülgen Gülnihal's father were found in a mass grave.

Maria Yeorgiadis talks about her father, mother, sister and brother who all went missing in 1974 from Değirmenlik (Kitrea) village. Maria says, "the only thing I want to find out is the bones of my family…I want to do a proper burial ceremony for them…This is a humanitarian wish, nothing else… What has happened in the past has happened. The river cannot flow back" (Uludağ, 2006b, pp. 140-141).

Cemaliye Şoforel lost her husband and her son in 1974. They were taken from the village of Dohni with other 72 men and boys on the 15th of August by the Greek Cypriots as the prisoners of war. They were put in two buses to a destination—a mass grave near Muttayaga—to be killed and buried (Uludağ, 2006b, pp. 146-147). Cemaliye Şoforel remembers her son's last wish: "Mama! Come and kiss me for the last time please! Come and kiss me one last time" (Uludağ, 2006b, p. 146).

Spiros Hacinikolau was five years old when his father disappeared from Yialoussa (Yeni Erenköy) village in 1974. His father, Takis Hadjinikolaou was a judge. He was taken from the village with 8 other people (Uludağ, 2006b, pp. 36-44). Spiros' answer to the question, "why is it important to find out what happened to the missing persons?" is important to understand the psychology of the people who have never had the chance of learning what happened to their missing: "Because this is logical. It's common sense. Until you get the bones of your loved one back, you must not believe that he or she is dead. You need to see proof for that. And culturally, you need a grave, you want to visit that grave, light a candle, bring some flowers" Uludağ, 2006b, pp. 41-42).

Costas Kunduris talks about his father who disappeared from Stroncilo village on the 14th August in 1974. Sevgül Uludağ wrote: "Some men, coming from outside the village, collected the 8 Greek Cypriots from Stroncilo. Among them was Yiannis Kunduris, the father of Kostas and two of his uncles. According to rumors, they were not Turkish soldiers but Turkish Cyprot soldiers from the village of Sinda (Inonu)...Like all missing stories, there is no way to confirm what exactly happened. People are silent, people don't talk, people fear that if they utter a word, they would be in trouble" (Uludağ, 2006b, pp. 46-47). She quotes Costas Kunduris as saying: "If I found out that a Turkish Cypriot was responsible for the disappearance of my father, I would not want to take revenge. Because I know that this happened during a period when nationalism was very strong. That is why I am not thinking of taking revenge from anyone" (Uludağ, 2006b, p. 49).

The third series: Persons Who Returned From the Edge of Death

In 2004, she interviewed a number of people who were shot and wounded, but had the luck to survive. Suat Hüseyin Kafadar was lucky to escape from a massacre in 1974. He is from Dohni. On the 15th of August that year, Greek Cypriot gunmen came to the village, collected all men and put them in a bus. The bus stopped near Ayafila village. Then Greek Cypriots began shooting all the prisoners of war. He was wounded, but he played dead (Uludağ, 2004a).

Costas Panayotu Artemiu was shot to dead with 15 other Greek Cypriots in 1974, but he succeeded to survive. Sevgul Uludağ asks him: "Did you believe that you were alive?" He replies: "When they lined us up in front of a wall to shoot, I believed that I couldn't survive. Then I was only lucky" (Uludağ, 2004b).

Petros Souppouris was ten years old when he succeeded to survive a massacre in Balikesir in 1974. He was wounded, but all of his family was killed in the massacre (Uludağ, 2004c).

Huseyin Akansoy was taken from Murataga as a prisoner of war by Greek Cypriots. However, his family was killed in the massacre in 1974 (Uludağ, 2004d).

Hüseyin Hasn Kuzuli is a sepherd from Sandallar village. In 1974, he escaped from the massacre because he hid in a cave (Uludağ, 2004e).

Mustafa Şadanoğlu is from Atlılar village. He escaped from the massacre because he was a volunteer soldier in the 1974 war in Famagusta. He lost all his family (Uludağ, 2005f).

Yiannos Demetriou was eleven years old in 1974 when his village Aşşa (Paşaköy) was invaded by gunmen. Then they were allowed to go to the South. However, his grandfather is in the missing persons list (Uludağ, 2004g).

Christoforos Skarparis was living in Aşşa (Paşaköy) village during the war in 1974. He and his family drove to the South (Uludağ, 2004h).

Hasan Paşa was arrested in 1974 as a prisoner of war. He was beaten to death, but he succeeded to survive (Uludağ, 2004i).

Panikos Neocleous joined the war in 1974. He tells his story of how he escaped from Kyrenia to Larnaka (Uludağ, 2004j).

The fourth series: The Orphans of Nationalism

In 2005, Sevgül Uludağ conducted another series of interviews with the children and wives of those who were killed by underground organizations in both sides. Sevgül wrote in the introduction to the series: "They were the orphans or widows of nationalism. Those who killed their fathers or husbands were the death squads of nationalism" (Uludağ, 2005a).

Stella Mişaulis Dimitriu was 10 years old when her father Kostas Mişaulis was killed with Derviş Ali Kavazoğlu in 1965 by Turkish Cypriot underground organization, TMT.

Andreas Dimitriu Tofaris, husband of Stella Mişaulis Dimitriu, was only 5 years old when his father, Ilias Tofaris was killed by Greek Cyriot underground organization, EOKA, in 1958. Sevgul Uludağ asks Andreas, "why did they kill your father?" He replies, "It was certainly a political homicide. My father was a member of AKEL and

PEO. In those years, Grivas was killing the leftists. He was trying to terrorize everyone, because the leftist movement was growing, broadening, and improving its effectiveness. Grivas was trying to stop this" (Uludağ, 2005b).

Ayşe Zeytincioğlu was a two-years-old child when her father, Fazıl Önder was shot dead in 1958 (Uludağ, 2005c). Fazıl Önder was the owner of the newspaper *İnkılapçı* (The Revolutionary). According to Sevgül Uludağ, Fazıl Önder was killed by the Turkish Cypriot underground organization, TMT, because of his political views (Uludağ 2006b, p. 221).

Hıfsiye Hikmet was 4 years old when her father Ayhan Hikmet and his friend Muzaffer Gürkan were shot dead in 1962. His father and Muzaffer Gürkan were journalists and publishing a newspaper called *Cumhuriyet* (The Republic). Sevgul Uludağ asks Hıfsiye Hikmet: "You were 4 years old when your father was killed. Do you remember anything from that day?" She replies: "Yes, I remember almost everything." She asks: "What do you remember?" Hifsiye Hikmet answers: "That night, we had guests in our house...We slept after guests had left. Then I heard my mother's scream: Help! Help! They killed my husband... Then I remember, a lot of journalists came to our house. I was in my mother's arms. I barely remember seeing my father's dead body" (Uludağ, 2005d).

Sevgül Uludağ with Greek Cypriot journalist Makarios Drusiotis also interviewed Emin Hikmet (Uludağ, 2005e). Emin Hikmet was only two years old when his father Ayhan Hikmet was murdered. They ask him: "What happened that night? You were two years old. Do you remember anything from that night?" He answers: "This is a good question and the answer is, whatever I remember is the memories of a child. They are invalid, they are only memories. They may be correct, may be not. If you ask how it happened, I don't know. I don't know whether they are my dreams, or the reality."

Huriye Alpay is the wife of Alpay Mustafa. Alpay Mustafa was an active member of the Turkish Cypriot underground organization. He was murdered on 22nd of January in 1967 while under arrest in Nicosia polis station. According to Huriye Alpay, her husband was murdered by the head of TMT organization in order to silence him (Uludağ, 2005f).

Sevgül Uludağ also interviewed Bora Alpay, the son of Alpay Mustafa. Bora Alpay was only seven months old when his father was killed in the cell of the police station. She asks Bora: "What do you think happened? Everyone says something. You probably talked to a lot of people?" He answers: "I think, they tried to create an excuse. Simple reasons. The incident in Çağlayan that night was not very important. But that was the justification." "What could have been the real reason?" she asks. Bora Alpay says: "I don't really know. There could be a number of reasons. It could be that my father was trying to leave TMT. Because he was telling my mother that, 'I am fed up with this dirty job. I have to leave. I have a son now'. This could be the first reason. He wanted to leave the organization" (Uludağ, 2005g).

Olgun Dayıoğlu talks about his grandfather, Ali Fehim Osman who was murdered in 1966. But the perpetrator was not found. Ali Osman Fehim had been arrested three times by Turkish Cypriot authorities for not obeying orders (Uludağ, 2005h).

Petros Petru is the son of Mihalis Petru who was killed by EOKA, the Greek Cypriot underground organization in 1958. Petros believes that his father was killed to further the policy of dividing Cyprus (Uludağ, 2005i).

The fifth series: Cyprus Untold Stories

In 2006, Sevgul Uludağ has begun a new series which still continues today, and nobody knows how and when it will end. She started the series with an informer line for the witnesses. She says that this last series of interviews are totally under the control of the readers. While beginning the series, she made an announcement, writing that "if you know something, call me. If you don't want to talk to me, here is the telephone number of the Committee for the Missing Persons. Call them. If you know something, talk" (Irvan, 2007). This is a very creative way of doing peace journalism.

Conclusion

There have been several attempts to compare oral history with journalism (Feldstein, 2004; Tisdale, 2000). For Tisdale, both journalists and oral historians are "involved in compiling information that relies on the preparation of questions for witnesses to events, the accuracy of witness testimony, and the interpretations of what the witnesses experienced" (2000, p. 41). There are similarities and differences: "The journalist reports current events. The oral historian is more concerned with events long after they occurred" (Tisdale, 2000, p. 42). However, they are both concerned with accuracy and credibility (Tisdale, 2000, p. 44). Feldstein calls oral history as the kissing cousin of journalism. "The objective of both journalism and oral history is to record truth" (Feldstein, 2004, p. 5).

Although a journalist, Sevgül Uludağ's work is mostly oral history. Almost all interviews are life-story interviews, beginning from birth to today. Therefore, all of them are quite long. For example, interview with Sevilay Berk is 4688 words; Maria Georgiades' interview is 3226 words; Interview with Suat Kafadar is 3513 words. Secondly, she defines her position as the natural transmitter. She says in the last paragraph of her book: "Many would stop me in the middle of the street to whisper 'secrets', to point out a burial site or to share a story from their past...I have only been their 'mouthpiece', publishing what they want to say" (Uludağ, 2006b, p. 469).

Why should her work be counted as peace journalism? First reason I could give is her aim. She says: "I was uncovering the truth, the untold stories of ordinary people—I was trying to find out (and I am still trying to do that) what actually happened on this island that brought us to the point we are at today (Uludağ, 2006b, p. 23). However, she does not stop there. She acts as a self-appointed Reconciliation Committee to bring people from both communities together to share their past experiences and feelings. Because she believes that a true peace can only be established through reconciliation (Uludağ, 2006b, p. 197). For her, in order to move to a peaceful future, it is necessary to acknowledge what really happened in the past (Uludağ, 2006b, p. 35). As Desmond Tutu, the chairperson of the South African Truth and Reconciliation Commission put it, "however painful the experience, the wounds of the past must not be allowed to fester. They must be opened. They must be cleaned...Reconciliation based on falsehood, on not facing up the reality, is not true reconciliation" (Tutu, 1998, p. 7).

Second reason is her courage to uncover crimes in the past in both communities. As Andreas Paraschos, the editor of the Greek Cypriot newspaper *Politis*, wrote in the foreword to the Oysters with the Missing Pearls, "Sevgul Uludag, more courageous and much more correct, has done a radical movement. She has not looked for a door to enter the problem. She lifted the roof and saw it from above... She went down inside and started to walk it through" (Uludağ, 2006b, p. 12). In line with how Johan Galtung (2006), Jake Lynch and Annabel McCormick (2005) described peace journalism, she has not concentrated on the sufferings in only one side. Third reason is her understanding of journalism. She believes that instead of using every occasion to create more hatred and the feelings of vengeance, journalists from both sides of Cyprus should focus on the roots of the conflict, on the reasons behind what happened, on the people who were responsible for the crimes (Uludağ, 2006b, pp. 196-197).

As a conclusion, Sevgül Uludağ is a good example for journalists and journalism students who think journalism must have a mission to help establish peace. She also shows us how the method of oral history can be used to let ordinary people to tell their version of truth against the "official truth" (Uludağ, 2006b, p. 23).

References

Blee, K. M. (1993). Evidence, empathy, and ethics: Lessons from oral histories of the Klan. *The Journal of American History*, September, *80*(2), 596-606.

Cockburn, C. (2004). *The line: Women, partition and the gender order in Cyprus*. London: Zed Books.

Feldstein, M. (2004). Kissing cousins: Journalism and oral history. *Oral History Review*, *30*(1), 1-22.

Galtung, J. (2006). Peace journalism as an ethical challenge. *Global Media Journal: Mediterranean Edition*, Fall, 1-4.

Hoffman, A. M. (1974). Reliability and validity in oral history. *Today's Speech*, Winter, 23-27.

İrvan, S. (2006). Peace journalism as a normative theory: Premises and obstacles. *Global Media Journal: Mediterranean Edition*, *1*(2), Fall, 34-39.

İrvan, S. (2007). Unpublished oral history interview with Sevgül Uludağ, 17 January.

Lynch, J. and Annabel M. (2005). *Peace Journalism*. Howtorn.

Portelli, A. (1997). What makes oral history different. In R. Perks & A. Thomson (Eds.), *Oral History Reader*, pp. 63-74. London: Routledge.

Shinar, D. (2004). Media peace discourse: Constraints, concepts, and building blocks. *Conflict & Communication Online*, *3*(1/2), 1-8.

Thompson, P. (2000). *The voice of the past*. New York: Oxford University Press.

Tisdale, J. R. (2000). Observational reporting as oral history: How journalists interpreted the death and destruction of Hurricane Audrey. *Oral History Review*, *27*(2), 41-65.

Tutu, D. (1998). Foreword by chairperson. *Truth and Reconciliation Commission of South Africa Report*. Retrieved on April 25, 2007 from http://www.doj.gov.za/trc/report/finalreport /TRC%20VOLUME%201.pdf

Uludağ, S. (2004a). Ölümün kıyısından dönenler (1): Dohni'de yaşanan katliamdan sağ kurtulan tek Kıbrıslıtürk olan Suat Hüseyin Kafadar, yaşadıklarını anlatıyor. *Yeraltı Notları*, 10 October. Retrieved on April 25, 2007 from http://www.stwing.upenn.edu/~durduran/hamambocu/authors/svg/svg9_10_2004.html

Uludağ, S. (2004b). Ölümün kıyısından dönenler (2): Çocuklarımız böyle şeyler yaşamasın. *Yeraltı Notları*, 11 October. Retrieved on April 25, 2007 from http://www.stwing.upenn.edu/~durduran/hamambocu/authors/svg/svg9_11_2004.html

Uludağ, S. (2004c). Ölümün kıyısından dönenler (3): Onlara Kıbrıslıtürklerle birlikte yaşamak zorundayız diyorum. *Yeraltı Notları*, 13 October. Retrieved on April 25, 2007 from http://www.stwing.upenn.edu/~durduran/hamambocu/authors/svg/svg9_13_2004.html

Uludağ, S. (2004d). Ölümün kıyısından dönenler (4): Muratağa diye bir yer. *Yeraltı Notları*, 18 October. Retrieved on April 25, 2007 from http://www.stwing.upenn.edu/~durduran/hamambocu/authors/svg/svg9_18_2004.html

Uludağ, S. (2004e). Ölümün kıyısından dönenler (5): Sandallar'dan bir çobanın öyküsü. *Yeraltı Notları*, 20 October. Retrieved on April 25, 2007 from http://

www.stwing.upenn.edu/~durduran/hamambocu/authors/svg/svg9_20_2004.html

Uludağ, S. (2004f). Ölümün kıyısından dönenler (6): Atlılar diye bir köy. *Yeraltı Notları*, 24 October. Retrieved on April 25, 2007 from http://www.stwing.upenn.edu/~durduran/hamambocu/authors/svg/svg9_24_2004.html

Uludağ, S. (2004g). Ölümün kıyısından dönenler (7): Geceden sabaha 20-30 yaş birden büyümüştük. *Yeraltı Notları*, 29 October. Retrieved on April 25, 2007 from http://www.stwing.upenn.edu/~durduran/hamambocu/authors/svg/svg9_29_2004.html

Uludağ, S. (2004h). Ölümün kıyısından dönenler (8): Aşşa Kültür Derneği Başkanı Christoforos Skarparis, çocukluk anılarındaki Aşşa'yı (Paşaköy) anlatıyor. *Yeraltı Notları*, 29 October. Retrieved on April 25, 2007 from http://www.stwing.upenn.edu/~durduran/hamambocu/authors/svg/svg10_3_2004.html

Uludağ, S. (2004i). Ölümün kıyısından dönenler (9): Hasan Paşa - Savaş rüzgarlarının sürüklediği bir yaşam. *Yeraltı Notları*, 8 November. Retrieved on April 25, 2007 from http://www.stwing.upenn.edu/~durduran/hamambocu/authors/svg/svg10_8_2004.html

Uludağ, S. (2004j). Ölümün kıyısından dönenler (10): Tahtakaleli Panikos Neocleous'un öyküsü. *Yeraltı Notları*, 22 November. Retrieved on April 25, 2007 from http://www.stwing.upenn.edu/~durduran/hamambocu/authors/svg/svg10_22_2004.html

Uludağ, S. (2005a). Milliyetçiliğin öksüz bıraktıkları (1): Stella Mişaulis Dimitriu. *Yeraltı Notları*, 13 March. Retrieved on April 25, 2007 from http://www.stwing.upenn.edu/~durduran/hamambocu/authors/svg/svg2_13_2005.html

Uludağ, S. (2005b). Milliyetçiliğin öksüz bıraktıkları (2): Grivas'ın solcuları öldürdüğü bir dönemdi. *Yeraltı Notları*, 16 March. Retrieved on April 25, 2007 from http://www.stwing.upenn.edu/~durduran/hamambocu/authors/svg/svg2_16_2005.html

Uludağ, S. (2005c). Milliyetçiliğin öksüz bıraktıkları (3): Fazıl Önder'in kızı Ayşe Zeytincioğlu anlatıyor. *Yeraltı Notları*, 21 March. Retrieved on April 25, 2007 from http://www.stwing.upenn.edu/~durduran/hamambocu/authors/svg/svg2_21_2005.html

Uludağ, S. (2005d). Milliyetçiliğin öksüz bıraktıkları (4): Ayhan Hikmet'in kızı Hıfsiye Hikmet. *Yeraltı Notları*, 28 March. Retrieved on April 25, 2007 from http://www.stwing.upenn.edu/~durduran/hamambocu/authors/svg/svg2_28_2005.html

Uludağ, S. (2005e). Milliyetçiliğin öksüz bıraktıkları (5): Emin Hikmet. *Yeraltı Notları*, 10 April. Retrieved on April 25, 2007 from http://www.stwing.upenn.edu/~durduran/hamambocu/authors/svg/svg3_10_2005.html

Uludağ, S. (2005f). Milliyetçiliğin öksüz bıraktıkları (6): Alpay Mustafa'nın eşi Huriye Alpay. *Yeraltı Notları*, 11 April. Retrieved on April 25, 2007 from http://www.stwing.upenn.edu/~durduran/hamambocu/authors/svg/svg3_11_2005.html

Uludağ, S. (2005g). Milliyetçiliğin öksüz bıraktıkları (7): Bora Alpay. *Yeraltı Notları*, 20 April. Retrieved on April 25, 2007 from http://www.stwing.upenn.edu/~durduran/hamambocu/authors/svg/svg3_20_2005.html

Uludağ, S. (2005h). Milliyetçiliğin öksüz bıraktıkları (8): Faili meçhul bir cinayetin kurbanı olan Ali Fehim Osman'ın torunu Olgun Dayıoğlu anlatıyor. *Yeraltı Notları*, 13 May. Retrieved on April 25, 2007 from http://www.stwing.upenn.edu/~durduran/hamambocu/authors/svg/svg4_13_2005.html

Uludağ, S. (2005i). Milliyetçiliğin öksüz bıraktıkları (9): EOKA tarafından öldürülen Mihalis Petru'nun oğlu Petros Petru anlatıyor. *Yeraltı Notları*, 20 May. Retrieved on April 25, 2007 from http://www.stwing.upenn.edu/~durduran/hamambocu/authors/svg/svg4_20_2005.html

Uludağ, Sevgül (2006a). *İncisini kaybeden istiridyeler*. 2. ed. Nicosia.

Uludağ, Sevgül (2006b). *Oysters with the missing pearls*. Nicosia: Ikme.

Savaşa/Şiddete Dayalı Bir Toplumsal Gerçeklik Ortamının İnşasında Medyanın Rolü: Savaş, Görsel Medya ve Gerçeklik

Süreyya Çakır
Mersin Üniversitesi
sureyyacakir@mersin.edu.tr

"Artık hiçbir haritaya bakamıyorum. Kentlerin adları yanık et kokuyor." Canetti

Yirminci yüzyıldan savaş/şiddetle birlikte savaş/şiddet imajlarını da devralan yirmi birinci yüzyılın başlangında savaş/şiddet ve yıkım tüm hızıyla sürmekte. Buna koşut olarak, yüksek yıkım potansiyeline sahip şiddet araçlarının teknik gelişimi de akıl almaz boyutlara ulaşmış bulunmakta. Bu durumda barış, her zamankinden uzak bir ütopya olarak önümüzde durmakta.

Günümüzde gittikçe artan oranda toplumsal gerçekliğin kurucusu ve yönlendiricisi haline gelmiş olan görsel medyanın sembolik temsil biçimleri, savaşın, acının, sömürünün, çaresizliğin kol gezdiği, şiddete bel bağlayan bir dünyanın yeniden üretilmesinde oldukça etkin bir role sahiptir. Bugünün savaşlarının en önemli yanı, teknoloji ve medya ile yoğun bir işbirliği içinde ve inanılmaz derecede çoğalan savaş nesneleri ile yürütülüyor olmasıdır. İçinde bulunduğumuz "Yeni Dünya Düzeni" diye adlandırılan "İletişim Düzeni"nde şiddet/savaş, medyatik bir nitelik kazanmıştır. Buna koşut olarak, kitle iletişim araçları içinde hegemonik bir güce sahip olan televizyon ve bilgisayar teknolojileri aracılığıyla gerçek şiddetin/savaşın kurmaca haline geldiği, sanallaştığı ve gösteriye dönüştüğü bir kültürel ortam gündemdedir. Naklen, canlı savaş yayını pratiği, savaşı sanal bir olgu haline getirmekte; toplumsal bir eğilim olan sanallaşma olgusu, savaş/şiddet algısını değiştirmekte ve onu zaman-mekan koordinatlarının kesiştiği gerçeklik düzleminde sorunlu hale getirmektedir. Savaşın medyada estetize edilmiş sunumlarının, toplumsal ve bireysel düzlemlerde uzantıları olmakta; şiddet içselleşmekte, kapsam ve yaygınlık alanı genişlemekte, etik ve insani değerler devre-dışı kalmaktadır; ve şiddet şiddeti doğurmakta, korku kültürü egemen kılınmaktadır. Şiddeti uygulayandan yana olan şiddet sunumları, savaşın/şiddetin içselleşmesini ve onaylanmasını sonuçlamaktadır.

Bu saptamaları temel alarak şekillenecek olan bu çalışma, medyadaki savaş/şiddet imgeleri dolayımıyla nasıl savaşa dayalı bir toplumsal gerçeklik ortamı kurulduğu üzerine odaklanacaktır. Bu odaklanmayı, savaş olgusunu, savaşın medyadaki sunum biçimlerini ve savaşın sanallaşmasını, toplumsal bir eğilim olan sanallaşma olgusu ile ilişkilendirerek ve sanallaşma olgusuna koşut olarak gündeme gelen temsil sorunları üzerinden yapacaktır.

Gerçek, Temsili Gerçeklik , Medya ve Savaş

Toplumsal gerçeklik, 18. yüzyıldan itibaren gittikçe artan oranda simgesel/imgesel nitelikteki medyatik temsil biçimleri kanalıyla kurulmaktadır. 19. yüzyılın temsil sistemlerinde, hala nesnel gerçeklik ile ilişkinin somut temelleri mevcutken, 20. yüzyılın başından itibaren gittikçe yaygınlaşan görsel kültürün başat olduğu bir kültürel yapılanmada, temsil sistemleri gitgide nesnesinden uzaklaşır ve somut gerçeklik medya imgeleri tarafından kurulur ve düzenlenir hale gelir. Bu "Yeni İletişim Düzeni"ne özgü olan "yeni gerçeklik" dünyasında imaj ve gösteri, gerçeklik olur. Batı kültürel tarihinde temsilin ve imgelerin değişen yeri ve işlevine bağlı olarak meydana gelen ve toplumun genel eğilimini yansıtan bu süreci, "temsil sistemlerinden simülasyon ve baş dönmesi sistemlerine geçiş" olarak kavramsallaştırmaktadır Baudrillard. (2004a, s. 81). Zizek (2002) ise, tarihin belli bir dönemine özgü olan, televizyon, bilgisayar sistemleri ile derinleşen bu temsil sorununu, gerçekliğin kendisinin "görsel bir sanrı olarak algılan"dığı, medyanın bizi kuşattığı tüm imgesel alanlarda söz konusu olan bir "gerçeklik kaybı" olarak nitelendirmektedir (s. 168). "Gerçeklik kaybı"na ve gerçekliğin bulanıklaşmasına yol açan sanal gerçeklik, imaj ve taklit ile onların gölgesine dönüşmüş bulunan "gerçek" gerçeklik arasındaki farkı ortadan kaldırmaktadır. Bu durumda algılayan bireyin de deneyim alanı daralırken ortamıyla ilişkisi içinde kendi kimliğini kuramamakta; fantastik bir kurmaca dünyada parçalanmış bir kimlikle hayalet bir varlığa dönüşmektedir. Hakim medya niteliğiyle bir "gerçeklik yaratma aygıtı" haline gelmiş bulunan televizyon ve bilgisayar teknolojileri ile birlikte gerçeğin kurmacaya, kurmacanın ise gerçek haline geldiği ve bu nedenle gerçeğin sanallaştığı ve bulanıklaştığı 20. yüzyılın ikinci yarısından günümüze dek süren evrede, farklı bir gerçeklik, zaman ve mekan algısı hüküm sürer; gerçek deneyim alanı daralır ve sanallaşır. Sanallık üreten bir iletişim dizgesinde "görünüşler yalnızca deneyimin aktarıldığı ekranda olmakla kalmaz, deneyimin kendisi haline gelirler" (Castells 2002, ss. 212-213).

İmgenin, görünüşün, gerçeklik üzerinde başat bir etkiye sahip olduğu, imge ile toplumsal gerçeklik arasındaki ilişkinin bulanıklaştığı medya ile dolu günümüz dünyasında, bir toplumsal eğilim olarak sanallaşma olgusu koşutluğunda, savaş algısı ve savaşın gerçekliği de biçim değiştirmiş durumdadır. Savaşın ve savaş aletlerinin insandan ayrıldığı, teknoloji ve medya aracılığıyla yürütülen günümüz savaşları eski savaşlardan farklı bir niteliğe sahiptir. İnsanların, orduların, ölülerin ortalıkta görünmediği bu savaşlarda görüntüler ön plandadır. "Gerçek"in simgesel düzen tarafından uğratıldığı değişime koşut olarak gündeme gelen savaşı karşılama ve ona tanıklık etme biçimlerimizin değiştiği ve Körfez Savaşı'nın başlangıç noktasını oluşturduğu günümüzün "sıfır ölü stratejisi"ne sahip teknolojik "temiz savaş"larında, İkiz Kuleler vb. bütün olaylarda aklımızda daha çok görüntülerin kaldığını belirten Baudrillard (2002) şöyle sürdürmektedir: "Ve görüntülerin imge derinliğini ve büyücülüklerini unutmamamız gerek, çünkü istesek de istemesek de onlar bizim ilkel sahnemiz. New York olayları dünyanın durumunu değiştirdiği gibi, görüntünün gerçekle ilişkisini de değiştirmiş olacak" (ss. 73-75).

Savaşın tümüyle teknolojik bir içerik kazandığı; bilim, teknoloji ve sanayi işbirliği içinde yürütüldüğü, bilgisayar simülasyonları, sanal gerçeklik gibi bilgisayar teknolojilerinin kullanıldığı günümüzde savaş, elektronik ve bilgisayar savaşına dönüşmüş bulunmaktadır. Her şeyin gösteriye ve imaja teslim olduğu bugünün toplumu, savaşı da gösterinin bir parçası kılmış ve onu da seyirlik bir gösteriye dönüştürmüştür. Görüntüyle birlikte nesnesinden ayrılan ve kendi gerçekliğinden uzaklaşmış bulunan savaş olgusu, böylece anlam ve içeriğinden soyularak seyirlik bir nesne halini almıştır. Nitekim bu savaşlarda "kentler üzerinde füzeler ıslık çalarak uçuyor; füze yokediciler onları gökyüzünde karşılıyor. Gece karanlığında göktaşı yağmuru veya yıldız kayması seyrediyoruz sanki! Ekranda, uçağın hedefi vururken çektiği görüntülerden isabet derecesi üzerine hayranlıklarımızı dile getiriyoruz" (Bursalı 1995, s. 71).

Savaşın medyada—özellikle hakim medya olan televizyonda—sunum biçiminin, 20. yüzyılın başından beri söz konusu olan ve yukarıda kısaca değinilen görüntünün gerçekle ilişkisini temsil düzleminde sorunlu hale getiren yapısı, savaşın gerçeklik algısının değişmesinde bir eşik noktası oluşturmaktadır. Baudrillard'a (2004b) göre, verili haber düzeni olayları tözlerinden ayırmakta, daha sonra yapay bir "eş zamanlılık" ortamında onların tarihle bağını koparmakta ve politika-ötesi bir yer haline gelmiş bulunan haber sahnesi aracılığıyla izleyiciye sunmaktadır. İşte bu nedenle olaylar canlı yayın adı altında gerçekleştirilen üretim ve dağıtım ağında "haber adlı boşluk içinde kaybolup gitmektedirler". İmgeler ve yorumların gerçeğin yerini aldığı böyle bir ortamda, savaş dahil her şey başlamadan bitmektedir. "Tarihsel zaman süreci içinde ortaya çıkan (çıkmış olanla) naklen yayınlanan haber şeklindeki olay arasında çok büyük bir fark" meydana gelmektedir. Tarihsel zaman ve gerçek olay, canlı yayınla gerçekliğinden koparılmakta ve imgesel, soyut bir An'a indirgenmektedir. "Haber/olay bize bir anlamda gerçekten o anda bir olay oluyormuş illüzyonu sunmaktadır—bu aslında gerçek olayı ortadan kaldıran, canlı yayın aracılığıyla aktarılan medyatik bir dünya illüzyonudur" (Baudrillard 2004b).

Savaşın gerçeklik etkisinin nötralize edildiği, yanılsamaya dayalı bir ortam yaratıldığı, seyirlik bir gösteriye döndüğü günümüz savaşlarının Milat noktasını Körfez Savaşı oluşturmaktadır. İlk kez Körfez Savaşı ile birlikte sanal bir savaş izler insanlık. Sınırlandırılmış ve yönlendirilmiş bir haber ve enformasyon akışı içinde, ölümü ve savaşı an'ında ve yer'inde bir tanıklıkla naklen, canlı yayından seyreder. Ve ilk kez, güvenlikli mekanlarında bilgilenme isteği ve ahlaki kaygıların yerini ürpertici, heyecan verici bir hazza ve duygulanıma bıraktığı bir "temiz savaş" gösterisi yaşar. Acısı, kanı, insanı, ordusu olmayan, eğlencelik bir savaş, her türlü somut anlamından uzaklaşmıştır. Sanki yaşanmıyordur ve gerçek olan savaş değil, savaşın belleklerdeki görüntüsüdür. Açınca başlayan ve kapatınca kaybolan düğmelere bağlıdır savaş. Batılı bakma biçimini yansıtan bu savaşın medya ile bağlantısını şöyle kurar Belge (1995): "Bu savaşın sürdürülme biçimi, Batılıların bakış açısından, adeta bir manevra gibiydi – şu farkla ki hedefler gerçek nesneler ya da insanlardı. Medyanın bu savaşı izlemede benimsediği üslup da, harekatın neredeyse 'cerrahi' karakterini vurguluyordu. Ürpertici bir 'bilimsellik' ya da, daha doğrusu, 'kurgu-bilimsel'likte bir dil kullanılıyordu" (s. 45).

Enformasyon ve silah sistemlerinde, vizyon teknolojilerinin önemli bir role sahip olduğunu gösteren Körfez savaşı'nı Batılı imaj teknolojilerinin bir örneği olarak gören Robins ise, bu savaşın "izleyenler ve izlenen arasındaki savaş" olduğunu belirtir. Bu tarihten itibaren insanlığın savaşı yaşama ve algılama pratikleri, yüksek teknolojili sistemler ve medya kanalıyla oluşturulmuş; bu sistemlerin yarattıkları "teknolojik örtüklük" duygusuyla yönlendirdikleri algılama biçimleriyle birlikte insanlık, bilinç düzleminde başka bir düzeye geçmiştir. İzleyenler açısından teknoloji yoluyla "psişik bir dondurma süreci"nin yaşandığı, bilginin duygudan ayrıldığı, gerçeklikten ve gerçekliğin acı veren boyutundan uzaklaşmanın yaşandığı bu savaş, görüntü yoluyla körlük durumu yaratmıştır; bakılan, ama görülmeyen ve hissedilmeyen. Ekrandan-bakılan bu savaşa ilişkin şöyle söylemektedir Robins (1999): "Tıpkı bir video-oyun savaşıydı. Ama ekranlarımızdaki şey bir savaş idiyse gerçeği ekranda yoktu. Uzaktan gelen imajlar uzak gerçeklikleri soyutlaştırdı. İmajın kanıtlama gücüyle savaş hakkında bir şeyler öğrendik ama bildiğimiz şey, adeta gerçekleşmemiş bir savaşmaydı. Her şeyden önce bir görme ve görmeme biçimiydi. Sanki bir imajın röntgencisi olup, gerçekliğine karşı sağır olmak mümkün gibiydi" (ss. 111-114). Aşırı teknolojiye maruz kalmış yüksek bir körlük, sağırlık, edilginlik ve gizil şiddet durumuna gönderme yapan bu betimlemeler, Adorno'nun (1998) faşizm benzetmesinin toplum ve insanlık ölçeğinde yaygınlaşmış halini yansıtıyordu: "Faşizmin kendisi gibi robotlar da öznesiz çalışıyorlar. Tıpkı onun gibi robotlar da müthiş bir teknik kusursuzluğu mutlak körlükle birleştiriyorlar. Ve yine Faşizm gibi onlar da ölümcül bir korku yaratıyorlar ve tamamıyla etkisizler" (s. 57).

Sinematografik biçimin, toplumsal ve politik yaşamdan savaşa kadar hemen her şeyi ele geçirmiş bulunduğu günümüzde, Irak Savaşı ile ardından yaşanan savaşların ve şiddet/terör eylemlerinin, bir savaş mizanseni içinde yürütüldüğünü ve tıpkı bir filme benzediğini öne süren Baudrillard (2004b), sinema kuramı ve pratiğinin uzantısı olarak gördüğü Irak Savaşı'nı şöyle değerlendirmektedir: "Gördüğümüz şeyler oturduğumuz koltuklarda sürekli kasılmamıza yol açmıştır. Bu bir filme benzeyen bir şey değil, filmin ta kendisidir. Bu savaşın dekupajı yapılmış bir senaryosu vardır, bu yüzden sahneye koyma sürecinde bu metne uyulması bir zorunluluğa benzemektedir. Oyuncu seçimi, teknik ve mali olanaklar çok titiz bir çalışmanın sonucudur. Bu bir profesyonel işidir. Bu ekip filmin yayınlanması ve kanallara dağıtımı sürecinde de hakimdir. Sonuç olarak bu işlemsel savaş devasa bir özel efekte, sinema bir savaş paradigmasına dönerken, bizler, bu filmin gerçek olduğunu düşünüyoruz. Oysa bu yansımalar sinematografik bir varlığa dönüşmüş savaş imgelerinden başka bir şey değildir." Sanal savaşın metafor olmaktan çıktığı böyle bir durumda savaş gerçekliği düşsel bir nitelik kazanmakta, bir kurmacaya dönüşmektedir.

Günümüzde savaş ile içiçe geçmiş bulunan terör de biçim değiştirmiştir. Kökenlerinden uzaklaşarak "siyasal şiddetin yozlaşmış biçimi"ne dönüşen bugünün terörünün (Oktay 1995, s. 94) uyguladığı şiddetin en temel özelliği görüntüleri kullanmasıdır. Daha çok kurban etmeyle ilgili bulunan ilkel şiddetten farklı olarak, aşırı-modernliğin ürünü olan, ağırlıklı olarak ekrandan doğan, görüntülerle aynı yapıyı taşıyan ve "temsil sistemlerinden simülasyon sistemlerine geçiş"in uzantısı olarak gündeme gelen bugünün şiddetinin terör olduğunu belirtir Baudrillard (2004a): "Medya her zaman terörist şiddetin ön saflarındadır. Terörist şiddeti özellikle modern bir biçim haline getiren budur" (ss. 80-81). Terörist şiddetin, daha geniş bir yaygınlık alanına sahip olmak üzere, "korku gösterisini verili bir alanın tamamına yayacak bir aygıt" olarak medyaya ihtiyacı vardır. "Teröristin uyguladığı şiddet bu aygıtı sahiplenmesine ve onu kendisi için en elverişli gördüğü korku tipini yaymak için kullanmasına izin verir" (Critical Art Ensemble 2003, ss. 232-234). Örneğin, 11 Eylül'de New York'taki terör eylemi bu kullanımın en somutlaştığı göstergelerden biridir. "Teröristler, sistemin, sisteme yöneltikleri silahlarıyla birlikte, bir de görüntülerin zamansal olarak gerçekliklerini, bütün dünyada aynı anda canlı yayınlanmasını kullandılar. Görüntüleri, tıpkı borsa spekülasyonları, elektronik bilgilendirme ve hava trafiğinin başkaları tarafından sahiplenilmesi gibi, sahiplendiler" (Baudrillard 2002, s. 75). İkiz kulelerin bombalanmasının ardındaki kişi olduğundan şüphelenilen Ladin'in, James Bond filmlerinin çoğundaki baş suçlu olan Blofeld'in gerçek hayattaki muadili olup olmadığı şeklinde ironik bir soru soran Zizek de (2002), New York'taki manzaranın ve "çöken kulelerden yakaladığımız karelerin, Hollywood'un yozlaştırdığı bizlere, büyük felaket prodüksiyonlarındaki en nefes kesici sahneleri hatırlat"tığını belirtir (ss. 294-2950. Terörün medyada kurmacaya dayanan ve yanılsama üreten bu sunum özellikleri, gerçeklik ve algı düzleminde çarpıklığa ve siyasi düzlemde çarpıtma ve manipülasyona, şiddetin şiddeti doğurduğu bir dünyanın somutlaşmasına zemin hazırlamaktadır.

Bilgisayar ortamında üretilen, simülasyon (benzetim) teknolojilerine dayanarak yaratılan sanal-savaş senaryoları da, gerçek savaşın medyada sunumunun yarattığı çarpık ve kurmaca bir savaş algısına dayanan temsil krizini derinleştirmektedir. Körfez Savaşı'ndan beri yaşanan savaşların ve terör eylemlerinin gösterdiği gibi, günümüz askeri stratejilerinde benzetim teknolojileri ve gözetleme sistemleri önemli bir role sahiptir. Bir video oyun stratejisi içinde yürütülen benzetim teknolojileri, benzetim görünümüne bakarak gerçek dünya savaşlarının nasıl olabileceğini görmek açısından, gerçek-dünya karşılaşmaları için stratejik bir önem taşımaktadır. Bu teknolojilerle "savaşın siber alanda yürütülüyormuş gibi görünmesine yol açan bir gerçek dışına çıkma etkisi yaratıl"dığını söyleyen Robins (1996) şöyle sürdürür: "Benzetim adeta model aldığı gerçekliği silmektedir. Komutan da savaşçı da, heyecanlı, kanlı, yıkıcı bir savaş içindeymiş gibi değil, bir oyun mantığına hükmediyormuş gibidirler. Olay sanki bundan ibaretmiş gibi" demektedir (ss. 93-96).

Hızla gelip geçen ve yerini yeni savaşlara ve olaylara bırakan bir milat noktası oluşturan Körfez Savaşı'ndan sonraki geçen zamanda teknoloji de, habercilik anlayışı da gelişti ve bu gelişme, gerçek ile her türlü canlı teması silme şeklinde bir eğilim içinde oldu; yaşanan şeyin bildiğimiz savaşla alakası kesilmişti görüntü dünyasında. Nerdeyse insan elini ortadan kaldırma şeklinde derinleşti zihniyet; çünkü "olabildiği kadar el değmemiş, kusursuz haberi yakalamaya çalışıyordu insanlık. Bütün sorun "gerçek"teydi. Haber denilen şey gerçek olmalıydı. Gerçek ise "sahih," yani doğru olmalıydı. Bu, başından beri inanılan şeydi. Böylesi bir gerçeği yakalamanın yolu da insan elini işin içine sokmamaktı" (Kahraman 2003, ss. 167-168). Gerçekliği gerçek'ten kopararak varılan bu noktada, yalanın, yanılsamanın, taklidin, sahteliğin, sentetik olanın, imajların kol gezdiği bir kültürel ortamda, insanın bu kadar çok gerçek peşinde koşması da tarihin bir ironisi olarak karşımızda durmakta.

Ekranlardan süzülerek geldikçe silikleşen, kurmaca bir gerçeklik duygusu ile birlikte gündeme gelen ve şişirilmiş bir enformasyonla, propagandayla, aşırı görüntüyle görünmez kılınan günümüz savaşlarının bu gösteri odaklı yapılarının, toplumsal, kültürel ve siyasal yansımaları olduğu kadar psikolojik ve etik uzantıları vardır. Bu sorunlu alanlar, öncelikle, gerçeklik ilkesinin ve dolayısıyla savaşın yokluğu önermeleri ile bağlantılı olarak tartışılacak, ardından yarattığı toplumsal, bireysel ve etik sorunsallıklar üzerinde durulacaktır.

Savaş Gerçek Ötesi mi?

Ekranın gerçekliği gölgede bıraktığını, artık imaj, benzeşim ve gösteri dünyasında yaşadığımızı söyleyenlerin tespitlerinin, günümüz toplumlarını açıklayıcı boyutları saklı olduğu ölçüde doğruluk payları vardır. Ancak tarihin yoksandığı, onun sonunun ilan edildiği, ideolojinin dışlandığı, gerçek savaşın olmadığı şeklinde noktalara varan saptamalar (Baudrillard 2004b) gerçeğin bulanıklaşmasına daha çok katkıda bulunmakta, gerçekliği idrak etme ve onu dönüştürme iradesini ortadan kaldırmaktadır. Baudrillard'ın, gerçeklik ilkesinin yok olduğunu, tümüyle pasifize olmuş, yığınsal bir kitlesel varoluşa indirgenmiş bulunan bir insanlık durumunun toplumsalı ortadan kaldırdığını öne süren saptamaları, tavır almayı, karşı-duruş geliştirmeyi önlemekte, verili olana mahkum etmektedir insanlığı.

Savaşın sembolik temsilleriyle birlikte her ne kadar gerçeklik bulanıklaşsa ve gerçeklik ilkesi zedelense de, son kertede belirleyici olan gerçek dünyadır; dünyanın gerçekliği tek dayanak noktası ve nihai tartışma zeminidir. "Benzetimin gücü bizi savaşın yalnızca sanal bir olay olduğuna inandırmamalı" demektedir Robins (1999, s. 97). En nihayetinde gerçek, bizim bilme biçimimizden ve bizden bağımsız olarak orada durmaktadır. Üstü örtülen, bastırılan gerçeklik zamanı geldiğinde kusar kendini. Nihayet, Körfez Savaşı'nda savaş ilerledikçe bastırılmış gerçeğin kendini açığa vurduğunu ve "izleyen(in) izleneni de işe karıştırdı"ğını, gerçek yanma, sakatlanma ve ölüm görüntülerinin, kurbanların seslerinin ve yüzlerinin ekrana yansıdığını belirtir Robins (1999, s. 115). Ekran gerçeği uzaklaştırsa da, tam olarak onun yerine geçemez. Aşınıp yıpranan şey gerçeklik duygusu olsa da, gerçeğin ağırlığını hafifleten medya temsillerinden bağımsız olarak bir gerçeklik vardır; belki savaşın failleri ve onun medya tüketicileri olarak rehavete kapılmış seyredenler nezdinde daha seyreltilmiş ve nahoş bir karşılığı olsa da, en azından şiddete/savaşa maruz kalanlar cephesinde kendini olanca ağırlığıyla hissettiren travmatik, çıplak, kaskatı bir gerçeklik ortada durmaktadır. Son kertede gerçek olan, Körfez Savaşı ekranlarına yansımayan, katledilen 150.000 insanın varlığıdır. Ekranların süzgecinden geçerken onu algılama, içselleştirme, empati kurma ve tepki geliştirme yetilerimiz hafifletilmiş de olsa bu, savaşta tecavüze uğrayan kadınların gerçeğini değiştirmez. En nihayetinde gerçek olan da, şiddetin, savaşın, terörün onu yaratan hegemonik dünya güçleri ile bağlantısı olduğudur. Terörize edilen bir dünyanın ürünü olan, sanallıktan beslenen, gerçeği dillendirmekten çok örtmeye ve maskelemeye yarayan, terör üzerine kurulu bir söylemden yola çıkan metaforik bir söylem, verili olanın onanması ve meşruiyetine zemin hazırlamakta; "ütopyalar kadar hakikate ulaşımı da imkansızlaştıran bir tükenişi ele ver"mektedir (Aktaş 2001, ss. 41-42). Erk'in yayılma ve meşruiyet alanını sağlama alma çabalarının uzantısı olarak gündeme gelen şiddet- karşı-şiddet ilişkisi yeni savaşlara vesile olmakta, onlara gerekçe hazırlamaktadır. Örneğin, "fiziksel açıdan olduğu kadar imgesel açıdan da ürpertici" olan ikiz kulelere yönelik seyirlik saldırı sonrasında "bu metaforik bahanenin özrüne ya da sanrısına sığınılarak Afganistan, Filistin, Çeçenistan ve benzeri bir çok çıbanbaşında (!)" kitlesel katliamlara girişilmiştir ((Aktaş 2001, s. 38).

Gerçeklik gibi, tarihi ve ideolojiyi de dışlayan, "tarihsel olay"ın tıpkı gerçeklik gibi ortadan kalktığını ve Yeni Dünya Düzeni'nde, medyanın oluşturduğu, tarihi değil, tarih-ötesi olay tip'lerinin (11 Eylül gibi) karşımıza çıktığını öne süren Baudrillard'a (2004b) göre bu olaylar, sisteme özgü ani içsel sarsıntılara, "bilinçli bir düzensizlikten çok mutlak bir kargaşaya yol açan Kötülük adlı güçten esinlenmiş olaylara benzemektedirler". Bu iddialar, George W. Bush'un "kötüye karşı savaşmak için dünyanın cesareti var mı, yok mu" şeklindeki açıklamaları ile örtüşmekte ve gerçek siyasal amaçları maskelemeye yaramaktadır (Zizek 2003, s. 75). Tüm bu olayları belirsiz, rasgele olaylar dizisi olarak ele alan, hatta ne olduğu pek belli olmayan "Kötülük" adlı soyut bir güce havale eden bu iddialar, anlama yollarını tıkamakta, her türlü eleştirelliği ortadan kaldırmakta, verili olanı onaylayıcı bir tutum içine sokmakta ve onu sonsuzlaştırmakta, tavır almayı önlemekte, değişim, dönüşüm dinamiklerinin yolunu tıkamakta ve ütopyayı yok etmektedir. Oysa savaşın bu yaşanma biçimi, teknoloji-kapitalizm işbirliğinin bir uzantısı olarak gündeme gelmektedir ve bu nedenle savaşın/şiddetin ve savaş temsillerinin ideolojik boyutları ve işlevleri saklıdır. Son beş yüz yıldır Batı'nın refahının, Amerika'nın fethinden Kongo'daki katliama kadar acımasız şiddet ve yıkımın Dışarı'ya ihracıyla sağlandığını belirten Zizek (2002), DTM (Dünya Ticaret Merkezi) gibi saldırıların "gerçek etkisinin gerçek olmaktan çok daha büyük ölçüde simgesel olduğunu" belirtir (s. 296). Nitekim, Saraybosna'da, Ruanda'da, Kongo'da daha büyük çaplı şiddet biçimleri yaşanmıştır; ve DTM kurbanlarından çok daha fazla sayıda insan AIDS'ten ölmektedir (Zizek 2002, s. 296); ve hala Irak'ta, Filistin'de ve dünyanın başka yerlerinde şiddet ve savaş tüm acımasızlığıyla sürmektedir. Modernizm/kapitalizm ve teknoloji işbirliğine dayanarak savaş ve şiddet ortamı kurulmakta, ve medyada estetize edilerek meşrulaştırılmaktadır. Verili sistem medya teknolojilerini kullanarak savaşı sistemin yapısal unsurlarından biri haline getirirken, bir yandan sistemin alt-yapısal koşullarını oluşturmakta; öbür yandan korkuyu besleyerek onun ideolojik yeniden üretimine zemin hazırlamaktadır.

Sembolik olarak hükmetmenin ötesine geçip "bu dünyaya müdahale etme" hedefini taşıyan askeri benzetim teknolojileriyle bağlantılı olarak gündeme gelen "tele-temsilin ve tele-operasyonun işlevleri"nin çok önemli olduğunu belirtir Robins (1999): "Bilgisayar-benzetim teknolojisi, gerçek dünya durumlarını ve olaylarını uzaktan izlemeye ve uzaktan denetlemeye yarayan, duyargaları, silah sistemleriyle sibernetik sistemin bir parçasıdır" (s. 97). Dolayısıyla, kapitalist dokuyla bağlantıları kuvvetli olan imaj ve askeri vizyon teknolojilerinin sistemle bütünleşmiş işleyiş mekanizmalarıyla birlikte gözetleme ve müdahale olanağı sağlayan düzen-içi işlevlerinin ifşa edilmesini önleyen bu bakma biçimleri, karşı-müdahale olanağını dışlamaktadır. "Gerçekliğin inkar edilmesinin kurumsallaştırılması ve normalleştirilmesi"nin günümüz askeri enformasyon toplumunun belirleyici bir özelliği olduğunu ifade eden Robins (1999), "kurgusal seri-cinayet katilleri ile gerçek olanlar, gerçekten katledenler arasında bir ortaklık ilişkisi olduğunu göz ardı etmeme"k gerektiğini söylemektedir (ss. 134-135, 138).

Sanal Savaş, Toplumsal, Bireysel ve Etik Uzantıları

İmajın gerçek üzerindeki hegemonyasına bağlı olarak gelişen kurmaca gerçeklik evresinde gündeme gelen "yaşanan varlığın alt-üst oluşu" olarak da kavramsallaştırılabilecek genel temsil sorunlarının savaş alanındaki uzantılarının—savaş temsilinin görsel medyadaki sorunlu, illüzyonik doğası—toplumsal, bireysel ve etik sonuçları üzerinde de durmak gerekir.

Mitsel niteliklere sahip bir kitle iletişim aracı olan televizyondaki metaforik görüntüler ile göndermede bulunduğu gerçeklik arasında toplumsal uzlaşmaya dayalı sembolik bir ilişki vardır. Toplumda kodlanmış bulunan gerçeklik, belli bir seçme, kurgulama ve yorumlama işleminden geçirilerek televizyonda teknolojik olarak aktarılabilir, izleyici için uygun bir "kültürel metin" haline getirilmektedir. Bu kültürel metin, çekimler arasından seçilmiş, ayıklanmış, ses ve metinsel öğelerin de dahil edildiği bir müdahaleler alanı olduğu ölçüde gerçekliğin biçimlendirildiği ve aynı zamanda görüntülerin içerdiği gerçeklik algısının da değişime zorlandığı bir seyir mekanıdır. "Olayların doğasını 'formatlara' dönüştürme olanağına" dayanarak televizyonda belli teknikler yoluyla kurgusal/sentetik bir gerçeklik yaratılmaktadır. Bir "akış televizyonu" niteliğine sahip olan televizyonun bu özelliği sayesinde tüm gerçekler aynı potada değerlendirilmekte, her yeni görüntü bir öncekinin etkisini silmekte, her şeyi bir şakaya ve oyuna dönüştürmektedir. Öyle ki, "Hiçbir cinayet açıkça vahşi değildir, hiçbir doğa hareketi açıkça zarar vermez, ardarda gelen olaylar hiçbiri üzerinde fazla düşünmeye olanak vermez". Sınırlı bir rahatlamanın sağlandığı bu yolla, şiddet gösterimlerinin fantazya mı, yoksa yaşanan gerçekliğin uzantısı mı olduğunun ayırdedilmesi gittikçe güçleşmektedir (Türkoğlu 2004, ss. 256-258). Gerçeklik ile fantazya arasındaki sınırın ortadan kalkması ve gerçeğin bulanıklaşması, algının bulanıklaşmasına yol açmakta; bu da duyguların yalama olmasına ve körleşmesine neden olmaktadır. Bu durumda "gerçek ölüm ve acı artık, ekranda seyrettiğimiz sürece, bizi yapıntı ölüm ve acıdan daha fazla irkilt"memektedir (Uğur 2003, s. 31).

Gerçeklik duygusunu zedeleyen savaşı izleme pratiği, her şeyden önce izleyicinin psişik donanımını daha parçalı bir yapı haline getirmekte, duyuları birbirinden ayırmakta, bu da savaş pratiğini algılama, ona özgü bir kavrayış ve tepki geliştirme iradesini ortadan kaldırmaktadır. Savaşı algılama biçimlerimizi değiştiren yüksek teknolojili savaş sistemleri, izleyicilere "psişik bir dondurma süreci" yaşatmakta, bireysel aklı parçalara ayırmakta, bilgiyi duygudan koparmakta, ötekini hissetme, acı'yı içselleştirme duygusunu dumura uğratmaktadır. "Psikolojik yalıtım" özelliğine sahip olan uzun kamera çekimleri, "ahlaki ayrılma" duygusu yaratmaktadır. Askerlerin silahlarını tam olarak kullanabilmeleri için askeri bağlardan kopması ve kurbanların psikolojik olarak görünmez olması gerekmektedir. Ayrıca, "öldürme işlemi 'uzaktan' teknoloji dolayımıyla, doğrudan çatışma ve şiddet şokundan uzak olmalıdır. Ateşleme düğmesi ve bunu izleyen ölümler arasındaki nedensel bağlantının kırılması gereklidir". Nitekim Irak Savaşı'nda katil ve kurban arasındaki görsel mesafe artmış; görünür olan, sesten, acıdan, kandan ayrılmıştır. "Hareketi yakın çekimde (zoom yaparak) görsek de düşman, yüzü olmayan bir yabancıdan başka bir şey değildi. Biz, gözetleyenler için, onların ölümlerinin gerçekliği gerçekleşmiyordu" diyen Robins'e (1999) göre "video-oyun fantazyalarının bir uzantısı" olan, gerçek insanları soyutlayan bu savaşla birlikte, insanlığın gerçek dünyayla, savaşı hissetmenin ve ona karşı bir tepki geliştirmekle bağlantısı koptu; vicdan ve sağduyuya karşı eşik algısı düştü; ve izleyicinin kendisi ile bağı kopmuş olan savaş, ahlaki bir yükümlülük konusu olmaktan çıktı (ss. 111-116).

Öldürülen insanların katleden insanlar tarafından izlenmesi de sorunun ayrı bir boyutunu oluşturmaktadır. Hem izleyici failler, hem de izleyiciler nezdinde "seyirci olarak şiddet gösterilerine müdahale etmeden bakmak, ister sanatsal, ister gerçeklik olsun gösterinin elemanlarını nesneleştirme yoluyla rasyonellik kazanmaktadır" (Türkoğlu 2004, s. 241). Karşındakini nesne kılmakla bağlantılı olan şiddetin tepkisizce seyredilmesi olgusu, röntgencilik eylemine dönüşmekte, bu da eylemin failleri nezdinde ahlaki bir ikileme yol açmamaktadır. "Sadizm röntgenciliğe dönüştüğü zaman kendisini nötrleştiriyor" demektedir Robins (1999). Ekranın teşvik ettiği hastalıklı röntgencilik, gerçeklik ile imajı ikame edilir şeyler haline getirmekte; öldürme olayının aslını, gerçekliğini ekran dışında tutarak öldürenleri ahlaki bir ilişkiye girmekten uzaklaştırmaktadır. Peki bu nasıl mümkün olmaktadır? En güçlü savunma mekanizmalarından biri olan benliğin bölünmesi mekanizması ve bu bölünmeyle birlikte gündeme gelen benliğin parçalanmasıyla faillerin hem katil, hem de normal insan olabilmesi durumu, açıklayıcı bir pencere sunmaktadır. Tıpkı bunun gibi, içinde bulunulan "denetim ve gözlem teknolojilerinin bir çeşit video-oyunu senaryosu üretmesi"nin neden olduğu bir iletişim düzeni de, oyuncu-benliğin, gerçek dünyayla cebelleşen benlikten daha gerçek olduğunun düşünülmesine yol açmaktadır. Gerçeklik ve fantazya arasındaki sınırların bulanıklaştığı böyle bir durumda ortaya çıkan "esriklik hali"nde, oyuncu-benliğin, savaşın gerçekliğiyle olan ahlaki bağlantısı yitip gitmektedir. İzleyici röntgencilerin durumuna gelince, her ne kadar onların durumu farklılıklar içerse ve sadistlikten uzak, alışkanlığa ve dışsallık yaratan görüntü sunumlarına bağlı izleme biçimleri olsa da, "yine de, patolojik durumun uzantısının normale gölge düşürdüğünü; şiddet ve ıstırapların 'sıradan' seyircisinin, fantastik, sapkın, ürkütücü uçlardan çok da uzak olmadığını" söylemektedir Robins (1999, ss. 134-137). Böylelikle izleyiciyle olduğu kadar savaş failleriyle de bağı kopmuş bulunan ve röntgencilik eylemine dönüşen savaş olgusu, ahlaki bağlantıyı da ortadan kaldırmaktadır.

Böylelikle, imaja teslim olunmuş, ahlak ise devre-dışı bırakılmıştır. Savaş/şiddet sunumlarının gerçekle ilişkisinin sanal bir nitelik kazanmasının yarattığı Etik düzlemdeki en önemli sorun, savaşı/şiddeti etiğin alanının dışına çıkarması, onu etiğe karşı bir noktaya konumlaması, gerçeklik gibi etiğin de yok sayılmasıdır. Erk'in meşruiyetini sağlama almak için her şeyin mübah olduğu, başarının tek ölçüt halini aldığı verili durumda, Kahraman'ın (2003) sanat için söylediği şey, tüm bir hayat için olduğu gibi gerçek savaş için de geçerli hale geliyor: "Hayat popülerleştikçe sanallığın önemi de düzeyi de gelişiyor. Bu denklemin ters değişkeni ise ahlaki değerler, onlar sürekli düşüş kaydediyor" (s. 170).

Ahlaki olarak nötrleşmiş bir kitlenin savaş karşısındaki yaptırım gücü de zayıf olmaktadır. Bu durum, savaşa karşı engelleyici gücü yüksek, bilinçli bir karşı-duruş geliştirmekten ziyade, tepkimeci, duygusal ve şiddet içeren yanıtlarla savunma psikolojisi içine girmeyi sonuçlamaktadır. Şiddetin şiddeti tetiklediği böyle bir ortam ise şiddete, dehşete ve vahşete dayalı bir dünyanın kanıksanmasına ve onun yeniden-üretilmesine zemin hazırlamakta, korku kültürünü beslemektedir. Gerçek dünyanın olaylarına referansta bulunmayan, sorumluluk yüklemeden arzuları tatmin eden, korkutucu ve ürkütücü deneyimleri yansıtma potansiyeline sahip olan ekran, "ahlaki benliklerimiz yerine temel korkularımıza" seslenmekte, kaygıya hakimiyet alanı sağlamaktadır. İçimizdeki saldırganlık, öfke ve korku duygularının aracısına dönüşen ekran, dışsal bir tehdit yanılsaması yaratarak korkuyu beslemekte, daha sonra da "savunmacı şiddet"i harekete geçirmekte (Robins 1999, s 123); şiddet bir öz-savunma aracı olarak gündeme gelmektedir. "Korkunun boy gezdirdiği ilişki ortamlarında şiddetin su yüzüne çıkması ise an meselesidir" (Uğur 2003, s. 43).

Gerçeğin metaforik bir nitelik kazandığı, çarpık temsiliyetin ve metafor'un gerçek'i yıprattığı ve tükettiği, tüketilen simgeler tarafından anlamların kurulduğu yapay ve sanal bir üst-gerçeklik ortamında, şiddetin karşılığı olarak şiddet meşruiyet zemini bulmaktadır. Şiddetin ve korkunun şiddeti beslediği bir ortamda suç ve terörün yaygınlık alanı genişlemektedir. Görüntüler aracılığı ile yumuşatılarak olağanlaştırılan şiddet, estetik bir kurgu malzemesine dönüştürdüğü suçu meşru kılmakta ve onu içselleştirmekte, suç ile boşalma yaratmakta, suçun kanıksanması ona yönelimi kolaylaştırmaktadır. Hayatını suçların ve suç işleyenlerin kapladığını düşünmeye başlayan insan, duyarlık yitimine uğramakta, suça yönelme olasılığı artmaktadır (Oskay, 1992, ss. 58-59).

Böylelikle ekran bir yandan, şiddete/savaşa/suça yaslanan dünyayı pekiştirirken ve insanı olan bitenlerin tanığı kılarak korkuya malzeme olurken, öte yandan korunaklı bir ortamda, fiziksel savaşın/şiddetin uzağında bir izleme pratiğiyle güvenlik duygusu zerk etmekte, rahatlatıcı bir etkiye yol açmaktadır. "John Berger'in söylediği gibi ekran röntgenciliği, hayata karşı şimdiye dek eşi benzeri görülmemiş bir acımasızlığa ve kayıtsızlığa geçit vermektedir: 'Ekran gerçekliğin yerine geçmektedir. Bu yer değiştirmenin çifte işlevi vardır. Çünkü gerçeklik olaylarla bilincin karşılaşmasından doğar. Gerçekliği reddetmek yalnızca nesnelliği reddetmek değildir. Öznel olanın da temel bir parçasını reddetmektir.' Ekranın gücü ahlaki tepki vermeyi daha çok zorlaştırmaktadır" (Robins 1999, ss. 123-124).

Kuşkusuz bu her zaman böyle olmuyor. Acı çekenleri görüp o çöküntüyü hissettiğimiz de oluyor. Ancak, gerçekliğin yerine geçen, onun çelişkin, oynak doğasını yansıtmayan, kontrolün ve gücün bizde olmadığı ve kendimizi güven içinde hissetmediğimiz bir dünyada güç, kontrol ve güven duyguları zerk eden ekrandaki imaj, ahlaki davranışları güçleştirmekte, ahlaki yapımıza belli zorluklar yüklemekte, gerçek ve karşılıklı bir diyalog sürecine girmeyi önlemektedir (Robins 1999, s. 138). Gerçek acı çekmeyi gösteren ancak sonra da tecrit eden, ahlaklı, merhametli ve karşılıklı ilişkilere girmeyi sağlayamayan fotoğrafik imajın yol açtığı ahlaki uçurumun video ekranlarında ve elektronik imajlarda daha da büyüdüğünü belirtir Robins (1999, s. 125). Her ne kadar televizyon imajlarının uzaklığı "düşman"ın kaderine karşı her zaman kayıtsız kalmayı sonuçlasa da, televizyonun belgesel niteliğinin öne çıktığı eski zamanlarda imajı ahlaki nedenselliğe yaklaştırabilme olanağı daha fazla iken, savaşa video-oyun muamelesi yapmak, bu olanağı iyice ortadan kaldırmaktadır. İmajı belgesel niteliğinden soyutlamak, görüntü olgusuyla bağlantılı ancak bilince ait olmayan süreç üzerinde görüntüyü daha etkin kılmaktadır. Bunun sonucunda "ekran, içsel itkilerimizin doğrudan bir işlevi haline gelir." Çocuksu terör ve savunma biçimlerini harekete geçiren video oyunları, oyuncuların, sürekli olarak kendilerini yok etmeye çalışan yıkıcı güçlerden korunmaya çalıştığı "paranoyak bir ortam" yaratır. Nitekim Körfez Savaşı sırasında da, video-oyun imajları, bizi, fiziksel ve toplumsal bütünlüğümüzü ve düzenimizi tehdit eden tehlikelerin ikamesiyle bağlantılı bir konuma yerleştirmiştir.

Umuttan Söz etmek Hala Mümkün mü?

Bu durumda, daha önceleri hiç bilmediğimiz bir biçimde şiddet imajları ile kuşatılmış bulunduğumuz bir dünyada, aşınan vicdan ve merhamet duygularının, yıpranan gerçeklik duygusunun, sorgulanmaya ve restore edilmeye; bölünmüş benliklerin ise parçalarının yerine oturtulmaya ve ilişkilendirilmeye hiç olmadığı kadar ihtiyacı vardır.

Bu çıkışsız tabloda yeni bir başlangıç noktası kaçınılmaz görünüyor veya topyekun bir yokoluş. Yukarıda resmi çizilen günümüzün toplumsal gerçeklik ortamında savaşsız, şiddete dayanmayan bir dünya umudu hala mümkün mü? Resim iç açıcı olmasa da, eğer hala umuttan söz etmek için bir neden varsa, bu, Walter Benjamin'in sözünü ettiği "umutsuzlar adınadır " (aktaran Jay 1989, s. 305).

Bu durumda gerçek/gerçeklik yokluğuna dayalı, benzeşim ve gösteri dünyasında yaşadığımızı söyleyenlerin eleştirel boyutlarından beslenerek, ancak onların kıyamet senaryolarına fazla prim vermeden yapılabilecekler üzerine odaklanacak yeni, daha insani, etik bir senaryoya ihtiyacı var insanlığın. Bu senaryoda "dünyadaki organik varoluş tekrar gerçekliğin odağı haline getirilmeli, sanal alem benzeti sıfatıyla uygun yerine oturtulmalıdır. Sanal ortam ancak böyle bir durumda ütopik bir işlev görebilir." Yoksa sanal olan, günümüzde kazanmış olduğu hegemonik varoluş biçimine uygun olarak bir kontrol aygıtı olarak durur önümüzde (Critical Art Ensemble 2003, s. 235).

Savaş adına yaşananların hepsi, Adorno'nun (1998) dediği gibi, "deneyimin...kuruyup büzüşmesinin bir başka ifadesidir...Olayların şeyleşmiş, katılaşmış, alçıdan kalıpları, olayların yerini almıştır sanki" (s. 57). Bu durumda "gerçeklikten kaçışı toplumsal olarak kurumsallaştıran teknolojik sistem" karşısında, görsel deneyimlerin alanını genişletirken gerçek deneyim alanlarından uzaklaştıran ve topyekün yok edici bir boyut kazanan teknolojik rasyonalizasyonu bir kenara bırakıp, teknolojik gelişmelere yüklediğimiz anlamları, yitirdiklerimiz açısından da ele almalıyız. Görsel deneyim alanı ile gerçek deneyim alanı arasındaki açı farkının büyük olduğu düşünüldüğünde, deneyim alanı kumandaların düğmelerini açıp kapamaya indirgenmiş bulunan insanlık için, deneyim önemli bir sorun olarak karşımızda durmaktadır. "Modern kültürde deneyimlerin inkarı, reddedilmesi, modern yaşam deneyimlerini hafifletmek üzere vizyon teknolojilerinin yaşamımıza uyarlanması zihinlerimizi meşgul ediyor. Öncelikle bunlar üzerinde durmadan, deneyimin yeniden geçerlilik kazanma yolları hakkındaki olasılıkları düşünemeyiz." demektedir Robins (1999, s. 51).

Yine Robins'in dediği gibi, günümüzde imaj alanı içinde yaşıyor olmamızdan daha da önemli olan şey, bölüntülenmiş yaşam deneyimlerine dayalı modern kültürün, imaj ortamlarının etkisiyle benlik de dahil olmak üzere birbiriyle uzlaşmaz parçalara ayrılmış olmasıdır. Seyirci ve oyuncu benlik arasındaki bağlantı kopuktur. "Seyirci-benlik ahlaki olarak hiçbir yere bağlı değildir, şiddet imajları okyanusunda başıboş yüzmektedir. Oyuncu-benlik ahlaki olarak katlanılmaz bir şiddet gerçekliğine kapılıp gitmektedir." Kültürün genel niteliği olan "kolektif, toplumsal bölünme mekanizması"nın ortadan kalktığı bir dönüşüm, seyirci benlik ile oyuncu benlik arasındaki yabancılaşmayı ortadan kaldırmanın zeminini oluşturacağından "benliğin ve ötekinin karşılıklı olarak dönüştürdüğü ve dönüştüğü bir diyalog ve müzakere sürecinin yaşanması zorunludur" (Robins 1999, ss. 137-138).

Bu noktada Canetti'nin kendi yaşamı için söyledikleri bütün bir hayat için umutsuz bir umut vaadi taşıyor gibi: "Bütün yaşamım, her şey kafamda bir araya gelsin ve yeniden bir bütün oluşturabilsin diye, işbölümünü ortadan kaldırmaya ve her şeyi düşünmeye yönelik, çaresiz bir çabadan başka bir şey değil. Her şeyi bilmeyi değil, parçalanmışı yeniden biraraya getirmeyi istiyorum. Böyle bir girişimin başarıya ulaşamayacağı, neredeyse kesin gibi. Ama başarıya ilişkin küçücük olasılık bile her türlü çabaya değer" (Canetti 1994, s. 144). Kaybedecek daha fazla şeyi olmayan umutsuzlar için denemeye değer görünüyor...

Kaynakça

Adorno, W. T. (1998). *Minima Moralia* (Çev. Orhan Koçak, Ahmet Doğukan) İstanbul: Metis.

Aktaş, Ü. (2001). Metaforik savaş ya da herkesin imtihanı. *Birikim 151*, 38-42.

Baudrillard, J. (2002). Terörizmin mantığı. *Cogito 30*, 67-78.

Baudrillard, J. (2004a). *Kötülüğün şeffaflığı* (Çev. Işık Ergüden, 3. Basım). İstanbul: Ayrıntı.

Baudrillard, J. (2004b). Sanal evren ve haber dünyası. http://izinsizgosteri.net/asalsayi07/baudrillard_07.html (Son ulaşım 01.05.2004).

Belge, M. (1995). Soğuk savaş sonrası çatışmalar. *Cogito 3*, 43-54.

Bursalı, O. (1995). Yeni dünya düzeni, bilim ve savaş. *Cogito 3*, 71-77.

Canetti, E. (1994). Notlar'dan. *Cogito 2*, 136-145.

Castells, M. (2002). Gerçek sanallık kültürü. *Cogito 30*, 212-215.

Critical Art Ensemble. (2003). İnternette terörizm mitolojisi. *Cogito 34*, 203-235.

Jay, M. (1989). *Diyalektik imgelem* (Çev. Ünsal Oskay). İstanbul: Ara.

Kahraman, H. B. (2003). *Kitle kültürü kitlelerin afyonu*. İstanbul: Agora.

Oktay , A. (1995). *Şiddet, söz, yaşam*. Ankara: Ark.

Oskay, Ü. (1992). *İletişimin ABC'si*. İstanbul: Simavi.

Robins, K. (1999). *İmaj* (Çev. Nurçay Türkoğlu). İstanbul: Ayrıntı.

Türkoğlu, Nurçay. (2004). *Toplumsal iletişim*, İstanbul: Babil.

Uğur, A. (2003). *Kültür kıtası atlası* (2. Basım). İstanbul: YKY.

Zizek, S. (2002). *Kırılgan temas* (Çev. Tuncay Birkan). İstanbul: Metis.

Zizek, S. (2003). Irak savaşı: Gerçek tehlike nerede? *Birikim 169*, 71-77.

Miscommunication: The Other of Communication or the Otherness of Communication?

Tuğrul İlter
Faculty of Communication and Media Studies
Eastern Mediterranean University, North Cyprus
tugrul.ilter@emu.edu.tr

Introduction

Communication is commonly defined as a pre-destined, goal-driven, purposeful act, whose completion is marked by the realization of its purpose when the predestined destination is reached. Examples range from textbooks to advertising to mission statements of schools of communication.[1] Often it is understood as an intended (by a Subject) signified in transit between origin and end, one whose origin aims for its destination, as leading to an understanding that is (finally) cleansed of the otherness of mediation and representation. At other times it is the transcendental signifier, such as Lacan's "phallus," that dictates this fateful journey to the subjects, over whom its chain of command/signification rules. Because its destination is predestined, its origin is its end. However, this end/origin is to be reached after an alienating diversion or detour through an Other, not only because communication involves always more than one within the person in the case of so called "intra-personal communication" (consider the split between our consciousness and our unconscious or between the signifier(s) and the signified of the person) as well as more than one person in other forms of communication involving subjects, but also because it is supplemented by signifiers, mediators, representatives, translations that are other than the aimed for destination.

The task of communication is then understood as making sure that no miscommunication obstructs and obscures communication, that the transmission from origin to end is not derailed by miscommunication, that the end intended, or destined, by the Subject and/or the transcendental signifier is finally reached, following an alienating detour from itself. Accordingly, miscommunication is understood either as having no place within communication proper, being alien and other to it, and hence as an external threat to its taking place like "noise," or as a diversion off course, which, however, is destined to get back on the course proper to it.[2] The diversion in the latter, therefore, also has its eyes set on the telos of communication, is internal to the working of communication, assuring its fateful end, acting like a relay that leads us to its end, and therefore, assuring communication itself. Nevertheless, the fact that this "alienating detour" through the other(s) of communication (signification, mediation, representations, translation—writing in the generalized Derridean sense) is necessary, that it has to occur everytime there is communication, should alert us to other possibilities of understanding communication. Using the resources of deconstruction and taking into consideration the irreducible gap between the signifier and the signified as well as the irreducible necessity of mediation through an other, and the disseminating, differing and deferring character of such "detours" in any communication, which makes their "return to course" a re-turn, that is to say, a new and different heading, a dissemination, I attempt to rethink communication in this paper without reducing its complexity. I contend that miscommunication, misunderstanding, and the misses of communication in general, cannot be absolutely and definitively separated from communication proper as they *are* part and parcel of communication, the very reference setting up its condition of possibility, indicating communication's difference-within, its differential make-up.

1 For example, Belch and Belch (1999) argue that "for effective communication to occur, the message decoding process of the receiver must match the encoding of the sender. Simply put, this means the receiver understands and correctly interprets what the source is trying to communicate" and inform us that "advertisers spend millions of dollars every year...pretesting messages to make sure consumers understand and decode them in the manner the advertiser intended" (p. 143).

2 Metaphor is called a metaphor because it is thought that it has carried you away from the signifier's goal of the primary or literal meaning, which stays as the referent of its definition as metaphor. Although Jacques Lacan has displaced the signified as the point of reference of the signifier, he describes a similar relationship regarding the journey of the signifier: In discussing the title of "The Purloined Letter" he writes: "we are quite simply dealing with a letter which has been diverted from its path; one whose course has been *prolonged*... since it can be diverted, it must have a course *which is proper to it:* the trait by which its incidence as signifier is affirmed" (1988, p. 43).

Models of Communication

It is not possible to refer to a strictly canonical definition of communication in the field of communication and media studies, because the field is inter- or trans-disciplinary, and is thus conspicuously intertextual in its weave, as well as being informed by perspectives like Cultural Studies that resist disciplinary canonization or attempt to make such resistance canonical. One of the first things that students of communication learn is that there are (too) many, and often incompatible and incommensurable definitions of communication. In his dictionary of communication, for instance, Erol Mutlu (1998) states that there are close to two-hundred different definitions of communication (1998, p. 168). What comes closest to a canonical definition of communication, the one that seems to have the most popular appeal, in and out of the field of communication and media studies, relies on the use of, basically similar, "models of communication." Referring to the basic structure that they share, these models are commonly referred to, in the singular, as the "S=>M=>R" model, where S stands for the Sender, M stands for the Message, or the Meaning of the Message, and R stands for the Receiver. The M originates from the S and is aimed at the R, hence the model posits a unidirectional "line of communication." Perhaps the best known is Harold Lasswell's "5W Formula," so called because the model is made up of five questions that start with the letter W, which then serves as a mnemonic device: *Who (says) What (to) Whom (in) What Channel (with) What Effect?*

A similarly popular model is provided by Claude Shannon's "schematic diagram of a general communication system" (Figure 1). Shannon's model introduces additional complications to Laswell's model. First a non-human Transmitter and a corresponding Receiver are introduced in between Laswell's Sender and Receiver, which translate the message into a signal and then the signal back to the message. Although with this complication the new model seemingly introduces the problem of translation as an irreducible part of communication, this opening is foreclosed by Shannon's (1948) framing of communication as an engineering problem, for he writes: "Frequently the messages have *meaning*...[but] these semantic aspects of communication are irrelevant to the engineering problem" (1948, p. 1). Second, the model introduces an external source of "noise" that interferes with the line or aim of communication from completing itself and reaching its end. "Noise" is thus identified as the culprit responsible for miscommunication. Since noise interferes from outside the line of communication in the model's representation, the solution that will overcome miscommunication and achieve communication is to keep noise out where it belongs, by insulating and isolating the "inside" of communication to make it one with itself, and to make it impermeable to "outside" interference, so the two will not end up in a relationship, get mixed up, hybridize, become heterogeneous, and contradict each other.

Yet this representational excommunication of miscommunication to communication's outside can hardly be successful and needs to be seen as what it is, an excommunication of something inside. However much Shannon enframes and tries to limit his discussion of communication within an "engineering" framework, the engineers too will have experienced, at least some of the time, along with the rest of us, miscommunication and misunderstanding even with the reception of a perfectly clear "signal," and the "exact" or "approximate" reproduction of a message that is not the least bit or little corrupted by "noise." That miscommunication can still occur despite keeping noise out of the line of communication indicates that, perhaps, the source of miscommunication lies within communication itself, and that it is only projected to the outside in such representational stagings of communication like Shannon's. That is why I referred to this projection as an excommunication. Instead of treating such representations as transparent "models" that let us see the really real beyond them, we need to focus on the materiality of such stagings that *are* communications that communicate, the very thing we are trying to understand.

How, then, does communication accommodate what is projected from the inside, the miscommunication? There is, for example, the polysemy of (whichever) language used in every communication, with one signifier leading to many signifieds, which tells us that no communication is one with itself, undivided and self-same. Accordingly, we do not have only one line aimed like an arrow for only one destination but a dissemination, a division and dispersal of lines without the fateful guarantee of a final convergence on a singular goal, the reason of a higher plan, or a Hegelian *Aufhebung*.[3] We observe this differential excess that overflows a simple unity at the other end also. Despite structuralist representations such as "primary meaning" (denotation or literal meaning) and "secondary meaning" (connotation or metaphorical meaning), polysemic difference and plurality is irreducible to an indivisible, self-same, in-different origin/end. "Literal" is itself a metaphor whose metaphoricity we have forgotten, that is to say, what is represented as the primary or original meaning itself rests on difference, and is the product of a displacement, a deviation from an earlier, more "original" heading. In discussing metaphor, which "is determined by philosophy as a provisional loss of meaning...a certainly inevitable detour...with its sights set on...the circular reappropriation of literal, proper meaning," Jacques Derrida (1982) argues that "de-tour is a re-turn" (1982, p. 270).

Furthermore, meaning is always in process. Its being is always in the process of becoming. Thus, meaning is always yet-to-come and constantly differs from and defers itself in what Jacques Derrida has referred to as the "play of *differance*."[4] The previously mentioned polysemy is,

3 As Colin Gordon (1980) puts it, in a different context: "Our world does not follow a program, but we live in a world of programs" (1980, p. 245).

4 In response to structuralism's synchronic exclusion of diachrony to convey

indeed, the result of this differance. What this means is that, despite teleological projections of a particular destination, the message/meaning is always already off course, missing its teleological destination, and its future heading is not fixed and given but is yet-to-come. Therefore, we can never say with unshakeable certainty that what has been communicated has finally, fully arrived. In what Friedrich Nietzsche (1974) has called "the eternal return of the same", and what Jacques Derrida (1988) refers to as "iterability" in "Signature, Event, Context," each communication keeps re-communicating, and re-communicating differently every time. If we recall Roland Barthes' (1974) notion of a "writerly text," for example, with every re-reading of a book or a re-watching of a film, what is communicated arrives again. What is delivered in communication is always haunted by its future arrival, and lives in the undecidable, spectral state of having arrived and yet to arrive.

The S->M=>R model of communication has been criticized extensively for its one-way linearity, and for assuming a passive, non-interpretive stance for the receiver, which is then derided by likening it to a "hypodermic needle," or a "magic bullet." The critiques then call for a two-way exchange and interaction to replace the model's one-way linearity. In its revision, neither the sender nor the receiver are exclusively such, and they alternate in assuming those roles, with the direction of communication changing accordingly, rather like an alternating electric current changing polarity. While these critiques have been useful in hinting at the irreducible complexity of communication and opening up new areas of research such as "audience research," the fundamental teleological structure in question is left intact and is reproduced at various other levels. Even with the above mentioned alternation added, for instance, the model is still singularly linear, S⇔M⇔R, and the message or the meaning of the message still originates in the conscious intention to mean or the hermeneutic ability to interpret of a simple, undivided subject. In fact, such simplicity applies to all the other elements of these models and seems to heed Denis McQuail and Sven Windahl's (1993) definition of a model of a communication process as "a consciously *simplified description* in *graphic form* of a piece of reality" (1993, p. 2).

What I find most remarkable about these models that purport to explain what communication is, is that they completely ignore language or at most reduce it, to the extent that it is implied, into a neutral carrier of communication. For these models, language seems to be a transparent vehicle of transport without any effectivity of its own on communication and what is communicated by communication. I will now take a different turn and change my heading to discuss a couple of older theories that make up for this deficiency and take the productivity and effectivity of language to be of central importance in communication.

a timeless, basic, original sense of "structure," Derrida (1982) spells difference as "differance" (with an *a*) to indicate both a spatial difference (differing) *and* temporal difference (deferring), and how they rely on each other in a supplementary relationship (1982, pp. 1-27). For a discussion of his notion of "to-come" regarding spectrality and a democracy-to-come see *Specters of Marx* (Derrida, 1994).

John Austin's Speech Act Theory

If we recall McQuail and Windahl's definition of a communication model quoted earlier, it sets up a certain relationship between "a piece of reality" and a "description" of it. Such statements can then be factually verifed and judged to be "true" or "false" by reference to their referent. This is because in a "reality versus representation of reality" relationship, the description here is taken to be dependent on and correspond to a pre- and self-existing reality, which is assumed not to need a representation, a mediation, or a communication to make itself fully and completely self-present. The description is thus seen as originating from and aiming for that reality's self presence in a relationship of correspondence and adequation.[5] Therefore, such a judgment could also be used to determine whether a communication has reached its destination and fulfilled itself. John L. Austin calls such statements "constatives" and tells us that they are the typical statements of a philosophical discourse that he has "an inclination to play old Harry with."[6] Austin's work is of interest here for us primarily because of another kind of communication, the "speech acts" that he calls "performatives," which do not depend on a previously present reality, and, therefore, problematize its originality vis-à-vis the speech act.[7] His work thus represents an interesting departure from the concept of communication as a purely semiotic, linguistic, or symbolic concept.

According to Austin (1975), performatives "do not 'describe' or 'report' or constate anything at all," they "are not 'true or false'" but they "are a part of the doing of an action" and he stresses that they are not "just saying something," that is to say, the performative utterance "is not to *describe* my doing of what I should be said in so uttering to be doing or to state that I am doing it: it is to do it" (1975, pp. 5, 6). When the official says "I now pronounce you man and wife" in a marriage ceremony,

5 Ann Game (1991) discusses how "in sociological discourse critique is framed in terms of adequation" (1991, p. 7). This notion of the accuracy of representation suggests the phrase "mirror of nature" to Richard Rorty (1980), an understanding of knowledge that he questions.

6 More precisely he writes: "I admit to an inclination to play Old Harry with, viz. (1) the true/false fetish, (2) the value/fact fetish" (Austin, 1975, p. 151).

7 Although Austin (1975) starts with the performative-constative distinction, as a distinction between "doing and saying" (p. 47), that distinction turns out to be leaky, and he soon introduces questions about the tenability of an air-tight distinction after observing "our initial and tentative distinction…breaking down" (p. 54), with "a shift from descriptive to performative utterance and wavering between them" (p. 85), and concluding that "unhappiness nevertheless seems to characterize both kinds of utterance, not merely the performative; and that the requirement of conforming or bearing some relation to the facts, different in different cases, seems to characterize performatives, in addition to the requirement that they should be happy, similarly to the way which is characteristic of supposed constatives" (p. 91), and that "statements *are* liable to every kind of infelicity to which performatives are liable" (p. 136). So there is something about his work on speech acts that problematizes and complicates the received understanding of constatives as well. The discussion of performatives, thus, turns out not only to be about another kind of communication but also about another way of understanding communication.

for example, the pronouncement makes the couple man and wife, it is not a description of "man and wife." Other examples Austin provides include "I name this ship the *Queen Elizabeth*" uttered in a naming ceremony, "I give and bequeath my watch to my brother" as in a will, and "I bet you sixpence it will rain tomorrow" uttered to make a bet (p. 5).

Performatives, thus, cannot be deemed true or false by reference to pre-existing facts in the way language is theorised "in the favourite philosophical sense" as "an utterance of certain noises with a certain meaning…i.e. with a certain sense and with a certain reference" (p. 94). In other words, the performative does not have its referent outside of itself. It is a reference without a referent (that predates it, is external to it, etc.). Against this "descriptive fallacy," which is "too prone to give explanations in terms of 'the meaning of words'," Austin argues that "the occasion of an utterance matters seriously and that the words used are to some extent to be 'explained' by the 'context' in which they are designed to be or have actually been spoken in a linguistic interchange" (p. 100). Therefore, "what we have to study is *not* the sentence but the issuing of an utterance in a speech situation," indeed what we need to consider is "the total situation in which the utterance is issued—the total speech act" (pp. 52, 139).[8] This is because "a good many other things have as a general rule to be right and to go right if we are to be said to have happily brought off our action," otherwise the utterance will be "infelicitous" or "unhappy" and will fail to bring about the fact of its action (p. 14).

Austin then lists the "necessary conditions" that define the "context in which [speech acts] are designed to be" and will make them happy:

> "There must exist an accepted conventional procedure having a conventional effect, that procedure to include the uttering of certain words by certain persons in certain circumstances, and further, the particular persons and circumstances in a given case must be appropriate for the invocation of the particular procedure invoked. The procedure must be executed by all participants both correctly and completely. Where, as often, the procedure is designed for use by persons having certain thoughts or feelings, or for the inauguration of certain consequential conduct on the part of any participant, then a person participating in and so invoking the procedure must in fact have those thoughts or feelings, and the participants must intend so to conduct themselves, and further must actually so conduct themselves subsequently" (pp. 14-15).

Unless these conditions are met, and met "completely" to the last detail, the speech act will fail. This is a very tall order to meet, especially as Austin also tells us that "infelicity is an ill to which *all* acts are heir which have the general character of ritual or ceremonial, all *conventional* acts" (pp. 18-19). But this is not all that is required. Even more is needed to keep speech acts happy and clear of the infelicity of misunderstanding, "a type of infelicity to which all utterances are probaly liable" (p. 39). All "parasitic" uses of language, which are parasitic upon its "normal use," and which fall under "the doctrine of the *etiolations* of language" are to be excluded from consideration because they are not serious and genuine in their intention but are pale imitations. Austin thus argues that "a performative utterance will…be…hollow or void if said by an actor on the stage, or if introduced in a poem, or spoken in soliloquy" because in such cases language is not used "seriously" (p. 22). While it may be easier to distinguish the above examples by their settings, even when the "appropriate circumstances" are there, the speech act could still end up as a "misfire" (p. 16), "misinvocation" or "misapplication" (p. 17) for lacking the seriousness that separates it from a pallid imitation. I could, for instance, "say, 'I promise' and have no intention of keeping it" (p. 16).

Austin's theory of speech act thus recognizes the myriad ways that a speech act could go wrong, and hence requires that an overwhelming number of conditions are met, and met to the last detail, as well as spotting and excluding the etiolations when those conditions are seemingly, phenomenally met, so we don't end up with a miscommunication still. Yet, while trying to establish the required distinctions and exclusions, Austin also recognizes that "these distinctions [between 'purported' and 'professed'] are not hard and fast" (p. 16), "the boundary between 'inappropriate persons' and 'inappropriate circumstances' will necessarily not be a very hard and fast one" (p. 34), "the distinctions [between 'feelings,' 'thoughts,' and 'intentions'] are so loose that the cases are not necessarily easily distinguishable" (p. 41), "there [is] certainly no one absolute criterion [to distinguish the constative from the performative]: and…very probably it is not possible to lay down even a list of all possible criteria; moreover, they certainly would not distinguish performatives from constatives, as very commonly the *same* sentence is used on different occasions of utterance in *both* ways, performative and constative" (p. 67), "these formulas are at best very slippery tests for deciding whether an expression is an illocution as distinct from a perlocution or neither" (pp. 131-132).

Despite the porous and leaky borders that make the "distinct" identities "indistinct" and rift by difference, however, Austin still wants to maintain that "words used are to be explained by the context in which they are designed to be" (p. 100). The leaky, contaminating, hybridizing ambiguity and ambivalence of these communication acts is thought to be reducible by the limits of a "context," a

8 As is becoming clear from these statements, the title of his book, and the footnote that says: "still confining ourselves, for simplicity, to *spoken* utterance," Austin's (1975) discussion of language is limited to the spoken language, giving speech a privileged, exemplary status (1975, p. 114).

context that is teleologically determined in terms of the conscious intention of the speaking subject that centers the totality of his speech act. The difficulty in distinguishing unhappy, pallid imitations that are not serious from serious and happy utterances is that "no criterion that is simply *inherent* in the manifest utterance is capable of distinguishing an utterance when it is serious from the same utterance when it is not" (Derrida, 1988, p. 68), and "as marks do not constitute their contexts by themselves, nothing prevents them from functioning in another conttext" (Derrida, 1988, p. 12). These problems do not go unnoticed by Austin as the above qualifications from him demonstrate. He thus looks behind the phenomenal utterance to find what he is looking for, the telos of intention. Before examining further this "solution" to the problems he encounters, let us note how ironic and self-defeating this is for Austin as a solution. It is ironic in that Austin defines himself as the theorist of "ordinary" speech but ends up considering the inescapable possibility as well as occurrence of "infelicities" and "etiolations" of ordinary speech as "accidental" by means of an idealization where "ordinary" is determined by reference to an ideal purity. It is also self-defeating in that, as Jacques Derrida (1988) points out, Austin's solution "is rather remarkable and typical of that philosophical tradition with which he would like to have so few ties" (1988, p. 15). For example, it takes us back to the phenomenological simplification of the "ideal model" of communication discussed earlier. There too the complexity of communication, its polysemy or dissemination for example, was reduced to a simplicity cleansed of the play of differance, contradiction, aporia—in a word, of miscommunication.

In reading Austin's work, which interests and excites him because it represents a novel departure from the conventional understanding of communication but whose project is troubled by the "tenacious and most central presuppositions of the *continental* metaphysical tradition" (p. 38), Derrida (1988) notes how Austin's procedure in dealing with the difficulties encountered consists "in recognizing that the possibility of…failure is an essential risk of the operations under consideration," that failure is "in fact a structural possibility," while at the same time excluding "that risk as accidental, exterior, one which teaches us nothing about the linguistic phenomenon being considered" (p. 15). Austin's "ordinary language" is thus marked by the exclusion of the "non-serious," the "parasitism," the "etiolation," and the "non-ordinary" as we noted earlier. Derrida then notes how "it is as just such a 'parasite' that writing has always been treated by the philosophical tradition" (p. 17). We have already noted how Austin had confined himself, "for simplicity, to *spoken* utterance," and excluded writing (See note 7). The reason(s) for this exclusion, not elaborated by Austin but taken up by a self-declared follower, John Searle, and which are a main concern for Derrida, is ambivalent and is worth going over. On the one hand, as far as the simplicity argument is concerned, writing is understood as being no more than an extension in space and time, without alteration, of voice or of gesture and, as such, is thought to have "no effect on either the structure or the contents of the meaning it is supposed to transmit" (p. 4). While it is noted that writing communicates in the absence of the sender or of the receiver, this absence is thought to be "a progressive extenuation of presence, not as a break in presence," and "idealized in its representation as distant presence," where representation is understood in turn "not as supplanting presence but as its continuous reparation," one that uses "analogy" to link presence to absence as we have seen in the so called models of communication in the first section (pp. 5, 7, 6). In such an understanding, writing is phonetic and, thus, reducible to speech. Therefore, there is no need to take up writing as exemplary to understand communication. Writing is thought to be genetically derived from speech, so if you know about speech, you know about writing too. But if this were true, and writing was genetically derived from speech, it would not hurt us to use writing as an example—a useful example even—of communication together with other examples. But writing is also actively excluded because of the danger(s) it poses to the idealized property of communication.[9] In Austin's case, it would be excluded as that which prevents the taking place of proper communication, as an *etiolation*, a pale imitation far removed from the presence to self of a conscious intention. Why is that? How can writing be both an extension and simple derivative of communication on the one hand, and an obstacle to it at the same time?

We may look for clues in Austin's "solution" which relies on a metaphysics of consciousness and its teleology of conscious intention, where the presence to self of a conscious intention constitutes the "utterance origin." As Derrida (1988) points out, conscious intention is what Austin considers to be the "organizing center" of an "exhaustively definable context" thus making possible a "teleological jurisdiction of an entire field" leading Derrida to conclude that "performative communication becomes once more the communication of an intentional meaning, even if that meaning has no referent in the form of a thing or of a prior or exterior state of things" (p. 14). A context exhaustively determined via a teleological jurisdiction means that "no irreducible polysemy," that is to say, "no dissemination" escapes "the horizon of the unity of meaning" (p. 14). There is to be no remainder that does not add up to a unified totality for a speech act to be happy.

It is precisely here, in the constitution of that exhaustive contextual totality, that writing proves to be troublesome,

9 Consider the following pronouncements: Aristotle of Stagira (384-322 BC): "Spoken words are the symbols of mental experience, and written words are the symbols of spoken words." Jean-Jacques Rousseau (1712-1778): "Languages are made to be spoken. Writing serves only as a supplement to speech" and "Writing is derivative. It merely represents speech. It is a poor substitute, a weak extension. It's not essential. Do without it if you can." Ferdinand de Sausssure (1857-1913): "The spoken word alone is the object of linguistic study. Writing is a trap. Its actions are vicious and tyrannical. All its cases are monstrous. Linguistics should put them under observation in special compartments" (Quoted in Collins & Mayblin, 1997, p. 42).

leading to its excommunication. First of all, "a written sign carries a force that breaks with its context" and "ruptures presence" (p. 9). The dreaded absence "is originary in writing," and this is not an absence that can be understood as a modification of presence but is a radical absence, an irreducible absence of intention, since it is what enables the written sign to break with any given context and still to act and to communicate in a structure of *iterability*, that is to say repetition with or as alterity (p. 7). To be read as such, a written sign must be repeatable, but be repeatable with a difference, which is to say that it must be recognizable in displacement from another context, that it must already be a citation "out of context," that it must be a parasitic imitation, an *etiolation* of itself. The differance of iterability thus means "the irreducible absence of intention" (p. 18). This does not mean that signs of communication are "valid outside of a context," for "there are only contexts," but that contexts lack a governing center that can exhaustively constrain and control their intertextuality (p. 12).

It should thus be clear why a speech act theory that relies on an exhaustive context determined in terms of a teleology of conscious intention would not want to consider written utterances as exemplary. However, Derrida's analysis of writing with regard to speech acts have implications that go much farther, for he argues that the "absence attributed to writing is proper to every communication" (p. 7), and that iterability "is generative of all marks" (p. 11). Speech, like writing, is also differant and iterable, it too is always-already citable and quotable, repeating itself in duplicity, differing from and deferring itself every time. So writing, after all, turns out to be exemplary. This is not to say that speech is writing, for difference, including the speech-writing difference in the classical sense, is irreducible and is generative of their respective identities—as of all identities—and we should not erase their difference. However, this necessitates for Derrida "a certain generalization and a certain displacement of the concept of writing" (p. 3), leading in turn to a generalized understanding of "text," and he uses the term "archi-writing" elsewhere in his work for this notion of a general writing. Thus, what Austin wants to exclude as etiolations turns out to be the condition of possibility of all utterances, all marks of communication. Derrida points out, for example, that "what Austin excludes as anomaly, exception, 'non-serious' *citation* (on stage, in a poem, or a soliloquy) is the determined modification of a general citationality—or rather, a general iterability—without which there would not even be a 'successful' performative" (p. 17).

As we noted earlier, Austin acknowledges that *all* conventional acts are exposed to failure, but wants, nonetheless, to exclude such failure, without reflecting on the consequences of that exposure as a *necessary* possibility that could teach us about communication as necessarily divided, duplicit, and impure. Noting Austin's acknowledgement that there is no "pure" performative, Derrida then concludes that "a successful performative is necessarily an 'impure' performative" because what makes a performative utterance possible is a "citational doubling" that comes "to split and dissociate from itself the pure singularity of the event" (p. 17).

Jacques Lacan and Edgar Allan Poe's "The Purloined Letter"

Jacques Lacan has devoted a seminar to Edgar Allan Poe's story, "The Purloined Letter," and has selected this seminar as the opening piece of his *Ecrits* (Selected Writings), because, it seems, he uses Poe's story as a parable to advance his own conception of psychoanalysis.[10] Thus, in Derrida's (1987) words, "psychoanalysis finds itself...in the text that it deciphers" and, furthermore "the deciphered text inscribes in itself...the scene of the deciphering" (Derrida, 1987, pp. 419, 414). The "parergonal logic" that frames Poe's story—whereby a literary fiction puts truth on stage such that "the literary example yields a message to be deciphered on the basis of Freud's teaching" is made transparent by Lacan's use of the story as "an example destined to 'illustrate'...a law," where his "demand for truth leads [him] to putting aside the scene of writing"—is taken up by Derrida in his reading of Lacan's seminar (pp. 425-426, 427, 436).

However, Lacan's reading of Poe is of interest for us here because it rests on a critique of semanticism that would jump over the signifier and hastily go after the signified content of a text as the teleological end of communication like we observed in the logic of the "models." Lacan (1988) thus takes the organization of the signifier into account, arguing that "the signifier is not functional" (Lacan, 1988, p. 40), positing the signifier to be prior "in relation to the signified" (p. 42), and attempts to demonstrate, through Poe's story, "the decisive orientation which the subject receives from the itinerary of a signifier" (p. 29). The latter point is especially promising as regards our problematization of the teleology of conscious intention as in Austin's speech act theory that we looked at in the previous section.

Poe's story (1988) tells, within a narrative frame, of the displacements of a letter. The Queen is perusing a letter in the royal *boudoir* when the King interrupts with his entrance. She wants to conceal the letter from him, and, in her haste, is forced to put it on a table with the address uppermost, the contents thus unexposed. At this juncture Minister D enters, perceives the letter, recognizes the handwriting of the address, observes the Queen's confusion, and fathoms her secret. While transacting his business with the royal couple, he produces a similar letter, places it casually next to the Queen's letter and proceeds

10 "Seminar on the Purloined Letter" is not included in the English translation of Lacan's *Ecrits*. Alan Sheridan, who translated that work into English states in a note that Lacan had selected the essays to be included in that volume. So it may be that, for whatever reason(s), Lacan has later changed his mind about the exemplary status of this seminar. Whether Derrida's critique had anything to do with this is a matter of conjecture.

to take her letter while leaving behind his unimportant replacement, and exits the room when he finishes his transaction. The Queen observes the robbery but cannot dare call attention to the fact in the King's presence. The Queen then employs the Prefect of Police to reclaim the letter from the Minister in question. The Prefect of Police searches the Minister's office and home thoroughly when he is not around, going through every possible secret hiding place, but is unable to find the letter. This is when he brings the matter to the attention of Dupin who is the friend of our narrator in the story and asks for his help in return for sharing the very large sum of reward money. The Prefect of Police complains that the matter is simple and yet has baffled them, to which Dupin responds with remarks like "Perhaps the mystery is a little *too* plain" and "A little *too* self-evident" (p. 7), which the policeman finds amusing and odd. The story continues with the friends discussing the antics of "policial action in searches for articles" (p. 19) based on the assumption that "*all* men proceed to conceal a letter" (p. 16), comparing mathematical reasoning and poetic foolishness, and betting that had the Minister been a "mere mathematician, he could not have reasoned at all, and thus would have been at the mercy of the Prefect" (p. 17), and observing how "over-largely lettered signs and placards of the street escape observation by dint of being excessively obvious" (p. 20). With these insights Dupin is convinced that "the Minister had resorted to the comprehensive and sagacious expedient of not attempting to conceal it at all" (p. 20) and is then able to rob the letter from the Minister by substituting a facsimile regarding external details but with a quotation inside that will let the Minister know who did it.

Jacques Lacan (1988) begins his seminar by asking us to recognize that "the repetition automatism (*Wiederholungszwang*) finds its basis in…the *insistence* of the signifying chain," this being "a correlate of the ex-sistence (or eccentric place) in which we must necessarily locate the subject of the unconscious," since "psychoanalytic effects…such as foreclosure (*Verwerfung*), repression (*Verdrangung*), denial (*Verneinung*)…follow so faithfully the displacement (*Entstellung*) of the signifier" whereupon we observe "the specific law of that chain that governs those psychoanalytic effects" (1988, pp. 28, 29). He then proceeds to tell us that he has "decided to illustrate" for us "today the truth…that it is the symbolic order which is constitutive for the subject—by demonstrating in a story the decisive orientation which the subject receives from the itinerary of the signifier" (p. 29).

Lacan (1988) divides the story into "two scenes," one designated as "the primal scene" and the other considered as "its repetition in the very sense we are considering today." The *quotient* of the primal scene is that "the Minister has filched from the Queen her letter and that…the Queen knows that he now has it, and by no means innocently" with "the letter abandoned by the Minister" being the scene's significant "*remainder*" (p. 30). The quotient of the second scene "is that the Minister no longer has the letter, but far from suspecting that Dupin is the culprit who has ravished him, knows nothing of it" and, again, "what he is left with is far from insignificant" (p. 31).

What makes the two scenes "similar," and one a repetition of the other, for Lacan, is "the intersubjectivity in which the two actions are motivated…as well as the three terms through which it structures them" (p. 31), thus there are "three moments, structuring three glances, borne by three subjects, incarnated each time by different characters" (p. 32). Hence in the story, (I) "a glance that sees nothing: the King and the police," (II) "a glance which sees that the first sees nothing and deludes itself as to the secrecy of what it hides: the Queen, then the Minister," and (III) a glance which "sees that the first two glances leave what should be hidden exposed to whoever would seize it: the Minister, and finally Dupin" (p. 32). In order to let us "grasp in its unity" this "intersubjective complex" Lacan offers a "model" that he names "the politics of the ostrich" (involving a word play in French that may also mean "the politics of the other"), which is explained as "the second believing itself invisible because the first has its head stuck in the ground, and all the while letting the third calmly pluck its rear" (p. 32). What Lacan finds interesting in this intersubjective complex "is the manner in which the subjects relay each other in their displacement during the intersubjective repetition" and how "their displacement is determined by the place which a pure signifier," like the purloined letter of Poe's story, "comes to occupy in their trio," and it is the determining place occupied by the pure signifier that confirms the status of what is going on as "repetition automatism" (p. 32).

Lacan then reminds us how Martin Heidegger "discloses to us in the word *aletheia* the play of truth" whereupon "we rediscover a secret to which truth has always initiated her lovers, and through which they learn that it is in hiding that she offers herself to them *most truly*" because Lacan discerns such a "trick" in Poe's tale: "so perfect a verissimilitude that it may be said that truth here reveals its fictive arrangement" (pp. 37, 34). To illustrate, he begins with a question: "What could be more convincing…than the gesture of laying one's cards face up on the table?" (p. 36). That would persuade us "momentarily…that the magician has in fact demonstrated…how his trick is performed, whereas he has only renewed it in still purer form: at which point we fathom the measure of the supremacy of the signifier in the subject" (p. 36). Then a suspicion and a further question:

> Is not the magician repeating his trick before our eyes, without deceiving us this time about divulging his secret, but pressing his wager to the point of really explaining it to us without us seeing a thing? *That* would be the summit of the illusionist's art: through one of his fictive creations to *truly delude us* (p. 37).

Now, Dupin's insinuation in his dialogue with the Prefect of Police assumes a new significance: "Because a problem is too simple, indeed too evident, it may appear obscure" (p. 37). Lacan describes their dialogue as "played between a deaf man and one who hears," presenting "the complexity of what is ordinarily simplified, with the most confused results in the notion of communication" (p. 34). This confusion comes about because "an act of communication may give the impression...of allowing in its transmission but a single meaning," and theorists too often stop at this impression, considering "the highly significant commentary into which he who understands integrates it" null because it is "unperceived by him who does not understand it" (p. 34). Therefore, if we approach a dialogue as a report of meaning, "its verissimilitude may appear to depend on a guarantee of exactitude" whereas "dialogue is more fertile than it seems," which necessitates a "transition...from the domain of exactitude to the register of truth" which is situated "at the very foundation of intersubjectivity" (pp. 34, 35).

To clear up the confusion regarding the communication-by-letter in the story, Lacan asks: "For a purloined letter to exist...to whom does a letter belong? Might it be that the [adressee] was never the real receiver?" (p. 41). Reaffirming the signifier's "priority in relation to the signified," (p. 42), he answers: "we are quite simply dealing with a letter which has been diverted form its path; one whose course has been prolonged (etymologically the word of the title)" (p. 43). Because "it can be diverted, it must have a course *which is proper to it*" leading us into an "alternating operation, which is its principle, requiring it to leave its place, even though it returns to it by a circular path" the very "repetition automatism that the Seminar began with (p. 43).

Thus, in this alternating operation of the "repetition automatism:

> The subject must pass through the channels of the symbolic...it is not only the subject, but the subjects, grasped in their intersubjectivity, who line up, in other words our ostriches... more docile than sheep, model their very being on the moment of the signifying chain which traverses them.... The displacement of the signifier determines the subjects in their acts, in their destiny, in their refusals, in their blindness, in their end and in their fate, their innate gifts and social acquisitions notwithstanding, without regard for character or sex, and that, willingly or not, everything that might be considered the stuff of psychology, kit and caboodle, will follow the path of the signifier (pp. 43, 44).

Because for Lacan, repetition automatism proceeds according to a predestined destination, he concludes that "what the 'purloined letter'...means is that a letter always arrives at its destination" (p. 53), and he even changes the first part of the note Dupin leaves in his substitute letter at the Minister's office from "Un dessein si funeste" (so sinister a plan) to "Un destin si funeste" (so sinister a destiny) (p. 52).

In reading Lacan's Seminar, Derrida (1987) argues that "the displacement of the signifier is analysed as a signified" for "the signifier has its place in the letter, and the letter refinds its proper meaning in its proper place" (1987, pp. 428, 436). This is a re-finding and a reconstitution of the proper because we are dealing with a purloined letter, that is, "the proper, the place, meaning, and truth have become distant from themselves for the time of a detour" (p. 436). There is an itinerary that is proper to this detour which then enables a readequation. That is why "the letter is found in the place where Dupin and the psychoanalyst expect to find it: on the immense body of a woman, between the 'legs' of the fireplace...the terminus of its circular itinerary" (p. 440). Therefore, according to Lacan's theory of the proper place, "the signifier must never risk being lost, destroyed, divided, or fragmented without return" (p. 438). And yet, for Derrida, this risk is constitutive of all signifiers as marks of communication. Indeed, "there is no destination" but rather *adestination* for "within every sign... there is distancing" (p. 29), a difference and deferral. Thus no instance of communication can escape adestination. That is to say, "the condition for it to arrive is that it ends up and even begins by not arriving" (p. 29). While every communication arrives somewhere, they do not arrive at a pre-destined, intended destination but they are always off course by the measure of a difference, a gap, a division, a re-turn. In the iterable structuration of difference and deferral discussed earlier, the communication is always haunted by its future arrival, and lives in the undecidable, spectral state of having arrived and yet to arrive.

(In)conclusion

To recall, I started with the conventional, "norm"al communication of communication as a pre-destined transfer of meaning from origin to end, focusing on the example of "models of communication." Here, the completion of the gap between origin and end constitutes communication, a reductive operation that reduces their difference to one: communication—so that communication excludes miscommunication. I then argued that these models were miscommunicating, in that miscommunication was in fact being excommunicated from within communication, that miscommunication was inside communication, not outside of it.

I then, looked at two promising theories that ruptured and divided the line of communication that led the origin to the end, or vice versa, reducing one to the other. Austin's speech act theory, by introducing the notion of "the performative," ruptured that reductive journey by questioning the adequation or correspondence relation between a statement and the real fact identified by that statement. Lacan's discussion of "The Purloined Letter" ruptured the line of communication enabling the reduction of a signifier to its signified, by doing away with the signified altogether. In both cases, the alleged heading of communication, its destination, is displaced by those divisions.

However, we also saw that these two theorists were no less reductive in their respective displacements. In Austin's case, polysemy was reduced by its proper context, defined in terms of the presence-to-self of a conscious intention. In Lacan's case the fateful journey of communication was dictated by the transcendental signifier, the Phallus, hence the "phather" of all signifiers. The misdirection—from the signified—of Lacanian communication was nonetheless given the directions of a return to course, to the course that was proper to it, and towards which it was destined. And because the directions for the correction of a prolonged course to the proper course were given by the chain of signifiers, governed by the Phallus, we could, perhaps , rename that chain "the Phallic chain of command."

What these very different examples illustrate, perhaps, is that the displacement of the destination of communication by itself is not enough to overcome the problems observed by those examples themselves. What we need to be concerned about could rather be that very search for a predestination itself, whose aim is to reduce the play of differance, and to close the gap of difference and alterity. I find Derrida's notions of *dissemination* as irreducible polysemy, and of an irreducible *adestination* indicating the structural necessity of non-arrival conditioning every communication, useful in this regard.

In the London underground, when the train approaches a station, an announcement is made, "mind the gap," referring to the gap between the train and the platform, which is irreducible even when the train has reached its *temporary* destination. So I would like to end with that slogan from the London underground that says: "Mind the Gap!"

References

Austin, J. L. (1975). *How To Do Things With Words* (Second Edition ed.). Cambridge, Massachusetts: Harvard University Press.

Barthes, R. (1974). *S/Z* (R. Miller, Trans.). New York: Hill and Wang.

Belch, G. E., & Belch, M. A. (1999). *Advertising and Promotion: An Integrated Marketing Communications Perspective* (4 ed.). Boston, Massachusetts: Irwin McGraw-Hill.

Collins, J., & Mayblin, B. (1997). *Introducing Derrida.* New York: Totem Books.

Derrida, J. (1982). *Margins of Philosophy* (A. Bass, Trans.). Chicago: The University of Chicago Press.

Derrida, J. (1987). *The Postcard: From Socrates to Freud and Beyond* (A. Bass, Trans.). Chicago: The University of Chicago Press.

Derrida, J. (1988). *Limited Inc* (S. Weber & J. Mehlman, Trans.). Evanston, IL: Northwestern University Press.

Derrida, J. (1994). *Specters of Marx: The State of the Debt, the Work of Mourning, & the New International* (P. Kamuf, Trans.). New York and London: Routledge.

Game, A. (1991). *Undoing the Social: Towards a Deconstructive Sociology.* Toronto and Buffalo: University of Toronto Press.

Gordon, C. (1980). Afterword. In C. Gordon (Ed.), *Power/Knowledge: Selected Interviews & Other Writings 1972-1977 by Michel Foucault* (pp. 229-260). New York: Pantheon.

Lacan, J. (1988). Seminar on "The Purloined Letter" (J. Mehlman, Trans.). In J. P. M. a. W. J. Richardson (Ed.), *The Purloined Poe: Lacan, Derrida, and Psychoanalytic Reading* (pp. 28-54). Baltimore and London: The Johns Hopkins University Press.

McQuail, D., & Windahl, S. (1993). *Communication Models for the Study of Mass Communications.* London and New York: Longman.

Mutlu, E. (1998). *İletişim Sözlüğü* (3 ed.). Ankara: Bilim ve Sanat Yayınları/ARK.

Nietzsche, F. (1974). *The Gay Science: With a Prelude in Ryhmes and an Appendix of Songs* (W. Kaufmann, Trans.). New York: Random House, Inc.

Poe, E. A. (1988). The Purloined Letter. In J. P. Muller & W. J. Richardson (Eds.), *The Purloined Poe* (pp. 6-27). Baltimore and London: The Johns Hopkins University Press.

Rorty, R. (1980). *Philosophy and the Mirror of Nature.* Oxford: Blackwell.

Shannon, C. E. (1948). A Mathematical Theory of Communication. Retrieved April 10, 2007, from http://en.wikipedia.org/wiki/A_Mathematical_Theory_of_Communication

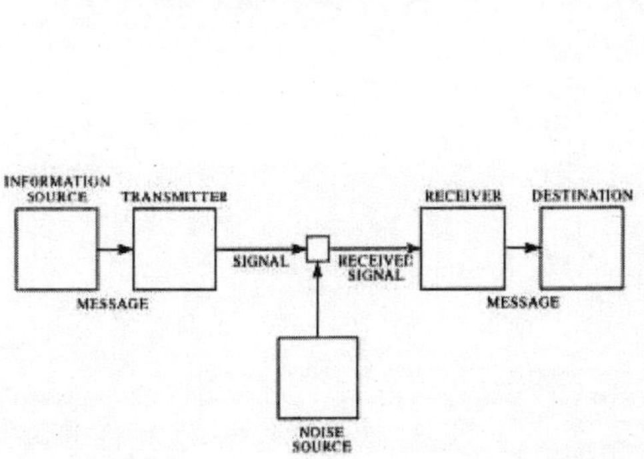

Figure 1. Schematic diagram of a general communication system

"Biz" and the "Business" of Peace: An evaluation of the only bi-communal, bi-lingual TV Programme in Cyprus

Vasvi Çiftçioğlu
Faculty of Communication and Media Studies
Eastern Mediterranean University
avanaktv@gmail.com

Introduction

> Only when they open up to a process of democratization on all levels—to the so called International Information Order—will the mass media fulfill their function as contributors to a peaceful society… Until such time, every analysis of "communication and peace" must of necessity turn into an analysis of "communication and the prevention of peace" (Jörg Becker, 1982, p. 238)

Becker, in his article entitled "Communication and Peace: The Empirical and theoretical relation between two categories in social sciences", criticizes the assumptions about the positive impacts of communication on peace. For him these kinds of assumptions that are predominantly highlighted in the 1978 mass media declaration of UNESCO[1] are almost impossible to achieve. Becker argues, "if mass-medial reception, as well as production at once expression and motor of structural violence; if the communications technology can be understood, historically, only as an integral part of the military complex, if the access to and the power over the mass media are unequal and unbalanced; if, indeed the 'law of universal violence' (Adorno and Horkheimer) obtains, then the mass media can filled their original hoped for function as 'peace bringers' under rare and exceptional circumstances" (p. 227).

For critical scholars like Edward Herman and Naom Chomsky, mass media has some functions, but not "peace bringing". According to Herman and Chomsky (1988), the functions of mass media are, "…to amuse, entertain and inform and to inculcate the individuals with the values, beliefs, and codes of behavior that will integrate them into the institutional structures of a larger society". Furthermore, they argued that mass media makes a "systematic propaganda" to serve the interests of elite groups (p. 1).

There are many authors who argue that mass media support conflicts/wars either to serve their economic/politic interest or the interests of elite groups/ governments. However, the discussions/arguments about the role of media in peace processes and peace building are currently more positive, compared to 20 years ago. This positive movement is directly related with "Peace Journalism" approach which is created by Johan Galtung during 1970s, but become popular in the recent decade. It can be defined as, "when editors and reporters make choices –of what stories to report and about how to report them- that create opportunities for society at large to consider and value non-violent responses to conflict" (Jake Lynch and Annabel McGoldrick, 2005, p. 5). Briefly, "the basic premise of peace journalism is that if the media play a negative role in terms of increasing the tensions between and among the sides of the conflict, it can also play a positive role by promoting peace and reconciliation" (İrvan, 2006, p. 34). Against a background of increased dialogue over the possibility that media could participate in the promotion of peaceful resolutions to conflicts, this paper argues that there are significant political, economic, and cultural barriers to an effective use of media in promoting peace.

Situation in Cyprus

Like most of their colleagues in the world, majority of the journalists in Cyprus, are more interested with conflict oriented stories. Although a current study, which was based on a questionnaire applied to journalists in North

1 http://www.unesco.ru/files/docs/shs/decl_on_smi_eng.pdf

Cyprus, concludes that 76.6 % of journalists support peace journalism (Ersoy, 2006), some journalists and newspapers in Cyprus have serious ethnocentric intensions and their reports are conflict oriented[2]. A current example of this can be seen in the news stories about the "a Greek Cypriot gang attacks Turkish Cypriot students in the English School" on the 22nd of November. As expected this event occupied the front page headline of all the newspapers—Greek and Turkish—in Cyprus. The argumentation in the majority of the newspapers, with the exception of "Afrika" and "Yenidüzen", was conflict oriented. And also it was written that, *Simerini* an extreme right wing Greek Cypriot newspaper, provoked this event.[3] A week after this event there was a "Turkish poem night" in the English school. It was of no surprise that this event was not on the front page of any Turkish or Greek Cypriot newspaper because it did not contain any conflict. "Turkish Cypriot students read poems to a Greek and Turkish Cypriot audience in a peaceful atmosphere", did not attract the attention of news editors. Most of the newspapers presented the story, but compared to them, BİZ/EMEIS program broadcast on CyBC 2 gave much more space/attention to this event. BİZ/EMEIS is the only bi-communal and bi-lingual programme in the world—produced by both Turkish Cypriots and Greek Cypriots, broadcast by Cyprus Broadcasting Corporation which is a semi governmental institution in South Cyprus. However, this program did not present anything about the first event—"a Greek Cypriot gang attacks Turkish Cypriot students in the English School"—because it was deemed too "sensitive/dangerous". To better understand the reasons behind this, it is vital, first to introduce the "Cyprus problem," and then the general approach of Turkish and Greek Cypriot media to the "Cyprus problem".

Cyprus Problem: a Brief Overview

Cyprus problem is a very big, complicated, unsolved historical issue between Turkish Cypriots and Greek Cypriots, which can be, and is, the subject of academic thesis or books. Thus, the arguments presented here about the Cyprus problem, constitute a brief summary of the problem. There are so many books and articles written about the Cyprus problem. Majority of them are supporting either the views of Turkish Cypriots or Greek Cypriots by using the historical terminology of the respective side. Here, the arguments of both sides are presented[4].

Turkish Cypriots and Greek Cypriots lived together under the control of different empires (1571-1878 Ottoman Empire, 1878-1960 United Kingdom). In 1960, following the international Zurich and London agreements, Cyprus obtained its independence from the British Rule. In place of the British Colony of Cyprus emerged a new, bi communal state, the "Republic of Cyprus". The independence and sovereignty of the Republic was placed under the guarantee of the three parties involved in its establishment, namely Turkey, Greece, and Great Britain. It should be noted, however, that the establishment of the Republic of Cyprus was the result of a compromise. This is a very important point in evaluating the events that followed. In 1955 some Greek Cypriots formed a paramilitary organization called EOKA and started a guerrilla war against the British Rule demanding ENOSIS (Union with Greece). As a reaction to the Greek Cypriot action the Turkish Cypriots in 1957 put forward their demand for TAKSIM (Partition) and they also formed a paramilitary organization called TMT. In 1958, there were inter communal clashes between EOKA and TMT. Seen this way, it is clear that neither Greek Cypriots nor Turkish Cypriots saw the newly formed Republic as a fulfillment of their "National Aspirations". More importantly, the leaderships of both ethnic groups never really accepted this arrangement. In the new state the executive and legislative powers were distributed proportionally between the two ethnic groups according to their population. The president of the Republic was to be Greek Cypriot whilst the Vice-president Turkish Cypriot. The relation of the deputies in the parliament was 1 Turkish Cypriot and 2 Greek Cypriots. The percentages of civil servants in official departments were: 30 % Turkish Cypriots and 70 % Greek Cypriots.

In 1963, the president of the Republic of Cyprus proposed 13 points for the amendment of the constitution. The proposal was perceived by the Turkish Cypriots as an attempt of the Greek Cypriots to negate the bi-communal status of the Republic on the way to achieving ENOSIS. Their reaction was to resign their posts. Later, when they decided to return to there duties they were refused by the Greek Cypriot authorities.

Following a period of tension, in December 1963 erupted the "inter communal clashes". Turkish Cypriots accused the Greek Cypriots of wanting to achieve ENOSIS. Greek Cypriots on the other hand, blamed the Turkish Cypriots as "rebelling against the state wanting to achieve TAKSIM". (It is not clear which side actually started the fighting). After 1963 Turkish Cypriots never returned to their positions in the parliament, but United Nations declared in 1964, that the Republic of Cyprus was still recognized as the "legal government" of the island. During 1963-1974 inter communal clashes (periodically) continued between the Greek Cypriot "National Guard" and EOKA on the one hand, and the Turkish Cypriot paramilitary organization TMT on the other hand. The dominant discourse of each community defined their organization as that of "freedom fighters" and the other as a "terrorist organization".

In 15th of July 1974, a military coup controlled from Greece, attacked the "leader" of the Republic of Cyprus, Makarios. In 20th of July Turkey, as a guarantor, made a

2 http://www.cirkef.com/7/pages/15%20-%20antimedya.htm
3 *Cyprus Mail*, Thursday, November 23, 2006.
4 In order to be sure that the historical arguments presented under this topic are impartial, I made focus group discussions with two Turkish Cypriots and one Greek Cypriot journalist.

military operation to the island, "to re-assign the Republic of Cyprus constitution and to protect Turkish Cypriots". After this military operation all Turkish Cypriots immigrated to the Northern part of the island, and all Greek Cypriots immigrated to the Southern part of the island. Until today, the island is still divided into two parts. Greek Cypriots called this division and the military operation of Turkey as an "invasion" and also they named the northern part of the island as "occupied territories." Turkish Cypriots on the other hand, used to call the operation the "Happy Peace Operation". Majority of the Turkish Cypriots do not call it an "invasion". After 1974, the Republic of Cyprus continued to be recognized as the only legal government on the island.

In 1983 the Turkish Republic of Northern Cyprus (TRNC) was declared, but it is still only recognized by Turkey and there are two UN statements which prohibits recognition of the TRNC. The Republic of Cyprus and/or dominant Greek Cypriot discourse, called TRNC and all its institutions/representatives as "fake/so called". On the other hand, TRNC and/or dominant Turkish Cypriot discourse called the Republic of Cyprus as "Greek Administration" and its institutions/representatives as "Greek", and also declared that this government does not represent the Turkish Cypriot community.

There was a dramatic change in the Cyprus problem during April, 2003. The "borders" opened on that date, and the Turkish Cypriots and the Greek Cypriots got the chance to visit the "other" part of the island, to communicate with their old friends, to make new friends, to find new jobs, but the island is still divided. The last chance for "peace" was missed in April 2004. There was a Referendum for re-uniting the island based on the Annan plan, but 76 % of Greek Cypriots rejected it, while 65 % of Turkish Cypriots accepted it.

General Approaches of the Turkish and Greek Cypriot Media to the Cyprus Problem

Almost all Greek Cypriot media institutions use the official language of their government, and this terminology—occupied territories, fake state, so called prime minister etc.—is accepted/used by all Greek Cypriots. Opposition to this terminology is not socially accepted and those who use different terminologies are called traitors[5]. Kostas Themistokleus, who is a Greek Cypriot deputy of EDI, once offered to use a more positive terminology about North Cyprus and TRNC, but the reaction of the media and the public was very destructive for him[6]. On the other hand, the terminology used in the Turkish Cypriot media is not strictly fixed and identical as in the Greek Cypriot media, but sometimes there is a commonality of terminology because of their dependence on the state news agency TAK (Turkish News Agency Cyprus) which is their main news provider[7]. Although, there is a Turkish Cypriot newspaper *Afrika* which sometimes uses a very different terminology than other Turkish Cypriot newspapers such as "occupation of the Turkish military", it can be said that Greek Cypriot and Turkish Cypriot media mainly do not use each other's terminology while presenting the Cyprus problem. For example, one can never witness an expression like "fake prime minister of TRNC" on any Turkish Cypriot media—including Africa—or one can never witness an expression like "Ministry of Education of TRNC" on any Greek Cypriot media. And it is obvious that state controlled channels, TAK and BRTK (Bayrak Radio Television Institution) on the North, and CyBC and CNA (Cyprus News Agency) on the South are more and more dependent on the official terminologies used by the governments. It is argued that if Turkish or Greek Cypriot Media use the exact terminology of the "other side" it means to destroy the existence of its community[8]. The commonality of the terminology used in either the Greek or Turkish Cypriot media can be explained as the result of "elite consensus" on the issues (Wolfsfeld, 2001) and/or "collective memory" of the societies (Halbwachs, 1980 cited in Holtrof, 1998). It is also argued that the terminology like "occupied territories" used by Greek Cypriots became a "natural" part of their language[9].

Biz/Emeis: a Bi-Communal, Bi-Lingual TV Program Broadcasted on CyBC

While the approaches and terminologies of media/journalists in the two communities are almost opposite of each other, the Republic of Cyprus decided to have a bi-communal, bi-lingual program. BİZ/EMEIS is the first and only bi-communal program on Cyprus Broadcasting Cooperation (CyBC)[10]. The official aim of the program in the very beginning was to create a "Turkish Zone" for the Turkish Cypriots[11]. This official aim suits the ideals of the Republic Of Cyprus which always claims that all the Turkish Cypriots are its citizens. Before introducing BİZ/EMEIS in detail, it is important to discuss the characteristics of the institution—CyBC—which hosts it.

In 1956 the British Government formed the Cyprus Broadcasting Service (CBS) as a Public Service Radio channel which has Turkish and Greek Radio Departments (frequencies) working independently from each other. In 1959, CBS started to have television broadcasts. Turkish Cypriots and Greek Cypriots were working together, and

5 This argument is based on the interview with Hasan Tuna, who is an expert translator. He translates Greek newspapers to Turkish for TRNC Presidency.

6 Interview with Hasan Tuna.

7 This argument is based on interviews with, Hüseyin Yalyalı—who is an experienced journalist working for TAK and also member of Board of Directors in BASIN-SEN (Journalist's Union)—and Sami Özuslu, who is the ex-news manager of Sim Fm, currently a columnist in *Yenidüzen* newspaper and producer/presenter of a current affairs program in *Genç TV*.

8 Interview with Hüseyin Yalyalı.

9 Interview with Hasan Tuna

10 It is also known as the "Greek State TV" by Turkish Cypriots, This naming is related with the terminology about Cyprus Problem.

11 President of the Board of directors of CyBC Andreas Aloneftis, announced this, in the 2nd program of BİZ/EMEİS broadcast on 2nd of March, 2004.

in the beginning it was like a "test" broadcast that mostly included programs in English—actually a summary of these programs were also broadcast in Greek and Turkish. It is said that during those days, Greek Cypriot programs were broadcast on Tuesdays and Turkish Cypriot Programs were broadcast on Fridays. Both CBS Radio and TV had limited time periods for broadcasting—there weren't full day broadcasts in those days[12].

In 1960, with the constitution of the Republic Of Cyprus, the control of CBS was given to the Ministry of the Interior—belonging to the Greek Cypriot part of the cabinet—and its status changed to "Corporation"—semi governmental—, thus it was re-named as the Cyprus Broadcasting Corporation (CBC). Later on they re-named it again as CyBC. Turkish Cypriots and Greek Cypriots worked together until 21st of December 1963. When the inter-communal clashes started at that time, Turkish Cypriots left their positions in CyBC. It is said that during the 1960-1963 period the Greek Cypriot authorities used to control the materials prepared by Turkish Cypriots for the celebration of national days, and sometimes the materials were censored[13]. After December 1963, the Turkish programs broadcast in CyBC were reduced, and the institution hired some Cypriot Armenians who knew Turkish for presenting Turkish news. There were also some Turkish Cypriots and Greek Cypriots who were working for Turkish departments, but it is said that their pronunciation was very insufficient, even funny. Furthermore, the news bulletins mainly included "propaganda" against Turkish Cypriot Leadership and TMT; they used to call Turkish Cypriots who left their positions in the Republic of Cyprus as "rebellions/terrorists". Those who left CyBC formed a Turkish Cypriot Radio called "Bayrak – Flag" in 1963 in order to make "counter-propaganda".[14] Bayrak is still considered the "illegal channel of so-called state" by the Republic of Cyprus authorities. From December 1963 till April 2003, CyBC Television continued its "Turkish language" broadcast in a very limited sense, only having 10 minute Turkish News bulletins everyday. There were also some short current affairs programs in Turkish, but these were broadcast very rarely. The personnel preparing these programs were mainly Cypriot Armenians. There were also few Turkish speaking Greeks from Istanbul and Turkish Cypriots who preferred to live in the South. As it was mentioned before, news bulletins used the official terminology of the Republic of Cyprus.

In April 2003, after the "borders" opened, CyBC asked Hüseyin Halil—a Turkish Cypriot Journalist who lived in South Cyprus since 1994—to produce a current affairs program including Turkish Cypriot guests. Hüseyin Halil produced a 1-hour, weekly program called "Ayna/Mirror" broadcast in CyBC 2 for 9 months. This program included discussions mainly with Turkish Cypriot guests—and sometimes both with Turkish and Greek Cypriot guests—about a solution for the Cyprus problem and the reunification of the island. "Ayna" was the first TV program broadcast on CyBC with Turkish Cypriot guests after 1963. As Hüseyin Halil put it, "it was the only program where Turkish Cypriot—politicians—could reach both the Turkish Cypriot and the Greek Cypriot communities through the CyBC. And also it was the first time that Turkish Cypriots attended a program in an institution totally controlled by Greek Cypriots."[15]

During February 2004, CyBC started to search for Turkish Cypriot and Greek Cypriot professionals to hire for "BİZ/EMEIS". As it was mentioned before, the official aim of the program in the beginning was to create "a Turkish Zone" in CyBC for the Turkish Cypriot audience. As President of the Board of directors of CyBC Andreas Aloneftis said, "you can not have public Radio-TV aiming only at the Greek Cypriots, and neglect 18-20 % of the population—Turkish Cypriots"[16].

The crew consists of 12 people from both the Turkish Cypriot and Greek Cypriot communities. Their capacities cover all aspects of television production and their output is a magazine program aired one hour every weeknight on the CyBC2 from 7-8 pm since 1st of March 2004. The program has two regular presenters—Turkish Cypriots—and two journalists (one Turkish Cypriot, one Greek Cypriot). The program is guided by the presenters who provide a light approach to the program. They inform the viewers of what will be expected in the program and introduce guests and film documentaries. The journalists (and often the presenters) interview guests. Ideally there are two guests, one from each community. The interviews are conducted in the individual's ethnic language. Ear pieces linked to radio transmission provide live translation for all guests and journalists, and the program is broadcast either with Greek or Turkish subtitles.

Topics tackled on the program deal with historical, political, cultural and traditional issues as well as current events. They are handled in the live studio interviews and the film documentaries made specifically for the program.

"A Turkish Zone targeting the Turkish Cypriot audience" imagined by the officials, became a "peace bridge between the two communities" as its workers used to call it. Although the workers of this program do not call themselves "peace journalists", the program is considered to be a "peace bridge" between the two communities. In the following pages, I will discuss possibilities and impossibilities of the media's role in peace building, by using BİZ/EMEIS as a case study. While doing this, I will focus on my personal experiences as producer/director working for BİZ/EMEİS

12 The information in this paragraph is based on the interview with Artam Diren, who worked for CBS and CyBC Turkish Radio Department during 1959-1963 as a producer, and Mustafa Akalın who worked for CBC Turkish Radio Department during 1956-1959 and the Turkish Department of CyBC TV during 1959-1963.
13 ibid
14 ibid.

15 Interview with Hüseyin Halil.
16 President of the Board of directors of CyBC Andreas Aloneftis, announced this, in the 2nd program of BİZ/EMEİS broadcast on 2nd of March, 2004.

and the interviews I conducted with all the workers of the program.

The Peace Journalism Approach and the Role of Media in Peace Building

> "All other things being equal, journalists prefer to tell stories about conflict. News is first and foremost, about conflict and disorder. Protests, violence, crime, wars, and disasters provide the most natural material for news reports. Journalists become famous and win awards for covering such stories" (Wolfsfeld, 2004, p. 15).

The above characteristics of journalism presented by Wolfsfeld, are usually defined as "war/conflict journalism," which mainly focuses on the conflict/violence side of the events supporting one of the parties involved—win/lose approach—, without conflict analysis. As discussed before, Johan Galtung offered an alternative approach—peace journalism—against war journalism. Hanitzsch (2004) identifies peace journalism as "a special mode of socially responsible journalism" (p. 284). It is important to mention that, the peace journalism approach not only differs from war/conflict journalism but it also differs from good/truth journalism. As Galtung[17] discusses, that "good reporting... should be truthful, is obvious. But truth journalism alone is not peace journalism. And truth does not come easily given the tendency to take sides once the 'who wins' perspective has been adopted".

Peace Journalism approach offered by Johan Galtung, became very popular in the academic and public debate. Galtung himself formed a peace and development network called TRANSCEND. This network has a web page including dozens of articles introducing peace journalism and useful guides for its practical applications. Furthermore, authors of this network also offer peace oriented solutions for worldwide conflicts.

After the rise of discussions about peace journalism in the public and academic arena, it was argued that the media can also promote peace, but it was obvious that wars and conflicts were attracting the journalists and news media more than peace and peace building. Ozgunes and Terzis (2000) argued that, "Media... can not be blamed for creation of ethnic/national conflicts but play an important role in their conduct" (p. 407). There are various reasons for the media to be interested in conflicts; some argue that it is related with economic interests (Becker, 1982; Tehrenian, 2002), or "with the media professional standards [and] conventional discourse" (Shinar, 2003, p. 3).

One of the main tasks of peace journalism is not to play a role in conducting conflicts, As Annabel McGoldrick and Jake Lynch (2001) argue, "Peace Journalism seeks to minimize the rift between opposed parties by not repeating 'facts' that demonize or set the stage for conflict" (p. 6). Furthermore McGoldrick and Lynch (2001) define peace journalism as a "broader, fairer, and more accurate way of framing stories, drawing on the insights of conflict analysis and transformation... it opens up a literacy of non violence and creativity as applied to practical job of everyday reporting" (p. 6). According to Galtung[18], the approaches of peace journalism and dominant media to conflicts are very different from each other. He argues that:

> In general there seem to be two ways of looking at a conflict, the high road and the low road, depending on whether the focus is on the conflict and its peaceful transformation, or on the meta-conflict that comes after the root conflict, created by violence and war and the question of who wins...The low road, by far dominant in the media, sees a conflict as a battle and the battle as sports arena and gladiator circus. The parties, usually reduced to the number 2, are combatants in the struggle to impose their goals... The high road, the road of peace journalism, would focus on conflict transformation... in conflict there is also a clear opportunity for human progress, using the conflict to find new ways, being imaginative, creative, transforming the conflict so that the opportunities take the upper hand. Without violence. In this there is no argument that violence should not be reported.

It's crucial to mention that, conflict analysis and transformation method of peace journalism is also used for non violent conflicts and conflicts which do not include the possibility of violence. Thus, peace journalism approach is a "practical tool" in reporting political, cultural, social conflicts in order to build a peaceful basis for resolving them.

Apart from the discussions about the peace journalism approach in the public and academic debate there are also some academicians, policy makers and media professionals who focus on the "role of media in peace building". As Gadi Wolfsfeld (2001) argues, "the news media can play a central role in the promotion of peace. They can emphasize the benefits that peace can bring, they can raise the legitimacy of groups or leaders working for peace, and they can help transform images of the enemy (p. 5)." With similar lines Shinar (2003) argues that, "the media must take the crucial and necessary step in full: to internalize the cultural meanings the conflict, to transmit these meanings to the public, in order to raise the consciousness of their significance and consequences; and to encourage public debate, first on peacemaking under constraining cultural conditions and secondly, on the choice between interminable violent feud and a great but acceptable burden imposed by the transformation of

17 Johan Galtung, Chapter 5: Media: Peace Journalism. Retrieved from http://www.crnetwork.ca/programs/PeaceJournalism.htm.

18 Johan Galtung, Chapter 5: Media: Peace Journalism. Retrieved from http://www.crnetwork.ca/programs/PeaceJournalism.htm.

conflict" (p. 9). Eytan Gilboa (2005) on the other hand, goes one step further and introduces a new role model for the media as, "Media-Broker Diplomacy—which typically occurs when there is no contact between the enemies and no third party to help them to resolve their problems" (p. 99). Furthermore, there are different peace institutes either governmental or non governmental, which trains journalists for "peace reporting" and/or assisting media institutions for "peace building" in conflict areas—different EU countries spend enormous amounts of money for this purpose every year.[19]

As the arguments presented here clearly show, there is a great hope for the practice of "peace journalism" to transform conflicts. And also there is a great hope for strengthening the "peace building" role of the media in conflict areas. However, these approaches have several weaknesses in practice. Before discussing these points, I want to honestly focus on my own experiences related with peace journalism. Although I call my self a "critical journalist", I did not know anything about peace journalism before I took the COM 602[20] course this semester. As I started to read and learn the key concepts and guides about peace journalism, I realized that although I have a critical approach to events, my approaches are "conflict" oriented. Personally I am very sensitive about not using any racist/ ethnocentric arguments in my news stories but before getting familiar with peace journalism, my approach to Cyprus problem was conflict oriented. With "conflict orientation", I mean highlighting the negative aspects and/or problems about events. Majority of journalists in Cyprus—both North and South—use a conflict oriented approach including racist/ethnocentric arguments. This may have several reasons, which can be the subject of a new article, but I think basically it depends on the way they teach journalism in universities—"conflicts/ problems have more news value." With the help of the peace journalism approach, now I have a better understanding of conflicts, and the way that, as a journalist, I can present them. The last example of this that I experienced was a follow up story I covered about the situation of the Turkish Cypriot students in the English School, after a Greek Cypriot gang attacked them on the 22nd of November 2006. I reported it for *Yenidüzen* newspaper as a free lance journalist, and I was very lucky that the news editor did not censor/edit it, because in the past they changed the headlines of my reports. Censorship/re-editing of news stories written by peace journalists are one of the main institutional obstacles that we face in practice. And it is very interesting that, this issue is rarely discussed in the academy. In the following pages, I am going to introduce some weaknesses of the peace journalism approach and also some practical difficulties about its application.

Weaknesses of Peace Journalism Approach

Although it offers a very useful approach to transform conflicts, the peace journalism approach also has several weaknesses. Some of them are related with its theoretical assumptions, and some of them are related with the problematic aspects of its application.

Tomas Hanitzsch (2004), in his article entitled "Journalists as Peacekeeping force? Peace journalism and mass communication theory," argues that peace journalism is based on the assumption that media have "powerful, causal and linear effects" on audiences (p. 483). Furthermore Hanitzsch (2004) argues that:

> The willingness of proponents of peace journalism to assume powerful media effects connects readily with an implicit conceptualization of the audience which revives early conceptualizations from the first half of the 20th century. The audience is seen as a mass, as aggregate composed of dispersed individuals whose characteristics are only of modest consequence for the understanding of mass communication. (p. 489).

I am not going to discuss in detail, the problematic sides of the assumption about audiences "as passive masses". Briefly, I want to note that the understanding of audiences as "passive masses" is seriously criticized. For example, Ang (1995), who totally rejects passive audience assumptions, argues that, "audiences are active in the ways in which they use, interpret and take pleasure in media products" (p. 219). Similarly, Ambercrombie (1999) argues that "audiences are not blank sheets of paper on which media messages are written" (p. 141). Therefore, I want to mention that peace journalism approach which assumes that news stories—either written from peace journalism or war journalism approach—directly effects audiences is wrong.

Hanitzsch (2004) also argues that "it cannot be the primary task of journalism to free the world from crises, conflicts and other evils, since this is the task of other social systems such as politics and the military" (p. 491). I don't agree with Hanitzsch's argument here, because we know that media/ journalists who use war journalism approach have important roles in the creation of conflicts. Thus, journalists who use peace journalism approach can take part in transforming conflicts.

Liz Fawcett (2002), in her article "Why Peace Journalism Isn't News," focuses on "a case study involving a nationalist and a unionist newspaper in Northern Ireland which joined together in a 'peace journalism' initiative" (p. 213). Drawing on this case study she concludes that in order to support the peace journalism approach, these newspapers behaved like "politicians and storytellers". I think this was only an example of the wrong application of peace journalism It will be very reductionist to conclude that all

19 Spurk (2002). Media and Peace building: concepts, actors and challenges. Retrieved from http://www.swisspeace.org

20 A PHD course in the Faculty of Communication and Media Studies—Eastern Mediterranean University.

the newspapers applying the peace journalism approach will behave like storytellers or politicians.

Finally, I want to discuss the weaknesses of the arguments which claim that media can promote peace building. Theoretically speaking yes, media can promote peace. But why do they have to promote it? To put it more clearly, what will be their profit to support peace? One can not ignore the nature of media institutions. As Tehrenian (2002) states, "in national as well as international media politics, whoever pays the piper calls the tune" (p. 77). Furthermore he argues that:

> Both government and commercial systems have a strong, built-in bias in favor of two different kinds of propaganda, namely political and commercial advertising.Media contents thus tend to present either government propaganda or programs catered to the lowest common denominator of taste attracting the largest possible audiences and profits. (p. 75).

Briefly, broadcasting policy of media institutions depend on profit making and/or serving their own political/ ideological interests. Thus media institutions are not freely waiting for us to call them to promote peace. As Wolfsfeld (2001, 2004) argues, if there is an "elite consensus" on the peace process, the media will more likely to support it.

One of the main weaknesses of the discussions related with peace journalism and the role of the media in peace building is their lack of focus on the ideologies of media institutions. This will be my critical point in evaluating both BİZ/EMEIS and peace journalism. The discussions about peace journalism mainly focus on the application of "(ethical) codes of peace journalism". According this view, if majority of the journalists internalize peace journalism, this will directly affect the news media in a way that they start to cover news stories from the peace journalism perspective. This is a very naïve approach. I argue that journalists do not have absolute freedom in reporting events, exactly the way they want, because of institutional obstacles. This is a major blind spot of both traditional journalism and peace journalism that is rarely discussed in the academic debates.

The stories covered by journalists are controlled by editors. The editors in newspapers have the authority to change/ edit the news stories and also to decide for their headlines. In Cyprus, like most of the other countries, this editing process is a routine of media institutions[21]. Furthermore, beside the editor's interference in the news stories, there are several factors which influence news like ownership. Journalists are not free floating individuals in media institutions who can use any approach they like. They are part of institutions, which have their own policies, ideologies, interests etc. which they have to obey in order not to be fired.

21 Interview with Sami Özuslu.

Evaluation of BİZ/EMEIS as a Peace Project

First of all, it is crucial to state that, BİZ/EMEIS as a program is broadcast on a semi-governmental TV channel—CyBC—, "naturally" uses the official terminology of the state about the Cyprus Problem, and sometimes this terminology is very offensive against Turkish Cypriots. Second important point is that, although there are significant differences between the Greek Cypriot workers' and the Turkish Cypriot workers' evaluations about the program, they all agree that it serves more or less the function of a communication bridge between the two communities. In the following sections I will compare and evaluate the interpretations of Turkish Cypriot and Greek Cypriot workers about the program.

While majority of Turkish Cypriots think that the aim of CyBC for broadcasting this program is to make propaganda aimed at the Turkish Cypriot audience, Greek Cypriot's mainly think that CyBC as a public service institution has to broadcast this program. Here it is obvious that the official terminology used in the program which supports the Greek Cypriots' political views about the Cyprus problem makes Turkish Cypriots to think that the main aim of the institution is to make propaganda. I believe that this program is an international advertisement for the image of CyBC and the Republic of Cyprus that says they care about Turkish Cypriots.

All Turkish Cypriots in the program believe that the program does not show enough attention for the sensitivities of the Turkish Cypriot community. Majority of the Greek Cypriots also share the same thought. However some of them said that the program shows enough attention to the sensitivities of both Greek and Turkish Cypriot communities. The program broadcast in a semi-governmental state channel in the South, naturally is more sensitive about the issues concerning Greek Cypriots. The main example of this is the property issues. There were several films and studio discussions made about the "Greek properties" in the North—"occupied territories". But the program never deals with the Turkish properties in the South—"Free territories". When we have filming to do in the North, we have to be careful not to shoot a Greek Cypriot property used by Turkish Cypriots. We were told this by the director of the program, in the very beginning of the program.

According to the Greek Cypriot workers of the program, there were no differences between them and the Turkish Cypriots in terms of advantages/disadvantages. They argued that all the workers have equal working conditions. Turkish Cypriots on the other hand, believe that they have some disadvantages compared to Greek Cypriots such as being a numerical minority in CyBC, using an official language that disturbs the Turkish Cypriot audience and them. Furthermore, Turkish Cypriots believe that Greek Cypriots have several advantages of being the host, because they, the Turkish Cypriots have to cross the border everyday to come to work. And from the very beginning they have to get familiar with the official terminology used by the CyBC. As a producer I am still having problems about finding the Greek names of the villages in the North, because it is prohibited to use the Turkish names given after 1974.

There are many other prohibitions in the program for Turkish Cypriots. We can not interview official persons from TRNC. We can not film any event called international—because it means recognition of TRNC. Furthermore, we cannot use the terminology that we use in our daily lives—like North Cyprus, South Cyprus etc. We have been working for this program for almost three years now, so we are socialized into the routines of CyBC. In the very beginning they controlled every film that we made in order to be sure that it did not include anything against the Republic of Cyprus and/or the wrong terminology about the Cyprus problem. During these three years, they censored some films that we made because they thought that these films included something offensive for the Greek Cypriot audience. But actually they don't need censorship, because we internalize the terminology of the institution. Thus we self-censor ourselves. We learned what we can say in the program. And there is an advantage that the institution did not force us to use their terminology on every issue. For example I have two choices when I present something happening in North Cyprus; either I can say "...In the Occupied territories"—official terminology— or I can say "Turkish Cypriot Community..."—value free representation which may be decoded by the Greek Cypriot audience as "Occupied territories", and it may decoded by the Turkish Cypriot audience as "North Cyprus". Who knows? We, as the Turkish Cypriot workers of this program, cannot go beyond the boundaries of official terminology, but we try to use value free expressions in order not to disturb the Turkish Cypriot audience. Greek Cypriots mainly use the official terminology because it's natural for them. And it is important to mention that the Turkish Cypriot guests attending the live discussions in the program can use their own terminology but what they say will translated in quotation marks.

The discussions made in the studio, and the films prepared for the program are selected very carefully by the workers. We are not dealing with too sensitive issues related with the Cyprus Problem—like the news story about "a Greek Cypriot gang attacks Turkish Cypriot students in the English School"—but if we deal with sensitive issues it is expected that we mainly analyze it through the official perspective of the institution.

Briefly, all my colleagues believe that this program has created a bridge for peace enabling communication between the two communities, but it can not be a truly peace building project because of institutional obstacles.

Conclusion

> "But the owner will stay, and may not like what is going on"[22]

This sentence is the only one that I read in Galtung's discussions about the role of the owner in the application of peace journalism. Actually he doesn't continue to discuss this issue. I think he left it unfinished. In my opinion the ownership—either commercial or (semi) governmental— of the media institutions is the main factor that is going to effect the practice of peace journalism. The owners never like what is going on about the peace process or the practice of peace journalism, if it is not politically imposed on them. As I said before, journalists are not free floating individuals who are reporting whatever they want. The institutions that they work in have political/economic interests to be served. Furthermore, I want to argue that there isn't any opportunity for the workers of BİZ/ EMEİZ program to become peace journalists, because for applying a peace journalism approach one needs to have an independent and/or non-profit media organization. I think like this because, Hüseyin Gürşan the director of BRTK, argues that, "if we have a bi-communal, bi-lingual program like BİZ/EMEIS on BRTK we can not accept any violation of the official terminology of the TRNC. I mean the possible workers of this program must use the official terminology of the TRNC"[23]. Briefly I argue that being obliged to use the official terminology of one side destroys the possibility of the peace building function of any program.

References:

Abercrombie, N. (1999). *Television and society.* USA: Blackwell Publishers.

Ang, I. (1995). The nature of the audience. In Downing, J., Mohammadi, A. and Sreberny-Mohammadi, A. (Eds.), *Questioning the media: A critical introduction*, (pp. 207-227). Newbury Park CA.: Sage.

Becker, J. (1982). Communication and peace. The empirical and theoretical relation between two categories in social sciences. *Journal of Peace Research*, *19*(3), 227-240

Edward, S. H. & Chomsky N. (1988). *Manufacturing consent: Political economy of the mass media.* New York: Pantehon Books.

Ersoy, M. (2006). Peace journalism in Cyprus. Retrieved April 30, 2007, from http://mediaif.emu.edu.tr/metin

Fawcett, L. (2002). Why peace journalism isn't news. *Journalism Studies, 3*(2), 213-223.

Gilboa, E. (2005). Media-broker diplomacy: When journalists become mediators. *Critical Studies in Media*

22 Johan Galtung, Chapter 5: Media: Peace Journalism. Retrieved from http://www.crnetwork.ca/programs/PeaceJournalism.htm

23 Interview with Hüseyin Gürşan, directtor of BRTK- State channel of TRNC

Communication, 22(2), 99-120.

Hanitzsch, T. (2004). Journalists as peace keeping force? Peace journalism and mass communication theory. *Journalism Studies, 5*(4), 483-495.

Lynch, J. & McGoldrick A. (2001). What is peace journalism. *Activate, Winter,* 6-9.

Lynch, J. & McGoldrick A. (2005). *Peace journalism.* London: Howtorn Press.

İrvan, S. (2006). Peace Journalism as a Normative Theory: Premises and obstacles. Retrieved April 30, 2007 from: http://globalmedia.emu.edu.tr/fall2006/Fall_2006_Issue2/7Suleyman_Irvanpdf.pdf

Ozgunes, N. & Terzis G. (2000).Constraints and remedies for journalists reporting national conflict: The case of Greece and Turkey. *Journalism Studies, 1*(3), 405-426.

Shinar, D. (2003). The peace process in cultural conflict: The role of media. *Conflict and Communication Online, 2* (1), 1-10.

Spurk, C. (2002). Media and peace building: concepts, actors and challenges. Retrieved April 30, 2007, from http://www.swisspeace.ch/typo3/fileadmin/user_upload/pdf/KOFF/Reports/medienstudie.pdf

Tehranian, M. (2002). "Peace journalism: Negotiating global media ethics. *Press/Politics, 7*(2), 58-83.

Wolsfeld, G. (2001). *The news media and peace process: The Middle East and Northern Irleand.* Washington: USA Institute of Peace.

Wolfsfeld, G. (2004). *Media and path to peace.* Cambridge: University Press.

The Fairy-tale Like Story of Cyprus in the Eyes of Turkish Cypriot Youth: Re-Memorizing the "Past" as a Communication Tool Between Generations

Yetin Arslan
Faculty of Communication and Media Studies
Eastern Mediterranean University
yetin.arslan@emu.edu.tr

"If you go to our village after my death, please carry my photograph on your neck"!

These were the words of my grandfather. He, and also I, thought that he would never have the opportunity to go to his village. In those days, before 2003, it seemed almost impossible. However, the run of events did not go in the way that we thought. Before his death, he was able to visit *his village* (the one which he had to left in 1974), only once. Later, I was in *our present village* (the one which my family moved to in 1974), waiting for the return of my grandfather in order to see how he felt. My grandfather's face was not what I expected. He was so "unhappy", "ruined", "confused" and "shocked". I couldn't say anything. And he said to me; "my child they [Greek Cypriots] have all demolished our place". I had been there before my grandfather and I did not understand what he meant. Because everything had seemed fine to me and I did not see any ruins.

This is my personal story, which was the first time I have met with the feeling of "frustration" experienced as a result of "returning back to the other side". Like lots of Turkish Cypriot youth, I grew up listening to such stories, which were full of desire and wish to see or/and to *return* to the places that our families had to leave in 1974. It was also a wish and desire for us to visit our families' "old" places because we inherited these memories by listening to these stories of longing. And then, the frustration that our families experienced after they visited their places was puzzling for us, as listeners and witnesses of these "returns."

Post-1974 generation Turkish Cypriots were born into a country which was/is divided into two. For a long time, we had no chance to see the other part of our country and we could experience only one half of Cyprus. The south was "prohibited" and "unreachable" for the post-1974 generation: "As you grow old, you start to question things much better, as why don't I step on the gas and cross to the south. Everyone has an east, a west, a north and a south. South is forbidden, it is cursed" (Financial consultant)[1]. The border was an aporetic border which made the south as the unknown part of our country, the part that the older generations have always dreamed of going back to.

Today, Cyprus is divided into two, with a "Green Line", as northern and southern Cypruses. This "so-called" Green Line divides the island into two not only geographically, as the south and the north, but also ethnically in terms of Turkish Cypriots and Greek Cypriots[2]. When we talk about Cyprus, the "border"—and automatically division—is the first issue that comes to our minds, the border as a signifier of division, which separates the north and the south, Turkish and Greek, European and non-European[3], legitimate and illegitimate, the East and the West and also the past and the present[4].

1 In Güngör, Ç. (2002). *Kıbrıslı Türk Gençleri Konuşuyor*. İstanbul: Metis.

2 But there are some exceptions. There are some Greek Cypriots who live in the north, mostly on the Karpas Peninsula, and some Turkish Cypriots who remained in the south. And also there are other minorities who live in both parts; Armenians, Maronites, Kurds, Germans, English, Philippines, Latinos, etc.

3 After the accession of the Republic of Cyprus into the European Union, the Republic of Cyprus as a representative of the whole island became a member of the EU (1st May 2004) and "the Green Line of Cyprus became the EU's uncertain border in the east" (Papadakis, Peristianis & Welz, 2006, p. 4). Today, Cyprus is the last country whose capital is divided into two with a border/wall/line going through it and which has two municipalities. Furthermore, as a result of a new change, it is also the only country whose half is in the European Union and the other half is not.

4 However, here, we should keep in mind that with the changing circumstances and conjunctures it became a "third place" which enabled the transcultural and intercultural interactions, exchanges and communications. Here I do not preclude/exclude different significations of this very same border; it became a meeting place for the bi-communal group members, and then with the partial opening of the border (23rd April 2003) it became a passage that allowed the face to face communication of the two main communities.

The border has been established in 1974. Although this division has a long story it can be summarized as the "result" of contending nationalisms in Cyprus which has started as the anti-colonial struggle of Greek Cypriots against the British Colonialism with the aim of ENOSIS (Unification with Greece) and ends with the intervention of Turkey in 1974. During this period and after the partition of the island with a "green line", many Greek and Turkish Cypriots had to leave the placed that they used to live in. After these compulsory migrations forced by changing circumstances, Cyprus became a space in which the two main communities on the island live separately, side by side.

When the subject is Cyprus and migration we should talk about different displacements in different time periods. However, the main displacement that I will take into consideration in this paper is the displacement of Turkish Cypriots in 1974—Turkish Cypriots who had to leave their homes, their homeland in the southern part of Cyprus, moved to the northern part of the island, and did not have the opportunity to see/visit their homes/homelands until the opening of the border in 23rd April 2003[5]. In this study, I focus on the Turkish Cypriot youth whose families were displaced in 1974, ones who were born or/and grew up after the division/partition of the island—those who grew up in a divided country and whose identity is/was defined/constructed according to the compass "direction" of where they were born.[6] For the post 1974 generation Turkish Cypriots, the very simple question "Where are you from?" has always been a very complex and confusing one, in contrast to our parents who generally answered this question by referring to their "old" places as their homeland. For instance, I was born after 1974 in Esentepe (one of the "old" Greek villages, Ayios Ambrosios), and my father always told me that "This house is not ours; we are just living in it". In such a condition, it was really difficult to say I am from Esentepe. The answer to this question has always started with "My father is from Ayios Nikolaos and my mother is from Knodhara (Gönendere)". Or as Meltem says; "How can I explain where I am from? Who lives in Cyprus? Is my house really my house?".

Communication/Miscommunication with the "Other"

For a long time after the island was divided into two, the two main communities on the island lived separately and in isolation from each other. The communication between the partitions was cut, and since then, from 1974 until the end of the 1990s there were no "direct" communications between the two main communities. During that time, "the partition of Cyprus has been an extraordinarily complete barrier to communication. Not only has the fence been difficult to penetrate and the two crossing points rigorously policed, with all movement subject to a forbidding bureaucracy, but other forms of contact has been frustrated too" (Cockburn, 2004, p. 172). For instance, there is/was no direct telephone line between the two parts of Cyprus since 1974[7]. Thus, the communications between the two communities were very limited and it can be said that the only significant communication between the two main communities on the island was through the mass media[8] which generally were in support of the official discourses of their respective governments. Referring to different studies (see also Arslan, 2002 & Güresun, 2001), I can say that the discourse of Northern Cyprus' media was largely nationalistic which constructed the other main community on the island—Greek Cypriots—as an external "other". This form of communication is also controlled, censored and is generally a *biased* communication.

Hence, communication between the two main communities was very limited—except for political communications. However, for us—Turkish Cypriot youth—Greek Cypriots as a community were beyond the "border"; they were beyond the present, in our "past", in "stories". They were in newspapers, TV news, sometimes in our albums or/and on the walls of houses. But at the same time, they were nowhere. Their *traces* were everywhere but as a community they were ghost-like. We were connected and disconnected at the same time. The only communication was the narratives about them by third parties while we did not have any social, mutual communication. We were aware of each other without having any direct communication. The border that separated us also reminded us that there is another community behind the border. So, it was also a facilitation of contact. The border as a signifier also functioned as a unifying signifier, which pointed out and connected with the other side. It became a reminder, which reminded us of the existence of the Greek Cypriot community beyond it. Thus, its function became undecidable between separation and connection: it separated and connected; it neither separated nor connected, all at the same time. Inadvertently, the communication or the lack of communication of the two main communities became *ambivalent*. Here I mean the presence of two contradictory meanings about the communication or/and lack of communication of two main communities on the island.

Those who are Born Into the *Unrecognized* Part of the Divided Country

Like lots of other Turkish Cypriots, I grew up in a Greek Cypriot's house; we used their furniture, TVs, plates, even

5 The opening of the gates was announced on 21st April 2003 by the Turkish Cypriot authorities, just after the signing of Cyprus' EU Accession Treaty (16th April 2003).

6 I interviewed 12 people, 8 women and 4 men between the ages of 24-32. In this text they appear as; Ebru, Deniz, Güliz, Meltem, Ahmet, Osman, Dilek, Sevgi, Ali, Gamze.

7 The only telephone network between the two communities is/was the telephone lines that were assembled through a project by the United Nations High Commissioner for Refugees (UNCHR). It is a network in which telephone lines from both sides (16-20 lines) of Cyprus are connected to one another at Ledra Palace. At the beginning (1974) there were only 2 lines.

8 There are broadcasts on government TVs in the other's language in both parts. Both communities could watch each other's television broadcasts. They have news about each other in their media and they could also read translated press articles of each other in their own newspapers.

their clothes. We could travel everywhere in the world [9](but with a Turkish passport), but not to the "other" side; we could call and send/receive mail to/from every place in the world (but through Turkey) but not to/from the south[10]; "On the way to Budapest, I realised that my passport was good for nothing. I had a separate country but I had to get a Turkish passport. Passport is something which represents national idendity but mine is not valid around the world" (PR person)[11].

Our access to the world's communication network was possible only through Turkey, because, the part of Cyprus, to which we belong communally, is unrecognized internationally. The north of Cyprus is considered "illegal" as it is not recognized by other countries except Turkey and "Cypriots have long grown used to the fact that letters with an address in the 'wrong' part of Cyprus are often 'lost' in the post" (Cockburn, 2004, p. 172). That is to say, the border which separated us from the southern part of our country was, in one of its disguises, the line which separated us as the "unknown", "unreachable", "prohibited" and also "unrecognized" part[12]. Hence, the border for Turkish Cypriots also served as a retaining wall which separated us from the world. There have been social, cultural and economic isolations and embargoes for the north of Cyprus since the establishment of the Turkish Republic of Northern Cyprus in 1983. And the border of separation became a symbol which separated the legitimate and the illegitimate. That's why it is not only a "Green Line" that separated us from the "other side". As Deren Derya[13] (a Turkish Cypriot youth) puts it, referring the opening of the border, "I don't call it the green line I could call it the black line. Because it was like the line separating me from the world"

Stories of the *Past*

The post-74 generation grew up by listening to different stories about the "past" and the South—both official and personal. These stories sometimes supported and at other times contradicted each other. We inherited the Cyprus problem/issue and we need to construct and re-construct the meaning of who we are by hearing the older generation's narratives—official and personal stories. These narratives can be interpreted as having been the main communication tool between the youth and the South or/ and the past.

The official narrative was generally based on the positing of an ontological difference between the Greek Cypriots and Turkish Cypriots and it was nourished by the education system and also the media which are the most influential agencies of Ideological State Apparatuses[14]. Within the official story/history of Turkish Cypriot authorities, the border is/was the symbol of sovereignty. The educational policy in northern part of Cyprus, was mainly based on the "re-membering" of the Turkish Cypriot in the "new" geography—North Cyprus. Within this system, the past was "monumentalized". The "new" *imagined community*[15] for Turkish Cypriots was constructed by taking the "new" geography after the migration in 1974 as its basis—which was the northern part of the island. This way of imagining a "new" nation by referring to a new geography, excludes the other main community—Greek Cypriots—on the island. The Greek Cypriot community is represented as "Other", which is monsterized, and is removed from the "common" life between the two main communities before and during the ethnic conflict. As one Turkish Cypriot youth says; "When I was a child, I used to think that Greek Cypriots were much more different from us. That they would somehow look different than the Turkish Cypriots. I also thought that all the Greeks in the world were men, I somehow could not imagine a Greek Cypriot as a woman or a child" (Housewife)[16]. Of course, this is because these stories are militarized stories. Men's stories generally focus on wars of ethnic conflict and thus the relation between the two main communities was reduced to war in the official/educational narratives. And generally Greek Cypriots were represented as EOKA fighters or/ and priests. I can say that, this narrative is selective, and it selects to remember the hostilities and obliges us to forget the peaceful coexistence before and also during the ethnic war among the two main communities of Cyprus.

What interests me in personal memories is that they provide alternative discourses to the official story telling in most of the cases. The south and the past can be likened to a nostalgic picture which is taken and then framed by the older generations. The older generations became the mediators/narrators between the south/past and the young generations. I believe that these stories split and divide the discursive unity of official (hi)stories and representations, and they were bridges for a possible "peace" on the island—especially for the young generation who had no chance to communicate with the other main community on the island, and only had the opportunity to experience one half of Cyprus.

Within the Turkish Cypriot official narrative "returning back to the south" was not a common theme[17]. But within

9 With TRNC's passport, Turkish Cypriots can travel to very few countries with special visas. For most of the countries we need to have Turkish Republic's passport.

10 The postal adress is through Turkey, routed through "Mersin 10 Turkey," and the international call for the north of Cyprus is 0090 which is also via Turkey.

11 In Güngör, Ç. (2002). *Kıbrıslı Türk Gençleri Konuşuyor*. İstanbul: Metis.

12 I think this is the most important point which distinguishes us from the Greek Cypriot youth.

13 In the documentary titled "Which Cyprus?" directed by Rüstem Batum (2004).

14 The Ideological State Apparatuses is the term which is used by Louis Althusser to refer to the agencies of the state such as the educational system, the family, the legal system, religious institutions, the political system and also the media (1989).

15 Imagined community is a concept which is used by Benedict Anderson (1991) who argues that natioanl identity is an abstract and symbolic imagination of our belongingness.

16 In Güngör, Ç. (2002). *Kıbrıslı Türk Gençleri Konuşuyor*. İstanbul: Metis.

17 However, in the official story of Greek Cypriots it is not the same. Their story is both based on forgetfulness and on returning back (see also Gregoriou, 2005). Turkish Cypriot authorities did not position themselves as "owners" of the whole island. But, "the wall of a Greek Cypriot military post at the west end of

the personal stories, which produced cracks within the official story, "returning back" and "the dreaming of a return" were the most emphasized themes. These were repeated again and again; they became coded memories and then transferred to the new generation by the older generations. These stories can be likened to the fairy tales which are narrated by the older generations to the younger generation. Like fairy tales which "develop maps for coping with personal anxieties, family conflicts, social frictions, and the myriad frustrations of daily life" (Tatar, 1999, p. xi), these stories that we have heard from our parents/grandparents helped us to "frame" the places that they had to leave; "South: like a story that I will always listen to" (Dilek). Thus, these stories became the main communication tool, and older generations became mediators between us and the south and the past; "I always feel like my grandmother was the link between the South and me. She raised me up and she was always telling me stories about her past and her life in the South" (Güliz).

The Partial Opening of the Border and "Experiencing" the Impossible

The opening of the "gates" on 23rd of April, 2003, gave the opportunity to all Cypriots to visit and experience the "other" side. Now several gates are open and the south is not an inaccessible space anymore. As a result many previously displaced Cypriots became *guests* in their *own* houses. With the exception of a few undesirable cases, this strange experience can be interpreted as a civilian negotiation between the two migrant communities. It helped the migrant Cypriots from both communities to see and try to understand the "other"; "It was the first time that my father gave his place in the dining table to someone else" (Ebru). Ebru's father gave his place to the "ex owner" of his house. There were many examples of empathy like this. "This kind of dialogue is an example of people-to-people reconciliation whereby the one puts himself in the position of the other" (Hadjipavlou, 2007, p. 65). Here, Ebru's father was welcomed to another migrant Cypriot.

The opening of the border, made face to face communication possible and at the same time, it enabled the possibility of an "archeological excavation". It made it possible to go beyond the border to the "lost past" of the communities of Cyprus. It also enabled the youths to experience the "other" part of their country which they had not have the chance to experience. Many memories of Turkish Cypriot migrants were constructed in terms of displacement. For the migrant Cypriots the past, as a time and the south, as a place were/are always attached to each other, and they have taken this displacement as the central point of their narratives. The past always reminded them of the places that they had to leave in 1974 and earlier. From that view, the border can also be defined as a time line in the memories of Cypriot communities, especially for migrant Cypriots. The past is "like the child's relation to the mother,[...]always already 'after the break'" (Hall, 1990, p. 226). When we talked about the "past" in Cyprus, we always speak after the break; after the division, after the time line, after the displacement; which is after the "border". The division has different stories and different "break" points for the Greek and Turkish communities. However, the partition of the island in 1974 has another significance in terms of communication, especially for the youth. Because, it did not only limit the crossing or the traveling to the other part of the country, but also cut off all ways of communication which made the other main community, Greek Cypriot community, a ghost-like community for the Turkish Cypriot youth.

Before the opening, the border was an *aporia* for the Cypriot peoples which was a "dead end" and allowed no passage. Since 1974, "the hope of returning", "the dreaming of 'old' houses/villages/places", "the longing", etc were the most remarkable motifs in the individuals' stories. The opening of the border enabled Cypriot peoples' *dream to come true*. After the partial openings, the border was not aporia anymore[18]. After 2003, there were holes in it which enabled the individuals' stories to come alive. Within this time period, Cyprus happened to be a country that the Cypriots wanted to visit more than any other "foreign" country, because, it parts had been "forbidden" and "closed" for those years.

The "past" in the memories of the Cypriot peoples were fantasized. "The displacement leaves an empty or absent space that defines the [Cypriot identities] in an imagined, fantastic space" (Romero, 2006, p. 158). And maybe that's why these stories always started with "those were the days", "our weather/our sun/our water was extremely better", "the apples from our region were more beautiful/delicious", etc. It was like a fantasy beyond reality; beyond the border, beyond the time line. The border as an aporia made their pasts' fantastic. Because going beyond the border was impossible, dreaming/narrating was the only way of going back. These individual stories were constructed as fantasies of the individuals' pasts. And "to go beyond the border" was the common *social* dream for the migrant Cypriot people. That's why the south became the most desired/dreamed part of the world for Turkish Cypriots[19]; "It was the part of the island that my grandmother always dreamed of going back and to live" (Güliz)[20].

We grew up listening to stories about the places that our parents had to leave and how beautiful they were; "I

Nicosia....bears the inscription "Our borders are not here. They are in Kyrenia" (Gregoriou, 2005). This indicates that the Greek Cypriot's "official" discourse does not accept that "border" [the green line] as the identifying margin of their identity construction.

18 Today 5 check points are open to crossings from the north to the south and vice versa.

19 After the opening of the border, with referring the crossings from the north to the south and vice versa, Afrika newspaper's headline was; "Cyprus, the most desired country that the Cypriots want to go/visit" (25th April, 2003, p. 7, Günlük)

20 Here, I should note that although there were differences in the interpretation of the Cyprus issue, ethnic conflict in leftist and rightist families, the narrations related to their "old" places were not different.

created images that were of course very Mediterranean, maybe some scenes from an Italian movies..." (Meltem), "The narratives about the places in the south side always described as somewhere beautiful" (Ahmet)

The narratives of our parents/grandparents resemble the fairy tales which start with the words "once upon a time"[21]. The "once upon a time" for Cypriot people implied the time before the division of the island, before the immigration, before 1974; before the border. The post-74 generation is the listeners of these stories. Everyone that I interviewed for this study visited their parents' "old" houses (including me). We really *wanted* to go and visit those places because we had also "memories" of those places. And listening to the repeated stories related to the past and about returning back created a wish and curiosity in our minds related to our parents' places.

We are the postmemorial generation who grew up listening to stories about these fantastic, unreachable and beautiful places. These narratives of the south constitute and energize an inherited memory in Turkish Cypriot youth. This can be explained with the term "postmemory" which "defines the familial inheritance and transmission of cultural trauma" (Hirsch, 2001, p. 7). Here, I use the term "post memory" in order to designate our familial inheritance of these memories; however, I believe it is also notable that every memory is a creation and representation. And every memory is always after the break and it is has developed from the notion of "afterwardness" (see also King, 2000). Thus, I prefer to use the term re-memorizing in order to highlight this aspect of the youth's memory. Through narration and representation of the south by the older generations we re-memorized the "past" and the "south". The frustration that we experienced when visiting *our elders' previous* houses is because of the stories whose referent was not experienced or lived; but what we had inherited through listening. These stories were the mediums of our re-memory, and while experiencing returns as re-turns we are disappointed for ourselves and for our parents/grandparents;

> I went to my parent's village with my mother. I was shocked; the village was not inhabited after 1974. So most of the houses were destroyed; only very few houses still existed. In fact my parents' house is still there, it was very disappointing to see the size of the house, the narrow streets of the village and also the location of the village....my grandmother always wanted to visit her village again, but she passed away before the border was opened so she didn't have the chance to see her village again. But I am glad that she didn't; it would have been very disappointing for her (Güliz).

21 Here again, I want to mention that when the subject is Cyprus and migration we should talk about different displacements in different time periods. Then, "once upon a time" refers to different time/place/lives. However, in this study I focus on the displacement of Turkish Cypriots in 1974. Some Turkish Cypriots had to move 3 times between the years 1957 and 1974.

Marianne Hirsh uses the term postmemory "as a response of the second generation to the trauma of the first (2001, p. 8). The south in the minds of migrants' children was equal to the stories that they listened to, as told by the previous generations. These stories, narratives, created re-memories of the post-74 generation. We developed ties with those places through the stories that we heard. Under these feelings/expectations, the frustration that we experienced is due to our way of remembering these stories that we had listened to.

Until the opening of the border, we have listened to different stories of "returning home again". These stories could be interpreted as the "melancholia" of this returning to home/homeland. The opening of the border enabled Turkish Cypriot migrants to travel to the places that they had left, but the melancholia persisted. The experiencing of the "returning home" of the Turkish Cypriot youth, as witnesses of these returns, created an "emptiness" in their sensations. I remember the first time that we went to my father's place. I was so excited. But at the moment that we arrived at my father's previous home I was confused. I did not know what I should say and feel. That moment created an unbridgeable distance that separates the narrator and the listener of the stories (see also Hirsh, 2001).

> I was not very moved to be in the house of my family which I visited after the border opened. I just felt unexplainable feelings when I thought that I would have been born in that house and lived in that area if incidents had not broken out. But I felt different things when I followed the conversations and movements of my father while we were visiting his village. As I tried to understand him, I saw that as a person who never lived around here, I would never be able to understand his feelings (Ali).

As Ali tries to tell what he feels, his feeling is arrested by the "emptiness" and the "unexplainability". This is not only because of the unlived memory but the ambiguity in Ali's sensations while trying to understand his father's loss. "Unless, what they experienced was not a feeling of historical alienation and emotional disengagement but another kind of displaced presence, essential to *their* re-turn as different from that of their parents, also constitutive of their historical experience as witnesses" (Gregoriou, 2005, p. 17).

For migrant Turkish Cypriots, the saturation that "the places may have been reached one day" has been surpassed after visiting their "old" places. In some cases, the melancholia was turned into mourning. Deniz's grandfather became reticent after he visited his house and garden after the opening of the border;

> After 1974, my grandfather took very good care of his house and garden. He always thought that the Greek owner of his [previous] house and garden also took very good care of his places in the south;

> because he thought that one day anyone would return to his/her place. But after he visited and saw his garden which was not used and was not cared for he was very disappointed. He always thought that one day we would have peace in Cyprus and he would reach his garden. But at the time that he visited his garden and found them squalid he was frustrated (Deniz).

Here, the melancholia of Deniz's grandfather has turned into mourning because he lost his dream of "returning back and found out that he could not find his garden as he left". In the melancholia there is still identification with the lost object, however the mourning is the acceptance of the loss of the object (Zizeck, 2000, pp. 659-663)[22]. Or, as Butler puts it; "the melancholic refuses the loss of the object, and internalization becomes a strategy of magically resustaining the lost object, not only because loss is painful, but the ambivalence felt toward the object requires that the object be retained until differences are settled" (1999, pp. 78-79). In the melancholia the subject refuses to accept the loss of the object, and the relationship between the subject and the object is ambivalent and unresolved. In Deniz's grandfather's case, until he visited his places he refuses to accept/face up to the loss of these places and lived melancholia towards his places. But after he visited his places and couldn't find them as he left, he lost his tie with those places and this made him to mourn; the lack has turned into a loss in his emotions. This again reminds us that there is no actual "return" to the past or/and going "home" again (Hall, 1993). Here, Deniz's grandfather had to come to terms with the loss and the change because the time transformed the place; you can not *return* to the past both spatially and timely.

After the opening of the border, after traveling to the "old" places, we heard many different stories—of both Turkish and Greek Cypriots. In these stories migrant Cypriots found their homes "smaller", "older" even "closer or further to the mosques or/and churches". These narratives of the "homes" were all constructed by taking the impossibility of the opening of the border. These stories can be likening to the melodramas. As Steve Neale (1986) points out, the root of the melodramatic pleasure lies in its poignancy. The melodrama always plays to the feeling of the "impossibility" of going back, to the feeling of being "too late". The feeling of "too late" grows out of the running of the two different emotional states together. And the base which makes the running of these two different emotional states together is the (empty) ground of desire: "if only" (Abisel, et.al. 2005, p. 39). The longing, the yearning and the dreaming of a return back was so "powerful" because of this "if only" or the impossibility. In the Cyprus case this "if only" refers/referred to the wish; "*if only* the war would not have happened". And with the opening of the borders the gap between this "impossibility" and the Cypriots' dream was not closed down, it is still there. We might not have the right words to define it right now.

Our parent/grandparents were disappointed because they did not find the places "as they were". And we are disappointed because the image that is constituted by these imaginary, representational narratives did not match with the *reality;* "I went to my parent's village with my mother. I was shocked; the village was not inhabited after 1974. So most of the houses were destroyed, only very few houses still existed. In fact my parents' house is still there, it was very disappointing to see the size of the house, the narrow streets of the village and also the location of the village" (Güliz).

But, after the opening of the border, we did not experience the feelings that we expected; "I have accepted Girne always as home and it still is. As a fact, I come from Limassol and I do not have anything to do with Limassol and I feel that I would not be able to increase my sense of belonging towards it. I thought that if I spent time there, Limassol would have more meaning for me. But it didn't happen that way" (Dilek). Here, Dilek's memories of the place as home clashed with what she experiences in the present.

Today, 4 years after the opening of the border, the visits to the "old" places are not on the agenda anymore. My father says "I do not want to visit my house often. Because, every time that I visit, I feel farther apart from my house". Migrant Cypriots have dreamed 29 years (from 1974—division—to 2003—opening of the borders) to see and visit their places, but now they are not as desirous as they were before the opening of the border, for a number of reasons. The first one is their disappointment in every visit, because of the contradiction or/and discrepancy of the *image* in their minds and the *real. T*he second reason is their "new attachments" on the other side (Papadakis, 2005). Furthermore, the stories are *silenced* nowadays. The south is not unavoidable anymore, and the impossibility which enabled these fairytale like stories and kept them alive also faded away. Every visit kills the migrant Cypriots' memories and transforms their melancholies to the mourning.

Closing Notes

Today, we are experiencing a "new" Cyprus, new, in terms of communication. With the opening of the "gates", the two main communities on the island finally had the opportunity to have mutual, face-to-face and line-to-line communication with each other. However, we are still living in a divided country. Before the opening of the border, the opening of the border meant "solution", "peace" on the island, an event which would also bring about the "legitimacy", "recognition" and also freedom for the Turkish Cypriots. Today, although we are individually recognized, the part of our country that we are living in is still "unrecognized". Our citizenship in terms of world

22 Here, I would like to thank my friend Pembe Behçetoğulları, for her valuable suggestions for my discussion on melancholia and mourning.

citizenship is still undecidable. Many Turkish Cypriots have the passports of the Republic of Cyprus[23] which makes us individually recognized, but the part of our country that we are living in is unrecognized. And the crossing to the "other" part of our island became a site of transformation of our identities; from illegitimate to legitimate, from non-European to European; from TRNC citizenship to Republic of Cyprus' citizenship. In every crossing, Turkish Cypriots who have Republic of Cyprus' IDs, first show their TRNC's IDs to the Turkish Cypriot policemen. They cross the Northern Cyprus' check points as citizens of TRNC and then, enter the buffer zone or "no man's land". When entering the southern part they show their Republic of Cyprus' IDs to the Greek Cypriot policemen and enter as the citizens of the Republic of Cyprus. Here, I believe, it is not exaggerated to say that we are still in-between.

The people that I talk to define themselves differently as; Turkish Cypriot, Cypriot, Cypriotturk and Turkish speaking Cypriots. However, there are not illustrated differences in their narratives related to their families' places or/and the way that they are experiencing the "new" Cyprus. Their ambivalent sensations can be accepted as the most remarkable motif in the youth's sensations; "It was an unbelievable feeling. It is the place that you always listen about and even 'know' but the first time that you see it...I felt like a stranger and at the same time as belonging there. It was an unbelievably confusing feeling" (Ebru).

Many of Cypriots experience Cyprus as "two different countries on the same island". When I went to the South I felt like I actually traveled to another country...nowadays I think the border is just like any other border between two countries (Güliz). Today, many Turkish Cypriot youth go to the southern part of their island for shopping, entertainment, to see the touristic places...etc. their/our way of experiencing the part of Cyprus in our "memories" just like another country in somewhere else in the world; "I go there to see the other part of the island, or for shopping, or enjoyment. I feel like a stranger instead of a citizen" (Gamze).

I don't want to deny the positive role of the opening of the border in a probable peace in Cyprus, but the traces of the division can be seen in everywhere in our country; "We still need peace, peace, and peace!!! We still have borders, guns, bombs, soldiers, tanks... So if we still have this between us. I think we are not even half-way there" (Meltem). Although we did not experience any violence since the opening of the border, we have a long way to go for peace in Cyprus. And it can be said that, the lack of communication between the two main communities has turned into a "controlled communication" (see also Anastasiou, 2002), and today the border in Cyprus functions as a border between two different countries; "The border is something which continuously reminds me of the division of the island and that we have a state which is not recognised. This has always disturbed me" (Deniz).

Few words more...

Today, Cyprus is still a divided country. And we are experiencing our country as two different countries, with different IDs and identities. And I can say that, peace in Cyprus is a *utopia.* Here I am not using the negative meaning of utopia. I am vesting a positive meaning to it rather than the negative meaning vested by Hercules Milas; "I see the dream of reaching to utopia as not accepting the present situation in the name of 'realism' but the struggle to end up in better tomorrows, which is not present now, but can be obtained with belief and efforts of people. The dream when people can not reach it, they stay where they are and never go forward" (2007). That's why we should keep dreaming of peace in Cyprus.

23 Here I should also note that issuing passports to Turkish Cypriots is necessary for the *legitimacy* of the Republic of Cyprus. If the Republic of Cyprus did not do this it would be Greek Cypriot Republic and would thereby become *illegitimate.* Because Turkish Cypriot community was the founding partner of the Republic of Cyprus in its establishment in1960.

References

Anastasiu, H. (2002). Communication across conflict lines: The case of ethically divided Cyprus. *Journal of Peace Research, 39*(5), 581-596.

Arslan, Y. (2002). Re-construction of Turkish Cypriot sense of self in selected newspapers in TRNC (Unpublished MA Thesis). EMU: Famagusta.

Abisel, N., Arslan, U.T., Behcetoğulları, P., Karadoğan, A., et. al. (2005). *Çok tuhaf çok tanıdık.* İstanbul: Metis Yayınları.

Althusser, L.. (1989). *İdeoloji ve devletin ideolojik aygıtları* (Çev. M. Özışık & Y. Alp). İstanbul: İletişim.

Anderson, B. (1991). *Imagined communities: Reflections on the origin and spread of nationalism.* London: Verso.

Butler, J. (1999). *Gender trouble feminism and the subversion of identity.* New York & London: Routledge.

Cockburn, C. (2004). *The line.* London: Zed Books.

Gregoriou, Z. (2005). Crossing the green line: The re-turn home and the unwitnessed traumas of the youth's unlived memory. *Proceedings of the 10th International Cultural Symposium* (May 4-6), Ege University: İzmir.

Güngör, Ç. (2002). *Kıbrıslı Türk gençleri konuşuyor.* İstanbul: Metis.

Güresun, H. (2001). Representation of the "Other" and the reconstruction of national identity in news discourses: A critical discourse analysis of "KIBRIS" (Unpublished MA Thesis). EMU: Famagusta.

Hadjipavlou, M. (2007). Multiple stories: The "crossings" as part of citizens' reconciliation efforts in Cyprus. *Innovation: The European Journal of Social Science Research, 20(1)*, 53-73.

Hall, S. (1990). Cultural identity and diaspora. In R. Jonathan, (Ed.), *Identity: Community, culture, difference* (pp.

222-37). London: Lawrence and Wishart.

Hall, S. (1993). Culture, community, nation. *Cultural Studies, 7*(3), 349–363.

Hirsh, M. (2001). Surviving images: Holocaust photographs and the work of postmemory. *The Yale Journal of Criticism, 14*(I), 5-37.

King, N. (2000). *Memory, narrative, identity*. Edinburgh: Edinburgh University Press.

Milas, H. (2007, Spring, Special Version on Peace Journalism). Kıbrıs'ta sözde sorun mu?, *Gündem*, p. 3. Gazimağusa: FCMS, EMU.

Papadakis, Y. (2005). *Echoes from the Dead Zone: Across the Cyprus divide.* London/New York: I.B. Tauris & Co. Ltd.

Papadakis, Y., Peristianis, N. & Welz, G. (2006). *Divided Cyprus*. Bloomington and Indianapolis: Indiana University Press.

Romero, R. E. (2006). Amusement parks, bagpipes, and cemeteries: Fantastic spaces of Galician identity through emigration. *Journal of Spanish Cultural Studies, 7*(2), 155-169.

Tatar, M. (1999). *The classic fairy tales*. Harvard University.

Zizek, S. (2000). Melancholy and the Act. *Critical Inquiry, 26* (Summer), 657-681.

Visual Reference:

Batum, R. (Director). (2005). *Which Cyprus?* [Docementary].

1990 Sonrası Türk Sinemasında Etnik Kimliklerin Temsili

Zehra Yiğit
Afyonkarahisar Kocatepe Üniversitesi
z_akbulut@yahoo.com

Giriş

Türkiye yapısı itibariyle bir çok alt kimliğin buluştuğu bir toplumsal yapı sergilemektedir. Bununla beraber AB süreci ve son 20-25 yıldır Türkiye'de yaşanan çeşitli olaylar neticesinde etnik kimlik unsuru, sık sık gündeme yansıyan bir konu görünümündedir. Coğrafi açıdan Doğu ve Güneydoğu Anadolu bölgeleri her ne kadar Türkiye'nin doğusunda yer alsa da bugün söz konusu kavramların içini dolduran özellikler yalnızca bölgelerin konumlarından ibaret görülmemektedir. Doğulu ve Batılı olmaya yeni anlamlar yüklenmektedir.

Toplumu yansıtan bir sanat dalı olan sinema çeşitli şekillerde; önce üstü örtük bir halde etnik kimliklerin kültürlerine ve yaşamlarına dair pek çok şeye değinmekte iken, 1990 sonrası bu etnik kımlikler—sayıları az da olsa—açıkça sinemaya yansımaktadır. Araştırma, özelde Kürt etnik kimliğe dair, sinemanın sunduğu kimlik inşalarını "ben" ve "öteki" çerçevesinde değerlendirmeyi amaçlamaktadır. Böylece insanların birbirlerini tanıdıkça birbirlerini anlayacağından hareketle farklı bakış açıları ile Kürtlerin kültürleri, yaşam tarzlarını ve düşüncelerini sunan bu filmlerin, bu etnik alt kültürü tanıtma ve anlatmadaki öneminden bahsedilecektir.

Türkiye'de Etnik Kimlik ve Kürt Kimliği

Etniklik bir çok farklı ölçütler dikkate alınarak tanımlanabilecek bir kavramdır. *"Genel olarak, benimsedikleri soy (köken), dil, din ve sahip oldukları kültür itibariyle diğer gruplardan farklı olan gruplar etnik olarak nitelenebilir"* (Önder, 2007, s. 1). Etnik kimlik, başta dil ve dini inanç olmak üzere, örf, adet, gelenek ve töreler gibi ortak sosyal değerler tarafından belirlenen "kültürel" bir olgu olarak tanımlanmaktadır. Etnik kimlik, doğuştan kazanılan bir nitelik, genetik, biyolojik yada ırksal bir özellik değildir. Bu nedenle de etnik kimlik kültürel yapıya bağlı olarak niteliksel ve niceliksel anlamda değişebilir nitelikte görülmektedir. Bruinessen (2000, ss. 26-27) durumu şöyle ifade etmektedir: *"Etnisite akışkandır ve en azından bir dereceye kadar kişisel tercihlere bağlıdır; doğuştan kazanılan, değişmez bir kimlik değildir ve bir kimsenin yalnızca tek bir etnik gruba mensup olması şart değildir. Herkesin kısmen örtüşen farklı kimlikleri vardır ve kişinin hangi kimlikleri öne çıkaracağı hangilerini geri plana iteceği duruma bağlıdır."* Örneğin Zazaca konuşan bir Sünni, Zaza, Sünni Müslüman, Türkiye vatandaşı gibi kimliklere sahip olmaktadır. Ayrıca bir sosyal sınıfa, örneğin aşirete mensup olabilmekte, belirli bir köyden yada kasabadandır. Bu kimliklerinin her birini kullanacakları anlar mevcut bulunmaktadır (Bruinessen, 2000, s. 27).

Dil ve din her ne kadar etnik nüfus için önemli bir öğe olsa da asla tek başına yeterli durumda görülmemektedir. Anadil her zaman etnik kimlikle örtüşmeyebileceği gibi diğer yandan dini inanç için de aynı durum söz konusu olmaktadır. Türkiye'de halkın çoğunluğunun (% 95) Müslüman olması, ülke içindeki etnik gruplar arasında kaynaşmayı ve bütünleşmeyi kolaylaştıran bir unsur olarak durmaktadır. Ayrıca din ve dil dışında, alt grupların tanımında önem taşıyan başka grup nitelikleri de mevcut bulunmaktadır: *"Bunlara örnek olarak, örgütlenme yapısı, aşiret organizasyonu, mensubiyet algılaması, meslek-uğraş benzerliği, dilleri soyları farklı toplulukların ortak bir kaderi paylaşmış olmalarının yarattığı dayanışma, birlik duygusu sayılabil[mektedir]"* (Önder, 2007, s. 3). Önder (2007) bu duruma Çerkez'leri örnek vermektedir (s. 3). Birbirinden farklı kökene ve dile sahip olan Adige, Abhaz, Dağıstanlı, Balkar, Karaçay gibi grupların her biri farklı etnik gruplar olmalarına rağmen kimliklerini bu isimle anmaktadırlar.

Türkiye'de karışıklık yaratan bir diğer kavram da üst kimlik kavramıdır. Üst kimlik çeşitli şekillerde tanımlanabilmektedir: Etnolojik olarak aynı kökene sahip alt grupların ana kimliğidir. Kırgızlar yada Özbeklerin Türk olarak tanımlanması üst kimliğe örnek olarak verilebilmektedir. Bazen de üst kimlik aynı coğrafya paylaşan benzer kültürlere sahip, tarihi paylaşımları olan, aynı kaderi paylaşmış grupların temsili kimliği olarak tanımlanmaktadır. Çerkez olarak tanımlanan Karaçaylar ve Balkarlar da Türk üst kimliği içerisinde yerini almaktadır. Siyasi anlamda da üst kimlik, farklı etnik gruplara mensup kişilerin, vatandaşlık bilinci ve bağıyla benimsediği temsili ulusal kimlik olarak ifade edilmektedir. TC anayasasının 66. maddesi kendisine vatandaşlık bağı ile bağlı herkesi Türk olarak kabul etmektedir. Bugün Türkiye'nin yaklaşık % 90 oranını Türkler oluştururken Kürtler, Zazalar, Araplar, Çerkezler, Lazlar, diğer yandan azınlık olarak tanımlanan Ermeni, Rum ve Yahudiler nüfusun ortalama % 10'luk kısmını oluşturduğu ifade edilmektedir. Kürt özelindeki sorunlar ise özellikle 1990'lar da Türk toplumun gündem maddesi durumuna geldiği görülmekte, Kürtlerle ilgili fikirler değişmeye, duyulan haberlere bağlı olarak farklı bir konuma yavaş yavaş taşınmaya başladığı düşünülmektedir.

Batının Kürtlüğe gösterdiği ilginin nedeninin ise Batılıların büyük enerji kaynağı ve jeopolitik öneme sahip Orta Doğu kendi çıkarlarına hizmet edecek yeni bir etnik unsur yaratma isteklerinden kaynaklandığı düşünülmektedir. Birsen Gökçe (2004) *"1990'lı yıllar Sovyet bloğunun dağılmasına koşut olarak Türkiye'de sağ-sol çatışmasının anlamsızlaştığı veya bu ayrımın bulanıklaştığı ve etnik/dinsel kimliklerin patladığı bir dönem olmuştur"* (s. 46) diyerek düşüncelerini ifade ederken Ali İhsan Gültekin (1994) de *"Ne garip tecellidir ki; SSCB'nin dağılmasıyla sonuçlanan ve Dünya'da böylesine olumlu barış rüzgarlarının estirilmeye çalışıldığı günlerde, Ülkemizin başına Ermeni terörünün akabinde PKK terörü musallat edilmiş ,... terörist şiddetin boyutları büyürken, yeni ekonomik darboğazlarla yüz yüze gelinmiştir.* (ss. 6-7) demektedir. Çokkültürlülük gibi yaklaşımlarla üçüncü dünya ülkelerini içten bölmek Batının siyasi yaklaşımlarından birisi olarak ifade edilmekte, tüm bu çalışmalar ise Kürtlerin Kürdistan kurma ve da özerk olma hayallerini teşvik edip, bölücü terör örgütleri ile bir sorun haline dönüştüğü düşünülmektedir. Terör, Doğu ve Güneydoğu Anadolu bölgelerinin önemli bir sorunu olmakla beraber "doğu"lu kimliği üzerinde büyük etki yapan, zaman zaman anlamını değiştiren bir kavram olarak görülmektedir.

Türk Sinemasında Kürt Etnik Kökeni

Türkiye'de son 20-25 yıla damgasını vurmuş olan etnik kimlik özelinde Kürt meselesi ve güneydoğuda yaşananlar, savaşın sinema tarihinde nasıl bir iz bırakacağını söylemek için henüz erken olduğu düşünülmektedir. Sinema ilk yılları boyunca toplum adına çok da fazla bir şey yapmadığı, daha çok melodram filmleri ile gerçekliği çok da olmayan bir hayat tarzı sunduğu görülmektedir. Sinemacılar çağının bu ilk yıllarının (1950'li yıllar) melodram örnekleriyle dolu olmasına rağmen sosyal ve siyasal ortamın etkisiyle çekilen *Susuz Yaz, Gurbet Kuşları, Karanlıkta Uyananlar, Acı Hayat* gibi gerçekçi filmlerin de çekildiği görülmektedir. Sinemacılar Dönemi, 27 Mayıs 1960 İhtilali ve paralelinde 61 Anayasası ile bir dönüm noktası yaşayan bir sürece denk gelmekte, bu anayasaya paralel toplumsal yapıda görülmeye başlayan değişik fikir ve düşünüşlerden sinemanın da payını aldığı düşünülmektedir. *"1961 Anayasasının getirdiği özgürlük havası, sinemamızın o döneme kadar neredeyse "sırtını döndüğü" toplumsal gerçeklerle nihayet ilgilenme fırsatını getirmiştir"* (Güçhan, 1992, s. 81).

1967 yılında çektiği *Hudutların Kanunu* filmiyle gerçekçilikte önemli bir aşama almış olan Ömer Lütfi Akad'ın çizgisini sürdüren, geliştiren Yılmaz Güney ise 70'lere damgasını vurmaktadır. Döneme damgasını vuran çeşitli görüşler -toplumsal gerçekçilik, halk sineması, devrimci sinema, ulusal sinema, milli sinema gibi- bu döneme hakim düşünceler olarak görülmektedir. Kürt kökenli bir yönetmen olan Yılmaz Güney filmleri ise Doğu ve Güneydoğu Anadolu sorunlarını Kürt kimliğini belirtmeden, en gerçekçi haliyle yansıtmaktadır. Güney, *Seyithan, Sürü, Yol, Duvar, Ağıt* gibi filmlerde değişen toplumsal yapı, kapitalizmle beraber ağalık, eşkıya, töre, kan davası, çete, kaçakçılık ve daha çok bir çok öğeyi kullanarak Kürtlere ait değerlere sayısız gönderme yaparak eleştirisini sunmaktadır. Bu filmlerin neredeyse tamamı mekan olarak Güneydoğu Anadolu'yu kullanmaktadır.

1990'lara gelene kadar, Türk sinemasında etnik kimliklerin daha çok milliyetçi bir söylemle ekranlara yansıtıldığı, Kürt etnik kimliğine dair ise direk olarak bir şey söylenmediği görülmektedir. *Malkoçoğlu, Karaoğlan, Kara Murat* sonrası 50'li yıllarda Kore, 1974 sonrası Kıbrıs Barış Harekâtı Yeşilçam'a bazı grupları yada etnik kimlikleri ötekileştirerek malzeme yapmaktadır. 2000'lere gelindiğinde ise milliyetçi söylemde öteki durumuna Kürt etnik kimliğinin geçtiği görülmektedir. *"Deli Yürek-Bumerang Cehennemi" Kurtlar Vadisi-Irak, Emret Komutanım: Şah Mat, Son Osmanlı-Yandım Ali*'de farklı bakış açılarından benzer söylemler yaratmaktaydı Diğer yandan Türk sinemasında Doğu ve Güneydoğu Anadolu'da öyküsünü kurmuş bir çok filmde bu filmlerden farklı üstelik gerçeğinden zaman zaman uzak bir mit yaratılmaktadır; *Eşkıya*"nın sular altında kalmış Güneydoğu Anadolu köylerinden, *Vizontele*'nin kahramanlarına mistik bir doğu yaratılmaktadır .

1991 yılında iki film; *Mem-u Zin* (Ümit Elçi-1991), *Siyabend-i Heco* (Şahin Gök -1991) Kürtlerin yaşamlarına dair hikayeler anlatmaktaydı. Artık *"... uzun yıllar Güneydoğu'ya—her ne kadar "Kürt" kimliği açıkça belirtilmese de—ya "medeniyetten uzak" karakterlerle, dağ kanunlarıyla, çetelerle özdeşleştirilen fütursuz göndermeler yapan veya sadece törelerin veya kaçakçılığın fon olarak kullanıldığı melodramların içinden "oryantalist" bir bakışla yaklaşan Türk sinemasında, bu bakışın kırıldığını söyleyebiliriz"* (Maktav, 2006, para. 33). Euroimages destekli bu filmler Kürt etnik kimliğine, onların yaşamlarına ve kültürlere has değerleri bireylerle paylaşmak için yapılmaktadır. Araştırmalar Türk toplumunun kendisiyle ilgili gerçekleri tam olarak bilmediğini, üstelik Türk halkını oluşturan toplulukların da birbirlerini yeterince tanımadığı ve birbirlerine karşı ön yargılı olduğunu göstermektedir. *Siyabed-i Heco* ve *Mem-u Zin* bu grupların birbirlerini tanıması için bir fırsat yaratmaktadır. Diğer yandan *Gönül Yarası* filminde *"Bir türküye ağlamak için Kürtçe bilmek şart mıdır?"* diyen Dünya aracılığı ile Yavuz Turgul mesajını iletmektedir.

Kürt sorunu üzerine film çeken yönetmenlerden bir diğeri Gani Rüzgar Şavata olarak görülmektedir. Şavata *Sınır* (1999), *Doz* (2001), *Dava* (2002), *Kardakiler* (2002), *Azad* (2002) gibi çektiği filmlerde koruculuk, aşiretler arası sürtüşme, namus davaları, ağalık, aşiretler arası sürtüşme, koruculuk, eşkıyalık devrimci karakterli kızlar, Kuzey ırak, Saddam zulmü, peşmergeler gibi genişletebilinecek geniş bir alanda filmlerinin öyküsünü kurmaktadır. Kürt temalı filmler konusunda çalışmalar yapan iki isimde Almanya'da yaşayan Yüksel Yavuz'da (*Nisan Çocukları, Küçük Özgürlük*) bulunmaktadır.

1990'lar Türkiye'de PKK sorunun gündeme oturduğu ve Kürt etnik kimliği üzerinde yoğun bir etki yapan değişimin yaşandığı yıllar olarak görülmektedir. Türkiye'deki bu çatışmalar ve etnik kimlik mücadelesi bağlamında devlet eliyle barışı özendirecek filmler yapılması ise uzlaştırıcı çabalar olarak görülmektedir. Bu bağlamda yapılan filmler, *Işıklar Sönmesin* (Reis Çelik, 1992), *Güneşe Yolculuk* (Yeşim Ustaoğlu, 1999), *Büyük Adam Küçük Aşk* (Handan İpekçi, 2001), *Fotoğraf* (Kazım Öz, 2001), *Yazı-Tura* (Uğur Yücel, 2004) olarak görülmektedir.

Araştırmanın Yöntem ve Örneklemi

Türk sineması, 1990'lı yıllar sonrasında var olan toplumsal şartların yansıması olarak, Kürt temasını konu alan filmlerle etnik köken olgusunu farklı bakış açıları ile izleyicisine sunmaktadır. Çalışmaya seçilen filmlerde—*Işıklar Sönmesin* (Reis Çelik, 1992), *Güneşe Yolculuk* (Yeşim Ustaoğlu, 1999), *Büyük Adam Küçük Aşk* (Handan İpekçi, 2001), *Fotoğraf* (Kazım Öz, 2001), *Yazı-Tura* (Uğur Yücel, 2004)—Kürt kimliği, Türk kimliğinin karşısında konumlandırılmakta, yaratılan ötekilik ve zıtlık kimliklerin sunumunu kolaylaştırmaktadır. Kürt etnik kimliği, Türk kimliğinin bir alt kimliği olmasına rağmen çalışma bu karşıtlıkları temel alarak Türk ve Kürt etnik kimliğinin temsilini incelemektedir. Bu eserler, etnik kimlik sorunsalını açıktan açığa eleştiren kurgusal filmler olarak, çoğunluğu Güneydoğu'daki sorunların biraz daha düzlüğe çıkmasından sonra Eurimages ve Kültür Bakanlığı destekli olarak "barış", "uyum", "birliktelik", "ötekilik", "farklılık" gibi duygular temel alınarak çekildiği görülmektedir.

Bu çalışmada filmlerin analizinde kullanılan ilk veri toplama tekniği, göstergebilim yaklaşımının içerisinde yer alan "Eyleyenler Örnekçesi"dir. Greimas'ın kuramına göre önemli olan işi yapan (eyleyen) kişi yani özne olarak görülmektedir. Örnekçeye göre filmlerimizdeki özne durumundaki bireyler ortaya çıkarılacak onlara içerik analizi uygulanacaktır. Böylece iki yöntem birbirlerini desteklemiş ve konuya bir bütünlük getirmiş olacaktır. Ayrıca analizlerde filmlerin teker teker parçalara bölünmesi daha sonra ise bu parçalardan bütüne gitmek; tüme varmak söz konusu olabilecektir. İçerik analizi ile genel hatlarıyla öznelerin cinsiyetleri, isimleri, dilleri, doğum yerleri gibi özellikleri ortaya konulmaya çalışılırken ayrıca Türklük ve Kürtlük bağlamında yaratılan ötekilik kavramı varsa filmlerin sundukları çözüm önerileri ortaya konmaya çalışılacaktır.

Temsil, bir nesnenin (sözgelimi bir kavram, kişi yada zamanın) yerine bir başkasını koyma, geçirme veya ikame etme anlamına gelmektedir. Diğer yandan temsil, bir şeyin, bir olgunun yada nesnenin, dışsal bir gerçekliğin başka bir düzlemde, dil yada düşüncede, aynen hiçbir anlam veya içerik kaybı olmadan yansıtılması, betimlenmesi anlamına gelmektedir (Cevizci, 1999, s. 839). Yani bir nesne (sözgelimi bir kavram, kişi yada zamanın) hakkındaki bir resim, fotoğraf yada herhangi bir görüntü, yazılı bir metin asla gerçekten o nesne değil o nesnenin görünüşünün yada onu temsil etme çabasındaki kişiye ifade ettiği şeyin yeniden kurulması olarak görülmektedir. Ayrıca temsil kavramı *"Göstergelerin anlamlarının yerine geçirilmesi"* (Cevizci, 1999, s. 839) durumunu da ifade etmektedir. Yani *"Temsil; imge ve metinlerin, temsil ettikleri orijinal kaynakları doğrudan yansıtmalarından ziyade onları yeniden kurmalarını anlatan bir terimdir"* (Marshall, 1999, s. 725).

Temsiller, içinde yer alınan kültürden öğrenilmekte, kültürün daha önceden tanımlamış olduğu şekliyle de içselleştirilmektedir. *"Walter Lipmann, önce görüp sonra tanımlamayız, önce tanımlar sonra görürüz diyor"* (Mutlu, 1998, s. 55). Böylece stereotip (basmakalıp) yargılar oluşturulmaktadır. *"Kültürel temsiller yalnızca psikolojik duruşları şekillendirmekle kalmaz, toplumsal gerçekliğin nasıl inşa edileceğine ilişkin olarak da, yani, toplumsal yaşamın ve toplumsal kurumların şekillendirilmesinde hangi figür ve sınırların baskın çıkacağı konusunda da çok önemli rol oynar"* (Ryan & Kellner, 1997, s. 37). Doğal algılamada anlam birey tarafından üretilmektedir. *"Medya gerçekliğin ses (dil) ve görüntü (resim) unsurlarına dayalı soyutlamaları kullanarak, gerçekliği kendisinden bağımsız bir mesaja (temsil) dönüştürür"* (Güneş, 1996, s. 102). Bu temsiller ise belirli ideolojiler çerçevesinde, her zaman gerçekliği yansıtmadığı gibi zaman zaman eksik yansıtabilmekte, gerçekliği temsil etmeyip yok sayabilip ya da yanlışlarıyla izleyiciyi yönlendirebilmekte böylece de stereotip yargılar oluşturabilmektedir.

Temsiller olumlu ve olumsuz kurularak gerçek saptırılabilmektedir. Ayrıca gerçekin temsili nitel yada nicel anlamda yanlış ve/veya yoğun yada düşük olarak temsil edilebilmektedir. Yanlış yansıtılmak kadar yansıtılmamanın yani mevcut bulunmamanın da anlam ifade ettiği görülmektedir. Toplumdaki grupların (yaş, ırk, meslek ve cinsiyet) temsil edilme biçimleri medyada belirginleşmekte, oluşmakta sonrada yinelenmelerle ve diğer yandan alternatif düşüncelerin engellenmesiyle bize sunulmakta birey ise sunulanı sorgulamadan kabul etmeyi öğrenmektedir. Temsiller bize neyi düşünmemiz gerektiğini çoğunlukla üstü kapalı olarak söylemek kullanılarak da hayatımızın birer parçası haline gelmektedir. Bu anlamda

Kürt etnik kimliğinin bu filmlerde nasıl kurulduğu ve insanların bilinçlerini nasıl şekillendirdiğinin de ortaya çıkarılması önem kazanmaktadır

Araştırmanın Veri ve Bulguları

Işıklar Sönmesin (1992, Reis Çelik): Güneydoğu'da olaylar henüz oldukça sıcak bir seyirde devam etmekteyken 1992 yılında yapılan *Işıklar Sönmesin* bu konuda yapılan ilk film olma önemini taşımaktadır. İki benzemez karakteri bir araya getirip, onların birbirlerinin mevcudiyetine bir anlamda mecbur kalmalarından yola çıkarak, illaki geliştirmek zorunda kaldıkları ilişkilerinin hikayesi, bu zıt ve uyumsuz karakterlerin kaçınılmaz olarak birbirlerini anlamaya başlaması, birbirlerine karşı hoş görülerini arttırmalarını sağlaması ve barış mesajları içermesi anlamında önemli yere sahip olmaktadır. Filmde askerler takip ettikleri örgüt mensuplarını yakalamak üzereyken çığ düşmekte, askerlerden Murat hariç, karşı taraftan ise Zazan ve örgüt lideri hariç herkes ölür. Böylece Yüzbaşı Murat (Tarık Tarcan) ile Seydo (Berhan Şimsek) zorunlu bir şekilde bir arada kalmak durumunda kalmaktadır.

Güneşe Yolculuk (1999, Yeşim Ustaoğlu): Film, gözaltında kaybolan babasını bulmak için İstanbul'a gelen ve bazı yasal olmayan işlere bulaşan Zorduç'lu Kürt Berzan ile su borularındaki kaçakları bulan Tire'li Mehmet'in İstanbul'da bir tesadüf sonucu karşılaşmaları sonrası gelişen dostluklarının hikayesi olarak görülmektedir.

Büyük Adam Küçük Aşk (2001, Handan İpekçi): İpekçi, ikinci filminde, toplumsal çalkantıların ortasında kalan küçük bir çocuğun dramını işlemekte, bu vesileyle 90'larda ülkemizde yaşanan ortamın bireyler üzerindeki etkilerini beyazperdeye yansıtmaktadır. "Handan İpekçi *Büyük Adam Küçük Aşk*'ta birbirini anlamamakta direnen iki toplumun, bir arada yaşamasının koşullarını sorguluyor. Karşı tarafa, kendi değerlerini, kendi kültürünü dayatmak yerine, onu anlamaya çalışmanın meziyetleri üstünde duruyor" (Sayar, 2001). Film ailesini kaybetmiş Hejar'ın yanına bırakıldığı avukatın polis baskınında öldürülmesinden sonra, küçük kızı Rıfat beyin yanına alması ve ardından onlar arasında gelişen sevgiyi anlatmaktadır.

Fotoğraf (2001, Kazım Öz): İstanbul otogarından otobüse binen iki gencin öyküsünü anlatan film, bu iki gencin daha sonra bir çatışmada karşı karşıya gelişiyle sonuçlanmaktadır. Biri asker olan diğeri Kürt milliyetçisi olan gençlerin içinde bulundukları durumun nedenleri yada aralarında gelişen dostluklarını derinlemesine incelemeyen film nesnel olmaktan çok öznel tavrıyla dikkatleri çekmektedir.

Yazı-Tura (2004, Uğur Yücel): Filmin iki kahramanı Güneydoğu'da askerliğini yapmış iki gazi olan Şeytan Rıdvan ve Hayalet Cevher'dir. Yönetmen *"Türkiyeli bir insan olarak, duygularımın, sorumluluğum bir yansıması"* (Dursun, 2004) dediği filmini 1999 yılında çekmiştir. İki karakterin öyküleri ayrı ayrı epizotlar halinde anlatılmaktadır. Birinci epizotta iki öykü birlikte ilerlemekte, yaklaşık 13 dakika süren bölümde, öyküleri anlatılacak karakterlerden kısa kesitler sunulmaktadır. İkinci epizot Rıdvan'ın öyküsü olarak karşımıza çıkmaktadır. Daha sonra üçüncü epizotta ise Hayalet Cevher'in öyküsü anlatılmaktadır. Çalışmada Hayalet Cevher'in öyküsü işlenmemektedir. Çalışma Rıdvan'ın öyküsünü Türklük-Kürtlük çerçevesinde incelemektedir. Filmde Rıdvan askerden sakat olarak gelmiştir üstelik psikolojisi de bozuktur. Rıdvan'ı intihar sürecine taşıyan olayların anlatıldığı film, Türk sinemasında, Türk askerinin de kaybedebileceği, sakat gelebileceği yada psikolojisinin bozulup onu intihara sürükleyen nedenler üzerine kafa yormakta bu anlamda kaybeden askerler üzerine çekilen ilk film olma özelliğiyle önemli bir yere sahip olmaktadır.

Filmlerin Analizi

Özneler ve Meslekleri:

Kimlik, Hegel'in köle-efendi diyalektiğinde yaptığı çözümlemeye benzer olarak toplumsal bir olgu olarak görülmektedir. Yani Hegel'in kişilerin kimlik kazanmasını birbirleriyle olan ilişkilerine bağlamasına benzer bir şekilde, toplumların kimlik kazanması da aynı ilişkiye bağlanabilmektedir. Toplumlarında kimlik edinmesi ancak başkaları vasıtasıyla olabilmektedir. *"Başkalık olmadan kimlik olmaz. Diğer bir deyişle, aidiyet ve kimlik, başkalık ve öteki ile tanımlanır anlamlanır"* (Yurdusev, 1997, s. 20). "Ben ve öteki" ayrımı, bütün kimlik kategorilerinde bulunmaktadır. Bir şeyin kimliği, başka bir şeyin kimliğine bağlı bulunmaktadır. Hegel'in köle-efendi diyalektiği ve ben-öteki ayrımı, bireyi tüm kimlik kategorilerinde yapılabilecek bir ötekileştirmeye götürmektedir. Türk kimliği de ötekini yaratarak kendini tanımlayabilmektedir. "Ben" Türk ve "Öteki" Türk olmayan olarak kendini tanımlayabilen farklılığı yaratan bu ikili düalizm olarak düşünülmektedir. Filmlerdeki eyleyenler, filmlerde yaratılan ötekilik bağlamında; Türk ve Kürt etnik kökeni olarak seçilmiştir. *Işıklar Sönmesin*'de özneler; Murat ve Seydo, *Güneşe Yolculuk*'ta Mehmet ve Berzan, *Büyük Adam Küçük Aşk*'ta Rıfat bey ve Hejar, *Fotoğraf*'ta Faruk Öztürk ve Ali Türkoğlu, *Yazı–Tura*'da Rıdvan ve Elif olarak saptanmaktadır. Bundan sonraki analizler bu ikililer baz alınarak yapılacaktır.

Özneler ve Meslekleri	Türk	Kürt Etnik Kimliği
Işıklar Sönmesin	Murat – Yüzbaşı/asker	Seydo /Örgüt mensubu
Güneşe Yolculuk	Mehmet	Berzan
Büyük Adam Küçük Aşk	Rıfat Bey – Emekli Yargıç	Hejar
Fotoğraf	Faruk Öztürk - Asker	Ali Türkoğlu /Kürt
Yazı-Tura	Şeytan Rıdvan–Asker (gazi)	Elif –Kürt terörist

***Tablo 1:** Özneler ve Meslekleri*

Filmlerden *Işıklar Sönmesin* Yüzbaşı, *Fotoğraf* Asker, *Yazı Tura* da Gazi/asker kullanılmakta, *Büyük Adam Küçük Aşk* ise emekli yargıç kullanılmaktadır. Ryan ve Kellner özellikle muhafazakar bakış açısına göre, ulusal azametin askeri güç kullanımından geçtiğini ifade etmektedir (Ryan & Kellner, 1997, s. 302). Ulusal eril itibari temsil eden askerlerin dayanıklılığı ve cesareti bu noktada önemli bir veri olarak karşımızda durmaktadır. *Işıklar Sönmesin*'de Yüzbaşı Murat karakteristik yapısı itibariyle kibar, sevimli, yakışıklı, ince, anlayışlı, uzlaşmacı, adil, becerikli bir Türk askeri olarak sunulmaktadır. *Fotoğraf* ise birbirlerine benzer yaratılan askerlerin İstanbullu, neredeyse aynı yaşlarda (1975 ve 1973) olduğu görülmekte ayrıca ikisinin de gelecekten korktuğu, kaygılandığı, yaşayacaklarından dolayı heyecan içerisinde yolculuklarına devam ettiği görülmektedir. *Yazı-Tura* filminde ise iktidarını kaybetmiş (bacağı yok) bir gazi karşımıza çıkmaktadır. *Büyük Adam Küçük Aşk*'ta ise Rıfat bey, emekli yargıçtır. Afyonkarahisar'lı oluşu, Cumhuriyet okuması ise onun demokratik ve milliyetçi yapısını destekler niteliktedir. Diğer yandan var olan tek oğlunun yurtdışında olması ise bu durumla çelişki içindedir. Asker motifine uymayan tek film *Güneşe Yolculuk*'taki Mehmet karakteridir.

Kürt etnik kimliğini temsil eden Seydo, görünüm itibariyle esmer, bıyıklı, başında poşusu olan biridir. Diğer yandan kızgın, öfkeli kendisini milleti uğruna feda edecek biri olarak gösterilmektedir. Seydo'daki kızgınlık Berzan'da da bulunmaktadır. Berzan dışlanmış, itilmiş, yoksul, çaresiz ama umutları olan, kendi haklarını savunacak bilinç düzeyine erişmiş biri olarak görülmektedir. Yapı itibariyle o da esmer, kara kaş kara gözdür. Ali ve Berzan rolünü oynayan Nazmi Kırık'tır. Ali sakin görünümlü, kibar, temkinli birisidir. Hejar, beş yaşında bir Diyarbakır'ın Lice ilçesinde doğmuş bir Kürt kızıdır. Bildiği tek dil Kürtçe'dir. Görünüş olarak da etnik kimliğini yansıtacak özelliklere sahiptir; kara kaş, kara göz, esmer uzun saçları arkadan ikiye örülmüştür. Kırmızı elbisesi onun altında sarı tişörtü ile rengarenk görülmektedir. Elleri kınalı, kulağında ekonomik durumunu ifade eden altın küpe yerine takılmış ipler vardır. Elif'in karakterine dair özelliklerinden bahsedilmemekte ancak diğer karakterler gibi esmer biri olarak karşımıza çıkmaktadır. Diğer yandan filmde bu karakterleri karşı tarafta konumlandıran onların siyasi duruşları olarak görülmektedir. Seydo kendini örgüt mensubu olarak tanımlamakta, Berzan'ın ölüm oruçlarına onay verdiği, eylemlerde bulunduğu görülmekte, Ali ve Elif bir çatışmada askerlerin karşı safında yer almaktadır.

Yeşim Ustaoğlu, *Güneşe Yolculuk* filminde Kürt sorununu ötekilik kavramı içerisine sıkıştırmaktadır. Böylece Kürtleri, Türklerin karşısına koymakta; zenciler, eşcinseller, çingeneler, göçmenler gibi Kürtleri de öteki olarak almakta ve bir çözüm yolu önermemektedir. Bir kimlik arayışı içinde olan Tire'li Mehmet'in aksine Kürt Berzan'ın böyle bir kimlik arayışı söz konusu görülmemektedir. Üstelik filmin sonunda Tire'li Mehmet'in kimliğini yavaş yavaş değiştirmesi de ilginç görülmektedir. Mehmet, Kürt arkadaşları ile tefler eşliğinde halay çekerken, acemi şekilde sallanmakta, bariz bir şekilde oyuna eşlik edememektedir. Ancak arkadaşını kaybettiğinde canı yanmakta, acı çekmekte, öfkelenmekte, isyan etmektedir. Bir sonraki sahnede ise aynı seslerle artık onlar gibi halay çekebilmektedir. Bunun nedeni ise olsa olsa hayatına kattığı acılar olabilmekte, tüm yaşananlar onu, arkadaşlarından birisi yapmaktadır. Bu düşünce filmin sonunda iyice vurgulanmaktadır. Diğer yandan Mehmet'in teni onun ötekiliğini arttıran bir öğe olarak sık sık vurgulanmakta, *"Nerelisin?"* tarzı sorularla sık sık karşılaşmaktadır. Öteki olarak vurgulanan Tire'li Mehmet filmde saçını sarıya boyamak zorunda kalmaktadır.

"Abi senin saçın niye sarı?

Senin saçın niye siyah?

Allah yaratmış.

Allah benim saçımı da böyle yaratmış.

Ne biçim yaratmış ya?"

diyen çocukla Mehmet'in konuşmasından, onun ötekilikten kurtulamadığını, bu haliyle de Batıda olduğu gibi Doğuda da dışlandığı görülmektedir. Böylece ona da bu durumu kabul etmekten başka çare kalmamaktadır. Sonunda saçının boyasını çıkarmakta kendisine nereli olduğunu soran komandoya da Zorduç'lu olduğunu ifade etmektedir.

Tarihin ilk dönemlerinden beri toplumlar kendilerini diğer toplumlardan farklılıklarıyla tanımlamışlardır. Bir kimlik ötekinden ayrılan özellikleriyle tanımlanırsa, bu farklılıklar çok fazla vurgulanırsa, bu vurgu, ötekinin olumsuz bir biçimde nitelenmesine, dışlanmasına, aşağılanmasına ve inkarına götürür (Yurdusev, 1997, s. 22). Buna göre bu ötekileştirme çerçevesinde Mehmet'in teni, kendisiyle aynı kimliğe sahip diğer şeylerle ortak yanlarına bakmaktan çok kendisini ötekinden ayıran yanlarına bakarak kendisine tam zıt bir ten rengi yaratmaktadır. Mehmet'i Kürtleştirerek tanımlamakta Mehmet, Kürt olmasa da Kürt olmayı kabul etmektedir. Tunca Arslana *göre Güneşe Yolculuk* bu anlamda kardeşlik ve birliktelilik gibi bir mesaj vermemektedir. "Ezilenlerin, hep birlikte 'en ezilen'in kimliğine bürünmesinden başka çözüm olmadığını savunuyor, 'Ben de zenciyim', 'Ben de çingeneyim', 'Ben de eşcinselim' gibi 'Ben de Kürdüm' denmesini öneriyor. Bu 'bilince' erişmemiş 'alt tabaka' ise sağa sola saldıran milliyetçi futbol fanatikleri ya da gözaltından çıkan Mehmet'i kovan oda arkadaşlarından ibaret gösteriliyor filmde" (Arslan, 2000, para. 3).

Öznelerin Cinsiyeti ve Dilleri:

Tüm filmlerde Türk kimliğinin temsilcisi durumundaki karakterler, erkek cinsel kimliği ile görülmektedir. Temsil; göstergebilim, dilbilim, Marksizm ve feminizm içinde önemli bir kavram durumunda, anlamın kurulması yönüne işaret etmektedir. Feministler temsilin stereotip toplumsal cinsiyet rollerini yarattığını, eril söylemin oluşturduğu kadının ikincil konumunu onayladığını öne sürmektedirler. Onlara göre tüm medya imgeleri örneğin televizyon dizileri, reklamlar ve haberler bu yönde bilinçaltımızı ve hareketlerinizi şekillendirmektedir. Kürt etnik kimliği *Büyük Adam Küçük Aşk*'ta 6 yaşında Kürt bir kız, *Yazı-Tura*'da sevdiği kız olarak bir Kürt genç kız olarak seçildiği görülmektedir. Böylece etnik kimliği ile öteki olan Kürt birey, diğer yandan cinsel kimliği olan kadınlıkla da öteki durumu bir kez daha vurgulanmaktadır.

Öznelerin Cinsiyeti	Türk	Kürt Etnik Kimliği
Işıklar Sönmesin	Erkek	Erkek
Güneşe Yolculuk	Erkek	Erkek
Büyük Adam Küçük Aşk	Erkek	Kadın
Fotoğraf	Erkek	Erkek
Yazı Tura	Erkek	Kadın

Tablo 2: *Öznelerin Cinsiyeti*

Yazı–Tura filmi ise "… Güneydoğu'daki savaşı, 'erkekliği kanıtlamaya olan ihtiyacı' ile ilişkilendiriyor ve nasıl bulunacağını bilmediğimiz o büyük gücün, tezahür ettiği hallerden biri. Bir yerde iktidarı sağlamlaştırmanın başka yolu kalmayınca sürekli kanıtlanmaya çalışılan tek şey de erkeklik oluyor" (Radikal.com.tr., cumartesi eki, Erkekler de ağlar!, 2.10.2004). Filmler Türk karakterlerin hepsini Türkçe konuştururken öteki kabul edilen Kürt etnik kökenli bireyleri hem Türkçe hem de Kürtçe konuşturmaktadır. Karakterlerimizden bir tek Hejar, Türkçe bilmemekte ana dili olarak Kürtçe'yi kullanmaktadır. Böylece etnik kimliği ile öteki olan karakterler dilleri ile de ötekiliklerini sürdürmektedir. Fotoğraf filmi bu anlamda diğerlerinden farklı seyirde gitmekte, filmin açılış sahnesinde söylenen 10. yıl marşına Kürtçe alt yazı yazarak filmin dilinin Kürtçe olduğuna gönderme yapmaktadır.

Öznelerin Dilleri	Türk	Kürt Etnik Kimliği
Işıklar Sönmesin	Türkçe	Kürtçe - Türkçe
Güneşe Yolculuk	Türkçe	Kürtçe - Türkçe
Büyük Adam Küçük Aşk	Türkçe	Kürtçe
Fotoğraf	Türkçe	Kürtçe - Türkçe
Yazı Tura	Türkçe	Türkçe – Bilinmiyor

Tablo 3: *Öznelerin Dilleri*

Bir iletişim aracı olarak dilin önemini vurgulayıp kültürel dayatmacılık yerine kültürlerarası iletişimi öneren Handan İpekçi, *Büyük Adam Küçük Aşk*'ta, Kürtçe'ye karşı ön yargılı olan Rıfat bey tarafından defalarca kez *"Türkçe konuşacaksın Türkçe! Bu memlekette Türkçe konuşulur"* yaptırdığı ikazlar sonrası karakterine yavaş yavaş Kürtçe öğretmeye başlarken diğer yandan Hejar'a Kürtçe öğretmektedir.

Öznelerin Doğum Yerleri:

Filmlerde karakterlerin doğum yerleri ise Doğulu ve Batılı kimliği çerçevesinde yerleştirilmiştir. *Büyük Adam Küçük Aşk*'ta yargıç, Afyonkarahisar doğumludur. Kurtuluş savaşının önemli cephelerinden birinde doğmuş olması ise onun kimliğini bütünleyen parçalardan biri haline gelmiştir. Diğer yandan Küçük Hejar Diyarbakır'ın Lice İlçesinin Zenge köyünde doğmuştur. Özellikle bir dönem yoğun çatışmaların yaşandığı yer olarak her gün haberlere yansıyan şehir doğumlu olması ise onun kimliğinin bir diğer tamamlayanı olarak görülmektedir. *Güneşe Yolculuk* da bu zıtlığı yaratmaktadır. İzmir'e yakın bir ilçeden Tire'den olan Mehmet ile Irak sınırına yakın olduğu belirtilen bir köy; Susuz /Zorduç doğumlu olan Berzan'ın dostluğu anlatılmaktadır. *Yazı–Tura* filminde de Nevşehir-Göreme'nin karşısına Bingöl şehrindeki bir Kürt kız denk düşmektedir. Doğu-Batı zıtlığı bozmak isteyen ve bu vatan hepimizin demek isteyen *Işıklar Sönmesin* ise Yüzbaşı Murat'ı Ardahan doğumlu yapmakta diğer Örgüt mensubunun nereli olduğuna dair direk bilgi vermemektedir. Bununla beraber *Fotoğraf* ise İstanbul'dan yola çıkan iki arkadaşı ters gruplara oturtmaktadır.

Öznelerin Doğum Yerleri	Türk	Kürt Etnik Kimliği
Işıklar Sönmesin	Ardahan	Belirtilmemiş/ Doğulu
Güneşe Yolculuk	Tire	Susuz / Zorduç
Büyük Adam Küçük Aşk	Afyon	Diyarbakır-Lice-Zenge köyü
Fotoğraf	İstanbul	İstanbul
Yazı Tura	Göreme/ Nevşehir	Bingöl

Tablo 4: *Öznelerin Doğum Yerleri*

Filmlerde Güneydoğu olarak tabir edilen mekan çoğunlukla karlı, kıraç, dağlarla temsil edilmektedir. *Fotoğraf* filminde Doğu temsili, yüksek dağlar, ovalar, sürekli araba bekleyen yolcular, yıkık-dökük evler, panzerler, dar sokaklar yoksul insanlar gösterilmekteler. *Güneşe Yolculuk* filmi ise Doğu-Batı tezadını İstanbul'dan Susuz'a yapılan yolculuk sırasında daha da net ortaya çıkarmaktadır. Bu yolculuk sırasında iklimler değişmekte, yolda yağmur yağmakta sonra ise karlı yollar görülmektedir. Kıraç topraklardan, geniş ovalardan, pamuk tarlalarından, yüksek dağlardan geçilmektedir. Mehmet doğuya giderken pek çok ulaşım aracı değiştirmektedir. Önce pikapla başlayan yolculukta sırasıyla dolmuş,tren, at arabasıyla devam etmektedir. Araçlar modern olandan ilkel olana doğru değişmektedir. Yolda bir kamyonete yanaşıp nereye gittiklerini sorduğunda aldığı cevap oranın yokluğunu, çaresizliğini de anlatmaktadır. *"Babamın Türkçe'si yok! İstanbul'a gidilecek."*

İstanbul'a yapılan göç ve büyük şehirden beklenen umutlar, koca bir aileyi yerinden yurdundan etmektedir. Yolda gördüğü yasak gazete satan Kürt çocuklar, boşalmış köyler, yıkılmış binalar, sular altında kalmış evler, panzerlerin dönüp durduğu şehirler, beklenen ama çok seyrek gelen araçlar, korkan insanlar da güneydoğu temsili olarak karşımıza çıkmaktadır.

Güvenlik Güçlerinin Temsili; Asker, Polis, vd.:

Güvenlik güçlerinin temsili anlamında filmler (*Işıklar Sönmesin* hariç) zıtlıklardan faydalanmış görülmektedir. Böylece siyahın yanında beyazın daha kolay seçilmesine benzer kötü gösterilen güvenlik güçleri karakterlere dair pek şeyin netleşmesini sağlamış gözükmektedir. *Güneşe Yolculuk* filminde iyi tek bir güvenlik gücüne bir istisna hariç rastlanmamaktadır. O istisna ise *"Keşke asker olarak gönderilmeseydim"* diyen Tireli komanda olarak görülmektedir. Filmde haberlerde görülen güvenlik güçleri dışında karakterlerin muhatap olduğu polis, askerler vd. söz konusu olmaktadır. Baskıcı, sert ve kötü gösterilen polislerin işlerini tam olarak yapamadığı da ekranlara yansımaktadır; Örneğin Şanlıurfa'ya giderken aramalarda polis görevini eksik yapmakta Berzan'ın sakladığı kimliğin olmadığını fark etmemektedir. Arzu, Mehmet'i ararken karakola gittiğinde, oradaki polisler de sevimsiz gösterilmektedir. Arzu Berzan'a; *"Niye kendin gitmedin? Yoksa korkuyor musun onlardan?"* diyerek polisleri kastetmektedir. Güvenlik güçlerinden korkuya dair başka cümleler de filmde bulunmaktadır; Mehmet gözaltında kalıp çıktıktan sonra arkadaşları onu bu korku yüzünden istememektedirler: *"Kalmaya devam ederlerse hepimizin anasını bellicekler."*cümlesine ek olarak sorulan *"Ne demek oluyor ki bu?"* sorusunun cevabı olarak da *" Hepimizin götü belada oluyor"* cevabı gelmektedir. Adli morgdaki çalışan da bu korkuyu desteklemektedir: *"Sonra beni, bu içeri gördüklerinden beter ederler."* demekte sonraki cümlesinde ise *" .. olmaz sen beni ipe mi göndereceksin".* diye söylemektedir. Zorduç'a arkadaşını götürmekte olan Mehmet ise lavabo dönüşünde bir polis tarafından aracının arandığını görmekte üstelik *"Geç bakalım beni önümüzdeki kasabaya bırak"* diye emreden polise cevap verememektedir. Yolda önünü kesen askerler de yine oldukça sert olarak yansıtılmaktadır. Tren de yine arama yapan polisler de korku unsuru olarak çıkmaktadır. Diğer yandan yollarda durmadan Mehmet'i takip eden kırmızı renkli X işareti de devletin varlığını göstermekte, gözetleme kuleleri de bunu onaylıyor görülmektedir.

Büyük Adam Küçük Aşk filminde ise polis *"3 şahıs ex bir arkadaşımız yaralı"* diye telsizle durumu bildirdikten sonra avukatın *"ateş etmeyin"* dediği duyulmakta, sesin arkasından gelen bir el silah sesi yargısız infaza örnek teşkil etmektedir. Filmde polis, çatışmada ölmemesine rağmen herkesi öldü diye bildirmekte, üstelik yaşayan birini yargısız vurulmaktadır. Polisler evi ararken, sevimsiz tavırlar içerisinde gösterilmekteler; kaba, umursamaz, duyarsız ifade edilmektedir. Örneğin radyoyu kurcalamakta "Cumhuriyetin 75. yılında" oynanan Beşiktaş maçına kulak kesmekte, sanki biraz önce yaşanan hiçbir şeyi o yaşamamış hiç etkilenmemiş gibi gösterilmektedir. Polislerin yargısız infazına tanık olan yargıç küçük kızın kurtarılmasını şaşkınlık içinde karşılamaktadır *"İnanmıyorum, görmemişler".* (Biraz sonra çocuğu azarlarken de *"polise git de aklın başına gelsin"* demektedir.) Polise ait olumsuz tavır polisin elinde taşıdığı silahla güçlendirilmekte; Rıfat beyi duvara dayadığında elinde olan silah, kapıyı açtığında da elinde görülmektedir. Diğer polis ise alt komşuyu *"Nereye teyze? Sonra teyze! Hadi"* diye tersleyerek emrivaki bir şekilde eve sokmaktadır. Polis *"Yoksa tanıyor muydun karşıdakileri?"* diye ön yargı kalıpları içerisinde karşısındaki yaşlı bir kadını suçlamaktadır. Bir diğer sahnede daktilo başında *"Polis devletindeki hukuk devleti mi..."* diye daktilo başında yazdığı yazıyla durum üzerinde izleyiciyi düşünmeye davet etmektedir. Küçük Hejar'ın otomatik tavırları, korkuları, dışarıya çıkmaya cesaret edemeyişi, telsiz seslerinden korkuşu, ve üniformalı askerin fotoğrafını (Rıfat Beyin oğlu) onun daha önce yaşanmışlığı ile ilişkilendirilmekte, polise karşı olumsuz tavrı desteklemektedir.

Işıklar Sönmesin filminde ise askerler oldukça kibar özenli konumlandırılmaktadır. *"Teslim ol çağrısı yapmadan kimsenin ateş etmesini istemiyorum."* diyen duyarlı asker *"Ben infaz mangası değilim. Suçunuzun hesabını mahkemede verirsiniz. Sizin hukukunuzla, devlet hukukunu bir mi tutuyorsunuz?* diyerek adil, diğer yandan *"Herhalde bu arkadaşını bırakacak değiliz al arkadaşını"* diyerek Zazan'ı kurtarma çalışmalarında destek olması ile de iyi niyetli, insancıl olarak gösterilmektedir. *Fotoğraf* filminde ise askerler ayak çekimiyle kıyafetleri gibi tek tip haline getirilmektedir. Üstelik girdikleri çatışmada ölenlerin yanında fotoğraf çektirecek kadar hasta olarak sunulmaktadır. Diğer yandan asker çekildikleri fotoğrafları "Savaş" adlı kardeşine göndermekte, yeni bir nesil bu fotoğraflarla ve "şavaş, savaş" diye büyütülmekte olduğu ekranlara yansımaktadır. *Yazı-Tura* filminde ise gazi kazandığı yerde kaybetmeye başlamıştır. Buradaki askerin psikolojisi bozuktur, üstelik iktidarını kaybetmiştir.

SONUÇ

Yapılan içerik analizi sonucu seçilmiş olan filmlerde Türklük ve Kürtlük birbirlerinin ötekisi olarak temsil edilmektedir. Cinsel kimlik olarak Kürt etnik kökenli birey, filmlerin üçünde erkek, ikisinde kadın olarak konumlandırılmaktadır. Ayrıca temsil edilen Kürtler –Hejar hariç- bir örgütte, siyasal bir eylemde, dağ başında bir çatışmada gösterilmektedir. Bu bireylerden üçü ise film sonunda öldürülmektedir. Görünüm itibariyle esmer, kara kaş kara göz temsil edilen Kürt etnik kimliğine dahil bireyler çoğunlukla poşu kullanan bireyler olarak sunulmaktadır.

Güneşe Yolculuk filmi ötekilik temelli oturttuğu öyküsüne herhangi bir öneri sunmamakta aksine insanlara bu durumu kabullenmeyi çözüm olarak sunmaktadır. *Büyük Adam Küçük Aşk* filmi ise insanları hümanist bir bakış açısıyla ön yargılardan uzak, birbirlerini sevmeye ve kabullenmeye çağırmaktadır. *Işıklar Sönmesin* Türkler ve Kürtler arasında olması gereken kardeşlik, barış ve dayanışmayı önermektedir. *Fotoğraf* filmi Türk- Kürt barışından ve kardeşliğinden çok Kürt yanlısı bir tutum çizmektedir. *Yazı-Tura* filmi Türk askerine dair var olan imajın görüldüğü gibi olmadığına işaret ederek, onların da kazandığı yerde başlayan yenilgilerinden bahsetmektedir.

Çalışmada temsillerin toplumsal yapıyla paralel işlediği, çekilen filmlere yönetmenlerinin hayat görüşlerinin yansıdığı görülmektedir. Film sayısındaki azlık Kürtlük ve temsili konusunda genellemelere varmayı güçleştirdiği görülmektedir. Hollywood sinemasının Amerikan toplumsal yapısını, çeşitli görüş açıları ile eleştirilebildiği görülmektedir; Amerika'nın katılmış olduğu savaşlar, giden ve dönen askerlerin psikolojileri, barışçıl veya ırkçı yaklaşımları ya da farklı etnik kültürlerin sinemaya yansımasına sıklıkla rastlanılmaktadır. Türkiye'de de etnik kökenlere dair çeşitli bakış açıları ve temalarda filmlerin yapılması da konunun tabu olarak algılanmasının yok olmasına neden olacağı gibi insanların birbirlerini tanıması daha barışçıl çözüm önerilerin oluşması neden olacaktır.

Kaynakça

Arslan, T. (2000, 7 Mart) Gerçek ve güneş yanığı. *Radikal*, http://www.radikal.com.tr/2000/03/07/kultur/ger.shtml (Son erişim 1 Ocak 2007).

Bruinessen, M. V. (2000). *Kürtlük, Türklük, Alevilik* (Çev. H. Yurdakul). İstanbul: İletişim Yayınları.

Burton, G. (1995). *Görünenden fazlası; medya analizlerine giriş* (Çev. Nefin Dinç). İstanbul: Alan Yayıncılık.

Cevizci, A. (1999). *Paradigma, felsefe sözlüğü*. İstanbul: Ekin Yayınları.

Dursun, E. (2004, 18 Ekim). Paramparça hayatlar üzerine ihtimal hesapları. *Aksiyon 515* http://www.aksiyon.com.tr/detay.php?id=16901 (Son erişim 1 Ocak 2007).

Güneş, S. (1996). *Medya ve kültür, sessiz yığınların kültürel intiharları*. Konya: Vadi Yayınları.

Gökçe, B. (2004). *Türkiye'nin toplumsal yapısı ve toplumsal kurumlar*, (Güncelleştirilmiş ve genişletilmiş 2. Baskı). Ankara: Savaş Yayınevi.

Güçhan, G. (1992). *Toplumsal değişme ve Türk sineması*. Ankara: İmge Kitabevi.

Gültekin, A. İ. (1994). *Kürt gerçeği*. Ankara: Aktuğ Matbaası.

Maktav, H. (2006). Vatan, millet, sinema. *Birikim 207*, 71-83. http://www.birikimdergisi.com/birikim/dergiyazi.aspx?did=1&dsid=323&dyid=4852 (Son erişim 1 Ocak 2007).

Marshall, G. (1999). *Sosyoloji sözlüğü* (Çev. Osman Akınhay, Derya Kömürcü). Ankara: Bilim ve Sanat Yayınları.

Mutlu, E. (1998) *İletişim sözlüğü* (3. Basım). Ankara: Ark Yayınları.

Önder, A. T. (2007). *Türkiye'nin etnik yapısı* (25. basım, genişletilmiş). Ankara: Fark yayınları.

Erkekler de Ağlar! (2004). *Radikal Cumartesi eki*, (2.10.2004).

Ryan, M & Kellner,D. (1997). *Politik kamera* (Çev. Elif Özsayar). İstanbul: Ayrıntı Yayınları.

Yurdusev, A. N. (1997). *Avrupa kimliğinin oluşumu ve Türk kimliği* (Yayıma Haz: Atila Eralp). Ankara: İmge Yayınevi.

Rahatlatıcı ve Rahatsız Edici Filmler

Zeynep Özarslan
Yabancı Diller Yüksek Okulu
Yıldız Teknik Üniversitesi
zeynep.ozarslan@gmail.com

Giriş

Sinema tarihi boyunca üretilen filmlerin "rahatlatıcı" ya da "rahatsız edici" olarak adlandırılması, genel sınıflandırma yöntemlerinin, yani ülkeye, akıma, yönetmene ya da türe göre yapılan sınıflandırmaların yanısıra ideolojik bir bakışı da gerektirmektedir. Toplumsal iletişim sürecinde toplumsal ve kültürel pratik olarak sinema, toplumdaki egemen ve muhalif kültürlerin mücadele ettiği bir alan olarak yorumlandığında "rahatlatıcı ya da rahatsız edici filmler" başlığında belirleyici olan aslında egemen veya muhalif grupların filme bakışıdır. Bu bağlamda, anaakım sinema içinde yer alan filmler, varolan toplumsal sistemin varolması muhtemel sistemlerin içinde en iyisi olduğu yönünde telkinlerde bulunduğundan, o toplumda egemen olan sınıfın bakışına göre oldukça "rahatlatıcı" bir işleve sahiptir. Diğer bir deyişle, bu filmler toplumdaki iki farklı kesimi, yani halkı ve iktidardaki güçleri rahatlatmaktadır. Çünkü bu rahatlatıcı filmler, bir yandan insanların gündelik sıkıntılarını unutup eğlenmesine, zaman geçirmesine olanak tanıyarak "toplumsal huzur"a katkıda bulunmakta, diğer yandan da egemen sınıfların ideolojisini ve kültürünü yeniden üreterek egemenin iktidarını sağlamlaştırmaktadır. Ancak, iktidarın bakışına göre rahatlatıcı olan bu filmler muhalif söylem ve eylemler geliştirerek iktidarla mücadele eden insanlar için "rahatsız edici" olabilmektedir. Çünkü muhalif bakışla aslında bu filmler genellikle mikro yaşam alanlarından seçtiği öykülerinde sanal gerilimler yaratarak filmin sonunda bu sanal gerilimleri çözüme kavuşturduğundan izleyicilerine yanılsamalı ve anlık rahatlamalar sağlamaktadır. Başka bir ifadeyle, bu filmler mikro yaşamları yani bireysel yaşamları, makro yaşamla yani toplumsal yaşamla ilintilendirmediği için, varolan toplumsal sorunları ve de bu sorunların olası çözümlerini sunmadığı için, yaşamın sorgulanmasını engellemekte ve daha güzel bir toplum hayalini üretmediği için kalıcı bir rahatlamaya hizmet etmemekte, bu nedenle de "rahatsız edici filmler" olarak yorumlanabilmektedir. Benzer şekilde muhalif öğeler taşıyan filmler de egemen sınıfı temsil eden ya da destekleyen insanlar için "rahatsız edici" olabilmektedir. Çünkü muhalif filmler, hergün deneyimlenen ekonomik, politik, kültürel sıkıntıları, yaşanan acıları göstererek, içinde yaşanılan toplumsal sistemin aslında varsayıldığı gibi sorunsuz olmadığını gösterdiklerinden iktidara göre toplumsal huzuru tehdit etmektedirler. Ayrıca bu filmler, egemen güçlerce kurgulanan ve de yaşantılanan gerçeklik olmak üzere iki farklı gerçeklik olduğunu anlatmakta ve iktidarın kurgusunu parçalamaya ve yeniden kurgulamaya yardımcı olmaktadır. Yani toplumsal sorunların çözülmesi ya da gerçeklerin dönüştürülmesi durumunda yaşanması muhtemel gerçekleri anlatarak varolan toplumsal yapıların ötesinde daha insani bir toplum hayalini desteklemekte ve böylelikle toplumsal bilinçte farkındalık geliştirilmesine katkıda bulunmaktadır. Bu nedenlerle de muhalif öğeler taşıyan filmler toplumda muhalif düşünceye, yaşayışa sahip olan insanlar için oldukça "rahatlatıcı" olabilmektedir. Kısacası muhalif öğeler barındıran filmlerin üretim, dağıtım ve gösterim aşamalarında ideolojik ve kültürel olarak toplumdaki egemen güçleri rahatsız ettiği ileri sürülebilir.

Sinemada İktidar Mücadelesi

Her devlet toplumsal yapıyı belirleyebilmek ve toplum üzerinde hegemonyasını kurabilmek için yaşanan zamana, yaşam koşullarına ve üretim biçimlerine göre farklı iktidar biçimleri, uygulamaları ve mekanizmaları geliştirir. Bu bağlamda toplumsal yaşamda tek bir iktidar ve de tek bir muhalefet yoktur, yani tarihe, coğrafyaya, üretim ilişkilerine ve toplumsal ilişkilere göre değişen iktidarlar ve muhalefet etme biçimleri vardır. Yaşanan döneme ve coğrafyaya göre iktidarın uygulamaları, ilişkileri ve yönlendirmeleri değişir ve bu durum bir anlamda da bunlara denk gelen direniş biçimlerinin oluşmasına da yol açar. Aynı şekilde yine farklı direniş biçimleri de iktidarın sürekli kendini sorgulamasına ve yenilemesine neden olur. Kısacası iktidar ilişkileri süreklidir, değişken ve dinamiktir ve karşılaştığı ya da karşılaşması muhtemel direniş biçimlerine karşı sürekli kendini yenileyen bir yapıdadır.

İnsanlık tarihi boyunca muhalif hareketler toplumsal yaşamın ekonomik, ideolojik, kültürel vb. alanlarında iktidarla mücadele eder. Yani muhalifler eşitsiz üretim ve güç ilişkilerine ve de dayatılan yaşam kouşullarına karşı bütünlüklü bir mücadele yürütmeye çalışır, bunun için tarihsel, ekonomik ve coğrafik koşullara göre farklı stratejiler geliştirir. Bu bağlamda tıpkı iktidar ilişkileri gibi muhalefet etme biçimleri de sabit ve değişmez değildir, akışkan ve dinamiktir, kendini sürekli sorgular ve yeniler. Kısacası muhalif hareketler iktidarın sunduğu gerçeklerin aslında yaşantılanan gerçekler değil iktidarın bir kurgusu olduğunu göstermek ve karşı-hegemonya geliştirmek için kendi kurumlarını, uygulamalarını ve mekanizmalarını kurar. Bu bağlamda da toplumsal yaşamın bir parçası olarak kültürel yaşam da iktidar mücadelesinin yaşandığı bir alan haline gelir. Günümüz kapitalist toplumlarında sinema hem bir sanat hem de bir endüstri olarak toplumların kültürel yaşamlarında bu mücadelelerin yoğun olarak yaşandığı bir alandır. Çünkü "Film bir yanıyla halihazırdaki ekonomik ilişkiler sistemi içinde üretilen bir üründür, ... bu onu değişim değerine sahip olan bir metaya dönüştürür. Diğer yandan da sistemin maddi ürünü olması nedeniyle sistemin ideolojik bir ürünüdür de" (Comolli ve Narboni, 1976, s. 24).

Sinemada egemen ideolojiyi destekleyen sinemasal üretimler anaakım –egemen, ticari, popüler- sinemayı oluşturur. Tüm dünyadaki sinemasal üretimler incelendiğinde Hollywood sinemasının anaakım sinema olduğu ileri sürülebilir, ayrıca her toplumda popüler olan ticari sinemalar da yine egemen sinema olarak yorumlanabilir. Ancak anaakım sinema sinemasal üretimlerin tümünü kapsayan bütünlüklü homojen bir yapıda değildir. Tıpkı toplumsal yaşamda iktidarın boşluklarından sızarak iktidarın yapısını parçalamaya çalışan muhalif güçler gibi anaakım sinema dışında sinemasal üretimler yapan sinemacılar da içinde bulundukları döneme, coğrafyaya ve yaşam koşullarına göre farklı muhalif öğeler barındıran filmler yaparak muhalif sinemaların gelişimine katkıda bulunurlar. Hem anaakım sinemacıları hem de egemen güçleri rahatsız eden muhalif sinema kısaca muhalif ideolojinin üretildiği sinemadır. Muhalif sinema, iktidardaki ideolojinin kurgusu olan toplumsal gerçeklerin hergün deneyimlenen hakikatler olmadığını gösterir ve iktidarın kurgusunu parçalayarak, bozarak varolan toplumsal hakikatler doğrultusunda yeniden kurgular. Yani yaşananlara eleştirel bir bakışla yaklaşır. Egemen ideolojinin yoksaydığı ya da "öteki", "normal dışı" olarak adlandırdığı bütün sınıfsal, etnik, cinsel, kültürel kimlikleri kucaklar, herkesin eşit olduğunu savunur. Kısacası daha insani bir yaşam için çağrıda bulunur. Sonuç olarak, egemen ideolojinin söylem ve uygulamalarına karşı toplumun farkındalık düzeyini geliştirmeyi amaçlayan muhalif filmler egemen ideolojiyi temsil edenleri ve destekleyenleri rahatsız eder.

Sinemanın İdeolojik İşlevi

İdeoloji sadece düşünce, uslamlama bağlamında değil aynı zamanda toplumdaki üretim ve mülkiyet ilişkileri bağlamında da değerlendirilmesi gereken bir sorunsaldır. Çünkü üretim biçimi yani ekonomik altyapı üstyapıyı da belirler. Bu bağlamda örneğin günümüz kapitalist toplum sisteminde maddi üretim araçlarına sahip olan egemen güçler toplumun düşünsel gücünü de belirler.

> "Egemen sınıfın düşünceleri, bütün çağlarda, egemen düşüncelerdir, başka bir deyişle, toplumun egemen *maddi* gücü olan sınıf, aynı zamanda egemen *zihinsel* güçtür. Maddi üretim araçlarını elinde bulunduran sınıf, aynı zamanda, zihinsel üretimin araçlarını da emrinde bulundurur, bunlar o kadar birbirinin içine girmiş durumdadırlar ki, kendilerine zihinsel üretim araçları verilmeyenlerin düşünceleri de aynı zamanda bu egemen sınıfa bağımlıdır. Egemen düşünceler, egemen maddi ilişkilerin fikirsel ifadesinden başka bir şey değildir, egemen düşünceler, fikirler biçiminde kavranan maddi, egemen ilişkilerdir, şu halde bir sınıfı egemen sınıf yapan ilişkilerin ifadesidirler; başka bir deyişle, bu düşünceler, onun egemenliğinin fikirleridirler" (Marx, Engels, 1992, s. 75).

Toplumda egemen olan güç toplum üzerinde hegemonyasını kurmak ve kendini yeniden üretmek için ideolojik aygıtlara gereksinim duyar. Althusser (2003) devletin ideolojik aygıtlarının tümünün üretim ilişkilerini yeniden üretmeyi hedeflediğini ve her birinin "kendine özgü yoldan" bu amaca katkıda bulunduğunu belirtir (s. 180). Ancak egemen gruplar toplum üzerinde tam olarak bütünlüklü bir hegemonya sağlayamaz, çünkü her zaman bir direniş vardır. Böylece muhalif ideolojiler egemen ideolojinin boşluklarından sızarak karşı-hegemonya geliştirilmesi yönünde mücadele eder. Bu bağlamda günümüz toplumlarının kültürel yaşamında önemli bir yere sahip olan sinema sanatı ve endüstrisi, toplumsal bilincin ve belleğin oluşturulmasında ve dönüştürülmesinde egemen ve muhalif ideolojilerin mücadelesini yansıtan bir alan olarak yorumlanabilir. Wasko (2003) da sinema endüstrisindeki ideolojik işleyişi anlatır ve sinemasal çözümlemelerin ekonomi politik ilişkiler bağlamında yapılmasını gerektiğini ifade eder:

> "Örneğin, Amrikan film endüstrisinin önemi sadece filmlerinin dünya çapında popüler olmasından kaynaklanmaz. Aslında, bu sadece buzdağının görünen kısmıdır. Hollywood'un başarısını kutlamaktansa ekonomi politikçiler Amerikan filmlerinin uluslararası film pazarını nasıl egemenliği altına aldığıyla, bu pazar egemenliğini güçlendirmek için hangi mekanizmaları kullandığıyla, bunlara devletin ne kadar dahil olduğuyla, film ihracının diğer medya ürünlerinin pazarlanmasıyla ne kadar ilişkili olduğuyla, diğer ülkelerdeki yerli film endüstrileri üzerinde ne gibi sonuçlar doğurduğuyla ve bu durumdan kaynaklanan politik/kültürel sonuçların ne olduğuyla ilgilenirler. Daha da

önemlisi, bu ekonomik düzenlemelerin politik ve ideolojik sonuçlarının birbiri ile ilişkili olmasıdır, çünkü film tüm bir toplumsal, ekonomik ve politik bağlama yerleştirilmeli ve iktidarın yapısını koruma ve yeniden üretmeye katkısı bağlamında çözümlenmelidir" (s. 227).

Toplumsal iletişim sürecinde sinemanın ideolojik işlevinin gözlemlenebildiği alanlardan biri sinemasal üretimlerdeki tarihin sunumudur. Anaakım sinema egemen mitleri, öyküleri, kahramanları, imgeleri yeniden üreterek egemen ideolojinin ve resmi tarihin estetik bir biçimde yeniden üretilmesine ve böylelikle toplumsal bilincin egemenden yana şekillenmesine katkıda bulunur. Ancak "kamusal alana ulaşmayı başaran her tarihi temsil 'egemen' değildir. Bu alan geçmişin birbiri ile savaş halinde olan, çatışan yapılarıyla kesişir. Egemen bellek bu mücadeleler sürecinde oluşur ve her zaman çekişmeye açıktır" (Popular Memory Group, 1982, s. 207). Bu bağlamda muhalif ideolojiler de toplumsal bilinç ve bellek üzerinde belirleyici olabilmektedir. O halde muhalif ideolojilerin üretildiği muhalif filmler de muhalif bir kültürün yaratılmasına katkıda bulunmaktadır. Muhalif filmler egemen güçlerin unutturmaya çalıştığı olayları, kişileri, imgeleri yansıtır, yaşananların unutulmaması için mücadele eder ve tarihte bir iz bırakır. Ancak bu durum, egemen ideolojiyi temsil edenleri ve destekleyenleri rahatsız etmektedir. İktidar kimi zaman söylemleriyle kimi zaman da uygulamalarıyla bu rahatsızlığını ifade eder. Yani muhalif sinemacılar ve filmler çeşitli karalama kampanyalarıyla, sansürle ya da filmin tümünün gösterimine izin verilmemesi gibi durumlarla karşılaşabilir. Nitekim bu rahatsız ediciliğin son örneklerinden biri yönetmenliğini Çayan Demirel'in yaptığı *38* adlı belgeselin gösteriminde yaşanmıştır. Yönetmenin ifadelerine göre belgesel, toplumdaki farklı grupların birarada kardeşçe yaşamasına katkıda bulunmayı amaçlayan bir resmi tarih eleştirisidir.

> "Tarih yazımının değişmesi bence barışa atılacak ilk adımdır. Bizim bu derdi işlememizdeki ve altını çizmemizdeki neden de budur. Yoksa halkları birbirine düşman etmek gibi bir derdimiz yok. Çünkü halklar birbirine düşman değil. Belgeselde katliama maruz kalmış yaşlı bir ana, 'Derdime yanan yok. Biz de halkız. Halk halka ağlasın' diyor. Demek ki halkların birbirinden bir beklentisi var. Resmi ideolojiyi oluşturan kurumların, kişilerin halkları birbirine düşürme istencini kaldırabilmenin yolu da bu resmi tarihle hesaplaşma kanımca." (İlgün, 2006, para 6).

1937-1938 Dersim olaylarının eleştirel bir şekilde anlatıldığı belgeselde Demirel, orada yaşayan insanların yaşananları unutmadığını ve bu "travma"nın geleneklerinde yaşadığını ve aslında filmi Dersimlilerden çok "Anadolu'da yaşayan halklara izlettirmek gerektiğini" sözlerine ekliyor. Bu bağlamda *38* toplumsal bellekte yer eden olayları ve kişileri egemen ideolojiden farklı bir bakışla değerlendirmekte ve toplumsal bilincin ve belleğin muhalif bir yönde değiştirilmesi ve dönüştürülmesine katkıda bulunmayı ve toplumsal farkındalığı geliştirmeyi de hedeflemektedir. Ancak 6 Nisan 2007 tarihli *Radikal* gazetesinin haberine göre daha önce yurtdışında gösterilen ve hiçbir sorun yaşamayan belgeselin bu yılki Munzur Barış ve Kültür Günleri'ndeki gösterimi engellenmiştir. Habere göre polis belgesel için "önizleme" talep etmiş, daha sonra da eser işletme belgesinin olup olmadığını sormuştur. Ancak "ticari amaçlarla çekilmemiş belgesele 'eser işletme belgesi' gerekmemek"tedir. Yasalara aykırı herhangi bir durum olmamasına rağmen belgesel, "organizasyon komitesi tarafından 'provokasyon korkusuyla' programdan çıkarıl"mıştır. (Mavioğlu, 2007, para.1). Bu örnekte olduğu gibi resmi tarihi eleştiren bir film iktidarı rahatsız edebilmekte ve filmin tümüyle gösterimden kaldırılması bile mümkün olmaktadır.

Sinemada iktidar mücadelesini yansıtan alanlardan biri de toplumsal gerçeklerin sunumudur. Sinema toplumsal gerçeklikleri göstermek için kültürel temsilleri kullanır. Anaakım sinema iktidardaki güçlerin gerçekliğini topluma aktarmak için egemen kültürel temsilleri kullanır. Ancak, "egemen temsiller belki de en çok ideolojik olanlardır, en açık şekilde mitlerin basmakalıplığına uygun hareket edenlerdir" (Popular Memory Group, 1982, s. 207). Böylelikle egemen ideolojinin "normal" "meşru" kabul ettiği kimlikler, imgeler sorgulanmadan izleyici tarafından onaylanır. Yani anaakım sinema ile egemen güçlerin tasarımı, kurgusu ve hatta yanılsaması olan gerçeklikler topluma tekrar yansıtılır. Buna göre kurmacanın replikası gibi işleyen anaakım filmlerin karşısında muhalif filmler kurgunun gerçekliğiyle toplumsal yaşamdaki yanılsamaları gösterir ve toplumsal gerçekliklerin dönüştürülmesi durumunda yaşanması muhtemel gerçeklikleri, güzellikleri anlatır. Ryan ve Kellner (1997) sinemadaki kültürel temsiller ve ideoloji arasındaki ilişkiyi şöyle açıklamaktadır:

> Temsiller, içinde yer alınan kültürden de devralınır ve içselleştirilerek benliğin bir parçası haline getirilir. ... Kültürel temsiller yalnızca psikolojik duruşları şekillendirmekle kalmaz, toplumsal gerçekliğin nasıl inşa edileceğine ilişkin olarak da, yani toplumsal yaşamın ve toplumsal kurumların şekillendirilmesinde hangi figür ve sınırların baskın çıkacağı konusunda da çok önemli bir rol oynar. Kapitalizmin, güçlünün güçsüzü yuttuğu bir cangıl gibi mi, yoksa özgürlükçü bir ütopya olarak mı kavranacağını (hissedilip yaşanacağını) bu temsiller belirler. Bu yüzden, kültürel temsillerin üretimi üzerinde söz sahibi olmak toplumsal iktidarın muhafazası açısından kritik önem taşıdığı gibi, toplumsal dönüşümler amaçlayan ilerici hareketler için de vazgeçilmez bir kaynak oluşturur. Sinema, günümüzde, bu tür politik mücadelelerin yürütülmesi açısından özel önem taşıyan bir kültürel temsil arenası oluşturur. Filmler, muhtelif temsil biçimlerinin,

toplumsal gerçekliğin nasıl kavranacağını, daha da fazlası ne olacağını belirlemek için birbirleriyle yarıştığı bir kapışma zeminidir (s. 37).

Buna göre örneğin anaakım sinema içinde yer alan filmlerde kültürel kimlikler egemen ideolojinin bakışıyla yansıtılır. Egemen ideoloji toplumsal bir bütünlük yaratabilmek için toplumu homojenleştirmeye çalışır. Toplumsal yaşamda, simgesel yapıdaki farklı kültürel kimlikler özneye "öteki" üzerinden kendisini tanımlayabilmesi için olanak sunar, ancak bu "öteki" bir eksiğe de işaret eder, bu bağlamda da gerçekte tüm toplumsal yapılar tamamlanmamıştır, eksiktir, ancak iktidar bu homojenleştirme polikasıyla eksiğin üzerini örtmek ister. Ne var ki bunu tümüyle başaramaz. Sonuçta da aslında toplumsal bütünlük sağlamak için iktidar tarafından "öteki"leştirilen kimlikler yüzünden toplumsal ayrıcalıklar doğar, güçlenir. Diğer bir deyişle, "... ayrımcılığın günlük toplumsal pratikleri Ötekiler hakkındaki olumsuz inançların bilişsel temelini önvarsayar: Irkçı ideolojiler tarafından yapılandırıldıkları için kalıplaşmış fikirler, önyargılar, ırkçı tutumlar ya da diğer toplumsal olarak paylaşılan düşünceler" (van Dijk, 2003, s. 53). Bu durum "öteki"ni yoketmeye ve tek kimliğin geçerli olduğu imkansız bir toplum yaratma istemine de yol açar. Bu düşünce –ideoloji- ve uygulamalar anaakım sinema sayesinde yeniden üretilir. Örneğin neredeyse sinema tarihinin başından bu yana anaakım Hollywood filmlerinde siyahiler genellikle "öteki" olarak temsil edilir, bu bağlamda beyaz ırkın üstünlüğünü öven ve ırkçı öğeler barındıran D. W. Griffith'in *Bir Milletin Doğuşu* (1915) filminin sinema tarihinin ilk filmlerinden olması da dikkat çekici bir örnektir. Anaakım Hollywood sinemasının egemen ideolojinin "öteki"leştirme politikasını yeniden üreten türüne bir örnek de western filmleridir. Western filmlerinde genellikle beyaz adam uygar, ama kızılderililer vahşiler olarak sunulur. Böylelikle western filmleri yeni Amerikan değerlerinin ve düşünüş biçimlerinin üretilmesine ve de "Batı toprakları ve kaynaklarının ticari sömürüsü için bahane yaratılmasına" (Altman, 2003, s. 332) yardımcı olur.

Anaakım sinemada cinsel kimliklerin ve cinselliğin sunumunda da egemen ideolojinin bakışı yeniden üretilir. Anaakım filmlerde heteroseksüel ilişki "normal" olarak sunulmakta ve böylelikle toplumsal bilinçte meşrulaştırılmaktadır, buna karşın homoseksüel ilişki "anormal, ahlak dışı, hastalık" vb. olarak sunulmakta ve olumsuzlanmaktadır. Yani anaakım sinemanın en belirgin özelliklerinden olan geleneksel in meşruluğu ve farklı olanın kötülenmesi cinsel kimliklerin sunumunda da tekrar edilmektedir. Ayrıca anaakım sinemada heteroseksüel ilişkide kadın genellikle erkeğin zevk nesnesi olarak sunulur, kadının cinsel obje olarak sunumu cinselliğin sömürülmesini de doğurur. Anaakım sinemadaki bu yaklaşımlar, günlük sıkıntılardan kaçmayı isteyen, sorunların üzerini örtmeye çalışan ya da suçu kendisinde değil "öteki"nde arayan sıradan izleyici için oldukça rahatlatıcı olabilmektedir.

Muhalif sinemacılar filmlerindeki muhalif temsil kodlarıyla anaakım sinemanın bu rahatlatıcı işlevine karşı koyarlar, geleneksel, muhafazakar düşünce ve tavırları reddederek egemen ideolojiyi temsil edenleri ve destekleyenleri rahatsız ederler. Muhalif filmler toplumda "öteki" olarak tanımlanan, dışlanan, karalanan, düşmanca davranılan kültürel kimliklerin sorunlarını ele alır, bu sorunları neden-sonuç ilişkisi bağlamında ve toplumsal ve iktidar ilişkileriyle ilintilendirerek çözmeye yardımcı olur. Farklı kimliklerin, kültürlerin ayrımcılık değil zenginlik getirdiğini ve "öteki" ve "normal dışı" olanların da insani olabileceğini anlatır, "normal"i, meşru kabul edileni sorgular. Örneğin muhalif bir filmde kızılderililere ve kültürlerine saygıyla yaklaşılır ve hatta kızılderililerin "batı"lılardan bile daha insani olabildikleri anlatılır ya da kadın sorununu ele alan feminist fimlerle cinsel kimlikler egemenden farklı bir şekilde yorumlanır. Kısacası muhalif filmler daha insani ve eşitlikçi bir dünya için çağrıda bulunur.

Anaakım filmler anlatım dilleriyle de sıradan izleyici için oldukça rahatlatıcı olabilmektedir. Popüler filmlerde toplumsal bağlamından kopuk, öznel ve de genellikle mükemmel yaşamlar, çok fazla karakterin yer almadığı, basit ve yüzeysel bir şekilde anlatılır. Bu öykü yapısı içinde birbirinden bağımsız, küçük, sanal gerilimler yaratılır ya da küçük öznel sorunların nedeni sorgulanmadan sonuçlarına odaklanılır ve çoğunlukla da filmin sonunda tüm bu gerilimler, sorunlar çözüme kavuşturularak izleyici rahatlatılır. Böylelikle aslında günlük yaşamdaki ekonomik, toplumsal ve de iktidar ilişkilerinin çok katmanlı yapısı saklanır, izleyicinin yaşamı, iktidarı ve de bu ilişkileri algılayışı basitleştirilir, gerçek yaşamda filmlerde sunulanlara benzeyen olaylarla, sorunlarla karşılaşıldığında neden-sonuç ilişkisinin algılanması da bir parça engellenir. Kısacası genellikle tek katmanlı ticari filmler tek boyutlu bir yaşam yaratılmasına da yardımcı olur. Buna karşın muhalif filmlerde anlatım dili, yapı, öykü, kurgu genellikle çok katmanlıdır. Yine sıradan yaşam öyküleri ya da birey psikolojisi anlatılsa bile bu öyküler toplumsal gerçekliklerle ilişkilendirilerek sunulur. Basit, sade yaşamları olan karakterlerin içinde bulunduğu ilişkiler ve de bu ilişkilerin ortaya çıkardığı nedenler ve sonuçlar derinlikli ve karmaşıktır. Popüler filmlerde olduğu gibi yaşananların neden ya da sonuçları irrasyonel değildir. Böylelikle yaşamın bir bütün olarak algılanmasına da katkıda bulunulur. Kısacası, anaakım sinemanın eğlendirmek, rahatlatmak gibi işlevlerine yardımcı olan öğelerden biri de anaakım filmlerde çoğunlukla izleyicilerin entelektüel değil duygusal katılımının yeterli olmasıdır. Buna karşın muhalif sinema izleyicilerini sadece duygusal değil entelektüel yani bilinçli katılım için de çağırır ve bu durum da iktidardaki grupları rahatsız eder.

Anaakım sinemanın rahatlatıcılığı geçici ve yanılsamalıdır. Bu bağlamda anaakım sinemanın ve geçmiş dönemlerdeki karnavalların yarattığı rahatlamalar arasında bir benzerlik olduğu ileri sürülebilir. Karnavallarda insanlar toplumsal kimliklerinden sıyrılır, kurallar kısa bir süre için askıya alınır, sembolik de olsa herkes dilediğini yapmakta özgürdür, toplumsal olarak geçici bir delilik durumu sözkonusudur. Popüler filmlerde de karakterlerin toplumsal yaşamdan soyut olarak sunulması ve ekonomik ve toplumsal zorlukların gösterilmemesi, gösterilse bile bunların irrasyonel bir şekilde çözüme kavuşması izleyicilerini karnavallardaki gibi mutlu eder. Gündelik yaşamın sıkıntılarıyla boğuşan insanlar karnaval dönemlerinde şenlikli bir rahatlığa kavuşur.

> "Karnaval, sahneye çıkmaksızın ve icracılarla izleyiciler arasında bir ayrım yapılmaksızın gerçekleşen bir törendir. Karnavalda herkes etkin bir katılımcıdır, karnaval edimine herkes katılır. Karnaval izlenmez, hatta daha doğru bir dille icra bile edilemez; katılımcıları karnavalın içinde yaşarlar; yani, karnavalesk bir yaşam sürerler. Karnavalesk yaşam alışıldık seyrinden çıkmış bir yaşam olduğu için de, bir ölçüde "ters yüz edilmiş bir yaşam"dır, "dünyanın tersine çevrilmiş tarafı"dır" (Bakhtin, 2001, s. 238).

Bu ters yüz edilme sayesinde toplum iktidarın baskılarından kurtulur, toplumsal bilinçte bastırılmış olan geri döner ve katılımcılar geçici, yanılsamalı bir özgürlük yaşar. Bu sayede karnavallarda iktidarı temsil eden herşey aşılağılanabilir, hatta sembolik de olsa bir şiddet uygulanabilir. Örneğin Babil şenliklerinde "... bu beş gün içinde efendiler ve köleler yer değiştirir, köleler emir verir, efendiler bu emirleri yerine getirirdi. Ölüme yargılı bir mahkuma kralın giysileri giydirilir, kralın tahtına oturtulur ve yemek, içmek, eğlenmek ve kralın cariyeleriyle yatmak gibi istediği emirleri vermesine izin verilirdi. Ama beşinci günün sonunda krallık giysileri üzerinden çıkarılır, kamçılanır ve haça gerilirdi" (Frazer, 1991, s. 222). Bu ters yüz edilme, toplumsal irrasyonellik ve geçici rahatlama anaakım Hollywood romantik komedi türüyle örneklenebilir. Bu tür filmlerde genellikle üst sınıftan insanların "mükemmel" yaşamları sunulur, karakterlerin neredeyse hiçbir sorunları yoktur, ya da küçük, önemsiz sorunları vardır ve bunlar hemen çözülür veya—Yeşilçam melodramlarında da olduğu gibi—zenginle fakirin imkansız gibi görünen aşkı bütün zorlukları aşar ve film mutlu bir evlilikle biter. Böylelikle ekonomik ve toplumsal sorunlara dayanmayan sanal gerilimler, yanılsamalar filmin sonunda aşılır, izleyici de bu kısa süreli boşalma anları ile rahatlamış olur. Bu durum anaakım Hollywood sinemasından bir örnekle açıklanabilir. Yönetmenliğini Garry Marshall'ın yaptığı *Pretty Woman* (1990) (Pretty Woman, "Plot Outline" bölümü, 2007) filminde üst sınıftan zengin bir işadamı alt sınıftan bir hayat kadınına aşık olur. Modern bir Cinderella masalını andıran filmde karakterler ve olaylar gerçek yaşamda karşılaşılmasına olanak olmayan bir şekilde sunulur. Örneğin Julia Roberts'ın oynadığı Vivian—hayat kadını—karakterinin neredeyse hiç sorunu yoktur. Gerçek yaşamda ekonomik ve toplumsal birçok sorunla boğuşan, dövülen, aşağılanan, sömürülen benzerlerine karşın filmde Vivian sadece bazı insanlardan kötü muamele görür ve bu durum da biraz para ve eğitimle hemen aşılır. Richard Gere'in oynadığı Edward karakteri gerçek yaşamın aksine filmde kendi konumunu, statüsünü, vb. sorgulamadan çok kısa bir sürede Vivian'a aşık olur ve film mutlu sonla biter. Filmde üst sınıftan birinin, Edward'ın, alt sınıftan birinin—ve üstüne üstlük hayat kadını olan Vivian'ın—peşinden koşması karnavallardaki gibi ters yüz edilmiş bir yaşama gönderme yapar, böylelikle izleyici anlık boşalmalar, doyumlar yaşayarak rahatlamış olur. Tıpkı karnavallarda olduğu gibi şenlikli geçici bir özgürleşme yaşanır. Bakhtin'in ifadeleriyle; "Bayram, tüm yasaklamaları ve hiyerarşik engelleriyle resmi sistemin tamamının geçici bir süre askıya alınması anlamına geliyordu. Kısa bir süre için yaşam alışıldık, meşrulaşmış ve kutsanmış akışlarından çıkıp, ütopik özgürlük alanına giriyordu. Tam da bu özgürlüğün kısalığı, geçiciliği, imgelerin festival atmosferinden doğan fantastik mahiyetini ve ütopik radikalizmini artırıyordu" (Bakhtin, 2001, s. 109). Gerçek yaşamda toplumsal bilincin kabul edemeyeceği söylemsel ve eylemsel pratikler üzerinden yürüyen ve aslında iktidarın denetimi altında gerçekleşen bu durumda içgüdüler, arzular tekrar hapsedilmek üzere bir süreliğine serbest bırakılır. Çünkü festivallerde "... bütün içgüdüler dizginsiz bırakılır, her türlü doyuma izin verilir... Festival, izin verilen, daha doğrusu zorunlu olan bir aşırılıktır, bir yasağın kutsal ihlalidir. İnsanlar aldıkları bir emir sonucunda mutlu oldukları için aşırılık yapmaz; festivalin özü aşırılıktır; festival duygusunu yaratan şey, kural olarak yasak olan şeyleri yapma özgürlüğüdür" (Freud, 1999, s. 206). Film bittiğinde ise izleyici anlık, yanılsamalı rahatlamadan çıkar, "gerçeğin çölüne" geri döner. Bu nedenle de egemen güçler insanlardaki bu geçici rahatlamayı kalıcı hale getirmek için toplumu sürekli bu tarz kültür ürünlerine maruz bırakmaya çalışır.

Muhalif filmler sadece seçtikleri öyküler ya da anlatım dilleri ile değil gösterim biçimleriyle de iktidardaki güçleri rahatsız edebilmektedir. Zaman zaman ticari sinemadan farklı gösterim biçimleri kullanan muhalif sinema izleyicilerine ortak bir muhalif kültür, gelenek ve tarih yaratılması için çağrıda bulunur. Benzer duygu ve düşüncede olan insanların biraraya gelmesi, dayanışması ve birlikte mücadele etmesi için fırsatlar yaratabilir. Böyellikle sinema kar getiren gösterim alanları dışında bu düşünce ve duyguların geniş halk kesimlerine ulaşabileceği gösterim biçimleri düzenler. Hatta küresel ve enternasyonel mücadelelerin olumsal olduğunu anlatarak bu yönde kamuoyu oluşturulmasına katkıda bulunabilir. Örneğin Türkiye'de 1 Mayıs 2006 İşçi Bayramı etkinlikleri kapsamında Uluslararası İşçi Filmleri Festivali düzenlenmiştir. Festivali düzenleyenler festivalin önemini şöyle anlatmaktadır:

> "Seçilen filmler farklı coğrafyalardan işçi sınıfı öykülerini anlatmaktadır. Coğrafi ve kültürel farklılıklarına rağmen filmlerin ortak bir vurgusu ve meselesi vardır. İşçi sınıfının mücadelesinin evrensel olduğu konusunda ikna yeteneğine sahip filmlerdir. Filmlerin gerek ülke sinemalarındaki gerek dünya sineması içindeki yerleri bakımından

nitelikli ve dikkate değer filmler olmasına özen gösterilmiştir. Gerçekten de bu filmler sadece temaları ya da işçi sınıfının sorunlarından bahsetmeleri anlamında değil belki daha da önemlisi, sinema anlatımlarındaki ustalık, yenilik, gözüpeklik ve evrensellikleri ile Godard'ın bir sözünü hatırlatırcasına, "sadece içerikleriyle değil biçimleri ile de politik olabilen filmler"dir. (Uluslararası işçi filmleri festivali, "1. Uluslararası işçi filmleri," 2006).

Ayrıca, festival kapsamında yer alan filmler İstanbul ve Ankara'dan sonra Mayıs ayından itibaren Bolu, Artvin, Adana, Mersin, Bursa, Eskişehir, İzmir gibi değişik illerde de gösterilmiştir (Uluslararası işçi filmleri festivali, "Festival Anadolu'da," 2006). Festivali düzenleyenler "maddi üretim araçlarının mülkiyetine sahip olan" egemen güçlerin bütün toplum kesimleri üzerinde ideolojik hegemonya kurduğunu, buna bir üst yapı kurumu olarak kültürel hayatın ve "son yarım yüzyıldaki en etkin unsurlarından biri" olarak sinemanın da dahil olduğunu belirtirler. Festivalin amacını ise şöyle açıklamaktadırlar: "Özetle söylemek gerekirse, festivalle, dünyayı sosyal, bireysel ve çevresel özellikleriyle insanca yaşanabilir olmaktan çıkaran neoliberalizme karşı direniş öykülerini görsel bir anlatımla sergileyelim istedik." Festival sayesinde Türkiye'deki işçilerin hem ülke içindeki hem de dışındaki kendi (işçi) sınıfından insanlarla iletişim kurmalarına katkıda bulunmasının amaçlandığını da eklemektedirler. "Sınıf bilincinin yokluğunun ya da zayıflığının yol açtığı toplumsal dejenerasyonun etkisizleştirilmesine" katkıda bulunmayı ve "işçilerin kendi gerçeklikleriyle yüzleşmelerine yardımcı" olmayı amaçlamışlardır. Ayrıca festival sayesinde anaakım sinemanın tercih etmediği "sosyal gerçeklik" akımının "yeniden değer bulmasına katkı sunmak" da amaçlanmıştır (Uluslararası işçi filmleri festivali, "Neden işçi filmleri", 2006). Bu örnekte de görüldüğü gibi muhalif filmler muhalif söylemin yaratılmasına ve bu söylemin geniş halk kesimlerine ulaştırılmasına katkıda bulunur. Böylelikle enternasyonel bağlamdaki küreselleşme karşıtı, kapitalizm karşıtı, neo-liberal politikalar karşıtı söylem ve eylemler, yani tüm iktidar karşıtı mücadeleler desteklenir ve bu konuda kamuoyu oluşturulmasına yardımcı olunur. Bu durum ise toplum üzerinde tam bir hegemonya yaratmaya çalışan egemen güçler için rahatsız edici olabilmektedir.

"Rahatsız Edici" Bir Film: *Die Fetten Jahre Sind Vorbei (The Edukators -Eğitmenler)*

Yönetmenliğini Hans Weingartner'ın yaptığı *Eğitmenler* (2004) muhaliflerin iktidardaki güçleri "rahatsız ettiğini" somut bir şekilde ironik bir dille göstermektedir. Filmde Berlin'de yaşayan, kendilerini "Eğitmenler" olarak adlandıran devrimci iki genç arakadaş, Jan (Daniel Brühl) ve Peter (Stipe Erceg), klasik yaklaşımlardan farklı bir muhalefet etme biçimi geliştirmişlerdir. Jan ve Peter zenginlere kızgındırlar ve bu nedenle zengin insanların ve villalarının bir listesini yaparlar ve sahipleri tatile gittiğinde bu seçtikleri villalara gizlice girip evdeki eşyaların yerini değiştirirler, yaratıcı düzenlemeler yaparlar ve evsahiplerini "rahatsız eden" "Çok fazla paran var", "Varlıklı günleriniz sayılı" yazılı, "eğitmenler" imzalı notlar bırakırlar. Jan ve Peter bu "eğitici projelerini" Peter'ın kız arkadaşı Jule'dan (Julia Jentsch) bile gizlerler. Peter kısa bir tatile gittiğinde, Jule ile Jan arasında duygusal bir yakınlaşma olur. Jule, bir süre önce Golf marka arabasıyla zengin işadamı Hardenberg'in (Burghart Klaußner) Mercedes Benz marka arabasına çarpar ve açılan davadan sonra Hardenberg'e yaklaşık 100.000 euro borçlanır. Bunu öğrenen Jan, Jule'e Peter ile yaptıkları aktiviteleri anlatır ve intikamını alması için Jule'u Hardenberg'in evine girmeye ikna eder. Eve girerler, eşyaların yerini değiştirirler, harika vakit geçirirler ve ayrılırlar, ancak Jule cep telefonunu orda unutmuştur. Bunu üzerine tekrar Hardenberg'in evine giderler fakat bu sefer Hardenberg'e yakalanırlar, Peter'ı yardıma çağırırlar ve hep beraber Hardenberg'i bir dağ evine kaçırırlar. Burada Hardenberg kendisinin de gençlik yıllarında onlar gibi idealleri olduğunu, yani 68 kuşağından olduğunu, ancak yaşamın onu değiştirdiğini anlatır. Bir süre sonra üçlü Hardenberg'i serbest bırakır. Hardenberg, dağ evinde onları ele vermeyeceğine söz verdiği halde serbest kaldıktan sonra polise haber verir. Ancak üç arkadaş ondan daha zekice bir plan yapmıştır ve film "bazı insanlar hiç değişmez" yazılı bir notla sona erer.

Filmde, küreselleşmeye, kapitalist dünya düzenine, fakir insanların ve halkların sömürülmesine, mülkiyete yani kısacası üretimden elde edilen kazancın eşitsiz dağılımı yüzünden ortaya çıkan toplumsal eşitsizliklere ve adeletsizliklere karşı olan üç arkadaş bu fikirlerini ifade etmek için kendilerine has, "zararsız" ve etkili bir mücadele etme biçimi geliştirmişlerdir. Zenginlerin evlerinden hiçbir şey çalmayan ve kimseyi incitmeyen "eğitmenler"in amacı sadece zenginlerin hırslarının, yaşamlarının toplumun geri kalanını nasıl incittiğini göstermektir. Ekonomik eşitsizliklerin toplumsal eşitsizliğe, huzursuzluğa ve öfkeye yol açtığı mesajını verirler. Filmde üç arkadaş gerçekte "başaşağı duran" yaşamı tekrar ayakları üzerine oturtmak, yani yaşamı ters yüz etmek için girdikleri villalardaki eşyaları yeniden düzenlerler. Böylelikle zenginlere bir tür ders verirler. Yüklü miktar paralar harcayıp evinin güvenliğini sağladığını zanneden zenginler tatil dönüşü evlerini tam bir kaos içinde ve "Çok fazla paran var", "Varlıklı günleriniz sayılı" notlarını bulduklarında gerçekten "rahatsız" olmaktadır. "Dünya nüfusunun % 10'u zenginliği paylaşıyor, geri kalan % 90 açlık ve yoksulluk içinde yaşıyor. Dünyada her insanın günlük ihtiyacı olan 2000 kaloriyi karşılayabilecek kadar buğday var. Fakat eşit olarak dağıtılmıyor. Dünyanın % 90'ı açlıktan ölüyor ve geri kalan % 10'u diet yapıyor. Herkes mutsuz" (Weingartner, 2007, "The affluent society" bölümü, para.1). Filmin yönetmeninin de ifade ettiği gibi toplumun büyük kesiminin gerçek yaşamda huzursuz ve rahatsız bir yaşam sürmesi bu üç arkadaşı kızdırmakta ve onlar da kendi yöntemleriyle varlıklı kesimden intikam almaktadır. Kendi izole, rahat dünyalarında zenginler de rahatsız olmalıdır. Yönetmen bu durumu şöyle anlatmaktadır:

"Filmdeki temalardan biri de kişinin korkularından kurtulmasıdır. Güvenlik ve emniyet ile ilgili endişelere, kaygılara son vermek önemlidir. Özgürlük güvenlikten daha çok çaba gerektirir, ama aynı zamanda daha heyecan vericidir. Mükafatları daha büyüktür. İnsan olmanın ne olduğuna dair kendime özgü bir kavramım var. Bence insanlar göçebedir. Özgür olmaya ihtiyaçları var. Ve bugünlerde çok azımız böyleyiz. Birçok insan Hardenberg gibi, kendi mülkiyetlerinin tutsakları. Biri şöyle demişti: Sahip olduğun şey bir gün sana sahip olur" (Weingartner, 2007, "Prisoners of their own possessions" bölümü, para.1).

Bu bağlamda Peter, Jan ve Jule'ün zenginleri aslında rahatsız etmediği tersine ironik bir şekilde rahatlattığı bile ileri sürülebilir. Film bir çeşit özgürlük mücadelesini anlatmaktadır ve birlikte mücadele etmeye teşvik etmektedir. "Direnişin ilk adımı özgür olmaktır, ikinci adımı ise benzer gereksinimleri olan, benzer değerleri paylaşan insanlarla bağlantı kurabilmek için müttefikler bulmaktır." Çünkü "eğer yalnız olursan, kaybolursun" (Weingartner, 2007, "Strength within a group" bölümü, para. 1). Yönetmen Weingartner üç arkadaşın mücadelesini "şiirsel bir direniş" olarak görmektedir.

Filmde kadın erkek ilişkilerinin sunumu da egemen, muhafazakar düşüncede, inançta olan insanları rahatsız edebilir. Jule özgürlüğüne düşkün biridir ve Jan ile yakınlaşarak aslında kimseye ait olmadığını da göstermektedir. Bu bağlamda film, iki erkek ve bir kadın arasındaki üçlü aşkı anlatan *Jules et Jim*'e de gönderme yapar. Yönetmen (Weingartner, 2007, "Strength within a group" bölümü, para. 2) Jan ve Jule'un ihanetine inanmanın zor olduğunu ancak Peter'ın arkadaşlığın burjuva ahlak değerlerinden daha değerli olduğunu anladığını belirtir ve böylelikle üçlü toplumsal kısıtlamalara, şekillenmelere de karşı çıkmış olur.

Sonuç olarak *Eğitmenler* zenginlerin güvende olduklarını zannetikleri bir anda aslında hiç de güvende olamayacaklarını, toplumun yoksul olan % 90'ı rahatsızken bu zengin % 10'un da rahatsız olması gerektiğini anlatmaktadır. İzleyicilerini sorgulamaya, eşitsizliklere başkaldırmaya ve özgürlük için dayanışmaya çağırır. Bu nedenle de toplumsal farkındalık geliştirmeyi hedefleyen muhalif bir film olarak iktidardaki güçleri de rahatsız etmektedir.

Sonuç

Sonuç olarak toplumun tüm kesimlerine seslenmeyi hedefleyen, iktidarın kültürel pratiklerini yeniden üreterek toplumu şekillendirmeyi amaçlayan, toplumsal gerçekliklerden ve yaşamdan kopuk öznel öyküler anlatan anaakım sinema varolan toplumsal gerçekliklerin değiştirilemeyeceği, dönüştürülemeyeceği mitini yeniden üretir. Egemen ideolojinin varsayımı, yani varolan sistemin varolması muhtemel sistemler içinde en iyisi olduğu ve küçük aksaklıklar olsa da herşeyin yolunda olduğu anlayışı onaylanır, onaylatılır. Geleneksel olanın devam ettirilmesi ve yaşananların kabulu yönünde telkinlerde bulunur. Buna karşın muhalif filmler, gerçek toplumsal yaşamdan üretilen sıradan bir öyküyle izleyicilerin o ana dek belki de çok fazla bilincinde olmadıkları ama yaşamlarında deneyimledikleri sorunları, sıkıntıları, gerçekleri ve de güzellikleri anlatarak toplumsal bilinçte egemen güçlerin gerçekliklerine karşı bir farkındalık, tepki geliştirilmesine ve egemen ideolojik şekillenmelerin parçalanmasına katkıda bulunur. Kısacası muhalif filmler yaşanılanların aslında kader olmadığını göstererek, toplumsal gerçekliklerin daha insani bir yönde değiştirilmesi, dönüştürülmesi için çağrıda bulunarak, başka bir dünyanın mümkün olduğunu anlatarak egemen güçleri rahatsız etmektedir.

Kaynakça

Althusser, L. (2003). *İdeoloji ve devletin ideolojik aygıtları.* İstanbul: İthaki Yayınları.

Altman, R. (2003). Sinema ve tür. G. Nowell-Smith (Ed.), *Dünya sinema tarihi* içinde (ss. 322-333). İstanbul: Kabalcı Yayınları.

Bakhtin, M. (2001). *Karnavaldan romana.* İstanbul: Ayrıntı Yayınları.

Comolli, J.-L. & Narboni, J. (1976), Cinema/Ideology/ Criticism. B. Nichols (Ed.) *Movies and methods.* Cilt 1 içinde (ss. 22-30). Berkeley: University of California Press.

Frazer, J. G. (1991). *Altın dal: Dinin ve folklorun kökleri I.* İstanbul: Payel Yayınları.

Freud, S. (1999). *Dinin kökenleri.* Ankara: Öteki Yayınları.

İlgün, S. (2006, Ekim). Resmi tarihle hesaplaşma. http://www.evrensel.net/06/10/10/kultur.html#1 (Son erişim 10.04.2007).

Marx, K. & Engels, F. (1992). *Alman ideolojisi.* Ankara: Sol Yayınları.

Mavioğlu, E. (2007, 6 Nisan). Dersim belgeseli polise takıldı. *Radikal* http://www.radikal.com.tr/haber.php?haberno=217666&tarih=06/04/2007 (Son erişim 07.04.2007).

Popular Memory Group, (1982). Popular memory: Theory, politics, method. Johnson, R., McLennan, G., Schwarz, B. and Sutton, D. (Eds.) *Making histories* içinde (ss. 205-252). Minneapolis: University of Minnesota Press.

Pretty Woman. (1990). http://www.imdb.com/title/tt0100405/ (Son erişim 12.04.2007).

Ryan, M. & Kellner, D. (1997). *Politik kamera.* İstanbul: Ayrıntı Yayınları.

Uluslararası İşçi Filmleri Festivali (2006). http://www.laborfest.sendika.org/index.php?eylem=yazi&yazi_no=7 (Son erişim 05.04.2007).

van Dijk, T. (2003). Söylem ve ideoloji:Çok alanlı bir yaklaşım. Çoban, B. & Özarslan Z. (Ed.) *Söylem ve ideoloji* içinde (ss. 13-112). İstanbul: Su Yayınları.

Wasko, J. (2003). The political economy of film. T. Miller & R. Stam (Ed.) *A Companion to film theory* içinde, (ss. 221-233). Blackwell Reference Online.

Weingartner, H. (2004). *The Edukators* (Die Fetten Jahre Sind Vorbei) http://www3.ifcfilms.com/theedukators/edukators.html (Son erişim 13.04.2007).

Author Index